Windows XP™ All-in-One Desk Reference For Dummies®

Cheat Sheet

Don't PANIC!

WITHDRAWN

The five most common causes of computer-induced insanity — and their cures:

5. If there's no mouse cursor on the screen or the cursor won't move no matter how much you move the mouse, shut the computer down, make sure the mouse is plugged in, and restart the computer. If that doesn't work, flip the mouse over and use your fingernail to scrape off built-up gunk, pull the ball out if there is one, and clean the inside with a cotton swab and a touch of isopropyl alcohol. If the cursor still won't move, throw the stupid thing away. Mice are cheap. Sheesh.

4. If you suddenly can't get at your e-mail or get on the Web even though you could get to it yesterday and you haven't changed anything at all, chill. Chances are good that your Internet Service Provider (the place your computer dials into) is having problems. Come back in a few hours. DON'T CHANGE YOUR SETTINGS.

3. If you can't find a file that was sitting around yesterday, chances are good it's either in the Recycle Bin or you dragged it somewhere weird. Double-click the Recycle Bin icon. If your file is there, double-click it and then click Restore. If your file isn't there, choose Start➪Search, click the kind of file you're looking for, and ask Rover (yes, that's his name) to go look for it.

2. If you spend the money to buy an expensive piece of hardware — a new video card, a second hard drive, a fancy force-feedback mouse, or a different cable modem — spend a little bit more money and have the retailer install it. Life's too short.

1. If the stupid computer won't work right, turn it off. Go read a book or watch a movie. Get some sleep. Come back when you're not so tied up in knots. Few pursuits in the history of humanity are as frustrating as trying to get a recalcitrant computer to behave itself.

Three Fatal Flaws

Every single Windows XP user — from the first-time novice to the most grizzled veteran — needs to understand three vital points about Windows XP:

- Windows XP hides a key piece of information from you that can help you identify and avoid viruses. The next time you use Windows XP, take a few seconds and make it show you "file name extensions" — the little piece at the end of each file's name, usually three characters long (for example, doc or exe or bat), that dictates how Windows treats the file. See Book I, Chapter 2 for complete details on showing file extension names.

- Windows XP will beg, bully, and cajole you into divulging all sorts of information about yourself, and *you don't have to give in*. From the Registration Wizard to Windows Messenger, to .NET Passport and MSN and a dozen places in between — *all* of that information is optional. Don't hand out any more than you feel comfortable giving. There's nothing illegal, immoral, or habit-forming about telling Windows Messenger, for example, that your name is William Gates III. Read Book IX, Chapter 3 for more on this.

- Windows XP does not have built-in anti-virus protection. You need to buy, install, frequently update, and religiously use an anti-virus package. Choosing one specific manufacturer's package over another's isn't nearly as important as getting AV software installed, updated, and working. All of the major anti-virus packages work well.

For Dummies: Bestselling Book Series for Beginners

Windows XP™ All-in-One Desk Reference For Dummies®

Windows Media Player

Choose which song to play

Click here to see the normal Windows menu

The "Media Guide" is Microsoft's Web site

Bill would be happy to take your money

If they called it a "User Interface" you'd never touch it, true?

Burn a custom CD, or copy to your MP3 player

For Web radio stations. Snore.

The contents of the My Music and Shared Music folders

"Rip" a CD (convert music on the CD into files on your PC)

Make Windows Run Faster

If Windows XP runs too slowly, buy more memory.

If you're up to 256 MB of memory and Windows XP *still* runs too slow, buy a new PC, bucko. Don't bother trying to upgrade: It's expensive, time consuming, and you won't be happy with the results. Give the old PC to the kids or a worthwhile charity or use it as a boat anchor. The PC won't mind.

Hungry Minds™

For Dummies: Bestselling Book Series for Beginners

Windows XP™
ALL-IN-ONE DESK REFERENCE
FOR
DUMMIES®

by Woody Leonhard

Hungry Minds™

Best-Selling Books • Digital Downloads • e-Books • Answer Networks • e-Newsletters • Branded Web Sites • e-Learning

New York, NY ◆ Cleveland, OH ◆ Indianapolis, IN

Windows XP™ All-in-One Desk Reference For Dummies®

Published by
Hungry Minds, Inc.
909 Third Avenue
New York, NY 10022
www.hungryminds.com
www.dummies.com

Copyright © 2002 Hungry Minds, Inc. All rights reserved. No part of this book, including interior design, cover design, and icons, may be reproduced or transmitted in any form, by any means (electronic, photocopying, recording, or otherwise) without the prior written permission of the publisher.

Library of Congress Control Number: 2001096625

ISBN: 0-7645-1548-9

Printed in the United States of America

10 9 8 7 6 5 4 3 2

1B/TQ/RR/QR/IN

Distributed in the United States by Hungry Minds, Inc.

Distributed by CDG Books Canada Inc. for Canada; by Transworld Publishers Limited in the United Kingdom; by IDG Norge Books for Norway; by IDG Sweden Books for Sweden; by IDG Books Australia Publishing Corporation Pty. Ltd. for Australia and New Zealand; by TransQuest Publishers Pte Ltd. for Singapore, Malaysia, Thailand, Indonesia, and Hong Kong; by Gotop Information Inc. for Taiwan; by ICG Muse, Inc. for Japan; by Intersoft for South Africa; by Eyrolles for France; by International Thomson Publishing for Germany, Austria and Switzerland; by Distribuidora Cuspide for Argentina; by LR International for Brazil; by Galileo Libros for Chile; by Ediciones ZETA S.C.R. Ltda. for Peru; by WS Computer Publishing Corporation, Inc., for the Philippines; by Contemporanea de Ediciones for Venezuela; by Express Computer Distributors for the Caribbean and West Indies; by Micronesia Media Distributor, Inc. for Micronesia; by Chips Computadoras S.A. de C.V. for Mexico; by Editorial Norma de Panama S.A. for Panama; by American Bookshops for Finland.

For general information on Hungry Minds' products and services please contact our Customer Care Department within the U.S. at 800-762-2974, outside the U.S. at 317-572-3993 or fax 317-572-4002.

For sales inquiries and reseller information, including discounts, premium and bulk quantity sales, and foreign-language translations, please contact our Customer Care Department at 800-434-3422, fax 317-572-4002, or write to Hungry Minds, Inc., Attn: Customer Care Department, 10475 Crosspoint Boulevard, Indianapolis, IN 46256.

For information on licensing foreign or domestic rights, please contact our Sub-Rights Customer Care Department at 212-884-5000.

For information on using Hungry Minds' products and services in the classroom or for ordering examination copies, please contact our Educational Sales Department at 800-434-2086 or fax 317-572-4005.

For press review copies, author interviews, or other publicity information, please contact our Public Relations Department at 317-572-3168 or fax 317-572-4168.

For authorization to photocopy items for corporate, personal, or educational use, please contact Copyright Clearance Center, 222 Rosewood Drive, Danvers, MA 01923, or fax 978-750-4470.

Hungry Minds™ is a trademark of Hungry Minds, Inc.

About the Author

Curmudgeon, critic, and self-described "Windows Victim" **Woody Leonhard** publishes a handful of fiercely independent electronic newsletters covering Microsoft products: Woody's Windows Watch and Woody's Office Watch lead the way. Under Editor-in-Chief Peter Deegan, the free weekly newsletters — with 600,000 subscribers — rate as the most widely read source of Windows news, tips, and information you can't find anywhere else: www.woodyswatch.com.

With a couple dozen computer books under his belt, Woody knows where the bodies are buried. He was one of the first Microsoft Consulting Partners and a charter member of the Microsoft Solutions Provider organization. He's a one-man major Microsoft beta testing site and delights in being a constant thorn in Microsoft's side. Along with several co-authors and editors, he's won an unprecedented six Computer Press Association Awards and two American Business Press Awards.

Woody currently lives with his son and two dogs in Phuket, Thailand, where he's working on an action-adventure novel set in Saudi Arabia. Most mornings you can see him jogging on Patong Beach with the dogs, then guzzling a latte at Starbucks. Feel free to drop by and say, "Sawadee krap!" Microsoft hit squads, please take a number and form a queue at the rear of the building.

About the Contributors

Katherine Murray has been using technology to write about technology since the early 80s. With more than 40 books to her credit (spanning genres from technical to trade to parenting to business books), Katherine enjoys working on projects that teach new skills, uncover hidden talents, or develop mastery and efficiency in a chosen area. Katherine gets the biggest kick out of writing about technologies that help people communicate better — in person, in print, by e-mail, or on the Web. For the last 14 years, Katherine has owned and operated reVisions Plus, Inc., a publishing services company that uses many different programs — one of which, of course, is Microsoft Windows.

Jonathan Sachs discovered computers as a freshman at Oberlin College. He worked as a student staff member of the college computer center for three years and graduated with an A.B. in Physics. He moved on to DePaul Law School, graduated, passed the Illinois bar, and relocated to the San Francisco area, where he's currently employed as a programmer. He lives with two cats in a house in the East Bay hills. Jonathan has published three books and several magazine articles on computer topics — and one science fiction story. In his spare time he grows vegetables, reads, and, in a small way, sells used books through eBay.

Justin Leonhard drew recognition as the first teenager to publicly crash Office XP. He put together the main peer-to-peer network used in this book, tested it with the toughest applications Windows XP handles — games — and generated several interesting bug reports in the process. He recently completed his Advanced Open Water scuba certification and spends his spare time playing video games and building robots.

Dedication

I would like to dedicate this book to Justin, who keeps asking such insightful questions, and to Add — Duangkhae Tongthueng — who helped me in more ways than she will ever know and made my life so happy.

Author's Acknowledgments

I would like to thank Andrea Boucher, who at this very moment is pulling her hair out, bringing the final manuscript together; Jill Schorr, the only Acquisitions Editor who's "acquired" me for a new project in the past five years; Claudette Moore and Debbie McKenna, the best agents in the biz; Kathy Murray and Jonathan Sachs, contributors of the first degree; and all of the production people who made the book — er, books — work. Pulling together a project like this involves an enormous amount of hard work from dozens of talented, experienced people. I hope you have as much fun reading this tome as we did creating it.

Publisher's Acknowledgments

We're proud of this book; please send us your comments through our Hungry Minds Online Registration Form located at www.dummies.com.

Some of the people who helped bring this book to market include the following:

Acquisitions, Editorial, and Media Development

Project Editor: Andrea C. Boucher

Acquisitions Editor: Jill Schorr

Technical Editor: Vince Averello

Editorial Manager: Constance Carlisle

Permissions Editor: Carmen Krikorian

Media Development Manager: Laura Carpenter VanWinkle

Media Development Supervisor: Richard Graves

Editorial Assistant: Amanda Foxworth, Jean Rogers

Production

Project Coordinator: Maridee V. Ennis

Layout and Graphics: Gabriele McCann, Jill Piscitelli, Jacque Schneider, Betty Schulte, Brian Torwelle, Jeremey Unger, Erin Zeltner

Proofreaders: Joel K. Draper, David Faust, John Greenough, Andy Hollandbeck, Susan Moritz

Indexer: TECHBOOKS Production Services

General and Administrative

Hungry Minds Technology Publishing Group: Richard Swadley, Senior Vice President and Publisher; Mary Bednarek, Vice President and Publisher, Networking; Joseph Wikert, Vice President and Publisher, Web Development Group; Mary C. Corder, Editorial Director, Dummies Technology; Andy Cummings, Publishing Director, Dummies Technology; Barry Pruett, Publishing Director, Visual/Graphic Design

Hungry Minds Manufacturing: Ivor Parker, Vice President, Manufacturing

Hungry Minds Marketing: John Helmus, Assistant Vice President, Director of Marketing

Hungry Minds Production for Branded Press: Debbie Stailey, Production Director

Hungry Minds Sales: Michael Violano, Vice President, International Sales and Sub Rights

Contents at a Glance

Cartoons at a Glance

By Rich Tennant

page 7

page 495

page 385

page 453

page 281

page 317

page 231

page 577

page 667

Cartoon Information:
Fax: 978-546-7747
E-Mail: richtennant@the5thwave.com
World Wide Web: www.the5thwave.com

Table of Contents

Introduction

Windows XP marks a return to the mother ship for all Windows users: after many years of living with two very different versions of Windows — a flaky version that crashed all the time but ran games and a stable version that could only talk business and wouldn't fraternize with fun things like cameras — we're all back together again.

For most people, Windows XP rates as the first must-have version of Windows ever. If you're like me, BXP (Before XP) you used Windows because you had to. Now, with all the new things XP can do, you may catch yourself *enjoying* Windows. At least on odd-numbered days.

It's okay. Group therapy helps.

About Windows XP All-in-One

Windows XP All-in-One Desk Reference For Dummies takes you through the Land of the Dummies — with introductory material and stuff your grandmother could (and should!) understand — and then continues the journey into more advanced areas, where you can really put Windows to work every day. I don't dwell on technical mumbo-jumbo, and I keep the baffling jargon to a minimum. At the same time, though, I tackle the tough problems you're likely to encounter, show you the major road signs, and give you a lot of help where you'll need it the most.

Whether you want to set up a quick, easy, reliable network in your home office or you want to cheat at Solitaire, this is your book. Er, I should say *nine* books. I've broken the topics out into nine different books so you'll find it easy to hop around to a topic — and a level of coverage — that feels comfortable.

I didn't design this book to be read from front to back. It's a reference. Each chapter and each section is meant to focus on solving a particular problem or describing a specific technique. Sections toward the beginning are more tutorial. Sections near the end take the bull by the horns and squeeze.

Windows XP All-in-One Desk Reference For Dummies should be your reference of first resort, even before you consult Windows XP's Help and Support Center. There's a big reason why: Windows Help was written by hundreds of people over the course of many, many years. Some of the material was written ages ago, and it's confusing as all get-out, but it's still in Windows Help for folks who are tackling tough "legacy" problems. Some of the terminology in the Help files is inconsistent and down-right misleading, largely because the technology has changed so much since some of the articles were written. The proverbial bottom line: I don't duplicate the material in the Windows XP Help and Support Center, but I will point to it if I figure it'll help you.

Conventions

I try to keep the typographical conventions to a minimum:

✦ The first time a buzzword appears in text, I italicize it and define it immediately. That makes it easier for you to glance back and re-read the definition.

✦ When I want you to type something, or press a specific key, I'll put the letters or key name in bold. For example: "Press the **Ctrl, Alt,** and **Del** keys simultaneously to initiate a Vulcan Mind Meld."

✦ I set off Web addresses and e-mail addresses in monospace. For example, my e-mail address is `talk2woody@woodyswatch.com` (true fact), and my newsletter's Web page is at `www.woodyswatch.com` (another true fact).

There's one other convention, though, that I use all the time. I always, absolutely, adamantly include the file name extension — those letters at the end of a file name, like `doc` or `vbs` or `exe` — when talking about a file. Yeah, I know Windows XP hides file name extensions, unless you go in and change it. Yeah, I know that Bill G Hisself made the decision to hide them, and he won't back off. (At least, that's the rumor.)

I also know that hundreds — probably thousands — of *Microsoft employees* passed along the ILOVEYOU virus, primarily because they couldn't see the file name extension that would've warned them. Bah. Bad decision, Bill.

(If you haven't yet told Windows XP to show you file name extensions, take a minute now and hop to Book I, Chapter 2, and get Windows XP to dance to *your* tune.)

What You Don't Have to Read

Throughout this book, I've gone to great lengths to separate out the "optional" reading from the "required" reading. If you want to learn about a topic or solve a specific problem, follow along in the main part of the text. You can skip the icons and sidebars as you go, unless one happens to catch your eye.

On the other hand, if you know a topic pretty well but want to make sure you've caught all the high points, skip down the icons and make sure they register. If they don't, glance at the surrounding text.

Sidebars stand as "graduate courses" for those who are curious about a specific topic — or stand knee-deep in muck, searching for a way out.

Foolish Assumptions

I don't make many assumptions about you, dear reader, except for the fact that you're obviously intelligent, well-informed, discerning, and of impeccable taste. That's why you chose this book, eh?

Okay, okay. Least I can do is butter you up a bit. Here's the straight scoop. If you've never used Windows before, bribe your neighbor (or, better, your neighbor's kids) to teach you how to do three things:

+ Play solitaire
+ Get on the World Wide Web
+ Shut down Windows and turn off the computer

That covers it. If you can play solitaire, you know how to turn on your computer, use the Start button, click, and double-click. Once you're on the Web, well, heaven help us all. And if you know that you need to click Start in order to Stop, you're well on your way to achieving Dummy Enlightenment.

And *that* begins with Book I, Chapter 1.

Organization

Windows XP All-in-One Desk Reference For Dummies contains nine books, each of which gives a thorough airing of a specific topic. If you're looking for information on a specific Windows XP topic, check the headings in the Table of Contents or refer to the index.

By design, this book enables you to get as much (or as little) information as you need at any particular moment. Want to know how to jimmy your Minesweeper score to amaze your boss and confound your co-workers? Look at Book I, Chapter 5. Worried about cookies? Try Book IX, Chapter 3. Also by design, *Windows XP All-in-One Desk Reference For Dummies* is a reference that you reach for again and again whenever some new question about Windows XP comes up.

Here are the nine books, and what they contain:

Book I: A Windows XP Overview: What Windows can and can't do. What's inside a PC, and how does Windows control it? Do you really need Windows XP? How do you upgrade? What is activation, and why you should be concerned. Adding users. Manipulating files. Using the Windows Taskbar and shortcuts. Getting help. Performing searches. Cheating at the Windows games. Burning CDs. Maintaining a Windows XP system. The care and feeding of disks. Using the built-in applications for word processing and image manipulation. How is XP/Pro different from XP/Home?

Book II: Customizing Your Windows eXPerience: Personalizing the desktop with themes, colors, backgrounds, and the like. Avoiding Active Desktop. Mouse Pointers. Screen Savers. ClearType. Changing the Start menu. Using the Quick Launch toolbar.

Book III: Windows XP and the Internet: Expanding your reach through the Internet. Outlook Express: your tool for managing e-mail and newsgroups. Chatting and more with Windows Messenger.

Book IV: Adventures with Internet Explorer: Connecting to the Internet. Working with Internet Explorer. Working with Web pages intelligently. E-mailing, saving, and printing Web pages. Using the History folder. Maintaining favorites. Searching. Personalizing Internet Explorer. Speeding it up. Blocking undesirable content.

Book V: Touring the Services of America Online: Up and running with AOL. Screen names and passwords. Setting your profile. Creating and sending messages. Sending and receiving files. Using the Address Book. Filtering spam. Newsgroups, Chat, and Instant Messenger.

Book VI: Connecting with Microsoft Network: How MSN Explorer compares to AOL. Using Passport to get an ID and set your password. Setting up your own home page. E-mail and newsgroups.

Book VII: Adding and Using Other Hardware: Cameras, scanners, printers, audio, memory, monitors, and more. Choosing the right products and getting them to work.

Book VIII: Joining the Multimedia Mix: Windows Media Player, Windows Movie Maker, digital cameras, and other video devices. Ripping from audio CDs. Burning your own CDs. Digital licensing. Printing and sharing pictures.

Book IX: Setting Up a Network with Windows XP: Concepts behind peer-to-peer and client/server networking. How to build your own network quickly, easily and reliably. Details on viruses and other things that go bump in the night. Firewalls. Protecting your privacy on the Internet.

Icons

Some of the points in *Windows XP All-in-One Desk Reference For Dummies* merit your special attention. I set those points off with icons.

When I'm jumping up and down on one foot with an idea so absolutely cool I can't stand it any more, that's when I stick a Tip icon in the margin. You can browse through any chapter and hit the very highest points by jumping from Tip to Tip.

You don't need to memorize the stuff marked with this icon, but you should try to remember that there's something special lurking about.

Achtung! Cuidado! Thar be tygers here! Any place you see a Warning icon, you can be sure that I've been burnt — badly — in the past. Mind your fingers. These are really, really mean suckers.

Okay, so I'm a geek. I admit it. Sure, I love to poke fun at geeks. But I'm a modern, new-age sensitive guy, in touch with my inner geekiness. Sometimes I just can't help but let it out, ya know? That's where the Technical Stuff icon comes in. If you get all tied up in knots about techy stuff, pass these by. (For the record, I managed to write this whole book without telling you that an IP Address consists of a unique 32-bit combination of network ID and host ID, expressed as a set of four decimal numbers with each octet separated by periods. See? I *can* restrain myself sometimes.)

Where to Go from Here

That's about it. Time for you to crack the book open and have at it.

Don't forget to sign up for my newsletters. They'll keep you up-to-date on all the Windows XP news you need to know — including notes about this book — and you're sure to find a tip or two in every issue that you can use right away. The Woody's Watches are free and worth every penny. Hit www.woodyswatch.com.

See ya! talk2woody@woodyswatch.com.

Book I

A Windows XP Overview

The 5th Wave   By Rich Tennant

Before installing Windows XP,
Dwayne prepares to partition
the hard drive.

Contents at a Glance

Chapter 1: Introducing Windows XP

In This Chapter

✔ **Where Windows XP fits into The Grand Scheme of Things**

✔ **What Windows can (and can't) do for you**

✔ **Dissecting your computer**

✔ **Installing and activating Windows**

✔ **Getting help**

So you're sitting in front of your computer, and this thing called Windows XP is staring at you. The screen you see — the one with the peoples' names on it — is called a Welcome screen, but it doesn't say "Welcome" or "Howdy" or even "Sit down and get to work, bucko." It says only that you have to click your user name in order to start, but you don't have any idea what a user name is, why you have to have one, what Windows has to do with anything, and why in the %$#@! you can't bypass all this garbage, log on, and get your mail.

Good for you. That's the right attitude.

Someday, I swear, you'll be able to pull a PC out of the box, plug it into the wall, turn it on, and get your mail — bang, bang, bang, just like that, in ten seconds flat. If you want the computer to do something, you'll pick up the mouse and say, "Computer, get me my mail," just like Scotty in the *Star Trek* movies. Except you won't need the mouse. Probably won't have to plug the computer into the wall, either.

No matter what anyone may tell you, computers are still in their infancy. Maybe my son will see the day when they're truly easy to use, when the marketing hype about "intuitive" and "seamless" and "user friendly" actually comes true. I doubt that I will.

In the meantime, those of us who are stuck in the early 21st century have to make do with PCs that grow obsolete before you can unpack them, software that's so ornery you find yourself arguing with it, and Internet connections that surely involve turtles carrying bits on their backs.

Windows XP is one of the most sophisticated computer programs ever made. It cost more money to develop and took more people to build than any computer program, ever. So why is it so blasted hard to use?

Why doesn't it do what you want it to do the first time? For that matter, why do you need it at all?

That's what this chapter is all about.

What Windows Does (And Doesn't)

Some day you'll get really, really mad at Windows. I guarantee it. When you feel like putting your fist through the computer screen, tossing your XP CD in a bonfire, or hiring an expensive Windows expert to drive out the devils within (insist on a Microsoft Certified System Exorcist, of course), read through this section. It may help you understand why and how Windows has limitations. It also may help you communicate with the geeky rescue team that tries to bail you out, whether you rely on the store that sold you the PC, the smelly guy in the apartment downstairs, or your eight-year-old daughter's nerdy classmate.

Hardware and software

At the most fundamental level, all computer stuff comes in one of two flavors: either it's hardware, or it's software. *Hardware* is anything you can touch — a computer screen, a mouse, a CD. *Software* is everything else: e-mail messages, that letter to your Aunt Martha, pictures of your last vacation, programs like Microsoft Office. If you have a roll of film developed and put on a CD, the shiny, round CD is hardware — you can touch it — but the pictures themselves are software. Get the difference?

Windows XP is software. You can't touch it.

Your PC, on the other hand, is hardware. Kick the computer screen and your toe hurts. Drop the big box on the floor and it smashes into a gazillion pieces. That's hardware.

Chances are very good that one of the major PC manufacturers — Dell, Compaq, Gateway, IBM, Toshiba, Sony, HP, and the like — made your hardware. Microsoft, and Microsoft alone, makes Windows XP. The PC manufacturers don't make Windows. Microsoft doesn't make PCs, although it does make other kinds of hardware — video game boxes, keyboards, mice, and a few other odds and ends.

When you first set up your PC, Windows had you click "I accept" to a licensing agreement that's long enough to wrap around the Empire State Building. If you're curious about what you accepted, a printed copy of the End User License Agreement is in the box that your PC came in or in the CD packaging (if you bought Windows XP separately from your computer). If you can't find your copy, choose Start➪Help and Support. Type **eula** in the Search box and press Enter.

When you bought your computer, you paid for a license to use one copy of Windows on the PC that you bought. The PC manufacturer paid Microsoft a royalty so that it could sell you Windows along with your PC. You may think that you got Windows from, say, Dell — indeed, you may have to contact Dell for technical support on Windows questions — but, in fact, Windows came from Microsoft.

Now you know who to blame, for sure.

Why do I have to run Windows?

The short answer: You *don't* have to run Windows.

The PC you have is a dumb box. (You needed me to tell you that, eh?) In order to get the dumb box to do anything worthwhile, you need a computer program that takes control of the PC and makes it do things such as show Web pages on the screen, respond to mouse clicks, or print ransom notes. An *operating system* controls the dumb box and makes it do worthwhile things, in ways that mere humans can understand.

Without an operating system, the computer can sit in a corner and count to itself, or put profound messages on the screen, such as `Non-system disk or disk error. Insert system disk and press any key when ready`. If you want your computer to do more than that, though, you need an operating system.

Windows is not the only operating system in town. The single largest competitor to Windows is an operating system called Linux. Some people (I'm told) actually prefer Linux to Windows, and the debates between pro-Windows and pro-Linux camps can become rather heated. Suffice it to say that, oh, 99 percent of all individual PC users stick with Windows. You probably will, too.

A terminology survival kit

Some terms pop up so frequently that you'll find it worthwhile to memorize them, or at least understand where they come from. That way, you won't be caught flatfooted when your first-grader comes home and asks if he can download a program from the Internet.

A *program* is *software* (see preceding section) that works on a computer. Windows, the *operating system* (see preceding section), is a program. So are computer games, Microsoft Office, Microsoft Word (which is the word processor part of Office), Internet Explorer (the Web browser in Windows), the Windows Media Player, those nasty viruses you've heard about, that screen saver with splatting suicidal bungee jumping cows, and so on.

If you really want to drive your techie friends nuts, the next time you have a problem with your computer, tell them that the hassles occur when you're "running Microsoft." They won't have any idea if you mean Windows, Office, Word, Outlook, or any of a gazillion other programs.

A special kind of program called a *driver* makes specific pieces of hardware work with the operating system. For example, your computer's printer has a driver; your monitor has a driver; your mouse has a driver; Tiger Woods has a driver. Several, actually, and he makes a living with them. Would that we were all so talented.

Sticking a program on your computer, and setting it up so that it works, is called *installing*.

When you crank up a program — that is, get it going on your computer — you can say you *started* it, *launched* it, *ran* it, or *executed* it. They all mean the same thing.

If the program quits the way it's supposed to, you can say it *stopped, finished, ended, exited,* or *terminated*. Again, all of these terms mean the same thing. If the program stops with some sort of weird error message, you can say it *crashed, died, cratered, croaked, went belly up, GPFed* (techspeak for "generated a General Protection Fault" — don't ask), or employ any of a dozen colorful but unprintable epithets. If the program just sits there and you can't get it to do anything, you can say the program *froze, hung, stopped responding,* or *went into a loop*.

A *bug* is something that doesn't work right. (A bug is not a virus! Viruses work right far too often.) Admiral Grace Hopper often repeated the story of a moth being found in a relay of an old Mark II computer. The moth was taped into the technician's log book on September 9, 1947, with the annotation "1545 Relay #70 Panel F (moth) in relay. First actual case of bug being found."

The people who invented all of this terminology think of the Internet as being some great blob in the sky — it's "up," as in "up in the sky." So if you send something from your computer to the Internet, you're *uploading*. If you take something off the Internet and put it on your computer, you're *downloading*.

That should cover about 90 percent of the buzzwords you hear in common parlance.

And then you have *wizards*. Windows comes with lots of 'em. They guide you through complex procedures, moving one step at a time. Typically, wizards have three buttons on the bottom of each screen: Back, Next (or Finish), and Cancel (see Figure 1-1). Wizards remember what you've chosen as you go from step to step, making it easy to experiment a bit, change your mind, back up, and try a different setting, without getting all the check boxes confused.

A brief history on booting

You probably know that the process of getting your computer started — from the time you hit the On button until the time the computer starts responding — is called *booting*, but do you know why? It's an old term, dating back to the dawn of computing history. When a computer starts, it has to bring in a teensy-tiny program that, in turn, brings in all the other programs that make the computer work. The process resembles pulling yourself up by your own bootstraps — the tiny program is called a bootstrap loader, whence *boot*. The name stuck.

Figure 1-1:
The Add
Printer
Wizard
helps you
connect
printers
to your
computer.

Where We've Been

Unlike Windows ME (which is a barely warmed over remake of Windows 98) and Windows 2000 (which should've been called Windows NT 5.0) Windows XP is quite different from anything that has come before. To understand why XP works so differently, you need to understand the genetic cesspool from which it emerged.

Let's start at the beginning.

Microsoft licensed the first PC operating system, called DOS, to IBM in late 1981. MS-DOS sold like hotcakes for a number of reasons, not the least of which is that it was the only game in town. None of this sissy graphical stuff; DOS demanded that you type, and type, and type again, in order to get anything done.

The rise of Windows

The 'Softies only started developing Windows in earnest when the company discovered that it needed an operating system to run Excel, its spreadsheet program. Windows 1.0 shipped in November 1985. It was slow, bloated, and unstable — some things never change, eh? — but if you wanted to run Excel, you had to have Windows.

Excel 2.0 and Windows 2.0 shipped in late 1987. This breathtaking, revolutionary new version of Windows let you overlap windows — place one window on top of another — and it took advantage of the PC/XT's advanced computer chip, the 80286. Version 2.1 (also called Windows 286) shipped in June 1988, and some people discovered that it spent more time working than crashing. My experience was, uh, somewhat different. Windows 286 came on a single diskette.

Do you have Macintosh friends who like to taunt you about the ways Microsoft "stole" ideas from the old Mac systems? The next time those revisionist historians start kicking sand in your face, make sure you set the record straight. The fact is that both Apple and Microsoft stole many of their ideas from Xerox — specifically the Star machine built at Xerox's Palo Alto Research Center in the late 1970s and early 1980s. The Star had a desktop, with icons and overlapping windows. It used a mouse, supported "point and click" interactions, popped up menus, ran on dialog boxes, used an Ethernet network just like the one you swear at today, and introduced the laser printer.

Windows 3.0 arrived in May, 1990, and the computer industry changed forever. Microsoft finally had a hit on its hands to rival the old MS-DOS. When Windows 3.1 came along in April 1992, it rapidly became the most widely used operating system in history. In October 1992, Windows for Workgroups 3.1 (which I loved to call "Windows for Warehouses") started rolling out, with support for networking, shared files and printers, internal e-mail, and other features you take for granted today. Some of the features worked. Sporadically. A much better version, Workgroups for Windows 3.11, became available in November 1993. It caught on in the corporate world. Sporadically.

eNTer NT

At its heart, Windows 3.x was built on top of MS-DOS, and that caused all sorts of headaches: DOS simply wasn't stable or versatile enough to make Windows a rock-solid operating system. Bill Gates figured, all the way back in 1988, that DOS would never be able to support an advanced version of Windows, so he hired a guy named Dave Cutler to build a new version of Windows from scratch. At the time, Dave led the team that built the VMS operating system for Digital Equipment Corp's DEC computers.

When Dave's all-new version of Windows shipped five years later in August 1993, Windows NT 3.1 ("New Technology"; yes, the first version number was 3.1) greeted the market with a thud. It was awfully persnickety about the kinds of hardware it would support, and it didn't play games worth squat.

NT and the "old" Windows

For the next eight years, two entirely different lineages of Windows co-existed.

The old DOS/Windows 3.1 branch became Windows 95 (shipped in August 1995, "probably the last version of Windows based on DOS"), Windows 98 (June 1998, "absolutely the last version of Windows based on DOS, for sure"), and then Windows ME (Millennium Edition, September 2000, "no, honest, this is really, really the last version of Windows based on DOS").

On the New Technology side of the fence, Windows NT 3.1 begat Windows NT 3.5 (September 1994), which begat Windows NT 4.0 (August 1996). Many companies still use Windows NT 3.51 and NT 4 for their servers — the machines that anchor corporate networks. In February 2000, Microsoft released Windows 2000, which confused the living daylights out of everybody: In spite of its name, Windows 2000 is the next version of Windows NT and has nothing at all in common with Windows 98 or ME.

Microsoft made oodles of money milking the DOS-based Windows cash cow and waited patiently while sales on the NT side gradually picked up. Windows NT 5.0, er, 2000 still didn't play games worth squat, and some hardware gave it heartburn, but Windows 2000 rapidly became the operating system of choice for most businesses and at least a few home users.

Merging the branches

Windows XP — in my opinion, the first must-have version of Windows since Windows 95 — officially shipped in October 2001. Twenty years after Microsoft tip-toed into the big time with MS-DOS, the Windows XP juggernaut blew away everything in sight.

Some people think that Windows XP (the XP stands for eXPerience, according to the marketing folks) represents a melding or blending of the two Windows lineages: a little ME here, a little 2000 there, with a side of 98 thrown in for good measure.

Ain't so.

Windows XP is 100 percent, bona fide NT. Period. Not one single part of Windows ME — or any of the other DOS-based Windows versions, for that matter, not to mention DOS itself — is in Windows XP. Not one.

That's good news and bad news. First, the good news: If you can get XP to work at all on your old computer, or if you buy a new PC that's designed to use Windows XP, your new system will almost certainly be considerably more stable than it would be with Windows ME or any of its progenitors. The bad news: If you learned how to get around a problem in Windows ME (or 98 or 95), you may not be able to use the same tricks in Windows XP. The surface may look the same. The plumbing is radically different.

Microsoft went to a lot of effort to make Windows XP look like Windows ME. But that similarity is only skin deep. Beneath the façade, Windows XP is a gussied up version of Windows NT/2000. XP is *not* a descendant of Windows ME or Windows 98, even though it's marketed that way. Tricks that work in Windows ME or 98 may or may not work in Windows XP.

The future of Windows

Another big shift is afoot in Redmond, Washington (Microsoft's headquarters), and it has more to do with marketing than anything else. In a nutshell, Microsoft wants to get out of the business of selling software and into the business of renting it. Along the way, Microsoft wants to sink its teeth into a lot of lucrative markets by acting as an electronic go-between and charging for the service.

That's where the next Microsoft initiative — called .NET ("dot net") — is headed. Before too long, Windows as we know it won't be nearly as important (or as profitable!) as it currently is. Control of the Windows desktop will take a back seat to control of the glue that holds the Internet together. And you can bet that Microsoft will be in the glue business.

Some of the features you see in Windows XP — NET Passport being a good example — represent Microsoft's first steps in the new direction. Many of the battles that left their scars on Windows XP — the tussle over various digital audio standards, say, or the ongoing battle between AOL and Microsoft, waged on both the Web browser and instant messaging fronts — will affect our computing future in profound ways.

Now's a great time to dig into Windows XP and get to know it. Future versions of Windows may well seem anticlimactic, compared to this one.

Anatomy of a Computer

Here's how it usually goes. You figure you need to buy a new PC. So you spend a couple of weeks brushing up on the details — bits and bytes and kilobytes and megabytes and gigabytes — and comparison shopping. You end up at your local Computers Were Us shop, and this guy behind the counter convinces you that the absolutely best bargain you'll ever see is sitting right here, right now, and you'd better take it quick before somebody else nabs it.

Your eyes glaze over as you look at yet another spec sheet and try to figure out one last time if a RAM is a ROM and how a CD-R differs from a CD-RW. In the end, you figure the guy behind the counter must know what he's doing, so you plunk down your plastic and pray you got a good deal.

The next Sunday morning you look in the paper and discover you could've bought twice as much machine for half as much money. The only thing you know for sure is that your PC is hopelessly out of date, and the next time you'll be smarter about the whole process.

If that describes your experiences, relax. It happens to everybody. Take solace in the fact that you bought twice as much machine for the same amount of money as the poor schmuck who went through the same process last month.

In this section I'm going to try to give you just enough information about the inner workings of your PC to be able to figure out what you have to do with Windows. The details will change from week to week. But these are the basics.

Inside the big box

The big box that your computer lives in is sometimes called a *CPU,* meaning Central Processing Unit (see Figure 1-2). Right off the bat, you're bound to get confused, unless somebody clues you in on one important detail: The main computer chip inside that big box is *also* called a CPU. I prefer to call the big box "The PC" because of the naming ambiguity, but you have probably thought of a few better names.

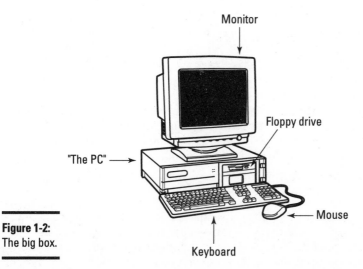

Figure 1-2:
The big box.

Monitor

Floppy drive

"The PC" →

Mouse

Keyboard

The big box contains many parts and pieces (and no small amount of dust and dirt), but the crucial, central element inside every PC is the *motherboard* (see Figure 1-3). Attached to the motherboard you'll find:

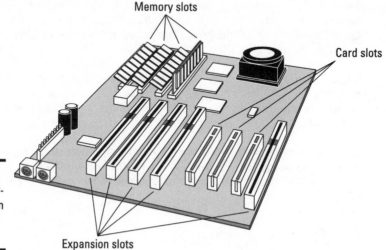

Memory slots

Card slots

Expansion slots

Figure 1-3:
The mother-
board sits in
the middle
of it all.

✦ **The *processor* or CPU:** This gizmo does all the computing. It's probably from Intel or AMD or one of their competitors. People who sell comput-ers rate the processors by speed, measured in MHz (megahertz) or GHz (gigaherz, 1 GHz = 1,024 MHz). Windows XP runs like a slug on anything slower than 300 MHz or so.

If you're buying a new computer, the speed really doesn't mean much, unless you're designing airplane wings or reshooting *Jurassic Park.* Ignore the salesperson. If you want to improve Windows XP perform-ance, your money should go to more memory (see next) or a fast Internet connection.

✦ **Memory chips and places to put them:** Memory is measured in MB (megabytes). Windows XP runs on a machine with 64 MB — I've done it — but you usually want 128 MB or more. Most computers allow you to add more memory to them, and boosting your computer's memory to 128 MB from 64 MB makes it much snappier.

✦ **Lots of other stuff:** You'll never have to play with this other stuff, unless you're very unlucky.

Never let a salesperson talk you into eviscerating your PC and upgrading the CPU: A 900 MHz PC doesn't run a whole lot faster than a 500 MHz PC. Memory upgrades don't mean much beyond 256 MB: You'll see a noticeable improvement in performance up to the 256 MB mark, especially if you run multiple memory-hungry applications at the same time (I won't mention Office 2000 and Office XP by name), but very little improvement beyond that. Instead of nickel-and-diming yourself to death on little upgrades, wait until you can afford a new PC, and give away your old one.

If you decide to get more memory, have the company that sells you the memory install it. The process is simple, quick, and easy — if you know what you're doing. Having the dealer install the memory also puts the monkey on their back if a memory chip doesn't work or a bracket gets snapped.

What you see, what you get

The *computer monitor* or *screen* — you may think of it as a hoity-toity TV — uses technology that's quite different from what you have in your television set. A TV scans lines across the screen from left to right, with hundreds of them stacked on top of each other. Colors on each individual line vary all over the place. The near-infinitely variable color on a TV combined with a comparatively small number of lines makes for pleasant, but fuzzy, pictures.

By contrast (pun absolutely intended, of course), a computer monitor works with dots of light, called *pixels*. Each pixel can have a different color, but the maximum number of different colors that can appear on the screen at one time is limited. As a result, computer monitors are much sharper than TV tubes, but if the number of on-screen colors is restricted, pictures shown on the monitor won't look as good as they would on a TV set.

Although it's theoretically possible to use a TV set as a makeshift computer monitor, the result leaves much to be desired. So-called *scan converters* allow you to plug a TV set into the back of your computer, but text ends up so murky that it's hardly readable. Very expensive converters sharpen text — but in the end usually cost more than the price of a new monitor.

Most people set up Windows XP to run at 1024 x 768 pixels — that is, their monitors show 1024 pixels across the screen, with 768 running up and down. Some folks have screens (and eyes!) that are good enough to run 1280 x 1024. Others limp along at 800 x 600. The more pixels you can cram on a screen — that is, the higher the *screen resolution* — the more information you can pack on the screen. That's important if you commonly have more than one word processing document open at a time, for example. At 800 x 600, two open Word documents placed side-by-side look big but fuzzy, like viewing them through a dirty magnifying glass. At 1280 x 1024, those same two documents look sharp, but the text may be so small that you have to squint to make it out.

A special-purpose computer stuck on a board called a *graphics adapter* creates everything that's shown on your computer's screen. The graphics adapter has to juggle all the pixels and all the colors. People who sell graphics adapters rate them in accordance with both their resolution and their *color depth,* and the two are interrelated: A graphics adapter that can handle 1024 x 768 pixels on the screen with 64,000 colors showing simultaneously may be able to show 1280 x 1024 pixels, but only 256 simultaneous colors.

If you don't like the graphics adapter that shipped with your computer, you can always buy a new one. But beware of one big potential problem. The drivers that ship with new graphics adapters — the programs that allow Windows XP to control the graphics adapter — are notorious for being buggy and unstable. Think twice before buying a new graphics adapter, and always update the driver to the latest version by following the instructions on the manufacturer's Web site.

Flat panel displays — the thin screens used universally in portable computers and increasingly on desktops — work differently, but also have limitations on their resolution and color depth.

Computer monitors are sold by size, measured diagonally, like TV sets. Just like TV sets, the only way to pick a good computer screen over a run-of-the-mill one is to compare them side by side or to follow the recommendation of someone who has.

Managing disks

Your PC's memory chips hold information only temporarily: Turn off the electricity, and the contents of main memory goes bye-bye. If you want to re-use your work, keeping it around after the plug has been pulled, you have to save it, typically on a disk. The following are the most common types of disks:

✦ **Floppies:** Hard to believe they're still alive after all these years, but the ubiquitous 1.44 MB floppy disk drive is still going strong.

You probably know how to put a floppy disk into a drive (right-side up with the slidey-metal-thing pointing into the PC). You may not know how to get a recalcitrant floppy out of the drive. Sometimes the slide starts bowing, and the floppy hangs when you press the eject button. If that happens to you, get a long pair of thin tweezers — stamp collector's tongs work great — turn off your PC, unplug it, grab the diskette between the prongs of the tweezers and gently pry the diskette out. You have to get the tweezers all the way down beyond the tip of the slide, so longer is definitely better.

✦ **Hard drives:** Get the biggest, cheapest one(s) you can; electronic pictures swallow up an enormous amount of space. Speed doesn't matter much, and the technology (ATA, EIDE, SCSI) matters even less.

If you buy a new hard drive, have the dealer install it. You have to worry about lots of permutations and combinations, and it simply isn't worth the effort. Life's too short.

✦ **CD and DVD drives:** Of course, these drives work with CDs and DVDs, which can be filled with data or contain music or movies. Although Windows XP will play an audio CD automatically, you may have to jump through some extra hoops to get it to play DVDs. See the section on "Multimedia galore," later in this chapter, for details.

✦ **CD-R drives:** These drives let you create *(burn)* your own CDs. Once burned, twice shy. Uh, after you burn a CD in a CD-R drive, you generally can't re-burn it.

✦ **CD-RW drives:** These drives not only allow you to burn CDs; they're also reusable. The CD-RW drive, in conjunction with CD-RW disks, lets you burn and re-burn to your heart's content.

Most audio CD players — like the one you probably have in your car, or in your room — will play only CDs that are burned with a CD-R drive. You can't re-burn audio CDs.

✦ **CD-R/CD-RW drives:** Many drives nowadays can create both CD-R disks and CD-RW disks, just to confuse everybody. You need CD-R disks if you're going to burn audio CDs. You probably want CD-RW disks for everything else, even though the blank disks themselves cost more than CD-R disks.

This list is by no means definitive: There are Jaz disks, Zip drives, and recordable media that sing till the cows come home.

Making PC connections

Your PC connects to the outside world using a bewildering variety of cables and connectors. The most common are as follows:

✦ **USB or Universal Serial Bus cables:** These cables have a flat connector that plugs into your PC. The other end is usually shaped like a D, but different pieces of hardware have different *terminators*. ("I'll be back...") USB is the connector of choice for just about any kind of hardware — printers, scanners, MP3 players, Palm/pocket computers, portable disk drives, even mice. If you run out of USB connections on the back of your PC, get a USB hub and plug away.

✦ **RJ-45 connectors:** These are the most common kind of network connectors. They look like overweight telephone plugs (see Figure 1-4). One end plugs into your PC, typically into a *NIC* (Network Interface Card, say "nick"), a network connector on the motherboard, or a network connector on a card that slides into a portable (a so-called "PC Card" or "PCMCIA Card"). The other end plugs into your network's hub (see Figure 1-5), or possibly into a cable modem, DSL box, or other Internet connection sharing device.

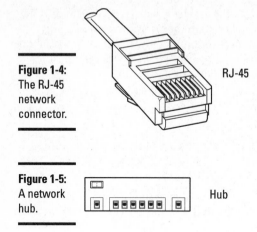

Figure 1-4:
The RJ-45
network
connector.

RJ-45

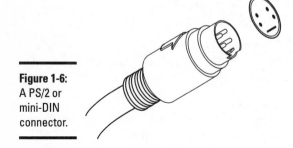

Figure 1-5:
A network
hub.

Hub

✦ **PS/2 or mini-DIN connectors:** These are round connectors with six pins and a plastic hump that prevents you from getting the connector twisted around in the wrong direction (see Figure 1-6). Ancient technology that works great. Commonly found on keyboards and mice.

Figure 1-6:
A PS/2 or
mini-DIN
connector.

TECHNICAL STUFF

If you have a mouse and a keyboard, both with PS/2 connectors, but your PC sports only one PS/2 slot, not to worry! Most cable manufacturers have Y connectors that allow you to attach two PS/2 devices to a single port. Surprisingly, both the mouse and the keyboard can co-exist with nary a hiccup. Try www.cablestogo.com.

✦ **Parallel and serial ports:** These are the long (parallel, 25-pin, with 13 pins on top and 12 on the bottom) and short (serial, 9-pin, five on top and four on the bottom) connections on the back of your computer. The serial port is notoriously slow, and both kinds sometimes fall apart — which is particularly disconcerting when you unscrew a connector and a nut falls off inside your computer. If you have a choice, choose USB.

Futzing with sound

If you plug your computer's speakers directly into the back of the PC, the whole process won't strain any little gray cells (see Figure 1-7).

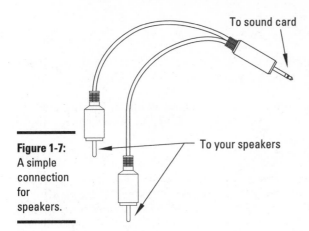

To sound card

To your speakers

Figure 1-7:
A simple
connection
for
speakers.

Most Windows XP users care about sound, and many find that tiny, tinny speakers meticulously paired with an under-aspirated amp sound about as bad as Leonard Nimoy singing *The Star Spangled Banner*. (No offense, Leonard, okay?)

Chances are pretty good that you are running Windows XP on a PC with at least a little oomph in the audio department. If so, you have to be concerned about four different sound jacks, because each one does something different. Your machine may not have all four. (Are you feeling inadequate yet?) Here's how they are usually marked, although sometimes you have to root around in the documentation to find details:

✦ **Line in:** A stereo input jack. Feeds a stereo signal into the PC. Not used very often, but it can be handy if you need to record a radio program or digitize something on audio tape.

✦ **Mike in:** Almost exclusively used for voice-recognition systems, where you speak into the mike and the computer attempts to convert your speech into text. There are lots of gotchas, particularly when selecting microphones. See `www.woodyswatch.com/office/archtemplate.asp?v6-n30` for details.

✦ **Line out:** A stereo output jack that bypasses the computer's internal amplifier. This is the source for the highest-quality sound your computer can produce.

✦ **Headphone or speaker out:** Goes through the internal amplifier. Use this jack for headphones or speakers, but avoid it in all other situations.

PC manufacturers love to extol the virtues of their advanced sound systems, but the simple fact is that you can hook up a rather plain-vanilla PC to a home stereo and get great sound. Just connect the "line out" jack on the back of your PC to the "Aux in" jack on your home stereo. Voilà!

Do You Need Windows XP?

If you haven't yet decided whether Windows XP is worth the plunge, this section should help you make up your mind.

You can safely skip this section, unless you have to justify the upgrade to the boss — or your spouse. Trust me. You want Windows XP. Here's why:

It just works

In the vast majority of cases, Windows XP works far more reliably than any other version of Windows. One of the main reasons why: Windows XP successfully protects itself from programs that try to overwrite its crucial files. The end — or at least the severe curtailing — of "DLL hell" goes a long way toward increasing Windows XP's reliability.

Although rooting around inside Windows XP is certainly an order of magnitude more complex than in Windows 98 or ME, you're much less likely to dig into the bowels of XP, unless you're running some really weird, relatively old hardware or trying to coax a hopelessly ancient game into action.

Multimedia galore

If you want to use your computer for music, pictures, video, and the like, Windows XP has plenty of good news for you: Microsoft finally gets it. Well, more than it used to, anyway.

One of the most controversial parts of XP is its limited support (some would say "lack of support") for the MP3 audio format. A lot of misinformation is floating around about XP and MP3, so let me set the record straight:

✦ If you have MP3 files, Windows XP will play them, no hassle, no sweat. You can e-mail MP3 files, burn CDs full of them, copy and trade them to your heart's content, and XP helps you every inch of the way.

✦ On the other hand, if you are trying to convert audio CD tracks to MP3 format (a process called *ripping*), Windows XP won't help much — for many reasons, but two stand out:

  • Microsoft would have to pay a royalty for the technology that allows audio CD tracks to be converted to MP3. Microsoft doesn't want to pay a royalty for every copy of Windows XP that's sold, so it doesn't ship fully functional MP3 ripping technology in the box with Windows XP. You have to pay extra for it, find the ripper somewhere else and install it on your machine, or get the ripper some other way — perhaps along with your MP3 player.

- Microsoft has no incentive for building MP3 ripping technology into Windows XP. Some wags (this one included) feel that Microsoft could've done something more to support MP3 ripping if it wanted to badly enough. But it doesn't want to. Microsoft wants the world to change to its own WMA audio file format, for a bunch of reasons, not the least of which is the fact that WMA discourages piracy, and Microsoft wants to discourage piracy.

✦ No matter where you stand on the ethical questions surrounding piracy, Microsoft can clearly make a lot of money helping companies sell (non-pirated) music files. It doesn't make squat from pirated copies.

Windows XP does not include DVD support, straight out of the box. Again, licensing considerations take the brunt of the blame. Unless DVD playback software came with your DVD player or PC, you have to find, pay for, and install DVD playback software before Windows XP will play DVDs.

Windows XP also includes digital camera support that's automatic, full-featured, and probably better than the software that shipped with your camera. Add the slide show feature built into Windows Explorer, and digital imaging takes a giant leap forward.

Easy multi-user support

Windows XP/Home makes setting up multiple users on the same machine very easy:

✦ Each user can have his or her own password or decide not to use a password at all.

✦ With XP/Home, you don't have to memorize user names or passwords: one click and you're in.

✦ You can switch among users quickly and easily. So if your daughter wants to check her Hotmail quickly while you go get a sandwich, all it takes is a click.

✦ Your programs keep running when you switch users, unless you specifically close them down.

Windows XP/Pro, straight out of the box, retains the old you-gotta-know-yer-user-id-and-password-to-get-in bias, and it won't allow you to switch quickly between users, but in a corporate environment with centralized access controls that makes sense. (You can change XP/Pro to make it act like XP/Home, though — and vice-versa.)

Workgroups and domains

When you attach computers to each other, you can choose from two inherently different ways to go. In a *client/server network*, which Microsoft calls a *domain*, one computer (the server) controls access to all the others (the clients). On the other hand, in a *peer-to-peer network*, which Microsoft calls a *workgroup*, all of the computers are equal, with no single computer standing out above all the rest.

Client/server networks abound in large companies, where central control is crucial. Network Administrators set up security rules, grant access where needed, allow new users to get onto client PCs, and generally ride herd on the entire network. Usually the server(s) hold important corporate files and backup copies of key files on the client computers. Usually the major networked printers hang off of the server(s). Usually all Internet access goes through the server(s).

Usually.

Peer-to-peer networking, on the other hand, doesn't get hung up in the kind of security and central administration that client/server networks take for granted. For example, a typical user on a typical peer-to-peer network can share a disk drive so that anybody on the network can see it. On a client/server network, you'd usually have to call in the Network Administrator.

At the risk of over-simplifying, peer-to-peer networking works best in homes and small offices where security isn't a major concern. Client/server networking works best in larger companies with significant security needs — and a budget to match. Network Administrators don't come cheap.

Making networks easy

Windows XP finally delivers on Microsoft's promise to make simple networking simple. That's no small accomplishment, as anyone who's struggled with assembling and maintaining a network can readily attest. In most cases, putting together a small network of Windows XP, 2000, ME, and 98 PCs is as easy as connecting the wires and running a Wizard. Really.

The good news extends well beyond the mechanics of pulling together a network. Windows XP makes sharing an Internet connection among many machines easy, whether they're running Windows XP, 2000, ME, or even lowly Windows 98. Sharing a printer with any other computer on a network takes a few clicks. Sharing a disk drive takes even less effort.

Do you need Windows XP/Pro?

Windows XP/Pro costs a whole heckuvalot more than Windows XP/Home, but for many folks, both at home and at the office, XP/Home beats the pants off XP/Pro. The arguments, both, uh, Pro and Con, may get esoteric and techie very quickly. What's a Dummy to do?

Fortunately, the situation isn't nearly as difficult as you may think. In most situations, if you get to pick the version of Windows XP that's right for you, you want XP/Home. If somebody else makes the decision — presumably a corporate IT department or some such — they probably choose XP/Pro, simply because it fits into the existing PC network better.

You should buy XP/Pro if:

✦ You want to set up a secure, client/server network (see sidebar "Workgroups and domains"). If you think XP/Pro itself is expensive, wait until you see the bill for this one.

✦ Your company wants you to use XP/Pro. They probably have good reasons to spend the extra bucks, mostly centered around security, central administration, and automated backup.

✦ While you're on the road, you need to dial into your computer at work and use it directly from your laptop. That takes a feature called Remote Desktop, which runs only with XP/Pro.

✦ The machine you're currently using runs Windows 2000 Pro (or Windows NT 4), and you want to upgrade it directly to Windows XP, carrying across all of your settings.

You can upgrade directly from Windows 98 or Windows ME to either Windows XP/Home or XP/Pro, and bring all of your settings with you. See the next section, "Upgrading — A Brain Transplant."

XP/Pro comes in handy in a corporate environment in a few minor ways. For example, it handles Roaming Profiles, which let you log onto any computer on the network and retrieve your settings, and it has built-in security hooks that let you get at folders even when the server is not working (so-called Offline Folders) — but none of the other XP/Pro features are show stoppers.

Upgrading — A Brain Transplant

If your current machine runs Windows 98 or ME, you can upgrade to Windows XP by simply starting Windows, inserting the Windows XP CD into your CD drive and following the instructions.

If you decide that Windows XP isn't your cup of tea, you can remove it and restore your old Windows 98 or ME system, intact. Here's how:

1. **Choose Start➪Control Panel.**

2. **Click Add and Remove Programs.**

3. **Click Windows XP, and then click Add/Remove.**

4. **Pick the option to Uninstall Windows XP, and click Continue.**

If your current machine runs Windows NT 4 or Windows 2000, you can upgrade to Windows XP/Pro directly with the CD. However, you will not be able to automatically uninstall XP and reinstall NT 4 or 2000.

If your current machine runs Windows 95 or NT 3.x, you won't be able to upgrade. Your only option is to erase Windows from your hard drive (never a simple proposition) and perform a clean install, from scratch (see the section "Considering a clean install" for sobering enlightenment). Chances are good that your Windows 95 or NT 3.x system isn't powerful enough to run XP very well anyway. Far better to wait until you can afford a new PC, and get Windows XP pre-installed.

Windows Upgrade Advisor / Hardware Compatibility List

Microsoft keeps a master list of all hardware that's passed muster for Windows XP. The so-called Hardware Compatibility List ("HCL" to techies) contains the names of products that have received Microsoft's seal of approval. If you're thinking of upgrading your current computer to Windows XP or if you want to add new hardware to an existing PC, Windows XP compatibility is a bit, uh, important. You can browse through the list at `www.microsoft.com/hcl/default.asp`.

The hardware compatibility list must be taken with at least a small grain of salt. While it's true that hardware manufacturers sweat blood to meet Microsoft's stringent standards, the fact remains that any randomly chosen piece of hardware may refuse to behave itself, whether the cause is a conflict in another piece of hardware, in a lousy device driver, or the phase of the moon.

Before you upgrade an existing PC to Windows XP, you should check the machine to make sure there are no known problems. Microsoft distributes a program called the Windows XP Upgrade Advisor that reaches into the inner-most parts of your PC and reports on potential problems with the upgrade. You can download the XP/Home Upgrade Advisor from `www.microsoft.com/windowsxp/home/howtobuy/upgrading/advisor.asp`. The XP/Pro advisor is at `www.microsoft.com/windowsxp/pro/howtobuy/upgrading/advisor.asp`. You may also find a copy of both advisors on a free CD at your friendly local computer shop.

Considering a clean install

Windows XP is an enormously complex program. In the best of all possible worlds, if you upgrade from your current version of Windows — be it 98, ME, NT 4, or 2000 — to Windows XP, the upgrade routines successfully grab all of your old settings, get rid of the extraneous garbage that's floating around on your old machine, and install a stable, pristine copy of Windows XP, ready for you to take around the block.

Unfortunately, the world is not a pretty place, and your hard drive probably looks like a bit-strewn sewer. Historically, Windows has been considerably less stable for upgraders than for those who perform a *clean install* — wiping out the contents of the hard drive and starting all over again. All the flotsam and jetsam left from an old version of Windows invariably mucks up the works with the new version.

A clean install is not for the faint of heart. No matter how hard you try, you will lose data, somewhere, somehow — it always happens, even to those of us masochists who have been running clean installs for a decade. If you value everything on your computer, go for the simple upgrade. If you want your PC to run smoothly, think about a clean install.

The following is my general procedure for a clean install, on computers that can start from the CD drive, in very broad terms:

1. **Download and install Revelation from SnadBoy software at** `www.snadboy.com` **(see Figure 1-8).**

Use Revelation for a few days (or weeks!) to retrieve any passwords that you may have stashed away.

Figure 1-8: SnadBoy's Revelation lets you see passwords that appear as ***** on the screen.

2. **Make sure that you have current CDs for all the software that you normally use.**

If the programs require passwords/installation keys, you need the passwords, too.

3. **Back up everything. Twice.**

If you have a Windows XP computer handy, and you can attach it to the PC that you're upgrading through a network or a direct-connect cable, you may want to try a Vulcan Mind Meld, er, the Windows XP Migration Wizard. Use it to transfer all your files and settings over to the other PC, temporarily. Follow the instructions in the next section, "Using the

Migration Wizard," to pick up the settings before you perform the upgrade and stick them on the temporary machine. Then follow the instructions again to move them from the temporary PC back to your (freshly upgraded) original PC.

4. **Insert the Windows XP installation disk in the CD drive, and then choose Start⇨Shut Down to go through a full shut down.**

   Windows XP may offer to install itself while you're trying to shut down. If it does, click Cancel. Power off the PC and wait at least a full minute.

5. **Turn the power on.**

   If the PC is capable of starting ("booting") from the CD, you see a line on the screen that says something like `Press any key to boot from CD`. Press the Enter key.

6. **Go through the steps indicated by the installer to delete the primary partition.**

   That wipes out all the data on the hard drive.

7. **Pick your jaw up from the floor, kick yourself twice for being so obstinate, pat yourself on the back for starting out fresh, and follow through with the rest of the installation.**

   Windows XP does a good job of taking you through the steps. Just follow along. The only really tricky part of the installation: Windows XP has to restart your PC early in the installation process. When that happens, you'll probably get that `Press any key to boot from the CD` message again. This time — the second time you see the message — ignore it. Let Windows XP start itself from the hard drive.

Clean installs rate right up there with root canals and prostate exams. Nobody in their right mind will try one, unless they really want to make sure that Windows will run smoothly.

Using the Migration Wizard

Windows XP's Files and Settings Transfer Wizard (better known as the Migration Wizard) makes transferring certain kinds of settings and data files between two computers comparatively easy. It sounds great and works well, as long as you don't expect too much. You need to be aware of several limitations:

✦ The PC you're transferring files and settings "to" must be running Windows XP. If at all possible, it should be connected to the PC that you're transferring settings "from." The "from" PC can be running just about any version of Windows — Windows 95, 98, ME, NT 4, 2000, or XP.

The Files and Settings Transfer Wizard can send a humongous amount of data from one PC to another. You can schlep diskettes from one machine to another, if you have a few spare hours or days. Far better, though, is if you can get both PCs talking to each other on a network. Failing that, you can buy a special cable called a "Serial PC to PC Transfer Cable" that plugs into the serial slots on both PCs (the slots you may be using for printers). The Wizard will work with any of 'em.

✦ The Wizard can't install your old programs on your new PC. You have to do that yourself, manually, one at a time, generally from the original CDs that the programs came on.

If you use the Files and Settings Transfer Wizard but you don't install all of your old programs on your new PC, weird things may happen on the new PC. You may double-click on a file in Windows Explorer, for example, and have Windows XP say that it can't find the program associated with the file. Outlook may have trouble displaying a file attached to a message. Nothing earth-shattering will happen, mind you, but it can be annoying.

✦ The Wizard picks up only data files and some Windows Registry entries. That means you can't expect it to pull across all of your passwords, and some copy protection schemes (on games, for example) may go haywire.

On the plus side, though, the Files and Settings Transfer Wizard doesn't pick up much of the garbage that seems to accumulate in every Windows PC, which means you can use it without fear of gumming up your new computer.

Here are the kinds of things you can expect to go across in a transfer:

✦ Data files from your Windows Desktop, the My Documents folder (including My Pictures and My Sounds, if you have those in the My Documents folder), and the Shared Desktop and Documents folders.

✦ Other files scattered around your hard disk(s), as long as Windows recognizes them as common data files.

The Files and Settings Transfer Wizard really chooses which files to transfer based on the filename extension. It looks for filename extensions that are commonly associated with data files, such as .doc or .jpg. See the section on showing filename extensions in Book I, Chapter 2 for a lengthy tirade on this topic.

✦ Settings for Windows (desktop, screen savers, Taskbar options, and the like), Windows Explorer, Internet Explorer (including your list of Favorites), and Outlook Express.

✦ All of your Microsoft Office settings.

To use the Migration Wiz… er, the File and Settings Transfer Wizard:

1. **Make sure Windows XP is up and running on the "to" PC.**

   Get your hardware installed, set up your users, and run Windows XP long enough to be familiar with it.

2. **Log on the "to" PC as the user who's supposed to receive all the files and settings from the "from" PC.**

   If both the "to" and "from" PCs are connected to your network, choose Start⇨My Network Places or Start⇨My Computer to make sure that the network connection is up and kicking. If they aren't connected to the same network, get a Serial PC to PC Transfer Cable and attach it to the serial ports on both PCs.

3. **Choose Start⇨Files and Settings Transfer Wizard, if it's on the Start menu.**

   If it isn't, choose Start⇨All Programs⇨Accessories⇨System Tools⇨Files and Settings Transfer Wizard.

4. **Follow the steps in the Wizard (see Figure 1-9).**

   The exact steps vary depending on the method you're using to transfer the data. If you have many large documents or picture files, plan on spending a few hours. If you're transferring by diskette, don't be surprised if it takes a day.

Figure 1-9:
The Files
and Settings
Transfer
Wizard can
send most
(but not all!)
of your
important
information
from an old
PC to a
new one.

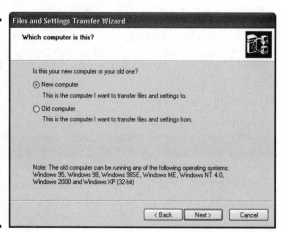

If you perform a scorched-earth clean install of Windows XP (see the preceding section), you can use the Files and Settings Transfer Wizard twice to drag most of your data (but none of your programs!) through the upgrade, even though you delete everything on your hard disk in the process of upgrading. All it takes is an intermediary machine running Windows XP that holds your settings while the old PC is wiped clean. For the first run of the Files and Settings Transfer Wizard, use the intermediary machine as the "to" machine. Then upgrade the old PC. Finally, run the Files and Settings Transfer Wizard again, this time using the intermediary machine as the "from" machine. Works like a champ.

Product Activation

When you buy a copy of Windows XP in a shrink-wrapped box, you're allowed to install it on one — and only one — PC.

When you buy a new PC with Windows XP pre-installed, Windows stays with the PC. You can't transfer Windows XP from the original, bundled machine to a different machine. Microsoft uses a technique called "BIOS locking" to make sure that the copy of Windows XP that ships with a PC stays tied to that specific PC, forever and ever. See Fred Langa's expose at www.langa.com/newsletters/2001/2001-09-10.htm for a detailed explanation of what's involved.

There are some if's, and's, and but's floating around (for example, what if you upgrade to Windows XP and the next day your PC suddenly dies?), but in general, you can't copy Windows XP and pass around pirate CDs to your buddies or install a single copy on all the machines in your home. If you have three PCs, and you want to run Windows XP on all of them, you have to buy three copies of Windows XP, either in shrink-wrapped boxes or pre-installed on new machines.

Corporate licenses are a little different. I talk about them at the end of this section.

Windows XP enforces this one-Windows-one-PC licensing requirement with a technique called *Windows Product Activation*, or WPA. Here's how WPA works:

1. **The Windows XP installer makes you type the unique 25-character code that's printed on the case of your Windows XP CD.**

   Later, the Product Activation program looks at various serial numbers inside your PC — the processor, network card, and disk drives, among others — mixes them together, and produces a second 25-character code that identifies your PC. Those 50 characters, taken together, are called the *Installation ID*.

2. **When you *activate* Windows XP (see Figure 1-10), you give Microsoft that 50-character Installation ID.**

   Microsoft checks to see whether anybody else has submitted the 25-character code from the case of the Windows XP CD.

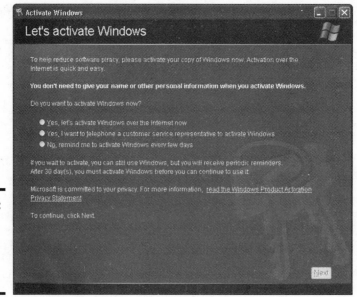

Figure 1-10:
The
Windows
Product
Activation
Wizard.

- If nobody else has activated that 25-character code from the CD case, or if the 25-character code has been activated with that specific Installation ID (which means you activated this particular copy of Windows XP from the same PC twice), Microsoft sends back a 42-character *Confirmation ID*. Both the Installation ID and the Confirmation ID are stored on your PC.

- If that 25-character code has already been used on a different PC, though, you get a polite message on your machine saying, `According to our records, the number of times that you can activate Windows with this product key has been exceeded. Please enter a different product key, and then click Retry.` You're given further instructions for contacting Microsoft, if you feel the need.

3. **Every time Windows XP starts, it recalculates the 25-character code that's based on the various serial numbers inside your PC.**

   If the code matches the one that's stored on your PC, and the Confirmation ID is good, Windows takes off.

4. **On the other hand, if the recalculated 25-character code doesn't match your original code, pandemonium breaks loose.**

   Your hard drives start spinning at twice their normal speed, your keyboard gets short-circuited with your PC's power supply, and the local constabulary receives an urgent fax from Redmond with a pre-approved no-knock search warrant. Okay, okay. I'm exaggerating a little bit. Here's what really happens:

- If Windows decides that you've only made a few changes to your PC — replaced a hard drive, say, or even changed the motherboard — it lets you start Windows anyway.

- On the other hand, if Windows determines that you've made too many changes, it refuses to start, and insists that you contact Microsoft for a new Confirmation ID. That starts the activation cycle all over again. Microsoft has full details at www.microsoft.com/piracy/basics/ xp_activation.asp and www.microsoft.com/TechNet/ prodtechnol/winxppro/evaluate/xpactiv.asp

If you bought your PC with Windows XP pre-installed, it was activated before you ever got it.

If you bought and installed Windows XP yourself, though, the activation time clock takes over. From the day you install Windows XP, you have 30 days to activate it. Windows tries to get you to activate it while you're installing. Failing that, it continues to remind you, relentlessly, as the 30 days tick away. Reinstalling Windows XP won't bypass the activation requirement.

Activating via the Internet makes the whole process of generating, sending, and receiving ID codes invisible: All you know is that the process worked, and you can continue to use the software you bought. If you activate by telephone, though, you have to be sitting at your computer with your Windows XP installation CD handy. You get to read a bunch of numbers to the rep on the other end of the phone line, and she reads a bunch of numbers back to you so that you can type them into the WPA Wizard.

Surprisingly, Windows XP still works a little bit, even after the activation period has expired, and even though it won't start. For example, a modem attached to a PC that hasn't been activated can still dial out, if it's set up for Internet Connection Sharing.

As the Activation Wizard screens emphasize (see Figure 1-11), activation is not the same as registration. When you activate Windows XP, your computer sends Microsoft a 50-character Installation ID — *and nothing else*. When you register Windows XP, you send Microsoft your name, address, telephone number, and any other information that the screens can extract from you.

Activation is a given: You have to activate Windows XP or it dies. Registration, on the other hand, is entirely optional — and basically useless for Dummies everywhere. (What? You think Microsoft wants your mailing address to send you a product recall? A birthday card? Sheeesh.) You have no reason in the world to register Windows XP. Don't do it.

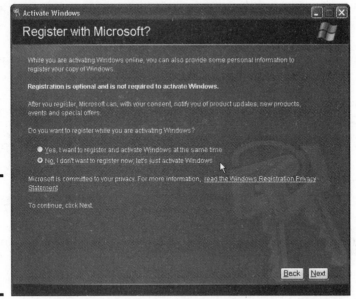

Register with Microsoft?

While you are activating Windows online, you can also provide some personal information to register your copy of Windows.

Registration is optional and is not required to activate Windows.

After you register, Microsoft can, with your consent, notify you of product updates, new products, events and special offers.

Do you want to register while you are activating Windows?

● Yes, I want to register and activate Windows at the same time
○ No, I don't want to register now; let's just activate Windows

Microsoft is committed to your privacy. For more information, read the Windows Registration Privacy Statement.

To continue, click Next.

Back   Next

Figure 1-11: You can (and should!) activate without registering.

Big companies with big bucks don't have to put up with Windows Product Activation. (One guess why.) Any company that buys Windows XP via a site license — that is, buys many copies at a time — gets a special version that doesn't require activation.

If you hear rumors on the Internet about a pirate version of Windows XP that magically bypasses Windows Product Activation, chances are very good that it's a corporate copy.

What if the Wheels Fall Off?

So what should you do if Windows XP dies?

✦ If you got Windows XP bundled with a new PC, scream bloody murder at the vendor who sold you the %$#@! thing. Don't put up with any talk about "it's a software problem; Microsoft is at fault." If you bought Windows XP with a new PC, the company that sold you the machine has full responsibility for making it work right.

✦ If you upgraded from Windows 98 or SE to Windows XP, you can always uninstall XP and go back to your old operating system, as unpalatable as that may seem. Follow the instructions in the section called "Upgrading — A Brain Transplant."

✦ If you upgraded from Windows NT 4 or 2000 and you didn't go through a clean install, try that. You don't have much to lose, eh? Follow the instructions in the section called "Considering a clean install."

✦ If you've done a clean install and Windows XP still falls over and plays dead, man, you have my sympathies. Check with your hardware manufacturer and make sure you have the latest BIOS version installed. (Make sure you get an instruction book; changing the BIOS is remarkably easy, if you follow the instructions.) Hit the newsgroups online, or drop by my WOPR Lounge, www.wopr.com/lounge, to see if anybody there can lend a hand. If all else fails, admit defeat, and reinstall your old operating system. Again, life's too short.

Chapter 2: Finding Your Way from Start to Finish

In This Chapter

➤ Logging on

➤ Adding users

➤ Moving around the desktop

➤ Working with windows (that's "windows" with a wittle...uh, small...w)

➤ Taking control of your files

➤ A button named Start

➤ Logging off

This chapter explains how to get Windows kick-started, and what you should (and shouldn't!) do to tell the beast where you want it to go. If you're an old hand at Windows, you know most of this stuff — such as using the Taskbar and interacting with dialog boxes — but I bet some of it will come as a surprise. If you're new to Windows, this is the place where you start paying your dues. In particular, you find out things such as how to add and delete users, and why you may want to avoid Microsoft Passport. Not to worry. When you get past the terminology, the concepts won't hurt a bit.

This chapter also includes the most important tip I have to offer new Windows users, a tip that will pay for this book, all by itself, if it keeps you from getting infected by just one virus. Details are in the section called "Showing filename extensions." Read it. Believe it. Tell your friends about it. Tattoo it on the inside of your eyelids.

Controlling Who Gets On

Windows XP assumes that, sooner or later, more than one person will want to work on your PC. All sorts of problems crop up when several people share a PC. I get my screen set up just right, with all my icons right where I can find them, and then my son comes along and plasters the desktop with a shot of Alpha Centauri. He puts together a killer teen Media Player playlist, and "accidentally" deletes my Grateful Dead list in the process.

It's worse than sharing a TV remote.

Windows helps keep peace in the family — and in the office — by requiring people to *log on*. The process of logging on (also called *signing on*) lets Windows keep track of each person's settings: You tell Windows who you are, and Windows lets you play in your own sandbox.

Having personal settings that activate when you log on to Windows XP isn't heavy-duty security, at least in the Home version of Windows XP. (Windows XP/Pro beefs up security substantially, but makes you jump through many more hoops.) In XP/Home, your settings can get clobbered, and your files deleted, if someone else tries hard enough. But as long as everybody sharing the PC cooperates, the XP logon method works pretty darn well.

The Welcome screen

When it's ready to get started, Windows XP greets you with a *Welcome screen* — variously called a "Logon screen" or a "Signon screen" as well — like the one shown in Figure 2-1. The screen lists all the users who have been signed up to use the computer. It may also show a catch-all user called "Guest." (I guess that sounds better than "Other" or "Hey, you!")

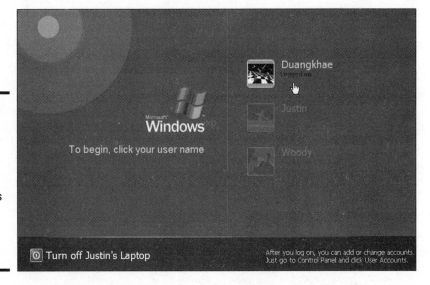

Figure 2-1: The Welcome screen helps Windows keep users from bumping into each other.

You can set up a Guest account to grant very limited capabilities to anyone who hasn't been formally set up on that specific PC. (I explain how to set up the Guest account and new users in the next section, "Adding users.") Of course, nothing prevents a guest — friend, foe, or mother-in-law — from clicking on one of the other icons and logging on under an assumed identity: Windows XP/Home relies on the gentlemanly conduct of all participants to keep its settings straight.

And if you can't rely on gentlemanly conduct, you need to set up a password. I talk about how you do that in the section "Changing user settings."

Adding users

After you log on by clicking your name on the Welcome screen, you can add more users quite easily. Here's how:

1. **Choose Start⇨Control Panel⇨User Accounts.**

You see the User Accounts dialog box, as shown in Figure 2-2.

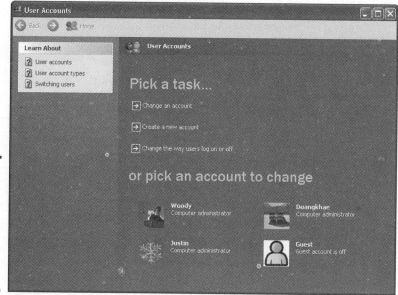

Figure 2-2: Perform all kinds of account maintenance in the User Accounts screen.

2. **Click the task marked Create a New Account.**

3. **Enter a name.**

You're done. Rocket science.

The name now appears on the Welcome screen.

A note on account names. You can give a new account just about any name you like: first name, last name, nickname, titles, abbreviations. No sweat. Even weird punctuation marks make it past the Windows censors: The name "All your base@!^" works fine.

To make the Guest account available on your computer, click Guest Account on the User Accounts screen (refer to Figure 2-2). Then click Turn On the Guest Account.

Changing user settings

If you pick an account from the User Account screen, which you bring up by choosing Start⇨Control Panel⇨User Accounts, Windows immediately presents you with five options. (See Figure 2-3.) Click on any of these options to begin the chosen task. Here's what the options entail:

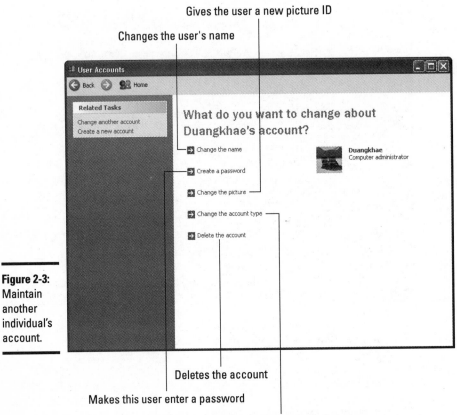

Gives the user a new picture ID

Changes the user's name

Deletes the account

Makes this user enter a password

Lets you put on user restrictions

Figure 2-3:
Maintain another individual's account.

♦ **Change the name:** Modifies the name displayed on the Welcome screen and at the very top of the Start menu, while leaving all other settings intact. Use this option if you want to change the name on the account only — for example, if "Bill" suddenly wants to be called "William."

✦ **Create a password:** Requires users to enter a password whenever they start Windows. They can't get past the Welcome screen (using their own account) without it. This is a weird setting because you can change it for other people — you can force "Bill" to use a password when none was required before. Worse, you specify the initial password when you set up an account this way, so Bill would have to pry the password out of you before he can log on.

Passwords are cAse SenSitive — you must enter the password, capitals and all, precisely the way it was originally typed. If you can't get the computer to recognize your password, make sure the Caps Lock key is off. That's the number one source of logon frustration.

If you decide to put a password on your account, take a couple of minutes to run the Forgotten Password Wizard (choose Start➪Help and Support and type **forgotten password wizard**). This nifty little program creates a diskette that you can use to unlock your password and get into your account, even if your precocious seven-year-old daughter changed it to MXYPLFTFFT. You have to run the wizard just once; the diskette it creates will always unlock your account.

✦ **Change the picture:** Changes the picture that appears next to the user's name on the Welcome screen, the Start menu, and in the User Accounts areas. You can choose a picture from any of the common file types: GIF, BMP, JPG, or PNG. Windows offers a couple dozen pictures to choose from, but you can reach out and grab any picture, anywhere. If you pick a big picture, Windows automatically scales to size.

✦ **Change the account type:** Lets you change accounts from Computer Administrator to Limited and back again. The implications are somewhat complex; I talk about them in the next section.

✦ **Delete the account:** Allows you to deep-six the account, if you're that bold (or mad, in all senses of the term). Windows offers to keep copies of the deleted account's My Documents folder and Desktop, but warns you quite sternly and correctly that if you snuff the account, you take along all the e-mail messages, Internet Favorites, and other settings that belong to the user. Definitely not a good way to make friends.

Okay, I fibbed — you can't make all of those changes to other peoples' accounts if you're a lowly Limited user. In fact, you must be a designated Computer Administrator before Windows grants you such power. But therein lies a different, mottled story, which I relate to you in the next section.

Using account types

All Windows XP/Home users can be divided into two groups: the haves and the have-nots. The haves are called *Computer Administrators*. The have-nots are called *Limited*. That's it. "Limited." Kinda makes your toes curl just to think about it.

A Limited user, running his Limited account, can only do, uh, limited things:

✦ Run programs that are installed on the computer (but he can't install new programs)

✦ Use hardware that's installed on the computer (but he can't install new hardware)

✦ Create and use documents/pictures/sounds in his My Documents/My Pictures/My Music folders, as well as in the PC's shared folders

✦ Change his password or switch back and forth between requiring a password for his account and not requiring one

✦ Change the picture that appears next to his name on the Welcome screen and the Start menu

On the other hand, Computer Administrators can change anything, anywhere, at any time, with the sole exception of getting into folders marked Private. Computer Administrators can even change other users' passwords — a good thing to remember if you ever forget your password.

In order to mark a folder as Private — and thus keep other users from getting into it — you must be using the Windows NT file system, known as *NTFS*. If Windows XP was installed on your computer when you bought it, chances are good that it's using NTFS. If you upgraded from Windows 98 or ME to Windows XP/Home, though, there's a very big chance you aren't using NTFS. To find out if you're using NTFS, and to mark a folder as Private if it's possible, follow the steps detailed later in this chapter in the section called "Making a folder private."

When you install Windows XP/Home, every account that's set up is considered a Computer Administrator account. That's why other people can make Windows suddenly require you to enter a password: Everybody is an Administrator.

What's an Administrator?

Back in the days of locked-up file servers, when the guys who held the keys to the Corporate Black Boxes wore white lab coats, the alpha net-techs identified themselves to their computers by signing with the ID "Administrator." Each PC had one Administrator account called, uh, "Administrator" (these guys were relentlessly creative), and that account could do just about anything: take the printer offline, crash all of the system disks, jumble your settings beyond recognition with a single slipped finger. The name stuck, even after the lab coats disappeared. Nowadays, an Administrator account is one that can do anything, to anyone, at any time.

Avoiding Microsoft Passport

On the surface, *Microsoft Passport* dazzles as a wonderful idea: a central location where you can put all the consumer-related information you'll need to interact with vendors over the Web, not to mention chat with other people using Windows Messenger, download stock prices, customize weather predictions, send and receive e-mail using Microsoft's own Hotmail e-mail service, open a bank account, trade stock, and on and on.

If you choose Start➪Control Panel➪User Accounts and then select your own account in the User Account screen, you have the option of signing up for Microsoft Passport — or linking your local PC to your existing Passport — as shown in Figure 2-4.

How much do you trust Microsoft to protect your privacy? That seems to be the root question when any discussion of Microsoft Passport hits the ether. Most people don't trust Microsoft much farther than they can throw a cow. With a tractor and two barns attached.

On the face of it, the Passport seems innocuous: Type in your name, pick an ID and a password, and suddenly all of these wonderful features become available.

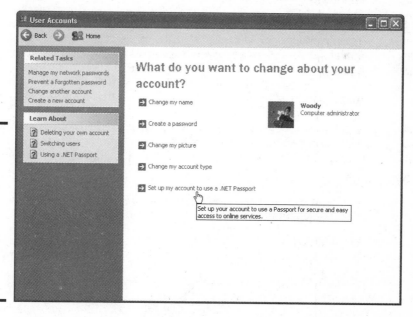

Figure 2-4:
When you bring up your account, you have the choice of hitching up to Microsoft Passport.

Beneath the surface, though, you have to realize that Microsoft holds the keys to all of the Passport data. If you trust Microsoft (and, personally, in this case, I do), the only real problem with Passport is a growing sense of Big Brother's imminent arrival. If you don't trust Microsoft, you'd be a fool to hand over your personal information — even something as simple as a list of your favorite stocks.

On the third hand, if you don't sign up for Passport, you can't use Windows Messenger for instant chatting, can't use Hotmail for e-mail on the Web, can't ask someone to take over the controls at your computer and help you with Remote Assistance, can't put Microsoft's neat stock ticker on your Windows desktop, and on and on.

What's a person to do?

Many folks strike a balance between privacy and convenience by getting a Passport, but being very vigilant about the kinds of information they hand over to Microsoft's ever-expanding database. You may find that a workable solution, too. Just be aware that Passport data collection can be a two-way street: If you use a Passport to get onto a site, there's a chance that the site will send gathered information back to Microsoft. I don't mean to make you paranoid, but almost anything that you enter on any Web page hooked up to Passport could end up sitting in a Microsoft database.

I cover Microsoft Passport extensively in Woody's Windows Watch (my free e-mail newsletter, www.woodyswatch.com), and each time I learn something new about Passport, the new info seems to fall into the Big Brother category. If you decide to use Passport, understand that Microsoft will hold any information you enter. And make sure you stay on top of the latest developments with Passport. It's another one of those areas that requires constant vigilance.

Don't be too surprised if you see reference to ".NET Passport" and maybe "Windows Passport" in various trade publications. Passport has gone through more skin changes than a rattler. Version 1.1 shipped in the original Windows XP, but Version 2.0 came online shortly afterward, and Version 3.0 seems poised to strike not long after that. No matter what you call it — Microsoft Passport, Windows Passport, .NET Passport — and no matter what version you're using, the basic idea behind Passport hasn't changed.

At any rate, if you want to sign up for Microsoft Passport and have your account on your PC linked to that big MS Passport logbook in the sky, follow these steps:

1. **Choose Start⇨Control Panel⇨User Accounts.**

2. **Choose your own account**

3. **Click Set Up My Account to Use a .NET Passport**

   You are transported to Microsoft's Web site, where you can consummate the relationship.

Deleting yourself

AHA! I bet you saw it.

Did you compare Figure 2-3 to Figure 2-4? Bonus Dummies Merit Points if you noticed the subtle difference. (One hundred Dummies Merit Points are redeemable for one Severe Bragging Right at any local Dummies store. Tell 'em Woody sent ya.)

You can't delete your own account.

Windows has to protect itself. Every PC must have at least one user signed up as Computer Administrator. If Windows XP lost all of its Administrators, no one would be around to add new users or change existing ones, much less to install programs or hardware, right?

Although you and I could probably think of a few dozen ways to ensure that a PC always has at least one Computer Administrator, Microsoft has chosen a rather straightforward approach. First, you can't turn yourself into a Limited user if you're the only Computer Administrator left. Second, you can't delete your own account.

Betwixt the two of those requirements, Windows XP is assured of always having a minimum of one Computer Administrator available at its beck and call.

The Basics

As soon as you log onto the computer, you're greeted with an enormous expanse of near-nothingness, cleverly painted with a pretty picture of a wheat field.

Or is it Bill's front yard? Hard to tell.

The desktop

Your Windows destiny, such as it is, unfolds on the computer's screen. The screen that Windows shows you every time you start is called the *desktop*, although it doesn't bear much resemblance to a real desktop. Try putting a pencil on it.

The first time you start Windows, your desktop looks something like the one in Figure 2-5.

Figure 2-5:
The bone-
stock
Windows
XP/Home
desktop.

Stores deleted files

The current time, if
you set the clock right

System status
information

Recycle Bin

11:13 AM

Although the number and appearance of objects scattered on your computer monitor varies depending on who sold you the computer and what was included when you bought it, chances are pretty good that you have only a few pictures — they're called *icons* — sitting on the desktop. In Figure 2-5, one icon appears, the Recycle Bin icon, where Windows sticks everything you threw away.

Your desktop probably looks different from the one in Figure 2-5. For one thing, you're bound to have a handful of icons sitting around. If you bought a new computer with Windows XP installed, chances are good that the manufacturer sold some desktop real estate to a software company or an Internet Service Provider. (Oh yeah, the AOLs and Nortons of the world compensate the Dells and Compaqs for services rendered. Don't you ever doubt it.) If you see an icon you don't like, right-click on it and choose Delete. Good riddance to bad rubbish.

Yeah, yeah, I know. The terminology stinks: The Windows desktop doesn't look anything like your desktop. Mine, neither. And calling those little pictures "icons" seems a bit, uh, iconoclastic, given that real icons rate as exquisite *objets d'art,* rendered in paint on wood. The price of progress, I guess.

When you get past the verdant fields rolling across your screen, the rest of the desktop isn't very inspiring, although plenty of surprises await as you begin clicking:

✦ **Windows taskbar:** Runs all along the bottom of the screen, keeps you posted on what your computer is doing — which computer programs are running, where you're visiting on the Internet, and almost anything else that requires your attention.

✦ **Notification area:** Also known to techies as the *system tray.* This area sits on top of the taskbar on the right side and tells you the time, but it also lets you know what Windows is doing behind the scenes. For example, if you're using a modem to connect to the Internet, little modem lights down here reassure you that the connection hasn't frozen. At least, that's the theory. Other tiny icons in the notification area may control your speaker volume or tell you if you're logged on to Windows Messenger.

✦ **Start button:** Located in the lower left of the desktop. This button gives you access to everything your computer can do. Click it and you see the Start menu — *menu* being geekspeak for a list of things that you can click. Look for all the details in the "Starting with the Start Button" section, later in this chapter.

The Windows desktop looks simple enough, but don't fool yourself: Underneath that calm exterior sits the most sophisticated computer program ever created. Hundreds of millions of dollars went into creating the illusion of simplicity — something to remember the next time you feel like kicking your computer and screaming at the Windows gods.

Mousing

Your computer's mouse serves as the primary way of interacting with Windows, but you already knew that. You can click on the left mouse button or the right mouse button, or you can roll the wheel down the middle (if you have one), and the mouse will do different things, depending on where you click or roll. But you already knew that, too.

You can interchange the action of the left and right mouse buttons — that is, you can tell Windows XP that it should treat the left mouse button as if it were the right button, and the right button as if it were the left. The swap comes in handy for some left-handers, but most southpaws I know (including my son) prefer to keep the buttons as-is, simply because it's easier to use other people's computers if your fingers are trained for the "normal" setting. To switch left and right mouse buttons, follow these steps:

1. **Choose Start⇨Control Panel⇨Printers and Other Hardware⇨Mouse.**

2. **Choose the Buttons tab.**

3. **Check the box marked Switch Primary and Secondary Buttons.**

4. **Click OK.**

Making the mouse behave

Here are a few important rodent things you may not know:

✦ To move an item on the Windows desktop — a process called *dragging* — click the left button, move the mouse, and then release the button. On laptops with a touch pad, you can tie your fingers up in knots trying to replicate the click-move-release shuck 'n' jive. Chances are good that the touch pad recognizes a swift tap as the beginning of a drag. Check the documentation and practice a bit.

Windows has a feature called ClickLock that can come in handy if you have trouble holding down the left mouse button and moving the mouse at the same time — a common problem for laptop users who have fewer than three hands. When Windows uses ClickLock, you hold down the mouse button for a while (you can tell Windows exactly how long) and Windows "locks" the mouse button. To turn on ClickLock

1. **Choose Start⇨Control Panel⇨Printers and Other Hardware⇨ Mouse.**

2. **On the Buttons tab, check the box marked Turn on ClickLock.**

3. **Immediately click the Settings button and adjust the length of time you need to hold down the mouse button for ClickLock to kick in.**

Note that you can test the ClickLock time length setting by clicking next to Settings for ClickLock and dragging the box around.

✦ You can roll over items on the desktop too quickly! When you're spelunking around Windows XP trying to get a feel for what's happening, go slowly. The word for it is *hovering* — that's when you let the mouse pointer kind of sit in one place for a spell. You'll be surprised at how often Windows flashes information on the screen in response to hovering.

✦ Although almost everyone catches on to single-clicking, given a few tries, many people have trouble with double-clicking, and here's the reason why: Windows ain't that smart. If you click twice, Windows has to figure out if you wanted to make two single-clicks or one double-click — and that's surprisingly difficult. Windows watches as you click. You have to click twice, quickly, without moving the mouse very far in between clicks for Windows to identify the two clicks as a double-click. If you have trouble getting Windows to recognize your double-clicks, you're probably moving the mouse just a bit too far between the clicks for a double-click to "take."

If you have consistent problems with Windows recognizing your double-clicks, try adjusting the double-click speed:

1. **Choose Start➪Control Panel➪Printers and Other Hardware➪ Mouse.**

2. **Click the Buttons tab.**

3. **Double-click the folder on the right side, as a test to see how much leeway Windows gives you.**

4. **Adjust the Double-click speed slider as needed to suit your leisurely lifestyle.**

✦ The best way to get the feel for a new mouse? Play one of the games that ships with Windows. I recommend Minesweeper and Solitaire. Try clicking in unlikely places, double-clicking, or right-clicking in new and different ways. Bet you'll discover several wrinkles, even if you're an old hand at the games.

Inside the computer, programmers measure the movement of mice in units called *mickeys.* Nope, I'm not making this up. Move your mouse a short distance and it has traveled a few mickeys. Move it to Anaheim, and it's put on a lot of mickeys.

Pointers on pointers

When you move the mouse around on your desk, the *pointer* on the screen (see Table 2-1) moves around in concert. Click one of the mouse buttons while the pointer is sitting on something and it may (or may not) react.

Table 2-1		Standard Windows Mouse Pointers
When a pointer looks like this:	*It means:*	*And Windows is trying to tell you this:*
	Normal	The mouse is ready for action. Move it around the screen, and point and click to get work done.
	Hot	Windows has found a "hot" spot — a *hyperlink* in geekspeak — and if you click while this pointer is showing, you are transported to the linked location.
	Ready to resize	Hold down the left mouse button and move the mouse forward and backward on your desk ("up" and "down" as you're looking at the Windows desktop) to make a window taller or shorter.
	Ready to resize	Same as the preceding pointer, except it makes the selected window fatter or skinnier as you move the mouse left and right.
	Expand or shrink to fit	Click and drag on a window's corner, and the picture expands or shrinks to fit.
	Kinda busy	You can keep doing whatever you're doing, but Windows may be a bit slow following along because it's working on something else. If Windows gets to be too slow to keep up with you, do yourself (and Windows) a favor and go grab a latte.
	Out to lunch	Windows is really, really busy and doesn't want to be disturbed. You may be able to move the pointer around a bit, but you won't get much done.
	Pick a pic	Windows expects you to draw or choose a part of a picture (for example, if you're selecting Uncle Ernie's head for cropping). When the pointer is like this, click in the upper left corner of the picture, hold down the mouse button, and release it when you get to the lower right corner. Don't be too anal about it: When you're done selecting with this pointer, you always have an opportunity to use the resizing arrows to fix your mistakes.
	Move	Instead of resizing the selected area (see the preceding), if you see a four-headed arrow like this one, you know that Windows is going to move the entire selected area, all at once.

(continued)

Table 2-1 *(continued)*

When a pointer looks like this:	It means:	And Windows is trying to tell you this:
	Help	Click on something to get help. If you don't want help, press Esc on the keyboard and the pointer returns to normal.
I	*Text allowed*	Click where the mouse pointer looks like an I-Beam and you can type text where you clicked.
⃠	*No way*	Windows shows you this pointer if you're trying to do something that can't be done — trying to move a printer into a word processing document, for example.

 One other thing to note are what's called *skid pads*. If you see a faint stair-step triangle in the lower right corner of a window, you can probably use the four resizing arrows to make the window larger or smaller.

 If Windows shows you one of its "busy" pointers, you go out to have a latte, and lunch, and run through a quick 18 holes, and come back only to discover that the busy pointer is still there, chances are pretty good that Windows is *hung.* (That's a technical term, okay? Don't laugh. You can also say that Windows *went belly up* or that it *crashed* or *froze* or *died* or *bit the big one.*) If Windows hangs, hold down the Ctrl key and, without letting go of it, press the Alt key and, without letting go of the preceding two, press the Del key. (That's called a *three-finger salute* or a *Vulcan Mind Meld* or, uh, several entirely unprintable things.) The Windows Task Manager appears, and you can (usually) use it to close down whatever is ailing Windows.

 If you encounter one of the resizing pointers while working with a picture, remember that different programs use the resizing pointers differently: Some may cut off ("crop") parts of a picture as you resize it, while others may stretch or shrink the picture as you drag the mouse. Usually you can use some combination of the Shift and Ctrl keys to convince the program to behave itself: Hold down the Ctrl key while resizing, for example, and the program may start stretching the picture instead of cropping it. Experiment. If all else fails, you can always start over again.

The point where typed text gets inserted onto the screen is called the *insertion point* (more rocket science). Various word processors show the insertion point differently, but Word uses a solid vertical line. Don't be too surprised if some old cuss — yours truly included — calls the insertion point a "cursor." That's a throwback to the Cro-Magnon days when word processors worked more like typewriters, and the blinking cursor kept track of where text would go.

Using the right button

Windows XP allows you to right-click just about anywhere and choose from a list of actions to be performed on the item you've clicked. For example, you can right-click on a disk drive and choose to search the disk drive; you can right-click on a printer and make the printer stop printing. The choices that appear when you right-click on an item are called a *shortcut menu* (sometimes also called a *right-click menu* or a *context menu*). In Figure 2-6, you can see an example of the context menu that appears when you right-click on a blank portion of the Windows desktop.

Figure 2-6:
The right-click shortcut menu for the Windows desktop, with Microsoft Office installed.

Mice need to be cleaned! If you start having problems with a sluggish mouse — one that jumps, stalls, or doesn't move around the screen the way it should — you should immediately turn the beast upside down and clean it. If you see a rubber ball, pop the lid off, take out the ball, blow on it, and clean off the roller contacts inside (you may need a cotton swab and some iso-propyl alcohol). Regardless of whether the mouse has a ball, the feet need to be cleaned from time to time — use your fingernails and scrape gently.

Windows

Most of the time that you spend working with Windows is spent working with, uh, windows. The kind with the little "w" — the rectangles that appear all over your screen. Each part of a window has a name and a specific function.

Many people spend most of their time on the computer working in Word 2002, which is the word processor in Office XP and the word processor used by Outlook 2002 for composing e-mail messages. You may have a copy of it on your machine. Look at Figure 2-7 for an overview of the components of the Word 2002 window, and what they represent.

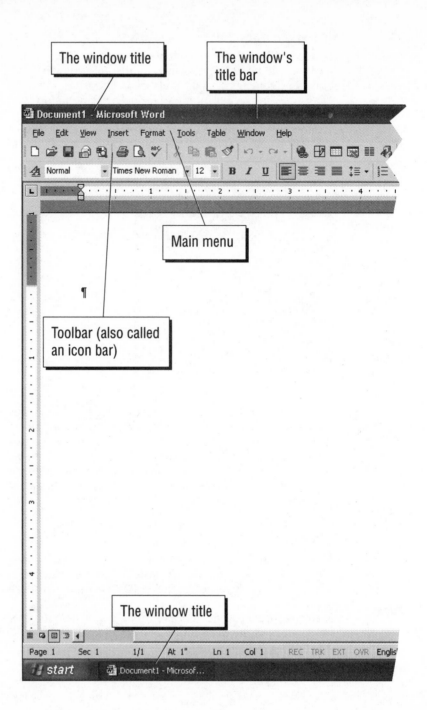

The window title

The window's title bar

Main menu

Toolbar (also called an icon bar)

The window title

Figure 2-7:
Word 2002's
window.

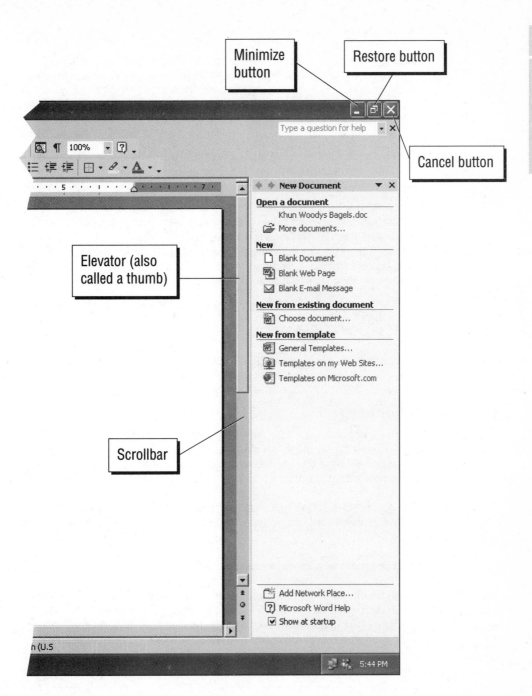

Minimize button

Restore button

Cancel button

Type a question for help

Elevator (also called a thumb)

New Document

Open a document
Khun Woodys Bagels.doc
More documents...

New
Blank Document
Blank Web Page
Blank E-mail Message

New from existing document
Choose document...

New from template
General Templates...
Templates on my Web Sites...
Templates on Microsoft.com

Scrollbar

Add Network Place...
Microsoft Word Help
Show at startup

h (U.S

5:44 PM

A few details worth noting:

✦ The window title appears both in the title bar — that is, the bar
  across the top of the window — and (usually) in the Windows taskbar,
  way down at the bottom of the screen. That makes it easy for you
  to identify which window is which and to switch among them by clicking
  on the taskbar. (I say "usually" because sometimes the boxes in the
  taskbar get stacked up; see the section called "Windows Taskbar.")

✦ Clicking the Minimize button makes the window disappear but leaves
  the title down in the Windows taskbar, so you can bring the window
  back with just a click.

✦ Clicking the Restore button "restores" the size of the window. That is,
  if the window doesn't take up the whole screen and you click the
  restore button, it expands to take up the full screen. On the other
  hand, if the window is taking up the whole screen and you click on
  the restore button, it reduces in size to occupy a portion of the screen.
  I have no idea why that's called restoring.

✦ Clicking the Cancel button removes the screen entirely — even from the
  Windows taskbar — most commonly by shutting down the program
  that's using the window.

Many windows can be resized by clicking and dragging an edge or a corner.
See the preceding section on "Mousing" for details.

Dialog boxes

When the computer interacts with you — that is, when it has a question to
ask, or when it needs more information in order to complete a task — it
usually puts a *dialog box* on the screen. A dialog box is nothing more or less
than a window that requires your attention.

Figure 2-8 shows a dialog box that illustrates how the various standard
Windows components can be used to extract information from unsuspecting
Dummies.

Each of the parts of a window has a name:

✦ **Title:** A dialog box's *title* appears at the top of the dialog box, but the
  title rarely appears in the Windows taskbar. This is one of the ways that
  a dialog box is different from a garden-variety window (see the preceding section): You can usually hop directly to a regular ol' window by
  clicking in the taskbar. To find a lost dialog box, you frequently have to
  hunt around.

The dialog box's title

Dialog tabs   Click to close the window

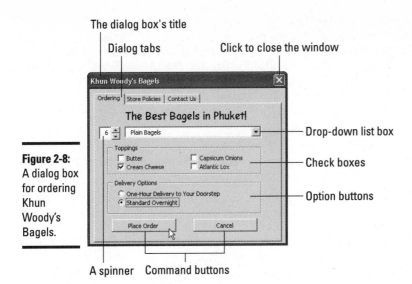

Drop-down list box

Check boxes

Option buttons

Figure 2-8:
A dialog box
for ordering
Khun
Woody's
Bagels.

A spinner   Command buttons

Those "things" that appear on dialog boxes are called *controls*. (Sounds a whole lot better than "things," true?) Windows comes with many controls, and most of the controls you see from day to day are drawn from the standard control toolbox. Standard controls are a real boon to us Dummies because they work the same way, all the time, no matter where you are in Windows.

✦ **Cancel button:** The Cancel button almost always appears on a dialog box, but the other two buttons that you often see on a regular window — Restore and Minimize — rarely show up on dialog boxes. Clicking the Cancel button almost always makes the dialog box go away.

✦ **Tabs:** Those funny-looking index tabs (usually just called *tabs*) are supposed to remind you of filing tabs. Click on a tab, and you bring up a whole bunch of settings, which are usually related — at least, some programmer somewhere thought they were related.

You can usually hop from one part of a dialog box to the next by pressing the Tab key. Press Shift+Tab to move backwards. If you see an underlined letter in a dialog box — called an *accelerator key* — hold down the Alt key and press the letter, and you go directly to that location. In some dialog boxes, pressing Enter is the same as clicking OK (unless you've used the Tab key to move around). In other dialog boxes, though, pressing Enter doesn't do anything.

✦ **Spinners:** These are almost always placed right next to numbers, with the number hooked up so that it increases when you click the up arrow and decreases when you click the down arrow. Sometimes you can bypass the spinner entirely, select the number, delete it, and type whatever you want.

+ **Drop-down lists:** These lists come in two different flavors. With one kind, you're limited to the choices that appear in the drop-down list: If the item you want is in the list, you just pick it; if the item isn't there, you're up the ol' creek without a paddle. The other kind of drop-down list lets you type in whatever you want if your choice doesn't appear in the list. Programmers hate that kind of drop-down list because it lets you do things like order anchovies and pepper sauce on your bagels.

+ **Check boxes:** *Check boxes* let you say "yes" or "no," independently, to a whole bunch of choices; if you see a bunch of check boxes, you can pick one or none or all of 'em. *Option buttons,* on the other hand, only let you choose one out of a group — no more, no less

Back in the good old days (he says, stroking his long, white beard), option buttons were called *radio buttons.* They act like the buttons on a radio: Push one, and a station plays; push a different button, and a different station kicks in. You can't have two different buttons pushed in at the same time. Old-fashioned radios had mechanical buttons that would pop in and out, reminiscent of the way Windows radio buttons work. But you aren't old enough to remember those old radios, are you? Me, neither.

+ **Command buttons:** These buttons tell the dialog box to get on with it. Click a command button, and the dialog box does something.

Usually it's pretty obvious when you can change things in a dialog box: Text that can't be changed generally appears against a gray background, for example, whereas text that can be changed frequently appears on a white background. Unfortunately, programmers aren't the most consistent folks in the world, and sometimes what you see on the screen is a bit, uh, nonstandard.

Utterly random, in some cases.

Files and folders

"What's a file?" Man, I wish I had a nickel for every time I've been asked that question.

A file is a, uh, thing. Yeah, that's it. A thing. A thing that has stuff inside of it. Why don't you ask me an easier question, like "what is a paragraph?" or "what is the meaning of life, the universe, and everything?"

A file is a fundamental chunk of stuff. Like most fundamental chunks of stuff (say, protons, or Congressional districts, or ear wax), any attempt at a definitive definition gets in the way of understanding the thing itself. Suffice it to say that a Word document is a file. An Excel workbook is a file. That photograph your cousin e-mailed you the other day is a file. Every track on Nine Inch Nails' latest CD is a file, but so is every track on every audio CD ever made. Trent Reznor isn't *that* special.

File and folder names can be very long, but they can't contain the following characters:

/ \ : * ? " < > |

Files can be huge. They can be tiny. They can even be empty, but don't short-circuit any gray cells on that observation.

Three things I know for sure about files:

✦ Every file has a name.

✦ Files — at least, files that aren't empty — contain bits, the 1s and 0s that computers use to represent reality (a tenuous concept under the best of circumstances).

✦ Windows lets you work with files — move them, copy them, create them, delete them, and group them together.

Folders hold files and other folders. Folders can be empty. A single folder can hold millions — yes, quite literally *millions* — of files and other folders.

Three things I know for sure about folders:

✦ Every folder has a name.

✦ Windows creates and keeps track of a whole bunch of folders, like

• **A My Documents folder** for each user on the PC. That's where Windows and Microsoft Office usually put new documents that you create.

• **My Pictures and My Music folders**, inside each user's My Documents folders. Windows — including the Media Player — tend to store your pictures and music files in these folders.

• **A Shared Documents folder**, which includes Shared Pictures and Shared Music folders, to make it easy to share documents, pictures, and music with other people who use your PC or other people on a network, if you have one. For more info on sharing documents, see the section called "Sharing Folders."

✦ Windows lets you move, copy, create, delete, and put folders inside of other folders.

If you set them up right, folders can help you keep track of things. If you toss your files around higgledy-piggledy, no system of folders in the world will help.

To look at the files and folders on your machine that you're most likely to bump into, choose Start⇨My Documents. You see something like the list shown in Figure 2-9.

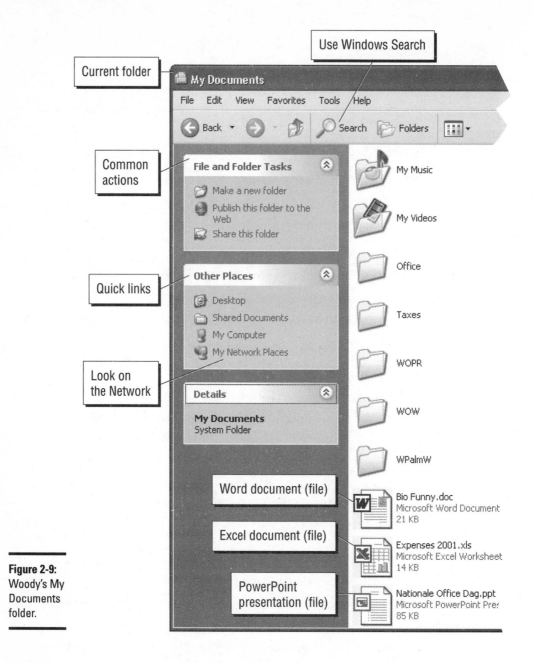

Figure 2-9:
Woody's My
Documents
folder.

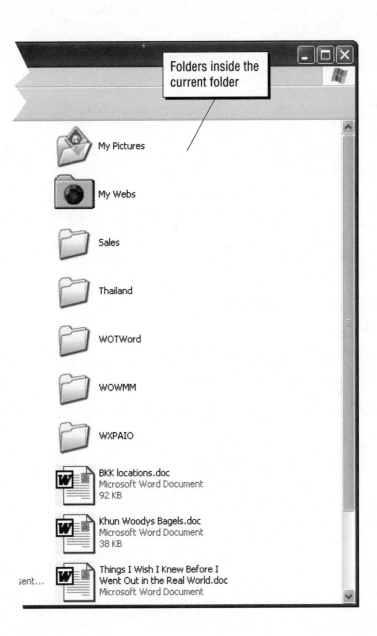

Folders inside the current folder

The picture of My Documents that you see in Figure 2-9 comes from a part of Windows called *Windows Explorer*, which can help keep your files and folders organized. Many of the things that you can do in Windows Explorer, you can also do elsewhere. For example, you can rename files in the File⇨Open dialog box in Word — but it's hard to beat the way Windows Explorer enables you to perform powerful actions quickly and easily.

I talk about Windows Explorer in the section called "Using Windows Explorer."

If you're looking at My Documents on your computer, and you can't see the three-letter ends of the filenames (such as "doc" and "xls") that are visible in Figure 2-9, don't panic! You need to tell Windows to show them — knock Windows upside the head, electronically, if you will. I explain how in the section called "Showing filename extensions." In that section, I also get on my soapbox and rant about the importance of every Windows user keeping Windows from hiding full filenames. In my opinion, this forced game of hide 'n seek qualifies as one of Windows' worse features.

Starting with the Start Button

Microsoft's subverting the Rolling Stones classic *Start Me Up* for advertising may be ancient history by now, but the royal road to Windows XP still starts at the Start button. Click it, and you get the Start menu, which looks something like the one shown in Figure 2-10.

The Start menu looks like it's etched in granite, but it isn't. You can change almost anything on it:

✦ To change the name or picture of the current user, see the section called "Changing user settings."

✦ To remove a program from the "pinned" programs list or the recently used programs list, right-click on it and click Remove from This List.

✦ To add a program to the "pinned" programs list, use Windows Explorer to find the program (see the section called "Using Windows Explorer"), right-click on the program, and click Pin to Start Menu.

If you bought a new computer with Windows XP installed, the people who make the computer may have sold one of the spots on the Start menu. Think of it as an electronic billboard on your desktop. Nope, I'm not exaggerating. I keep expecting to bump into a Windows XP machine with fly-out Start menu entries that read, oh, "Surveys have shown⇨Near and far⇨That people who drive like crazy⇨Are⇨Burma Shave." You can always delete those pesky Start menu billboards by right-clicking on them and choosing Remove from This List.

Recently used programs

"Pinned" programs

Current user's name

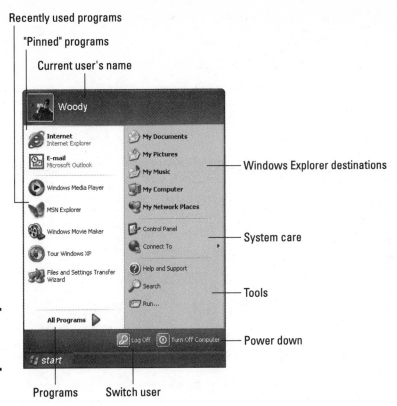

Figure 2-10:
Woody's
Start menu.

Windows Explorer destinations

System care

Tools

Power down

Programs   Switch user

Don't expect a whole lot of consistency in the way adjacent Start menu items behave.

You may expect that the Recently used program part of the Start menu would list the programs you've used most recently. And it does. Sorta. Partly. Now and then. Microsoft stacks the deck, so MSN Explorer (which connects to Microsoft's for-pay MSN service) may stay on the list a whole lot longer than other programs.

Some programs are more equal than others, eh?

Internet

Windows XP ships with Internet Explorer 6 (IE6), Microsoft's flagship Web browser. To bring up IE6, choose Start⇨Internet/Internet Explorer, and you'll be surfing on the Web, as shown in Figure 2-11.

Move to the last viewed page

Title of the current Web page

Type Web address here

Stop trying to retrieve the page

Show history

Try to get the page again

Send page as an e-mail message

Edit (change) the page

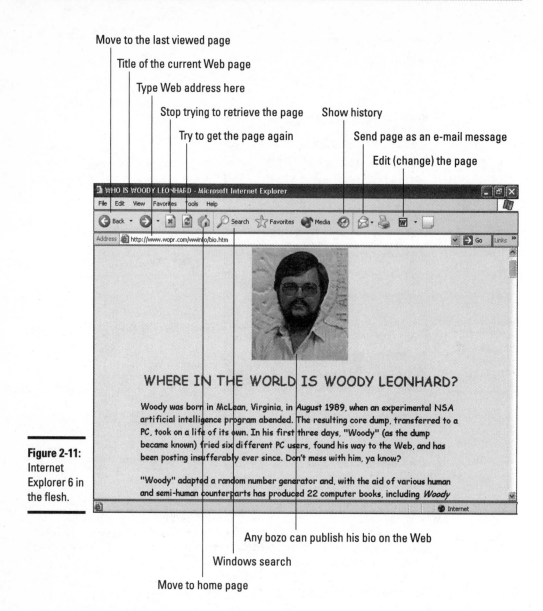

Figure 2-11:
Internet
Explorer 6 in
the flesh.

Any bozo can publish his bio on the Web

Windows search

Move to home page

Internet Explorer is so important that we've included an entire book on the subject. See Book IV.

E-mail

Windows XP ships with a versatile e-mail program called Outlook Express. Outlook Express also handles *newsgroups,* the places on the Internet where people can freely exchange ideas, gossip, tips, and fertilizer. Choose Start⇨E-mail/Outlook Express and it appears, as shown in Figure 2-12.

If you bought a PC with Microsoft Office installed, you are undoubtedly using Outlook — which, in spite of the sound-alike name and superficial similarities in appearance, is very different from Outlook Express. Trying to understand Outlook by reading about Outlook Express is like trying to understand cars by reading about incarnation. This Dummies book covers Outlook Express. It doesn't cover Outlook. No way, no how.

Book I
Chapter 2

Finding Your Way
from Start to Finish

Find an e-mail message or an address

This is Outlook Express

Connect to Internet newsgroups

Send and retrieve messages

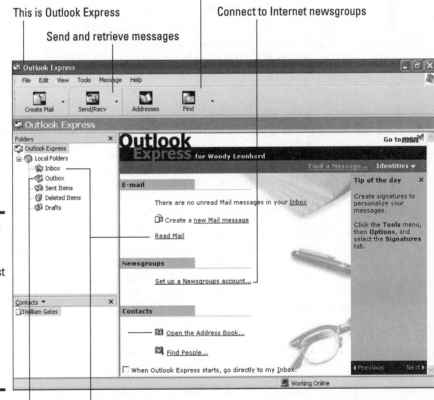

Figure 2-12: Outlook Express — the free, fast e-mail program, with an address book and newsgroup reader.

Look at new messages

Your written messages wait in Outbox

Outlook Express lets you compose and read e-mail messages. It also has an address book and a program for reading Internet newsgroups. I talk about Outlook Express at length in Book III, Chapter 2.

Media Player

Windows XP includes Microsoft's Media Player, a multi-faceted tool for playing, organizing, ripping, and burning audio and video files.

If you're new to the topic, don't be flummoxed. The terminology is a bit obtuse, but if you've lived with computers for more than a few days, you're already accustomed to clear-as-mud jargon. Here are the biggies:

✦ **MP3:** A way of storing digital music that's become very popular because it allows you to squeeze big audio files into tiny MP3 files, without much degradation in sound quality. MP3 stands for MPEG3, but nobody cares about that anyway. My son insists that MP3 means "Mario Party 3." It does.

✦ **WMA:** Microsoft's challenger to MP3 (short for Windows Media Audio). A typical WMA file is about half the size of a corresponding MP3, so you fit about twice as many songs into the same amount of room. In addition, music publishers can use WMA to limit the number of times a file is copied or the period of time a WMA track can be played. Copyright protection is the number-one reason why music publishers love WMA, and the number-one reason why many normal folks aren't really happy about it.

✦ **Ripping:** The process of converting audio CD tracks into MP3 or WMA format computer files. You stick an audio CD into your PC, and Windows Media Player (or another ripper) pulls the audio tracks off the CD and converts them into MP3 or WMA files.

✦ **Burning:** What you do when you create — or write to — a CD. It's also what you do if you are trying to make a living from music that's being ripped off by copyright abusers.

Choose Start⇨Windows Media Player, and you see the odd-shaped amoeba shown in Figure 2-13.

All of these rely on WindowsMedia.com, a Web site owned by (you guessed it!) Microsoft Corp.

My Documents, Pictures, Music

Figure 2-9, earlier in this chapter, shows you the contents of my My Documents folder. (I guess that makes it a list of my My Documents

documents, right?) Windows Explorer lets you look at your folders in various ways, called *views*, and you can switch from view to view depending on what you're trying to do, your mood, or the phase of the moon.

The Ripper

Connects to the Media Guide

Lists tracks, shows groovy "visuals"

Change "skin" appearance to a regular window

A "skin"

Playlist

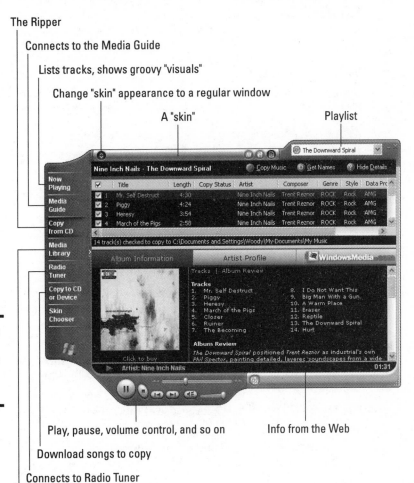

Figure 2-13:
Windows
Media
Player,
Version 8.

Play, pause, volume control, and so on

Info from the Web

Download songs to copy

Connects to Radio Tuner

Organize My Music folder

The view shown in Figure 2-9 is called Tiles view; it is, at once, the most visually impressive and the most cumbersome view Windows offers. If you get tired of seeing those big icons and you choose View⊅Details, you get the succinct list shown in Figure 2-14.

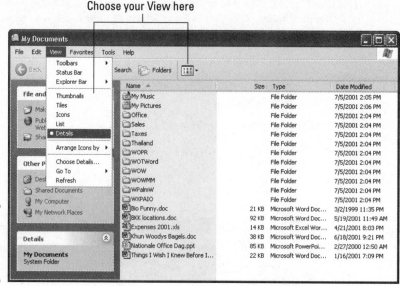

Choose your View here

Figure 2-14:
My
Documents,
details view.

The following are the views you can use:

✦ **Thumbnails:** Shows small versions (called *thumbnails*) of graphics files, along with a few surprises: tiny pictures of the first slide in PowerPoint presentations, small pictures of enclosed graphic files on file folders, even album cover art on identified My Music albums.

✦ **Tiles:** Gives large icons but makes no attempt to show you a small version of picture files. Documents are identified by what application "owns" them and how big they are.

✦ **Icons:** Trims down the large size of the Tiles but sacrifices document details.

✦ **List:** Simply lists filenames. This view is a good choice for looking at folders with lots and lots of files.

✦ **Details:** Shows filenames, sizes, and types. In most folders, the Details list also includes the date when the file was created, but for music and pictures, artist names and titles appear.

In Details view, you can sort the list of files by clicking on one of the column headings — name, size, and so on. You can right-click on one of the column headings and click More to change what the view shows (get rid of Type, for example, and replace it with Author).

✦ **Filmstrip:** Shows thumbnails of pictures across the bottom of the screen, with a Play button below the selected picture, as shown in Figure 2-15. (This view is available only in picture folders.)

Within the My Documents folder sit two more folders that you can get to directly from the Start menu. If you choose Start➪My Pictures, the Windows Explorer appears with the My Pictures folder open. Choose View➪Filmstrip and your pictures look like the ones shown in Figure 2-15.

Pictures appear full-screen

Moves up one level

Figure 2-15:
My Pictures.

Particulars on selected file   Previous/Next picture   Rotate

Double-click on a picture and it appears in the Windows Picture and Fax Viewer. At that point, you can easily zoom in and out on the picture, print it, copy it to a floppy, or even change the picture.

If you choose Start➪My Music, and then choose View➪Thumbnails, you see the My Music folder (shown in Figure 2-16), which appears with its own special set of actions in the pane on the left.

Windows Media Player

Moves up one level   Album cover art

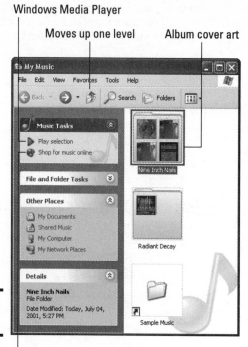

Figure 2-16:
My Music.

Buy an album

If you use the Windows Media Player to rip audio CDs, it places all the songs from a single CD into a folder, tucks each of those folders into a big folder for each artist, and puts the artists' folders into My Music. The covers appear, up to four on a folder, when you use Thumbnail view.

My Recent Documents

Windows keeps track of documents as you open them, maintaining a list of documents that you have opened most recently. Taking a leaf from the "HUH?" School of Computer Design, Microsoft's Usability Lab decided that Windows XP/Pro users should see the list on the Start menu, whereas Windows XP/Home users should not. If you like, you can tell Windows that you want to be able to get at that list. Here's how:

1. **Right-click Start and click Properties.**

2. **Click the Customize button.**

3. **Click the Advanced tab.**

4. **Check the box marked List My Most Recently Opened Documents, and then click OK twice.**

When the Most Recently Opened Documents list is enabled, an entry called My Recent Documents appears on your Start menu. If you choose Start⇨My Recent Documents, Windows presents you with a list of the 15 documents that you opened most recently (see Figure 2-17). If you want to open a listed document again, pick it from the list, and Windows does the rest.

Figure 2-17: The documents that you opened most recently can appear on your Start menu, if you know how to set it up.

Take this list with a grain of salt. Windows doesn't always get all of the files listed correctly.

If you want to wipe out the list of files that you've opened recently — hey, ain't nobody's business but your own — try this:

1. **Right-click Start and choose Properties.**

2. **Click the Customize button.**

3. **Click the Advanced tab.**

4. **Click Clear List, and then click OK twice.**

All of the entries in your My Recent Documents menu disappear.

My Computer

Choose Start⇨My Computer, and Windows shows you the highest level of folders on your machine, in addition to a list of all the drives (see Figures 2-18). You can use this bird's-eye view to "drill down" to various nooks and crannies in your folders and in the folders of all the other people who use your PC.

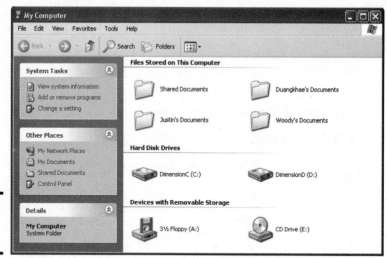

Figure 2-18:
My
Computer.

For a traditional (that is, pre-Windows XP) view of the contents of your computer that enables you to easily navigate down to the lowest level, click the Folders icon. You see all of your folders and how they're interrelated in the pane on the left (see Figure 2-19).

Click the Folders icon to see the full hierarchy of folders

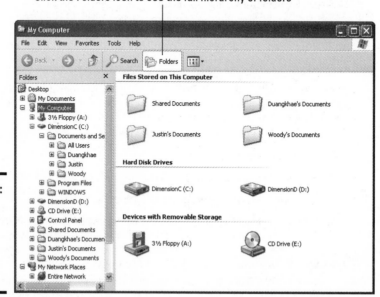

Figure 2-19:
My
Computer,
showing
folders in
the left
pane.

Control Panel

The inner workings of Windows XP reveal themselves inside the mysterious (and somewhat haughtily named) Control Panel. Choose Start⇨Control Panel to plug away at the innards (see Figure 2-20).

Makes Control Panel look like it did in Windows 98, ME, and 2000

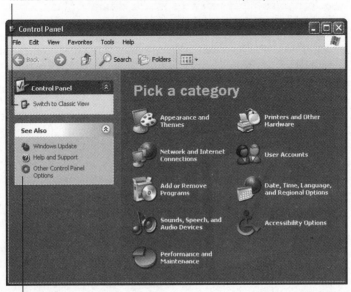

Figure 2-20:
The Control
Panel.

Outlook Express options are down here

I cover various Control Panel components (they're called *applets*) at various points in *Windows XP All-in-One Desk Reference For Dummies,* but the lion's share of the discussion appears in Book I, Chapter 6.

The main components of the Control Panel are as follows:

✦ **Appearance and Themes:** Change what your desktop looks like — wall-paper, colors, mouse pointers, screen saver, icon size and spacing, and so on. Set screen resolution (for example, 1024 x 768 or 800 x 600) so that you can pack more information onto your screen — assuming your eyes can handle it. Make the Windows taskbar hide when you're not using it, and change the items on your Start menu. Change what Windows Explorer shows when you're looking at folders.

✦ **Printers and Other Hardware:** Add or remove printers and connect to other printers on your network. Troubleshoot printers. Set up and modify Windows faxing. Install, remove, and set the options for scanners and digital cameras. Control the options on mice, game controllers, joysticks, and keyboards. Set up dialing rules and other modem arcana.

If you use a modem for your Internet connection, Windows faxing may not do what you expect. You may have to disconnect from the Internet before you send or receive a fax, for example. Many Dummies use J2 fax (www.j2.com) because it treats faxes like e-mail. Outbound faxes are converted to e-mail on your PC using J2's programs, and then they are sent to J2, which routes the fax to a local fax machine at your destination, thus bypassing long-distance telephone charges. Inbound faxes get delivered to your e-mail inbox.

✦ **Network and Internet Connections:** Set up a network. Configure Internet Explorer and its startup page, history files, cookies, AutoComplete, and so on. Set up Internet connections, particularly if you're sharing an Internet connection across a network, or if you have a cable modem or DSL.

✦ **User Accounts:** Add or remove users from the Windows welcome screen. Enable the "Guest" account (see "Adding users" in this chapter). Change account characteristics, such as the picture, password requirement, direct connection with .NET Passport, and so on.

✦ **Add or Remove Programs:** Add and remove specific features in some programs (most notably Windows XP).

✦ **Date, Time, Language, and Regional Options:** Set the time and date — although double-clicking the clock on the Windows taskbar is much simpler — or tell Windows to synchronize the clock automatically. Here you can also add support for complex languages (such as Thai) and right-to-left languages, and change how dates, times, currency, and numbers appear.

✦ **Sounds, Speech and Audio Devices:** Control volume, muting, and so on, but those functions are usually better performed inside the Windows Media Player. You can also choose a Sound scheme, which is something like a desktop theme, except that it involves the pings and pongs you associate with Windows events (for example, the music that plays when Windows starts, or the cling! you hear when you try to click on something you shouldn't). Speech choices cover only text-to-speech output — the "Warning, Will Robinson!" voice you hear when the computer tries to read something out loud.

✦ **Accessibility Options:** Change settings to help you see the screen, use the keyboard or mouse, or have Windows flash part of your screen when the speaker would play a sound.

✦ **Performance and Maintenance:** Use an enormous array of tools for troubleshooting and adjusting your PC, and making it work when it doesn't want to. Unfortunately, it also includes all the tools you need to shoot yourself in the foot, consistently and reliably, day in and day out. Use this part of Control Panel with discretion and respect.

Help and Support

Windows XP includes an online help system that's quite good in places, marginal in some areas, and very, uh, in tune with the Microsoft Party Line everywhere. To bring up the system, choose Start➪Help and Support. The help system (shown in Figure 2-21) connects to the Internet, if possible, and updates its "hot topics" list.

I cover the help system inside and out in Book I, Chapter 3.

TIP

Setting the time

Windows XP/Home synchs the clock on your PC with the clock maintained at time.windows.com once a week. If your modem suddenly starts dialing the phone for no apparent reason, Windows is possibly trying to set its clock. Sometimes the clock doesn't get set — hey, stuff happens on the Internet. If you want to make Windows XP set your PC's clock:

1. **Double-click on the time on the Windows taskbar in the lower right corner of the desktop.**

2. **Choose the tab marked Internet Time. (Yes, it's true: In the future, everything will run on Internet time.)**

3. **Click Update Now.**

   If that doesn't do the trick, follow the link on the Internet Time tab to look up the time

synchronization topic in the Windows Help and Support Center.

If you're paranoid about allowing your PC to phone Uncle Bill once a week — time.windows.com is owned lock, stock, and barrel by Microsoft, natch — follow the preceding three steps, but before you click Update Now, choose the time server at time.nist.gov. That site is run by the National Institute of Standards and Technology, which is a division of the U.S. government. Of course, if you're *really* paranoid, you probably think that NIST is a small division of Microsoft's R&R organization, and that Bill G. talks to Martians on alternate Wednesdays, but I digress.

Keywords only (not full sentences)   All of these do about the same thing

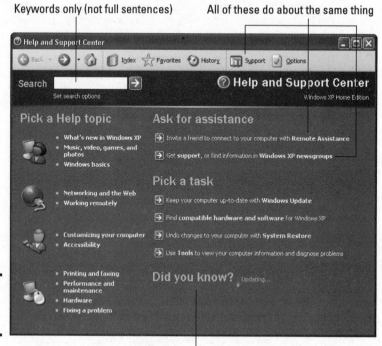

Figure 2-21:
Help and
Support.

Help connects to the Web to fill in this area with the latest

Search

Windows XP jumbles an odd assortment of "searchables" in the Search feature. Choose Start⇨Search and you see what I mean (see Figure 2-22).

I talk about Search extensively in Book I, Chapter 4.

Run

Harkening back to a kinder, gentler age, where you had to type (and type and type and type) to get anything done at a computer, the Run box lets you type program names and have Windows run the programs. It also recognizes Web addresses.

What's that I hear? Scoffing? Perhaps a little snort and a rejoinder about buggy whips and five cent cigars? Oh ye of little faith!

Here. Try this. Choose Start⇨Run, type **calc** (see Figure 2-23), and press Enter.

Search for any kind of file   Files that meet the search criteria

Limits the search to specific kinds of files

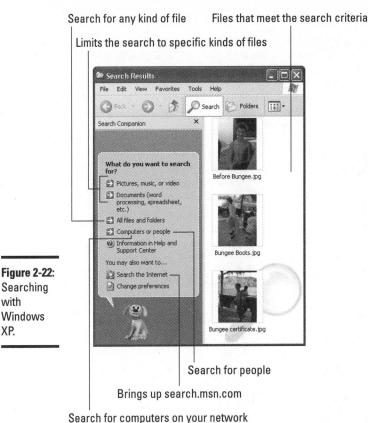

Figure 2-22:
Searching
with
Windows
XP.

Search for people

Brings up search.msn.com

Search for computers on your network

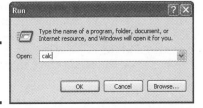

Figure 2-23:
The
Run box.

I defy you to find a quicker, easier way to run the Windows calculator.

Okay, okay. That calc thing isn't much more than a parlor trick that you can try at home. In fact, the Run box is pretty thoroughly outdated and something you don't want to use on a regular basis. You may find unusual situations where you need it, but with any luck you'll never encounter one of them.

All Programs

Almost all of the programs on your computer are accessible through the All Programs menu. To see it, choose Start⇨All Programs. Figure 2-24 shows you what the Games folder in All Programs looks like.

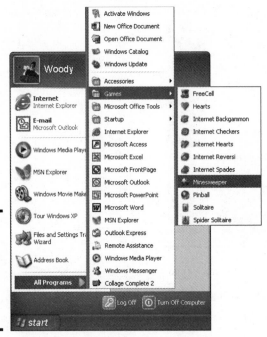

Figure 2-24: The Games folder in the Start Menu's All Programs menu.

Those right arrowheads that you can see to the right of Accessories, Games, Microsoft Office Tools, and Startup in Figure 2-24 simply indicate that you have more choices to make. You can let your mouse pointer hover over an arrowhead-endowed Start menu entry and the *pop-out menu* appears. Or if you're the impatient type, you can click on the menu entry to make the pop-out appear faster.

Are you an inveterate Windows 98/ME/NT/2000 user who misses her old Start menu — the single-column menu, with its little icons, that automatically tucked away menus items you didn't use very often? You can bring the old buzzard back to life, if you insist, and have it replace this new-fangled version of the Start menu. Here's how:

1. **Right-click Start and click Properties.**

2. **Click the Start Menu tab.**

3. **Choose the button marked Classic Start Menu, and click OK.**

   Personally, I prefer the new Start menu to the old one, but it's nice to know that you can go back to the classic version, if you like.

   Organizing the contents of the All Programs menu is very easy:

   ✦ To copy or move an item on the All Programs menu to a different location on the All Programs menu, right-click it, drag it to the new location (you can navigate anywhere on the menu, even into the pop-out menus), release the right mouse button, and choose Copy or Move.

   ✦ To sort all of the items on the All Programs menu alphabetically (with folders sorting higher than programs), right-click on any folder or program and choose Sort by Name.

Getting Around

Your PC is a big place, and you can get lost easily. Microsoft has spent hundreds of millions of dollars to make sure that Windows points you in the right direction and keeps you on track through all sorts of activities.

Amazingly, some of it actually works.

Using Windows Explorer

If you're going to get any work done, you have to interact with Windows. If Windows is going to get any work done, it has to interact with you. Fair 'nuff.

Computer geeks refer to the way Windows interacts with people as the *human interface*. As far as I'm concerned, that jargon's more than a little presumptuous. We poor, downtrodden Windows victims should refer to people-machine interactions as the *stupid computer interface*. About time to put the horse before the cart, sez I.

Now that we have the terminology turned right-side-out, you can easily understand where Windows Explorer fits into the Grand Scheme of WinThings. Windows Explorer lies at the center of the stupid computer interface. When you want to work with Windows — ask it where it stuck your wedding pictures, show it how to mangle your files, tell it (literally) where to go — you usually use Windows Explorer.

If you choose Start➪My Documents or Start➪My Computer or Start➪My Pictures or My Music or My Network Places, Windows Explorer jumps to your command like an automated bird dog, pointing at whatever location you selected. When you run a search with Start➪Search, Windows Explorer takes the reins.

This book is littered with pictures of Windows Explorer. If you look through this chapter, you see Windows Explorer in many of its guises: working on the My Documents folder (refer to Figures 2-9, 2-14, 2-26, 2-27), My Pictures (refer to Figure 2-15), My Music (refer to Figure 2-16), My Computer (refer to Figures 2-18 and 2-19), and viewing the results of a search (refer to Figure 2-22).

Windows Explorer takes a snapshot of your hard drive and presents that snapshot to you. If the contents of the disk change, the snapshot is *not* automatically updated, which can be a real problem. Say you're using Windows Explorer to leaf through the files in My Documents. You suddenly realize that you need to write a letter to your Aunt Emma, so you start Word and write the letter, saving it in My Documents. If you switch back to Windows Explorer, you may not be able to see the letter to Aunt Emma: The snapshot may not be updated. Disconcerting. To force Windows Explorer to update its snapshot, you can close it down and start it again, or you can press F5.

The following are some Windows Explorer high points:

✦ **The name of the current folder appears in the title bar.** If you click once on a file or folder, details for the selected file or folder appear in the Details box in the lower left corner. If you double-click on a folder, it becomes the current folder. If you double-click on a document, it opens. (For example, if you double-click on a Word document, Windows fires up Word and has it start with the document open and ready for work.)

✦ **Almost any actions that you want to perform on files or folders show up in the File and Folder Tasks list in the upper left corner of Windows Explorer.** Provided you know the secret, that is! You have to click once on a folder before the list of folder actions becomes visible; and you have to click once on a file before you can see the list of file actions. So if you're trying to copy a file, and you don't see Copy File in the list of File and Folder Tasks, click the file you want to copy first. When you do, Copy This File shows up in the list of Tasks.

✦ **You can open as many copies of Windows Explorer as you like.** That can be very helpful if you're scatterbrained like me ... er, if you like to multi-task, and want to look in several places at once. Simply choose Start⇨My Documents (or My Computer, whatever), and a totally independent copy of Windows Explorer appears, ready for your finagling.

Creating files and folders

Usually you create new files and folders when you're using a program; you make new Word documents when you're using Word, say, or come up with a new folder to hold all of your offshore banking spreadsheets when you're using Excel. Programs usually have the tools for making new files and folders tucked away in the File⇨Save and File⇨Save As dialog boxes. Click around a bit and you'll find them.

But you can also create a new file or folder directly in My Documents quite easily, without going to the hassle of cranking up a 900-pound gorilla of a program:

1. **Move to the location where you want to put the new file or folder.**

   For example, if you want to stick a new folder called Revisionist Techno Grunge in your My Music folder, choose Start⇨My Documents and double-click on the My Music folder. (If you want to show off, you could just choose Start⇨My Music, which does the same thing.)

2. **Right-click a blank spot in your chosen location.**

   By "blank" I mean "don't right-click on an existing file or folder," okay? If you want the new folder or file to appear on the desktop, right-click any empty spot on the desktop.

3. **Choose New (see Figure 2-25) and pick the kind of file you want to create.**

   If you want a new folder, click Folder.

4. **Windows creates the new file or folder and leaves it with the name highlighted, so that you can rename it by simply typing.**

Figure 2-25: Right-click in an empty location and pick New to create a new file or folder.

Creating new folders is fast and easy. If you choose Start⇨My Music, right-click an empty location in the My Music folder, choose New⇨Folder, immediately type **Revisionist Techno Grunge**, and hit Enter, you become the proud owner of a new folder called Revisionist Techno Grunge, located inside the My Music folder.

Modifying files and folders

Modifying files and folders is easy — rename them, delete them, move or copy them — if you remember the trick: Click once and wait.

The whole world's in a rush. When I'm learning something new, I tend to try a lot of different things all at once, and that plays havoc on computers. They're only human, ya know? When it comes to working with files and folders, it's important that you wait for the computer to catch up with you. In particular, when you're trying to rename, move, copy or delete a file, *click once and wait* while the computer figures out what you can do and shows you the legal choices in the File and Folder Tasks area.

If you double-click on a file, Windows interprets your action as an attempt to open the file and start working on it. Double-click on a Word document, for example, and Word springs to life with the document loaded, ready to rumble.

If you simply click on a file, though — just click once, and wait until the computer catches up — Windows offers a whole range of options for your consideration. In Figure 2-26, I clicked once on a Word document, and Windows gave me all sorts of choices in the File and Folder Tasks area, over on the left.

Figure 2-26: Click once and wait to perform minor surgery on a file.

If you want to copy or move more than one file (or folder) at a time, select all of the files (or folders) before choosing the action in the File and Folders Tasks area. To select more than one file, hold down the Ctrl key while clicking, or click and drag around the outside of the files and folders to "lasso" them. You can also use the Shift key if you want to choose a bunch of contiguous files and folders — ones that are next to each other. Click the first file or folder, push the Shift key, and click the last file or folder.

The options for folders (see Figure 2-27) are a little bit different from those for files. In particular, Windows allows you to share a folder but not a file — Windows isn't set up to share individual files. Windows allows you to print a file but not all the files in a folder; to print all the files in a folder, you have to go into the folder and print each file individually. But even though the details are ever-so-slightly different, the principle remains the same: If you want to muck around with folders or files, *click once and wait.*

Figure 2-27: Folder tasks vary just slightly from file tasks.

Click once and wait is, far and away, the easiest way to rename, move, copy, delete, e-mail, or print a file. It's also the least error-prone, because you can see what you're doing, step by step.

Showing filename extensions

I've been fighting Microsoft on this topic for many years. Forgive me if I get a little, uh, steamed — yeah, that's the polite way to put it — in the retelling.

Every file has a name. Almost every file has a name that looks more or less like this: `Some Name or Another.ext`.

The part to the left of the period — Some Name or Another, in this example — generally tells you something about the file. The part to the right of the period — ext, in this case — is called a *filename extension,* the subject of my diatribe.

Filename extensions have been around since the first PC emerged from its primordial ooze. They were a part of the PC's legacy before anybody ever talked about "legacy." Somebody, somewhere decided that Windows wasn't going to show filename extensions any more. (My guess is that Bill G. himself made the decision, about five years ago, but it's only a guess.) Filename extensions were considered dangerous: too complicated for the typical user; a bit of technical arcana that novices shouldn't have to sweat.

Garbage. Pure, unadulterated garbage.

The fact is that nearly all files have names like Letter to Mom.doc or Financial Projections.xls or ILOVEYOU.vbs. But Windows, in its infinite wisdom, shows you only the first part of the filename. It cuts off the filename extension. So you see Letter to Mom, without the .doc (which brands the file as a Word document), Financial Projections without the .xls (a dead giveaway for an Excel spreadsheet), and ILOVEYOU without the .vbs (which is the filename extension for Visual Basic programs). Table 2-2 lists many common filename extensions.

Table 2-2	Common Filename Extensions
Extension	*Type of File*
bat*, exe, com, dll, vbs, vbe, js, jse	Different kinds of programs
txt, asc	Text
ini, inf, pif	System files
htm, html	HTML files, typically for Web sites or formatted e-mail
bmp, gif, jpg, wmf, mpg, avi	Various kinds of graphic files
mp3, wav, wma, mid	Sound files
doc, dot	Microsoft Word
xls, xla, xlt	Microsoft Excel
ppt, pot	Microsoft PowerPoint
pst	Microsoft Outlook

* *Italicized* names indicate file types that have been used to propagate viruses and other malware. This is far from an exhaustive list, and the guys in black hats are finding new approaches every day.

Every time you see a file mentioned in Windows, you see a little icon next to the filename. For example, Word documents have an icon that looks like a sheet of paper with a flying W on top. Excel worksheets sport grids with a big X. PowerPoint Presentation icons look like Pac Man in drag, but you get the point. (Take a close look at Figure 2-26, and you'll see what I mean.) The icon is directly tied to the filename extension. All .doc files have the flying W icon. All .xls files get grids with Xs. All .ppt files get Pac Man. Uh, Pac Men. Whatever. Graphics files — .gif and .jpg and .bmp among others — sometimes use a small rendition of the picture inside for the icon.

I really hate it when Windows hides filename extensions, for four big reasons:

✦ If you can see the filename extension, you can usually figure out what kind of file you have at hand (refer to Table 2-2). That can be really important when, for example, you get an e-mail message with a file called ILOVEYOU attached to it. Millions of people — even experienced Microsoft geeks, who should know better — received bogus messages, opened the ILOVEYOU file, and got infected with the ILOVEYOU virus. Many of those people would've been tipped off if they had told Windows that they wanted to see the full filename, ILOVEYOU.vbs.

✦ It's almost impossible to get Windows to change filename extensions if you can't see them. For example, while writing this book I wanted to create a new text file called White.htm. I couldn't do it. Finally, I had to haul in Windows Notepad and use an undocumented trick in the File Save dialog box to get the extension changed.

✦ Microsoft Outlook forbids you from sending or receiving specific kinds of files, based solely on the filename extension. If you can't see the filename extension, you don't stand a snowball's chance of figuring out why Outlook is being so draconian.

✦ You bump into filename extensions anyway. No matter how hard Microsoft wants to hide filename extensions, they show up everywhere — from the Readme.txt files mentioned repeatedly in Microsoft's official documentation, to discussions of .jpg file sizes on Web pages, and a gazillion places in between.

To make Windows show you filename extensions, curl your right hand into a ball, extend your index finger, and stick your thumb straight up in the air. Point your index finger at your computer's screen, make your eyes bulge waaaaay out like Jim Carrey, and shout as hysterically as you can, "Show me filename extensions, sucka, or I'm gonna getcha!"

Oops. Wait a second. I got carried away a bit. Sorry.

To make Windows show you filename extensions, follow these steps:

1. **Bring up Windows Explorer (by, say, choosing Start⇨My Documents).**

2. **Choose Tools⇨Folder Options and click the View tab.**

   You see the Folder Viewss Advanced Settings dialog box, as shown in Figure 2-28.

3. **Uncheck the box marked Hide Extensions for Known File Types.**

4. **Click Apply to All Folders at the top of the dialog box, click Yes, and then click OK.**

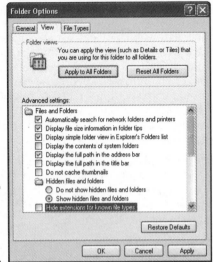

Figure 2-28: Show me the filename extensions!

While you're here, you may want to change two other settings if you can avoid the temptation to delete or rename files that you don't understand. Click the button marked Show Hidden Files and Folders if you want Windows to show you all of the files that are on your computer. Also consider unchecking the box that says Hide Protected Operating System Files (Recommended).

Sharing Folders

Sharing is good, right? Your Mom taught you to share, didn't she? Everything you need to know about sharing you learned in kindergarten — like how you can share your favorite crayon with your best friend and get back a gnarled blob of stunted wax, covered in mysterious goo.

Windows XP/Home supports four kinds of sharing. Unfortunately, "sharing" means different things in different contexts, and the devil (as you surely know by now) can be in Windows' details. Here's a quick guide to the four kinds of sharing that you find lurking in various parts of Windows, how to make them work, and what they really entail.

Sharing on one computer

The simplest form of sharing is with other people who use your computer: They log on with a user name that's different from yours, and you want them to be able to get a specific file or folder. In fact, in Windows XP/Home, just about anybody can get to any of your files, at any time. Sharing with other people on your computer is more about making it easy for them to find the files they need, as opposed to preventing them from seeing files that they shouldn't see. Thus, I think of this simple approach to sharing as "sticking your file or folder in a place where other people may think about looking for it." It's all about location, location, location.

Windows has a folder called Shared Documents that looks and acts a lot like My Documents. Inside Shared Documents, for example, you find folders called Shared Music and Shared Pictures.

The Shared Documents folder has three cool but minor characteristics that make it a special place:

✦ Windows Explorer makes it easy to get to the Shared Documents folder with a link to Shared Documents in the Other Places box on the left side of the screen. You can see it in Figures 2-9, 2-14, 2-18, and 2-26. A Shared Music link shows up on the left when you're in My Music (refer to Figure 2-16), and Shared Pictures appears in My Pictures, too (refer to Figure 2-15). You get the idea.

✦ The Shared Documents folder is shared across your network (if you have one). I talk about sharing among computers on a network in the next section.

✦ Limited users, such as the Guest account, can get into the Shared Documents folder but not into other My Documents folders (see the section on "Using account types" for details).

Aside from those three minor points, the only real advantage to putting a file or folder in Shared Documents is the location: People may think to look there when they go rooting around looking for stuff.

To put a file or folder in the Shared Documents folder — and thus make it "shared" in this sense of the term — you have to physically move it. The following is the easiest way to do that:

1. **Bring up Windows Explorer (choose, say, Start⇨My Documents), and click on the files and/or folders that you want to put in the Shared Documents folder.**

2. **In the File and Folder Tasks box on the left, choose Move this file or Move this folder.**

3. **In the Move Items dialog box (see Figure 2-29), pick a location in or under the Shared Documents folder where you want the chosen files and/or folders to go, and then click Move.**

Click here   Select the file(s) and/or folder(s) you want to share

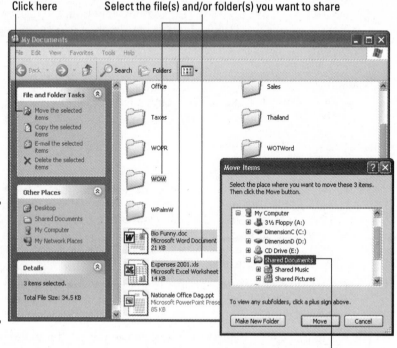

Figure 2-29:
Moving files
and folders
to the
Shared
Documents
folder.

Navigate to the Shared Documents folder, and click Move

The Windows XP documentation suggests that you click and drag the file(s) and/or folder(s) that you want to share to the Shared Documents folder in the Other Places box on the left of the Windows Explorer screen. I strongly recommend that you NOT follow those instructions. Dropping the files in the wrong "Other" place is too easy. More than that, using drag and drop gives you no opportunity to see any folders that may be sitting underneath the Shared Documents folder. That's a sure way to stack tons of unrelated files in one messy folder. It's also an invitation to disaster — or at least massive confusion — if Windows encounters duplicated folder names.

After you move the file or folder, you may have a hard time finding it! For example, if you use Word to create a document and then you move the document to the Shared Documents folder, Word isn't notified that the file has been moved. In Word, if you choose File and then click the name of the document, Word won't be able to find it. Ditto if you use Word's Task Pane to try to open the document. The only way you can open the document is via the File⇨Open dialog box.

Sneak-in-any-time-you-like sharing

The Windows Shared Documents approach to sharing files on a single computer works, but it really doesn't do much, particularly in Windows XP/Home where any user (except a Limited user; see "Using account types") can get into any folder (except those marked Private; see the section "Making a folder private") with a couple of clicks.

I get a big kick out of Microsoft's description of the Shared Documents folder, in the Windows Help file. It goes like this: "Billy can put his homework in Shared Documents so that dad can check his work. And mom can put digital pictures from the family vacation in Shared Pictures so that the whole family can see them."

Gawrsh. I can smell the bread baking in the oven. Or is that the family cat frying in the microwave? *BILLLLYYYYYY!*

Time for a dose of reality here, folks. If Billy is using Word to type up his homework, he'll probably save the work in his My Documents folder. (In fact, if Billy's as smart as I think he is, he'll use a separate folder inside of My Documents for each class's assignments.) Dad won't have any problem finding the homework file. All he has to do is choose Start⇨My Computer, double-click Billy's Documents, and double-click the homework file.

Mom can put the family photo album in Shared Pictures if she wants, but Billy and dad can find the pictures almost as easily in mom's My Pictures folder. Again, they only have to choose Start⇨My Computer, double-click Mom's Documents, and double-click Mom's Pictures, and they're in like Flynn.

Unless you take very specific steps to make a folder private (described in the section called "Making a folder private"), any file you put on a computer running Windows XP/Home is immediately and easily available to anyone who can stumble up to the mouse. Other people who use your computer may take a gander inside the Shared Documents folder to find what they're looking for, but Shared Documents is only a convenient dumping ground. There's no security, no privacy, no way, no how.

Sharing on your network

This is real sharing.

Windows XP lets you identify specific folders (or entire disk drives) that are to be shared with other people on your network. You can also tell Windows whether those other people should be able to only read the files in the folders, or whether they are also allowed to change the files.

Windows XP does not allow you to share individual files across a network. You can either share a folder (which may include other folders and certainly includes files), or you can share an entire drive. But single files won't work.

With Windows XP/Home, the sharing choices are quite straightforward: A folder (or drive) is either shared or it isn't. A shared folder (or drive) can be read-only or read-write. That's it. Anybody on the network can get at a shared folder or drive. There's no additional authorization, no secret password, no clandestine handshake, no list of who can get in and who can't.

In Windows XP/Pro, security options are legion — and chances are very good that you have little choice about security settings. That's why there are network administrators, eh?

Windows sets up the Shared Documents folder, detailed in the preceding two sections, for network sharing. So any files or folders that you move into the Shared Documents folder are "automagically" shared across the network — you needn't lift a finger.

Before you try to share a folder or drive on your network, you have to set up the network. D'OH! For instructions, see Book IX, Chapter 2.

If you don't mind lifting a finger once or twice, you can easily share a folder on your network:

1. **Bring up Windows Explorer (for example, choose Start⇨My Documents).**

2. **Right-click on the folder that you want to share, and choose Sharing and Security.**

3. **In the folder's Properties dialog box (see Figure 2-30), check the box marked Share This Folder on the Network.**

4. **Type a name that other people on the network will find enlightening.**

   Officially, that name is known as a *share name*, but any ol' moniker will work.

5. **If you want to give read-write access to every Tom, Dick, and Harry who can get on the network, check the box marked Allow Network Users to Change My Files.**

Click OK, and the shared folder becomes accessible from all the computers on your network. For example, if I choose Start⇨My Network Places on a computer connected to the computer that holds the folder shown in Figure 2-30, Windows Explorer lets me get into the newly shared folder, as shown in Figure 2-31.

When you share a folder on your network, all of the files and folders inside the shared folder are shared, too.

Figure 2-30:
Share a
folder called
WOW by
using the
Properties
dialog box.

Figure 2-31:
The new
shared
folder
WOW,
accessible
from the
network.

The process for sharing an entire drive is only slightly more difficult, but considerably more intimidating, than sharing a folder:

1. **Choose Start⇨My Computer to bring up My Computer in Windows Explorer.**

2. **Right-click the drive that you want to share.**

   Note that you can share CD drives, diskette drives, and just about any kind of drive.

3. **Choose Sharing and Security.**

   Windows responds with a rather odd statement: To protect your computer from unauthorized access, sharing the root of a drive is not recommended. If you understand the risk but still want to share the root of the drive, click here. (Bafflegab alert: The *root* of a drive is the whole drive, including all the folders on the drive.)

Setting up an entire drive for sharing (by right-clicking the drive choosing Sharing and Security) elicits a message from Windows about "the risk" of sharing an entire drive. Somewhat predictably, I've never found an explanation of "the risk" or its presumably dire consequences in any Windows documentation. Suffice it to say that granting access to an entire drive lets anybody on your network get at everything on the drive. If you're sharing your C: drive, granting access to the drive probably includes the Windows folder (which contains Windows itself), the Program Files folders (which contain most of the programs on your computer), settings for everybody on the computer — the whole enchilada.

4. **Click "If you understand the risk but still want to share the root of the drive, click here."**

5. **Check the box marked Share This Folder on the Network. Type a name for the drive that's intelligible to other people.**

   If you want to give everyone on the network write access, click the box marked Allow Network Users to Change My Files. Click OK and the drive becomes accessible from anywhere on the network.

When sharing CD drives, Jaz drives, and even diskette drives, including a description of the drive in the share name is often a good idea. That way, you know what the drive can handle before you try to use it, so you won't find yourself frustrated by repeated attempts to, oh, transfer your 2.3 MB resume to a 1.44 MB diskette.

"Sharing" files on the Internet

When you put a file on the Internet, Microsoft calls it "sharing" sometimes (see, for example, the Windows Help file on sharing) and "publishing" other times (see the Windows Explorer File and Folder tasks box). I call it "storing." There's a difference, but I'll spare you the semantic argument.

Several companies on the Internet rent out storage space. Sometimes the space is free — you pay by viewing all the ads — and sometimes there's a charge. In all cases, you must have access to the Internet in order to retrieve your files.

The files can be for your use only. Or you can give your friends and neighbors your site ID and password, and they can get at your files, too. That's where "sharing" comes into the picture: Store a file on the Internet, give your buddy a password, and he can retrieve the file and stick it on his computer.

Sharing a file on the Internet — I call it "saving" a file on the Internet — has nothing to do with making your own Web site or cranking out a home page. The sharing that's accessible from Windows Explorer (Windows also calls it "publishing") is nothing more or less than the ability to store a file on the Internet, much the same way as you would store the file on your own hard drive — except that a hundred billion people can get at it, if they know the password.

The two largest purveyors of Internet storage space are a company called Xdrive (www.xdrive.com) and — you guessed it — Microsoft Corporation (www.msn.com). Windows XP has a direct connection to sharing with Xdrive and MSN. Details about the service, how to get it, and how much it costs change from day to day, so I won't include them here. Suffice it to say that the services have a reputation for being reliable and secure, although you'll probably need to activate Microsoft's .NET Passport in order to use them (see the section on "Avoiding Microsoft Passport").

Making a folder private

Under the right circumstances, Windows XP/Home allows you to designate certain folders as *Private*. Private folders aren't accessible to anyone other than their owner.

In order to mark a folder as private, you must meet the following criteria:

◆ You must be using *NTFS* (the Windows NT File System) on the drive that contains the folder. NTFS contains numerous security enhancements that weren't around in earlier Windows file systems. If you bought your PC with Windows XP installed, it's likely (but not certain!) that you're using NTFS on all of your drives. If you upgraded from Windows NT or Windows 2000 to Windows XP, it's likely (but again, not certain) that all of your drives use NTFS. If you upgraded from Windows 98 or ME, you probably *aren't* using NTFS.

To see whether a drive uses NTFS, choose Start⇨My Computer. Right-click on the drive and pick Properties. The File System entry near the top of the Properties dialog box should say NTFS.

◆ The folder has to be one of your folders. You can mark My Documents as private, or you can mark any folder inside of My Documents (such as My Pictures or My Music) as private. You can also mark any folder inside your branch of the Documents and Settings folder. When you mark a folder as private, every folder inside of that folder automatically becomes private.

◆ You should assign a password to your account. Windows allows you to mark a folder as private even if you don't have a password-protected account, but it warns you that you're trying to do something very silly. If your account is not password protected, anybody can pretend to be you when they log on and simply open the private folder.

✦ As soon as you have a password, you should run the Forgotten Password Wizard and create a diskette that allows you to log on to the PC if you forget your password! Make sure the diskette is stored in a secure place. For more information on passwords and the Forgotten Password Wizard, see "Changing user settings" earlier in this chapter.

Windows Taskbar

If you have more than one program running, the fastest way to switch from one program to another is via the Windows Taskbar, shown in Figure 2-32.

Figure 2-32:
The
Windows
Taskbar
makes
switching
among
programs
easy.

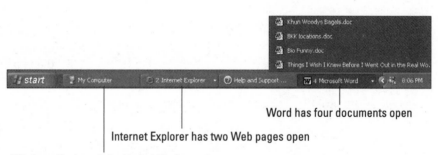

Word has four documents open

Internet Explorer has two Web pages open

Windows Explorer is looking at My Computer

With a few small exceptions, each running program carves out a chunk of space on the Windows taskbar. If more than one copy of a program is running (not an unusual state of affairs for Windows Explorer, among others) or if a program has more than one file open (common in Word, for example) and Windows runs low on real estate in the Taskbar area, the chunks are grouped together, with the number of open documents in front of the program name.

If you click on the button marked 4 Microsoft Word (as shown in Figure 2-32), for example, you see a list of the four documents that Word currently has open. Click on one of those documents, and Word comes up, loaded for bear.

The Windows Taskbar has many tricks up its sleeve, but it has one capability that you're likely to need. *Auto-Hide* lets the Taskbar shrink down to a thin line until you bump your mouse way down at the bottom of the screen. As soon as your mouse hits bottom, the Taskbar pops up. Here's how you teach the Taskbar to Auto-Hide:

1. **Right-click an empty part of the Taskbar.**

Usually the area immediately to the right of the Start button is a good place.

2. **Click Properties.**

The Taskbar tab should be visible.

3. **Check the box marked Auto-Hide the Taskbar, and click OK.**

If you don't want to hunt around for the mouse — or if your mouse has suddenly gone out to lunch — Windows XP has a feature called Coolswitch that lets you switch among running programs, while (insert your best W.C. Fields impression here) your fingers never leave your hands ... er, your fingers never leave the keyboard. Wink, wink. Just hold down the Alt key and press Tab. When you get to the program you want, release the Alt key. Bang.

Shortcuts

Sometimes life's easier with shortcuts. (As long as the shortcuts work, anyway.) So, too, in the Windows XP realm, where shortcuts point to things that can be started. You may set up a shortcut to Word and put it on your Desktop. Double-click on the Word shortcut, and Word starts, the same way as if you chose Start⇨All Programs⇨Microsoft Word.

You can set up shortcuts that point to the following:

✦ Programs, of any kind

✦ Web addresses such as www.woodyswatch.com/signup

✦ Documents, spreadsheets, databases, PowerPoint presentations, and anything else that can be started in Windows Explorer by double-clicking on it

✦ Specific chunks of text inside documents, spreadsheets, databases, presentations, and so on (they're called *scraps*)

✦ Folders (including the weird folders that are inside electronic cameras), even the Fonts folder and others that you may not think of

✦ Drives (hard disks, floppies, CDs, Jaz drives, the works)

✦ Other computers on your network, and drives and folders on those computers

✦ Printers (including printers on other computers on your network), scanners, cameras, and other pieces of hardware

✦ Dial-up network connections

Quick Launch Toolbar

While the Taskbar can get cramped at times, many Dummies are willing to give up a little bit of Taskbar room for a fancy one-click program launcher called the Quick Launch Toolbar. The Quick Launch Toolbar sits next to the Start button (see the following figure), and you can fill it with a handful of little icons that will start your favorite programs.

Click for more Quick Launch programs

Start Internet Explorer

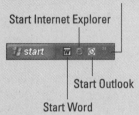

Start Outlook

Start Word

The Quick Launch Toolbar may be visible on your machine, depending on how it was set up. If it isn't visible, you have to turn it on manually. To turn on the Quick Launch Toolbar:

1. **Right-click a blank part of the Taskbar.**

   The area immediately to the right of the Start button is a good place.

2. **Click Properties.**

   You should see the Taskbar tab.

3. **Check the box marked Show Quick Launch, and click OK.**

The Quick Launch Toolbar first appears with three icons: Internet Explorer, Show the Desktop, and Windows Media Player. If you've installed Microsoft Office, Outlook probably shows up as an icon in the Quick Launch Toolbar, too.

You can add or delete icons on the Quick Launch Toolbar — and resize the toolbar, too, if you know the trick. Here's how to do both at the same time, after you use the preceding steps to show the Quick Launch Toolbar:

1. **Right-click a blank part of the Taskbar, and remove the checkmark in front of Lock the Taskbar.**

   That allows you to resize the Quick Launch Toolbar.

2. **Bring up Windows Explorer (choose Start⇨My Computer, for example) and find a program, document, or other file that you want to put on the Quick Launch Toolbar.**

   Hint: if you have Office XP installed, Word is probably C:\Program Files\Microsoft Office\Office10\winword.exe.

3. **Click the file that you want to put on the Quick Launch Toolbar and drag the icon to your preferred location on the Quick Launch Toolbar.**

4. **Right-click the new icon, and click Rename.**

   Whatever name you type appears above the icon when you hover your mouse over the icon.

5. **Repeat Steps 3 and 4 as many times as you like, to bring in as many Quick Launch Toolbar items as you like.**

6. **When you're done, click and drag the "perforated" line at the right edge of the Quick Launch Toolbar, resizing it to take as much (or as little) room as you like. Then right-click a blank part of the Taskbar and put the checkmark back on Lock the Taskbar.**

Judicious use of the Quick Launch Toolbar can save you gobs of time.

Shortcuts can do many amazing things. For example, you can set up a shortcut to a specific network printer on your desktop. Then, if you want to print a file on that printer, just drag the file onto the shortcut. Windows XP takes care of all the details.

There are many different ways to create shortcuts.

Say you use the Windows calculator all the time, and you want to put a shortcut to the Windows calculator on your desktop. Here's an easy way to do it:

1. **Right-click any blank spot on the desktop.**

2. **Choose New⇨Shortcut.**

The Create Shortcut Wizard appears (see Figure 2-33).

3. **Click Browse.**

Figure 2-33:
Use the
Create
Shortcut
Wizard to
put a
shortcut
to the
Windows
Calculator
on your
desktop.

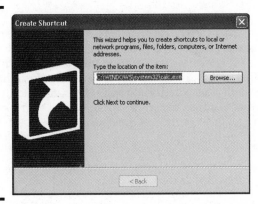

4. In the Browse for Folder dialog box, click My Computer, click the C: drive, click Windows, and then click System32.

Scroll way down to calc.exe (if you haven't told Windows that you want to see filename extensions, you see only "calc" — follow the instructions in the earlier section called "Showing filename extensions" to get full filenames showing).

5. **Click calc.exe and click OK.**

6. **Click Next, type a good, descriptive name like** Calculator, **and click Finish.**

Any time you double-click the Windows Calculator shortcut on your desktop, the Calculator comes to life.

You can use a similar procedure for setting up shortcuts to any file, folder, program, or document on your computer or any networked computer.

Often, the hardest part about setting up a shortcut is finding the program that you want the shortcut to refer to. In the preceding example, you saw how the Windows Calculator is located in the system32 folder, which in turn sits inside the Windows folder (techie shorthand is C:\Windows\system32). Many other Windows programs are in the system32 folder. If you're looking for the Microsoft Office XP programs, they're probably in C:\Program Files\Microsoft Office\Office10, while Office 2000 programs are most likely in C:\Program Files\Microsoft Office\Office. The Fonts folder sits in C:\Windows. In general, if you're looking for programs, your best bet is to look in the Program Files folder first and then in Windows.

You have many other ways to skin the shortcat ... uh, skin the shortcut cat. When you're working in Windows Explorer, you can right-click many types of files and folders, drag them to new locations — other folders, the desktop, even the Start menu or the Quick Launch Toolbar — release the mouse button, and click Create Shortcuts Here.

Believe it or not, Windows thrives on shortcuts. They're everywhere, lurking just beneath the surface. For example, every single entry on the Start menu is a (cleverly disguised) shortcut. The icons in the Quick Launch Toolbar are all shortcuts. Most of Windows Explorer is based on shortcuts — although they're hidden away where you can't reach them. So don't be afraid to experiment with shortcuts. In the worst-case scenario, you can always delete them. Doing so gets rid of the shortcut, but doesn't touch the original file at all.

Here's yet another way to create a shortcut. Say you want to put a shortcut to a network printer on your desktop. Try this:

1. **Choose Start⇨Control Panel and click Printers and Other Hardware.**

2. **Click View installed printers or fax printers.**

3. **Right-click the printer that you want to be shortcutted. (Uh, the printer you want the shortcut to go to? The shortcuttee? Somebody run and get me the Funk and Wagnalls.)**

4. **Click Create Shortcut.**

   Windows displays the dialog box shown in Figure 2-34. You'll find that "Create Shortcut" is a common option when right-clicking almost anything in Windows XP.

5. **Click Yes, and the shortcut that you wanted appears on your desktop.**

Figure 2-34:
The quick
and easy
way to put a
shortcut to
a network
printer
on your
desktop.

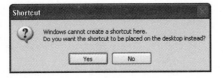

Recycling

When you delete a file, it doesn't go to that Big Bit Bucket in the Sky.

An intermediate step exists between deletion and the Big Bit Bucket. It's called *purgatory* — oops. Wait a sec. Wrong book. (*Existentialism For Dummies,* anybody?) Let me try that again. Ahem.

The step between deletion and the Big Bit Bucket is called the *Recycle Bin.*

When you delete a file or folder on your hard drive — whether by selecting the file or folder in Windows Explorer and pushing the Delete key, or by right-clicking and choosing Delete — Windows doesn't actually delete anything. It marks the file or folder as being deleted but, other than that, doesn't touch it at all.

Files and folders on floppy drives, and on network drives, really *are* deleted when you delete them. The Recycle Bin doesn't work on floppies or on drives attached to other computers on your network.

That's a good news, bad news state of affairs.

The good news: If you ever accidentally delete a file or a folder, you can easily recover the "deleted" file from the Recycle Bin.

The bad news: All of those deleted files take up space on your hard drive. The space won't be re-used until you go through the steps necessary to empty the Recycle Bin — and thus truly delete the files.

To rummage around in the Recycle Bin, and possibly bring a file back to life, double-click the Recycle Bin icon on the Windows desktop. Windows Explorer takes you to the Recycle Bin, as shown in Figure 2-35.

Figure 2-35:
The Recycle
Bin, where
all good files
go when
they kick the
bucket.

To restore a file or folder (sometimes Windows calls it "undeleting"), click
on the file or folder, and then click Restore This Item in the Recycle Bin
Tasks box in the upper-left corner. You can select a bunch of files or folders
by holding down the Ctrl key as you click.

To reclaim the space being used by the files and folders in the Recycle Bin,
click Empty the Recycle Bin in the Recycle Bin Tasks box. Windows asks if
you really, really want to get rid of those files permanently. If you say yes,
they're gone. Kaput. You can never get them back again.

After you empty the Recycle Bin, the deleted files and folders are permanently
gone. If you've been keeping backups, though, you might be able to resurrect
an old file or folder. See the section on backup in Book I, Chapter 6.

Logoff

Last things last, I always say.

Windows XP/Home allows you to have more than one person logged on to a
PC simultaneously. That's very convenient if, say, you're working on the
family PC checking Billy's homework when you hear the cat screaming
bloody murder in the kitchen, and your wife wants to put digital pictures
from the family vacation in the Shared Pictures folder while you run off to
check the microwave.

The ability to have more than one user logged onto a PC simultaneously is called *Fast User Switching*, and it has advantages and disadvantages:

✦ **On the plus side:** Fast User Switching lets you keep all of your programs going while somebody else pops onto the machine for a quick jaunt on the keyboard. When they're done, they can log off, and you can pick up precisely where you left off before you got bumped.

✦ **On the minus side:** All of the idle programs left sitting around by the inactive ("bumped") user can bog things down for the active user. You can avoid the overhead by logging off before the new user logs on.

If you want to disable Fast User Switching, choose Start⇨Control Panel and click User Accounts. At the bottom of the Pick a Task list, click Change the Way Users Log On or Off. Then clear the box marked Use Fast User Switching.

If you've used Windows for any time at all, you have undoubtedly discovered that you have to click Start in order to stop. That's one of the hallmark wonders of the modern Windows world, an oxymoron codified in code.

You probably won't be surprised to learn that you have to click Start in order to log off or switch users. Simply choose Start⇨Log Off, and then click Switch User or Log Off.

To further confuse matters, many computers — especially portables — can go into *Hibernate* or *Standby* mode (variously called Suspend, or Suspend to File, or any of a handful of Out-to-lunch synonyms). The primary differences between the two modes are as follows:

✦ In Standby mode, the PC shuts off the monitor and hard disks but keeps everything in memory so it can "wake up" quickly.

✦ In Hibernate mode, the PC shuts off the monitor and hard disks and shuffles a copy of everything in memory to the hard drive before going night-night. It takes longer to wake up from Hibernate mode because the contents of memory have to be pulled in from the hard drive.

If your portable runs out of power while in Standby mode, you're up the creek without a paddle. If it's in Hibernate mode (and Hibernate mode is working properly — not always a given!), running out of juice poses no problem at all: Plug the PC back into the wall and it comes out of Hibernate mode, brings its memory back from the hard drive, and picks up where you left off.

Not all computers support Standby mode or Hibernate mode. Some older computers don't handle either mode. Other computers can do both. If you have a choice, the guidelines are quite simple:

✦ If there's any chance that your PC will run out of power while in Standby mode, don't use it. Hibernate instead.

✦ If you have to bring your machine back up quickly (say, for a presentation, or to take sporadic notes), use Standby mode.

To go into Standby or Hibernate mode, choose Start⇨Turn Off Computer. You see a Dialog box with the recommended mode as your first option (see Figures 2-36 and 2-37).

Figure 2-36:
Go into
Standby
mode.

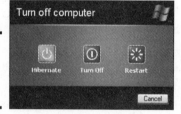

Figure 2-37:
Or use
Hibernate
mode.

If your PC supports both Standby and Hibernate mode, hold down the Shift key while the Turn Off Computer dialog box is on the screen. Windows obliges by changing back and forth between Standby and Hibernate.

You should always turn your computer off the "official" way, by choosing Start⇨Turn Off Computer⇨Turn Off. If you just flip the power switch off, Windows can accidentally zap files and leave them unusable. Windows needs time to make sure that everything is in order before turning the lights off. Make sure it gets the time it needs by using the official method for shutting down.

Chapter 3: Getting Help with Windows XP

In This Chapter

✔ Windows XP Help: a resource of first resort

✔ Remote Assistance

✔ Searching for help in all the right places

✔ More help when you're ready to give up

Think of this chapter as help on Help. When you need help, start here.

Windows XP ships with acres and acres — and layers and layers — of Help. Some of it works well. Some of it *would* work well, if you could figure out how to get to the right help at the right time.

This chapter tells you when and where to look for help. It also tells you when to give up and what to do after you've given up. Yes, killing your PC is an option. But you may have alternatives. No guarantees, of course.

This chapter also includes detailed, simple step-by-step instructions for inviting a friend to take over your computer, via the Internet, to see what is going on and lend you a hand *while you watch*. I believe this Remote Assistance capability is the most powerful and useful feature ever built into any version of Windows.

Here's what you can do when you're ready to tear your hair out.

Meet the Help and Support Center

When you choose Start⇔Help and Support Center, Windows XP presents you with a wide array of choices. Many of the top-level choices that you see in Figure 3-1 "drill down" to the same bits of information; by giving you many different ways to get to that information, Microsoft hopes to make finding what you need easier for you, even if you don't know the answer to your question in advance (a common problem in all earlier versions of Windows Help, which is somewhat improved in Windows XP).

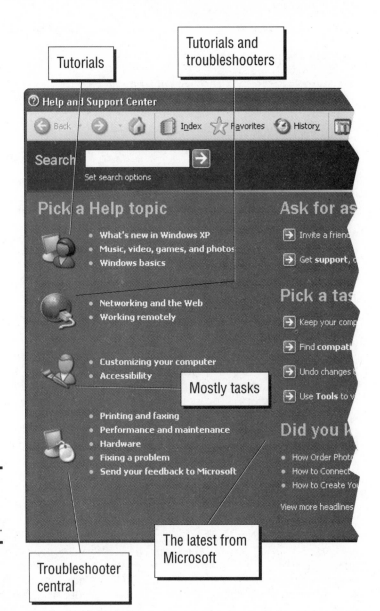

Figure 3-1:
Help and
Support's
cheery face.

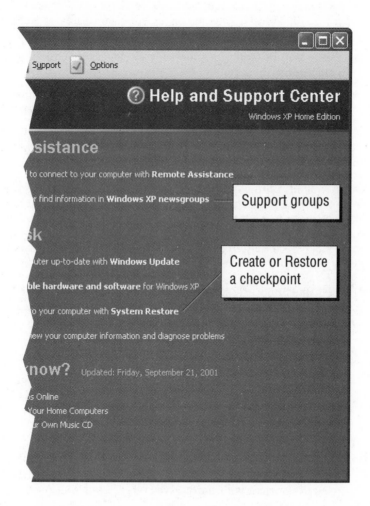

The Help and Support Center gives you only the Microsoft Party Line. If a big problem crops up with Windows XP, you find only a milquetoast report here. If you want searing insight or unbiased evaluations, look elsewhere. Like, oh, in this book, for example.

Windows Help morsels fall into several categories:

✦ **Overviews, articles, and tutorials:** Explanatory pieces aimed at giving you an idea of what is going on, as opposed to solving a specific problem.

✦ **Tasks:** Step-by-step procedures for solving a single problem or changing a single setting.

✦ **Walkthroughs:** Marketing demos ... uh, multimedia demonstrations of capabilities that tend to be, uh, light on details and heavy on splash.

✦ **Troubleshooters:** Take you through a series of (frequently complex) steps to help you identify and resolve problems.

The Help and Support Center exists primarily to reduce Microsoft's support costs, which is both good and bad. Microsoft has tried hard to enable you to solve your own problems. That's good. At the same time, Microsoft has made it pretty difficult to figure out how to pick up the phone and chat with somebody in Product Support Services. I spill the beans — and give you some much better alternatives — at the end of the section called "How to Really Get Help."

The Help and Support Center window puts a happy face on an otherwise sobering (and bewildering!) topic. After you click past the sugar coating, you find a few gotchas that you should know about:

✦ Few Dummies will want to jigger with the Search Options, except to increase the number of "hits" that are reported (see the section on "Running an Effective Search"). The Help and Support Center already looks in all the places it can; your only options are to cut off certain types of searches entirely — and any limitations you apply carry forward to the next search.

✦ Live, one-on-one support from Microsoft is notoriously uneven. One day you get a support rep who can solve your problem in the blink of an eye. The next day you spend hours on hold, only to be told that you need to reformat your hard drive and reinstall Windows.

✦ When Troubleshooters work they work well, but they cover only the most basic problems and the most direct solutions.

✦ Although Remote Assistance is a great idea, in practice the idea has plenty of problems: Both you and your assistant have to be connected to the Internet; you should probably establish a telephone connection prior to setting up the session; and if firewalls exist between you, Remote Assistance probably won't work at all. See the section on "Connecting to Remote Assistance," later in this chapter, for lots of details.

✦ Windows newsgroups on the Internet are unmoderated, which means anybody can post anything. Many well-meaning support group participants dole out utterly execrable advice.

✦ Sometimes Windows Updates are a little half-baked. I usually wait for an update to be in general circulation for at least a week before I apply it to my machine. And I wait at least a month to apply hardware driver updates, unless they solve a specific problem that's been killing me.

✦ The Hardware and Software Compatibility lists leave much to be desired. If a piece of hardware or software that you want to buy appears on the list, it's probably at least a little bit compatible. If it isn't on the list, you can't really draw much of a conclusion.

It never hurts to run a System Restore checkpoint when Windows is firing on all cylinders. The worst possible time to create a checkpoint? When your system has gone to the dogs. Right now, while you're thinking about it and Windows makes you smile from ear to ear, follow the instructions in Chapter 6 to run a checkpoint. That way, when the inevitable falling out occurs, you'll have something to fall back on.

How to Really Get Help

You use the Help and Support Center when you need help and support, right?

Well, yes. Sorta.

In my experience, the Help and Support Center works best when

✦ You want to learn about what functions big pieces of Windows perform, and you aren't overly concerned about solving a specific problem (for example, "What is Windows Media Player"?).

✦ You have a problem that's easy to define ("my printer won't print").

✦ You have a pretty good idea of what you want to do, but you need a little prodding on the mechanics to get the job done ("How do I change my desktop's picture?").

The Help and Support Center won't do much for you if you have only a vague idea of what's ailing your machine, if you want to understand enough details to think your way through a problem, if you're trying to decide on what hardware or software to buy for your computer, or if you want to know where the XP bodies are buried.

For all of that, and much more, you need an independent source of information. Like this book, for example.

My free e-mail newsletter, Woody's Windows Watch, can come in handy. Drop by www.woodyswatch.com and sign up.

If you can't find the help you need in the Help and Support Center, consider expanding your search for enlightenment in this order:

✦ Far and away the best way to get help involves simple bribery. Buttonhole a buddy who knows about this stuff, and get her to lend you a virtual hand. Promise her a beer, a pizza, a night on the town — whatever it takes. If your friend knows her stuff, it'll be cheaper and faster than the alternatives. If you can cajole your machine into connecting to the Internet — and get your friend to also connect to the Internet — Windows XP makes it easy for a friend to take over your computer while you watch with a feature called Remote Assistance, which I discuss in the next section, "Connecting to Remote Assistance."

✦ If your buddy is off getting a tan in Patong, you may be able to find help elsewhere on the Internet. See the section "Getting Help on the Web," later in this chapter.

✦ If all else fails, you can try to contact Microsoft by e-mail. You may qualify for free e-mail support, using something called Microsoft Online Assisted Support. The best way to find out if you qualify, and connect with a support droid if you do, is to jump through the prescribed hoops:

1. **Choose Start⇨Help and Support.**

2. **Under the Ask for Assistance list, click Get support, or find information in Windows XP newsgroups.**

3. **In the Support box, click Get Help From Microsoft.**

4. **You connect to Microsoft's support site on the Internet, and at that point you have a chance to review what support is available to you and how much it will cost.**

✦ As a last resort, you can try to contact Microsoft by telephone. Heaven help ya.

Microsoft offers support by phone — you know, an old-fashioned voice call — but some pundits (including yours truly) have observed that you'll probably have more luck with a psychic hotline. Be that as it may, the telephone number for tech support in the USA is (425) 635-3311; in Canada, it's (905) 568-4494.

Connecting to Remote Assistance

Raise your hand if you've heard this conversation.

Overworked Geek, answering the phone: "Hi, honey. How's it going?"

Geek's Clueless Husband: "Sorry to call you at work, but I'm having trouble with my computer."

OG: "What kind of trouble?"

GCH: "I clicked on the picture and it went into Microsoft, you know, and I tried to look at this report my boss sent me, but the computer said it couldn't."

OG: "Huh?"

GCH: "You're supposed to know about computers. C'mon, tell me. I'm sure you've seen this a hundred times. I clicked on the picture but the computer said it couldn't. How do I look at the report?"

OG: "Spfffft!"

GCH: "What's wrong? Why don't you say anything? You have time to help the other people in your office. Why can't you make time for me?"

OG wonders, for the tenth time that day, how she ever got into this bloody business.

At one time or another you may have been on the sending or the receiving end of that conversation — probably both, come to think of it. In the final analysis, one thing's clear: When you're trying to solve a computer problem — whether you're the solver or the solvee — being able to look at the screen is worth ten thousand words. Or more.

Windows XP includes a feature called Remote Assistance that lets you call on a friend to take over your PC. The interaction goes something like this:

1. **You create a special message inviting your friend to take over.**

2. **You send the message to your friend, either by standard e-mail, via Windows Messenger, or by giving your friend a file.**

3. **Your friend receives the message and responds by clicking on a specific link.**

4. **Your PC displays a message saying that your friend wants to take over.**

5. **If you give the go-ahead, your friend takes complete control of your machine. You watch as your friend types and clicks, just as you would if you knew what the heck you were doing. Your friend solves the problem, as you watch.**

6. **Either of you can break the connection at any time.**

The thought of handing your machine over to somebody on an Internet connection probably gives you the willies. I'm not real keen on it either, but Microsoft has built some industrial-strength controls into Remote Assistance. If you like, you can limit your friend to simply observing, instead of taking over the controls of your computer. You can also require your friend to type in a password before the session gets started. And you can put a time limit on the invitation: If your friend doesn't respond within an hour, say, the invitation gets cancelled.

Plenty of pitfalls lurk around the edges of Remote Assistance, but it mostly rates as an amazingly useful, powerful capability. The following are among the potential problems:

✦ Both of you have to be connected to the Internet. If you can't get connected to the Internet — especially if that's the problem you're trying to solve — you're outta luck.

✦ If you have a dial-up Internet connection, you have to *stay connected* from the time you create the invitation through the time you send the invitation, while your friend responds, and all the way until the time that the Remote Assistance session ends. You can't hop on the Internet, send an invitation, break your Internet connection, and then dial back an hour later to get the Remote Assistance session going.

✦ Both of you have to be running Windows XP or some other operating system that supports Remote Assistance.

✦ One of the following must be true so that you can send the invitation, and your friend can use the invitation to get connected to your PC:

• Both of you have to be logged on to Windows Messenger .

• You must be able to send, and your friend must be able to receive, e-mail with an attachment that includes a hot link.

• You must be able to send a file to your friend — possibly over a network or by simply handing your friend a floppy.

✦ If a firewall is between either of you and the Internet, it may interfere with Remote Assistance.

You — the person with the PC that's going to be taken over — must initiate the Remote Assistance session. Your friend can't tap you on the shoulder, electronically, and say something like — with apologies to Dire Straits — "You an' me, babe, how 'bout it?"

When you're ready to set up the connection for Remote Assistance, here's what you need to do:

1. **Make sure your friend is ready.**

   Call him or shoot him e-mail and make sure he's going to have his PC on, connected to the Internet, and running Windows XP. Also, make sure that he will have Windows Messenger cranked up, will be checking e-mail frequently, or will be waiting for you to hand him a file or make one available on your network.

   Make sure you can contact your friend using your selected method: If he's going to use Windows Messenger, make sure you're able to send messages back and forth; if you're using e-mail, make sure he's in your address book and send him a test message to make sure you have his e-mail address down pat; if you're going to send a diskette by carrier pigeon, make sure the pigeon knows the route and has had plenty of sleep.

2. **When you contact your friend, make up a password and give it to him.**

   It doesn't have to be anything fancy — a single letter or number will do — and it shouldn't be a password you use for anything else. It's a one-timer that will be valid only for this single Remote Assistance session.

3. **Get on the machine that will be zombified (that's a technical term I just made up — it's your computer, the one that your Remote Assistance friend will take over), and make sure it's connected to the Internet.**

4. **Choose Start⇨Help and Support to bring up the Help and Support Center (refer to Figure 3-1).**

5. **Under the Ask for Assistance list, click Invite My Worthless Brother-In-Law to Rummage Through All Of My Secret ... wait a sec ... wrong command ... here we go ... click Invite a Friend to Connect to Your Computer Using Remote Assistance.**

6. **In the Remote Assistance pane, click Invite Someone to Help You.**

7. **You have three choices for notifying your assistant, as shown in Figure 3-2.**

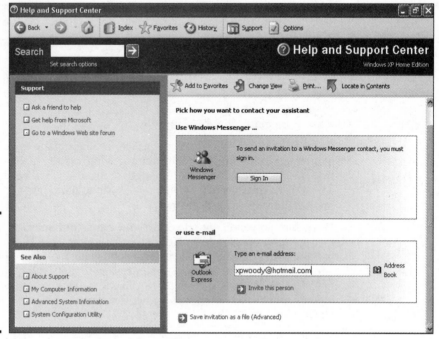

Figure 3-2:
The three
methods for
sending a
Remote
Assistance
invitation.

A. If your assistant has Windows Messenger running, and you have decided to contact each other that way, Sign In to Windows Messenger. You have to pick your friend's e-mail address and then click Invite This Person.

B. If your assistant is waiting for an e-mail message from you, type his address in the space provided and click Invite This Person.

It's important that you send a Remote Assistance invitation to the right person. You don't want to invite just anybody to take over your PC, eh? Because the potential security exposure is so great, I strongly recommend that you add your helper to your Address Book and test the Address Book entry a couple of times by sending trial messages before crunch time. Then use the Address Book to send your invitation.

C. If your assistant expects to get a file from you (and this option really isn't any more advanced than the other two, in spite of what the dialog box says), click Save Invitation As a File (Advanced).

8. **The Remote Assistance program asks you to type your name, to set a time limit for the invitation to expire (recommended: one hour), and to type a password (no limitation on length or form). If you're communicating via e-mail, you're also allowed to type a message to your friend. Just follow the easy steps.**

When the Remote Assistance program finishes, one of three things happens, depending on how you're communicating with your friend:

A. If you're using Windows Messenger, your friend (who's identified in the Windows interactions as, ahem, the *Expert*) receives a computer-generated instant message inviting him to help you, much like the message shown in Figure 3-3.

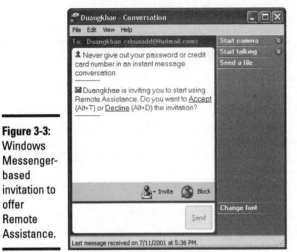

Figure 3-3:
Windows
Messenger-
based
invitation to
offer
Remote
Assistance.

B. If you're using e-mail, the Remote Assistance program generates an e-mail message destined for your friend. You probably get an e-mail warning message like the one shown in Figure 3-4, saying that some renegade program (like, Windows) is trying to send an e-mail message on your behalf. Just click Send.

Figure 3-4:
E-mail
security
rears its
ugly head in
the middle
of your
attempt to
send a
message to
the person
who's going
to help you.

If you create a Remote Assistance invitation that goes out via e-mail, using this B procedure, your e-mail program may *not* send the invitation automatically. As soon as you click Send, you should immediately start your e-mail program (choose Start⇨E-mail) and make sure that the invitation isn't languishing in your Outbox.

C. If you're working with a file, you need to tell Windows where to put the file called RAInvitation.msrcincident. The file easily fits on a diskette, or you may want to save it on a network drive. That's the file you should deliver to your friend.

9. **Your friend, the Expert, has to initiate the Remote Assistance session. The method for starting the session varies depending on how he got your invitation:**

A. If you're using Windows Messenger, your friend can start helping you by clicking Accept (refer to Figure 3-3).

B. If you're using e-mail, your friend receives a message that looks like the one in Figure 3-5. To initiate the Remote Assistance session, he must open the attached document and respond Yes to the Remote Assistance request shown in Figure 3-6.

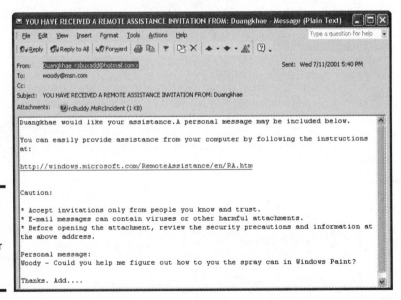

Figure 3-5: The e-mail message sent to your friend, the helper.

C. If your friend opens the file RAInvitation.msrcincident, he sees the message shown in Figure 3-6. Responding Yes initiates the Remote Assistance session.

Figure 3-6:
In order to start the Remote Assistance session, your friend has to respond Yes to this question.

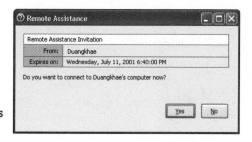

If your friend attempts to open the file RAInvitation.msrcincident and gets an error message saying that he must choose a program to open the file, he's not using Windows XP. As of this writing, only Windows XP can initiate a Remote Assistance session. At some point in the future, Microsoft possibly will make Remote Assistance available with other operating systems. For the latest information, choose Start⇨Help and Support, and type **Remote Assistance** in the Search box.

10. **After your friend, the Expert, initiates a Remote Assistance session, you need to allow him onto your machine.**

After he does his part (by clicking Accept in an Instant Message or clicking Yes in the Remote Assistance request), you see the message shown in Figure 3-7.

Figure 3-7:
You are given final authority on accepting or rejecting the Remote Assistance session.

11. Click Yes and two things happen simultaneously.

First, your computer sprouts a Remote Assistance dialog box, like the one shown in Figure 3-8.

Instant messaging history

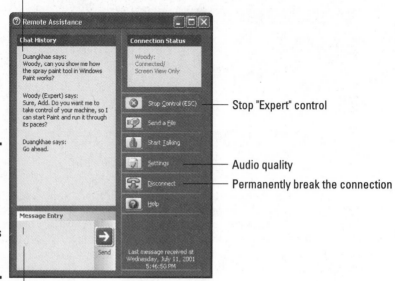

Figure 3-8:
The Remote
Assistance
control
dialog box
that appears
on your
machine.

Stop "Expert" control

Audio quality

Permanently break the connection

Type messages for your "Expert" here

Second, your friend's computer — which is to say, the "Expert's" computer — receives a Remote Assistance dialog box that looks a little bit like yours, but it also has a viewing box that displays everything on your screen. (See Figure 3-9.)

12. If your friend wants to take control of your PC, he needs to click the icon marked Take Control in the upper-left corner of the Remote Assistance window.

If he does that, your machine warns you that the "Expert" is trying to take control, displaying the dialog box shown in Figure 3-10.

Instant messaging history

Take control of the "Novice's" computer

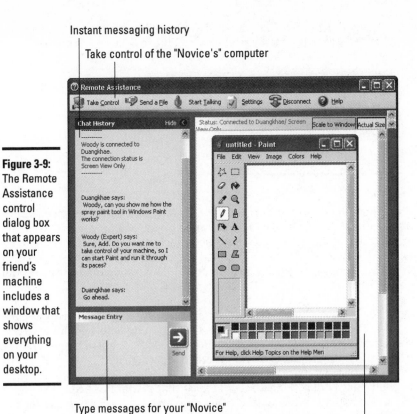

Figure 3-9:
The Remote
Assistance
control
dialog box
that appears
on your
friend's
machine
includes a
window that
shows
everything
on your
desktop.

Type messages for your "Novice"

Scroll to see the entire "Novice" desktop

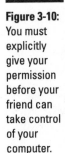

Figure 3-10:
You must
explicitly
give your
permission
before your
friend can
take control
of your
computer.

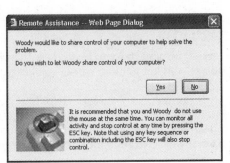

13. **When you (the "Novice") have given your blessing, your friend (the "Expert") sees the message shown in Figure 3-11 on his screen.**

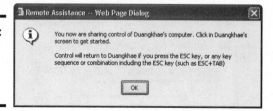

Figure 3-11:
Your friend
is in the
driver's
seat.

After a Remote Assistance session is under way and you've released control to your friend, your friend can do anything to your computer that you can do. Anything at all. Both of you have simultaneous control over the mouse pointer. If either or both of you type on the keyboard, the letters appear on-screen. You can stop your friend's control of your computer by pressing the Esc key.

Your friend can rest assured that this is a one-way connection. He can take control of your computer, but you can't do anything on his computer. He can see everything that you can see on your desktop, but you aren't allowed to look at his desktop at all. Who ever said life was fair?

All good things come to an end, or at least that's what I've been told. Remote Assistance sessions end when one or the other participant clicks the Disconnect icon, closes the Remote Assistance dialog box (for example, by clicking the X in the upper right corner), or when the Internet connection goes away.

Running an Effective Search

Windows Help has been set up for you to jump in, find an answer to your problem, resolve the problem, and get back to work.

Unfortunately, life is rarely so simple. So, too, with Help. Chances are good that you won't dive into Help until you're feeling very lost. And once you're there, well, it's like the old saying, "When you're up to your <insert favorite expletive here> in alligators, it's hard to remember that you need to drain the swamp."

Windows Help has a few tools that should help you to stay organized — to keep your <expletive> from being overwhelmed by 'gators — if you make a conscientious effort to learn about them and put them to use.

Understanding search limitations

If you're looking for sophisticated search capabilities, Windows Help isn't going to impress you. It has no natural language feature, so you can't ask a question such as "How do I install a digital camera?" and expect a decent response. All searches are for keywords. The words you type are the words that Windows Help uses.

Still, Windows Help has some flexibility and built-in know-how, as displayed in Table 3-1.

Table 3-1	Windows Help Search Combinations
If you search for	*Help returns*
mouse keyboard	All entries referring to either *mouse* or *keyboard*
mouse and keyboard	All entries that refer to both *mouse* and *keyboard*
mouse not keyboard	Entries that refer to only *mouse,* and do not refer to *keyboard*

Setting search options

The Windows XP Help and Support Center gives you surprisingly few options for controlling the destiny of your searches.

Although your choices are few, two Search changes make sense for most Dummies:

1. **Choose Start⇨Help and Support.**

2. **Click the Options icon in the upper-right corner of the screen.**

3. **In the Options box, click Set Search Options.**

   You see the Set Search Options dialog box, shown in Figure 3-12.

4. **If you want Windows Help to show you more than 15 results from each of its searches — a choice that slows down searches but increases your chances of finding an answer you need — consider setting the Return Up To XX Results Per Provider to 50.**

5. **If you dislike the way Windows Help highlights all the "matched" words when it shows you the results of a search, uncheck the box marked Turn On Search Highlighting.**

Collapsing the view

After you find the help you're looking for, you frequently want to keep the Help text in front of you, but you couldn't care less about the search pane, the index, or any of those fancy icons.

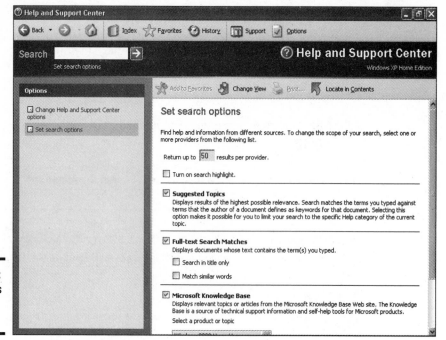

Figure 3-12:
Slim pickins
for search
options.

If you click the Change View icon, Windows Help retracts all of the unnecessary pieces, leaving the screen refreshingly uncluttered. Compare Figure 3-13
to Figure 3-12.

Figure 3-13:
Click the
Change
View
icon, and
Windows
Help pulls
in all the
unnecessary
appendages.

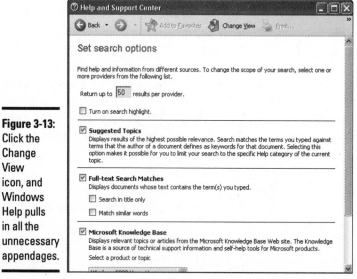

When you want the search box back, just click the Change View icon again, and Windows Help returns to its usual out-of-the-shell configuration.

Keeping your Favorites

Compared to Internet Explorer, Windows Help maintains a very unsophisticated list of Favorites. You have a couple ways to use Favorites:

✦ When you bump into a Help topic that you want to be able to find again, click the Add to Favorites icon (to the left of the Change View icon in Figure 3-14).

✦ To bring up your list of Favorites, click the Favorites icon at the top of the Help window.

Figure 3-14:
Windows Help's unsophisticated list of Favorites.

When you're running through a Troubleshooter that shuts down Windows, the Troubleshooter text warn you that a restart is imminent. Adding the Troubleshooter to your Favorites list before Windows shuts down is always a good idea, in case Windows Help has trouble finding its way back.

Hopping to the Table of Contents

Introducing one of Windows XP Help's great unsung features: the ability to jump from a Help topic straight to the topic's location in the Table of Contents.

What? You say you haven't seen the Help Table of Contents? Oh ye of little faith! There's a good reason why you haven't seen it. Microsoft goes to great lengths to hide it in Windows XP. Earlier versions of Windows made it very easy to leaf through the Table of Contents — there was a little Contents tab, prominently displayed in the Help panel, which brought up the TOC. Not so in Windows XP.

If you want to look at the Windows XP Table of Contents, you must first search for a topic using the techniques outlined in this section or find a topic in the Index (see "Working through the index" in this chapter) *before* you can jump to the Table of Contents. That's a lot like requiring you to pull a book off a library shelf before you're allowed to look at the card catalog, but sometimes Windows works in mysterious ways.

When you've found a topic that interests you, simply click the Locate in Contents button to jump to the TOC. From there you can leaf through related topics.

If you try to use Windows XP's Help to get help on, uh, Windows XP Help, you're in for a merry ride. For example, Windows XP Help goes to great lengths explaining how to use the Contents tab in Help (see the topic "Getting Help"). Of course, Windows XP doesn't *have* a Contents tab in Help. A foolish inconsistency is the hobgoblin of little minds, eh?

Working through the index

Just as this book has an index, so, too, does the Windows Help and Support Center. To find the index, click the Index icon. The index appears, as shown in Figure 3-15.

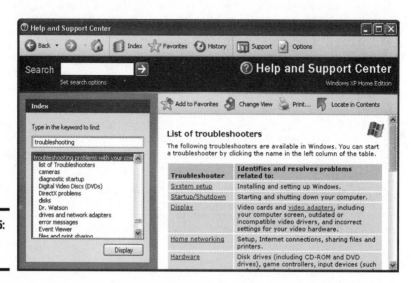

Figure 3-15: The Help index.

The Windows Help index is quite thorough but, like any index, relies heavily on the terminology being used in the Help articles themselves. That leads to frequent chicken-and-egg situations: You can find the answer to your question quite readily if you, uh, know the answer to the question. Or if you know the terminology involved (which is nearly the same thing, eh?).

Generally, Search is the best way to approach a problem, but the Index comes in handy from time to time. Don't hesitate to use it.

Getting Help on the Web

Of course, the single greatest source of information about Windows XP is the single greatest source of information about *everything* — the Web. The Windows Help and Support Center weaves in and out of the Web in a multitude of ways.

Whenever you use the Windows Help and Support Center to search for an answer to a question, it's vitally important that you get hooked up to the Web. Microsoft posts answers to its most-often-asked questions. Thousands of 'Softies are actively involved in keeping the answers as accurate as time and corporate discretion permit.

The following are the best sources I've found for Windows Help and information:

✦ **The Microsoft Knowledge Base:** This is the mother lode, the source of information that all of Microsoft's tech support people use. http://search.support.microsoft.com/kb/c.asp

✦ **Windows newsgroups:** These are a great source of information, but you have to remember that not everybody posting to the newsgroups knows whereof they speak. To get there, choose Start➪Help and Support and in the Ask for Assistance corner, click on Get Support or Find Information in Windows XP Newsgroups. Then in the Support box, click Go to a Windows Web Site Forum.

✦ **The Windows Update site:** You can get to this site by choosing Start➪Help and Support and, in the Pick a Task list, clicking Keep Your Computer Up-To-Date with Windows Update.

✦ **Product Support Options:** If you're curious about the tech support available directly from Microsoft, what you qualify for, and how much it will cost, hit www.microsoft.com and search for Product Support Options.

✦ **Woody's Windows Watch:** My free weekly newsletter focuses on the important issues and tough problems that tall Windows users face. Drop by `www.woodyswatch.com` and sign up.

✦ **User Web sites:** Several free user-helping-user Web sites focus on Windows problems (and even a few solutions!). My site, the WOPR Lounge (`www.wopr.com/lounge`) draws thousands of people every day.

Chapter 4: Searching Your Machine and Beyond

In This Chapter

✔ Secrets for powerful searches on your computer

✔ Automatic Indexing Service — less wait, more weight

✔ Search Companion strategy: throw Rover a bone

✔ Best ways to search the Web

Computers store lots and lots of stuff. As long as you're churning out the stuff, life goes along pretty easily. Sooner or later, though, the time comes when you have to find some stuff — the right stuff — and that's when the stuff hits the fan.

Windows XP includes a powerful search feature with a cute name — Search Companion — and a cloying mascot, a mutt called Rover.

This chapter explains how to make Rover sit up, heel, fetch, and ... play dead.

TIP

If you want to understand how Windows performs searches, you have to be able to see filename extensions — the short (usually three-letter) part of each file's name following the period that identifies the file's type, such as .doc and .jpg. Windows XP does not show you filename extensions unless you specifically tell it to. In order to make heads or tails out of anything in this chapter, make Windows show you filename extensions by following the steps outlined in Book I, Chapter 2.

Exploring the Search Companion

If you choose Start⇨Search, you bring the Search Companion to life, with Rover (see Figure 4-1) sitting ever-so-patiently at the bottom of the pane, tail wagging, waiting to help you fetch whatever you like.

Very few options

All do basically the same thing

Recognize Windows Explorer?   The folder that holds the file

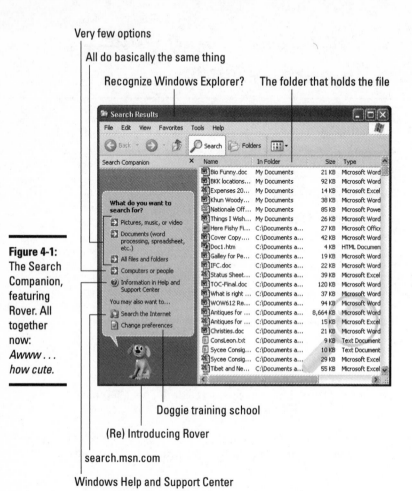

Figure 4-1:
The Search
Companion,
featuring
Rover. All
together
now:
*Awww . . .
how cute.*

Doggie training school

(Re) Introducing Rover

search.msn.com

Windows Help and Support Center

Rover exists solely to reduce your anxieties: a nice, cuddly pooch to reassure you that Windows XP is so friendly and helpful. Rover just wants to roll over and get scratched like a, well, like a Companion. C'mere Rover. Good boy.

Of course, Microsoft knows very well that if you're searching for something, you're probably in a panic — a file isn't where you put it, you need it now, and you're about ready to scream bloody murder at the stupid computer or commit some heinous act.

What about Bob?

Does Rover look familiar? You may have seen him in a shopping mall demo back in the mid-1990s. Rover was a "Friend of Bob" in Microsoft's ill-fated and much-maligned Bob operating system (born 1995, died 1996, sold 58,000). Microsoft Bob broke some new ground in computer obtuseness, drew universal ridicule, and spawned such evil as the Office 97 and 2000 Office Assistant, Clippy, a paper clip who managed to survive the turbulent 90s with no visible means of support. Bob has a fascinating history. According to Microsoft legend, possibly apocryphal, Bill G. first saw a test version of Bob dressed in a clown costume. Bill sat down and played with the new technology for quite some time and, at the end of the test session, declared that he wanted "to kill that %#$@ clown." On January 1, 1994, Melinda French —

one of Microsoft Bob's marketing managers — took on a new title: Mrs. Gates. Bob went on to become one Microsoft's worst disasters of all time: tons of boxes of Microsoft Bob languished in warehouses before the product was unceremoniously yanked. Five years later, Bob's on-screen canine friend, Rover, appears to have a new job as the Windows XP Search companion. (When Microsoft developers are forced to use their own tools while they're still being tested, they call it "eating your own dog food." I wonder if there's a parallel here?) In a major Microsoft marketing move, Bob's offspring Clippy was "retired" in Office XP — Office users no longer have to put up with the %$#@! paper clip, generally — and millions of dollars were spent on ceremoniously terminating the character. See www.officeclippy.com.

If you can't find a file or a folder, you crank up Search Companion. You probably figured that out. Search Companion also claims that it looks for computers, people, and places on the Internet. It does. Sorta.

You may not know that Search Companion can be jimmied to bypass Microsoft's proprietary Internet search site, search.msn.com — a trick that makes Internet searching a lot faster and more powerful. Details are in the section "Searching the Internet," later in this chapter.

If the Search Companion screen shown in Figure 4-1 looks familiar, it should. In fact, Search Companion is a pane inside Windows Explorer. You can see the striking similarities as shown in Figure 4-2.

What you can find

If you haven't yet told Windows XP to show you filename extensions — the usually-three-letter part of a file name that follows the last period — you better do so now, before you try to run a search. You don't stand a snowball's chance of understanding searches unless you have filename extensions showing. Windows XP's own Help and Support Center refers to filename extensions in many places, without explaining what they are or why you need them. You can be a Dummy, but don't be a Doormat. Read up on filename extensions in Book I, Chapter 2; then go into Windows Explorer and make Windows show them.

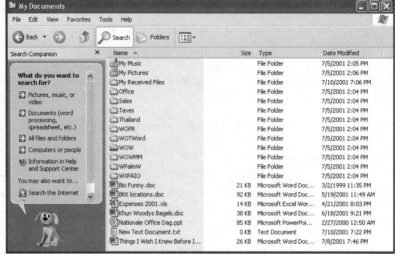

Figure 4-2:
Click the Search icon in Windows Explorer and the Search Companion appears.

When you bring up the Search Companion by choosing Start⇨Search (refer to Figure 4-1) or clicking the Search icon in any Windows Explorer window (refer to Figure 4-2), Rover offers to search for the following:

✦ **Pictures, music or video:** Choosing this option leads Rover (see Figure 4-3) to ask whether you want to limit your search to Pictures and Photos, Music, and/or Video. You can check as many boxes as you like; if you don't check any, Windows assumes that you want to check them all. Windows then runs a full search (as described in the next section, "Looking for Files and Folders") but narrows down the search to files with specific filename extensions, as shown in Table 4-1.

Note that the contents of the file don't matter: Windows XP doesn't look inside the file to see if it contains, oh, a JPEG image, for example. The Search Companion cares about only the filename extension.

✦ **Documents (word processing, spreadsheet, and so on):** Like the Pictures, Music, or Video option, choosing Documents leads to a full search, limited to the specific filename extensions shown in Table 4-1.

✦ **All files and folders:** This leads to the full search described in the next section, "Looking for Files and Folders."

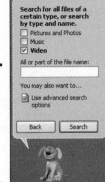

Figure 4-3:
Narrowing
down the
search
based on
filename
extensions.

✦ **Computers or people:** The computer side of this search (assuming you leave the computer name box empty) is identical to choosing Start⇨My Network Places and clicking View Workgroup Computers.

The people side of the search leads to your Outlook Express (not Outlook) address book. From there, you can also use OE's crude interface to look in the Bigfoot, VeriSign, or WhoWhere directories.

Don't bother using Start⇨Search to find people on the Internet. As of this writing, two of the three options don't work very well: The VeriSign directory is very tiny, and the Bigfoot directory automatically redirects to AT&T's AnyWho lookup site. If you're serious about finding somebody on the Web, use one of the standard search engines: www.anywho.com works well, as do people.yahoo.com and www.whowhere.lycos.com.

✦ **Information in Help and Support Center:** This option opens up the Help and Support Center, precisely the same as if you had chosen Start⇨Help and Support Center. See the preceding chapter for full details.

Table 4-1	Filename Extensions in Search
Choose this type of file	*And Windows limits the search to files with these common filename extensions**
Pictures and Photos	ANI, ART, BIT, BMP, CDR, CGM, CMP, DIB, EPS, GIF, JPG, TIF, PCX, PNG, PS, WMF
Music	AIF, AIFF, ASF, CDA, FAR, MID, MP3, RAM, RMI, WAV, WMA
Video	ASF, ASX, AVI, MMM, MPG
Documents	ASC, ASP, AW, CHI, CHT, DBF, DOC, DOT, HTM, HTML, MDB, MSG, OBD, PDD, POT, PPS, PPT, PUB, RTF, SAM, TIF, TXT, WRI, XLA, XLL, XLS, XLT

* This list is far from exhaustive; yes, TIF appears in two lists

The Search Companion also allows you to search the Internet. I go into details about this option in the section called "Searching the Internet," later in this chapter.

What you can't find

Surprisingly, Windows XP Search Companion doesn't search Outlook or Outlook Express e-mail messages unless you turn on the Indexing Service (discussed in the section "Indexing service," later in this chapter). If you want to look for text in a message, or even a message Subject line, Windows XP can't do it.

Office XP — specifically Word 2002 — can reach inside Outlook e-mail messages and search for text, Subject lines, senders, receivers, and the like. Word also supports AND/OR search arguments, narrowing searches to specific Outlook folders, and much more. If you have Office XP, you should use this vastly more powerful search tool:

1. **Start Word 2002.**

2. **If the task pane isn't visible on the right side of the screen, bring it up by choosing View⇨Task Pane.**

3. **Click the down-arrow to the right of the task pane title and select Search.**

4. **If Basic Search appears in the title, click Advanced Search at the bottom of the task pane.**

    The Word Advanced Search task pane appears. (See Figure 4-4.)

Figure 4-4:
If you need to search for Outlook e-mail messages, your only choice is the Office XP/Word 2002 Search task pane.

5. **To restrict the search to specific Outlook folders, click Search In and pick a folder.**

6. **Click Results Should Be and click Outlook Items/E-mail Messages.**

7. **Put together your search criteria in the upper part of the task pane, and click Search.**

Office XP can use Windows XP's Indexing Service to great effect. See "Indexing service," later in this chapter, for details.

Phrasing a search query

You have two different, almost mutually exclusive, ways to ask a computer to look things up:

✦ **Keyword searches:** These searches take the words you specify and look for those words. In some cases, keyword searches can be augmented by *qualifiers* LIKE, AND, or NOT. So you may have the Search Companion look for files with the names **blue or dolphin**, and you get back a list of files with either **blue** or **dolphin**, or both, in their names.

✦ **Natural language searches:** These searches, on the other hand, expect you to ask a question in the form of a question (with apologies to Alex Trebek). Thus, you might ask your computer, **What color are dolphins?** and get back a list of Web sites that discuss dolphins' colors.

Windows XP's Search Companion combines both search methods, but in a very specific way. If you're looking for Web sites, you're expected to ask a question — that is, Windows uses a natural language search approach when going out to the Internet. For everything else, you should type only keywords.

It's an odd dichotomy that you may find irritating, or confusing, or both.

Looking for Files and Folders

Maybe you need to find all of the handouts you typed for your Porcine Prevaricators seminar. Maybe you remember that you have a recipe with tarragon in it, but you can't remember where in the world you put it. Maybe you accidentally moved or deleted all of the pictures of your trip to Cancun, or Windows Media Player suddenly can't find your MP3s of the 1974 Grateful Dead tour.

Good. You're in the right place.

People generally go looking for files or folders on their computers for one of two reasons. Perhaps they vaguely remember that they used to have something — maybe a Christmas letter, a product description, or a great joke — and now they can't remember where they put it. Or they have been playing around with Windows Explorer, and whatever they thought was sitting in a specific place isn't there any more.

In either case, the solution is to make Windows XP do the work and go searching for your lost files or folders.

If you choose Start⇨Search, the Search Companion dog Rover (refer to Figure 4-1) gives you a chance to narrow down your search, in advance, by choosing Pictures, Music or Video, or Documents. If you know in advance what kind of file you're looking for, those choices can hone in on specific file types (refer to Table 4-1). If you don't know exactly what you're looking for, though, it's just as easy to go straight to the full-fledged search — the choice marked All Files and Folders.

Rover the Searching Agent

First things first.

You can get rid of the dog. Banish him to the dog house. Trade him in for a newer model — or at least a different one. You can simply tell him to get lost. He won't mind. Here's how:

1. **Bring up the little mutt by choosing Start⇨Search (see Figure 4-1).**

2. **Click Change Preferences at the bottom of the screen.**

   You see the question "How Do You Want To Use Search Companion?" (shown in Figure 4-5).

3. **To completely rid yourself of the critters, click Without an Animated Screen Character.**

4. **If you think you have a tiny chance of finding a character more to your liking, click With a Different Character, and peruse the ensuing rogues' gallery. If you find one you like, click OK.**

Do you really, really need to get a life? Here's how to tell. Right-click on Rover (or whichever cloying character you have chosen as your Search Companion), and click Do a Trick. Go ahead. I dare ya.

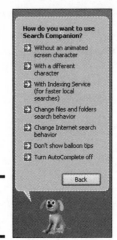

Figure 4-5:
Get rid of
Rover here.

Those little Search Companion characters — they're called *Agents* — are stored in ACS files. If you search for *.acs files (see "Using wildcards" later in this chapter), you can find a handful of them scattered in various places on your hard drive. If you come across other ACS files — Office XP has a bunch of them, for example — and put the files in the \Windows\ srchasst\chars folder, they are available for you to choose as an alternative to Rover.

Making the most of simple searches

Can you remember what's in the file you're looking for? Can you remember at least part of the file's name? Nine times out of ten, that's all you need.

Forgive me if you've read this a few times already, but you absolutely must make Windows XP show you filename extensions — the characters following the period towards the end of the file name, such as .exe or .bat. Read up on filename extensions, and why they're so important to see, in Book I, Chapter 2. Then follow the steps listed there to tell Windows XP to show you filename extensions.

The best approach to performing a simple search depends on whether you know for an absolute, dead-certain fact what kind of file you're dealing with. Here's how it works, in the best of all possible worlds:

Searching for pictures, music, or video

Here's what to do if you know for an absolute, dead-certain fact that the file you want is a picture, photo, music file, and/or video:

1. **Choose Start⇨Search.**

   You see Rover (refer to Figure 4-1) or something like him (or, if you're lucky, nothing at all!).

2. **Click Pictures, Music, or Video.**

   You see the Search pane (refer to Figure 4-3).

3. **Pick the kind of file you're looking for.**

   If you know anything at all about the file, type it in the box marked All or Part of the File Name. Windows is a whole lot smarter than this dialog box would have you believe. For example, if you search for Music files and you type **Ludwig** in the box, Windows will find Beethoven's 9th Symphony, even though Ludwig doesn't appear in the filename. Try it. You'll see.

   All of the advanced search options described in the section "Digging deeper with advanced searches" are available by choosing Use Advanced Search Options.

4. **If you don't find the file you want, crank up the Windows Media Player and see whether you can find it from there. I talk about Windows Media Player in Book VIII, Chapter 1.**

Searching for a document

Here's what to do if you are absolutely, completely certain that the file you want is a document — which is to say a text file (with the .txt filename extension), Word document (.doc), Excel workbook (.xls), PowerPoint presentation (.ppt or .pps), or one of the other documents listed in Table 4-1:

1. **Choose⇨Search.**

2. **Click Documents (Word Processing, Spreadsheet, and so on).**

   You see the dialog box shown in Figure 4-6.

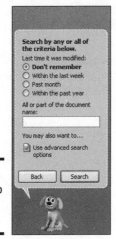

Figure 4-6:
Tell Rover to
search for
documents.

3. **Tell Rover how to narrow down the search.**

   If you can remember the last time that the document was modified —
   not created, or opened, but changed — click the appropriate button.
   There's no wiggle-room. If you check the button marked Within the Last
   Week, and you last modified the file eight days ago, it won't show up in
   the search.

   If you can remember any part of the filename, type it in the box. The
   Search Companion matches any file with a name that includes the characters you've typed. (See Table 4-2.)

Table 4-2	Simple Filename Matches	
Type this	*And you will match*	*But you will not match*
a	a.xls	b.xls
bug	bed bug.txt	abu ghanim.txt
add	madden.ppt	dad.ppt
wood	woody.doc	woo.doc

   Search Companion recognizes the key words OR and AND. If you type
   new or recent in the All or Part of the File Name box, Rover brings back
   files such as new pictures.jpg and recent songs.mp3. If you type
   two words in the All or Part of the File Name box, Rover assumes you
   mean AND.

   The search for filenames is quite literal, and filename extensions are
   included if you have Windows show filename extensions. So if you show
   filename extensions and search for the characters **txt**, you see all of
   your .txt text files.

All of the advanced search options described in the section "Digging deeper with advanced searches" are available by choosing Use Advanced Search Options.

4. **If you don't find the file you want, try the option called Change File Name or Keywords (see Figure 4-7). This option enables you to easily switch over to searching for text inside the documents (see Figure 4-8).**

Figure 4-7: Frequently people forget filenames but can think of keywords inside the document.

Figure 4-8: Type a keyword that's unique to the file, if you can think of one.

Searching for All Files and Folders

If you aren't absolutely, totally, utterly certain that you want to find a picture, photo, music file, video, or document, it's best to tell Rover to fetch everything matching your criteria, and sift through the results yourself. Here's how:

1. **Choose⇨Search.**

2. **Click All Files and Folders, and go for a full-fledged search.**

   When you do, you get the search dialog box shown in Figure 4-9.

Search by any or all of the criteria below.

All or part of the file name:

A word or phrase in the file:
Songkran

Look in:
Local Hard Drives (C:;

When was it modified?

What size is it?

More advanced options

Back   Search

Figure 4-9:
The full-fledged search.

3. **Help Rover find your file.**

   The filename part of the search is identical to the details I discussed in Table 4-2. If you have filename extensions showing, and you type **.doc** in this box, for example, you get a list of all the .doc files.

   The box marked A Word or Phrase in the File jumps through some interesting hoops. If you type a single word, Search Companion looks for that word, of course. If you type a phrase like **back in a minute**, Search Companion looks for that precise phrase, with spaces and punctuation exactly the way you specify.

   Search Companion also looks for information attached to a file — information you may not see if you open the file. It's called *metadata*, and I gave you an example of a metadata search earlier when I said that Search would find Beethoven's 9th if you look for **Ludwig**. Media files usually have metadata attached to them with information about the content. Microsoft Office documents always have metadata attached to them. You can see Office metadata by bringing up the Office application (such as Word, Excel, or PowerPoint) and choosing File⇨Properties. The file's metadata appears on the tabs marked Summary and Custom.

   The box marked Look In lets you pick the starting point of the search. If you want to search your entire network (a process that could take many hours!), click the down-arrow and choose Browse⇨My Network Places⇨Entire Network.

Windows XP warns you not to share an entire hard drive (see Book I, Chapter 2) for a reason, and this is it: Searching every shared hard drive on your network is as simple as firing up Search Companion and choosing Look In/Entire Network. And you can search for anything.

4. **Click Search and the Companion returns the names of files that match all of your criteria. (In geek terms, they're "ANDed" together.)**

   If you tell Rover that you want to see files with **woody** in all or part of the filename, with the phrase **blew it again** in the file, Search Companion returns only files with names that match AND contain the indicated phrase. So a file named **woodrow.doc** containing the phrase **blew it again** wouldn't make the cut. Nor would a file called **woody.txt** with the text **blewit agin**.

That's the lowdown on simple searches. Much more power awaits, in the next parts of this chapter.

Using wildcards

Windows XP's Search Companion lets you use *wildcards*, symbols that substitute for letters. The easiest way to describe a wildcard is with an example. **?** is the single-letter wildcard. If you tell Rover to look for files named **d?g.txt**, the mutt dutifully retrieves dog.txt and dug.txt (if you have files with those names), but it doesn't retrieve drag.txt or ding.txt. The **?** matches one — and only one — character in the filename.

Search Companion recognizes two wildcards. **?** matches a single character, and ***** matches multiple (zero or more) characters. (See Table 4-3.)

Table 4-3	Wildcards for Filenames	
This	*Matches This*	*But Not This*
d?g.txt	dog.txt, dug.txt	drag.txt, ding.txt
ne*w.mp3	new.mp3, neosow.mp3	ne.mp3, new.doc

Wildcards work with only file and folder names. The box marked A Word or Phrase in the File (refer to Figure 4-9) does *not* recognize wildcards.

Digging deeper with advanced searches

The full-fledged search dialog box(refer to Figure 4-9) has three buttons: When Was It Modified?, What Size Is It?, and More Advanced Options.

If you click on the (inappropriately named) When Was It Modified? button, you have a chance to specify when the file you're looking for was last changed (in computerese, *modified* means changed). As you can see in

Figure 4-10, though, you aren't limited to the modified date. In fact, Search Companion searches for files based on the date that they were created or last opened ("accessed" in computer lingo) as well.

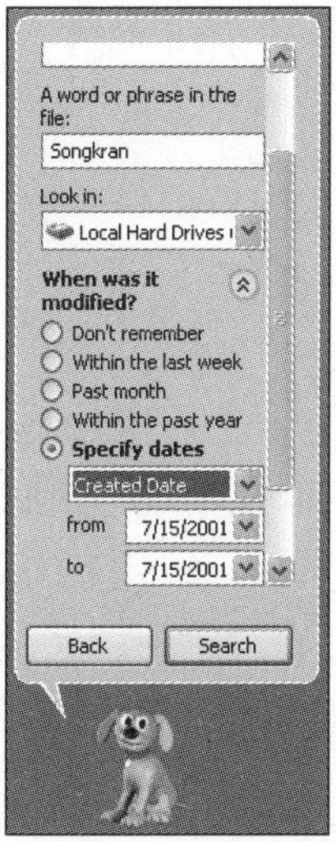

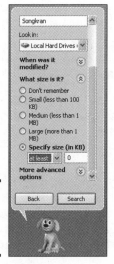

Figure 4-10:
Narrow
your search
based on
the date that
the file was
last
changed,
created, or
opened.

If you click on the What Size Is It? button, Search Companion lets you pick the file size (see Figure 4-11). In my experience, people are amazed at how big files get, so if you use this option, allow yourself lots of breathing room on the high side.

Figure 4-11:
Search
based on
file size.

Finally, the More Advanced Options selection (see Figure 4-12) holds six possibilities:

Figure 4-12:
A hodge-
podge of
additional
Search
criterion.

✦ Type of File lists all of the filename extensions that your computer recognizes, except that you don't get to see the filename extensions; you have to make do with the hokey names. If you have Microsoft Office installed, the list of Types starting with "Microsoft" goes on forever (my list includes one called Microsoft FrontPage Dont Publish — an all-time classic). If you know the filename extension that you're looking for, this is the worst place to tell Search Companion what kind of file you want. Type the filename extension in the All or Part of the File Name box (for example, ***.mpeg** or ***.ani**).

✦ Check the box marked Search System Folders, and Search Companion looks in the Windows, Documents and Settings, and Program Files folders.

✦ Check the box marked Search Hidden Files and Folders, and Search Companion looks in any files or folders that are marked Hidden.

Hidden files and folders aren't really hidden. They're just marked a certain way so that Windows Explorer won't show them — unless you tell Windows Explorer to show hidden files and folders. To hide a file or folder, choose Start➪My Documents to start Windows Explorer. Right-click on the file or folder, and click Properties. At the bottom of the Properties dialog box, in the Attributes area, check the box marked Hidden. Now your file or folder is hidden from view. To make Windows Explorer show hidden files and folders, follow the steps described in Book I, Chapter 2.

✦ The Search Subfolders box tells Search Companion that you want to look in the folder specified in the Look In box, as well as in all folders inside of the Look In folder. You almost always want to have this box checked.

✦ In spite of what you read in other books, the Case Sensitive box has nothing to do with filenames. If you check this box, Search Companion matches the case of the text you type in the A Word or Phrase in the File box. So if you type **Blue Mango** in the box and check this box, Search Companion looks for **Blue Mango** text inside files, but passes on both **blue Mango** and **BLUE mango**.

Filenames are never case sensitive. Ever. My Documents and my documents always refer to the same folder.

✦ Search Tape Backup applies only if you are using Windows XP's Backup feature.

If you've managed to read to this point, you're probably serious about searching. Good on ya, as they say Down Under. If you want the Search Companion cut to the chase, and stop bothering you with the "helping" screens that divert you to searching for specific kinds of files, do this:

1. **Choose Start➪Search and bring up Rover and the Search Companion (refer to Figure 4-1).**

2. **Click Change Preferences.**

3. **Click Change Files and Folders Search Behavior.**

4. **Click Advanced — Includes Options to Manually Enter Search Criteria. Recommended for Advanced Users Only (see Figure 4-13).**

Figure 4-13:
If you've
read this far,
you're an
advanced
user.

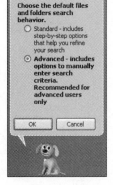

After you change to Advanced, the Search Companion always starts, ready for a full-fledged search (refer to Figure 4-9).

Saving a search

Do you find yourself repeating the same searches, over and over again? Maybe you need to look in BearShare's Download folder to see if those MP3s have finally arrived. Or you want to look at a list of invoices for your number-one customer. Only a real dummy would do the same thing over and over again when the computer can do the work. A *For Dummies* dummy, on the other hand, knows that he can save and reuse searches 'til the cows come home.

If he reads this book, anyway.

Here's how you save and reuse a search:

1. **Choose Start⇨Search to bring up the Search Companion.**

2. **Set up your search.**

In Figure 4-14, for example, I've instructed Rover to fetch all the MP3 files in the My Music folder that are less than a week old.

Figure 4-14: To save and reuse a search, set up a search the way you want it, and then run the search.

3. **Click Search and run the search.**

This is the trick. It doesn't matter whether or not you really want to run the search. You have to, if you're going to save the search to use in the future.

4. Choose File⇨Save Search.

Windows XP offers to save a file called `Files named @.mp3.fnd` or something equally obtuse. (See Figure 4-15.)

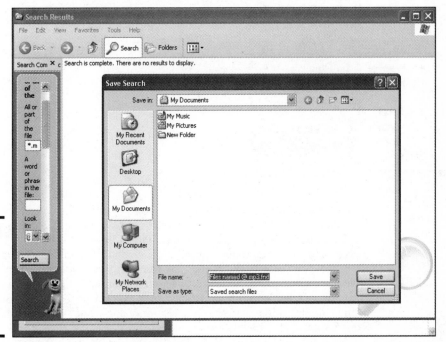

Figure 4-15:
The saved search has a strange filename, ending in .FND.

5. Navigate to a convenient location (if you put the search on your Desktop, it'll always be handy); give the search a more descriptive name, if you like; and click Save.

6. Any time you want to run the saved search, double-click on the .FND file and click Search. Voilà!

Indexing service

If you choose Change Preferences in any of the Search Companion dialog boxes, you see an option called With Indexing Service (For Faster Local Searches). Click that line and you enter a Search Companion dialog box (see Figure 4-16) that helps you turn on a feature called Indexing Service.

Figure 4-16:
The easy
way to set
up Windows
XP Indexing
Service.

Indexing is a fancy way for computers to scan documents, build and store indexes, and then retrieve documents based on the indexes in response to your searches. Sounds difficult? In principal, it's pretty simple: The computer waits until you aren't doing anything; then it starts looking, methodically, at every file on your hard drive(s). Say the computer's looking at a file called Woody da Dummy.doc. Inside the file, the computer discovers the words "jumping jack flash". It builds an index entry that says, among other things, "the word **jumping** is in Woody da Dummy.doc". Then it builds another index entry that says, "the word **jack** is in Woody da Dummy.doc". And so on. When you ask for all the files that contain the word **jack**, the Indexing Service realizes immediately that Woody da Dummy.doc should be included on the list.

In practice, indexing is one whole heckuvalot more difficult than you may imagine. The biggest problem Microsoft had, for years, was the intrusiveness of the bloody indexer: You'd be typing along, pause a few seconds to think, and WHAM! All of a sudden this crazy program had taken over your machine. Resume typing, and you had to wait an eternity to regain control of your PC. I'm very happy to say that, in Windows XP (and only Windows XP, in my eXPerience), indexing finally works.

If it's turned on, Windows XP Indexing Service hooks into Microsoft Office XP. So if you perform a search in Office XP, what you see is what Windows XP delivers.

You can really get your hands dirty with complex searches, providing the Indexing Service is running. For example, in Figure 4-17, I use the NEAR operator to ask the Indexing Service to return a list of all files where the word *read* appears within 50 words of the word *write*.

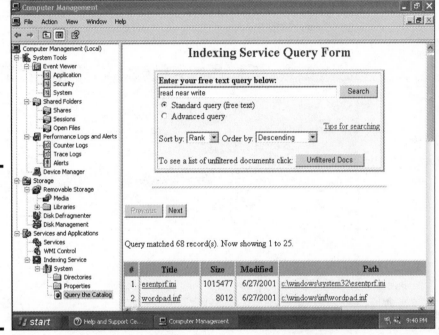

Figure 4-17:
You can make very complex searches with the Indexing Service's query language.

To learn more about the Indexing Service's query language and to run a query, follow these steps:

1. **To start the Windows Computer Management Console, choose Start⇨Control Panel, click Performance and Maintenance, click Administrative Tools, and then double-click Computer Management.**

2. **In the Computer Management Console, in the left pane, double-click on Services and Applications. Then click to expand Indexing Service; then System; then Query the Catalog.**

3. **Now you can run your search, or you can get help by choosing Action⇨Help and then clicking Indexing Service in the Help system.**

Searching the Internet

If you tell Rover to search the Internet, he tells you to type your question in a complete sentence. Press Search, and the Search Companion steers you directly to — you guessed it — Microsoft, Rover's master. In Figure 4-18, you can see that the question **What is the sound of one hand clapping?** was transformed by the Search Companion into **sound one hand clapping**, and then it was sent directly to search.msn.com.

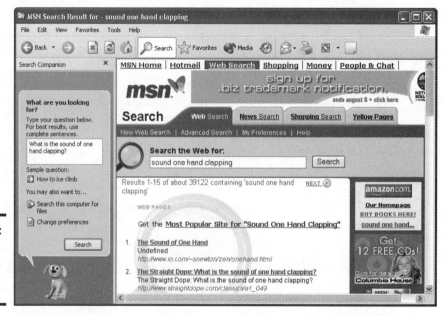

Figure 4-18: Rover goes directly to search. msn.com.

Nothing is particularly bad about search.msn.com, but I find it annoying. If you look at Figure 4-18, you see that well over half the screen is taken up with ads. What you can't see in Figure 4-18 is the *other* ad Microsoft tossed up on the screen, for good measure, in its own, separate Explorer window. *Pop-under ads* — the ones that appear automatically underneath the Web page you requested — should make your blood boil.

As far as I can tell, all the people who live in Redmond, Washington (the home of Microsoft) have cable modems or DSL in their offices and homes, and they aren't particularly concerned about how much, uh, offal gets shoved down their data pipes. If you happen to live just about anywhere else in the world, though, you may think differently.

The good news is that you can easily banish `search.msn.com` to the same dog house that Rover vacated and have your Internet searches use a Web site that doesn't bury half its screens in ads. Here's how:

1. **Choose Start➪Search to bring up the Search Companion (refer to Figure 4-1).**

2. **Click Change Preferences.**

3. **Click Change Internet Search Behavior.**

4. **Pick the Web-based search engine that you like best, and click OK.**

   In Figure 4-19, I chose Google.

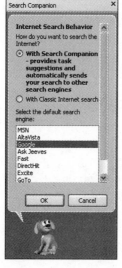

Figure 4-19: Change your default Internet search engine in the Internet Search Behavior screen.

After you change your default search engine, every time you ask Search Companion to search the Internet, it uses the engine you've chosen. See Figure 4-20 and note how little advertising and other useless information appears on the screen with a Google search. Wonder why I switched?

Web-based search engines change every day. I have no guarantee that my search engine of choice now will be the same six months from now. If you use the Search Companion to perform searches on the Web, be sure to check every few months to see whether a competing Web-based search engine works better than the one you're using.

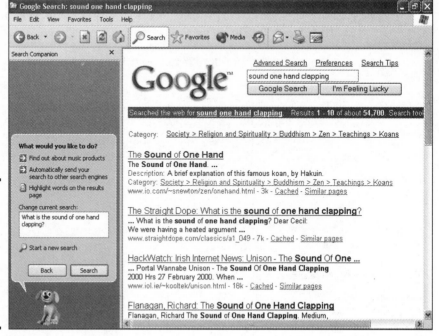

Figure 4-20:
A Google
search is
fast,
efficient,
and
wonderfully
devoid of all
those ads.

If you're serious about searching on the Web, Rover and the Search
Companion will irritate you sooner or later. To go directly to the Web and
take it on, mano a mano, see Book IV, Chapter 3.

Chapter 5: Getting the Basic Stuff Done

In This Chapter

✔ **How to cheat at the Windows games (I know that's what you're looking for)**

✔ **Burn your CDs but don't singe your fingers**

✔ **Take control of your PC when a program goes haywire**

✔ **... And lots of boring stuff you need to know anyway**

You bought your PC to get things done, right? I guess it depends on what you mean by "things." Certainly you need to know how to write a letter, even if you don't have Microsoft Office installed on your PC. Draw pictures. You should learn how to use the Windows Calculator, even if the thought of employing a $2,000 tool to solve a $2 problem leaves you feeling a little green.

Hey, I have to talk about that stuff somewhere.

On a somewhat less mundane level, this chapter also contains the most complete collection of Windows game "cheats" ever published, including many that have never been published before — in books, magazines, or on the Web. You read 'em here first. Give our readers their due, sez I.

This chapter also digs into the truly cool Windows XP support for burning CDs.

Beating Windows Games

You really bought this book because you heard it had all the game cheats, didn't you? C'mon, admit it. No, you can't find these cheats anywhere else: They're published here for the first time. Here ya go.

 What? Your boss doesn't like you having games on the company PC? Remind her that Windows games are, singularly, the best way to brush up on your mousing skills, take your mind off work for a brief spell, and take a break from all the typing. How do you spell Repetitive Motion Syndrome?

Windows XP ships with eleven games, many of which are quite good.

Solitaire

Venerable classic *Solitaire,* the oldest Windows game of all (see Figure 5-1) — dating back to the prehistory of Windows 3.0, with a copyright that reaches back to 1981, for heaven's sake — still captures the hearts and spare cranial cycles of millions. To get it going, choose Start⇨All Programs⇨Games⇨ Solitaire. But you've probably done that a hundred times already, haven't you?

Choose Game⇨Deck to change the card back

Click the deck to deal

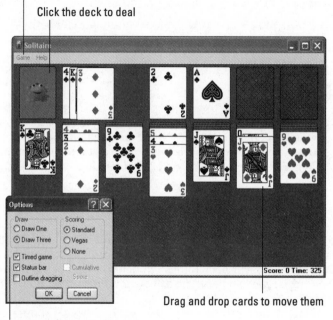

Figure 5-1:
Windows
Solitaire, the
mother of all
Windows
games.

Some decks show animations

Drag and drop cards to move them

If you don't know the rules for Solitaire in general, ask the guy sitting next to you on your next flight. The Windows version of solitaire

✦ Won't let you pull a card from inside a stack.

✦ Only lets you undo your last move. If you flip over a card that's face-down in one of the stacks, you can't undo the flip.

✦ Restricts you to putting Kings in open stacks.

Scoring a Solitaire game makes cricket look like child's play. To get the full details on Standard and Vegas scoring, choose Help⇨Contents, and then navigate to Solitaire⇨Choose a Scoring System.

One little cheat works if you have Solitaire set up to turn over three cards at a time. To make it turn over just one card, press **Ctrl+Alt+Shift** and click the deck. This is a particularly valuable cheat if you're using Vegas scoring. Vegas rules let you go through the deck three times if you have Solitaire set to turn over three cards at a time, but you can go through only once if Solitaire is set to turn over one card at a time. If you use the **Ctrl+Alt+Shift** trick and turn over one card at a time, you can go through the deck three times — a real boon for Vegas scorekeeping.

FreeCell

FreeCell, Microsoft's first Solitaire variant, mimics the card game of the same name. To get it going, choose Start➪All Programs➪Games➪FreeCell (see Figure 5-2).

Park your cards here   Stack the cards in order here

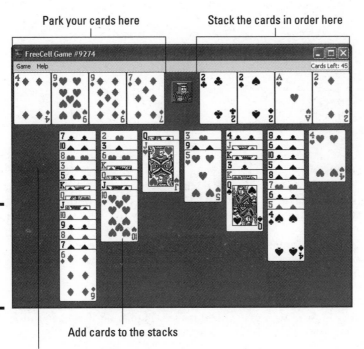

Figure 5-2:
FreeCell
should
stimulate a
few more
gray cells.

Add cards to the stacks

Any card can go in an open slot

The first page of the FreeCell Help file tells you that "It is believed (although not proven) that every game is winnable."

Ah, what fools these mortal Help files be.

FreeCell lets you replay the same hands, over and over, by assigning numbers to specific starting card combinations. To play hand number 50,000, for example, choose Games➪Select Game, type **50000**, and click OK. That's a nifty trick if you want to play the same hand at home and then do it again at work, or if you want to challenge a friend on a different machine to a duel.

All of the games numbered from 1 to 32000 are winnable, except for game 11982. Yes, there are people who study these things. No, they don't have lives. See `http://members.aol.com/wgreview/fcfaq.html` **for details.**

While a game is in progress, press Ctrl+Shift+F10. You receive one of the funniest dialog boxes in Windows (see Figure 5-3). If you click Abort and then click any card, you win immediately. Sorta. The cards are stacked in the correct slots, but not in the right order. Your score is updated to reflect a win.

Figure 5-3:
Pick Abort
to win at
FreeCell
every time.

FreeCell has two symmetric hands that you'll want to take a look at. Choose Games➪Select Game, and then type either **-1** or **-2**. The first option, **-1**, generates two rows for each suit, one of which runs A-3-5-7-9-J-K, from top to bottom; the other runs Q-10-8-6-4-2. The second option, **-2**, also generates two rows for each suit, but this time they run A-K-Q-J-10-9-8 and 7-6-5-4-3-2.

Oh. I better mention one tiny, little detail, before you defenestrate this book — that is, throw it out a convenient window. Both the **-1** and **-2** games are unwinnable. You can't beat either of them.

FreeCell keeps track of how many hands you've won and lost, and how long your current winning (or losing) streak may be. To get to the scores, choose Game➪Statistics. You see a list like the one shown in Figure 5-4.

Ah, but there's another trick — one I bet you've never heard about, no matter how much you love FreeCell. If you aren't afraid of getting your hands a little dirty, you can jigger your own statistics. Amaze your family and friends. Confuse your foes. Make your boss think that you have an IQ in the upper triple digits. Yes, you can do it.

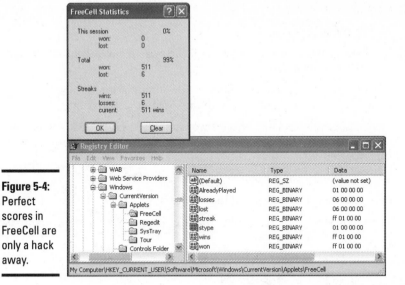

Figure 5-4:
Perfect
scores in
FreeCell are
only a hack
away.

FreeCell stores its scores in the Windows Registry. By switching a few numbers in the Registry, you can have FreeCell say that you've won thousands of hands, and lost few (or none!). How do you think I got the 511-hand winning streak shown in Figure 5-4?

To set your own scores in FreeCell, you have to go into the Windows Registry. No doubt you've been warned from the day you were born that the Registry is a dangerous, scary place. Balderdash. In fact, 99 percent of the Registry hacks that are published in the magazines and books don't do much in Windows XP. They aren't worth the effort. That's why you won't see any hacks in this book. Except for the game hacks. They work great.

You can set each of the four scores in FreeCell — Total Won, Total Lost, Streak Wins, and Streak Losses — to any number between 0 and 4,294,967,295. You can also tell FreeCell whether your Streak is a winning streak or a losing streak. Follow these easy steps:

1. **Choose Start➪Run.**

2. **Type** regedit **in the box marked Open and click OK.**

You see the Windows Registry Editor, the High Priest of Windows XP. I can see the beads of sweat on your forehead already. No, this isn't a scary place. At least, not *that* scary. Just be careful while you're here. Follow my instructions. Don't go changing anything willy-nilly, OK?

3. **Choose Edit⊅Find.**

   The Find dialog box appears.

4. **In the Find What box, type** FreeCell **(no space; capitalization doesn't matter) and press Enter.**

   The Registry Editor moves to a location that looks a lot like the place shown in Figure 5-4. This is where the FreeCell settings live.

5. **To see how the Registry entries work, change FreeCell's Total Won number to 511. On the right side of the screen, double-click on the line marked** won.

   The Edit Binary Value dialog box appears.

6. **Press Del on your keyboard four times.**

   That should wipe out any value that's currently sitting in the Value data box. (See Figure 5-5.)

Figure 5-5:
Use this dialog box (carefully!) to change values in the Registry.

7. **Type** ff010000 **and press Enter.**

   In case you were wondering, ff010000 is the value 511, written in a weird way. Table 5-1 gives you a bunch of common values, and their equivalents in FreeCell notation. The Registry Editor shows that you have changed the value of won to 511, er, ff010000. Great!

   The weird notation used by FreeCell is called *little-endian hexadecimal.* If you want to add more values to Table 5-1, you can. Convert the decimal number you want to 8-digit hexadecimal (using, say, the Windows Calculator, discussed in the section called "Calculating"). Take the last pair of hex digits and make them the first pair of the FreeCell value. Take the next-to-last pair and make them the second pair in the FreeCell value, and so on. Example: 511 in decimal is 00 00 01 ff in hexadecimal, so the FreeCell value for 511 is ff 01 00 00. Try it. You'll see.

8. Choose Start➪All Programs➪Games➪FreeCell to crank up FreeCell, choose Game➪Statistics to bring up the Statistics box, and verify that FreeCell honestly believes that you have won 511 hands!

9. Go back to the Registry Editor and change the values for Total Lost (Registry key lost), Streak Wins (key wins), and Streak Losses (key losses). Use Table 5-1 to pick some common values.

10. Tell FreeCell that your current streak is a winning streak.

   To do so, double-click stype (Streak Type, eh?), press Del four times, type 01000000, and press Enter. (If you want to make FreeCell think you're on a losing streak, type 00000000.)

11. Choose File➪Exit to get out of the Registry Editor.

Table 5-1		Values for FreeCell Registry Hacking	
Number	*What you should enter*	*Number*	*What you should enter*
0	00000000	255	ff000000
1	01000000	256	00010000
2	02000000	257	01010000
3	03000000	511	ff010000
10	0a000000	512	00020000
11	0b000000	1000	e8030000
15	0f000000	1001	e9030000
16	10000000	10,000	10270000
17	11000000	100,000	a0860100
100	64000000	1,000,000	40420f00
101	65000000	1,000,000,000	00ca9a3b
254	fe000000	4,294,967,295	ffffffff

Spider Solitaire

When you get the hang of it, Spider Solitaire is every bit as addictive as the two older Windows Solitaire siblings. Get Spider going by choosing Start➪All Programs➪Games➪Spider Solitaire.

The easiest way to learn Spider Solitaire is to start with a single suit — Spider gives you that option when you start. Basically, you have to move cards around in descending order (see Figure 5-6), and you can mix and match suits to your heart's content (pun intended). When you have a descending sequence (K to A) in a single suit, the entire sequence gets removed. When you get stuck, click the spider card deck and Spider Solitaire deals another row of cards.

Figure 5-6:
Spider
Solitaire
allows you
to mix
suits in
intermediate
steps, but
ultimately
you have to
match them
to win.

Spider Solitaire stores its scores in the Windows Registry, just like FreeCell. You can use a technique very similar to the one I described in the preceding section to hack the Registry and change your scores — it's almost identical to the method for Minesweeper as well. Look for the Registry values under `HKEY_CURRENT_USER\Software\Microsoft\Spider`. One bit of warning: Make sure that Spider Solitaire is *not* running when you change the Registry. Spider has a nasty habit of resetting Registry values when it finishes, regardless of whether you want it to.

Spider Solitaire has a boss button — push the Esc key when the boss comes by and Spider quickly minimizes itself.

Minesweeper

One of the most absorbing, simple games ever created — and a long-time personal favorite of Bill G. — is Minesweeper, which has been around since the days of Windows 3.1.

The concept is pretty simple: Click on a square and a number appears, indicating the number of adjacent squares that contain mines (see Figure 5-7). Click on a mine and you lose. Play against the clock.

The number of seconds since your first click

The number of unflagged mines on the playing field

Click to start a new game

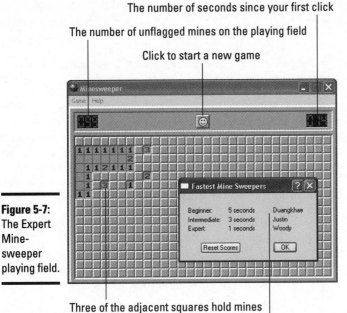

Figure 5-7:
The Expert Mine-sweeper playing field.

Three of the adjacent squares hold mines

Yes, you can hack the scores

If you've never tried Minesweeper, you're in for a treat — even inveterate computer-game-haters take a liking to this one.

Minesweeper holds oodles of options:

✦ Click Game and choose from Beginner (a 9 x 9 box playing field with 10 mines), Intermediate (a 16 x 16 field with 40 mines), and Expert (16 x 30 with 99 mines). Minesweeper automatically keeps high-score figures for each.

✦ Alternatively, you can choose Game➪Custom and tell Minesweeper how many squares you want to see and how many mines should be scattered on the field.

✦ If you think a square contains a mine, and you want to, uh, re-mined yourself of that fact, right-click on the square. A flag appears, warning you that once upon a time, you thought a mine might be here. Right-click on the same square a second time, and you see a question mark — probably to remind you that you once thought there was a mine here, but now you're not so sure, and maybe you really ought to click on the sucker to see whether it blows up. Right-click on the square a third time, and it goes back to normal.

Whenever you want to see the best times and who holds the records, choose Game⇨Best Times. The Fastest Minesweepers dialog box shown in Figure 5-7 appears.

There was a well-known cheat for Minesweeper that used to work in older versions of Windows, but doesn't appear to work in Windows XP. At least, we here at Dummies Central can't get it to work. Maybe you'll be luckier. In older versions, any time Minesweeper is running, you can type **xyzzy** and press Ctrl+Enter. From that moment on, every time you put the mouse over a "good" square — one that doesn't contain a mine — Minesweeper flashes a tiny, tiny, single white dot in the far upper left corner of the Windows desktop. And every time you put the mouse over a "bad" square, Minesweeper puts a single black dot in the far upper left corner. You may have to change your background or wallpaper to see it, but it's there. Click when you see the white dot, and you'll win every time.

Earlier versions of Minesweeper had a "stop-the-clock" cheat: Start the clock by clicking on a square; then hold down both mouse buttons and the **Esc** key at the same time. That stopped the clock. Unfortunately, that cheat doesn't work in Windows XP. At least, I couldn't get it to work.

Oh yes, you can hack the Windows Registry to set the Fastest Minesweepers names and times for the statistics box shown in Figure 5-7. As far as I can tell, this is the first time anybody has published this cheat. Pays to be a Dummy, eh? Here's how:

1. **Make sure Minesweeper is *not* running.**

2. **Choose Start⇨Run.**

3. **Type** regedit **in the box marked Open and click OK.**

   That brings up the Windows Registry Editor and, as I warned in the section on FreeCell, you have to be careful while you're here. Follow my instructions. Don't go changing anything willy-nilly.

4. **On the left side of the screen, click the + boxes and navigate to HKEY_CURRENT_USER⇨Software⇨Microsoft⇨winmine.**

5. **On the right side of the screen, double-click the line marked** Name1.

   You see a dialog box called Edit String, like the one shown in Figure 5-8.

6. **Type a new name in the Value Data box.**

   The new name shows up in the Statistics box as the fastest minesweeper in the Beginner category.

7. **Double-click the line marked** Time1, **click Decimal, enter the Beginner category winner's time (in seconds), and click OK.**

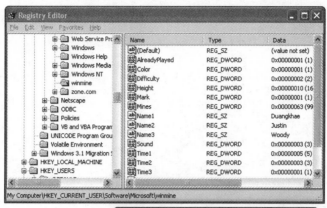

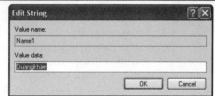

Figure 5-8:
The name of
the fastest
Mine-
sweeper
in the
Beginner
category is
stored as
Name1.

8. **Repeat the process for** Name2 **and** Time2 **(for the Intermediate winner) and** Name3 **and** Time3 **(for the Expert winner).**

9. **Choose Start⇨All Programs⇨Games⇨Minesweeper to get Minesweeper going, and click Game⇨Best Times to bring up the Statistics box and bask in the glory!**

10. **Get out of the Registry Editor by choosing File⇨Exit.**

You don't want to leave the Registry Editor open any longer than necessary.

Hearts

If you know how to play Hearts, the Windows one-player version will help you hone your skills. Windows XP plays a mean game of Hearts. Choose Start⇨All Programs⇨Games⇨Hearts to get it going.

The people who wrote the Hearts program insist that the computer doesn't "look" at your cards — or any other player's cards — when deciding what to play.

Believe it or not, you can cheat at Hearts and make Windows show you the contents of all your opponents' hands (see Figure 5-9). Follow these steps:

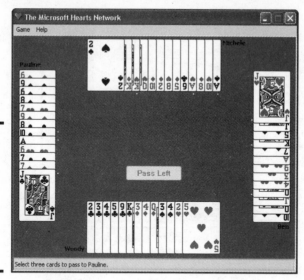

Figure 5-9:
The Hearts
cheat
shows you
all of the
cards in
your
opponents'
hands.

1. **You have to run Hearts on your computer at least once before you can make the changes necessary to cheat. If you've never run Hearts, choose Start⇨All Programs⇨Games⇨Hearts, enter your name, and click OK.**

2. **Choose Start⇨Run.**

3. **Type** regedit **in the box marked Open and click OK.**

   That brings up the Windows Registry Editor and, as I warned in the section on FreeCell, you have to be careful while you're here. Follow my instructions. Don't go changing anything you aren't supposed to be changing.

4. **On the left side of the screen, click the + boxes and navigate to HKEY_CURRENT_USER⇨Software⇨Microsoft⇨Windows⇨CurrentVers ion⇨Applets⇨Hearts.**

5. **Choose Edit⇨New⇨String Value.**

   The Windows Registry creates a new value called, imaginatively, New Value #1, and highlights the new value so that you can change its name.

6. **Type** ZB **and press Enter twice.**

7. **In the Value Data box, type** 42, **and press Enter.**

   Your Registry should have a new string value called ZB, with a value of 42, as shown in Figure 5-10. (Douglas Adams fans may pause to ponder whether Zaphod Beeblebrox and the ultimate answer to Life, the Universe and Everything may have a bearing on this setting.)

Figure 5-10:
This is what
you need to
make
Hearts
show you
everybody's
cards.

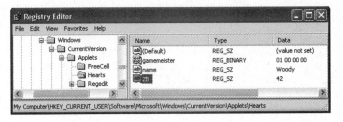

8. **Move back to Hearts (or start it if it isn't running, with Start⇨All Programs⇨Games⇨Hearts). Press** `Ctrl+Alt+Shift+F12` **all at the same time.**

   Your opponents' cards are now visible. To hide them, press `Ctrl+Alt+Shift+F12` again.

9. **Choose File⇨Exit to get out of the Registry Editor.**

   You don't want to leave the Registry Editor open any longer than necessary.

Hearts has a boss button — push the Esc key when the boss comes by and Hearts quickly minimizes itself.

Pinball

Although it will never come close to the real thing, Windows 3D Pinball - Space Cadet (that's the official name) does have some good graphics, decent sound, and "nudge" features that make it fun.

The game itself is far more complex than it appears at first blush. You're trying to advance from Space Cadet to Fleet Admiral by completing missions. Full details appear in the Pinball Help file, which you can see by choosing Help⇨Help Topics.

When you start Pinball for the first time, you have to hold down the Space bar on the keyboard to launch the ball, which isn't the least bit obvious. After you're over that hump, though, the game is pretty easy: The left flipper is the Z key and the right flipper is the / key.

Several locations on the Internet claim to have *trainers* for Space Cadet. A trainer alters the program itself, to give you extra capabilities. The Space Cadet trainers all claim to give you more than three balls — the major restriction in the game.

You can hack the Windows Registry to change Pinball scores and winners' names, but the technique is substantially more difficult than that for FreeCell, Spider Solitaire, or Minesweeper. Look in the Registry key HKEY_CURRENT_USER⇨Software⇨Microsoft⇨Plus!⇨Pinball⇨Space Cadet. The big trick: The key called Verification is supposed to contain the sum of all the high scores, plus the sum of the ASCII values of each character in all the names. (What's an ASCII value? If you have to ask, you don't want to know. Trust me.) Good luck.

Pinball also has a boss button — push the Esc key when the boss comes by and Pinball minimizes itself, and turns off the sound, in a split second.

Internet games

The five Internet games offered for free in Windows XP — Backgammon, Checkers, Hearts, Reversi, and Spades — all connect to zone.com, a gaming site on the Web. It probably won't surprise you one little bit to discover that zone.com is actually zone.msn.com, which (surprise!) is a division of Microsoft.

Many corporate Internet firewalls block access to zone.com. Can't imagine why, can you?

The Internet games have three big selling points: They're free; they hook you up with other players from all over the world, automatically, with no hassle; and they're decent (if uninspiring) versions of the games advertised.

The Internet games have one big disadvantage: They're really just ads. Microsoft wants you to play the games so that you'll be tempted to sign up for a zone.com membership. When you have a (free) membership, Microsoft tries to get you to pay for the more sophisticated games. Nothing is inherently wrong with zone.com, mind you, but you have many choices for online games. If you think you may be interested, start with the Multiplayer Online Games site, www.mpogd.com, or use any common Web search site to look for "online games."

Burning CDs

Windows XP includes simple, one-click (or two- or three-click) support for creating CDs. You need a CD recorder to make your own CDs, of course, but if you have a relatively modern recorder that attaches to your PC via a USB cable, your most difficult job will be pulling it out of the Styrofoam padding.

Understanding CD-R and CD-RW

Before you burn a CD, you should understand the fundamental differences between CD-R and CD-RW, the two most popular technologies. Most CD writers these days can burn both CD-R and CD-RW discs. You have to choose the kind that suits your situation.

✦ **CD-Recordable (CD-R) discs:** Can be played in audio CD players. Cannot be erased. You can record to a CD-R more than once (up to its capacity) if you use multi-session. See www.roxio.com/en/support/cdr/multisession.html for more information.

✦ **CD-Record/Write (CD-RW) discs:** Will not work in most audio CD players. Can be erased, and the erased area can be rewritten with new stuff. See www.roxio.com/en/support/cdr/howrecworks.html for more information.

Both CD-R and CD-RW discs can hold data or music. Both CD-R and CD-RW discs can be recorded multiple times, until they run out of space. Both CD-R and CD-RW discs can hold 74 minutes of music or 650 MB of data. Some CD-R discs can go all the way up to 80 minutes of audio, or 700 MB of data. (Yeah, yeah. Some CD-R discs are supposed to go way beyond that, but I don't trust 'em, and you shouldn't, either.)

DVD is not the same as CD-R or CD-RW. In general, unless the manufacturer very clearly states to the contrary, you can't create DVD discs in CD-R or CD-RW drives.

I talk about installing external CD-RW drives with USB cables in Book VII, Chapter 4. It's a piece o' cake.

There are some drives that will read DVDs/CD/CD-R/CD-RWs and write CD-Rs and CD-RWs but not write DVDs. DVD recorders are available but there are a plethora of formats & such; see www.dvddemystified.com/dvdfaq.html#4.3 for more information.

Burning with Windows

The first time you try to burn a CD with a new CD writer, work with data files instead of picture files or music. Start out with the easiest possible scenario (simple data files) before you work your way up to the most complex (audio CDs). That increases your chances of finding and solving problems when they're easiest to tackle.

When you have a CD-R or CD-RW drive installed and working, transferring your files to CD couldn't be simpler. Follow these steps:

1. **If you want to copy music files, don't follow these instructions. Use the Windows Media Player (WMP).**

   I tell you how to use Windows Media Player in Book VIII, Chapter 1. WMP has all sorts of bells and whistles that are specific to music, and it does a fine job of burning music CDs with all the ancillary information about artists, titles, and so on.

2. **For any other kind of file (picture, data, program, and so on), use Start⇨My Documents, Start⇨My Pictures, Start⇨My Computer, or Start⇨My Network Places to navigate to the files you want to copy.**

   Yes, you can pull files off your network.

3. **Select the files that you want to put on the CD.**

   All of the standard selection methods work:

   • Click once on a file to select it, or Ctrl+click to select multiple files.

   • Click on one file, hold down the Shift key, and click on a different file to select all the files in between.

   • Lasso a bunch of files and/or folders by clicking and dragging a box around them.

   • Use Ctrl+A to select all the files or folders sitting inside a folder.

   You may want to switch views so that you can see more files at once when selecting them. Choose View⇨List to see the largest number of files at once.

4. **After you select the files that you want to have transferred to your CD, you need to tell Windows where you want to put them:**

   • If the Copy to CD command is available in the task pane on the left — it is available if you are inside a folder that holds pictures (as shown in Figure 5-11) — click Copy to CD.

   • If the Copy to CD command is not available — which means that the current folder has documents and data files, for example — click Copy This File (or Copy This Folder, or Copy Selected Items, *mutatis mutandis*), and pick the CD-R drive as the destination.

   Each time you click Copy to CD, Windows copies the files you have selected into a temporary storage area, waiting for you to transfer the files, *en masse*, to the CD. As the files are being copied, Windows puts a CD-R icon in the notification area, near the time in the lower right of the screen, with a balloon that says `You have files waiting to be written to the CD. To see the files now, click this balloon.`

Figure 5-11:
Select the
files that
you want to
burn and
click Copy
to CD, if the
command is
available.

5. **Continue selecting files in this manner until you have all the files you want.**

6. **When you're done gathering files, click the balloon in the lower-right corner of the screen to see Windows' collection of files that are waiting to be burned on the CD.**

   Alternatively, choose Start⇨My Computer and navigate to the CD-R drive. You see the files you've chosen, grayed out to indicate that they're in a temporary waiting area (see Figure 5-12).

7. **Make sure that you want to burn all the chosen files. If you change your mind about any of them, just click on the file or folder and press Del.**

   You can move files around to different folders while in the temporary storage area, rename them — just about anything. When you have everything set up the way you want it, click Write These Files to CD in the CD Writing Tasks pane. Windows starts the CD Writing Wizard (see Figure 5-13).

8. **Follow the Wizard, inserting a CD when prompted (see Figure 5-14).**

   When the CD Writing Wizard is done, your files have been transferred to the CD. Probably. At least, that's the theory.

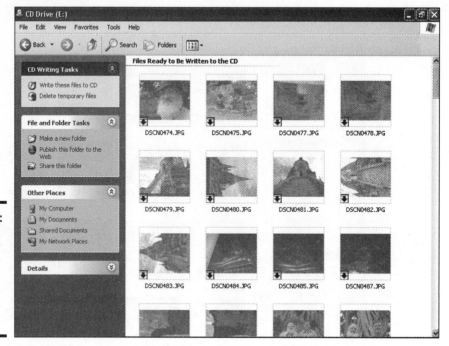

Figure 5-12:
Files being
held in a
temporary
area, prior
to being
copied to
the CD.

Immediately after the CD has been burned, take the CD out of the writer, and try to read it on a different machine. (If you have no other machine, take it out of the drive and try to read it on the same machine.) If you do this immediately, and the CD is screwed up, hopefully you can remember which files were supposed to be on it, and you should have a relatively easy time reconstructing the CD.

Figure 5-13:
After you
choose the
files, the CD
Writing
Wizard
steps you
through the
entire
burning
process.

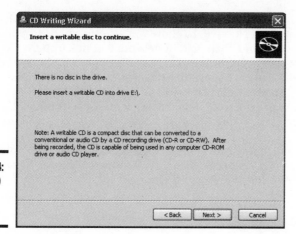

Figure 5-14:
Insert á CD
when
prompted.

Using the Free Word Processors That Come with Windows XP

If you're serious about word processing, you undoubtedly have Microsoft Office installed already. Office is a great program — I've been swearing at it for almost a decade; my first four books were about Office — and one that will serve you well.

On the other hand, if you only mess around the periphery of word processing, with an occasional letter to mom or a diatribe to the local newspaper, the word processing capabilities that come with Windows XP can help a little bit. As long as you don't have any great expectations, anyway.

Running Notepad

Reaching back into the primordial WinOoze, Notepad was conceived, designed, and developed by programmers, for programmers — and it shows. Although Notepad has been vastly improved over the years, many of the old limitations still pertain. Still, if you want a fast, no-nonsense text editor (certainly nobody would have the temerity to call Notepad a word processor), Notepad's a decent choice.

Notepad understands only plain, simple, unformatted text — basically the stuff you see on your keyboard. It wouldn't understand a **bold** or an embedded picture if you shook it by the shoulders, and heaven help ya if you want it to come up with links to Web pages.

On the other hand, Notepad's shortcomings are, in many ways, its saving graces. You can trust Notepad to show you exactly what's in a file — characters are characters, old chap, and there's none of this froo-froo formatting stuff to munge things up. Notepad saves only plain, simple, unformatted text; if you need a plain, simple, unformatted text document, Notepad's your tool of choice. To top it off, Notepad's fast and reliable. Of all the Windows programs I've ever met, Notepad is the only one I can think of that's never crashed on me.

To start Notepad, choose Start⇨All Programs⇨Accessories⇨Notepad, or double-click on any Text (.txt) file in the Windows Explorer. You see something like the file shown in Figure 5-15.

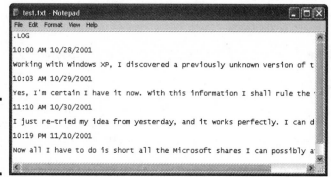

Figure 5-15: Notepad in its initial form.

Notepad can handle files up to about 48 MB in size. (That's not quite the size of the *Encyclopedia Britannica,* but it's close.) If you try to open a file that's larger, a dialog box suggests that you open the file with a different editor.

When you first start Notepad, it displays a file's contents in the 10-point Lucida Console font. That font was chosen by Notepad's designers because it's relatively easy to see on most computer monitors.

Just because the text you see in Notepad is in a specific font, don't assume for a moment that the data in the file itself is formatted. It isn't. The font you see on the screen is just the one Notepad uses to show the data. The stuff inside the file is plain-jane, unformatted, everyday text.

If you want to change the font that's displayed on the screen, choose Format⇨Font and pick from the offered list. You don't need to select any text before you choose the font, because the font you choose is applied to all the text on the screen — and it doesn't affect the contents of the file at all.

If you look at Figure 5-15, you'll notice that text extends way off the right side of the screen. That's intentional. Notepad, being ever-true to the file it's attached to, skips to a new line only when it encounters a line break — usually that means a carriage return (or "Enter key"), which typically occurs at the end of every paragraph.

Notepad allows you to wrap text on-screen, if you insist, so that you don't have to go scrolling all the way to the right to read every single paragraph. To have Notepad automatically break lines so that they show up on the screen, choose Format⇨Word Wrap.

Notepad has one little trick that you may find amusing — possibly worthwhile. If you type .LOG at the beginning of a file, Notepad sticks a time and date stamp at the end of the file each time it's opened.

Writing with WordPad

If you really want and need formatting — and you're too cheap to buy Microsoft Word — Windows XP's WordPad will do. If you've been locked out of Word 2002 by Microsoft's nefarious Office XP (De)Activation Wizard, you'll no doubt rely on WordPad to keep limping along until Microsoft can reactivate you.

If you find yourself reading these words because Office XP has slipped into "reduced functionality mode" (gawd, I love that phrase!), take heart, but be forewarned: If you aren't careful, you can really clobber your Word files by saving them with WordPad. If you have to edit a Word 97, 2000, or 2002 document with WordPad, always follow these steps:

1. **Make a copy of the Word document, and open the copy in WordPad.**

Do *not* edit original Word documents with WordPad. You'll break them as soon as you save them. Do *not* open Word documents in WordPad, thinking that you'll do a Save As and save with a different name. You'll forget.

2. **When you get Word 2002 back, open the original document, choose Tools⇨Compare and Merge Documents. Pick the WordPad version of the document, and click Merge.**

The resulting merged document probably looks like a mess, but it's a start.

3. **Use the Revisions Toolbar (which is showing) to march through your original document and apply the changes you made with WordPad.**

This is the only reliable way I know to ensure that WordPad doesn't accidentally swallow any of your formatting.

WordPad works much the same as any other word processor, only less so. Its feature set reflects its price — you can't expect much from a free word processor. That said, WordPad isn't encumbered with many of the confusing doodads that make Word so difficult for the first-time e-typist, and it may be a decent way to start learning how simple word processors work.

To get WordPad going, choose Start⇨All Programs⇨Accessories⇨WordPad (see Figure 5-16).

Like a Word document or a text file, Rich Text Format (RTF) is another type of file. RTF documents can have some simple formatting, but nothing nearly as complex as Word 97, for example. Many word processing programs from many different manufacturers can read and write RTF files, so RTF is a good choice if you need to create a file that can be moved to a lot of places.

If you're just starting out with word processing, keep these facts in mind:

✦ To format text, select the text you want to format; then pick the formatting you want from the Toolbar, or choose Format⇨Font.

✦ To format a paragraph, you can simply click once inside the paragraph and choose the formatting from the Toolbar, or choose Format⇨ Paragraph. Alternatively, you can select all the text in the paragraph, or in multiple paragraphs, before applying the formatting.

✦ General page layout (such as margins, whether the page is printed vertically or horizontally, and so on) is controlled by settings in the Page Setup dialog box. To get to the Page Setup dialog box, choose File⇨Page Setup.

✦ Tabs are complicated. Every paragraph starts out with tab stops set every half inch. You set additional tab stops with the Format⇨Tab dialog box, but the tab stops you set up work only in individual paragraphs: Select one paragraph and set a tab stop, and it works only in the selected paragraph; select three paragraphs and set the stop, and it works in all three.

WordPad treats tabs like any other character: A tab can be copied, moved and/or deleted, sometimes with unexpected results. Keep your eyes peeled when using tabs and tab stops. If something goes wrong, hit Edit⇨Undo immediately and try again.

WordPad lacks many of the features that you may have come to expect from other word processors: You can't even insert a page break, much less a table. If you spend any time at all writing anything but the most straightforward documents, you'll outgrow WordPad quickly.

Print Setup is under here

Separate options

Put a picture in a document

Paragraph formatting

Figure 5-16:
WordPad
working on
a Word 2000
document.

Character ("font") formatting

Taming Character Map

Windows XP includes a utility called Character Map that may prove a life-saver if you need to find characters that go beyond the standard keyboard fare — "On Beyond Zebra," as Dr. Seuss once said. Using the Character Map, you can ferret odd characters out of any font, copy them, and then paste them into whatever word processor you may be using (including WordPad).

Windows ships with many fonts — collections of characters — and several of those fonts include many interesting characters that you may want to use. To bring up the Character Map, choose Start➪All Programs➪ Accessories➪System Tools➪Character Map. You see the screen shown in Figure 5-17.

Click a character to see an enlarged view

Select a font

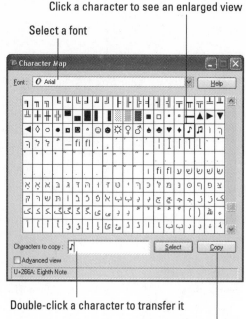

Figure 5-17:
Windows
Character
Map lets
you find odd
characters
in all of your
fonts.

Double-click a character to transfer it

Places the selected characters on the clipboard

You can use many characters as pictures — arrows, checkmarks, boxes, and so on — in the various Wingdings fonts (see Figure 5-18). Copy them into your documents, and increase the font size as you like.

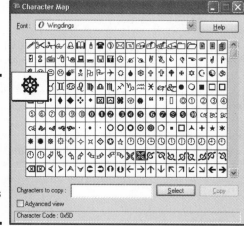

Figure 5-18:
Wingdings
contains
many
unusual and
useful
pictures,
disguised as
fonts.

Downloading document viewers

Although it won't compensate for a locked-out copy of Office XP, Microsoft has quite a number of free file viewers and format converters. You can't use a viewer to edit documents or even print them, but you will be able to see what the file contains.

The Word 97/2000 file viewer, in particular — a program called wd97vwr32.exe — allows you to view any Word 97, Word 2000, or Word 2002 ("Word XP") document. Best of all, the viewer is quite accurate — what you see is precisely what the author created. You don't have to buy anything; the viewer is free.

As of this writing, Microsoft distributes free document viewers for the following files:

+ Word 97, 2000, and 2002 ("Word XP") documents.

+ Excel 97, 2000, and 2002 ("Excel XP") spreadsheets.

+ PowerPoint 97, 2000, and 2002 ("PowerPoint XP") presentations. Think of this viewer as a slide show program that lets you see the presentation, regardless of whether you have a copy of PowerPoint installed.

To see the viewers that are available and download any viewers you or your friends may want, go to www.microsoft.com/office/000/viewers.htm.

Calculating

Windows XP includes a very capable calculator. Actually, it contains *two* very capable calculators. Before you run out and spend twenty bucks on a scientific calculator, check out the two you already own!

To run the Calculator, choose Start⇨All Programs⇨Accessories⇨Calculator. You probably see the Standard calculator, shown in Figure 5-19.

Figure 5-19:
The Standard, regular, calculator that you can use every day.

To use the calculator, just type whatever you like on your keyboard, and press Enter when you want to carry out the calculation. For example, to calculate 123 times 456, type **123 * 456** and press Enter.

The following are several calculator tricks:

+ You can use your mouse to "press" the keys on the calculator — an approach that's very slow and quite error prone.

+ Nope, an X on the keyboard doesn't translate into the times sign. I don't know why, but computer people have had a hang-up about this for decades. If you want "times" you have to press the asterisk on the keyboard — the * or Shift+8 key.

+ You can use the number pad, if your keyboard has one, but to make it work you have to get "Num Lock" going. Try typing a few numbers on your number pad. If the calculator sits there like a dodo and doesn't realize that you're trying to type into it, press the Num Lock key. The calculator should take the hint.

Of all the applications in Windows, you'd think that the %$#@! calculator would let you select the number in the read-out window so that you could copy it or paste over it, using any of the Windows-standard methods. Huh-uh. No way. Calculator limits you to copying the entire contents of the read-out (with Edit⇨Copy or Ctrl+C) or overwriting all of the read-out (with Edit⇨Paste or Ctrl+V). The Calculator doesn't even have the usual File menu, so you can save anything, print anything (like an audit tape), or even perform a File⇨Exit. Ahhhh! Don't get me started.

If you need to do some fancy-shmancy calculatin', choose View⇨Scientific to bring up the Scientific version of the Windows Calculator, shown in Figure 5-20.

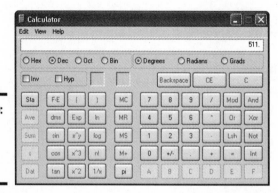

Figure 5-20: The full-functioned Scientific calculator.

The Scientific calculator slices and dices and cooks dinner, too. For details on all of the options, choose Help⇨Help Topics.

If you're hacking your Windows games, especially FreeCell, the way I explained in the "FreeCell" section of this chapter, you should know how to use the Scientific calculator to convert decimal numbers to hexadecimal, the same way as those guys in white lab coats. Here's how:

1. **Click Dec, so the Calculator knows you're typing a decimal number.**

2. **Type in the number.**

3. **Click Hex.**

That's all there is to it. Tough, huh?

I suppose you could always toss your tie over your shoulder, moan and groan about how hard converting these stupid numbers is, and then gnash your teeth a bit as you click. It would certainly impress the boss. Or the neighbors. The gnashing teeth would go a long way to cover that hex-eating grin on your face.

And I bet you always thought Computer Science was a difficult subject.

Painting

Nobody would ever mistake Windows Paint for a real graphics program. It's a good-enough application for manipulating existing pictures, and it helps you convert among the various picture file formats (JPEG, GIF, and so on), but it's certainly no competition for a real drawing tool like CorelDraw or a picture editing tool like Microsoft Photo Editor or Adobe PhotoShop.

That said, you can have a lot of fun with Windows Paint. To bring it to life, choose Start⇨All Programs⇨Accessories⇨Paint. You see a screen like the one shown in Figure 5-21.

Opening, saving, and closing pictures in Paint is a snap; it works just like any other Windows program. Where you're bound to get in the most trouble is in free-form drawing, which can be mighty inscrutable until you understand the following:

✦ You select a line color (used by all of the painting tools as their primary color) by left-clicking on the color on the palette (near the bottom of the window).

- You select a fill color (used to fill the inside of the solid shapes, such as the rectangle and oval) by right-clicking the color.
- Many of the painting tools let you choose the thickness of the lines they use — in the case of the spray can, you can choose the heaviness of the spray — in the box that appears after you select the tool.

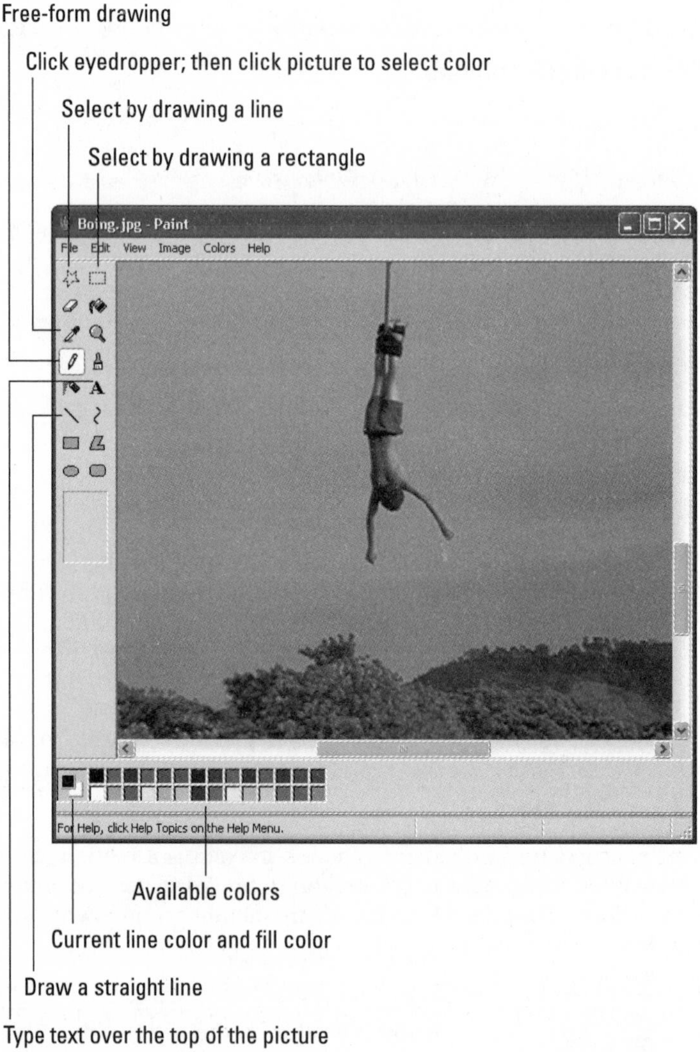
Free-form drawing
Click eyedropper; then click picture to select color
Select by drawing a line
Select by drawing a rectangle
Boing.jpg - Paint
File Edit View Image Colors Help
For Help, click Help Topics on the Help Menu.
Available colors
Current line color and fill color
Draw a straight line
Type text over the top of the picture

Figure 5-21: Don't let Windows Paint drive you off the deep end.

General rules for editing are a lot like what you see in the rest of Windows — select, copy, paste, delete, and so on. The only odd editing procedure I've found is for the free-form selection tool. If you click on this tool and draw an area on the picture, Paint responds by selecting the smallest rectangle that encloses the entire line that you've drawn. It's ... different.

You can specify the exact size of your picture by choosing View⇨Attributes.

Getting Older Programs to Work

Program compatibility rates as one of the big nightmares in Windows XP. So many programs have been written for the PC, for so many years, that Windows XP has absolutely no way to handle all of them in all circumstances.

The designers of Windows XP knew that they could never be all things to all people, so they built a very tricky safety net into XP. In essence, Windows XP can behave to a remarkable extent like any earlier version of Windows. So if you have a program that worked under Windows 95, say, and it doesn't work under Windows XP, you can tell Windows XP to pretend like it's Windows 95, and see if the offending program can be tricked.

The Program Compatibility Wizard doesn't work all the time, but it does trick squirrelly programs frequently enough to make the process worth the effort. It makes Windows XP act like Windows 95, 98, ME, NT 4, or 2000. Follow these steps to use the Program Compatibility Wizard:

1. **Choose Start⇨All Programs⇨Accessories⇨Program Compatibility Wizard.**

You awaken the Wizard, as shown in Figure 5-22.

2. **The Wizard searches for programs on your hard drive (or on CD) and asks you to pick the program that's giving you problems.**

3. **The Wizard then wants to know which version of Windows the program is expecting.**

This can be a bit of a turkey shoot. I have a trash can full of programs that never ran under *any* version of Windows, despite advertising to the contrary. But if you ever got the program to run under any earlier version of Windows, start with that version.

4. **The Wizard wants to know if the program was designed to run with specific color settings (256 colors) or screen resolutions (640 x 480, or 800 x 600).**

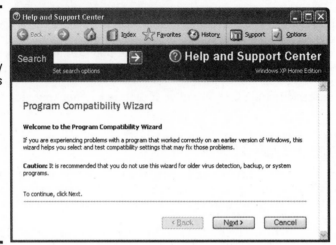

Figure 5-22: The Program Compatibility Wizard gives you a fighting chance to trick old programs into co-operating with Windows XP.

It also allows you to turn off Windows XP themes — the fancy graphics that XP uses to make it look different from earlier versions of Windows. In my eXPerience, it doesn't hurt to turn themes off on any program that's hiccupping with Windows XP.

5. **Try to run the program.**

   If it works, the Wizard enables you to easily have those settings kick in every time you run the program. If it doesn't work, the Wizard offers to try other settings.

Ultimately, if the program doesn't work, you're up a creek, unless you can convince the program manufacturer that Windows XP compatibility is the most important "new" feature that they can add to their product. Which it is.

Using Sneaky Key Commands

Windows XP includes two well-buried key commands that everyone should know about. Neither of the key combinations works if your machine is hopelessly frozen, but in most normal circumstances, they should help a lot, especially if a program isn't behaving the way it should.

Conjuring up the Task Manager

Windows XP has a secret command post that you can get to if you know the right handshake. Uh, key combination. Whatever. The key combination works all the time — unless Windows is seriously out to lunch — as long as you're a designated Administrator. If you use Windows XP/Home, you probably are an Administrator. If you use Windows XP/Pro, you probably are not. (For a discussion of Administrators, see the section on using account types in Book I, Chapter 2.)

To bring up the Task Manager, hold down the Ctrl, Alt, and Del keys simultaneously. Task Manager should appear with a list of all the applications that are currently running (see Figure 5-23).

Figure 5-23:
Task
Manager
gives you
absolute
control over
the running
applications.

With Task Manager, you can do the following:

✦ Click an application, and then click End Task to initiate an orderly shutdown of the application. Windows tries to shut down the application without destroying any data. If it's successful, the application disappears from the list. If it isn't successful, it presents you with the option of summarily executing the application (called End Now to the less imaginative) or simply ignoring it and allowing it to go its merry way.

✦ Click an application, and then click Switch To, and Windows brings up the switched-to application. This is very convenient if you find yourself stuck somewhere — in a game, say, that won't "let go" while it's taken control of your system — and you want to jump over to a different application.

✦ Click Shut Down on the menu. From that point, you can switch users, log off, hibernate, restart, or completely shut down the computer.

This is an orderly shutdown, so if you have an application that's hung so badly that it won't terminate itself, you have to tell Windows XP to End Now and risk losing all the unsaved data in the application.

Task Manager goes way beyond application control. For example, if you have a somewhat dominant techie gene (it runs in the family), you may be tickled to watch the progress of your computer on the Performance monitor, which is in the Task Manager, on the Performance tab (see Figure 5-24).

Figure 5-24: Performance monitor keeps track of every imaginable part of your computer — and some you probably couldn't imagine, in your worst nightmares.

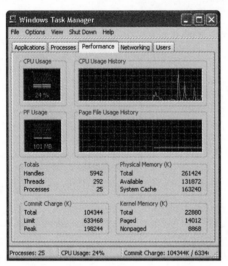

Switching coolly

Windows includes a quick, easy way to switch among running applications without diving for the mouse so that you can click on the Windows Taskbar. It's known as the CoolSwitch (yes, that's the technical term for it), and it works on any computer, any time, unless Windows is totally out to lunch.

Which happens sometimes.

To use the CoolSwitch, hold down the Alt key and press Tab. You see something like the screen shown in Figure 5-25.

A very important,
top-secret project

PowerPoint

Figure 5-25:
The
Windows
XP
CoolSwitch.

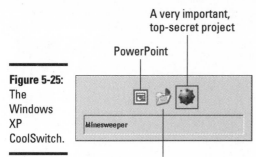

Windows Explorer with My Music open

As you press Tab over and over again, Windows cycles through the running programs. When you arrive at the program that you want to run, simply let go of the Alt key, and the selected program comes to life.

Cool, eh?

Chapter 6: Maintaining Your Windows XP System

In This Chapter

✔ Getting the latest version of XP

✔ Keeping track of the programs installed on your PC

✔ Working with disks

✔ Scheduling boring things so that your computer does them automatically

✔ Storing more and spending less with Zips

*I*nto every XP's life a little rain must fall.

Or something like that.

More than half a million people tested Windows XP. Real people, not Microsoft internal "testers." That's the main reason why Windows XP has a well-deserved reputation for working pretty darn well, on almost all computers.

Still, XP is a computer program, not a Cracker Jack toy, and it's going to have problems. The trick lies in making sure you don't have problems, too.

This chapter takes you through all of the important tools you have at hand to make XP do what you need to do, to head off problems, and to solve problems as they (inevitably!) occur.

Keeping Up to Date

One of the first times you start Windows XP, a little balloon appears in the notification area (the box on the lower right of the screen, where the clock sits) telling you "Stay current with automatic updates / Click here to learn how to keep your computer up-to-date automatically with important downloads from Windows Update."

Understanding Windows Update

Windows XP has many reasons to be so insistent in its desire to phone home and update itself. Windows Update helps you do the following:

✦ Avoid lockups and dodge other weird Windows gremlins by retrieving and installing the latest versions of various Windows programs, particularly drivers.

Drivers are computer programs that make specific parts of your computer work. You have a driver for your keyboard, mouse, modem, printer, USB port, camera, and on and on. Drivers are notorious for causing grief: In my experience, if Windows locks up on you, you have at least a 50/50 chance that a driver did the dirty work.

✦ Keep up with the latest security patches. Windows 98/ME had its share of security problems, but Windows XP introduced an entire genre of viruses, worms, and attack methods that the guys in black hats have only begun to exploit. See Book IX, Chapter 3 for details.

✦ Find more help. Microsoft continually refines (and in some cases improves) its Help system. Windows Update ensures that you have the latest Help files installed and ready to go the next time you dive into the Help and Support Center.

All of this benefit comes at no price: There's no charge (although you do have to be connected to the Internet); you needn't register your copy of Windows to take advantage of Windows Update; and no information about your machine is sent to Microsoft when you use it, aside from the obvious catalog of Windows components necessary for Update to do its job.

Setting up automatic updates

Here's how to start working with automatic update:

1. **If you want to change your Windows Update settings, you have to be an Administrator.**

   If you're running XP/Home (and using anything other than a Guest account), chances are very good that you are already an Administrator, and you don't have to worry about it. If you're running XP/Pro, you probably aren't an Administrator, unless you've convinced your company's network administrators to induct you into the club. See the section on using account types in Book I, Chapter 2, for advice and commiseration.

2. **Start the Windows Update Wizard by clicking the "Stay current with automatic updates" balloon.**

   You see a screen that looks something like the one shown in Figure 6-1.

Figure 6-1:
The
Windows
Update
Wizard.

3. **Tell Windows whether you want to have updates applied automatically or whether you want to look over the update candidates before (and after!) they're applied to your machine, as shown in Figure 6-2.**

Figure 6-2:
Setting
limits on
what
Windows
Update can
do to your
machine
without your
permission.

I strongly recommend that you tell Windows that you want to review changes to your system before they're applied (see Figure 6-2). Why? Because Microsoft has a long history of releasing updates that don't quite work right. In rare instances, you'll want to download and install an update immediately — if a major virus or worm starts making its way across the Internet, for example, and your machine is in its path. In most cases, though, you can afford to wait a week or two before changing major components on your machine, which gives you time to hear loud screams from other users (via sources such as the free Woody's Windows Watch newsletter, www.windowswatch.com) if something's awry.

4. Click Finish.

Windows connects to the Internet, following your instructions to look for the latest updates. If any updates are found, an icon appears in your notification area (near the clock).

 Choose Start⇨Control Panel⇨Performance and Maintenance⇨System and look at the Automatic Updates tab to change the update approach at any time.

Performing the update

 Unless you turn off Windows Update completely, each time you log on to the Internet, Windows checks to see whether any new versions of Windows files, drivers, Help files, and so on are available specifically for your computer. If new versions are available and you've told Windows to notify you and let you select updates, you see an icon in the notification area (near the clock) with a balloon message that says, "New updates are available from Windows Update. Click here to review these items and begin downloading."

 During the automatic updating process, you may be asked (several times) whether you want to allow Windows to download and install certain Windows components that handle the updating itself. It's a classic chicken-and-egg situation: You need these components in order to do the updating, but Windows can't automatically pull them down unless you give your permission. Say OK when asked about installing the components, if you want automatic update to work, uh, automatically.

Here's how the automatic update works, if you chose to review updates:

1. Choose Start⇨Help and Support, and under the Pick a Task heading, click Keep Your Computer Up-To-Date with Windows Update.

You see the Windows Update screen shown in Figure 6-3.

2. Click Scan for Updates.

Windows compares its database of available updates to the components installed on your machine and tells you what's available (see Figure 6-4).

 You can bypass Steps 1 and 2 by simply going to the Windows Update Web site, www.windowsupdate.Microsoft.com. If you click on the balloon in the notification area that says "New updates are available from Windows Update. Click here to review these items and begin downloading," you end up in Step 3. The final result is the same.

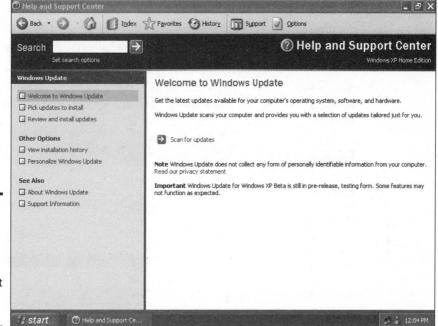

Figure 6-3:
Windows
scans your
machine
and finds
updates that
are specific
to your PC.

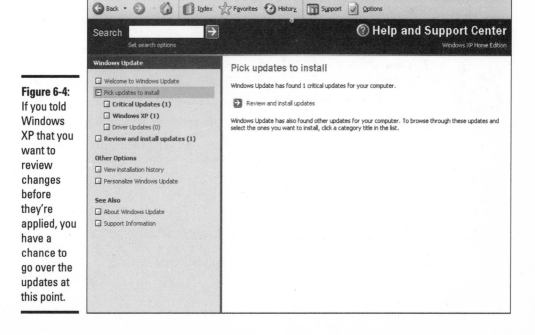

Figure 6-4:
If you told
Windows
XP that you
want to
review
changes
before
they're
applied, you
have a
chance to
go over the
updates at
this point.

3. Click Review and Install Updates.

You see a list of available updates. If you don't want to install a particular update, click Remove. If you want to install an optional add-on, click Add (see Figure 6-5).

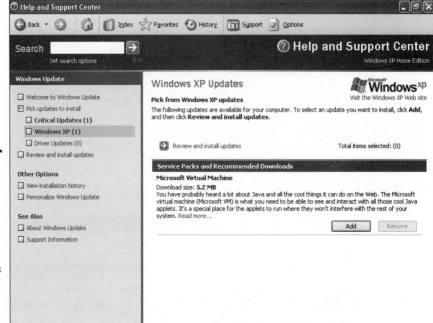

Figure 6-5: Windows Update offers to install non-critical Windows components that you may find useful.

Don't worry. Any Windows XP updates that you choose to Remove from the automatic updating machinery can be resurrected at a later date.

4. Windows downloads and installs the software you've selected.

You may be required to Accept a licensing agreement. You'll probably be required to restart your computer. But in the end, the updates almost always go smoothly.

Installing old updates

Like bad pennies that won't go away, Windows XP continues to bug — er, I mean *bother* — you about old updates that you've declined: The old updates appear on the Pick Updates to Install list for a long time.

Follow these steps to banish certain updates, so that they never darken your door again:

1. **Bring up the Windows Update screen. (Choose Start⇨Help and Support, and under the Pick a Task heading, click Keep Your Computer Up-To-Date with Windows Update.)**

2. **Click Personalize Windows Update.**

3. **Check the box marked Display the Option to Hide Individual Updates.**

   Doing so puts a box next to every offered update, which effectively hides the update from all further searches on your machine.

4. **If you change your mind and want Windows to show you all the pending updates, choose Start⇨Control Panel⇨Performance and Maintenance⇨System. Then, on the Automatic Updates tab, click Restore Declined Updates.**

Installing and Removing Programs

Windows XP includes a one-stop shopping point for adding and removing programs. To get to it, choose Start⇨Control Panel⇨Add or Remove Programs. You see the Add or Remove Programs dialog box, as shown in Figure 6-6.

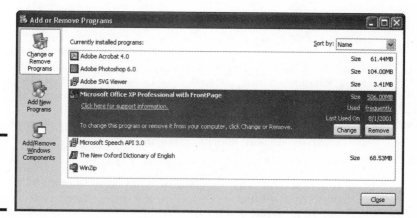

Figure 6-6:
Add or
remove
programs.

When Windows talks about changing programs, it isn't talking about making minor twiddles — this isn't the place to go if you want Microsoft Word to stop showing you rulers, for example. Add or Remove Programs is designed to activate or deactivate big chunks of a program — graft on a new arm or lop off an unused head (of which there are many, particularly in Office). If you look at Figure 6-7, you can see the kind of grand scale I'm talking about: In Add or Remove Programs, you may tell Excel that you want to use its Analysis Pack for financial analysis. Similarly, you may use Add or Remove Programs to completely obliterate Office's Speech Recognition capabilities. That's the kind of large-scale capability I'm talking about.

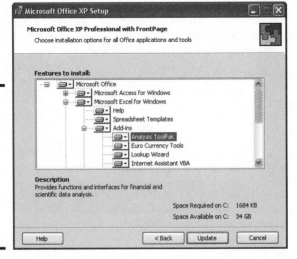

Figure 6-7:
The Office XP Setup dialog box, as seen from the Windows Add or Remove Programs.

Windows XP itself doesn't do much in Add or Remove Programs. The main function of Windows is as a gathering point: Well-behaved programs, when they're installed, are supposed to stick their uninstallers in Add or Remove Programs. That way, you have one centralized place to look when you want to get rid of a program. Microsoft doesn't write the uninstallers that Add or Remove Programs runs; if you have a gripe about a program's uninstaller, you need to talk to the company that made the program.

Several school-of-hard-knocks comments pertain:

✦ In practice, you never use Add or Remove Programs to add programs. If you want to install a program, do what savvy Dummies always do: Put the CD in the CD drive and follow the instructions. It's a whole lot easier that way.

✦ You rarely use Add or Remove Programs to remove parts of a program. Either you try to add features in a program that you forgot to include when you originally installed the program — most commonly with Office — or you want to delete a program entirely, to wipe its sorry tail off your hard drive.

Why sweat the small stuff? When you install a program, install all of it. Even Office XP, in all its bloated glory, only takes up 500 MB if you install every single far-out filter and truculent template. With hard disks so cheap they're likely candidates for landfill, it never pays to cut back on installed features to save a few megabytes.

✦ Many uninstallers, for reasons known only to their company's programmers — I won't mention Adobe by name — require you to insert the program's CD into your CD drive before you uninstall the program. That's like requiring you to show your dog's vaccination records before you kick it out of the house.

When you start a program's uninstaller, you're at the mercy of the uninstaller and the programmers who wrote it. Windows doesn't even enter into the picture.

Installing and Removing Parts of Windows

Most people never use big parts of Windows XP. Some parts are made with very specific functions in mind and, with two exceptions, the average Person on the Street rarely encounters the requisite specific situations.

Thank heaven.

The two exceptions? Fax support and automatic backup in Windows. Neither gets installed unless you make the trek to retrieve it. Fax is relatively simple and benign; I talk about it here. Backup is much meaner; I talk about it in the section called "Backup/Restore," later in this chapter.

Windows support for faxing has never been great. Although it's theoretically possible for you to get the Windows fax application working, one great Achilles' heel hampers you: If you have just one modem and it's connected to the Internet, you can't use it to send or receive faxes! Funny how Microsoft glosses over that detail, eh?

The smartest Dummies I know don't try to use Windows for faxing. Instead, they have a standalone fax machine (connected to its own telephone line, of course), or they use a fax service such as J2 Messenger (www.j2.com). J2's software lets you send faxes as easily as you print: Choose File⇨Print⇨Send with J2 Messenger, and the program turns your fax into an e-mail message. When you send the message to J2 headquarters — along with all your other e-mail — it's routed to a location close to the recipient, converted into a fax and then actually faxed for you, generally at a fraction of the cost for a long-distance phone call. J2 also offers inbound fax delivery: Your correspondent sends a fax to a specific phone number, the fax is converted to e-mail, and the e-mail is sent to you — all within a matter of seconds.

If the preceding caveat hasn't warned you off, here's how you install the Windows fax software. The same general procedure works for installing other obscure parts of Windows:

1. **Choose Start⇨Control Panel⇨Add or Remove Programs to bring up Add or Remove Programs.**

2. **Click Add/Remove Windows Components. to bring up the Windows Components Wizard (see Figure 6-8).**

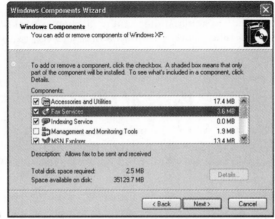

Figure 6-8:
Install unusual Windows components in Add or Remove Programs.

3. **Find the component that you want to add.**

   In this case, because you're trying to add fax support, check the box marked Fax Services. In general, you may have to click on a likely sounding component, and then click the Details button to see which subcomponents are available.

4. **Insert the CD that Windows came on, so that Windows can pull the component off the CD and install it on your PC.**

   You may be required to restart Windows. In any case, by the time the Wizard is done, your new component should be available and ready to use.

If you performed a typical installation of XP/Home, the following list covers the components that you installed and have available:

✦ All the Accessories and Utilities are installed.

✦ Fax Services aren't installed. Follow the instructions above to install Windows faxing, but make sure you understand the limitations.

✦ Indexing Service is installed.

✦ The only Management and Monitoring Tools available are for an obscure Internet network management standard called SNMP, or Simple Network Management Protocol. You can look up SNMP in the Windows Help and Support Center, but if you need to look it up, you probably don't need it.

✦ Internet Explorer and MSN Explorer are installed. You can get rid of them here, if you really want to.

If you read the fine print, you'll discover that Add/Remove Windows Components isn't really offering to remove Internet Explorer. This option, ahem, "Adds or removes access to Internet Explorer from the Start menu and the Desktop." In other words, you can get rid of the shortcut to IE from the Start menu (Windows XP, as it ships in plain-vanilla systems, doesn't have a shortcut to IE on the Desktop) using this option. Not exactly what you expected, eh?

✦ Under Networking Services, you can add three subcomponents — RIP Listener, which works with NetWare's Router Information Protocol Version 1; Simple TCP/IP Services, an obscure group that includes Quote of the Day; and Universal Plug and Play support, which comes into question only if you have UPnP devices installed (confusingly, UPnP isn't related to Plug 'n Play, the industry-wide standard for identifying hardware).

✦ Other Network File and Print Services includes support for only UNIX (and Linux) computers to print on printers connected to your PC.

✦ The software to automatically Update Root Certificates (digital security certificates for Microsoft products) is installed and running.

Maintaining Disks

E pur, si muove

Even so, it does move.

Galileo, to his inquisitors, April 30, 1633

Disks seem to cause more computer problems than all other infuriating PC parts combined. Why? They move. And unlike other parts of computers that are designed to move — printer rollers and keyboard springs and mouse balls, for example — they move quickly and with ultra-fine precision, day in and day out.

I go into details about the various kinds of disks and their plusses and minuses in the section on managing disks in Book I, Chapter 1. If you're unfamiliar with the inner workings of the beasts, that's a good place to start.

Like any other moving mechanical contraption, an ounce of disk prevention is worth ten tons of cure. Unlike other moving mechanical contraptions, a good shot of WD-40 usually won't cure the problem.

Formatting: NTFS versus FAT32

If you'll forgive a slightly stretched analogy, the surface of a floppy diskette or hard drive is a lot like a blank audio cassette tape. You know, the kind you can buy for 29 cents at a discount store. The surface of a floppy diskette is coated with some sort of magnetic gunk that somehow magically stores electrical impulses, holds onto them, and then spits them back when you want them.

Audio cassette tapes are amazingly forgiving — ever turn one into an accordion with a lousy capstan? — but diskettes and disks generally aren't so forgiving. Disks try to pack a lot of data into a small space, and because of that, they need to be calibrated. That's where *formatting* comes in.

When you format a disk drive, you calibrate it: mark it with guideposts that tell the PC where to store data and how to retrieve it. Every floppy diskette and every hard disk has to be formatted before it can be used. Chances are good that the manufacturer formatted your drive before you got it. That's comforting, because every time a disk gets reformatted, everything on the disk gets tossed out, completely, irretrievably. *Everything.*

If you feel like you have to completely wipe out everything on a disk and start over, you can reformat your hard drive in one of two ways:

✦ Choose Start⇨My Computer to bring up Windows Explorer, right-click on the drive you want to re-format, click Format, and click Start. As long as you're a designated Administrator (see the section on using account types in Book I, Chapter 2), you receive the dialog box and warning shown in Figure 6-9.

✦ Reformat your hard drive as part of a complete (re)installation of Windows XP. See the section on considering a clean install in Book I, Chapter 1, for details.

Reformatting a hard drive really does obliterate everything. You not only lose your documents, pictures, programs, and e-mail messages; if they're on the zapped hard drive, you also lose all of your settings, your passwords, and anything you've done to customize Windows. It's a drastic step.

Figure 6-9:
The
scorched-
earth
approach to
completely
obliterating
all the data
on a drive
and starting
over again.

The primary choice you have to make when formatting or reformatting a
hard drive — or even buying a preformatted hard drive — is which of the
two competing file systems you should employ:

- ✦ **FAT32:** Stands for 32-bit File Allocation Table, as if that means anything
  to an honest chap. FAT32 is the old DOS/Windows 98/ME method for
  storing data on a disk. You may want to use FAT32 if you have disk utility programs that you absolutely have to run that absolutely require
  FAT32 (check the manufacturer's Web site). You may also want to stick
  with FAT32 if you intend to run two different versions of Windows on the
  same machine (a process called *multiple booting,* which, thankfully, is
  way beyond the scope of this book), or if you find yourself occasionally
  using an ancient emergency Windows 95/98/ME boot diskette to bring
  an old system back to life: They understand only FAT.

If you really want to use one PC to start up with many different operating
systems — Windows 95, 98, ME, NT 3.51, NT 4, 2000, Linux, whatever —
I urge you to invest in a program called Partition Magic, from
PowerQuest, www.powerquest.com. Partition Magic slices and dices
multi-boot systems, making the entire process much simpler and more
easily controlled. Setting up a multi-boot system takes a fair amount of
know-how and perseverance. Partition Magic makes it less unnerving.

- ✦ **NTFS:** Stands for Windows NT File System. NTFS isn't quite as Neolithic
  as FAT32. NTFS includes built-in support for security and compression.
  It's the file system of choice in almost all circumstances.

As long as you're a designated Administrator (see Book I, Chapter 2 on using account types), formatting a drive for NTFS is as simple as choosing NTFS in the File System drop-down box in the Format dialog box (refer to Figure 6-9). You can also convert an existing FAT32 drive or *partition* (part of a drive) to NTFS by using an arcane command called `convert`. For details, search the Windows Help and Support Center for "convert ntfs." Windows has no analogous command to convert NTFS drives (or partitions) to FAT32.

If you install Windows XP on a PC that's running Windows 98 or ME, Windows offers you an opportunity to change any existing FAT32 drives (or partitions) to NTFS. Unless you have a very specific reason for sticking with FAT32, letting the system convert you is a good idea.

If you have a big hard drive, you may be forced to use NTFS. Windows XP won't format a drive larger than 32 GB for FAT32. Windows has good reasons for this restriction, but the upshot is that really big drives need NTFS.

Performing periodic maintenance

Drives die at the worst possible moment. A drive that's starting to get flaky can display all sorts of strange symptoms: Everything from long, long pauses when you're trying to open a file to completely inexplicable crashes and other errors in Windows itself.

Windows XP comes with a grab-bag of utilities designed to help you keep your hard drives in top shape. One of them runs automatically every time your system shuts down unexpectedly, like when the dog finally bites through the power cord: The next time you start your system, Windows scans your hard drives to see whether any pieces of files were left hanging around.

You can spend a lot of time futzing around with your hard drives and their care and feeding if you want, but as far as I'm concerned, just three utilities suffice. You have to be a designated Administrator (see the section on using account types in Book I, Chapter 2) to get them to work:

Running an error check

If a drive starts acting weird — for example, you get errors when trying to open a file, or Windows crashes in unpredictable ways — run the Windows error-checking routines:

If you're an old hand at Windows — or an even older hand at DOS — you probably recognize this as the venerable `CHKDSK` routine, in somewhat fancier clothing.

1. **Choose Start➪My Computer.**

2. **Right-click the drive that's malfunctioning and click Properties.**

3. **On the Tools tab, click Check Now.**

The Check Disk dialog box appears (see Figure 6-10).

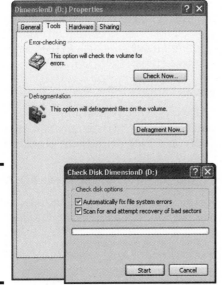

4. **In most circumstances, you want to Scan For and Attempt Recovery of Bad Sectors, so check that box, and click Start.**

If you don't want to sit and wait and wait (and wait) for Windows to finish, you probably want to check the box marked Automatically Fix File System Errors, too.

As long as you aren't using any files on the disk that Windows is scanning, Windows performs the scan on the spot and reports back on what it finds. If you are using files on the disk, however, Windows asks whether you want to schedule a scan to run the next time you restart your machine. If you say yes, you have to turn the computer off and then turn it back on again before Windows runs the scan. (Note that merely logging off isn't sufficient.)

Scheduling Cleanups

In addition to running an error check from time to time, I use the Windows Task Scheduler to periodically go through and remove temporary files that I don't need, with a utility called Cleanup. I tell you how to do that in the section "Scheduling Task Scheduler," later in this chapter.

Defragmenting a drive

Every week or so (or whenever I'm thinking about it), I run the Windows Disk Defragmenter on all my hard drives. This is quite different from the Check Disk routine (refer to Figure 6-10), which concentrates on the surface of the hard drive and whether it has been corrupted. Files become *fragmented* — scattered in pieces all over a hard drive — when Windows dynamically creates and deletes files. Having many fragmented files on a hard drive tends to slow down processing because Windows has to jump all over a disk to reassemble a file when you ask for it. Windows Disk Defragmenter focuses on putting the pieces of files back together, in contiguous slots, so that Windows doesn't have to scamper all over the disk to read an entire file. To run the Defragmenter, follow these steps:

1. **Choose Start⇨All Programs⇨Accessories⇨System Tools⇨Disk Defragmenter.**

   Alternatively, you can navigate to the drive in question, right-click it, click Properties, click Tools, and click Defragment Now (refer to Figure 6-10).

2. **Click the drive that you want to work on, and then click Analyze.**

   Windows XP checks to be sure that the files are put together properly, and then it advises you about whether a defragmentation run is worthwhile (see Figure 6-11).

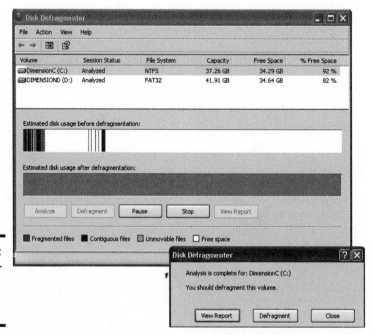

Figure 6-11: The Defragmenter's Analyze phase.

3. **To run the defragmenter, click Defragment.**

4. **Break out that novel you've always wanted to read. This can take a long, long time.**

   While Windows is defragmenting, it keeps you posted on its progress at the bottom of the Disk Defragmenter dialog box (see Figure 6-12), but don't be surprised if the "percent complete" figure freezes for a while and then jumps inexplicably.

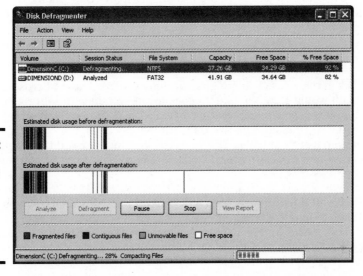

Figure 6-12:
Follow the progress of the defragmenter at the bottom of the dialog box.

Use those three tools regularly — Chkdsk, Cleanup, and Disk Defragmenter — and your disks will thank you. Profusely.

Backup/Restore

Windows XP/Pro comes with a very thorough (and very complex) backup and restore capability called Automated System Recovery, or ASR. The Backup part of ASR works through a Wizard. The Restore part can kick in, at your command, when you re-boot the computer — even if your system was so thoroughly messed up you had to replace the hard drive.

If you think you're going to click a couple of times and get automatic backups from Windows XP, you're in for a very rude awakening. While working with ASR isn't as complex as, say, setting up and maintaining a Big Corporate client/server Network, mastering ASR will certainly take you more than a day, assuming you already have a Ph.D. in Computer Science. Check the Windows XP Help and Support Center for the topic ASR and you'll see why.

Earlier versions of Windows let you boot your PC with a special diskette called an Emergency Repair Disk (or Emergency Boot Disk in very early versions). Windows doesn't have an ERD. All of the functions of the old ERP have been subsumed by ASR. Yes, that means you can't boot to Windows XP directly from diskette any more.

If you're using XP/Pro and you need automatic backups through your Big Corporate Network (you probably do!), and your network isn't already set up to handle backups, your only realistic choice is to bring in somebody who knows ASR and have them configure it for you. Usually, the designated stuckee is your favorite whipping boy, the Network Administrator. ASR kinda goes hand in hand with other Big Corporate Network chores.

What if you're using XP/Home? Ah, have I got a gotcha for you.

Back in the weeks leading up to Windows XP's release, Microsoft announced that it would ship ASR and its Backup subsystem with XP/Pro, but would *not* include any sort of automatic backup with XP/Home. That brought a hailstorm of criticism from two different perspectives: the "XP/Home users need backup just as much as XP/Pro users" contingency and the "Windows has always had a backup routine even if nobody ever used it" contingency. Both contingencies won.

Microsoft does, indeed, ship ASR Backup with XP/Home — if you know where to find it. Except, uh, well, er, there's no ASR Restore to go along with it. That makes XP/Home's Backup just about as useful as a Ferrari Testarossa with no wheels. Or a transmission, engine, seats, or brakes.

If you really, really want to install ASR Backup (better known as NTBackup) in XP/Home, even though there's no built-in Restore, put the XP/Home CD in a convenient drive and wait for the Welcome to Microsoft Windows XP screen. Choose Browse this CD⇨Valueadd⇨MSFT⇨NTBACKUP. Make sure you read (and understand!) the warning in the file readme.txt before running the installer.

Scheduling Task Scheduler

Windows XP has a built-in scheduler that runs just about any program according to any schedule you specify — daily, weekly, monthly, middle of the night, on alternate blue moons.

The scheduler comes in handy in two very different situations:

+ When you always want to do something at the same time of day. Perhaps you always want to dial up the Internet at 6:15 every morning, so that your machine is connected by the time you drag your sorry tail into your desk chair. Or maybe you want to run a PowerPoint presentation every morning at 7:30, so that your boss hears the tell-tale sounds as she walks by your cubicle. (And who said Dummies aren't Devious?)

✦ When you want to make sure that the computer performs some mundane maintenance job when it won't interfere with your work time. Thus, you may schedule disk cleanups every weekday at 2:00 in the afternoon, because you know you'll always be propped up in the mop closet taking a snooze.

Any discussion of scheduled tasks immediately conjures up the old question, "Should I leave my computer running all night, or should I turn it off?" The fact is — nobody knows which is better. You can find plenty of arguments on both sides of the fence. Suffice it to say that your computer has to be on (or suspended) for a scheduled task to run, so you may have to leave your computer on at least one night a week (or a month) to get the maintenance work done.

You find absolutely no debate about one "should I leave it on" question, though. Everybody in the know agrees that running a full surface scan of your hard drive daily is a bad idea. (Specifically Chkdsk, see "Performing periodic maintenance," in this chapter.) A full scan simply inflicts too much wear and tear on the hard drive's arms. It's kind of like forcing yourself to fly every morning, just to keep your shoulders in shape.

One of the most important uses of the Task Scheduler is driving a Windows file cleanup program called, imaginatively, Cleanup. I talk about it in this chapter's section on "Maintaining Disks." Here's how to get Cleanup scheduled — and how to use Scheduler in general:

1. **Choose Start⇨All Programs⇨Accessories⇨System Tools⇨Scheduled Tasks to get the Scheduler going.**

You see the (odd) Windows Explorer window shown in Figure 6-13.

Figure 6-13:
Scheduled
Tasks.

Yes, your instincts are correct if you looked at Figure 6-13 and thought something appeared familiar. All of Windows XP's Scheduled Tasks appear in a folder called Scheduled Tasks. The tasks themselves are just files, and the Add Scheduled Task icon that you see in Figure 6-13 is just a wizard. If you ever need to look at the Scheduled Tasks on a PC connected to your network, look for the Scheduled Tasks folder.

2. **Double-click the icon marked Add Scheduled Task.**

   The Scheduled Task Wizard appears with a frou-frou introductory screen.

3. **Click Next.**

   You see a list of some available programs, as shown in Figure 6-14.

Figure 6-14: To schedule regular Disk Cleanup runs, choose Disk Cleanup.

Does the list in Figure 6-14 look like an odd assortment of programs? It is. The Scheduled Task Wizard takes all the programs listed on the Start menu, alphabetizes them, and throws them all in this list. Literally. If you want to schedule a program that isn't on the Start menu, you have to click the Browse button.

4. **In this example, assume that you want to schedule regular Disk Cleanup runs, so click Disk Cleanup, and then click Next.**

   You can tell Windows how frequently you want to run Disk Cleanup (see Figure 6-15).

5. **Click Next again, and you can set the exact schedule — which days, what times.**

6. **Click Next again, and the Scheduled Task Wizard asks you to provide security information (see Figure 6-16).**

   This is an important screen because it reinforces the point that you aren't given any special security privileges just because you're scheduling a program. The program runs only if you have the authority to make it run. (See the section on using account types in Book I, Chapter 2.)

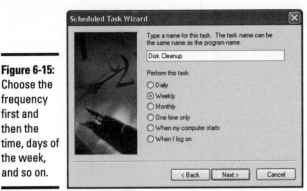

Figure 6-15:
Choose the
frequency
first and
then the
time, days of
the week,
and so on.

Figure 6-16:
A scheduled
program
runs only if
you have
sufficient
authority to
run it
manually.

7. **In the very last step, you can set "Advanced Properties" for the
scheduled task.**

   The advanced properties include telling Windows XP what to do if the
   task takes a verrrry long time to complete; whether the task should go
   into hibernation if something else happens on the computer (presumably you're awake in the wee hours, banging out an assignment); and
   whether Windows should wake up the computer if it's hibernating or
   run the task if the PC is using batteries at the time.

   The Windows Disk Cleanup program has a handful of settings that you may
   want to twiddle (see Figure 6-17). The System Schedule Wizard doesn't have
   any way to allow you to pick and choose your options for a scheduled program. The solution? Run Disk Cleanup once by hand (choose Start⇨All
   Programs⇨Accessories⇨System Tools⇨Disk Cleanup). Disk Cleanup
   remembers the settings that you applied when you ran it manually, and it
   uses those settings every time you run it with the Scheduler. Many other
   Windows programs work the same way.

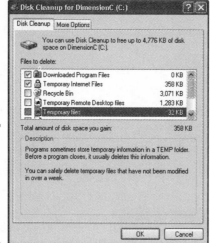

Figure 6-17:
Disk
Cleanup lets
you choose
what kinds
of files will
be deleted.

Zipping and Compression

Windows XP supports two very different kinds of file *compression*. The distinction is confusing but important, so bear with me.

File compression reduces the size of a file by cleverly taking out parts of the contents of the file that aren't needed, storing only the minimum amount of information necessary to reconstitute the file — *extract* it — into its full, original form. A certain amount of overhead is involved, because the computer has to take the time to squeeze extraneous information out of a file before storing it, and then the computer takes more time to restore the file to its original state when someone needs the file. But compression can reduce file sizes enormously. A compressed file often takes up half its original space — even less, in many cases.

How does compression work? That depends on the compression method you use. In one kind of compression, known as Huffman encoding, letters that occur frequently in a file (say, the letter *e* in a word processing document) are massaged so that they take up only a little bit of room in the file, while letters that occur less frequently (say, *x*) are allowed to occupy lots of space. Instead of allocating eight 1's and 0's for every letter in a document, say, some letters may take up only two 1's and 0's, while others could take up 15. The net result, overall, is a big reduction in file size. It's complicated, and the mathematics involved gets quite interesting.

Windows XP's two file compression techniques are as follows:

✦ Files can be compressed and placed in a "Compressed (zipped) Folder," with an icon to match.

✦ Files, folders, or even entire drives can be compressed using NTFS's built-in compression capabilities.

For a description of NTFS, see "Formatting: NTFS versus FAT32" in this chapter.

Here's where things get complicated.

NTFS compression is built into the file system: You can use it only on NTFS drives, and the compression doesn't persist when you move (or copy) the file off the drive. Think of NTFS compression as a capability inherent to the disk drive itself. That isn't really the case — Windows XP does all the sleight-of-hand behind the scenes — but the concept will help you remember NTFS compression's limitations and quirks.

Although Microsoft would have you believe that "Compressed (zipped) Folder" compression is based on folders, it isn't. A "Compressed (zipped) Folder" is really a file — *not* a folder — but it's a special kind of file called a Zip file. If you've ever encountered Zip files on the Internet (they have a filename extension of .ZIP and they're frequently manipulated with programs such as WinZip, `www.winzip.com`), you know exactly what I'm talking about. Zip files contain one or more compressed files, and they use the most common kind of compression found on the Internet. Think of "Compressed (zipped) Folders" as being Zip files, and if you have even a nodding acquaintance with ZIPs, you'll immediately understand the limitations and quirks of "Compressed (zipped) Folders". Microsoft calls them "Folders" because that's supposed to be easier for users to understand. You be the judge.

If you have Windows show you filename extensions — see my rant about that topic in the section on showing filename extensions in Book I, Chapter 2 — you see immediately that "Compressed (zipped) Folders" are, in fact, simple Zip files.

Table 6-1 shows a quick comparison of NTFS compression and Zip compression.

Table 6-1   NTFS Compression vs. "Compressed (Zipped) Folders" Compression

NTFS	*ZIP*
Think of NTFS compression as a feature of the hard disk itself	Zip technology works on any file, regardless of where it is stored
The minute you move an NTFS compressed file off an NTFS drive — by, say, sending a file as an e-mail attachment — the file is uncompressed, automatically, and you can't do anything about it: You'll send a big, uncompressed file.	You can move a "Compressed (zipped) Folder" (actually a Zip file, with a .ZIP file-name extension) anywhere, and it stays compressed. If you send a Zip file as an e-mail attachment, it goes over the ether as a compressed file. The person receiving the file can view it directly in Windows XP, or he can use a product such as WinZip to see it.
A lot of overhead is associated with NTFS compression: Windows has to compress and decompress those files on the fly, and that sucks up processing power.	Very little overhead is associated with Zip files. Many programs (for example, anti-virus programs) read Zip files directly.
NTFS compression is great if you're running out of room on an NTFS formatted drive.	"Compressed (zipped) Folders" (that is to say, Zip files) are in a near-universal form that can be used just about anywhere.
You have to have Administrator privileges in order to use NTFS compression	You can create, copy, or move Zip files just like any other files, with the same security restrictions
You can use NTFS compression on entire drives, folders, or single files. They cannot be password protected.	You can Zip files or folders, and they can be password protected.

If you try to compress the drive that contains your Windows folder, you won't be able to compress the files that are currently in use by Windows.

To use NTFS compression on an entire drive, follow these steps:

1. **Make sure that you are a full-fledged Administrator (see Book I, Chapter 2).**

2. **Choose Start⇨My Computer and right-click the drive that you want to compress. Click Properties and click on the General tab (see Figure 6-18).**

3. **If the drive is formatted with NTFS (see "Formatting: NTFS versus FAT32" in this chapter), you see a check box saying Compress Drive to Save Disk Space. Check this check box.**

4. **Click OK.**

Windows asks you to confirm that you want to compress the entire drive. Windows takes some time to compress the drive — in some cases, the estimated time is measured in days. Good luck.

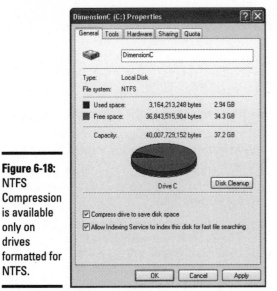

Figure 6-18:
NTFS
Compression
is available
only on
drives
formatted for
NTFS.

To use NTFS compression on a folder or single file, follow these steps:

1. **Make sure that you are a full-fledged Administrator (see Book I,
   Chapter 2).**

2. **Navigate to the folder or file you want to compress (for example.,
   choose Start➪My Documents or Start➪My Computer). Right-click on
   the file or folder you want to compress. Click Properties and click the
   Advanced button on the General tab.**

   The Advanced Properties dialog box appears (see Figure 6-19).

Figure 6-19:
NTFS
compression
for files and
folders is
available
only on NTFS
drives.

3. **Check the box marked Compress Contents to Save Disk Space and
   click OK.**

To uncompress a file or folder, go back into the Advanced Properties dialog box (right-click the file or folder, click Properties, and then click Advanced) and uncheck Compress Contents to Save Disk Space.

To use Zip compression, er, "Compressed (zipped) Folders," you must first create a Zip file, er, a "Compressed (zipped) Folder". Here's how:

1. **Choose Start⇨My Documents to navigate to the folder that you want to contain your new Zip file.**

2. **Right-click in any convenient empty location within the window and choose New⇨Compressed (Zipped) Folder.**

   Windows responds by creating a new Zip file, with a .ZIP filename extension, and placing it in the current folder.

   The new file is just like any other file — you can rename it, copy it, move it, delete it, send it as an e-mail attachment, save it on the Internet, or do anything else to it that you can do to a file. (That's because it *is* a file.)

3. **To add a file to your "Compressed (zipped) Folder," simply drag it onto the zipped folder icon.**

4. **To copy a file from your Zip file (uh, folder), double-click the zipped folder icon, and treat the file the same way you would treat any "regular" file (see Figure 6-20).**

Figure 6-20:
Zipped files can, with a few minor restrictions, be treated the same as any other files.

5. **To copy all of the files out of your Zip file (folder), click Extract All Files in the Folder Tasks Pane.**

   You see the Windows XP Compressed (zipped) Folders Extraction Wizard (see Figure 6-21), which guides you through the steps.

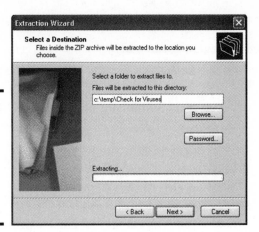

Figure 6-21:
To copy all
of the files
out of the
Zip file,
"extract"
them using
this Wizard.

 The Compressed (zipped) Folders Extraction Wizard places all the copied files into a new folder with the same name as the Zip file — which confuses the living bewilickers out of everybody. Unless you give the extracted folder a different name from the original Compressed (zipped) Folder, you end up with two folders with precisely the same name sitting on your desktop. Do yourself a huge favor and feed the Wizard a different folder name while you're extracting the files.

 Nico Mak's WinZip runs rings around Windows XP's built-in "Compressed (zipped) Folder" features. Check out `www.winzip.com` for details.

Creating Checkpoints and System Restore

Ever get the feeling that things were going right?

Moments later, did you get the feeling that something must be wrong *because* things are going right?

Now you understand the gestalt behind System Restore. If you take a snapshot of your PC from time to time, when things are going right, it's relatively easy to go back to that "right" time when the wolves come howling at the, uh, Gates.

 Windows XP automatically takes System Restore snapshots — called *checkpoints* — when it can tell that you're going to try to do something complicated, such as install a new network card. Unfortunately, Windows can't always tell when you're going to do something drastic — perhaps you have a new CD player and the instructions tell you to turn off your PC and install the player *before* you run the setup program. So it doesn't hurt one little bit to run checkpoints from time to time, all by yourself.

Here's how to generate a System Restore checkpoint:

1. **Wait until your PC is running smoothly.**

   No sense in having a checkpoint that propels you out of the frying pan into the fire, eh?

2. **Make sure you're set up as an Administrator (see Book I, Chapter 2).**

3. **Choose Start➪All Programs➪Accessories➪System Tools➪System Restore.**

   You get to choose between setting up a checkpoint and restoring to an earlier checkpoint.

4. **Pick Create a Restore Point (see Figure 6-22) and click Next.**

5. **Type a checkpoint name (such as Things Are Finally Working OK) and click Create.**

   Windows automatically brands the checkpoint with the current date and time.

6. **Windows creates a restore point with little fanfare and lets you go on your merry way.**

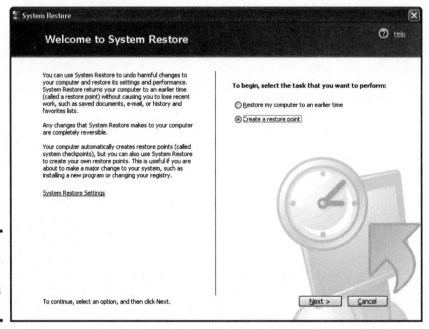

Figure 6-22:
Windows
XP creates
checkpoints
on demand.

If you ever need to restore your computer to a previous state, follow these steps:

1. **Close all running programs and save your work.**

System Restore doesn't muck with any data files, documents, pictures, or anything like that. It only works on system files. Your data is safe.

2. **Choose Start⇨All Programs⇨Accessories⇨System Tools⇨System Restore.**

3. **Pick Restore My Computer to an Earlier Time and click Next.**

4. **Select the date and specific checkpoint that you want to restore to (see Figure 6-23).**

5. **Windows shuts down, restarts, and restores itself to the point you chose.**

System Restore is a nifty feature that works very well.

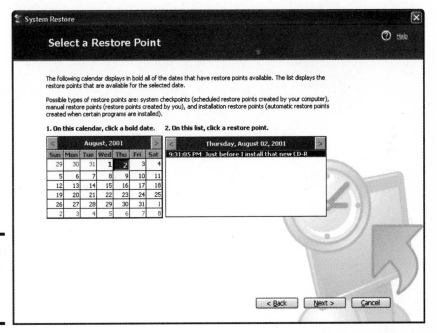

Figure 6-23:
Choose the
checkpoint
that you
need.

Chapter 7: Focusing on Windows XP/Professional

In This Chapter

✓ Do you need XP/Pro?

✓ What to do if you have XP/Pro and you want XP/Home

✓ What to do if you have XP/Home and you need XP/Pro

✓ Taking advantage of XP/Pro's features

*W*ith certain specific exceptions (for example, the discussion of client/ server networking, in Book IX, Chapter 1), *Windows XP All-in-One Desk Reference For Dummies* aims directly for Windows XP/Home.

Why?

With few exceptions, Windows XP/Pro — the other flavor of Windows XP — has nothing to offer the garden-variety Dummy.

This chapter looks at the exceptions — why you may want to pay extra for XP/Pro, and what to do with XP/Pro if you get it, either voluntarily or by corporate edict.

Differentiating XP/Pro and XP/Home

On the surface, Windows XP/Home and XP/Pro look very different. Just from the get-go, the installers make different assumptions about the kind of network that you want to establish. XP/Home sports a friendly point-and-click Welcome screen, while XP/Pro requires you to log on — and that, in turn, means you have to know your logon I.D. and password before you can even begin. In XP/Home, you can easily switch among multiple users on the same machine. In XP/Pro, switching users is about as easy as switching offices at CIA Headquarters.

Underneath the surface, though, the products are remarkably similar. Almost all of the features in Windows XP/Pro are also in XP/Home. Almost all of the features behave in precisely the same way. Even the CDs for XP/Home and XP/Pro are very nearly identical — only a handful of files differ. XP/Pro users can even tell Windows to use the easy Welcome screen and fast user switching, if they're so inclined, providing the PC isn't connected to a Big Corporate Network.

That's not accidental. Microsoft designed it that way, at least for this version of Windows. Redmond's Product Managers promise us that some future version of Windows will provide "more value" for the XP/Pro sucker, er, purchaser than the XP/Home purchaser. But for now the pickin's are slim indeed.

Weighing the advantages of XP/Home

XP/Home's main advantage lies more in what it *doesn't* have than in what it does have, if ya know what I mean.

XP/Home assumes that you don't want or need a lot of security. XP/Home won't tie into a sophisticated corporate security system. It doesn't recognize the heavy-duty security built into Windows NT Server or Windows 2000 Server (or Windows .NET Server or . . .).

Starting with Windows 2000 Advanced Server, security comes in the guise of the Active Directory, a comprehensive tool for managing computers on a client/server network, as well as managing users, system resources (such as printers and Internet connections), and the interactions among all of the pieces. Active Directory is a world unto its own, with so many technical nooks and crannies that it has spawned an entirely new breed of Network Administrators, charged specifically with the care and feeding of the AD beast.

On the flip side, most small business users don't want or need the overhead inherent in a heavy-duty security system — Network Administrators don't come cheap, and do-it-yourself network administration rates right up there with do-it-yourself proctology. Home users almost never want to subject themselves to the extra hassle.

XP/Home's lessened security requirements buy you a lot of extra goodies. The following are features that you will find in XP/Home, but won't find in XP/Pro:

+ Simple logon via the point-and-click Welcome screen.

+ No need to memorize a user name or password, unless you really want to use a password (see Book I, Chapter 2).

+ Fast switching among users, so that you can let little Billy surf the Internet real quick while you run and check on the cat. Billy gets full access to his own favorites, history, and settings. When you come back and bump Billy out of the driver's seat, you can pick up where you left off in a heartbeat.

If you have an XP/Pro system that is not connected to a client/server network (that's a Big Corporate Network, or a "domain" in Microsoft parlance), you can make XP/Pro treat users just like XP/Home. Choose Start➪Control Panel➪User Accounts➪Change the Way Users Log On or Off. Using the settings in the User Accounts dialog box, you can tell Windows to use the XP/Home-style Welcome screen, and/or allow fast switching among users.

All of the added XP/Pro security comes via client/server networking — which Microsoft calls a *domain*. For much more information about client/server and domains, see Book IX, Chapter 1.

Of course, the other big advantage to XP/Home is the price. If you're buying Windows in a shrinkwrapped package off the shelf, XP/Home costs about a hundred dollars less than XP/Pro. If you're buying a new PC, chances are very good that XP/Home comes free, while XP/Pro — if it's available at all — costs a pretty penny or two or ten. Thousand.

Weighing the advantages of XP/Pro

If you need XP/Pro, you probably already know it — or somebody in your company has told you, in no uncertain terms, that you need it, bucko, so you better get with the system.

There's a reason why corporate IT folks can be so, uh, insistent (that's the polite term, anyway) about you installing Windows XP/Pro. They're concerned about security, and for good reason. If you run XP/Home on your PC, and you manage to get hooked into the Big Corporate Network — you know, the one that runs on the Big Corporate Server — you and your PC represent a significant security risk.

Here's a common high-risk security scenario (computer security types love to use the term *scenario,* so I'm humoring them):

1. **You install Windows XP/Home on your portable computer at home; then you lug that computer into the office and plug it into the Big Corporate Network.**

2. **You get onto the Big Corporate Network using, say, the technique described in the section "Converting XP/Home to XP/Pro," later in this chapter.**

3. **You use your itty-bitty portable's modem to dial out to the big, bad Internet, and you don't use the Windows XP firewall. Ba-da-bing, ba-da-boom, you've suddenly opened a gaping hole into your company's network.**

That kind of security breach is hardly unique to Windows XP/Home — it's been around for a long time — but the widespread availability of Windows

XP/Home and its simple networking setup makes it a big, big target. Security folks, understandably, don't like having machines on "their" network that poke gaping holes in their carefully crafted protection plans.

Security concerns go beyond simple modem back doors. Windows XP/Pro sports all sorts of security features that XP/Home can't match:

✦ **Full integration with Active Directory:** That means, with XP/Pro, you can use Active Directory on the Big Corporate Network to control who uses your PC and what they can do on your PC (and on the network as a whole) — and official Network Administrators are in charge of the whole shootin' match.

✦ **Domains:** Even if your company doesn't use Active Directory, XP/Pro takes full advantage of the features Microsoft builds into all of its client/server networks *(domains)*. Lots of capabilities are associated with domains, including the ability to predefine access privileges for groups of users and assign each individual user to a specific group.

With Windows XP/Pro, if you have the Network Administrator's blessing, you can control access to individual files. With XP/Home, the lowest-level control is for entire folders.

✦ **Offline Folders:** XP/Pro can store copies of shared network files and folders on your portable PC's local hard drive, so you can take the files with you when you pull the PC off the network and take it on the road. When you plug the PC back into the network, XP/Pro handles all the file synchronization tasks (albeit in a rudimentary way — if you and another user have both made changes to the same file, you can save one or both copies, but there's no attempt to merge changes).

✦ **Encryption:** Windows XP/Pro lets you encrypt individual files and folders using the NTFS file system's built-in encryption routines (for a description of NTFS, see Book I, Chapter 2). Windows XP/Home lets you mark folders as Private, thus making it difficult for other people to get at them, but encryption goes one step further by scrambling the contents. NTFS encryption is notoriously difficult to crack.

Windows XP/Pro's file encryption capability strikes a resounding chord with many portable PC users who are concerned about losing their portables and having all of their data accessible to the cretin who ran away with the machine. If you carry around sensitive data, and you don't want to encrypt individual files (using, say, the Microsoft Office encryption routines), XP/Pro may be a good choice, based on this one feature alone.

XP/Pro also includes a couple of features, lacking in XP/Home, which make it easier to use in a corporate (read: client/server) environment:

✦ **IntelliMirror:** This feature makes it easy (well, at least *possible*) for Network Administrators to *push* installations of operating systems — force networked computers to install specific pieces of software. IntelliMirror allows push installs of entire operating systems, components, some applications, and their upgrades, onto all PCs connected to the Big Corporate Network.

If everybody comes into the office one morning and discovers that, oh, Word doesn't work right, chances are pretty good that somebody in IT pushed upgrades onto all the machines. Microsoft Office patches, in particular, are notorious for not working right the first time.

✦ **Roaming User Profiles:** Windows configures itself to your preferences, no matter which PC you use on the network.

Finally, XP/Pro has a grab-bag of additional features that a few users may want:

✦ **Remote Desktop:** This feature allows you to take over your office computer while you're on the road. The computer at the office has to be running Windows XP/Pro — XP/Home won't cut the mustard. The computer that's traveling can be running just about any version of Windows, from Windows 98 on.

If you're seriously considering Remote Desktop (see the Windows Help and Support Center topic "Remote Desktop"), make sure you take a look at Remote Assistance (see Book I, Chapter 3). Although the two are inherently different — for example, you have to explicitly initiate a Remote Assistance session from the "zombie" computer — in many respects they accomplish the same thing. Remote Assistance is much, much easier to install and use. It's also, arguably, more secure. Remote Desktop requires XP/Pro on the zombie computer — and any version of Windows can reside on the "controller" — and Remote Assistance requires XP (Home or Pro) on both computers.

✦ **Personal Web Server:** This feature lets you build a Web site on your XP/Pro machine. (It's actually Internet Information Services Version 5.1.) Anyone who has access to the files on your machine will be able to view your personal Web pages using a browser, just as if they were on the Internet.

✦ **Dual-CPU Support:** If you own a computer with two CPU chips, you need to run XP/Pro if you want to take advantage of both of them. XP/Home uses only one chip, no matter how many chips you have installed.

✦ **Multilingual User Interface:** Only XP/Pro can have its language changed on the fly, so you can see dialog boxes in different languages. Or so I'm told.

If you want to upgrade your current Windows 2000 PC to Windows XP — that is, install Windows XP on top of Windows 2000 and carry along all of your settings and applications — you have to pay for XP/Pro. Windows XP/Home won't install over the top of Windows 2000, although it will install over Windows 98 or ME. I have full details in Book I, Chapter 1.

Making a buying decision

Want to know which version of Windows XP to buy?

Here's *Woody's Tried-and-True Quick XP/Pro/Home Decision Tree For Dummies:*

✦ If you're going to install Windows XP on a computer that will be attached to a Big Corporate Network, chances are awfully good that the Network Administrator will insist that you use XP/Pro. Do it.

✦ If you decide that you really have to set up your own Big Corporate Network — with all the security capabilities that entails — don't buy XP/Pro or XP/Home just yet. Do yourself a favor and hire a Network Administrator with Active Directory experience and a long list of satisfied customers to scope out your situation *before* you open that particular vein and let it bleed. Uncle BillyJoeBob down at the local Computers Were Us shop doesn't make the grade.

You should consider becoming your own Network Administrator only if you seriously wish to pursue a new full-time career — and you have a very high tolerance for pain. It helps to have several screws loose, too.

✦ If you're going to install Windows XP on a portable computer and you're worried about somebody walking away with the computer and the data, get XP/Pro and immediately encrypt your sensitive folders. (You need to be using the NT File System, NTFS, in order to encrypt a drive. See the discussion in Book I, Chapter 2.)

To encrypt the My Documents folder with XP/Pro, choose Start➪My Documents. Click the Up icon on the toolbar. Right-click My Documents and click Properties. On the General tab, click Advanced. Then check the check box marked Encrypt Contents to Secure Data.

✦ If you need to be able to connect to your office computer while you're on the road, and nobody's around to push a couple of keys while you're gone (to get Remote Assistance going), you probably want Remote Desktop. Go ahead and buy XP/Pro.

✦ If the PC you're using right now has Windows 2000 or Windows NT 4 installed on it, and you want to upgrade to XP over the top of the old Windows, you need XP/Pro because XP/Home won't do the upgrade. Be very wary of this approach, though, because in-place upgrades are notoriously fragile.

✦ Look hard at the list of XP/Pro features in the section called "Weighing the advantages of XP/Pro." If you find a feature that you absolutely can't live without, you have to get XP/Pro. Unless you're besotted by an XP/Pro feature, you're best off getting XP/Home.

In the vast majority of cases, you either connect to a Big Corporate Network and will thus require XP/Pro, or you'll be happy as a dog in a butcher shop with XP/Home.

Changing Your Mind

What? You got the wrong version of XP?

Don't worry. Happens all the time.

Converting XP/Home to XP/Pro

By far the most common mismatch arises when someone (I'll raise my hand here) buys XP/Home for a particular machine, but decides he should've bought XP/Pro.

If you really need XP/Pro and all that it contains, Microsoft will sell you an upgrade kit, complete with CD, that fills in the gaps. Check `www.cheaper-windows.com` to get the best price.

In many cases, though, all you really need is an XP/Home machine that can get at stuff stored on the Big Corporate Network. If that's the case, not to worry. Have I got a trick for you. All it takes is a logon I.D. and password for the Big Corporate Network.

Say you have a portable PC that's running Windows XP/Home, and you want it to do double duty. At home — or, say, in a small field office — you want it to run on the regular, old, everyday XP/Home network. But when you plug it into the docking station at the main office, you want to use the portable to get into your Big Corporate Network.

No problem. Here's my favorite way to do it:

1. **Warn your Network Administrator that you're going to be sticking an XP/Home machine on the Big Corporate Network.**

2. **Get the PC working on the home (or field office) peer-to-peer network (which Microsoft calls a *workgroup*).**

   That may involve installing Windows XP/Home, or customizing it. Follow all the steps for installing a network in Book IX, Chapter 2.

3. **When the PC is working with the home or field office network, bring it into the main office and fire it up.**

4. **Attach the PC to the Big Corporate Network.**

   You probably plug in a cable or a card or both.

5. **Choose Start⇨My Network Places.**

6. **Click View Workgroup Computers.**

7. **In the Other Places pane, click Microsoft Windows Network.**

8. **Choose the Big Corporate Network.**

   In Figure 7-1, I chose the client/server network called SABAI. The alternative, MSHOME, is the default Windows XP/Home peer-to-peer network.

The standard XP/Home network (a peer-to-peer *workgroup* in Microsoft parlance)

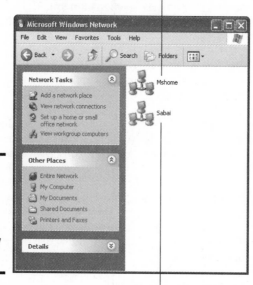

Figure 7-1:
Getting to
the Big
Corporate
Network
from an XP/
Home PC.

The Big Corporate Network (a client/server domain) at my company

9. **Windows requires you to enter a valid I.D. and password for the Big Corporate Network. Enter it, click OK, and you're in (see Figure 7-2).**

In some cases, this little trick may be all you need to run XP/Home on your Big Corporate Network.

Figure 7-2:
The
computers
on the
SABAI
client/server
network, as
viewed from
a Windows
XP/Home
PC.

Converting XP/Pro to XP/Home

What if you bought XP/Pro and all you want is XP/Home?

Hey, that's easy, too. You can't get your money back, but you can readily convince an XP/Pro machine to look and act pretty much like an XP/Home machine.

You may want to change two cosmetic differences between XP/Home and XP/Pro:

✦ XP/Home shows the Quick Launch Toolbar; XP/Pro does not. (The Quick Launch Toolbar is a bunch of little icons immediately to the right of the Start button.) To show the Quick Launch Toolbar, see Book I, Chapter 2.

✦ XP/Pro puts an item called My Recent Documents on the Start menu; XP/Home does not. See Book II, Chapter 2, if you want to turn it off.

If you install Windows XP/Pro rather blindly — or if you bought a new PC with XP/Pro installed — it may think that it should belong to a network called WORKGROUP. Unless you've changed the settings, XP/Home computers think that they belong to a network called MSHOME.

Here's how to convince a default XP/Pro machine to look for an XP/Home network:

1. **Choose Start⇨Control Panel.**

2. **Click Performance and Maintenance; then click System.**

3. **On the Computer Name tab (see Figure 7-3), click Change.**

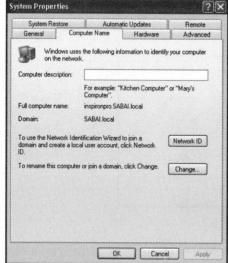

Figure 7-3:
Tell XP/Pro
to attach the
PC to a
different
network by
going
through the
Computer
Name tab.

4. **In the Computer Name Changes dialog box, click the button marked Workgroup and type in the XP/Home (peer-to-peer workgroup) network's name.**

Unless you've gone to Herculean lengths to change it, the name is MSHOME (see Figure 7-4).

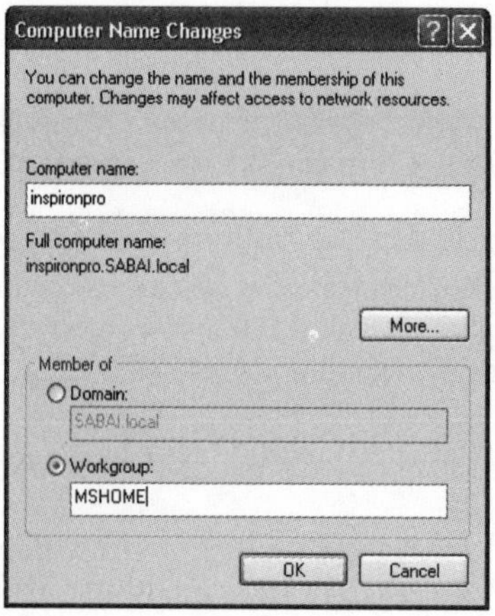

Figure 7-4:
Even if your
XP/Pro
machine
was part of
a Domain
(client/
server
network),
you can
easily
switch it to a
Workgroup
(peer-to-
peer
network).

5. Click OK twice.

The PC takes a few minutes to get its bearings, but if you have a peer-to-peer network running, you should be able to verify the change by choosing Start⇨My Network Places.

You can use this same technique to switch an XP/Pro machine back to a Big Corporate Network. When you get to the Computer Name Changes dialog box shown in Figure 7-4, simply click on Domain.

Even though it may not appear to be that way, the computer name field in the Computer Name Changes dialog box shown in Figure 7-4 is case sensitive. If you're trying to get connected to a domain called SABAI and you type **Sabai**, Windows XP won't be able to find it — at least, it didn't on my network. That's true, even if the name appears as all-caps in the dialog box.

Installing XP/Pro

Installation of XP/Pro proceeds almost identically to installation of XP/Home, with one key difference. (I discuss installing XP/Home at length in Book I, Chapter 1.)

The key difference: During installation, you encounter a dialog box that asks, "Do You Want to Make this Computer a Member of a Domain?" Although it may not be immediately obvious, you have three choices:

✦ Check the check box marked "No, This Computer is Not On a Network or On a Network Without a Domain." That sets the computer up for peer-to-peer (workgroup) networking. See Book IX, Chapter 2 for details.

✦ Check the check box marked "No, This Computer is Not On a Network or On a Network Without a Domain," and type a name in the area marked Make This Computer a Member of the Following Workgroup. This choice sets the computer up for peer-to-peer networking on the network that you pick. If you want the XP/Pro machine to get along with a typical XP/Home network, type **MSHOME** in that box.

✦ Check the check box marked "Yes, Make this Computer Part of the Following Domain," and type a domain name into the indicated area.

If you choose to make your computer part of a domain, and that domain is up and running, XP/Pro asks you to supply an Administrator I.D. and password for the domain. If you can do that, Windows XP/Pro reaches out to the server and makes all the changes necessary to add you to the network — er, domain.

Figures 7-5 and 7-6 show a newly installed XP/Pro machine that has added itself to the Active Directory on a server running Windows 2000 Advanced Server.

Figure 7-5:
If you can
supply an
Admin-
istrator I.D.
and
password
during
XP/Pro
installation,
your PC
will be
automati-
cally added
to the Active
Domain.

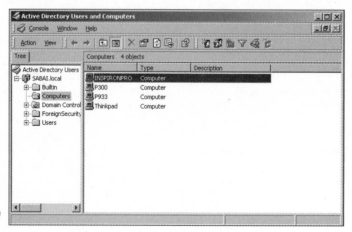

Figure 7-6:
Full details
from the
newly
installed
machine are
added to the
server's
Active
Domain
database.

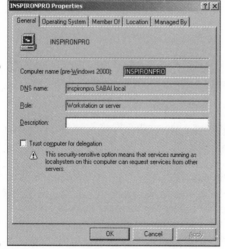

If you're installing Windows XP/Pro on a PC that's connected to a Big
Corporate Network, try to con the Network Administrator into looking over
your shoulder at the very end of the installation. She'll be able to provide
the appropriate logon I.D. and password at the key moment, so that your
machine gets added to the network with a minimum of fuss and bother.
"Please" works wonders. Bribery works better.

Index

Book II

Customizing Your Windows eXPerience

The 5th Wave By Rich Tennant

"Jeez—I thought 'Desktop Themes' just controlled the way things looked on the SCREEN of the computer."

Contents at a Glance

Chapter 1: Personalizing Your Desktop

In This Chapter

✔ Find the *real* story on how Windows puts together your Desktop

✔ Take control of each Desktop level

✔ See why you're better off ignoring some of the fancy stuff

✔ Establish a Super Boss Key — a key combination that immediately starts a screen saver

✔ Learn how to make your folders stand out

*I*t's your Desktop. Do with it what you will.

I've never bumped into a complete description of how the Windows Desktop gets tossed together, so you Dummies go to the head of the class. You may think it'd be easy for a computer to slap windows on the screen, but it isn't. In fact, Windows XP uses seven separate layers to produce that Windows eXPerience — and you can take control of every piece. I show you how in this chapter.

I've also included a discussion of Desktop Themes, backgrounds in Windows Explorer, and custom pictures for folders. Pretty cool stuff, especially when you see CD album covers plastered on My Music folders.

Most importantly, I've included instructions for creating a Super Boss Key in the section called "Selecting Screen Savers." When you push a key combination that you choose — say Alt+F10 — a Windows screensaver immediately springs into action. If you've ever been surprised when the boss walked in as you were dusting off your resume, day trading, or playing a mean game of Minesweeper, you now know how to cover your tracks. You're welcome.

Recognizing Desktop Levels

The Windows XP Desktop — that is, the stuff you see on your computer screen — consists of seven layers (see Figure 1-1).

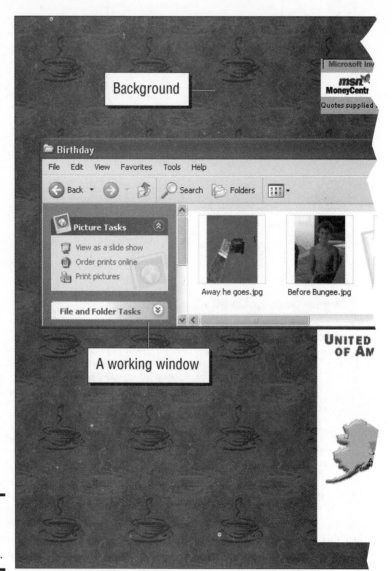

Figure 1-1:
The
Windows
XP Desktop.

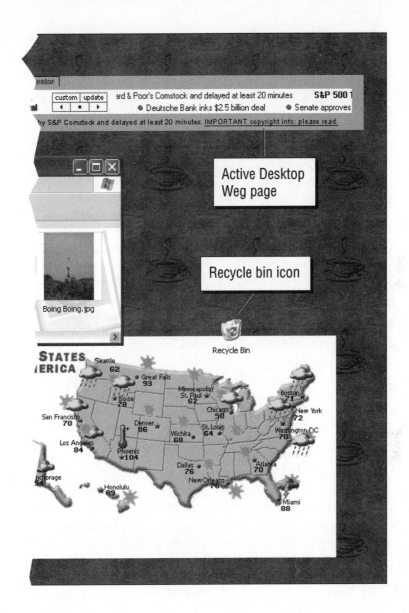

Active Desktop
Weg page

Recycle bin icon

For a quick change of pace, Desktop Themes change all seven layers, all at once. I talk about Desktop Themes in the section "Using Desktop Themes" in this chapter.

Here are the seven settings that control how Windows dishes up your Desktop:

✦ At the very bottom, the Windows Desktop has a *base color*, which is a solid color that you see only if you don't have a background or if your chosen background doesn't fill up the entire screen. Most people never see their Windows base color because the background usually covers it up. I tell you how to set the base color and all of the other Windows colors — for dialog boxes, the Taskbar, the works — in the section "Setting Colors in Windows XP."

✦ Above the base color lives the Windows *background*. You may be familiar with the rolling hills background — the one Microsoft calls Bliss — because it's the one that ships with Windows XP.

The people who sold you your computer may have ditched Microsoft's Bliss background and replaced it with some sort of dorky ad. I tell you how to get rid of the ad and replace it with a picture you want in the section called "Picking a Background."

✦ On top of the background, Windows lets you put pictures, Web pages, and just about anything you can imagine. Microsoft even has a little stock ticker and weather map that you can download and stick in this layer. This is the so-called *Active Desktop* layer and, by and large, it's a disaster. I tell you why in the section entitled "Avoiding the Active Desktop."

✦ Windows puts all of its Desktop icons on top of the Active Desktop layer. Bone-stock Windows XP includes only one icon — the Recycle Bin. If you bought a PC with Windows XP preinstalled, chances are good that the manufacturer put lots of additional icons on the Desktop, and you can easily get rid of them. I tell you how in the section "Controlling Icons."

✦ Above the icons you (finally!) find the program windows — the ones that actually do work. You know, little things like Word, Excel, and the Media Player.

✦ Then you have the mouse, which lives in the layer above the program windows. The complete lowdown on standard mouse pointers — how they work and what they do — appears in the section on pointers in Book I, Chapter 2. If you want to change the picture used for the pointer, I talk about fancy mouse pointers in the section called "Changing Mouse Pointers" in this chapter.

✦ At the very top of the Desktop food chain sits the screen saver. The screen saver kicks in only if you tell Windows that you want it to appear when your computer sits idle for a spell. I talk about that beast in the section called "Selecting Screen Savers."

If you have more than one user on your PC, each user can customize every single part of the seven layers to suit his or her tastes, and Windows XP remembers every setting, bringing it back when the user logs on. Much better than getting a life, isn't it?

Setting Colors in Windows XP

Windows XP ships with three designer color schemes: Blue (which you probably use), Olive Green (which looks just as bad as you might imagine) and silver (rather, uh, self-consciously techno-blah). To change color schemes:

Book II
Chapter 1

1. Right-click on any empty part of the Windows Desktop and choose Properties.

The Display Properties dialog box appears.

2. Click the Appearance tab (see Figure 1-2).

Figure 1-2: The three major Windows XP color schemes are accessible here.

3. From the Color Scheme drop-down list, choose Default (blue), Olive Green, or Silver, and click OK.

Windows changes the base color — that is, the color of the Windows Desktop when no background appears or the background doesn't fit (see the section "Picking a Background") — as well as the title bar color of all windows and dialog boxes, the color of the Windows Taskbar, menu highlight colors, and a dozen other colors, scattered in various places throughout Windows.

You aren't confined to Microsoft's three-color world. In fact, you can pick and choose many different Windows colors, individually, although some of them appear on-screen only if you tell Windows to use the Windows Classic Style of windows and buttons — the old-fashioned pre-XP style, where windows had squared off edges and OK buttons weren't so boldly sculpted.

If you're terribly nostalgic for old-fashioned Windows windows, choose Windows Classic Style from the Windows and Buttons drop-down box shown in Figure 1-2.

If you ever need to shoot pictures of the computer's screen, you will probably want to get rid of the distracting background and turn the Desktop itself white. (That's how all the screens in this book were shot.)

To set the Desktop's base color to white — regardless of whether you use Windows XP Style or Windows Classic Style windows and buttons — follow these steps:

1. **Right-click on any empty part of the Windows Desktop and choose Properties.**

The Display Properties dialog box appears.

2. **Click the Appearance tab (see Figure 1-2).**

3. **Click Advanced.**

You see the Advanced Appearance dialog box shown in Figure 1-3.

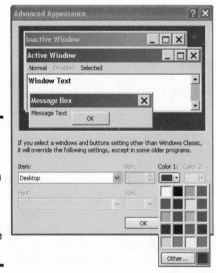

Figure 1-3: Individual color settings can be applied in the Advanced Appearance dialog box.

4. **Make sure that Desktop appears in the Item drop-down list; then click the down-arrow under Color 1, and click on the white color swatch in the upper left corner.**

5. **Click OK twice.**

   Your Desktop base color is now set to white, although you may have to change (or get rid of) your background in order to see it. I talk about strangling and axing the background in the next section. Stand back Lizzie Borden.

 The Advanced Appearance dialog box (refer to Figure 1-3) seems to be saying that you have to use Windows Classic windows and buttons in order to see changes made in the Advanced Appearance dialog box. At least, I *think* that's what the dialog box says. Sometimes this computer gobbledygook really confuses me. Read it and see what you think. Anyway, if you're spooked and think that you have to switch back to the old Windows Classic windows and buttons in order to change your base color, not to worry: Just follow the steps above and you'll be fine. Trust me.

Picking a Background

Windows XP, straight out of the box, ships with a picture of rolling verdant hills as the background. This background is peaceful and serene — Microsoft calls it "Bliss" — and it's booooooooring.

If you bought a PC with Windows XP preinstalled, chances are very good that the manufacturer has replaced Bliss with a background of its own choosing — maybe the manufacturer's own logo or something a bit more subtle, like "Buy Wheaties." Don't laugh. The background is up for sale. PC manufacturers can include whatever they like. You probably have an AOL icon on your Desktop. Same thing. Guess who bought and paid for that?

There's nothing particularly magical about the background. In fact, Windows XP will put *any* picture on your Desktop — big one, little one, ugly one, even a picture stolen straight off the Web. Here's how:

1. **Right-click on any empty part of the Windows Desktop and choose Properties.**

   The Display Properties dialog box appears.

2. **Click the Desktop tab (see Figure 1-4).**

   In the Background box, Windows XP lists pictures from the Windows folder and the My Pictures folder. (It also lists Web pages — files with HTM or HTML as filename extensions — in both of those folders.) Windows ships with lots of pictures in the Windows folder.

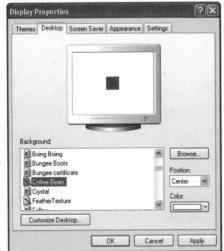

Figure 1-4:
Pick any
picture you
like on the
Desktop tab.

3. **Scroll through the Background box and pick the picture you want.**

If you don't see the picture you're looking for — surprisingly, pictures in
the Shared Pictures folder aren't included in this list, for example —
click the Browse button and go find the picture. A preview of the picture
appears in the little screen on the dialog box.

4. **If your picture is too big to fit on the screen, you need to tell
Windows how to shoehorn it into the available location. If your picture is too small to cover up the entire screen, you need to tell
Windows what to do with the extra room. You do both in the Position
box, as shown in Table 1-1.**

Table 1-1	How Windows Re-Sizes Desktop Pictures	
Position	*If the picture is too big*	*If the picture is too small*
Center	Windows carves a piece out of the middle of the picture and puts it on the screen.	Windows puts the picture in the center of the screen and fills the unoccupied part of the screen with the base color.*
Tile	Windows takes a suitably sized piece out of the upper left corner of the picture and uses it as the background.	Windows puts one copy of the picture in the upper left corner of the screen, and then "tiles" additional copies of the picture to fill up the remainder of the screen.
Stretch	Windows squishes the picture to fit the dimensions of the screen. If you're working with a photo, the effect is almost always horrible.	Windows stretches the picture so that it fits. Think Torquemada.

See the discussion of base color in the section "Setting Colors in Windows XP."

Selecting None for a background means that you don't want Windows XP to use a background at all: It should let the base color show through, unsullied.

5. **If you tell Windows to put your too-small picture in the Center of the screen in the Position box, you can use the Color box as a quick way to set the base color.**

6. **Click Apply.**

Windows changes the background according to your specifications but leaves the Display Properties dialog box open so that you can change your mind.

7. **Click OK.**

The Display Properties dialog box disappears.

Many people are mystified by the Color box on the Display Properties dialog box because it doesn't seem to do anything. In fact, Color kicks in only when you choose Center for the Position and when the picture you've chosen as a background is too small to occupy the entire screen.

Changing the base color in the Advanced Appearance dialog box (see Figure 1-3) also changes the color on the Desktop tab (refer to Figure 1-4) and vice versa.

Windows XP lets you right-click on a picture — a JPG or GIF file, regardless of whether you're using Windows Explorer or Internet Explorer — and choose Use as Desktop Background. When you do that, the picture appears as the background, with Position set to Stretch (if the picture is too big for the screen) or Tile (if the picture is not too big for the screen).

Avoiding the Active Desktop

You can read all the way through the Windows XP help files and never find a single mention of "Active Desktop," although it's featured prominently in Windows 98, ME, and 2000 product literature — touted as one of the big reasons to upgrade to those old dinosaurs, in fact.

There's a reason why. Active Desktop, introduced years ago in Internet Explorer 4, has a reputation for sucking up computer power and crashing Windows, inexplicably and unpredictably, with gleeful abandon. Believe me, you've never seen a program as gleeful as Active Desktop crashing Windows 98.

Microsoft has completely abandoned the terminology, but the technology remains in Windows XP. And if you use it right, you'll discover that it isn't as bad as it used to be.

I believe Alexander Pope called that "damning with faint praise."

The concept is simple enough: Windows XP lets you put pictures and Web pages (even tiny Web pages, called *live content*) on top of your Desktop background but underneath the Windows icons. In practice, you shouldn't have any problem at all putting static things — such as a picture, a calendar, or other stuff that doesn't change — on top of the background. But you're begging for trouble if you toss "live" things — such as stock market tickers — in there.

Static material sitting on top of the Desktop's background doesn't make many demands on Windows. Live things can tie up your PC, your Internet connection, and your life. If you want live content — news feeds, weather updates, commodities prices, Webcam shots of corn growing in Kansas — open up Internet Explorer and work directly with the source.

To put items on top of your Desktop's background but underneath the icons:

1. **Right-click on any open space on the Desktop and choose Properties.**

2. **In the Display Properties dialog box, click the Desktop tab (refer to Figure 1-4) and then click Customize Desktop.**

    The Desktop Items dialog box appears.

3. **In the Desktop Items dialog box, click the Web tab (see Figure 1-5).**

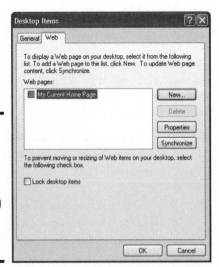

Figure 1-5:
Choose
Active
Desktop
items here
by checking
the box in
front of the
item.

Although the box is marked Web Pages, in fact you can put any picture or Web page (including any HTML file located on the Web or on your hard drive) in the Active Desktop layer. The way you do it is a little strange.

4. **Add the picture or Web page to the Web Pages list. Then check the box next to the picture or page, and Windows actually adds it to the Active Desktop.**

For example, My Current Home Page appears as one of the options in the Web Pages list, but it isn't actually shown on top of your Desktop background because the box in Figure 1-5 isn't checked. Confusing? You bet it is.

5. **Add new pictures or Web pages to the Web Pages list by clicking New.**

You see the New Desktop Item dialog box shown in Figure 1-6.

Book II
Chapter 1

Personalizing Your Desktop

Figure 1-6:
Preselect
Active
Desktop
items —
add them to
the Web
Pages
list — using
this dialog
box.

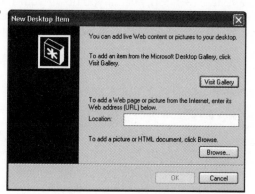

You can follow the New Desktop Item dialog box's suggestion and click Visit Gallery, but be forewarned: The mini-Web pages Microsoft offers in the Microsoft Desktop Gallery are very limited — the stock ticker and weather map you can see in Figure 1-1, plus a sports news page — and they haven't been updated in years. That's because they're "live content" and live content drags down your PC's performance and makes it less stable. Don't go there.

6. **Click Browse and navigate to any pictures that you want to put on top of your Desktop background. (Pictures are fine: they're *static* and won't hurt anything.)**

7. **When you're done gathering all the pictures you want, go back to the Desktop Items dialog box (refer to Figure 1-5), check the boxes in front of any pictures that you definitely want to put on the Desktop, and click OK twice.**

When you get back to the Desktop, you see a weird window with your picture inside of it — a window that's quite unlike any you've ever seen (see Figure 1-7). You may have to hover your mouse near the top of the picture to coax Windows into showing you the window's gray top part.

8. If you get tired of the picture, click the X in the upper-right corner of the window, as shown in Figure 1-7, or navigate back to the Web Pages list (see Step 5 in this list) and uncheck the box in front of the picture's name.

If you remove an Active Desktop picture by clicking the X in the upper-right corner of the weird window, the only way to bring the picture back is by bringing up the Web Pages list in the Desktop Items dialog box and checking the box in front of the picture's name.

If you check the box marked Lock Desktop Items in the Desktop Items dialog box (refer to Figure 1-5), Windows won't show the gray top part of any of the weird windows in the Active Desktop, even if you hover your mouse near the top of the pictures 'til the cows come home. Without the gray top part showing, you can't move or resize any of the weird Active Desktop windows, so they stay put.

Graphic positioning commands

Maximizes the picture

Expands the picture

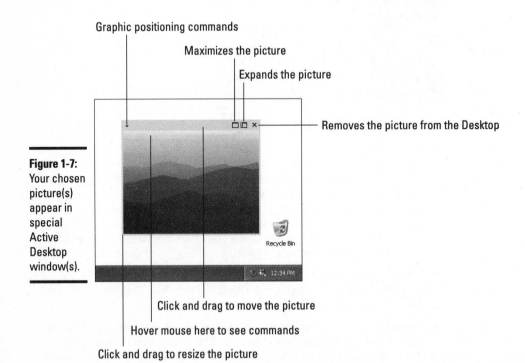

Removes the picture from the Desktop

Figure 1-7: Your chosen picture(s) appear in special Active Desktop window(s).

Click and drag to move the picture

Hover mouse here to see commands

Click and drag to resize the picture

Controlling Icons

Windows XP sticks icons above the Active Desktop items (see the preceding section, "Avoiding the Active Desktop") but below the real, working windows — the ones you use every day to get things done.

Windows XP, straight out of the box, ships with exactly one icon: the Recycle Bin. Microsoft found that most people appreciate a clean Desktop, devoid of icons — but they also found that hiding the Recycle Bin confused the living daylights out of all of their guinea pigs (uh, Usability Lab Test Subjects). So Microsoft compromised by making the Desktop squeaky-clean, except for the Recycle Bin: Bliss and a Recycle Bin. Who could ask for more?

If you bought a PC with Windows XP preloaded, you probably have so many icons on the Desktop that you can't see straight. That Desktop real estate is expensive, and the manufacturers get a pretty penny for dangling the right icons in your face. Know what? You can delete all of them, without feeling the least bit guilty. The worst you'll do is delete some shortcut to a manufacturer's tech support software, and if you really need to get to the program, the tech support rep on the telephone can tell you how to find it from the Start menu.

Windows XP gives you several simple tools for arranging icons on your Desktop. If you right-click on any empty part of the Desktop and choose Arrange Icons By, you see that you can do the following:

✦ Sort icons by name, size, type (folders, documents, shortcuts, and so on), or the date that the icon was last modified.

✦ *Auto Arrange* icons — that is, have Windows keep them arranged in an orderly fashion, with the first icon in the upper left corner, the second one directly below the first one, the third below it, and so on.

✦ If you don't want them arranged automatically, at least you can have Windows *Align to Grid*, so you can see all of them without one appearing directly on top of the other

In general, you can remove an icon from the Windows Desktop by right-clicking on it and choosing Delete, or by clicking on it once and pressing the Delete key. Unfortunately, PC manufacturers are wise to this trick, and they often disable the Delete function on icons that they want to remain on your Desktop.

Some icons are hard-wired: If you put a Word document on your Desktop, for example, the document inherits the icon of its associated application, Word. Same goes for Excel worksheets and text documents and recorded audio files.

Icons for shortcuts, however, can be changed at will. (I talk about shortcuts in Book I, Chapter 2.) To change an icon — that is, the picture — on a shortcut:

1. Right-click on the shortcut.

2. Click Properties.

3. In the Properties dialog box, choose Change Icon.

4. Pick an icon from the offered list, or click Browse and go looking for icons. Windows abounds with icons. See Table 1-2 for some likely hunting grounds.

5. Click OK twice and the icon will be changed.

Table 1-2	Places to Look for Icons
Contents	*File*
Everything	c:\windows\system32\shell32.dll
Computers	c:\windows\explorer.exe
Communication	c:\windows\system32\hticons.dll
Household	c:\windows\system32\pifmgr.dll
Folders	c:\windows\system32\syncui.dll
Old programs	c:\windows\system32\moricons.dll

Lots and lots (and lots and lots) of icons are available on the Internet. Use your favorite search engine.

Windows XP gives special treatment to five icons: the Recycle Bin (which can't be removed from the Desktop unless you go into the Windows Registry with a blunt axe), My Documents, My Computer, My Network Places, and Internet Explorer. To control the appearance of those icons:

1. Right-click on any open space on the Desktop and choose Properties.

2. In the Display Properties dialog box, click the Desktop tab (refer to Figure 1-4), and then click Customize Desktop.

3. In the Desktop Items dialog box, click the General tab (see Figure 1-8).

4. Check and/or uncheck each of the four boxes — My Documents, My Computer, My Network Places, and Internet Explorer — depending on whether you want the associated icon to appear on the Desktop.

5. To change an icon (that is, the picture itself), click on the icon and choose Change Icon.

Now you can look inside any files you want, looking for icons. Refer to Table 1-2 for some ideas.

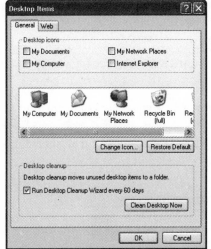

Figure 1-8:
Control
icons in the
Desktop
Items dialog
box.

Notice that one of the icons in Figure 1-8 is marked Recycle Bin (full). In fact, that isn't the icon for a full Recycle Bin. Ain't true. There *is* no icon for a full Recycle Bin. If the Recycle Bin gets full, Windows has apoplexy and shoots you a dialog box to ask whether it can empty the Bin. In fact, the icon shown appears when anything at all is in the Recycle Bin.

6. When you're done, click OK twice.

Your new icons appear on the Desktop.

The politically correct way to remove icons on the Desktop is via the Desktop Cleanup Wizard:

The Desktop Cleanup Wizard cleans up only shortcuts. (I talk about short-cuts in Book I, Chapter 2.) It doesn't touch data files, folders, or anything else you might be parking on your Desktop. Nor does it affect My Documents, My Computer, My Network Places, and Internet Explorer, which have to be handled individually, per the preceding instructions.

1. Right-click on any open space on the Desktop and choose Properties.

2. In the Display Properties dialog box, click the Desktop tab (refer to Figure 1-4), and then click Customize Desktop.

3. In the Desktop Items dialog box, click the General tab (refer to Figure 1-8).

4. Make sure that the box marked Run Desktop Cleanup Wizard Every 60 Days is checked.

You certainly want Windows XP to remind you every couple of months that you can tidy up.

5. Click Clean Desktop Now.

The Desktop Cleanup Wizard starts. You see a welcome screen. Ho-hum.

6. Click Next.

The Wizard presents you with a list of shortcuts on your Desktop, along with the dates that they were most recently used (see Figure 1-9).

The Desktop Cleanup Wizard doesn't pick up all shortcuts on the Desktop. But it does get the vast majority of them.

Figure 1-9: Take rarely-used shortcuts off your Desktop with the Desktop Cleanup Wizard.

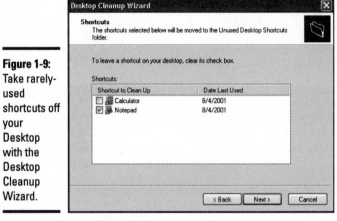

7. Check the boxes next to all the Shortcuts that you want to have removed from your Desktop, and click Next.

If it doesn't exist, Windows creates a new folder on your Desktop, called Unused Desktop Shortcuts, and moves all the checked shortcuts to that folder.

Changing Mouse Pointers

Believe it or not, Microsoft has spent many thousands of person-hours honing its mouse pointers. The pointers you see in a standard Windows XP installation have been selected to give you the best visual "clues" possible, without being overly distracting. I go into great detail on the standard mouse pointers and what they do in the section on pointers in Book I, Chapter 2.

What? You think they're boring? Yeah, me too.

You can control your mouse pointer destiny in three different ways:

✦ By choosing a new Desktop Theme, which replaces all of your pointers, along with the background, screen saver, and virtually everything else that can be customized. I talk about Desktop Themes in the section called "Using Desktop Themes."

✦ By selecting and changing individual pointers — so you can turn, say, the Windows "I'm busy but not completely tied up" mouse pointer (which Windows calls Working In Background) into, oh, a dinosaur.

✦ By changing all of your pointers, wholesale, according to schemes that Microsoft has constructed.

Book II
Chapter 1

To change individual pointers or to select from the prefab pointer schemes:

1. **Choose Start⇨Control Panel⇨Printers and Other Hardware⇨Mouse.**

2. **Click the Pointers tab (see Figure 1-10).**

3. **To change all the pointers at the same time, pick a new pointer scheme from the Scheme drop-down box.**

You can choose from purely functional sets of pointers (such as extra large pointers to use for presentations or pointers inverted to show solid black blobs) or fun sets (such as Conductor, Dinosaur, or Hands).

4. **If you want to bring back the original scheme, choose Windows Default (System Scheme), which is the one you started with.**

5. **To change an individual pointer, click on the pointer in the Customize box, and click Browse.**

Windows shows you all of the available pointers — which number in the hundreds. Choose the pointer you want, and click Open.

6. **If you want to change an individual pointer back to the original pointer for the particular scheme that you have chosen, click the pointer in the Customize box and choose Use Default.**

7. **When you've settled on a set of pointers that appeals to you, click Save As, and give your new, custom scheme a name, so that you can retrieve it at any time.**

8. **Click OK.**

Windows starts using the pointers you've chosen.

Personalizing Your Desktop

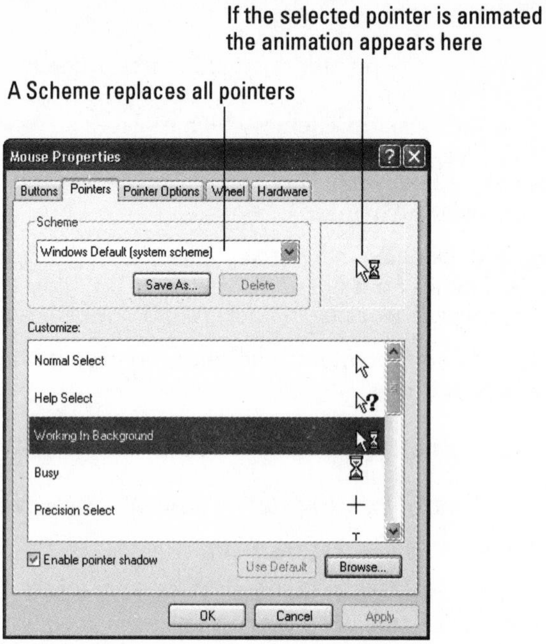

If the selected pointer is animated
the animation appears here

A Scheme replaces all pointers

Figure 1-10:
Mouse
pointers can
all be
changed.

Selecting Screen Savers

Windows screen savers are absolutely, totally, utterly, 100% for fun. Ten years ago, screen savers served a real purpose — they kept monitors from "burning in" the phosphors in frequently used parts of the screen. Nowadays, monitors aren't nearly as prone to burn-in (or burn-out — would that were the case with humans!), and saving screens rates right up there with manufacturing buggy whips on the obsolescence scale.

Still, screen savers are amusing, and if you follow the trick in this section, they serve one truly important function: A screen saver makes an excellent front for a "Super Boss Key" — a key that you can push whenever Da Boss makes an unexpected, unwanted appearance.

To select a screen saver:

1. **Right-click any empty part of the Desktop and click Properties.**

2. **Click the Screen Saver tab.**

You see the dialog box shown in Figure 1-11.

Choose a screen saver

Options specific to the screen saver

Start the screen saver immediately

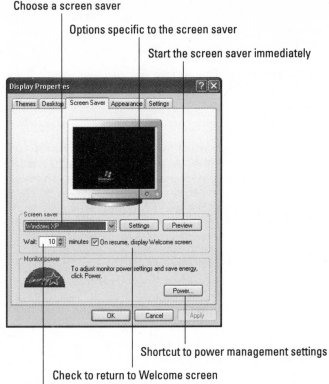

Figure 1-11:
Set Screen
Saver
attributes.

Shortcut to power management settings

Check to return to Welcome screen

Minutes of inactivity before the screen saver kicks in

Most of the settings are self-explanatory, but one can be a bit confusing: the box in Figure 1-11 marked On Resume, Display Welcome Screen. That box controls what happens when the computer "wakes up" after the screen saver has kicked in.

- If On Resume, Display Welcome Screen is checked, when the computer wakes up, it shows the Windows logon screen. If the user who was logged on has an account that requires a password, she will have to re-enter the password in order to get back into Windows. (I talk about passwords in the section on changing user settings in Book I, Chapter 2.)

- If On Resume, Display Welcome Screen is not checked, when the computer wakes up, it returns to the state it was in when the screen saver started. The user who was logged on remains logged on.

3. **When you're happy with your screen saver settings, click OK.**

In previous versions of Windows, bypassing the screen saver password protection scheme was relatively easy. Not so in Windows XP. If the On Resume, Display Welcome Screen box is checked, a potential cracker has to crack the Windows XP password itself — not an easy task.

If you want to get rid of your current screen saver, right-click an empty spot on the Desktop, click Properties, click Screen Saver, and click None in the Screen Saver drop-down box. Click OK, and your screen will never be saved again.

Here's the trick you've been waiting for — the reason why you read this chapter in the first place. You can use screen savers to create a Super Boss Key — a key combination, such as Alt+F10, that you can press to make the PC immediately switch over to running the screen saver. The Super Boss Key runs independently of the usual Windows screen saver stuff: The Super Boss Key doesn't affect the screen saver you set up to run on your computer when it's idle. The screen saver is just a handy program that won't look the least bit suspicious if your boss glances at your PC's monitor.

Setting up the Super Boss Key is really quite simple:

1. **Make sure that Windows is showing filename extensions.**

   I rant about that in the section on showing filename extensions in Book I, Chapter 2. You need to see filename extensions in order to find your screen saver programs.

2. **Bring up the Search Companion by choosing Start⇨Search; then click All Files and Folders.**

3. **Run a search for all** .scr **files — which are your screen savers.**

   To do so, type ***.scr** in the box marked All or Part of the File Name, and click Search. You end up with a dozen or more .scr files that correspond to the screen savers listed in the Display Properties box (see Figure 1-12).

4. **Decide on a screen saver that you want to use and look up the associated program's filename in Table 1-3.**

Table 1-3	Screen Savers and Their Program Files
Screen Saver	*File*
3D Flower Box	ssflwbox.scr
3D Flying Objects	ss3dfo.scr
3D Pipes	sspipes.scr
3D Text	sstext3d.scr
Beziers	ssbezier.scr
Blank	scrnsave.scr

Screen Saver	File
Marquee	ssmarque.scr
My Pictures Slideshow	ssmypics.scr
Mystify	ssmyst.scr
Starfield	ssstars.scr
Windows XP	logon.scr

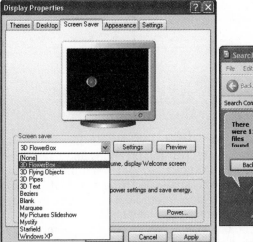

Figure 1-12: Screen Savers in the Display Properties box correspond to *.scr program files.

5. **In the Search Results window, right-click on the program's filename, and choose Create Shortcut.**

   Windows displays this message: `Windows cannot create a short-cut here. Do you want the shortcut to be placed on the desktop instead?`

6. **Click Yes.**

7. **Go to the Desktop, right-click on the new shortcut, and choose Properties (see Figure 1-13).**

8. **Click once inside the box that says Shortcut Key, and then press the key combination you want to use to activate the Super Boss Key, uh, screen saver.**

   In Figure 1-13, I chose **Alt+F10** (that is, I held down the **Alt** key, and pressed **F10**).

9. **Click OK and your Super Boss Key is complete.**

A few programs "swallow" certain odd key combinations — if such a program is running, it grabs the key combinations and doesn't hand them over to Windows, so Windows won't know that you want to run your Super Boss Key screen saver. I haven't found many programs that swallow Alt+F10, but some undoubtedly exist. So test your Super Boss Key in all of your favorite clandestine situations before you really need to use it, okay? If you find that your chosen key combination doesn't work with an important program (the worst offenders are games), try different key combinations until you find one that makes the Super Boss Key work.

If you want to gussy up your Super Boss Key screen saver, right-click on the shortcut and click Configure. You can change all of the screen saver's settings.

Seeing Desktop Text

If the characters you see on the Windows screen aren't good enough, Windows XP includes several options for improving the legibility of text on your Desktop. The five main options are as follows:

✦ Activate ClearType, which can make some text easier to read, especially on portable computers and flat panel displays

✦ Have Windows show Large Fonts, which increases the size of the font used for icon labels, window titles, Windows Explorer text, and menus (but nothing else)

✦ Change the "dpi" setting, an arcane zoom setting that's poorly documented and best avoided, particularly because, once changed, the new zoom factor applies to everyone who uses the PC, in all of their applications

Although you can find a few references to changing the dpi setting in the Windows XP Help and Support Center, only three people at Microsoft really understand the setting, and two of them are on sabbatical. (Okay, so I exaggerated a little bit. Not much.) Stay away from the dialog box (Display Properties⇨Advanced⇨General) and don't change the setting unless you're instructed to do so by someone who's willing to pay for all the therapy you'll need to cope with the aftermath.

✦ Use Magnification, which puts a strip on the screen that shows a highly magnified portion of the Desktop

✦ Try High Contrast, where Windows uses a coloring method that decreases details, but improves legibility, particularly at a distance, or for those with visual challenges

Windows, per se, doesn't control many of the font settings that you may imagine. For example, if you want to increase the size of the fonts in the Help and Support Center, Windows Large Fonts support doesn't do a thing. You have to bring up the Help and Support Center, click Options, and adjust the Font Size Used for Help setting.

Activating ClearType

Microsoft's ClearType technology uses a very strange color shading scheme — invented years ago — to make fonts look better on certain kinds of displays. If you choose to have Windows use ClearType, Windows employs the technology everywhere for showing text on the screen — on the Windows Desktop, inside your spreadsheet program, even inside Internet Explorer. Conventional wisdom says that ClearType works great on portable computers and flat-panel monitors.

My UWD (Unconventional Wisdom for Dummies) says that ClearType helps a bit with the labels under icons and small amounts of text scattered here and there on a screen, but I'd rather hang my eyeballs out to dry than force them to stare at a word processing screen that's been "enhanced" with ClearType. Yes, ClearType works much better on flat panel displays than on traditional computer screens. No, I don't use it.

Here's how to turn on ClearType. It's buried pretty well:

1. **Right-click any empty location on the Desktop and click Properties.**

2. **Click on the Appearance tab, and then click Effects.**

3. **Click the box marked Use the Following Method to Smooth Edges of Screen Fonts, and then choose ClearType (see Figure 1-14).**

4. **Click OK, and immediately start your word processor of choice. Work with it for a few minutes and see if you start getting a headache. If you do, head back to the Effects dialog box and turn ClearType off.**

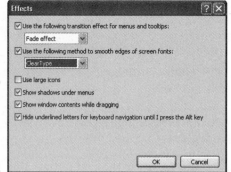

Figure 1-14:
Enable
ClearType in
the Effects
dialog box.

Showing large fonts

If you use the standard Windows Desktop Theme, you have an easy way to change the size of the fonts that Windows shows. Before you rush to your mouse, though, you should be aware of the limitations:

✦ The font size you select applies only to window title bars, labels for icons on the Desktop, in Windows Explorer, and in menus. It doesn't change anything else.

✦ When you apply a new Desktop Theme (see "Using Desktop Themes" in this chapter), your old font size settings are thrown away.

✦ Not all Desktop Themes support multiple font sizes. The only way to know for sure is to try to change the size and see whether it works.

Nope, I don't know how to change the size of the fonts in the Windows Explorer task panes.

To change to larger fonts:

1. **Right-click on any blank area on the Desktop and click Properties.**

2. **Click the Appearance tab.**

3. **Choose the font size you want in the Font Size drop-down box.**

Using magnification and high contrast

I won't belabor the point here, but two Accessibilities settings can come in handy, even if you don't normally think of Accessibility as a code name for "seeing text on the Desktop." The Magnifier puts a magnified strip along the top of the screen, which follows your mouse as you move it. High Contrast uses a modified color scheme to increase legibility of text.

To check out Magnification and High Contrast:

1. **Choose Start⇨Control Panel⇨Accessibility Options.**

2. **To work with High Contrast, choose Adjust the Contrast for Text and Colors on Your Screen under Pick a Task.**

3. **To start the Magnifier, choose Magnifier in the See Also section of the task pane.**

Using Desktop Themes

Windows XP Desktop themes incorporate many settings in one easy-to-choose package. The themes revolve around specific topics that frequently (and refreshingly) have nothing to do with Windows — say, cars with carapaces, cavorting carnivores, or carnal caruncles. A theme includes six of the seven Desktop levels I discuss in this chapter — a base color for the desktop, background, settings for fonts and colors of the working windows, pictures for the reserved Windows icons (Recycle Bin, My Documents, and so on), a set of mouse pointers, and a screen saver. A theme also includes a set of custom sounds that are associated with various Windows events. I've never seen a Desktop theme that includes Active Desktop items.

To bring in a new theme:

1. **Right-click any open spot on the Desktop and choose Properties.**

2. **Click the Themes tab.**

3. **Choose a theme from the Themes box.**

When you bring in a theme, it replaces all seven of the Desktop levels I discuss in this chapter, plus the sound scheme you may have had in place. The old background, icon pictures, mouse pointers, and screen savers all remain on your PC — the theme doesn't delete them — but if you want any of them back, you have to go through the customization steps you used earlier to reinstate them.

As we went to press, it appeared that Microsoft was going to peddle a selection of themes as an (extra-cost) adjunct to Windows XP. If you want to spend your money that way, by all means help yourself. But be aware of the fact that there are zillions of Windows Desktop themes available on the Web, and many of them are quite good. Simply instruct any half-sentient Web search engine to find "Windows Desktop theme" or try www.themeworld. com for thousands of free themes.

Customizing Folders

In some cases, Windows Explorer lets you change a folder's thumbnail by modifying the picture that's superimposed on a picture of a folder. You may have seen that startling capability if you used Windows Media Player to "rip" a CD — the cover art for the CD probably appeared on the folder that contains the CD. If you ripped more than one album by a single artist, chances are good up to four album covers appear on the folder that contains all of the albums.

To change the picture superimposed on a folder:

1. **Start Windows Explorer by choosing Start⇨My Documents; Start⇨ My Pictures, My Music, My Computer, or My Network Places; or by running a search with Start⇨Search.**

2. **Navigate to the folder that you want to change.**

3. **Make sure that you're viewing thumbnails by choosing View⇨Thumbnails.**

   Superimposed pictures appear only in Thumbnail View.

4. **Right-click on the folder.**

5. **If you want Windows to scan all the picture files inside the folder (including album cover art inside music folders) and place the four most-recently modified pictures on top of the folder, choose Refresh Thumbnail.**

6. **If you want to pick your own picture to superimpose on the folder, choose Properties and click the Customize tab.**

   You see the Properties dialog box shown in Figure 1-15.

   If you can't see the Customize tab, chances are good that you're trying to change the picture on a shortcut folder. Unfortunately, Windows won't let you change the picture superimposed on a shortcut folder.

7. **Click Choose Picture and choose any picture file — it need not be inside the indicated folder.**

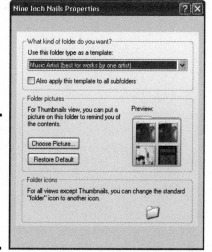

Figure 1-15:
Choose the pictures to be super-imposed on the folder in this dialog box.

8. **Click OK and the chosen picture will now appear superimposed on the folder while in Windows Explorer.**

Although Windows can put up to four pictures on top of a folder, you are allowed to put only one on top.

Chapter 2: Organizing Your Windows XP Interface

In This Chapter

✔ Harness the power of the Windows Start menu

✔ Get at your most recently used documents quickly

✔ Start your favorite programs with just a click

✔ Make workhorse programs start automatically

*W*indows XP contains an enormous variety of self-help tools that can make your working (and playing!) day go faster. As you get more comfortable with the Windows inner world, you will find shortcuts and simplifications that really do make a difference.

This chapter shows you how to take off the training wheels.

Customizing the Start Menu

I gave you a brief overview of the Start menu in Book I, Chapter 2. In this chapter, I'll take a look at the beast in far greater detail.

Your screen may not look exactly like the one shown in Figure 2-1. If you bought your PC with Windows XP preinstalled, chances are very good that the PC manufacturer stuck some programs on the Start menu that didn't originate with Microsoft. If you want to take control of your Start menu, follow the steps in this chapter to get rid of the stuff you don't want or need. It's your Start menu. You won't break anything. Take the, uh, bull by the horns.

In order to change the Start menu for everyone who uses your computer, you need to be a designated Administrator. Find out more about becoming an Administrator in the section on using account types in Book I, Chapter 2.

Recently used programs

"Pinned" programs

Current user's name

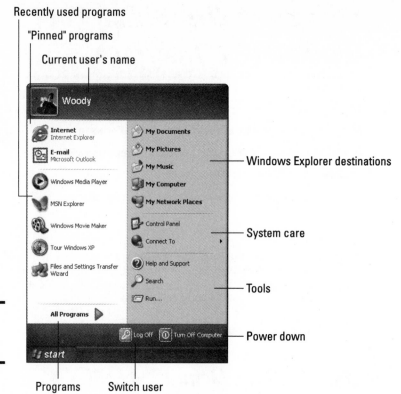

Windows Explorer destinations

System care

Tools

Power down

Figure 2-1:
Woody's
Start menu.

Programs   Switch user

Genesis of the Start menu

Although the Start menu looks like it sprang fully formed from the head of some malevolent Windows god, in fact Windows creates the left side of the Start menu on the fly, every time you click the Start button. That's why your computer takes a little while between the time you click Start and the time you see the Start menu on the screen. Here's where the various pieces come from, looking from top to bottom:

✦ The name and picture at the top are taken from the Windows sign on screen. You can change them by following the procedure described in the section on changing user settings in Book I, Chapter 2.

✦ You can *pin* a program to the upper left corner of the Start menu. Once pinned, it stays there until you remove it. Unfortunately, you can't pin a file. I go into details in the section "Pinning to the Start menu."

- ✦ The *recently used programs* list maintained by Windows goes in the lower left. Although you have a little bit of control over this list, Windows stacks the deck, loading its favorite programs first, whether you use them or not. Most of the time, you'll probably let Windows play with it — after you've learned how to unstack the deck. I talk about the way Windows maintains this list in the section "Reclaiming most recently used programs."

- ✦ Down at the bottom, *All Programs* actually connects to two folders on your hard drive. This is the part of the Start menu that was designed by Microsoft to be easy to modify. You can add fly-out menus and change and delete items to your heart's content — all of which is really pretty easy. I talk about these features in "Changing all programs."

Although you can make many little changes to the items on the right side of the Start menu (see "Making minor tweaks to the Start menu") — and you should definitely spend a few minutes deciding whether any of the changes are worthwhile for you — the one big change on the right side is the inclusion of a Most Recently Used Documents list. Some people love it. Some people hate it. Read "Showing recent documents" and decide for yourself.

Pinning to the Start menu

Do you have one or two programs that run your life?

Yeah. Me, too. Word and Outlook. I use them day in and day out. I dream in Word. Sad but true.

Windows XP enables you to easily put programs of your choice way up at the top, in the upper-left corner of the Start menu. That's the high-rent district, the place my mouse gravitates to every time I click Start.

I don't know why, but Microsoft calls this "pinning" — kind of a wimpy name for the most powerful feature on the Start menu, eh? If you have Office XP on your computer, chances are good that the Office installer pinned Outlook 2002 on your Start menu as your e-mail program.

Here's how you pin Word 2002 (the word processing program from Microsoft Office XP) on your Start menu. The procedure for any other program works similarly:

1. **Both Word 2002 and Outlook 2002 are on the All Programs menu, so pinning them is easy. Choose Start➪All Programs; then right-click on the program and choose Pin To Start Menu.**

   In Figure 2-2, I've pinned Word.

Figure 2-2:
Right-click
on any
program,
anywhere in
the Start
menu, and
pin it to the
upper-left
corner, in
the high-
rent district.

If the program you want to pin isn't on the Start menu already, you can use Windows Explorer or Search to find it. That isn't as easy as it sounds because many program filenames don't bear much resemblance to the program itself. For example, you can easily find Outlook.exe, Outlook's program file, with a standard Windows Search, but you may be hard-pressed to identify Winword.exe as the progenitor of Word. You can find many programs by choosing Start⇨My Computer, double-clicking on the main hard drive, and digging into the folder called Program Files. After you've found the program file, simply right-click on it and choose Pin To Start Menu.

If you pin a program on the Start menu by right-clicking on it and choosing Pin To Start Menu, Windows creates a second entry in the Start menu for the pinned copy. Your original — the program you right-clicked on — stays where it was.

You can also drag and drop a program from anywhere in Windows onto the pinned list.

When the program gets pinned, it appears at the bottom of the pinned pile — which is to say, below your Web browser and e-mail program. You can left-click on the program and drag it to any other spot in the pinned list that you like.

2. **Right-click on the program and click Rename; then give the program a name that you can live with. Figure 2-3 shows Word at the top of the pinned list, with the name Word 2002.**

If you pin a program on the Start menu by right-clicking on it and choosing Pin To Start Menu, both the original Start menu entry and the new pinned entry are linked. If you change the name on one (right-click and click Rename), the other copy is changed as well.

Figure 2-3: Word appears pinned at the top of the list.

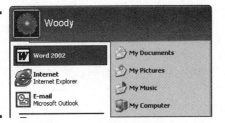

You can remove any program in the pinned part of the Start menu. If you right-click either of the built-in pinned programs (marked Internet and E-mail) and click Remove From This List, the program is removed. If you right-click any other pinned programs (presumably ones that you put up in the high-rent district, or ones that your computer's manufacturer so graciously added to the list), click Unpin From Start Menu and the item goes away.

Note that Unpinning a program removes it from only the pinned list in the upper-left corner of the Start menu. The program itself stays right where it is. So do any other shortcuts to the program, whether they're elsewhere on the Start menu or somewhere else in your computer, such as on your Desktop. Unpin with impunity, sez I.

You can change the Internet and e-mail programs listed at the beginning of the pinned list if you have more than one Web browser or e-mail program installed. (You probably do, because Windows XP installs MSN Explorer for both.) To change the Internet or e-mail program:

1. **Right-click on Start and click Properties.**

2. **On the Start Menu tab, make sure Start Menu is checked, and click Customize.**

3. **At the bottom, choose your favorite Web browser and/or e-mail program from the drop-down boxes.**

4. **Click OK twice.**

Reclaiming most recently used programs

Directly above the Start button, in the lower-left corner of the Start menu, you find a list of the programs that you've used most recently. This list is really handy: It is updated dynamically as you use programs, so you always have a very good chance to see the program you need right there on the list.

When you run a program that's pinned to the upper left corner of the Start menu (see the preceding section), it doesn't count: The most recently used list includes only programs that aren't up at the top of the Start menu.

At least, that's the theory. In fact, the Most Recently Used Programs list — like so many things in Windows XP — does a little bit more (or less?) than first meets the eye. Unless your hardware manufacturer has jiggered things, the first time you start Windows XP, you see these programs in the Most Recently Used box:

+ Windows Media Player

+ MSN Explorer

+ Windows Movie Maker

+ Tour Windows XP

+ File and Settings Transfer Wizard

That's an extraordinarily weird arrangement of most recently used programs, until you realize that Windows Media Player gives you, uh, lots of opportunities to purchase goodies from Microsoft; the folks in Redmond stand to make a lot of bucks if you sign up for MSN; and the XP Tour and the File and Settings Transfer Wizard greatly reduce the number of calls to Microsoft's Product Support Center. Make sense now?

In fact, the most recently used counter that controls what shows up in the most recently used programs box isn't quite kosher. If you play with the list for a while, you discover that the programs higher up in the list tend to stay on the list longer — whether you've used them or not. So Windows Media Player and MSN Explorer tend to hang around a whole lot longer than the Files and Settings Transfer Wizard (which you would expect), and many programs that you happen to run (which you probably wouldn't expect). I had to run one program a dozen times before it bumped the Media Player off the top of the list.

There's no reason on earth why you should keep Microsoft's advertising (or your PC manufacturer's either, for that matter, if your list varies from the standard one) on your Start menu. Fortunately, you can easily get rid of all the built-in most recently used programs and start out with a clean slate:

1. **Right-click on the Start button and click Properties.**

2. **On the Start menu tab, make sure that Start menu is checked, and click Customize.**

3. **On the General tab, in the middle of the Customize Start menu dialog box (see Figure 2-4), click Clear List.**

Figure 2-4:
Control the most recently used program list from here.

4. **While you're here, consider switching to smaller icons — which puts more programs on the Start menu in a smaller slice of real estate, although they'll be smaller and thus harder to hit with your mouse — and adding to the Number of Programs on the Start menu.**

The Windows Customize Start Menu dialog box says that you can set the Number of Programs on Start menu (refer to Figure 2-4). That isn't true. In fact, the number shown is actually the number of programs that appear in the most recently used box, in the lower-left corner of the Start menu.

5. **Click OK twice, and your most recently used program list starts to reflect the programs that, uh, you have most recently used.**

Windows maintains the most recently used program list on its own: You cannot drag and drop items on the list. You can, however, remove programs from the list. Just right-click on an offending program, and choose Remove From This List.

Changing all programs

When you choose Start⇨All Programs, Windows assembles the list of "all" programs by combining two separate folders on your hard drive: the Start Menu\Programs folder for you; and the Start Menu\Programs folder for All Users.

The programs that appear above the faint horizontal line on the All Programs menu actually live in the Start Menu folder. Programs below the line come from Start Menu\Programs and folders under there.

If you look at Figure 2-5, you see how the two folders get melded into the All Programs list: The All Users Start Menu\Programs folder is on the top; my Start Menu\Programs folder is on the bottom of Figure 2-5. Folders inside the Start Menu\Programs folders turn into fly-out menus on the All Programs list. Files inside the folders turn into menu entries. If you squint hard enough, you can see how Accessories shows up as a fly-out menu, with (among many others) the Calculator coming from the All Users side, and the Utilities folder coming from the Woody side.

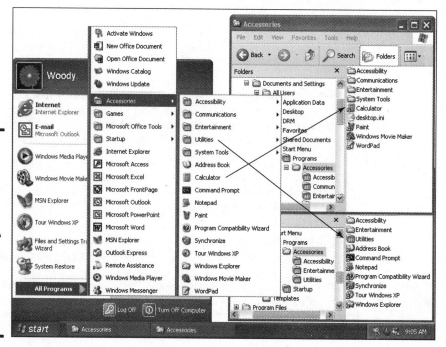

Figure 2-5:
The All Programs menu is assembled from the Start Menu\ Programs folders for All Users and for the logged-on user.

The following rule has no exceptions: Everything on the All Programs menu comes from one or the other of the two Start Menu\Programs folders.

Because all All Programs programs (say that ten times real fast) come from one of the two folders, you can easily change things around. For example, I've been complaining for years about the way Microsoft Office bullies its way onto the Start⇨All Programs menu. Every other set of programs from every other manufacturer has the good sense (and common decency) to install itself farther down on the All Programs line.

Take HP scanner software for example. To run HP scanner programs, you choose Start⇨All Programs⇨HP ScanJet Software, and then you pick one of the scanner programs. That's great: The programs are grouped together, they're easy to find, and they don't take up a lot of space on the All Programs menu.

Not Office.

If you have Microsoft Office installed on your PC, and you choose Start⇨All Programs, you immediately see all of the Office programs. Splat. Even if you use Microsoft Access once every 200 years, it still sits on your All Programs list, taking up space that could be better used by, oh, Total Annihilation. When you toss in New Office Document and Open Office Document — which I, for one, never use — and throw in the Office Tools fly-out menu for good measure, good ol' Microsoft Office takes up nine slots on the main All Programs menu (see Figure 2-6), when it should take one.

**Book II
Chapter 2**

Organizing Your
Windows XP
Interface

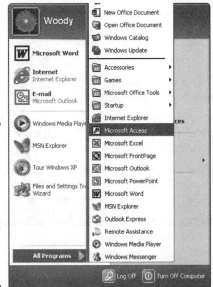

Figure 2-6:
Microsoft
Office, bless
its pointed
little head,
takes up
nine slots on
the main All
Programs
menu.

Time to get out your scalpel and dissect your All Programs menu:

1. **Navigate to the c:\Documents and Settings\All Users\Start Menu\Programs folder.**

   You can do that by choosing Start⇨My Computer and double-clicking your way down, but a much faster method is to right-click on the Start button, choose Explore All Users, and double-click on Programs (see Figure 2-7).

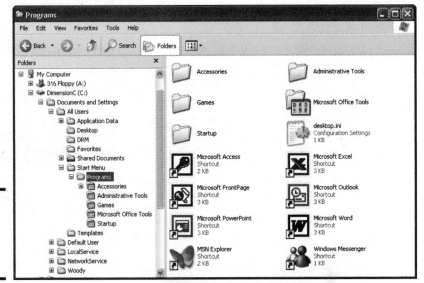

Figure 2-7:
The All Programs menu entries.

Next you want to create a fly-out menu called, simply, Office. It's easy.

2. **On the right side (which is to say, anywhere but in the Task pane), right-click any open spot and choose New⇨Folder. Then type Office and press Enter.**

   You now have a new folder called Office, and it shows up on the All Programs menu as an Empty fly-out (see Figure 2-8).

3. **Click on the Microsoft Access menu line and drag it into the Office fly-out menu — over the text (Empty). Release the mouse button and Microsoft Access moves to the Office fly-out menu.**

4. **One by one, click and drag all the rest of the Office programs to the Office fly-out menu.**

   Don't forget the New Office Document and Open Office Document entries at the top.

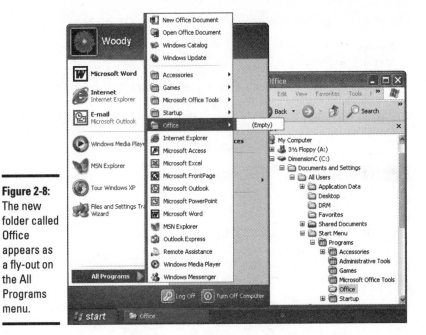

Figure 2-8:
The new folder called Office appears as a fly-out on the All Programs menu.

5. **Click on Microsoft Office Tools and drag the entire fly-out menu over to Office. Release the mouse button and you have put Office in its place (see Figure 2-9).**

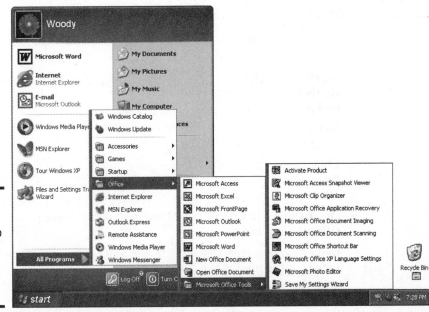

Figure 2-9:
Office relegated to its own fly-out menu, where it belongs.

Showing recent documents

Some people love the recent documents feature. Most people hate it. That's why Microsoft turned it off in the final, shipping version of Windows XP.

In most normal circumstances — with well-behaved programs that don't crash — Windows keeps track of which documents you've opened. You can have Windows show a list of those documents on the Start menu, just under My Documents (see Figure 2-10).

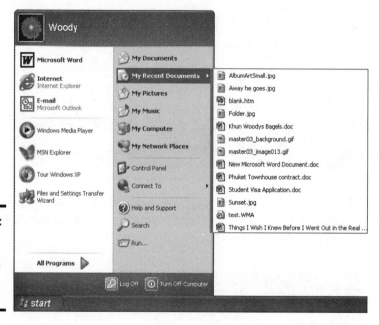

Figure 2-10:
The My
Recent
Documents
fly-out
menu.

Folks who like the feature appreciate being able to retrieve documents quickly and easily, without spelunking for the program that created them: Click on a Word document in the My Recent Documents folder, and Word comes to life, with the document open and ready to rumble.

Folks who hate the feature would just as soon open the application and use the application's most recently opened file list (typically on the File menu) to retrieve their documents. Some of the curmudgeons — present company definitely included — don't particularly want to leave (yet another) record of what they've been doing lying around for prying eyes.

To turn on My Recent Documents:

1. **Right-click Start and click Properties.**

2. **On the Start menu tab, make sure Start Menu is checked, and click Customize.**

3. **On the Advanced tab, check the box marked List My Most Recently Opened Documents (see Figure 2-11).**

   Note that you can return to this location to clear out the list. But clearing the list here does *not* clear similar lists in your applications, such as Word or Internet Explorer. For those, you have to refer to the application itself.

Book II
Chapter 2

Organizing Your
Windows XP
Interface

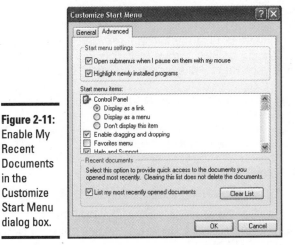

Figure 2-11:
Enable My
Recent
Documents
in the
Customize
Start Menu
dialog box.

Making minor tweaks to the Start menu

You can make a number of additional changes to the Start menu. Some of them are actually useful, particularly if you go into your computer fairly frequently to jiggle things. To tweak:

1. **Right-click Start and click Properties.**

2. **On the Start Menu tab, make sure Start Menu is checked, and click Customize.**

3. **Click the Advanced tab and check the features you want to enable, based on the following list. Click OK twice.**

The following six Start menu items can be turned into fly-out menus:

✦ **Control Panel:** This item can show all of the "classic applets" (read: all of the individual Control Panel applications) in a fly-out. That's the Display As a Menu option in the Start Menu Items list.

✦ **Favorites:** This item creates a menu that can appear above My Computer, with Favorites (primarily from Internet Explorer) listed on a fly-out menu. To show Favorites, check the Favorites box in the Start Menu Items list.

✦ **My Computer:** This item can have its own fly-out, listing your drives, as well as the Control Panel (which now appears twice on the Start menu), My Documents (again), and Shared Documents. Enable the fly-out by checking the Display As a Menu option on the Start Menu Items list.

✦ **My Documents, My Music, and My Pictures:** These items can all have their own fly-outs, listing files, and folders in each. Check Display As a Menu on the relevant Start Menu Items list.

If you're an inveterate twiddler (or twiddler in training), check the box in Start Menu Items called System Administrative Tools/Display on the All Programs Menu. The programs there will keep you occupied for years.

Do you install new programs rather frequently? Do you get really tired of Windows popping up its little yellow boxes, informing you that you've just installed a new program, when you know darn good and well that you just installed a new program? Here's a way to turn it off:

1. **Right-click Start and click Properties.**

2. **On the Start Menu tab, make sure that Start Menu is checked, and click Customize.**

3. **Click the Advanced tab and uncheck the box marked Highlight Newly Installed Programs. Click OK twice.**

I call it the D'OH switch.

Quick Launch Toolbar

Windows XP/Pro turns on the Windows XP Quick Launch Toolbar automatically. If you're using XP/Pro, you can skip the following section on "Activating" and jump directly to "Customizing."

Activating

Windows XP's Quick Launch Toolbar is a little tray of icons that sits next to the Start button, where you can stick shortcuts to start all of your favorite programs (see Figure 2-12). It's one of the handiest features in Windows — and if you are running Windows XP/Home, you may not even know that it exists.

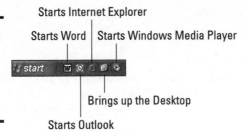

Figure 2-12:
The Quick Launch Toolbar I use every day.

Starts Internet Explorer

Starts Word | Starts Windows Media Player

Brings up the Desktop

Starts Outlook

To start the Quick Launch Toolbar, right-click on any open spot down on the Windows Taskbar, and choose Toolbars⇨Quick Launch. That's all there is to it. Your initial Quick Launch Toolbar includes icons for Internet Explorer, the Desktop, and the Windows Media Player.

Customizing

Adding your own icons to the Quick Launch Toolbar is very simple, too, but you immediately run into problems trying to squeeze more icons into that teensy-tiny space. Here's how to avoid the problem in the first place:

1. **Make sure the Quick Launch Toolbar is showing (right-click any open spot down on the Windows Taskbar and choose Toolbars⇨ Quick Launch).**

2. **Unlock the Taskbar, so that you can increase the size of the Quick Launch Toolbar.**

To do so, right-click any open spot on the Windows Taskbar, and uncheck the line marked Lock the Taskbar.

Windows shows two small drag handles, one to the left and one to the right of the Quick Launch Toolbar.

3. **Grab the drag handle on the right and stretch it out (to the right) a bit.**

4. **Find a program that you want to put in the Quick Launch Toolbar.**

For example, if you have Microsoft Office installed and you want to put Word down there, choose Start⇨All Programs, and look for Microsoft Word.

5. **Right-click on the program, and drag it down to the Quick Launch Toolbar.**

You see a big, black I-Beam in the Quick Launch Toolbar that indicates where the icon will go. When you release the icon, choose Copy Here.

When you drag icons to the Quick Launch Toolbar, right-click and choose Copy Here, so that the original program shortcut stays intact. If you left-click (or right-click and choose Move Here), the shortcut gets moved.

6. **Drag as many icons to the Quick Launch Toolbar as you like. When you're done, butt the right drag handle up against the rightmost icon, and then right-click on the Windows Taskbar and choose Lock Toolbar.**

You have more "play" with the Quick Launch Toolbar's resizing drag handles than you think. Try squishing the Quick Launch Toolbar by setting the right drag handle on top of the rightmost icon, and then lock the Toolbar. When you choose Lock Toolbar, chances are good that all of the icons appear anyway. It never hurts to tighten things up a bit, so Windows can use as much of the Taskbar as possible.

Custom Startup

Do you start a specific program just about every time you crank up Windows? Maybe you want to get the Windows Media Player going every time Windows wakes up. A friend of mine always starts the Windows Calculator. Of course, he's a hopeless drudge, so don't let him influence you.

You can easily tell Windows XP that you want to run a specific program every time Windows starts. You just have to put the program in the \Startup folder.

Say you want to start the Windows Calculator every time anybody logs on to Windows. You can make that happen if you put a shortcut to the Calculator into the All Users \Startup folder, like this:

1. **Right-click on the Start button and choose Explore All Users.**

2. **Double-click your way down to the c:\Documents and Settings\ All Users\Start Menu\Programs\Startup folder.**

3. **Go back to the Start button, and choose Start⇨All Programs⇨ Accessories.**

4. **Right-click on the Calculator, and drag it to the \Startup folder. When you release the Calculator, click Copy Here.**

   You see a shortcut to the Calculator go into the \Startup folder (see Figure 2-13).

   You're done. The next time anyone logs on to Windows, the Calculator will start.

Figure 2-13:
Put a
shortcut
to the
Calculator in
the \Startup
folder, and
it starts
every time
Windows
does.

If you want the Calculator to start for just one user, you need to put a shortcut to the calculator in that user's \Startup folder. The easy way: Have that user log on, right-click the Start button and click Explore. Then follow Steps 2 through 5 in the preceding list.

Index

Book III

Windows XP
and the Internet

The 5th Wave   By Rich Tennant

"He saw your laptop and wants to
know if he can check his Hotmail."

Contents at a Glance

Chapter 1: Expanding Your Reach through the Internet

In This Chapter

✔ Introducing the Internet

✔ Why you really do want to learn how to use it

✔ How much it will cost

✔ The truth behind all the bad things you've heard

✔ A quick run-down on getting connected

nternet this. Web that. E-mail today. Hair (or at least spam about hair products) tomorrow.

Windows XP makes it easy to get online. That means you can dash off a quick message to your daughter, send a birthday card to your mom, pick up the latest baseball scores and news headlines, glance at the stock market, look up show times and locations at a dozen local theaters, compare features and prices on the latest mobile phones, and check out the weather in Phuket (pronounced *Poo-KET*, by the way), Thailand, all in a matter of minutes — if your Internet connection is fast enough.

On the other hand, you probably know that the Internet is full of viruses, it isn't safe to use your credit card to order stuff from a Web site, pornographers lurk on every corner, and everything you do on the Internet is being monitored.

That's what the guy who works in the computer shop told you, isn't it?

What Is the Internet?

You know those stories about computer jocks who come up with great ideas, develop them in their basements (or garages or dorm rooms), release their product to the public, change the world, and make a gazillion bucks?

This isn't one of them.

The Internet started in the mid-1960s as an academic exercise — primarily with the RAND Corporation, MIT, and the National Physical Laboratory in England — and rapidly evolved into a military project, under the U.S. Department of Defense's Advanced Research Project Agency, designed to string together research groups working on ARPA projects.

By the end of the 1960s, ARPA had four computers hooked together — at UCLA, SRI (Stanford), UC Santa Barbara, and the University of Utah — using systems developed by Bolt Beranek and Newman, Inc. By the time Windows XP hit the stands in October, 2001, well over 100,000,000 computers were registered permanently on the Internet, and half a billion people could connect to the Internet with computers in their homes.

Ever wonder why you rarely see hard statistics about the Internet? I've found two big reasons: Defining terms related to the Internet is devilishly difficult these days (what do you mean when you say "X number of computers are connected to the Internet"?), and the Internet is growing so fast that any number you publish today will be meaningless tomorrow.

Inside the Internet

Some observers claim that the Internet works so well because it was designed to survive a nuclear attack. Not so. The people who built the Internet insist that they weren't nearly as concerned about nukes as they were about making communication among researchers reliable, even when a backhoe ate a phone line or one of the key computers ground to a halt.

As far as I'm concerned, the Internet works so well because the engineers who laid the groundwork were utter geniuses. Their original ideas from 30 years ago have been through the wringer a few times, but they're still pretty much intact. Here's what they decided:

✦ **No single computer should be in charge:** All the big computers connected directly to the Internet are equal (although, admittedly, some are more equal than others). By and large, computers on the Internet move data around like kids with a hot potato — catch it, figure out where you're going to throw it, and let it fly quickly. They don't need to check with some uber-computer before doing their work; they just catch, look, throw.

✦ **Break the data into fixed-size packets:** No matter how much data you're moving — an e-mail message that just says "Hi" or a full-color, life-size photograph of the Andromeda Galaxy — break the data into packets. Each packet gets routed to the appropriate computer. The receiving computer assembles all the packets and notifies the sending computer that everything came through okay.

✦ **Deliver each packet quickly:** If you want to send data from Computer A to Computer B, break the data into packets, and route each packet to Computer B using the fastest connection possible — even if that means some packets go through Bangor and others go through Bangkok.

Taken together, those three rules ensure that the Internet can take a lickin' and keep on tickin'. If a chipmunk eats through a telephone line, any big computer that's using the gnawed line can start rerouting packets over a different telephone line. If the Cumbersome Computer Company in Cupertino, California, loses power, computers that were sending packets through Cumbersome can switch to other connected computers. It all works quickly and reliably, although the techniques used internally by the Internet computers get a bit hairy at times.

Using the Internet

Big computers are hooked together with high-speed communication lines: the Internet *backbone*. If you want to use the Internet from your business or your house, you have to connect to one of the big computers first. Companies that own the big computers (Internet Service Providers) get to charge you for the privilege of getting onto the Internet through their big computers.

If you have a dial-up modem, here's how your connection to the Internet works:

1. **You pay.**

   You may find an Internet Service Provider by using one of the Windows XP sign-up options; you may receive a prepaid ISP account with AOL, MSN, or one of the other biggies when you buy your PC; you may talk to that kid in the computer shop; you may even see a "free three months" deal of some sort. In any case, you have to plunk down your credit card and pay the piper.

2. **Your Internet Service Provider may hand you some software, with instructions attached.**

   At the very least, your ISP gives you an I.D., a password, and a telephone number. Follow the ISP's instructions — using whatever software the ISP requires — to connect. (Windows XP's standard connection dialog box is shown in Figure 1-1.)

3. **When you connect, your computer dials your ISP's telephone number.**

   That pinging sound you probably hear ("ping-ping-ping-sssssssss") is the sound of your computer trying to talk to the ISP's computer over your modem. (See the sidebar, "What's a modem?")

What's a modem?

Your computer really, really wants to talk to other computers. If you hook your computer up to another computer with a fairly short cable, they can talk digitally, sending 1s and 0s over the cable to each other. Cool. But if your computer has to talk over the telephone line, that's another story entirely.

Back in the early days of telephones, all connections were analog: You talked into a mouthpiece, that caused a varying amount of electricity to travel through the telephone line; the earpiece on the other end of the telephone line picked up the electrical changes and converted the impulses back into sound. Those phones were a bit like tying a piece of string to two paper cups — the sound pulses in the cup on one end made the string vibrate, and the cup on the other end converted the vibrations back to sound.

Nowadays, telephone systems are entirely digital. Well, almost entirely digital. I'll come back to that in a second.

Computers are digital beasts — they talk in 1s and 0s. Telephones are analog beasts — they want varying pulses. Modems bridge the gap. They convert digits into pulses and vice versa. Think of it this way: Your computer has a string of 1s and 0s that it wants to send to your friend Moe's computer — let's say, 11001. You and Moe, being game Dummies, decide to play modem. (Bear with me, okay?)

You call Moe and exchange pleasantries. When you're both ready, you both tell your computers to have at it. Your computer starts flashing the 1s and 0s on the screen that it wants to send to Moe's computer. You see a 1 on your computer's screen and yell into the telephone, "ONE!" Moe hears you say "one," and types a 1 into his computer. You shout "ONE" again, and Moe types another 1. Then you shout "ZERO," and Moe

types a 0. "ZERO" again, 0 again. Then "ONE," and Moe types a 1. When your computer is finished, it flashes a message on the screen. You yell, "I'm done Moe, did you get it?" Moe yells back, "Yep, I got it!"

That's what a modem does. When it's sending data, it takes the 1s and 0s that the computer wants to send and shouts into the phone "ONE" or "ZERO." When it's receiving data, it listens for "ONE" and "ZERO" and relays the appropriate number to the computer. Some extra work is involved — exchanging pleasantries and making sure that all the data came through — but at its heart, a modem alternately yells and listens.

Here's the ironic part. Although the telephone system used to be entirely analog, these days it's almost entirely digital. The only analog part is the short distance — called the *local loop* — from your house to the closest telephone switch. Nowadays, when you talk into the telephone, a varying amount of electricity (an analog signal) is sent on the phone line that only goes as far as the switch — typically a few hundred yards. When your voice hits the switch, it's digitized and sent to the receiving switch, where it's converted back to analog so that it can travel the final few hundred yards to Moe's house. In essence, your slow-as-a-snail modem exists only to make the trip from your house to your local telephone switch. Everything else travels at blazing speeds.

DSL technology — the high-speed Internet access that you may be paying mountains of money for — simply leapfrogs that final few hundred yards. Instead of converting your PC's digital 1s and 0s to analog ONEs and ZEROs, the DSL box makes sure that the digital data that your PC generates gets patched directly into the already-digital network.

Figure 1-1:
If you
connect
directly to
the Internet,
you use a
dialog box
like this one.

4. **As soon as the modems are talking to each other, your computer sends your I.D. and password.**

   The ISP's computer makes sure that you have a valid account (which is to say, the computer makes sure you paid your bill).

5. **If the ISP's computer gives the okay, the connection is opened up, and you can start using your software — Internet Explorer, AOL, Outlook, Outlook Express, or one of the many others.**

6. **When you're done, tell the computer to hang up the modem.**

I have an extensive list of ISP sign-up options and the myriad ways you can spend your ISP bucks in Book IV, Chapter 1.

Other kinds of connections — DSL, cable modem, and satellite, in particular — don't work the same way. In the case of DSL and cable modem, your connection is probably "always on." The ISP computer verifies that you have a valid account once in a blue moon, and knocks you off if you don't.

What Is the World Wide Web?

People tend to confuse the World Wide Web with the Internet, which is a lot like confusing the dessert table with the buffet line. I'd be the first to admit that desserts are mighty darn important. Life-critical, in fact, if the truth be told. But they aren't the same as the buffet line.

In order to get to the dessert table, you have to stand in the buffet line. In order to get to the Web, you have to be running on the Internet.

Make sense?

The World Wide Web owes its existence to Tim Berners-Lee and a few co-conspirators at a research institute called CERN in Geneva, Switzerland. In 1990, Berners-Lee demonstrated a way to store and link information on the Internet so that all it took was a click to jump from one place — one Web page — to another. By the time Windows XP shipped in October 2001, almost 2,000,000,000 pages were on the Web.

Like the Internet itself, the World Wide Web owes much of its success to the brilliance of the people who brought it to life. The following are the ground rules:

✦ Web pages, stored on the Internet, are identified by an address such as www.dummies.com. Although you're probably accustomed to seeing addresses that start with www and end with com, org, or edu, plenty of addresses don't.

✦ Web pages are written in a funny kind of language called HTML, which is sort of a programming language, sort of a formatting language, and sort of a floor wax, all rolled into one. Many products claim to make it easy for novices to create powerful, efficient HTML. None of them do.

✦ In order to read a Web page, you have to use something called a *Web browser,* which is a program that runs on your computer. The browser is responsible for converting HTML into something you can read and use. The vast majority of people who view Web pages use Internet Explorer as their Web browser. Unless you live under a rock in the Gobi Desert, you know that Internet Explorer is part of Windows XP. Today, anyway. Heaven only knows what the courts will do.

One unwritten rule for the World Wide Web: All Web acronyms have to be completely, utterly inscrutable. For example, a Web address is called an URL, or Uniform Resource Locator, pronounced *earl.* HTML is short for Hypertext Markup Language. On the Web, a gorgeous, sunny, palm-lined beach with the scent of frangipani lilting through the air would no doubt be called SHS — Smelly Hot Sand. Sheeesh.

The best part of the Web is how easily you can jump from one place to another — and how easily you can create Web pages with hot links that transport the viewer wherever the author intends. That's the "H" in "HTML," and the original reason for creating the Web, so many years ago.

Who Pays for All This Stuff?

That's the $64,000,000,000 question, isn't it?

The Internet is one of the true bargains of the 21st Century. When you're online — for which you probably have to pay AOL, MSN, your cable company, or some other Internet Service Provider a monthly fee — the Internet itself is free.

Web sites

Most Web sites don't charge a cent. They pay for themselves in any of several ways:

+ **By reducing a company's operating costs:** Banks and brokerage firms, for example, have Web sites that routinely handle customer inquiries at a fraction of the cost of H2H (er, human-to-human) interactions.

+ **By increasing a company's visibility:** This means that the Web site gives you a good excuse to buy more of the company's products. That's why architectural firms show you pictures of their buildings and food companies post recipes.

+ **By drawing in new business:** Ask any real estate agent.

+ **By contracting advertising:** Some popular sites like www.newyorktimes.com sell ad spots outright.

+ **By using bounty advertising:** Smaller sites run ads, usually selected from a pool of advertisers. The advertiser pays a bounty for each person who clicks on the ad and views their Web site — a so-called *click through*.

+ **By affiliate programs:** Smaller sites may also participate in a retailer's affiliate program. If a customer clicks through and orders something, the Web site that originated the transaction gets a percentage of the amount ordered. Amazon.com is well-known for its affiliate program, but many others exist.

Some Web sites have an entrance fee. For example, if you want to use the Oxford English Dictionary on the Web (see Figure 1-2), you have to part with some substantial coin — $550 (U.S.) per year, the last time I looked. Guess that beats schlepping around 20 volumes.

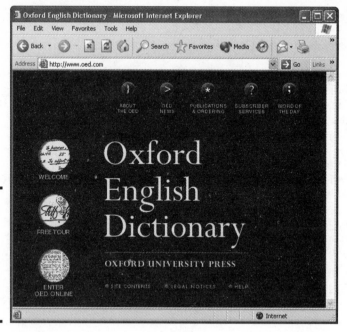

Figure 1-2:
The Oxford English Dictionary: venerable resource, pricey Web site.

E-mail

E-mail frequently comes free from your ISP. Keep these points in mind:

✦ Most ISPs limit the amount of mail that you can store for free.

✦ Most ISPs limit the size of individual e-mail messages, coming and going — you can't send or receive really big files.

✦ When your friends have your I.D., it's difficult to switch ISPs because you have to tell all your friends about your new I.D.

✦ Plenty of free e-mail services exist on the Internet. `www.hotmail.com` and `mail.yahoo.com` are among the more popular, but you can find hundreds of alternatives at `www.emailaddresses.com`

Other Internet products

E-mail newsletters are usually free, although an increasing number charge a small annual fee to help defray costs. Generally, the cost of creating and distributing a newsletter is not great — many newsletters rely almost solely on volunteer contributions — so newsletter publishers get by on small fees charged to advertisers. Many newsletters advertise products, services, or Web sites connected to the publisher.

Newsgroups are almost always free, providing your Internet Service Provider offers a news service. Unmoderated Usenet newsgroups — the kind of Internet newsgroup that has no human involved in filtering out the drivel — run themselves. Moderated newsgroups have volunteers who go over the postings before they get sent on to newsgroup members, removing the offal.

Internet Myths Exploded

The Internet is wild and woolly and wonderful — and, by and large, it's unregulated, in a Wild-West sort of way. Some would say it's unregulatable, and I'd have to agree. Although some central bodies control basic Internet coordination questions — how the computers talk to each other, who doles out domain names such as `dummies.com`, what a Web browser should do when it encounters a particular piece of HTML — no central authority or Web Fashion Police exists.

Being on the Internet doesn't absolve an individual or company of all restrictions, of course. An American company has to abide by American laws. An American company doing business in Germany has to abide by German laws, as well. Individuals can run afoul of regulations in one location while conforming to rules in another location. It's very confusing.

Most of the bad things you hear about the Internet, though, don't hold water. I wanted to put a bunch of them together, here in one place, so that you can grab your brother-in-law by the ear, whip out this book, and say, "There! I told you so!"

Viruses

"Everybody" knows that the Internet breeds viruses. "Everybody" knows that really bad viruses can drain your bank account, break your hard drive, and give you terminal halitosis — just by looking at an e-mail message with "Good Times" in the Subject line.

Right.

In fact, viruses (I use the term loosely) can hurt you, but hoaxes and lousy advice abound. Every Windows XP user should take these five steps:

1. **Buy, install, update, and religiously use one of the major anti-virus software packages. It doesn't matter which one.**

2. **Never, ever, ever open a file attached to an e-mail message until you do the following:**

   - Contact the person who sent you the file and verify that he did, in fact, send you the file intentionally. The most virulent and destructive attacks these days come in the form of files attached to e-mail messages that are automatically sent out by an infected system.

   - After you contact the person who sent you the file, don't open the file directly. Save it to disk and run your anti-virus software on it before you open it.

3. **Follow the instructions in Book I, Chapter 2, to force Windows XP to show you the full name of all the files that are on your computer.**

4. **If you get a virus warning in e-mail, take it with a grain of salt.**

   Check Rob Rosenberger's Virus Myths page, www.vmyths.com, to see whether it's a known hoax. Most of all, realize that if a killer virus is on the loose and attempting to overload the Internet and bring it to its knees, the worst possible way for you to notify your family and friends is by sending them e-mail!

5. **Flip to the very end of *Windows XP All-in-One Desk Reference For Dummies* — Book IX, Chapter 3 — for information about protecting yourself against virus attacks..**

You have to be careful. But your uncle's sister-in-law's roommate's hair-dresser's soon-to-be-ex boyfriend, who's a really smart computer guy (but kinda smelly) may not be the best source of unbiased information.

We regularly cover viruses and other kinds of destructive software — with a rather jaundiced eye, quite frankly — in *Woody's Windows Watch* and *Woody's Office Watch*. Sign up for the free electronic newsletters at www.woodyswatch.com.

Credit card fraud

A very large percentage of people who use the World Wide Web refuse to order anything because they're afraid that their credit card number will be stolen and they'll be liable for enormous bills. Or they think that the products will never arrive, and they won't get their money back.

If your credit card was issued in the U.S., and you're ordering from a company in the U.S., that's simply not the case:

   ✦ The Fair Credit Billing Act protects you from being charged by a company for an item you don't receive. It's the same law that governs orders placed over the telephone or by mail. A vendor generally has 30 days to send the merchandise, or they have to give you a formal, written chance to cancel your order. For details, go to the Federal Trade Commission's Web site, www.ftc.gov/bcp/conline/pubs/buying/mail.htm.

✦ Your maximum liability for charges fraudulently made on the card is $50 (U.S.) per card. The minute you notify the credit card company that somebody else is using your card, you have no further liability. If you have any questions, the Federal Trade Commission will help. See www.ftc.gov/bcp/conline/pubs/credit/cards.htm.

Some online vendors, such as Amazon.com, absolutely guarantee that your shopping will be safe. The Fair Credit Billing Act protects any charges fraudulently made in excess of $50. Amazon says it will reimburse any fraudulent charges *under* $50 that occurred as a result of using its Web site. For details, see www.amazon.com.

That said, you should still take a few simple precautions to make sure that you aren't giving away your credit card information:

✦ When you place an order online, make sure that you're dealing with a company you know. That's a common-sense precaution that you take in the physical world. Make sure to use the same common sense online.

✦ Only type in your credit card number when you're using a secure Web page. The easy way to tell whether a Web page is secure is to look at the address, and look for the "lock" icon at the bottom of Internet Explorer (see Figure 1-3). Secure Web sites scramble data, so anything that you type on the Web page is encrypted before it's sent to the vendor's computer.

✦ Don't send your credit card number in an ordinary e-mail message. E-mail is just too easy to intercept. And, for heaven's sake, don't give out any personal information when you're chatting online.

✦ If you receive an e-mail message requesting credit card information that seems to be from your bank, credit card company, Internet Service Provider, or even your sainted Aunt Martha, don't send sensitive information back via e-mail. Insist on using a secure Web site.

✦ You may be tempted to put your credit card information in a monster database such as Microsoft's Passport. Make sure that you understand the consequences of your actions before you type in your credit card number. See Book IX, Chapter 3.

The rules are different if you're not dealing with a U.S. company, using a U.S. credit card. For example, if you buy something in an online auction from an individual, you don't have the same level of protection. Make sure that you understand the rules before you hand out credit card information.

Book III
Chapter 1

Expanding Your
Reach through
the Internet

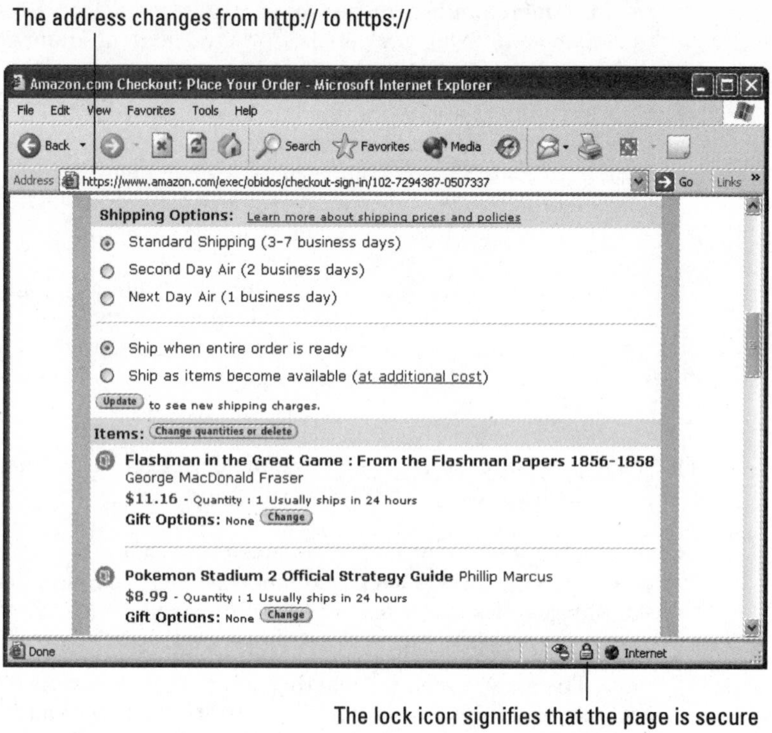

The address changes from http:// to https://

Amazon.com Checkout: Place Your Order - Microsoft Internet Explorer

File   Edit   View   Favorites   Tools   Help

Back ▾

Address   https://www.amazon.com/exec/obidos/checkout-sign-in/102-7294387-0507337   Go   Links »

Shipping Options: Learn more about shipping prices and policies

- ◉ Standard Shipping (3-7 business days)
- ○ Second Day Air (2 business days)
- ○ Next Day Air (1 business day)

- ◉ Ship when entire order is ready
- ○ Ship as items become available (at additional cost)

Update to see new shipping charges.

Items: (Change quantities or delete)

Flashman in the Great Game : From the Flashman Papers 1856-1858
George MacDonald Fraser
$11.16 - Quantity : 1 Usually ships in 24 hours
Gift Options: None (Change)

Pokemon Stadium 2 Official Strategy Guide Phillip Marcus
$8.99 - Quantity : 1 Usually ships in 24 hours
Gift Options: None (Change)

Done   Internet

Figure 1-3:
A secure
Web site.

The lock icon signifies that the page is secure

Identity theft continues to be a problem all over the world. Widespread availability of personal information online only adds fuel to the flame. If you think someone may be posing as you — to run up debts in your name, for example — see the U.S. government's main Web site on the topic, at www.consumer.gov/idtheft.

We'll just pass a law

Online pornography is big business — billions of dollars a year. It's one of the great success stories on the Internet.

Online gambling is big business, too — billions more. *Business 2.0* magazine (www.business2.com/articles/web/0,1653,12222,00.html) reports that consumers will lose about $3,000,000,000 (U.S.) to online gambling in 2001.

If there's a vice to be mined and a buck to be made, you can bet that somebody on the Internet is going at it, full tilt boogie, right now.

I wish I had a buck for every time I've heard some well-meaning person tell me that the U.S. Congress is at fault. If Washington would only pass a law, the sentiment goes, we could crush these pornographers (bookies, quacks, hatemongers, pill pushers, insert your favorite whipping boy here) overnight.

Uh, yeah. Sure.

Here's how the Internet works. Say the government of Moronovia decides that Internet sites shouldn't be allowed to show pictures of Minnie Mouse. There's a hue and cry in Parliament, a bill gets passed, and all the Moronovian Web sites featuring poor little Minnie are crushed into silicon dust, their Webmeisters marched off to serve 20 years at hard labor.

Halfway around the world in Enterprizistan, a Web designer is scanning the headlines and discovers that the Moronovian Web sites featuring Minnie Mouse are all down. He rummages around the Web for a day or two, dredges up some grainy pics of our favorite subversive mouse, throws together a Web page (www.minniemouse.ezn, anybody?), and he's suddenly in business.

That's how it works.

If you want to control where your kids can and can't go, consider using AOL. I've had very mixed success with Net Nanny (www.netnanny.com) and Cyber Patrol (www.surfcontrol.com). The problem, of course, is that the packages don't block some sites that should be blocked — and shut out perfectly good, even educational, sites.

Yes, some things can — and should — be done to curb Internet excesses. In some cases, legislation can make a difference. In many cases, it's just expectorating in the wind.

This legislation stuff cuts both ways. The Internet provides a hotbed of activity for subversive groups that oppose authoritarian regimes in many countries. In the end, widespread availability of Internet access may well end up being the most democratizing influence of our generation. Watch the People's Republic of China. Watch Burma, er, Myanmar.

Big Brother is watching

Psssst. For every copy of this e-mail message that you forward to a friend, Bill Gates will donate $100 to the National Furshlinger Society. Uh, Intel will send $5 to help a poor, starving dog get a first-rate education. Er, Dilbert will flip back his tie and scratch an unmentionable part of his anatomy. (Sorry, Scott. Couldn't resist.)

Oh. Did you know? Congress is going to impose a new tax of five cents for every e-mail message you read. And California is going to start charging 10 cents per minute for telephone calls placed to Internet Service Providers.

You can easily get caught up in the Big Brother hysteria. After all, the Net has reached into everyone's lives, and it's easy to get paranoid about something so big and so important. Still, you have to use a little common sense.

Some of the stuff that sounds like science fiction is true! Case in point: the FBI's Carnivore program, which monitors e-mail. Although the program was renamed DCS1000 more than a year ago (now *that* makes me feel more secure), the fact remains that the FBI is fully capable of monitoring e-mail, methodically and thoroughly.

Keep these facts in mind:

✦ No way exists for a person or company to monitor who receives copies of a text e-mail message (although a method called Web Bugs can be used in certain circumstances to monitor the destination of formatted e-mail messages; see www.privacyfoundation.org/resources/webbug.asp).

✦ No way exists for a company or the government to tell which telephone calls that you place originate from your computer's modem.

✦ Nobody can count how many e-mail messages you send or receive.

✦ If you use a program such as Outlook or Outlook Express, nobody can tell whether you've read an e-mail message or just deleted it.

✦ When it comes to large online data collection agencies accumulating personal information about you, as an individual, your worst enemy is . . . you. Don't give out any information that makes you uncomfortable.

The Internet is still a rather chaotic, anarchic place. A lot of people are fighting hard to keep it that way.

Chapter 2: Outlook Express: Your Tool for Managing E-Mail and Newsgroups

In This Chapter

✓ Using Windows XP's free e-mail program — Outlook Express

✓ Putting together decent e-mail messages with a minimum of hassle

✓ Keeping on top of your contacts

✓ Using Microsoft's *only* newsgroup reader — Outlook Express

*W*ho was it that said the best things in life are free? Whoever said it may have been thinking about Outlook Express. (Of course, I can't really say it's *free* if you consider it part of the price you paid for Windows XP.) Outlook Express is a surprisingly full-featured e-mail program that enables you to send messages in just about any form you want, receive messages from multiple accounts, and even work with newsgroups to find out what the buzz is on topics that are most interesting to you.

Outlook Express may sound like Outlook — part of Microsoft Office — but the two have very little in common. Outlook is the 800-pound gorilla of the personal information management game, with e-mail, task manager, calendar, scheduler, and more. Outlook Express focuses on e-mail and newsgroups — the two features that you're likely to want most in a daily e-mail program.

Getting Started with Outlook Express

Outlook Express is a great little program if you don't have any other way to get your e-mail. But if you use AOL or MSN for e-mail, or you're already hooked up to Outlook itself in Microsoft Office, you can skip this chapter (do not pass go, do not collect $200).

Even if you use the big Outlook (from Microsoft Office), you need Outlook Express to get into the Internet's newsgroups. Don't ask me why, but Microsoft still hasn't put newsgroup support in Outlook.

All you need in order to start Outlook Express is a connection to the Internet. When you're online, just click the little Outlook Express icon in the Windows taskbar at the bottom of your screen. The Outlook Express window appears, as shown in Figure 2-1.

The Outlook Express window is pretty easy to figure out. At the top of the window, you find the familiar title bar and menus; beneath that, you find the Outlook Express toolbar. Table 2-1 provides an overview of the Outlook Express tools. The screen is divided into four different panels:

✦ The Folders panel displays all of the folders you've created in Outlook Express and some you have not created — Inbox, Outbox, Sent Items, Deleted Items, and Drafts have been created automatically for you.

✦ The Contacts panel shows the contacts in the selected Address Book. This panel also lists any Windows Messenger contacts you've added to MSN.

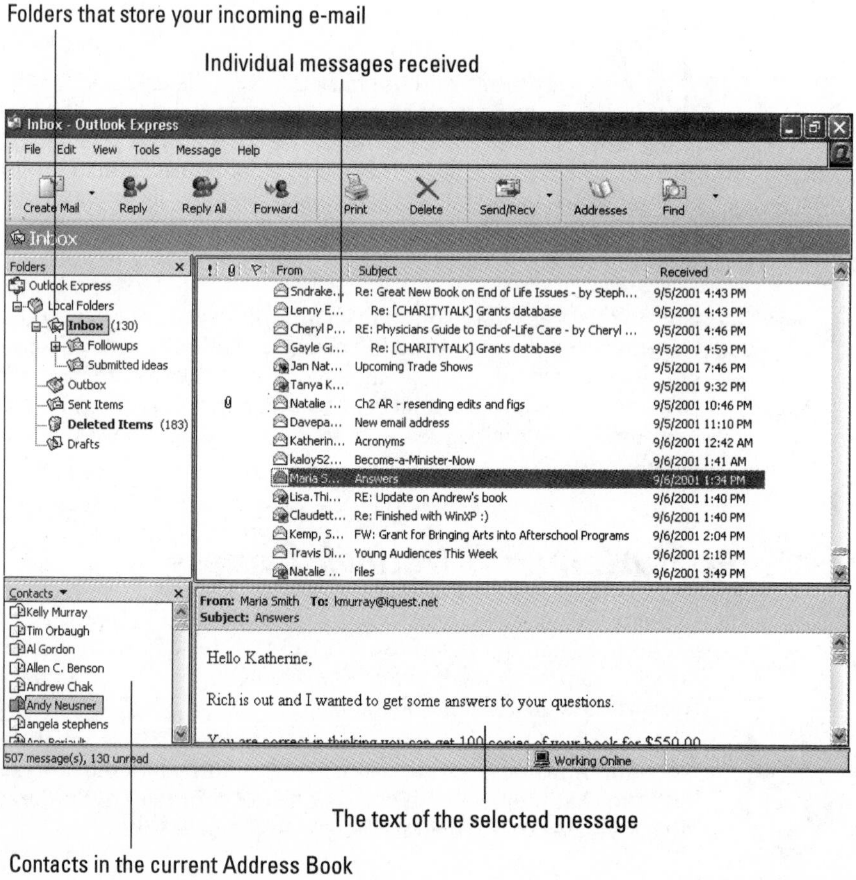

Folders that store your incoming e-mail

Individual messages received

Figure 2-1:
Checking out the Outlook Express window.

Contacts in the current Address Book

The text of the selected message

✦ The messages list in the top-right panel shows all the messages in the currently selected folder.

✦ The individual message panel shows the contents of the message highlighted in the messages list.

Table 2-1		Outlook Express Tools
Button	*Name*	*Description*
Create Mail	Create Mail	Displays the Create Mail window so that you can compose a new message
Reply	Reply	Enables you to respond to the current message
Reply All	Reply All	Lets you respond to all the recipients of the current message
Forward	Forward	Forwards the current message to the new recipient that you choose
Print	Print	Displays the Print dialog box so that you can print the current message
Delete	Delete	Deletes the current e-mail message
Send/Recv	Send/Recv	Sends any mail you've created and checks your mail server to see whether you have any new mail
Addresses	Addresses	Displays the Outlook Address Book so that you can add, edit, or delete contacts
Find	Find	Enables you to search for a message that you've sent or received, people on the Web, or specific text phrases

Book III
Chapter 2

Outlook Express:
Your Tool for
Managing E-Mail
and Newsgroups

Conversing with E-Mail

When you originally go through the "connecting to the Internet" stage of Windows XP installation, you are asked for the ISP information and e-mail account information. This info is plugged into Outlook Express automatically so that the first time you launch the program, the program should check your mail without any action from you.

The process of setting up mail accounts — and you can set up dozens, if you choose — is a simple one. Then you're free to create, send, and receive mail messages at will.

Setting up mail accounts

How many e-mail accounts do you need? Many people have more than one — perhaps one for work, one for school, one for business. And then let's not forget the kids.

If you want to add other e-mail accounts or modify your existing one, follow these steps:

1. **Start Outlook Express.**

2. **Choose Tools⇨Accounts.**

The Internet Accounts dialog box appears, as shown in Figure 2-2.

3. **Click Add, and then choose Mail.**

This act launches the Internet Connection Wizard (remember that?), which walks you through the steps involved in specifying your e-mail connection information and e-mail address. The POP and SMTP Server entries should come directly from your Internet Service Provider.

Later in this chapter, you find out how to work with newsgroups. When you want to add a newsgroup to Outlook Express, you use this same procedure to add the newsgroups that you want to work with.

Retrieving and reading messages

This is about as simple as it gets. When you want to check your e-mail, click Send/Recv in the Outlook Express toolbar. A dialog box opens, showing you the status as Outlook Express checks each e-mail account you use for new messages. If you want to only receive messages, you can click the down-arrow to the right of the Send/Recv button and choose Receive All from the menu.

Creating a message

```
Send and Receive All  Ctrl+M
Receive All
Send All
mail.iquest.net (Default)
pop3.concentric.net
```

When you're ready to create a message, click the Create Mail button in the Outlook Express toolbar. The New Message window appears so that you can create the message you want to send (see Figure 2-3).

The current default e-mail account

Choose Add⇨Mail to add a new e-mail address

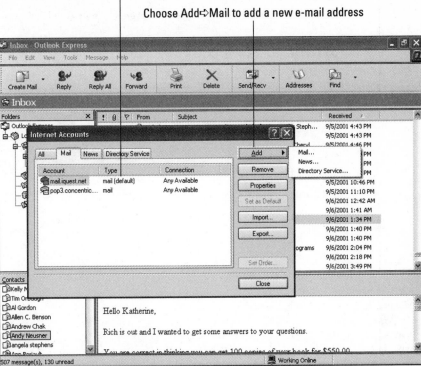

Figure 2-2:
Adding an
account.

Your first step involves choosing who you want to send the message to. You can enter the person's e-mail address in two different ways:

✦ You can type the e-mail address in the To line.

✦ You can click the Address Book icon to the left of the To line and select the recipient you want from the Address Book. (To select a recipient, click the contact from the list on the left, click To, and then click OK.)

Outlook Express then adds the contact name or e-mail address in the To line.

Next, enter a Subject for your message. For best results, keep it fairly short and make it descriptive.

Finally, type the body of your message. You've got a wide open space to do just that. You can enter the words the way you want them without any fancy formatting, or you can change the look of the text by choosing a different font and size, changing colors, indenting information, and more.

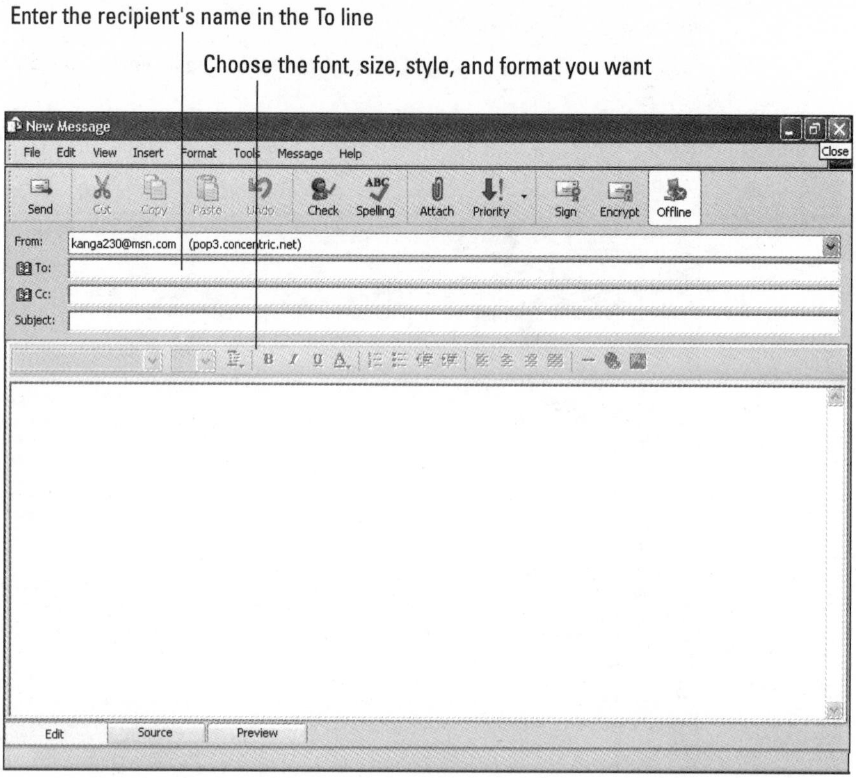

Enter the recipient's name in the To line

Choose the font, size, style, and format you want

Figure 2-3:
Writing a
new
message.

Formatting your text

If you've ever used a word processing program, you won't have any trouble figuring out Outlook Express's formatting tools. Just above the text area of the New Message window, you see a formatting toolbar with all the look-and-feel tools you'll ever need. Table 2-2 lists the various formatting tools and their functions.

Table 2-2	Formatting Tools for Your E-Mail Messages		
Button		**Name**	**Description**
Arial		Font	Allows you to choose the font for your message
10		Size	Determines the size of the font used
		Paragraph Style	Lets you assign a style to selected text

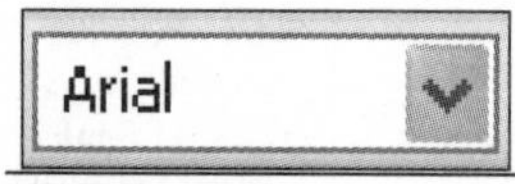

Button	Name	Description
B	Bold	Boldfaces selected text
I	Italic	Italicizes selected text
U	Underline	Underlines selected text
A	Font Color	Enables you to choose a new color for text
≔	Formatting Numbers	Creates a numbered list
≔	Formatting Bullets	Creates a bulleted list
≔	Decrease Indentation	Reduces the amount of space in the left margin
≔	Increase Indentation	Increases the spacing of the left margin
≣	Align Left	Left-aligns selected text
≣	Center	Centers selected text
≣	Align Right	Right-aligns selected text
≣	Justify	Justifies selected text
▬	Insert Horizontal Line	Adds a horizontal line at the cursor position
🔗	Create a Hyperlink	Enables you to add a hyperlink in the message
🖼	Insert Picture	Lets you add an image at the cursor position

**Book III
Chapter 2**

**Outlook Express:
Your Tool for
Managing E-Mail
and Newsgroups**

Adding a signature automatically

Many people have little catch-phrases, business mottos, and more that they like to stick on the end of their e-mail messages. If you're into these kinds of signatures, you can let Outlook Express add a signature for you automatically. Here are the steps for adding a signature:

1. **Choose Tools⇨Options.**

2. **Click the Signatures tab, and click New.**

3. **Enter your signature in the Edit Signature line or add the file that you want to attach by clicking File and selecting the file that you want to use (see Figure 2-4).**

4. **Click the Add signatures to all outgoing messages check box to apply the signature to all outgoing messages.**

Click to add signature automatically

Type your signature lines here

Create a new signature

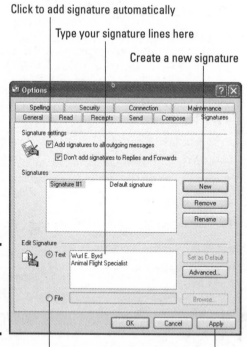

Figure 2-4: Adding a signature to outgoing e-mail.

To use a file as your signature   Add the signature

Checking spelling

Have you ever dashed off a quick e-mail message, only to discover later that you misspelled a critical word? You can avoid embarrassing moments like that by running Outlook Express's spelling checker before you send your messages. To check spelling, simply complete your message and then click Spelling (in the center of the Outlook Express toolbar) before you click Send. If the program suspects a misspelling, the Spelling dialog box appears and you can choose the spelling that you want or enter a new spelling. Click Cancel to close the dialog box.

Outlook Express doesn't have its own built-in dictionary. Instead, it hijacks the dictionary used by Microsoft Office. You can run a spell check only if you have Word, Excel, or PowerPoint installed.

Attaching files

A common operation for e-mail is the piggy-backing of files. When you need to get a report to an office in Vancouver, you send it attached to an e-mail message. When you need to get a chapter on an editor's desk in Indianapolis, you attach the file to an e-mail message.

When you want to attach files, the process is simple:

1. **Start Outlook Express as usual.**

2. **Click Create Message.**

   The New Message window opens.

3. **Choose the recipient and enter the subject line as usual. Type the body of your message and format as needed.**

4. **Click Attach in the Outlook Express toolbar.**

   The Insert Attachment dialog box appears, as shown in Figure 2-5.

5. **Navigate to the folder where the file is stored.**

6. **Click the file that you want to attach.**

7. **Click Attach to add the file.**

You can easily add more than one file to your e-mail message. If you want to select multiple files in the same folder, press and hold Ctrl while you click the mouse.

Sending a message

Okay, ready, set, send! Just click the Send button in the Outlook Express window. If you want to save the message that you created and send it later, choose File⇨Send Later. Outlook Express tells you that it is saving the message in your Outbox folder and you can send it when ready.

**Book III
Chapter 2**

Outlook Express: Your Tool for Managing E-Mail and Newsgroups

Navigate to the folder where the file is stored

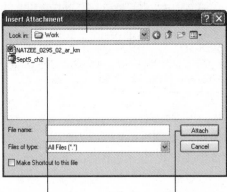

Figure 2-5:
Attaching a
file to your
message.

Choose the file   Click Attach to add the file

TIP

You If you want to save a message and work on it again before you send it, use File⇨Save. This places the message in your Drafts folder. When you want to continue working on it, simply open the Drafts folder and double-click the message.

Maintaining Your Contacts

You may already know about the Windows Address Book. It's that magical place that stores all your e-mail contact information — and then some. The Address Books stores not only e-mail addresses; it also includes mailing addresses, telephone numbers, and much more (see Figure 2-6).

Adding a contact

If you're a really popular person and you need to be able to add a new contact, you're in luck. The process is easy. Here are the steps:

1. **Start Outlook Express. Click the Addresses icon to bring up the Address Book.**

2. **Click New.**

3. **Choose your option:**

   - **New Contact:** An individual or organization.

   - **New Group:** A bunch of contacts, usually grouped together so that you can easily send one e-mail message to a whole group of people.

   - **New Folder:** Appears in the folder list.

Address Book toolbar

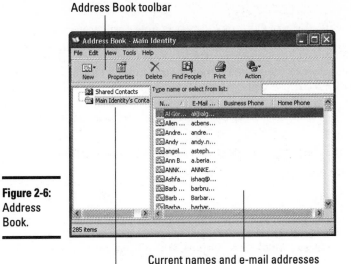

Figure 2-6:
Address
Book.

Current names and e-mail addresses

Contact lists available

4. **Click New Contact.**

   The Properties dialog box appears (see Figure 2-7).

Type the contact name

Select additional tabs to enter more contact info

Figure 2-7:
Entering a
new
contact.

Enter the e-mail address here

Book III
Chapter 2

Outlook Express:
Your Tool for
Managing E-Mail
and Newsgroups

Importing a contact list

One of the neat features of Outlook Express is how easily you can import contact lists that you've used in other applications or other programs. This means that if you've been growing a HUGE contact list on your other computer, you can now use the same contact list in Outlook Express. To import a contact list, follow these steps:

1. **Start Outlook Express. Click the Addresses icon to bring up the Address Book.**

2. **Choose File⇨Import and select one of the following options:**
   - Address Book (WAB)
   - Business Card (vCard)
   - Other Address Book

3. **Pick the Address Book File to Import From; then click Open.**

When you choose Other Address Book, the Address Book Import Tool dialog box comes up. Choose the program or file type that you used to create the contact list; then click Import. Outlook Express then imports your contacts.

Searching for contacts

You can search for people — either in your own Address Book or out there somewhere on the Internet.

To search for contacts, follow these steps:

1. **Start Outlook Express. Click the Addresses icon to bring up the Address Book.**

2. **In the Address Book window, click Find People.**

   The Find People dialog box appears, as shown in Figure 2-8.

3. **If you want to locate a user in your existing Address Book, leave the current selection in the Look In box. If you want to search for someone on the Web, click the Look In down-arrow and choose the people search engine that you want to use.**

4. **Enter any information about the person you want to find in the Name, E-mail, Address, Phone, or Other field.**

5. **Click Find Now to start the search.**

Know your people searches

Outlook Express offers you a number of helpful services when you want to find someone online. When you click the Look In down-arrow, you see services similar to the following:

- Bigfoot Internet Directory Service
- InfoSpace Business Directory Service
- InfoSpace Internet Directory Service

- VeriSign Internet Directory Service
- WhoWhere Internet Directory Service

You may show different services in the list on your machine, but they all do the same thing. Each of these services attempts to locate the person you're looking for and displays the findings in a results window.

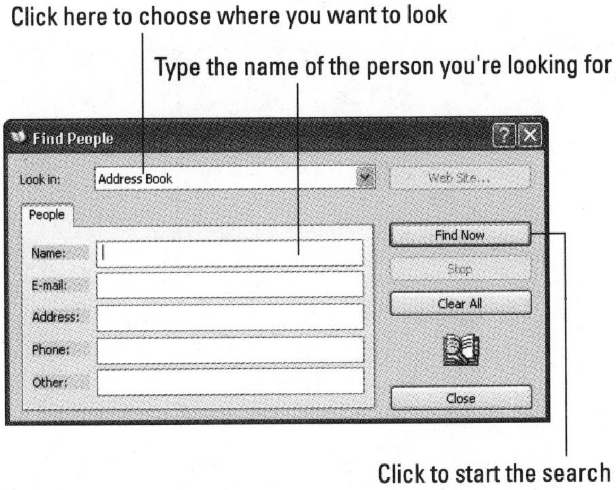

Click here to choose where you want to look

Type the name of the person you're looking for

Figure 2-8:
Finding
people near
and far.

Click to start the search

**Book III
Chapter 2**

**Outlook Express:
Your Tool for
Managing E-Mail
and Newsgroups**

Creating groups

If you often want to send e-mail to large groups of people at once, you can create a group in Outlook Express. For example, suppose that you want to send the latest Dilbert cartoon to all the people on your international sales staff. You would follow these steps:

1. **Display the Address Book by clicking Address Book in the Outlook Express toolbar.**

2. **Click the New button.**

A submenu appears.

3. **Click the New Group option.**

The Properties dialog box opens with the Group tab displayed (see Figure 2-9).

Enter the name for the group you want to create

Figure 2-9:
You can easily create a group to handle bulk e-mail.

Click Select Members to choose the people for your group

4. **Enter the name of the group that you want to create.**

5. **Click the Select Members button to choose the people that you want to include in your group.**

The Select Group Members dialog box appears.

6. **Select names by clicking the ones you want in the window on the left, and then click the Select button to add the names to the Members list on the right.**

If you want to select multiple names, press and hold **Ctrl** while you click additional names. When you click Select, all the highlighted names are copied to the list on the right.

7. **Click OK when you're finished.**

Your group is created.

Romping through Newsgroups

Outlook Express is also a newsreader, which means you can subscribe to and post to Internet newsgroups without ever leaving your e-mail program. A newsgroup is a bulletin-board-like list that may be organized around any number of different topics. Newsgroups are often unmoderated, which means that anybody can essentially say anything (and often they do).

Don't believe anything you hear and only half of what you see. And don't believe anything at all that you see posted on a newsgroup until you've had a chance to verify it ten ways from Tuesday.

Still, you can find some good information in newsgroups. You may be able to find a topic that interests you — professionally or personally. This section explains various ways to set up and work with newsgroups in Outlook Express.

Setting up Outlook Express News

When you first begin working with Outlook Express, the newsreader is not installed by default. You have to tell Windows XP that you want to use the newsreader before it is made available to you. Here are the steps to get things set up:

1. **Start Outlook Express.**

2. **Choose Tools⇔Accounts.**

   The Internet Accounts dialog box appears.

3. **Click the News tab.**

4. **Click the Add button and choose News.**

   This launches the Internet Connection Wizard.

5. **When prompted, enter the name of your news server (you may need to get this from your Internet Service Provider), and click Finish.**

   The news server is added to the News tab of the Internet Accounts dialog box.

   To stay on top of the latest on Windows XP and other Microsoft products, you may want to make sure that you have the "official" Microsoft newsgroups available. If your ISP doesn't have you covered already, add the news server called `msnews.microsoft.com`.

6. **Click Close to complete the operation.**

   A message appears asking whether you would like to download newsgroups from the news account you added. If you want to add newsgroups, click OK; otherwise, click No.

**Book III
Chapter 2**

Outlook Express:
Your Tool for
Managing E-Mail
and Newsgroups

TIP

Downloading all the newsgroups takes a few minutes, but it's worth the wait. You get the list that Outlook Express uses to let you know what's available, so you have to download it sooner or later if you want to subscribe to newsgroups.

Subscribing to newsgroups

After you set up Outlook Express to work with newsgroups, the name of your news server appears at the bottom of the Outlook Express list in the Folders panel. When you're ready to subscribe to newsgroups, click the news server name.

Outlook Express displays a message telling you that you have not yet subscribed to any newsgroups for this account. If you want to see a list of newsgroups, click Yes. The Newsgroup Subscriptions dialog box is displayed (see Figure 2-10).

You can use two different ways to find the newsgroups that you're interested in:

✦ Type a word or phrase in the text box at the top of the dialog box.

✦ Scroll through the list and hope that something catches your eye.

Click Subscribe to add the newsgroup to your list

Type a word or phrase you're interested in

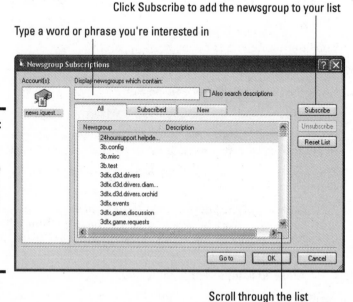

Figure 2-10:
You can
scroll
through the
newsgroup
list and see
what
captures
your
interest.

Scroll through the list

When you find a group that you want to join, click Subscribe. You can repeat the process for as many newsgroups as you want to add. When you're finished subscribing to newsgroups, click OK to close the dialog box.

Looking at messages

Now that you've set up the newsreader and subscribed to groups, you read messages whenever you want. The newsgroups are listed in the Outlook Express Folders panel, as shown in Figure 2-11.

To have Outlook Express check for new messages on your subscribed newsgroup, click Synchronize Account. The newsreader searches the newsgroups for new messages and lets you know which ones are unread.

To search for messages on specific topics, take advantage of the enormous database maintained by on the Web by Google at `groups.google.com`. It's one of the Internet's best-kept secrets.

To choose a newsgroup, double-click the newsgroup name. The messages appear in the panel on the top right of the newsgroup window.

Click Synchronize Account to download new messages

Book III
Chapter 2

Outlook Express:
Your Tool for
Managing E-Mail
and Newsgroups

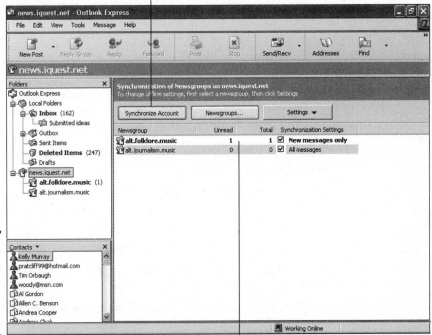

Figure 2-11:
Working with the newly subscribed newsgroups.

Double-click a newsgroup to view postings

Newsgroup manners

Some newsgroups are moderated (meaning that somebody's watching and sifting through the messages before they're made available at large), but most are not. As a result, newsgroups can get rude, raunchy, and mean. If you want to participate in helpful, respectful newsgroups, you can do your part by following these simple newsgroup rules:

- **Don't flame.** A flame is an inappropriately angry message directed at a specific person. Take a walk around the block. Do some push-ups. Don't flame.

- **DON'T SHOUT!** Typing in all uppercase is the same as shouting in the online world.

- **Don't answer inflammatory or obscene messages.** If your group has a case of the nasties, avoid making even sarcastic comments back. The less said to those kinds of postings, the better.

- **Don't get fancy.** Nobody wants to see decorative fonts, colorful backgrounds, or HTML messages in a newsgroup posting. Why? Because of the time they take the download (and the differences in our personal tastes). To stay on everybody's good side (which often isn't easy to do in newsgroups), keep it plain and simple with straight text.

To view a message in a newsgroup, double-click it. The message opens in a message window. You can then reply to the group, reply to the individual, forward the message to another person, print the message, move to the previous or next message, or display your Address Book.

Posting your own messages

After you've lurked for a while, you may decide to jump in the fray and cast your wisdom upon the waters. When you post a newsgroup message to the group, anyone who logs on to the newsgroup will be able to read it. To create a newsgroup message, follow these steps:

1. **Launch the newsreader by clicking the newsreader name in the Outlook Express Folders panel.**

2. **Select the newsgroup that you want to post to.**

   You may want to click Synchronize Account first to make sure that you've downloaded the most recent messages.

3. **Click New Post in the far left side of the Outlook Express toolbar.**

   What looks like a typical e-mail message window opens with the name of the newsgroup displayed in the top line.

4. **Enter a subject for the message and then type the body of the message.**

5. **Click Send to post the message to the group.**

Index

Book IV

Adventures with Internet Explorer

The 5th Wave By Rich Tennant

"This is amazing. You can stop looking for Derek. According to an MSN search I did, he's hiding behind the dryer in the basement."

Contents at a Glance

Chapter 1: Connecting to the Internet

In This Chapter

✔ **Before you connect**

✔ **Finding your modem**

✔ **Adding dial-up connections**

✔ **Making the connection**

✔ **Trouble spots and workarounds**

his chapter explains how to get connected with Internet Explorer (IE), the Web browser that comes (surprise, surprise) packaged with your version of Windows XP/Home Edition — at least until a Federal judge says otherwise.

Connecting with IE is, thankfully, a pretty straightforward process. You aren't likely to encounter many superhuman challenges along the way — perhaps an unrecognized modem or a misplaced password, but nothing insurmountable. This chapter walks you through the basics of making that initial IE connection and helps you anticipate and hopefully avoid any potential trouble spots on your path.

You may already be an old hand at making Internet connections (especially if you've already read Book III). If that's the case, go to the head of the class and move along to the next chapter.

Before You Connect

The idea that anyone in this day and Internet-age would own a computer without a modem is really unthinkable, but I suppose it's possible. If you have an older system (or you purchased one on the corner from a guy named Fingers), you may want to check and make sure that your system has what it takes to connect using Windows XP. This section shows you how to find your modem and ensure that you have what you need before connecting.

What types of modems are out there?

I'm old enough to remember the types of modems that you placed in little receiver cups (back in the days when our phones actually had curved mouthpieces and earpieces). Today, we have streamlined, small, and often invisible (that is, inside-the-computer) modems of varying speeds and styles. If you find that you're fascinated with modems and want to find out more about them, you'll discover a number of different modem types:

- **Internal modems** plug into the motherboard of your computer and provide a modem port somewhere on the back or side of your system unit or laptop. You plug the traditional phone cord into the slot and away you go.

- **External modems** are devices that are attached to your computer through a serial, parallel, or USB port on the back or side of the unit. You plug the modem into the computer at the appropriate point (your

computer's manual can tell you where), and then you plug the phone cord into the right spot on the modem.

- **Cable modems** can be either internal or external modems, and they enable our burgeoning cable television industry to offer us broadband connections that are usually faster and more reliable than traditional dial-ups through your average phone lines.

- **DSL** (Digital Subscriber Line) modems are special kinds of modems that allow for a broadband (wide and fast) connection. These modems can be internal or external; the external ones need a network adapter.

- **ISDN** modems are special modems created to work with ISDN lines — high-speed digital cabling that must be installed by your phone company or service provider.

Finding your modem

If you want to see what Windows XP thinks your modem of choice is, you can get a quick glimpse by getting into the Control Panel, like this:

1. **Choose Start⇨Control Panel⇨Printers and Other Hardware⇨ Phone and Modem Options.**

2. **Click the Modems tab.**

   Is a modem listed? Eureka! You're ready to rumble.

If you want to install drivers for another modem, you can click Add in the Modems tab of the Phone and Modem Options dialog box to start the process. Simply have the disk or CD that came with your modem handy (or know where the driver files are stored on your hard drive), and Windows XP prompts you for the information that it needs as the drivers are installed.

What's the big deal about bandwidth? If you're just now learning about the phenomena of pushing pictures, words, and sound through your phone lines into your PC, you may not understand the fuss over bandwidth issues. Put simply, *bandwidth* is the size of the channel through which the data can flow.

The larger the channel, the more data can flow through at the same time. When you hear people talking at parties about "increasing bandwidth" and dropping terms like "broadband connections," "ISDN," and "T-1 lines," realize that what they really want is more data, sent (and received) faster.

Do you have an ISP?

An ISP, or Internet Service Provider, is the mysterious link between you and all of the Internet world. This kindly, elderly person — er, large, hulking mainframe computer — is the presence that accepts your computer's incoming calls and passes the necessary data to and from the sites you visit and the e-mail accounts you use.

Before you begin to explore the Internet, you need to establish a relationship with an ISP. The Internet Service Provider will most likely give you the following:

✦ A phone number to use to dial in to the ISP's system

✦ A user name (also called a user ID) that you use to identify yourself

✦ A password, to ensure that other people can't use your user name

If you're going to use your ISP for e-mail, you should receive some more information:

✦ Your e-mail address, like woody@wopr.com or billg@microsoft.com

✦ The names of the computers that are used to send and receive mail (so-called POP3 and SMTP servers), such as pop3.email.msn.com or secure.smtp.email.msn.com

✦ Any special user names, passwords, or other instructions that you need to get connected to the computers that send and receive your mail

Frequently ISPs give you even more information — designed to help people running Macs or old versions of Windows — but you probably won't need it:

✦ The numeric IP addresses you need in order to log on to your ISP's server

✦ The domain name and DNS address

✦ A CD or disk with any software needed to log on to the ISP site

Some CDs are packed with junk. No, you don't need a seven-year-old version of Eudora, thank you very much. Other CDs, though, are designed to help you through Windows setup options, as detailed in the next section. That's the kind of CD worth having.

Many ISPs also give you a certain amount of Web storage space, in case you want to create your own Web page.

If you don't already have an account with an ISP, you can establish one through Windows — and give Bill G. the bounty — or you can go shopping for an account that you select yourself. You see how in the section, "Creating a New Connection," later in this chapter.

One of the best ways to find a reputable ISP is to ask friends, family, and coworkers who they use. Stay away from the ISPs everyone complains about — no matter how low their rates or how great their "free access" offers may sound. Remember: a day without Internet access is a day without sunshine.

Creating a New Connection

Ah, if only Windows were smart enough to apply plug-and-play technology to our phone lines, we'd never need to mess with setting up another Internet account. We could just plug in the phone line and let Windows figure the rest out for us. Windows XP doesn't make it quite that easy, but it does include a New Connection wizard that takes care of most of the dirty work. You simply follow the prompts on-screen, answer a few questions, click a few buttons, and you are online. Here's the process in a nutshell:

1. **Choose Start⇨My Network Places.**

2. **In the Network Tasks pane, choose View Network Connections.**

    The Network Connections window appears, showing existing dial-up and network connections on the current computer (see Figure 1-1).

3. **Click Create a New Connection.**

    This launches the New Connection Wizard.

At first glance, you may think that the choice you want in My Network Places is Add Network Place, but don't be fooled: The option you're looking for is Create New Connection. Add Network Place launches a wizard that signs you up for an online storage service — but it's not your doorway to the Internet.

The opening screen appears, telling you that the wizard will lead you through the steps necessary to connect to the Internet, connect to a private network, or set up a network in your home or small office. Click Next to get started with the fun stuff.

Click to launch the wizard   Existing dial-up connections

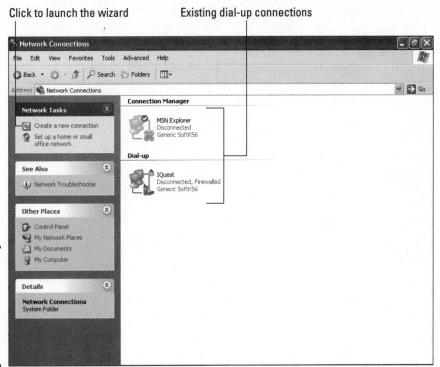

Figure 1-1:
Launch
the New
Connection
Wizard from
the Network
Tasks pane.

Four choices then greet you on the next page of the wizard. The first one is the one you want: Connect to the Internet. When you click it and click Next, the screen shown in Figure 1-2 appears.

The three different choices on the Getting Ready screen are important because they each launch different paths. Make your choice and click Next. Here's how they are different:

✦ **Choose from a List of Internet Service Providers (ISPs)** gives you the option of choosing MSN Explorer (not that you're in a captive audience or anything); if you opt out of that, you're presented with three additional choices (still the big three: America Online, Prodigy, and Earthlink). See the next section for more detail on choosing a new ISP.

✦ **Set Up My Connection Manually** takes you to a screen that gives you the choice of creating a standard dial-up connection (like the one you use if you have a regular-old modem in a plain-old PC). You can also elect to connect to a broadband connection or use a broadband connection that is always active (no sign-in required). Take a look at the section, "The ins and outs of dial-up configuration," later in this chapter, for specifics on completing this step.

Manually enter ISP information

Choose a new ISP from the list

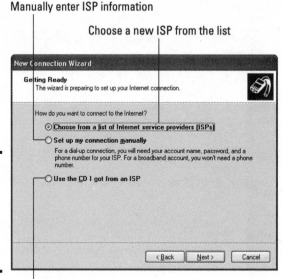

Figure 1-2:
Choose the
way in
which you
want to set
up your
connection.

Load the CD provided by your ISP

✦ **Use the CD I Got from an ISP** displays a screen that prompts you to
  insert the CD and click Finish; the setup program then launches and
  leads you through the connection process. This is so simple that your
  cat can do it — no further explanation necessary.

Depending on the configuration of your particular system, you may not see
these three options. If not, don't sweat it — the process will take you right
on into the next step.

ISP selection, Windows-style

If you decide that you want to choose one of the Windows-offered ISPs by
selecting Choose from a list of Internet Service Providers (ISPs) and clicking
Next, Windows displays a few additional options (see Figure 1-3).

If you're fine with setting up your Internet access through MSN, you can leave
the first option selected and click Finish to complete the wizard. MSN then
steps in with a message box asking whether you want to get on the Internet
with MSN Explorer. Click Yes to continue and establish your account.

If you want to see the other ISPs that are available to you (I'll give you a
hint — their nicknames are AOL, Prodigy, and Earthlink), click Select from
a list of other ISPs, and then click Finish. Folders appear for each of the
three ISP offerings; you also find a link that launches the Internet
Connection Wizard, which takes you online to find more ISPs.

Click to see other ISP possibilities

Click to use MSN Explorer as your ISP

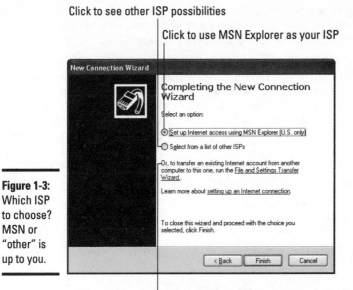

Figure 1-3:
Which ISP
to choose?
MSN or
"other" is
up to you.

Use a wizard that transfers an Internet account from another system

If you have an existing Internet account on another PC that you want to make available on this PC, and the two PCs are connected, click the File and Settings Transfer Wizard to launch a wizard that walks you through the process of transferring files. Before you start, make sure that the two PCs are connected, and close any open applications.

The ins and outs of dial-up configuration

No, this isn't as geeky as it sounds. If you have an existing Internet dial-up account and you want to use that information on this computer, you can simply enter the information manually and save all the fuss and bother. Don't sweat it — it's simple. Here are the steps:

1. **In the Getting Ready screen of the New Connection Wizard, click Set up my connection manually; then click Next.**

2. **When the Internet Connection screen appears, choose whether you want to use a dial-up modem, a broadband connection that you dial into, or a broadband connection that is always active. Again, click Next.**

3. **Enter the phone number that your modem will dial to access the ISP. (This step is for dial-up modems only.) Click Next.**

**Book IV
Chapter 1**

**Connecting to
the Internet**

4. **In the Internet Account Information screen (see Figure 1-4), enter the User Name for your account and the password you were given. Retype the password in the Confirm Password box.**

You may want to deselect one or all of the three options selected by default in the Internet Account Information window. If you need flexible settings for your connections that allow multiple users to use your system or that enable users to select from various ISPs, you may find these options more of a hindrance than a help. If you leave the options selected, the account name and password you entered will be used automatically for all users of your computer, the current Internet connection will be the one used for all connections, and the Internet Connection Firewall will be used for connections made using this account.

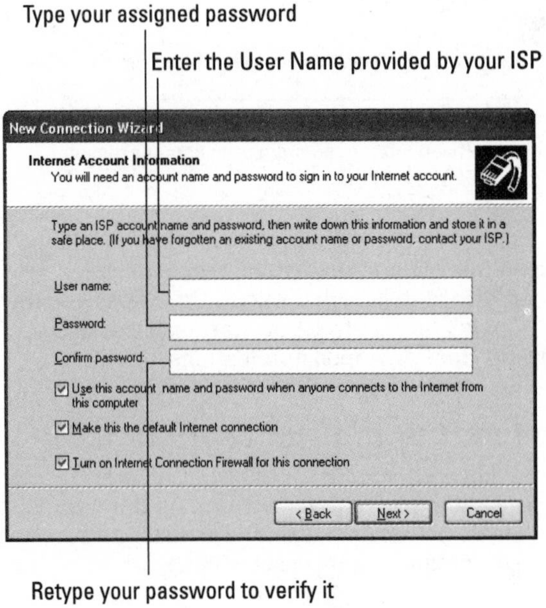

Type your assigned password

Enter the User Name provided by your ISP

Figure 1-4:
When
creating a
new dial-up
connection,
enter the
user name
and
password
provided by
the ISP.

> **New Connection Wizard**
>
> **Internet Account Information**
> You will need an account name and password to sign in to your Internet account.
>
> Type an ISP account name and password, then write down this information and store it in a safe place. (If you have forgotten an existing account name or password, contact your ISP.)
>
> User name:
>
> Password:
>
> Confirm password:
>
> ☑ Use this account name and password when anyone connects to the Internet from this computer
> ☑ Make this the default Internet connection
> ☑ Turn on Internet Connection Firewall for this connection
>
> [< Back] [Next >] [Cancel]

Retype your password to verify it

Click Next to move to the last screen of the wizard. Here you have the option to click a checkbox that creates an Internet shortcut on your desktop. If you want to create the shortcut, click the checkbox, and then click Finish.

This completes the New Connection Wizard, and Windows XP begins the process of making your dial-up connection.

Getting Connected

Okay, so you've finished the techie part. It's all downhill from here. At the end of the New Connection Wizard, Windows XP automatically displays the Connect Dial-up Connection dialog box so that you can enter the information that you need in order to make the connection (see Figure 1-5).

Click here to save the User Name and password
for subsequent dial-ups

Enter your password

Type your assigned User Name

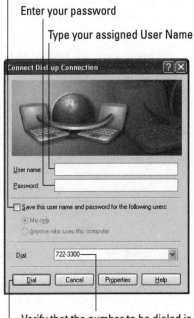

Figure 1-5:
To make the
connection,
just fill in the
info and
click Dial.

Verify that the number to be dialed is correct

Click dial

Enter the User Name and Password that your ISP provided. If you want the information to be retained so that you don't have to type it each time you go online, click the Save This User Name and Password for the Following Users checkbox. After you click the option, the sub-options become available; now you can choose whether you want the information to be saved for only you or for anyone who may use your computer.

Take a look at the Dial number to make sure that your modem will dial the right number. You can click the Dial down-arrow to see any other available access numbers; click the one you want.

Finally, click Dial. Your modem dials the number shown and establishes the connection to the Internet. Time to celebrate! Get up, walk around, tell your neighbor, open a Snapple — but don't forget to come back. The fun is just beginning!

Uh-Ohs and Their Answers

Even with all the best-laid plans in the world, sometimes unexpected glitches crop up. If your connection doesn't go smoothly the first time, don't despair. With a little trial and error, you'll be able to get around the difficulty and get online in no time. Here are a few possibilities that you can check out if things aren't going your way:

+ **"I'm not getting a dial tone."** This is a scary problem but usually something simple, such as a not-quite-connected phone line. First, check your hardware connections. Is the phone line plugged into the wall and all the way into the computer? Next, make sure you're using a functioning phone cord. Phone cords sometimes get a small stress break somewhere near the middle. You can also try plugging a phone into the connector to make sure the phone line is working the way it should. If none of those things is the problem, run the diagnostics on your modem (see "I don't think my modem is working properly," below) to sleuth out the problem.

+ **"My ISP isn't answering."** Was it something you said? If not, check the clock. If you are dialing into your ISP at a time of high traffic — usually between 8:00 a.m. and 10:00 a.m. and between 1:00 p.m. and 2:00 p.m. — your ISP may simply be swamped with incoming calls. Get yourself a cup of coffee and try again in a few minutes. If you try continually and are unable to get a rise out of your ISP, give their tech support line a call. The server may be down or — worst-case scenario — your modem could be failing and not giving the ISP's server the "handshake" it's looking for.

+ **"I can't connect."** Make sure that you've entered your User Name and Password correctly. (Most common source of problems: Caps Lock is turned on when you type your password.) Also, double-check the telephone number that your modem is dialing. Finally, check your ISP information, including the IP address or DNS, if your ISP insisted that you enter those numbers manually. When all else fails, call your ISP and ask them to walk you through the connection process. That's what tech support is for.

+ **"I don't think my modem is working properly."** If you fail to get a dial tone and your modem shows no signs of life, you can run diagnostics to take your modem's pulse and check its overall health. To test your modem, choose Start⇨Control Panel⇨Printers and Other Hardware. Next, click Phone and Modem Options. When the Phone and Modem Options dialog box appears, click the Modems tab. Your installed modem should be displayed in the Modem box. Double-click it to have Windows XP quickly run diagnostics. The results are displayed in the Device status area of the General tab (see Figure 1-6). If you have continuing problems, click the Troubleshoot button to have Windows help you explore further solutions.

Click the modem tab to run diagnostics

Results of the diagnostic test appear here

Figure 1-6:
You can easily run diagnostics if your modem is misbehaving.

1. **Select the Modem tab**

2. **Double-click the modem to start the test**

3. **Windows XP displays the results of the test**

4. **Click Troubleshoot to see more suggestions**

✦ **"My connection suddenly disconnects."** If you lose your connection repeatedly, the problem may be between your modem and your ISP. Check with your modem manufacturer to see whether software updates exist that would improve the consistency of the connection.

Book IV
Chapter 1

Connecting to
the Internet

Chapter 2: Finding Your Way around the Internet Explorer Window

In This Chapter

✔ Ready, set, browse!

✔ A walk around the IE window

✔ Finding your way around the Web

✔ Doing stuff with Web pages

✔ IE hide and seek

This chapter explains how to find your way around the Web using Internet Explorer (IE). The last chapter ended with that delicious moment when you heard your computer make contact with your ISP's computer. After that connection is made, the Connect box disappears (which means you're on!) and you're ready to make your computer actually *do* something. If that "something" involves browsing the Web, your next step is to launch Internet Explorer.

But before you go foraging in unknown worlds, stop a moment and reflect on what you've done. With a few simple clicks and a ready phone line, you've just joined with the Internet — a virtual world filled with just about any kind of information you may want (or not want) to find. All kinds of adventures are before you. But before you leave home, be sure to do two important things: (1) back up any files that are supremely important to you; and (2) install a virus checker that can net out any bugs you may catch while trading or downloading files. For more information on protecting your system from unfriendly inhabitants, see Book IX, Chapter 3.

Ready, Set, Browse!

As soon as you've made the connection with your ISP, you can begin your browsing session. You use Internet Explorer to do this. You have two different ways to launch IE:

✦ Click the Internet Explorer icon in the Taskbar.

✦ Choose Start⇨Internet (see Figure 2-1). Internet Explorer launches and fills your Windows work area.

Choose Start⇨Internet to start the program using menu sections

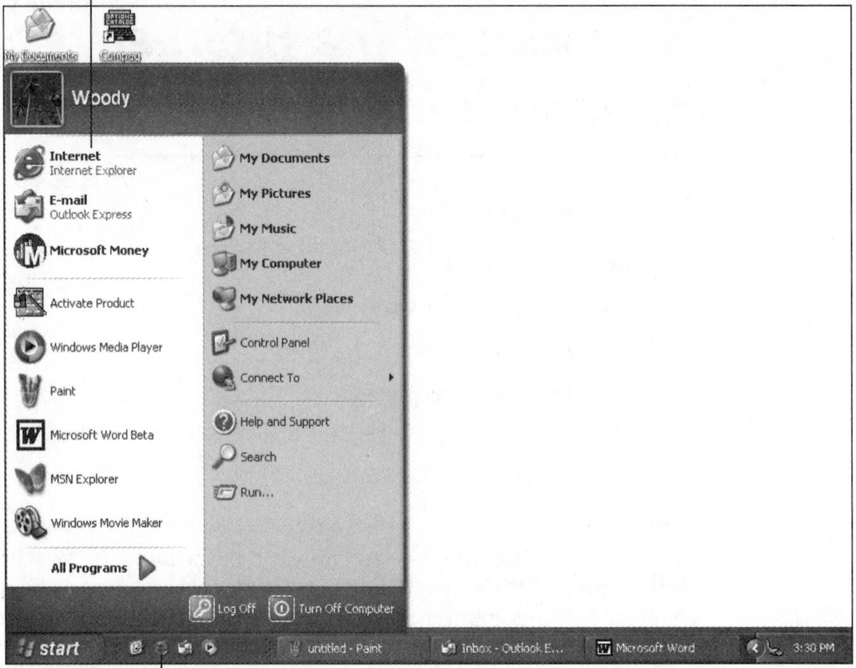

Figure 2-1:
Launch
Microsoft
Internet
Explorer
from the
Start menu
or the
Taskbar.

Click the Internet Explorer icon to launch the program

Internet Explorer launches, and after a relatively brief moment (depending on the speed of your PC), a page of Web information appears. What that page contains depends on whether your computer is set up to begin with a specific page, called a home page (most PC manufacturers set the home page display to something related to their systems). But not to worry — even if the initial page holds nothing of interest to you, you're almost ready to begin surfing the Web and visiting sites of your own choosing. (I show you how to change that pesky manufacturer's screen to a home page that you really want to see in the section called "Going Home.")

A Walk around the IE Window

One of the great things about Internet Explorer is that you can be an absolute no-clue beginner, and, with just a few hints about tools and such, you can find your way around the Web like a pro. Figure 2-2 gives you a diagram of the basic layout of the Internet Explorer window. As you can see, IE packs lots of possibilities in that small space. The items you'll use most often are these:

✦ **Menu bar:** Contains six menus: File, Edit, View, Favorites, Tools, and Help. Each menu includes a different set of commands related to working with Web sites. (See Table 2-1 for a description of the various menus.)

✦ **Standard toolbar:** Includes tools you use to find your way around on the Web and work with the Web pages that you find. (See Table 2-2 for an overview of the tools on the Standard toolbar.)

✦ **Address bar:** Enables you to enter the Web address of a page that you want to move to directly.

✦ **Links bar:** A customizable (meaning you can put your own favorite links on it if you choose) bar that gives you quick access to sites you visit often.

✦ **Browse window:** The part of the window that displays the Web pages you visit.

✦ **Status bar:** Displays information about Web pages, links, or actions that you can take while visiting a site.

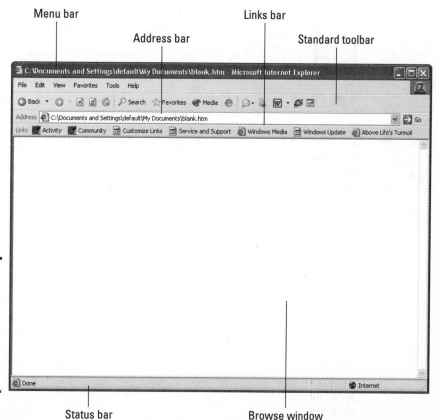

Menu bar

Links bar

Address bar

Standard toolbar

Figure 2-2: The IE window includes everything you need to work the Web.

Status bar

Browse window

Checking out IE menus

So who needs menus anymore? With all the buttons and links and clickable things on the screen, you may wonder why you need to spend time opening menus and selecting commands. Even though you can do many of the most common Web tasks right from the IE window — such as printing, adding Web pages to your Favorites folders, searching for information, and moving to new pages — you can carry out a number of operations only by using the IE menus. Table 2-1 gives you an introduction to the various menus, so that you know what to use when.

Table 2-1	The Fare on Internet Explorer Menus
Menu	*Description*
File	Contains commands that enable you to open, edit, save, print, send, and import and export "Favorites" entries and cookies to and from other browsers.
Edit	Lets you select, cut, copy, paste, and find text on the current Web page.
View	Houses the commands that control the display of the IE window. You can display and hide toolbars, change the text size, display the browser window in full-screen size, move to another page, and refresh the current page.
Favorites	Contains all the preset Favorites folders in which you can save the pages you visit. Additionally, you use the commands in this menu to add your own favorites and organize the existing favorites.
Tools	Includes the commands you use to send and receive mail, synchronize your data, update Windows, show links, search for other pages, and more.
Help	Provides help in whatever form you most need it — in the traditional contents and index display, as a tip of the day, or as online help.

There's no secret to using menus — just point your mouse at the menu that you want to open and click. If you're a keyboard person, you can press and hold the Alt key to see the underscored characters in the menu names. When the underscores appear, type the letter corresponding to the menu that you want to open, bypassing the mouse completely.

Unpacking the Standard toolbar

That bar of buttons stretching across the width of the IE window (just beneath the menu bar) isn't just a pretty, colorful collection of decorative items. Those are tools that you can use to accomplish things on the Web. Check out Table 2-2 to see what those colorful little buttons can do for you.

Table 2-2	The Right Tools for the Job	
Tool	*Name*	*Description*
Back ▾	Back	Moves to the previous Web page
➜ ▾	Forward	Moves to the page following the current one in the sequence you have selected
✖	Stop	Stops the loading of the current page
⟳	Refresh	Updates the display of the current page
🏠	Home	Returns to the page you have set as the home page for your system
Search	Search	Displays the Search Companion so that you can look for specific information
Favorites	Favorites	Opens the Favorites panel so that you can choose, add to, or organize your favorite Web site
Media	Media	Displays the Media panel so that you can sample music, radio, movies, and more
History	History	Opens the History panel so that you can select Web pages you've visited previously
Mail ▾	Mail	Enables you to send and receive e-mail and to send Web pages and links from IE
Print	Print	Prints the current Web page
W ▾	Edit	Launches an editor (such as Notepad or Microsoft Word)
Translate	Translate	Enables you to browse sites written in other languages
Full Screen	Full Screen	Hides the menu bar and toolbar, displaying the current Web page in full screen view

Right now you're just learning, but later on, you may be in the mood for a toolbar change. You can create your own custom toolbar buttons and rearrange the toolbars to appear the way you want them. To find out more, see Book IV, Chapter 4.

Displaying the Tip of the Day

If you're new to this whole browsing thing and you want to have a little help along the way, you can turn on IE's Tip of the Day feature. The tips appear in the bottom portion of your screen, which takes up a little real estate, but they provide simple suggestions that you can try as you work.

To display the Tip of the Day, follow these steps:

1. **Choose Help in the menu bar.**

   The Help menu opens.

2. **Click Tip of the Day.**

   A new pane opens just above the status bar at the bottom of the Internet Explorer window (see Figure 2-3).

3. **Review the tip and then, if you want to see another tip, click Next Tip.**

   If you want to close the tip box, click the Close button to the left of the tip area.

Exploring Web Pages

Everybody wants to be on the Web, and chances are — unless you've been living in a remote corner of the world somewhere — you've already had at least some experience with Web surfing. I see Web page addresses, called URLs (a geeky acronym for Uniform Resource Locator) plastered all over everything — from bumper stickers and mud flaps to billboards and gum labels. And this proliferation is the same all over the world. Web sites give us the ability to find out more about a company, a product, a person, or a place. We can find out about health issues, read news stories, make travel arrangements, and more. When you first begin to surf the Web, the possibilities seem limitless. And, believe me, unless you start out with a plan, you can float around out there in Massive Information Overload Land until the dog, the kids, or the alarm clock brings you back to reality.

So your best bet is to start with a plan. Where do you want to go and what do you want to find? You may want to do one (or all) of the following things:

✦ **Go to a specific site:** Want to check out the online presence of a new employer you're considering? Or perhaps you want to enter the Go-to-Greece! contest being offered by your local grocery store.

Display tips by choosing Help⇨Tip of the Day

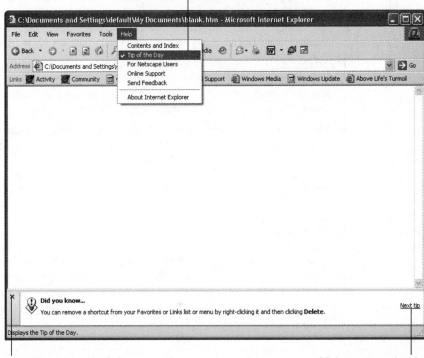

Figure 2-3:
You can
display tips
to help you
learn your
way around
IE faster.

Click here to hide the tip area

Click to see another tip

✦ **Search for information:** You can use various search engines to enter a word or a phrase and get the addresses of dozens — or hundreds — of Web sites with the information you seek.

✦ **Listen to Internet radio while you work:** A number of sites — some of them traditional on-air radio stations — now use Internet technology to broadcast radio programs through streaming audio.

✦ **Make travel arrangements:** All the major airlines — and numerous other travel companies — now offer travel packages online.

✦ **Check your stocks:** Again, you have your choice of brokerage firms — from the largest to the smallest — available online. Some Web sites offer you a stock ticker as a downloadable option, which enables you to check how your stocks are doing while you work (assuming, of course, you *are* working . . .).

✦ **Hold a business meeting:** Sound impossible? Not anymore. Web conferencing has made real the opportunity to meet with people in a virtual conference room and share ideas, review presentations, and even have private conversations that the rest of the group doesn't hear.

**Book IV
Chapter 2**

**Finding Your Way
around the Internet
Explorer Window**

✦ **Watch a preview of a new movie:** Not sure that you want to spend the exorbitant price on movie tickets without an ironclad guarantee that the movie will be worth the price of admission? You can now go to movie sites galore to watch trailers and behind-the-scenes clips of popular movies. (Check out www.catsanddogsmovie.com for a site that's *better* than a movie!)

✦ **Check up on your competitors:** Oh come on, admit it. That's the first site you visited, right? You have to keep tabs on the mom-and-pop store down the block that undercuts your price on lip balm.

✦ **Find new math games for your kids:** Who wants to sit and go through math drills with third graders all day long? Free, downloadable math games are out there on the Web for your choosing. Check them out, and load them up. Your kids will think they're fun — and maybe even learn something.

Web page basics

Depending on the sites you visit, you may be greeted by a variety of things: pictures, text, advertisements, and more. Those various elements enable you to interact with the sites in different ways: Some Web sites are there for your entertainment; others want to sell you something; others give you the opportunity to chat or play games; and still others offer links to additional information and services.

Figure 2-4 shows the screen that appears on my computer by default when Internet Explorer is launched for the first time. As you can see, this page offers lots of different experiences.

Understanding links

Clicking any of the items highlighted in Figure 2-4 causes an action to happen because each of those items are *links* — connections that take you to another page or carry out a programmed event (such as starting your e-mail program). You may notice a number of links that look different on Web pages that you visit, but most fall into one of two categories: text links or graphics links.

✦ A text link can be a word, phrase, tag, or menu item.

✦ A graphics link can be a picture, button, map, photo, drawing, or some other art item.

How can you tell a text link from regular text? Text links usually appear in a color different from the surrounding text, and, in many cases, the linked text is underlined. You can prove that a text phrase or an image is in fact a link by positioning the mouse pointer over the phrase. If the pointer changes to the hand pointer, you know you're hovering over a link. In Figure 2-5, a number of text links — both underlined and nonunderlined — appear. Additionally, several graphics links are used to take you to additional pages in the site.

Find out more about helping Red Cross

Click a category to find related information

Get help on using this page

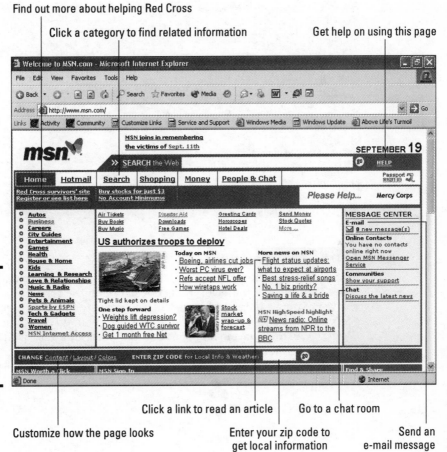

Figure 2-4: Internet Explorer starts by displaying the default page, MSN.

Customize how the page looks

Click a link to read an article

Go to a chat room

Enter your zip code to get local information

Send an e-mail message

Book IV
Chapter 2

Finding Your Way around the Internet Explorer Window

Text links   Graphics links

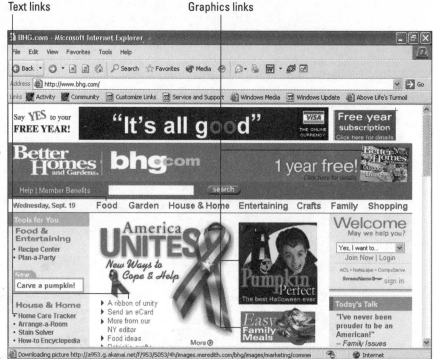

Figure 2-5:
This site,
which is
included
in the
Favorites
with
Windows
XP, includes
a number of
different
types of
links.

Scroll around the town

If you've used computers for any length of time at all, you've made your peace with the fact that everything doesn't fit on the screen at one time. If you're creating a letter, you have to scroll down to add your signature line. If you've been working on an Excel spreadsheet, you're accustomed to paging down to create a chart in an open area of the workbook. Now that you're becoming proficient at Web surfing, you'll find that more often than not, you have to scroll down to the bottom of the page in order to see all the text and graphics displayed there.

So how do you scroll? Two different ways:

✦ Press PgDn.

✦ Drag the scroll box in the vertical scrollbar (along the right edge of the IE window) downward, toward the bottom of the window.

You can maximize the amount of information on-screen by displaying IE in Full Screen view. To do this, choose View➪Full Screen or press F11. This removes all screen elements except the Standard toolbar. For more about working in Full Screen view, see Book IV, Chapter 4.

Moving to another page

When you've seen everything on the page and you're ready to move along, you can go to a new page by using one of several different options:

✦ Click in the Address text box and type the new Web page address; then click GO.

✦ Click a link on the current page to move to another page.

✦ Use one of the navigation buttons (Back, Forward, or Home), if they appear on the page, to move to another page relative to your current position.

Did you go to the wrong page? If you find that you entered the wrong address or you went to a page that wasn't where you meant to go, you can cancel the load operation by clicking the Stop button in the Standard toolbar. This halts the download process, during which IE transmits the text and graphics to your computer. As soon as you click Stop, you can re-enter the address of the Web page that you want to see.

Returning to a previous page

While you move from page to page, Internet Explorer remembers where you've been. Similar to dropping breadcrumbs, you don't ever have to worry about wanting to return to a Web place in your recent past. When you want to return to a page you saw previously, you can do so by clicking the Back button in the Standard toolbar (which takes you to the last page displayed before the current one).

If you want to return to a page that is further back in your memory than the most recent page, follow these steps:

1. Click the Address down-arrow.

A listing of previous sites appears.

2. Click the site that you want to see.

The site appears in the browser window.

When you search for past sites, you have another easy way to sift through pages that you saw weeks ago. You use the History button on the Standard toolbar to display folders storing the various pages from your recent history. For more about working with History folders, see Book IV, Chapter 3.

Going Home

Clicking Home in the Standard toolbar takes you back to the site that you entered as your home page — the page that appears automatically when you first launch Internet Explorer. If you didn't even know you *entered* a home page, you may still have the default configuration set up in your system. Want to take a look? The steps are simple:

1. **With Internet Explorer displayed on your screen, click Tools.**

   The Tools menu opens.

2. **Choose Internet Options.**

   The Internet Options dialog box appears (see Figure 2-6).

3. **If necessary, click the General tab.**

   You can then choose one of three options:

   • Click **Use Current** if you want to make the current Web page your home page.

   • Click **Use Default** if you want to return the home page selection to the page that was set on your computer when you first purchased it.

   • Click **Use Blank** if you want Internet Explorer to display no Web page at all — only a blank HTML page.

4. **Click Apply to apply the changes.**

5. **Click OK to close the Internet Options dialog box and return to the Web.**

Why would somebody want to load blankness? At first glance, it doesn't appear to make much sense to have a Web page load a screenful of nothing when you first log on. But some users prefer loading a blank page because the whole program loads faster, which puts you that much closer to doing the surfing you really want to do.

Doing Stuff with Web Pages

Now that you're beginning to find the pages you want to explore, you need to know what to do with them after you find them. When you find a page that you just can't let go — Aunt Edna in Des Moines just *has* to see that new gazpacho recipe! — you can do one of three different things with the page to make sure Aunt Edna enjoys the treasure you've found:

   ✦ E-mail the Web page to another person.

   ✦ Save the Web page for your own use.

   ✦ Print the Web page and mail, fax, or file it.

To save your current page as your home page

Type the home page you want here

To use original IE configuration

To use a blank home page

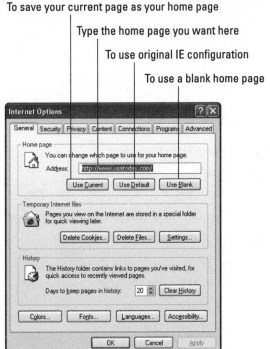

Figure 2-6:
You can
choose any
site on the
Web as your
home page.

The sections that follow take a closer look at each of these worthy goals.

E-mailing Web pages

What a boon — having e-mail capability right there in the IE Standard toolbar. When you've found a page you particularly like, you can e-mail the page to another user by clicking the Mail button and choosing Send Page from the drop-down submenu. This action launches your e-mail utility (which is most likely Outlook or Outlook Express, unless you've chosen something different). You can then select the To: recipient and click Send to send the page.

And that's not all. When you click the Mail button in the Standard toolbar, you see a number of different options: Read Mail, New Message, Send a Link, Send Page, and Read News. For more information on how to use your e-mail utility in Windows XP, see Book III, Chapter 1.

Saving Web pages

If you find one of those invaluable articles that backs up every argument you've ever made about buying quality running shoes (ammunition guaranteed to convince your mate), by all means, save it! Or — if you finally find

**Book IV
Chapter 2**

Finding Your Way
around the Internet
Explorer Window

that sparkling New! Icon you've seen on other peoples' sites, you can capture it to use on your own pages by saving the image to a file. This section explains how to save pages — and graphics items — for your own use later.

Saving to a file

There's no mystery to saving a Web page. It's not a whole lot different from saving any document in any program anywhere. Ready for the process? Don't blink — you may miss it:

1. **Display the Web page you want to save.**

2. **Open the File menu and click Save.**

   The Save Web Page dialog box appears (see Figure 2-7).

3. **Navigate to the folder in which you want to save the page.**

4. **Enter a name for the file if you want to change it.**

5. **Click Save.**

   Internet Explorer saves the file in the folder you specified.

Navigate to the folder in which you want to store the file

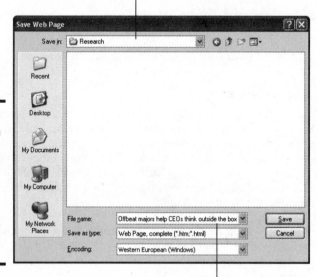

Figure 2-7: If you find a page that's particularly fetching, you can save it to your hard disk for later use.

Type a new name for the file if needed

Saving an image

Suppose that you run across a picture that you really love, or an icon that you must have, or a banner that you want to remember. You can save the image to your own hard disk by following these steps:

1. Right-click on the image that you want to save.

A shortcut menu appears (see Figure 2-8).

2. Click Save Picture As to display the Save As dialog box.

3. Navigate to the folder in which you want to save the file.

4. Enter a name for the file, if needed.

5. Click Save to save the file.

Right-click the image you want to save

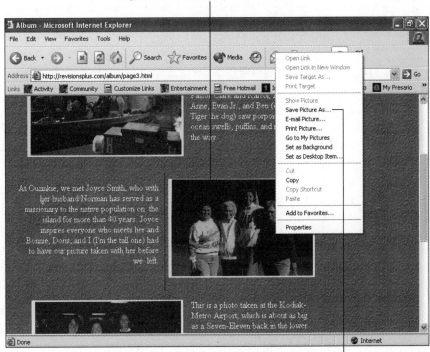

Figure 2-8:
Saving an image from a site

Select Save Picture As, enter a name, and click Save

A word about copyright. If you didn't create it yourself, it doesn't belong to you. Using images from the Web may be fine for your own personal use (sending a recipe to Aunt Edna is probably okay as well), but if you use images, text, ideas, pages, diagrams, music, or more as part of your business or as part of something you intend to make money on, you may be in danger of copyright violation. When in doubt, check it out.

Printing Web pages

Here's another simple one. When you display a page that you want to have a printed copy of, just click Print in the IE Standard toolbar, and Internet Explorer sends the current Web page to the printer. If you don't have a printer installed or connected, the program sends the file to the print queue where it sits, captive, until you connect the printer.

If you want to print only the current frame in a Web page that displays content in frames, simply right-click the frame and choose Print from the shortcut menu. The Print dialog box appears, and you can choose your printing options as needed. Click Print to send the frame to the printer.

Leaving and Returning to IE

Another great thing about working online is that you can easily move back and forth between applications in Windows XP. To minimize Internet Explorer while you go work on something else, click the Minimize button in the upper right corner of the window. Internet Explorer reduces to an item on the Taskbar.

When you want to restore the display of Internet Explorer, click the item in the Taskbar. If you have more than one Web page open, a shortcut menu of available pages appears (see Figure 2-9). Click the page that you want to see, and the IE window is restored to the screen. If you had only one page open, Internet Explorer opens as soon as you click its item in the Taskbar.

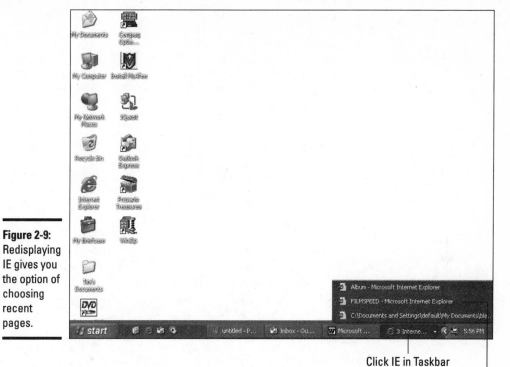

Figure 2-9:
Redisplaying
IE gives you
the option of
choosing
recent
pages.

Click IE in Taskbar

Choose the page you want to view

Chapter 3: Advanced Browsing and Searching with Internet Explorer

In This Chapter

✔ Reliving your past browses

✔ Saving sites for later

✔ Collecting your favorite things

✔ You'll never search alone

This chapter explains how to expand your Web horizons by capturing and organizing the sites you find and want to keep. You also discover how to look back over where you've been on the Web and find out how to search for your next leaps forward. The History, Favorites, and Search tools are the focus of this chapter, so get ready to take one step backward and two steps forward as you build up your IE muscles.

Going Back to the Past

Did you know that Windows knows where you've been on the Web? Depending on the sites you visit, this may be good or bad news for you (or for your kids). In its History folders, Internet Explorer keeps track of the pages you've landed on. Just in case that makes you curious — or nervous — skip right to the steps so that you can check out your past visits for yourself:

1. **Connect to the Internet.**

   Don't know how to connect to the Internet? See Book IV, Chapter 1 for details.

2. **Click the IE icon in the Taskbar or on your desktop to launch Internet Explorer.**

   Internet Explorer opens.

3. **Click the History button in the IE toolbar.**

   The History pane opens along the left side of the IE window (see Figure 3-1).

4. **Choose the item that you want to view.**

   If you want to see the sites that you visited last week, for example, click the Last Week selection. A list of visited sites appears.

5. **Click the site that you want to view.**

   Available pages within that site are displayed in the list.

6. **Click the page you want.**

   The selected page is displayed in the IE window.

If you're hoping to find a site that you visited more than two weeks ago, you're out of luck with History, although you can still use IE's Search capabilities to find the site you seek. See "The Secrets of Web Searching," later in this chapter, for more info on that.

Click the folder of the day of week you want to display

Click the history tool in the IE toolbar

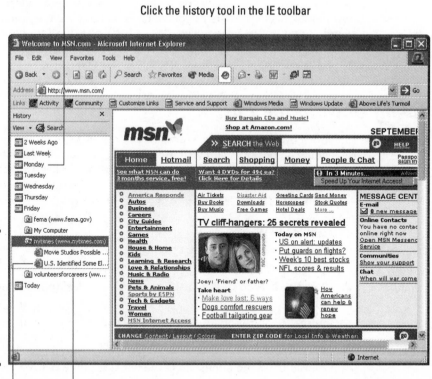

Figure 3-1: Click History in the IE toolbar to display your choices of sites to revisit.

Choose the page you want to see

Select the site to visit

History in the making

Some parents (okay, and maybe spouses) use the History files to make sure that other family members are surfing on the straight and narrow. Chances are, your employer is doing the same thing at work (but probably with a piece of software designed to spot policy infractions).

Whether your weakness is Dilbert, sports stats, or Martha Stewart home tips (oh, come *on!*),

remember that sneaking always shows up in the wash. The moral? Big Brother is watching. You're safest to stick with the sites that you would visit even if your mother were looking over your shoulder. And for those times when the temptation is just too great (everybody needs a good David Letterman fix once in a while), at least learn how to shred the evidence in your History folders.

Changing your view

Internet Explorer initially stores the pages you visit in nice, neat little time capsules, but you may want to change the view to something you're more comfortable with. You can organize past sites four different ways:

✦ **By date:** Arranges pages according to *when* you visited them. (Yes, you already saw this, unless you slept through the first part of this chapter.)

✦ **By site:** Displays a strict alphabetical listing of site names (which may or may not be helpful, considering that not all sites can be reduced to a single, alphabetizable word that makes sense).

✦ **By most visited:** Lists your past sites according to how many times you visited them. Have you checked out Dilbert more often than you've read *The New York Times*? The list shows you the answer (don't worry — I won't tell).

✦ **By order visited today:** Gives you a listing of the sites you visited today, in the order you visited them (with the most recent sites listed at the top).

You can also click My Computer in the History panel to view Web pages and documents you've accessed on your computer system.

To change the view displayed in the History pane, click the View button and choose the option you want to use. After you make your selection, IE redisplays the pages accordingly. Select the site that you want to see by clicking it; choose a specific page within a site by clicking that page. The page is displayed in the IE window, and you're free to move on to other things.

**Book IV
Chapter 3**

Advanced Browsing and Searching with Internet Explorer

When you want to close the History pane and recover the full display of the IE window, simply click the close symbol in the upper-right corner of the History pane.

Moving to another page

I know what you're saying to yourself: "There must be a better way. Do I have to mess with all of these folders and sites?" Until we, like our American Express cards, are endowed with smart card technology, we won't be able to simply remember all the sites we like — no matter how much ginkgo we take. But if you're looking for a faster, easier way to return to a site you've already typed in — oh, just a day or so ago — the answer is right under your mouse:

1. Make sure you're connected to the Internet (still or again).

2. Click the Address down-arrow.

Surprise! A list of previously viewed sites appears, as shown in Figure 3-2.

3. Click the site that you're looking for and you move there. Smooth, eh?

Choose the page you want to visit   Click the down arrow to display the list

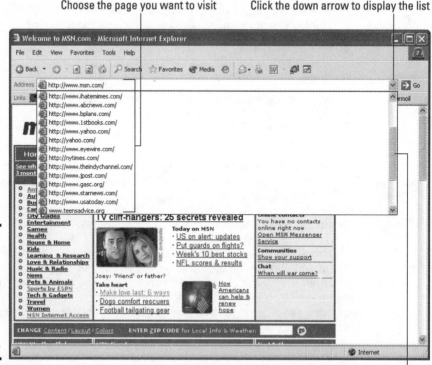

Figure 3-2: Click the Address down-arrow to display a list of recently viewed files.

Scroll down to see additional choices

One of the downsides of using the Address listing is that you don't know when you last visited the site or how high it ranks in your "most visited" category. (You don't even know *who* visited it, if several people in your home or office use your computer and you haven't figured out the new Windows XP feature that enables you to create different user accounts.) But if fast is what you want, this recall method is your best bet.

Increasing long-term memory

So how long does IE keep your past browsings in memory? By default, 20 days worth of wanderings are available to you through the History pane. If you want to up that number, you can increase your hold on the past all the way up to 99 days. If you want to reduce the amount of past baggage you carry, you can decrease the number all the way down to 0. To make the change, follow these steps:

1. Connect to the Internet and launch Internet Explorer.

2. Choose Tools⇨Internet Options.

   The Internet Options dialog box appears (see Figure 3-3). Click the General tab, if necessary.

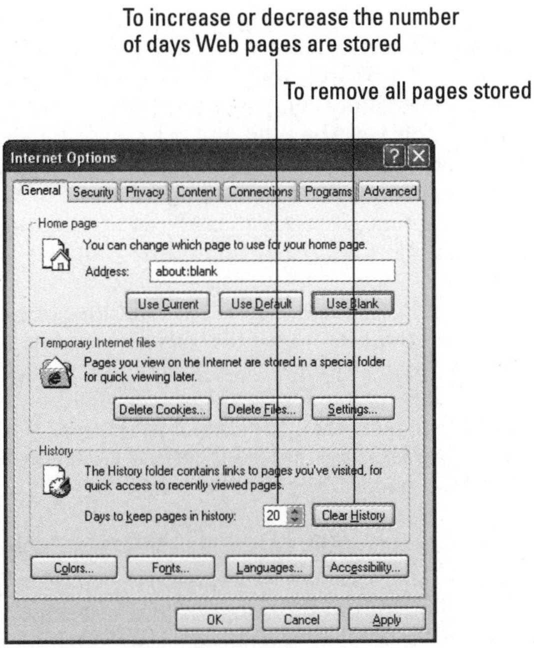

To increase or decrease the number
of days Web pages are stored

To remove all pages stored

Figure 3-3:
You can
increase or
decrease
the number
of days that
IE keeps
your Web
pages in the
History
folders.

[Internet Options dialog box showing General tab with Home page (Address: about:blank, Use Current, Use Default, Use Blank buttons), Temporary Internet files (Delete Cookies..., Delete Files..., Settings...), and History (Days to keep pages in history: 20, Clear History), with Colors..., Fonts..., Languages..., Accessibility... buttons, and OK, Cancel, Apply buttons.]

3. **In the History area, change the setting for number of days in one of three ways:**

   - Click the up-arrow to increase the number of days stored in memory.

   - Click the down-arrow to decrease the days.

   - Click in the text box and type the number of days you want to use.

4. **After you make the change, click Apply.**

   IE records your change and tracks the sites accordingly.

5. **Click OK to close the Internet Options dialog box and return to the Web.**

Yes, it's true that if we don't learn from the past, we're doomed to repeat it... But increasing the number of days that you store past Web pages to an exorbitant number (which in my view would be more than 20 to 30 days) puts a strain on your computer's available storage space. And as you know (or you will quickly learn), graphics-intensive Web pages can be real memory hogs, jamming their pork bellies into the space you need for other things — such as spreadsheet computations, report writing, or online chats.

Clearing your History folder

When I first learned about clearing out my History folders — years ago now — I was in the middle of a crisis. I was working on a project that required a hefty amount of research and I had a midnight deadline looming in front of me. If I ever needed my computer to function as fast as the sales literature said it would, this was the time. But my computer wasn't cooperating. In fact, it acted like someone had poured molasses into the phone lines. I watched, breathlessly frustrated, waiting for Web pages to load and graphics to appear. A few times, I received time-out errors; the page loaded so slowly that the server gave up. Other times, my computer simply locked.

I called my friendly, local PC-repair person (back in those days, such people existed and even answered their phones themselves), and he said, "Oh, that's simple. Just clear your memory."

A lifesaving bit of wisdom, just when I needed it most. You, too, will need it on a regular basis to keep your system from getting clogged with the plague of old, decomposing Web pages. Here are the steps:

1. **Launch Internet Explorer with, say, Start⇨Internet Explorer.**

   You don't have to be connected to the Internet to perform these steps.

2. **Open the Tools menu and choose Internet Options.**

   The Internet Options dialog box appears.

3. **In the History area, click Clear History.**

   A message box appears, asking, "Er... are you sure you want to do this?"

4. **Click Yes to continue.**

   Depending on how many files and days you are stored, your computer may be busy deleting files for several minutes. But when you're clean, you're clean.

5. **Click OK to close the dialog box and go on your merry way.**

Clearing your History is a bit like a lobotomy: You have no "oops!" factor giving you a chance to easily recover from a mistake. When those pages are gone, they're gone. So think twice or three times about what you're clearing before you click.

Playing Favorites

As your surfing savvy increases, you'll begin to find pages that are keepers — Web sites with information that you know you'll want to be able to find later. Internet Explorer gives you an easy way to collect and organize those sites in a feature called Favorites.

Window's preselected Favorites

When you load Internet Explorer for the first time, you notice that you only have to open the Favorites menu (in the IE menu bar) to display a whole slew of folders covering a variety of topics, from home and health to banking and sports (see Figure 3-4, which lists the Favorites found in a typical MSN online service installation). You also see a number of strategic alliances represented there: Many third-party vendors involved in "partnering" with Microsoft and hardware manufacturers get their links built right in to the default Favorites folders (a good gig if you can get it — and afford it!).

The Favorites displayed on your system will be different from the ones shown here — after all, this real estate is unabashedly for sale, and your PC manufacturer will no doubt wish to cash in. But the steps for displaying, selecting, adding, and organizing favorites all work the same way no matter how many pre-set Favorites you find in your folders.

To explore the favorites Microsoft has, uh, thoughtfully arranged for you, follow these steps:

1. **Connect to the Internet, if necessary, and start Internet Explorer.**

2. **Open the Favorites menu (or click Favorites on the IE toolbar).**

   A list of Favorites folders appears.

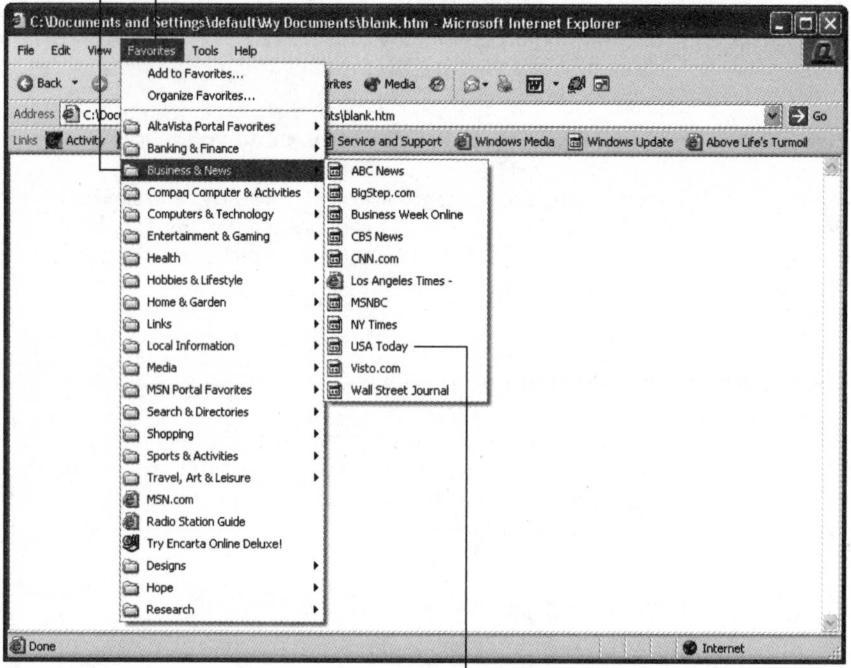

Point to the folder and it displays its Web pages

Click Favorites to display Favorites folders

Figure 3-4:
IE comes
with folders
full of preset
favorites,
ready for
exploring.

Click the page you want to display

3. **Click the folder that you want to see.**

   A submenu of sites appears.

4. **Select the site that you want to visit.**

   The home page for the site appears in the IE window.

Adding Favorites of your own

When you find yourself viewing a site that you want to save for later, you can add the site to your own Favorites folder. Internet Explorer enables you to add sites to the preset folders, or you can create a new folder that is specific to your own needs. These are the steps to add a favorite of your own:

1. **Open the Favorites menu or click Favorites in the IE toolbar.**

2. **Click Add to Favorites.**

   The Add Favorite dialog box appears, as shown in Figure 3-5.

What's wrong with Microsoft's Favorites?

Don't get me wrong — I'm not a Microsoft basher. I'm not one of those people who believe the rumors that the company has a master plan to take control of all PCs in the world and then sell us the access to our own data. But it's with Big Blue–like suspicion (remember the IBM of the 70s?) that we now regard Microsoft — all powerful, into everything, and expanding every minute (unless it's tempered by the current legal feeding frenzy). Sure, we love and use Microsoft's products. Some of us make livings writing about this stuff, after all. But do we really want this big company telling us *which* banking sites to visit or *which* entertainment companies to view? Isn't seeing a Disney link built right into IE's Favorites pretty unsettling? Talk about powerful marriages....

The best use of Microsoft's Favorites is, in "the world according to me," to simply treat them as suggestions — possible sites that you can visit *if* you're looking for that type of information. And then, using a discerning eye, you can decide for yourself. Do a few searches to find out who besides American Express may have what you're looking for. Let your kids play games on sites other than Disney's. When you find your own objective information on computer hardware and software reviews, save that site in your Computers & Technology folder.

The great power of the Internet is not in the "power" of the companies *on* the Internet. It's in the way you find, collect, store, and use the information that *you* want and need. Choice, flexibility, and personal control are the keynotes of this information age. So make sure that your Favorites are your own. Everything else is just marketing.

3. **Click the Create In button to display the folder list if it is not visible.**

4. **Click the folder in which you want to store the site.**

5. **Click OK to save the page and close the dialog box.**

If you want to create a new folder to store the Web page you're adding, click the New Folder button in the Add Favorite dialog box. The Create New Folder dialog box opens. Type a name for the folder (spaces and punctuation characters are okay) and click OK. IE adds the folder to the Create In list in the Add Favorite dialog box, and you can select it as you would any of the preset folders.

Making a site available offline

Some sites that you find you may want to hold for later reference. You can make a site *available offline* — that is, store it on your computer to make it available to you, in Internet Explorer, even when you aren't connected to the Internet. You can also control how much of the site you store on your computer by using the Offline Favorite Wizard. Here's how:

1. **Make sure that the site that you want to add appears in the IE window (which means that you must be connected to the Internet).**

2. **Choose Favorites⇨Add to Favorites.**

   The Add Favorite dialog box appears.

3. **Choose the name and folder for the page, as usual.**

4. **Click the Make Available Offline checkbox.**

   The Customize button becomes available.

5. **Click Customize.**

   The Offline Favorite Wizard starts.

6. **Click Next to start the process.**

   The Wizard's first question is whether you want to make pages linked to the current one available offline as well. If you click Yes, you can choose how many pages you want to download (see Figure 3-6).

Downloaded pages — especially those with photos, animation, and sound — can take up a huge amount of hard disk space. If you're trying to conserve space on your system, download only the pages you need.

Enter a name for the page or use the default

Click OK to add the page

Figure 3-5:
You can add
your own
favorites
and create
your own
folders in
the Add
Favorites
dialog box.

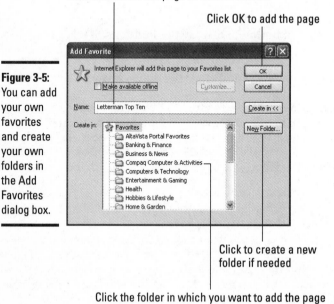

Click to create a new
folder if needed

Click the folder in which you want to add the page

Synchronized (Web) swimming

One of the problems of working with Web pages offline is that they can change without you knowing it. For that reason, Internet Explorer provides a synchronizing feature that enables you to make sure that you have the most recent content from the site. One of the stops in the Offline Favorite Wizard asks you to choose when you want to synchronize your pages. You can choose to synchronize pages manually or automatically.

To synchronize your pages manually, simply open the Tools menu and choose Synchronize whenever you are connected to the Internet. The Synchronize dialog box appears, and you can simply choose the page and click Synchronize to start the process.

To synchronize your pages automatically, you create a schedule that takes care of it for you. You can create the schedule while you're working with the Offline Favorite Wizard (select the option "I would like to create a new schedule" when it is presented). Specify how often (in days) you want the pages to be synchronized, select the time of day, and enter a name for the event if you choose. (You can simply leave the default name, My Scheduled Update, if you like.) Finally, click the checkbox in the wizard page to force IE to connect automatically if you are not online when your scheduled update time occurs.

To make linked pages available offline

Figure 3-6:
Use the
Offline
Favorite
Wizard to
tell IE how
much
information
you want to
store in your
favorite
pages.

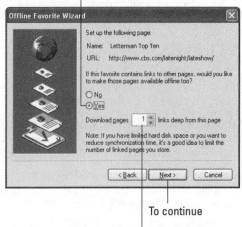

To continue

Tell IE the number of links to follow

7. **Choose when you want IE to synchronize the page you are adding, and click Next.**

   You can opt to do it manually (by opening the Tools menu and choosing Synchronize), or you can set up a schedule to do automatic synchronizing.

8. **If the site you added needs a password, click Yes in the next page of the wizard and enter your user name and password twice.**

9. **Click Finish to complete the wizard and return to the Add Favorite dialog box.**

10. **Click OK to close the dialog box and continue surfing.**

    Later, when you're offline, you can work with the page that you saved.

Organizing your Favorites

Sometimes surfing presents you with so many exciting things to look at that you may simply save pages right and left without taking the time to put them in folders. Over time, this creates a mess of pages in your Favorites menu and means you have to go scrolling through many pages in order to find the page you want.

To straighten your folders and your life, follow these steps:

1. **Click Favorites in the IE toolbar.**

   The Favorites panel opens.

2. **Click Organize.**

   The Organize Favorites dialog box appears (see Figure 3-7).

3. **In the folder list, select the folder containing the page(s) that you want to use.**

4. **Select the page that you want, and then click one of the following command buttons:**

   - **Create Folder:** Creates a new folder to store the page. A new folder appears in the list; you type the name for the folder and press Enter.

   - **Move to Folder:** Allows you to choose a new location for the page. The Browse for Folder dialog box opens so that you can select the folder to which you want to move the page (see Figure 3-8).

   - **Rename:** Allows you to enter a new name for the page (or folder). The page that you selected appears with the name highlighted; you simply type the new name and press Enter.

   - **Delete:** Removes the page (or folder). The Confirm Folder Delete message box appears so that you can confirm that you want to delete the selected page. Click Yes to continue.

Click Organize to get started   Navigate to the folder you want to view

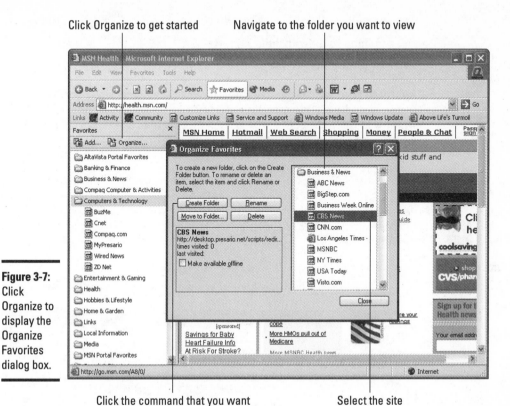

Figure 3-7:
Click
Organize to
display the
Organize
Favorites
dialog box.

Click the command that you want   Select the site

The Secrets of Web Searching

Internet searching can be a lonely business. You're out there, on the Internet range, with nothing but gleaming banner ads and text links to guide you. What happens when you want to find information on a specific subject but you're not sure where to start? IE has provided a helper to assist you with just this dilemma: the IE Search Companion.

Using the Search Companion

To scour the Web to find out more about a specific topic, person, place, or thing, start by clicking Search in the IE toolbar. The Search Companion opens in the left side of the IE window (see Figure 3-9).

To start a search, type a description of the item you want to find. The Search Companion suggests that you use complete sentences, but phrases work just as well. For example, you may search for

✦ Vacation cottages in Thailand

**Book IV
Chapter 3**

**Advanced Browsing
and Searching with
Internet Explorer**

✦ The music of Emerson, Lake, and Palmer

✦ Anything to do with Julia Roberts

✦ Low prices on DVD players

After you type your topic, click Search or press Enter. The companion begins searching and, after a few seconds, displays the results in the IE window in the right side of the window. To display a Web page with the information you seek, simply click the link of the page that you want to view. The Search Companion displays options that you can use to further focus your search (see Figure 3-10).

Okay, so the Search Companion isn't for everyone. If you want to have more control over your searches or take your pick from the various search possibilities that are out there, check out the section on browsing and searching the Internet in Book III, Chapter 2, for details.

Choose the folder to which you want to move the link to the page

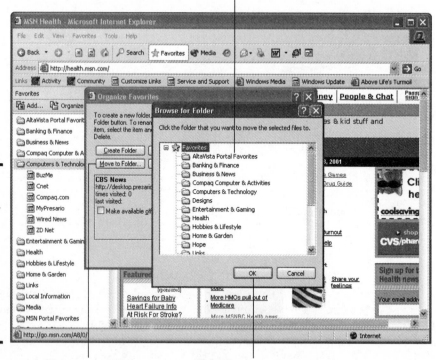

Figure 3-8:
Move the links to your favorite Web pages to a new location by using the Browse for Folder dialog box.

Click to move folder   Click OK to move the page

Type a phrase that tells IE what you want to find

Figure 3-9:
The Search
Companion
waits for
you to
confess
what you're
looking for.

Click search to begin looking

Click to customize the search companion

Customizing that Companion

On the first page of the Search Companion, click Change Preferences. A list of possibilities appears, giving you the following choices:

✦ **Without an animated screen character:** Is the companion an annoyance? Click the option to get rid of him (or her).

✦ **With a different character:** Rover, the animated dog, is your default companion. But you can also choose Merlin (the wizardly character from Windows ME), Courtney (an odd, automobile-driving character), or Earl, an all-mouth creation that frankly gives me the creeps. But suit yourself.

If you've installed Microsoft Office, you'll see the Office Assistants displayed in the lineup of characters you can choose for your helpers in IE.

✦ **With Indexing Service:** Selecting this option enables you to index the files on your computer so that searches on your local machine can be performed faster.

**Book IV
Chapter 3**

**Advanced Browsing
and Searching with
Internet Explorer**

Search options   Type a new search phrase

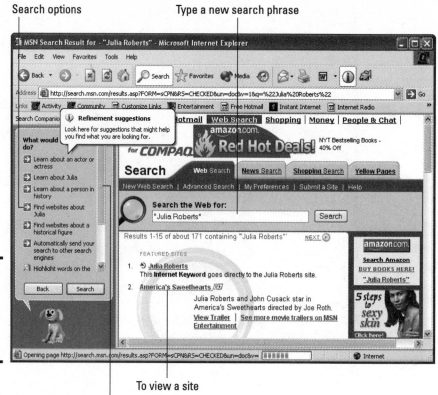

Figure 3-10:
Helpful
companion
or backseat
driver? You
decide.

To view a site

Scroll to see additional choices

✦ **Change files and folders search behavior:** This option allows you to refine the search for files and folders on your hard drive.

✦ **Don't show balloon tips:** This option does away with the display of popup tips while you search.

✦ **Turn AutoComplete off:** This option turns on the feature to display search strings that the companion recognizes.

Simply click the option that you want to change and follow the prompts on-screen. The Search Companion walks you through the necessary steps and brings you back to the initial search page when you're through.

For more information on what to *do* with Web info after you find what you're looking for, see Book IV, Chapter 2.

Chapter 4: Making Internet Explorer Your Own

In This Chapter

✔ **Nip, tuck, and tan: Changing IE's appearance**

✔ **Rearranging tools and toolbars**

✔ **Turbocharged surfing**

✔ **Make it easy on yourself**

✔ **Weeding out unwanted sites**

This chapter explains how to make some aesthetic and functional changes to Internet Explorer so that you can create the look and feel you want while surfing. If you're a late Internet bloomer and your eyesight isn't what it used to be, you can display LARGE text and LARGE buttons on the toolbars to help you find your way around the Web. If you're an Internet speed-demon and you want your system to function as fast as possible, you can use a few of the ideas in this chapter to streamline processing and make browsing an easier, low-effort endeavor. Finally, if you're a papa or mama bear worried about what the cubs may get into while you're away from the computer keyboard, you can use IE's Content Advisor to set up blockades for sites with questionable content. And — if all else fails and you've made a mess of things — you can return your IE settings to the way they were before you made all the modifications. At the end of this chapter, I'll tell you how.

A New Look for IE

Any marketing person at Microsoft will tell you: All users are not created equal. Some want a system that's fully customizable; others want everything done for them. If you're one of those people who like to play around with things to get them just right, you'll like the amount of flexibility IE gives you in deciding the way you want things to look.

Reading the fine print

Depending on the size of your monitor and the quality of the display, the Web content that you see may be a bit of a strain to read. Some site designers try to cram as much information as possible on a page, crushing paragraphs of text into a 13-inch diagonal space. You can control this to some degree by making the size of the text larger and easier to read. Here are the steps:

1. **Open the View menu and choose Text Size.**

2. **Select a new size for the text (see Figure 4-1).**

The display changes immediately. Don't like it? Change it again.

One trade-off when you enlarge the text size is that less information fits on the screen, which means that you have to do more scrolling to read through articles that capture (and hold) your interest.

Choose text size   The text size changes

Open the View menu   Select size

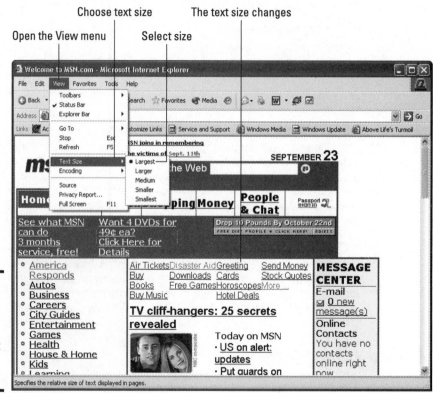

Figure 4-1:
You can choose five different sizes of text for IE's display.

Coloring IE

Another way to make IE your own involves changing the colors displayed in the browser window. For those pages that don't have any color preset in the coding of the page, you can change the color of the text or the background; you can also change the link colors used on the pages you visit, if those pages do not have link colors specified. Here are the steps:

What colors work?

Granted, not all Web page designers know what they're doing. Some companies and individuals seem to have a knack for online display — they seem to know how to balance pictures, text, headlines, colors, and animation to give us a page that's easy to read and delivers the information we're looking for. But often the design is intended to shock us. We are met by an overabundance of special swirling effects, clashing characters, animated text, and flashing buttons.

If you're a brave enough soul to want to make your own color improvements on the top of this visual cacophony, by all means give it a shot. But if your intent is to create a display that is easy (or at least not impossible) to read, remember these simple color guidelines:

- The higher the contrast, the better the readability. The contrast between the text and the background colors is important in helping the reader decipher the text. Use dark text on a light background whenever possible (or the reverse, light text on a dark background).

- Stay away from colors that may overwhelm the text (such as bright red for a page background).

- Use dark colors for skinny text. If the font used on the site is small and thin, letters may disappear (especially for those of us in the over-40 crowd) if the color selected for text is too light. If your background is light, stick with black, dark blue, green, or brown lettering for smaller text.

- Remember that they're *your* preferences. If other people will be using your computer, you may want to confer with other users before changing all backgrounds to pea green and all text to apricot. After all, one person's "pretty" is another's "egad!"

1. **Choose Tools⇨Internet Options.**

The Internet Options dialog box appears.

2. **Click Colors.**

The Colors dialog box appears (see Figure 4-2). Here you can select two different kinds of color controls:

- On the Colors side of the dialog box, you can choose whether you want to use the standard Windows colors (which is the default selection); or you can select the Text and Background colors yourself. If you want to set your own Text and Background colors, clear the Use Windows Colors check box. The Text and Background choices then become available and you can modify the colors by clicking the selection and choosing the new color from the displayed palette.

- On the Links side of the dialog box, you specify the colors of the links you have visited, the links you have yet to visit, and the color used to highlight the link when you "hover" over it with the mouse. Click the color selection that you want to change and choose the color from the displayed palette.

Book IV
Chapter 4

Making Internet Explorer Your Own

3. **Click the new color from the displayed Color palette.**

    If you want to create your own color, click the Define Custom Colors button and enter the specifications for the color you want to use.

4. **Click OK to close the palette, and then click OK again to close the Colors dialog box and make the changes to your browser settings.**

If you're convinced that your color scheme will work better than the color combinations other Web designers have put together, you can override the colors selected by other Web designers by clicking the Accessibility button in the Internet Options dialog box. When the Accessibility dialog box appears, click the Ignore Colors Specified on Web Pages check box to disable the Web colors selected. Click OK to close the dialog box; then return to the Colors dialog box and choose the colors you want.

Choose a hover color

Uncheck to change the colors   Change the colors of links

Figure 4-2:
Put your crayons away — you can color your screen any hue you want using IE's color options.

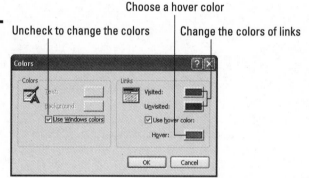

Getting the big picture with Full Screen view

As you get more comfortable surfing the Web (and more opinionated about what you do and don't like), you may want to do away with some of the toolbars in lieu of more screen real estate. Especially if you are working the Web primarily on a fact-finding mission (meaning you are finding and reading articles on various topics), having a maximum amount of space on screen means you do less scrolling.

You can choose from two easy ways to display your Web browser in full screen view: press F11 or click the Full Screen button in the toolbar. Everything except the navigation tools disappears, as Figure 4-3 shows.

When you want to jump to a new page, don't panic. You can restore IE to its traditional display by pressing F11 a second time.

Only the navigational tools remain   Click here to scroll the web page as usual

Figure 4-3:
Using Full
Screen view
gives you
maximum
screen real
estate.

If you want to display only the address bar in full screen view (so that you can jump from page to page while getting the greatest possible amount of room on-screen), press Alt+V to display the View menu, point to Toolbars, and select Address Bar. The address bar appears to the right of the navigational tools, as you see here:

Table 4-1 lists some keys you can use to quickly navigate a full screen.

Table 4-1	Quick Keys for Full Screen Navigating
Press	**To Do This**
Alt+F	Open the File menu
Alt+E	Display the Edit menu
Alt+V	Open the View menu

(continued)

Table 4-1 *(continued)*

Press	To Do This
Alt+A	Display the Favorites menu
Alt+T	Open the Tools menu
Alt+H	Show the Help options
Ctrl+F	Display the Find dialog box
Ctrl+P	Open the Print dialog box so you can print the current page

Tool Juggling for Everyone!

Whether you decide that you want to work in full screen view or you return to the traditional IE display, you have the choice of leaving the tools as they are or changing them around as you see fit. You can control which toolbars you want to display and even create your own custom toolbars while you're working the Web.

Hiding and redisplaying toolbars

Hiding a toolbar is so simple you may miss it. Ready? Right-click the toolbar you want to hide. When the shortcut menu appears, click the name of the toolbar, removing the checkmark. This also removes the toolbar from the IE display.

 When you want to redisplay the toolbar, simply right-click on another toolbar. The shortcut menu appears, complete with the name (but no checkmark) of the hidden toolbar. Click the name to redisplay it.

Changing the tool display

Want to go a step further? As your experience with IE grows, you notice that you use some tools to do lots of things and rarely use other tools at all. You may decide that you want to reorganize the tools so that the ones you use most are in the easiest-to-reach places on your toolbar. Use the Customize option to make these kinds of changes.

Right-click the IE toolbar and choose Customize. The Customize Toolbar dialog box appears, as shown in Figure 4-4. This dialog box displays the full list of available toolbar buttons on the left side and shows on the right the buttons used for the current toolbar. At the bottom of the dialog box, you see that you can change the placement of text and the size of the icons, if that floats your boat.

To add a new button to the toolbar, select it in the Available Toolbar Buttons list and click Add. The button is added to the IE toolbar list.

To move the button to the place on the toolbar where you want it (or to move other tools around), make sure that the tool is selected and then click Move Up or Move Down to put the button in the correct position. Click Close to save the change and return to the IE window.

Look silly? Click Reset to restore the toolbar to the way it was

Click here to add or remove tools from the toolbar

Figure 4-4:
You can do all kinds of decorative things with the Customize Toolbar dialog box.

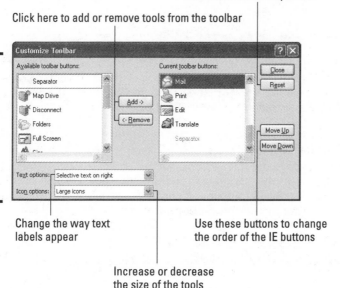

Change the way text labels appear

Use these buttons to change the order of the IE buttons

Increase or decrease the size of the tools

 Have you noticed the little divider line between the Home and Search buttons on the IE toolbar? That little line is called a *separator,* and it simply helps divide up different kinds of tools so that you can find them more easily. You can add separators to your toolbars, too. Just click Separator (at the top of the Available Toolbar Buttons list in the Customize Toolbar dialog box) and then click Add. This adds the separator to the current IE toolbar. You can then put the separator where you want it by clicking Move Up or Move Down.

What's in a text label?

How important is it to see the little labels that tell you what the button does? To some of us, labels are annoyances; to others, they're lifesavers. IE gives you the option of hiding text labels altogether or changing their position. Here are the steps:

1. **Right-click the IE toolbar and choose Customize to display the Customize Toolbar dialog box.**

2. **Click the Text Options down-arrow.**

   You have three choices:

   - **Show text labels** displays all the text labels beneath the buttons.

   - **Selective text on right** is the default selection, showing only some text labels to the right of the button

   - **No text labels** hides all text labels and displays only the buttons themselves.

3. **Click your choice and click Close.**

If you overhaul everything, moving buttons around and changing the text and size of the icons and then decide you were just running on low blood sugar and made an error in judgment, you can undo all your changes by clicking Reset in the Customize Toolbar.

Changing button size

You can change the size of *icons*, *buttons*, *thingies* — whatever you want to call them — in the Customize Toolbar dialog box. Display the dialog box by right-clicking the IE toolbar and clicking Customize; then click the Icon Options down-arrow. Your options are

- ✦ **Large Icons:** Displayed by default
- ✦ **Small Icons:** Reduce the size of the icons by half

Why would you want to reduce the size of the IE tool icons? Making the buttons smaller means that you can fit additional tools on the IE toolbar but still keep the toolbar as small as possible, giving you more screen space. This also helps if you intend to display the toolbar in Full Screen view — by adding buttons, you can load the toolbar with as much functionality as you can.

Increasing the Speed

It may take a while for you to accumulate enough files and cookies to slow your system down, but if you surf with any regularity, sooner or later your space for temporary Internet files will need to be cleaned out. Regular cleaning keeps your pages loading quickly. You can also turn off the display of graphic images on sites that you visit to reduce the time you spend waiting. Sure the pictures are nice, but if you find that they slow you down unnecessarily, you may want to try life without them for a while. This section gives you a few ways to increase the speed of your surfing.

Turning off graphics

If you decide that you want to try life without graphics, don't worry — your decision can be reversed with the click of a button. When you tell IE to load the page without the graphics, the browser displays an empty box where the image would be. To turn off graphics, follow these steps:

1. **Choose Tools⇨Internet Options.**

   The Internet Options dialog box opens.

2. **Click the Advanced tab, scroll down to the Multimedia section (shown in Figure 4-5), and clear the Show Pictures check box by clicking it.**

3. **Click Apply to save the change.**

4. **Click OK to close the dialog box.**

Just the facts, ma'am! If you're interested only in information, you can further reduce download times by clearing the check boxes for Play animations in Web pages, Play videos in Web pages, and Play sounds in Web pages. This reduces your Web pages to straight information, which may not be much fun but makes surfing much faster.

Even after you turn off the display of pictures, you can still view a picture if you choose. When the Web page appears, simply right-click the image placeholder (which usually is a small box surrounding a red X). When the shortcut menu appears, click Show Picture and the image appears on the page.

You turned the display of graphics back on, but they still aren't appearing. What gives? Press F5 to refresh the display and IE reloads the page, which includes downloading the graphics as expected.

Wiping away the cookie crumbs

What are cookies? *Cookies* are small text files that Web publishers store on your computer to keep information about your choices and preferences. Cookies are small files but, depending on the number of sites you visit (and the way in which you've set your preferences to allow cookies), they can quickly accumulate in the space reserved for your temporary Internet files.

Do you need cookies? Mostly, no. If you subscribed to a site (such as *The New York Times*) and provided a user name and password, that information is stored in a cookie on your computer. When you go to the site, the site reads the cookie and you are able to log on without entering the name and password each time. But the majority of cookies are simply files that Web pages put on your computer that have nothing to do with making things more convenient for you. Those are the ones you can delete without a second thought.

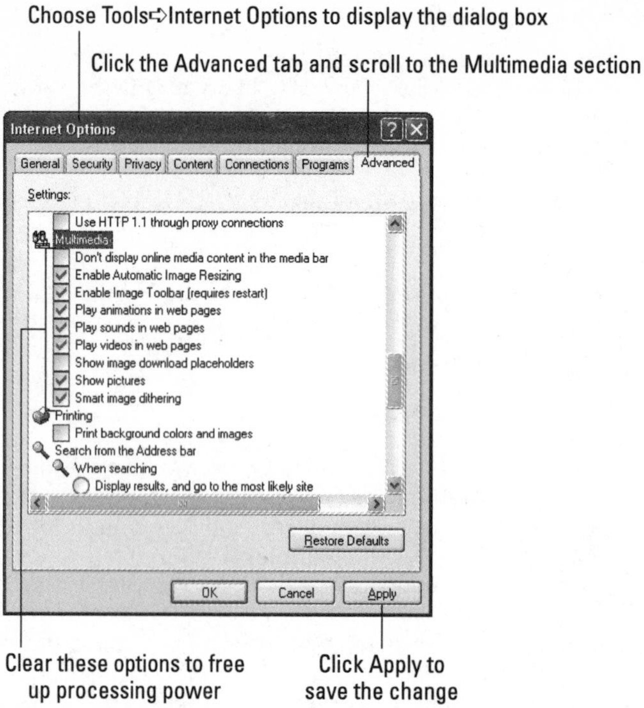

Choose Tools⇨Internet Options to display the dialog box

Click the Advanced tab and scroll to the Multimedia section

Figure 4-5:
If speed is
your issue,
you can
disable
graphics
and
multimedia
display to
allow text to
download
faster.

Clear these options to free
up processing power

Click Apply to
save the change

Deleting cookies

You can delete cookies individually or as a group. To delete all cookies,
choose Tools⇨Internet Options. In the Temporary Internet Files section of
the General tab, click Delete Cookies. A message box appears, asking
whether you want to proceed. Click OK to clear all cookies.

If you want to delete individual cookies, follow these steps:

1. **Choose Tools⇨Internet Options.**

   The Internet Options dialog box appears.

2. **In the Temporary Internet Files area of the General tab, click the
   Settings button.**

   The Settings dialog box appears.

3. **Click the View Files button to display the Temporary Internet Files
   window, in which all cookies and files are listed (see Figure 4-6).**

4. **Select the cookie that you want to delete and press Delete. Repeat as
   needed; then click the Close box to return to the Settings dialog box.**

Select the cookie and press delete

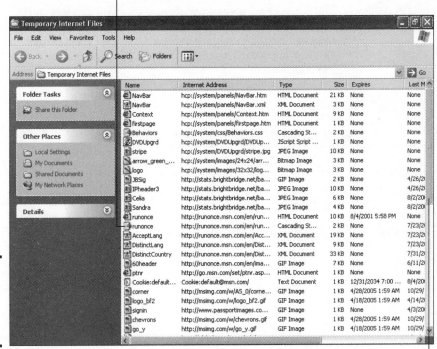

Figure 4-6:
Deleting
cookies
one by one
by one.

Scroll to the cookie or file you want to delete ────

5. **Click OK to close the dialog box, and click OK again to return to IE.**

IE stores files as well as cookies in temporary storage. You can delete all
files at once by clicking Delete Files in the General tab of the Internet
Options dialog box.

Controlling cookies

You can call the shots when it comes to cookie placement in IE. By default,
Internet Explorer alerts you when a Web page starts to put a cookie on your
system (see Figure 4-7). You can click Learn More About Cookies to display
help information on cookies; or click Settings to set additional options.

If you want to raise the bar on your privacy so that you accept fewer cookies, you can change your privacy settings. Here's how:

1. **Choose Tools⇨Internet Options.**

2. **Click the Privacy tab.**

   The Settings area displays a slider that you can use to raise or lower the settings for cookies. The default setting is Medium, but the range goes from Accept All Cookies to Block All Cookies. Each time you choose a new setting, a full description of the setting appears in the right side of the dialog box.

Figure 4-7:
This message appears when a site attempts to drop a cookie on your hard drive.

Cookie lesson 101

This button takes you to a dialog box where you can control these things

3. **Drag the slider to the setting that you want, and click Apply to save the change.**

4. **Click OK to close the dialog box and return to the IE window.**

Never no-how allow those cookies!

Some pesky sites dump all kinds of cookies on your hard drive and you want them to keep their crumbs to themselves. Other sites are Web friends and you want to allow their content, no matter what. You can be the one to make these choices by telling IE which sites to block and which to allow. You do this in the Per Site Privacy Actions dialog box.

To get to this dialog box, choose Tools⇨Internet Options. Click the Privacy tab and, at the bottom of the page, click Edit. This action takes you to the Per Site Privacy Actions page, in which you can enter the address of the sites that you want to block (simply type the URL and click Block) or allow (type the URL and click Allow). After you enter the address of the site, the site moves to the Managed Web Sites list in the bottom of the page. If you want to remove the site later, click it and click Remove.

After you finish entering the sites you want to manage, click OK to close the dialog box.

If you try a new setting and decide later that you don't like it, you can return the setting to the default by displaying the Privacy tab and clicking Default.

Adding more space for Web pages

One other way to give your computer more processing room is to increase the amount of storage space allowed for those temporary Internet files. You do this by choosing Tools⇨Internet Options (see a pattern developing here?), displaying the General tab, and clicking Settings.

In the Temporary Internet Files folder section of the Settings tab, drag the slider to the right to increase the amount of storage space reserved for Internet files. Of course, if you want to reduce the amount of space, drag the slider to the left. Alternatively, if you want to reserve a specific amount of space, you can click in the text box and type the number of megabytes you want to reserve for temporary storage.

If you have plenty of room to play with, upping your temporary storage is no big deal. But when you start to get worried about the amount of disk space you have left to use, you're better off to keep the space for temporary storage small and block a higher percentage of cookies.

Linking Your Way

One of my favorite ways to customize IE has little to do with speed or aesthetics — it's all about convenience. You can put the sites that you want to visit within reach of the mouse, anytime you're surfing anywhere on the Web. You do this using the Links bar.

IE comes preset with a number of links displayed in the Links bar, just beneath the Address Bar in the IE window. The labels are pretty generic — Activity, Community, Entertainment, and so on. But you can customize the Links bar to include your favorite sites so that you can get to them quickly without opening menus and folders to get there. The procedures are simple:

+ To add a new page, drag the address from the Address line to the Links bar.

+ To rearrange links on the bar, drag the link that you want to move to the new location.

+ To delete a link from the Links bar, right-click it and click Delete.

The shorter the link name, the more links you can add to your Links bar

Blocking Salacious (Or Questionable) Content

The final customizing issue to tackle in this chapter deals with the types of sites you want (or you want your kids) to browse. As access to the Internet has grown, so has the debate about filtering: Who has the right to view certain sites? How do we protect kids from lewd, threatening, frightening, or offensive information? And who decides just what "lewd" or "frightening" means?

Although schools, libraries, and offices have to develop their own policies about allowable content, you must decide what's right for your own home. IE includes the Content Advisor to help you enforce your decision after you make it.

To enlist the advisor, follow these steps:

1. **Choose Tools⇨Internet Options.**

   The Internet Options dialog box appears.

2. **Click the Content tab, and in the Content Advisor area, click Enable.**

   The Content Advisor dialog box opens, as shown in Figure 4-8

3. **Choose the category that you want to set the controls for (Language, Nudity, Sex, or Violence).**

4. **Move the slider to the level of control you want.**

   Drag the slider to the right to raise the allowable level; drag the slider to the left to decrease the allowable level.

5. **Repeat Steps 3 and 4 for each of the category areas that you want to set.**

6. **Click Apply to save the controls.**

   The Create Supervisor Password dialog box appears, asking you to provide a password (and confirm it) so that others can't undo the controls you set.

7. **Enter the password information and click OK to continue.**

   A message appears, telling you that the Content Advisor has been activated.

8. **Click OK twice to close the dialog boxes and return to browsing.**

Do you wonder who makes these determinations? You can click the More Info button in the Ratings tab of the Content Advisor to find out more about the rating service it uses.

Choose your concern ⌐

Click enable to start the content advisor

Who's standards are we using?
Click here to find out more.

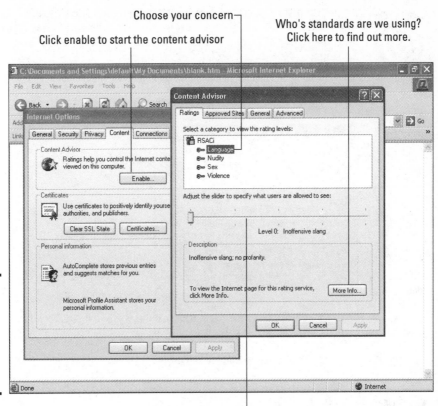

Figure 4-8:
The Content
Advisor
keeps an
eye out for
untoward
offerings.

Drag the change to the level of "advising"
on the various issues

After you enable the Content Advisor, it's likely to put the kibosh on things you'd rather it didn't. For example, when I tried to go out to Salon.com, the advisor wouldn't let me proceed because the site doesn't have a site rating. Check out the message in Figure 4-9.

The options in the Content Advisor dialog box give you the choice of always allowing the Web site (or the individual Web page) to be viewed. If you click either of those options, IE adds the Web site (or page) to the Approved Sites list, which means that IE will allow you to visit this site the next time you try.

To check out the Approved Sites list, choose Tools⇨Internet Options, click the Content tab of the Internet Options dialog box, choose Settings, and click Approved Sites.

If you want to visit the site on a one-time pass, click that option. Finally, enter the password that you assigned as the supervisor when you originally brought the Content Advisor to life. Then click OK to continue on to the site.

Book IV
Chapter 4

Making Internet
Explorer Your Own

If you are interrupted too frequently because of the Content Advisor's well-intentioned censorship, you may want to go back and change the Advisor settings. To do this, choose Tool⇨Internet Options, click Content, and click Settings.

The advisor tells you what's wrong

Figure 4-9:
When you visit a site that the Content Advisor doesn't like, expect an interruption.

Content Advisor - http://www.salon.com/

Sorry! Content Advisor will not allow you to see this site.   OK

This page may contain some or all of the following: Cancel

This page does not have a rating.

If you still want to see this site, someone must type in the supervisor password.

◯ Always allow this Web site to be viewed
◯ Always allow this Web page to be viewed
◉ Allow viewing only this time

Hint: same

Password: |

Click this option to add the site to your "approved" list

Going Back to Zero

Throughout this chapter, you've discovered how to make all kinds of changes — changes in the way things look, the way they operate, even the types of sites you're allowed to view. But what if you make all these changes and then decide that you liked the way things were in the good old days, way back before you added all these crazy colors and enlarged the text? Simple. Ready? Choose Tools⇨Reset Web Settings.

The Reset Web Settings dialog box offers to return all your Web settings to the way they were the first time you launched IE. All you need to do is click Yes. And if you want to return your home page to the original default, just leave the check box selected. What could be easier?

Resetting works great for those aesthetic changes, but getting rid of the Content Advisor takes another step. Choose Tools⇨Internet Options and click the Content tab. In the Content Advisor area, click Disable. IE prompts you for your password. A small popup box tells you that the Advisor has been disabled. Click OK to complete the process and then click OK again to close the Internet Options dialog box and return to the IE window.

Index

Book V

Touring the Services of America Online

The 5th Wave   By Rich Tennant

"It's a free starter disk for AOL."

Contents at a Glance

Chapter 1: Up and Running with AOL

In This Chapter

✓ The semi-straight scoop on AOL

✓ What you can expect from AOL

✓ From installation to startup

✓ A user by any other name

✓ Because I said so, that's why! (Setting Parental Controls)

This chapter explains how to decide whether AOL — that big Wal-Mart of the Internet world — is the right choice for your online service. What does it offer you and what does it cost? How do you find and install it (and get rid of it later if you choose)? This chapter skips the spin and goes right to the heart of the matter — telling you what AOL does and doesn't do, and showing you how to get the service up and running on your computer.

Using AOL is a choice. I cover AOL here simply because of its popularity — statistically, a fair percentage of you will be interested in signing up for AOL. If you choose not to use AOL and prefer instead to go your own way, whether you sign up with an independent Internet Service Provider or choose another well-pushed offering (such as MSN — surprise, surprise), you can skip this chapter and move on to the part that interests you.

What Is AOL?

America Online is an online service that you can choose to use as your Internet provider when you use Windows XP: You pay AOL for its services in connecting you to the Internet and for storing things like your e-mail and personal Web pages. You also pay AOL for its help in getting you connected — and keeping you connected. AOL is not Microsoft. It's Time-Warner. E-be-de-be-de-be-thaaat's all folks!

If you bought a PC with Windows XP installed, chances are very good that an AOL sign-up icon is sitting on your desktop. Lest you're of the Pollyannic persuasion, rest assured that the icon isn't there because the manufacturer thinks it's your best choice: AOL offers a "bounty" to your PC manufacturer for every sucker... er, new customer who signs up. Talk about incentive!

Top Ten AOL keywords

Want to know what other AOL users are looking for? Most of the top ten keywords used on AOL have something to do with finding something to buy, going somewhere, or playing games. Here's the list as of August 2001. You can find an updated list in AOL by clicking Keyword in the AOL toolbar or by entering the phrase **Keyword List** in the Keywords dialog box.

1. eBay
2. Slingo
3. Pogo
4. Love
5. Mapquest
6. Nascar
7. Games
8. Nickelodeon
9. What's Hot
10. Monster.com

That doesn't mean you have to *use* AOL — in fact, if you want to clear your desktop of the clutter and delete the icon altogether, you can simply click the icon once to select it and press Delete. That removes the shortcut on your desktop, but you can still install the service later if you choose by navigating in Windows Explorer to the folder storing the AOL setup utility and double-clicking it. (Most likely, the setup utility is stored in the \Program Files\Online Services\AOL folder.)

By the same token, you don't have to *avoid* AOL, either! Lots of folks use AOL and are quite happy with what they get. The Guys in White Lab Coats tend to look down their noses at AOL. That's okay. They have very big noses. Most AOL subscribers simply like the convenience, and they're willing to pay for it. My mom uses AOL. 'Nuff said.

America Online is basically an Internet Service Provider that attempts to be all things to all people. Want to check your stocks online? AOL offers it. Planning a family reunion? AOL can help you. Looking for love in all the wrong places? AOL has a thriving online matchmaking forum that allows you to post personal ads and review the ads of other romance seekers. You can search for information, make travel reservations, buy a new pair of shoes, and play games — all in the privacy and relative luxury of your own home.

America Online is both loved (as evidenced by a multimillion-strong subscriber base) and hated (as a search of industry gossip and newsgroup messages shows you). The love is understandable: AOL has been called "training wheels for new Internet users," making everything simple and in-your-face easy. The hate is predictable — a huge, ever-growing service that continues to capture a larger and larger share of the online market, at the same time partnering with many big companies also in that "suspectable" category. Whether you listen to the supporters or detractors, the only real way to determine whether AOL is worth your own time and money is to try it (or look over your friend's shoulder while *he* tries it).

What AOL Does Well

AOL must be doing something right in order to capture and hold so much of the online market. Since its inception way back in the dawn of the Internet age, AOL has been working to provide specific key features — features that help build the AOL brand, give customers what they want, and make sure that they keep coming back.

So what do customers want? Current AOL features give online customers specific things:

- ✦ **Flexibility and mobility:** AOL Anywhere lets users get to their AOL accounts from anywhere — over the Web, of course, but you can also use AOL on PDAs, cell phones, pagers, and TVs. You can check out `www.aol.com/anywhere/index.html` for more info.

- ✦ **Immediate, friendly contact:** AOL Instant Messenger (and its travel version, AOL Quick Buddy) is an instant chat that enables you to talk to friends and coworkers on the Internet. Through the use of this little pop-up message box, you can find out which of your friends is online and send them messages, photos, and more — instantly.

- ✦ **Easy access to information:** AOL Keywords enable you to find information quickly — with the use of a single word. Keywords are topics that bring up all kinds of information, from Web pages to newsgroup messages to articles, in response to the word that you enter in the Keyword box. The feature is designed to be intuitive so that even a guess is likely to result in something at least close to what you're looking for.

- ✦ **Bring people together:** AOL Chats enable you to have group discussions with others on a variety of topics, from faith to fun to families and more. And if you don't find a topic you like, you can create your own.

- ✦ **Make Web sites easy:** AOL makes having your own homepage a walk in the park. Using a feature called AOL Hometown, you can create your free homepage in three simple steps.

- ✦ **Keep surfing safe:** Parental controls enable you to choose the level of access that you want your kids to have while they surf with AOL. Not only can you set levels that determine the type of content allowed (levels include Kids Only, Young Teen, Mature Teen, and General), but you can also set an Online Timer to control the amount of time your kids can be online.

---

101 uses for AOL disks

If you haven't noticed, AOL is the direct mail marketing king. If you weren't inundated by little white disks — sometimes packaged in holographic packages, sometimes appearing in Tide-detergent-like envelopes — you are one of the few overlooked people in the country.

Clearly, someone at AOL received a mandate to "get the product into the customer's hands," purchased our names and addresses from an underground census agent, and proceeded to bombard us with diskettes (and now CDs) on a quarterly basis. It's not only humpbacked postal carriers and Greenpeace activists who decry this kind of wastefulness — some regular Joes on the Internet mind it, too. One site developer came up with a list of 101 ways to use the annoying mailbox stuffers. Here are just a few — but you can check out the whole list at `www.earthplaza.com/aoldisks/`.

1. Mini cutting board (great for the office or the car, use metal door for knife)

2. Attach it to a ruler and presto! — you've got a fly swatter

3. Construct a life-size replica of Stonehenge

4. At a restaurant, shove one under a wobbling table leg

5. Money clip (use metal door and discard the plastic case...the "rich nerd" look is in this year)

Why You May Consider Alternatives

Well, there are two sides to every story, and even though AOL tells you it's the greatest online service available, you may want to educate yourself from all the angles before you make a decision. AOL has had its share of problems, including these:

✦ Several times in the last few years, the glut of subscribers has overwhelmed the capacity of AOL's available telephone lines, causing service brown-outs in various places across the country and around the world. Is this maxxed-out bandwidth more serious or more annoying than the "busy-signal syndrome" experienced by many growing ISPs? Hard to say. You may want to talk to AOL users in your area to find out about local access challenges before you sign up.

✦ Hackers love to hate AOL. Whether AOL's security is easy to break or some of the best hacking minds have taken a particular liking to cracking their code, AOL has been the target of talented and sometimes twisted programmers. According to `www.aolwatch.org`, one hacker created havoc by greeting AOL subscribers with the message, "I've been hacking AOL since I was 11."

✦ Like many other Internet pioneers operating on the "build it and they will come" mentality, AOL had to figure out how to make a buck after it brought hoards of subscribers on board. Changes in pricing plans didn't sit well with many AOL users, who felt they were being nickeled and dimed when AOL charged for features that are free elsewhere on the Net.

www.aolwatch.org keeps a cynical eye on goings-on at AOL. In addition to lots of lampooning of Steve Case (including the parody, "How the Grinch Stole AOL"), you can find information on the latest hacks and mergers, new reviews, messages from users, feature-related articles, and more.

What's It Gonna Cost Me?

If you're like me, you always want to see in black and white what your bottom line costs will be before you make a decision as big as choosing a relationship with an online service provider. Here are AOL's pricing plans in the U.S., as of August, 2001. To keep an eye on the most current prices, go to www.aol.com/info/pricing.html.

✦ $23.90 per month gives you unlimited access to AOL and the Internet.

✦ $19.95 is your monthly charge if you're willing to pay the entire year in advance (which means a check for $239.40, if I've done my math right).

✦ $9.95 per month is your charge if you "bring your own access," meaning that you already have an Internet service with someone else and simply want to use AOL's features. (If you're on a budget, this won't be a cost-effective choice, because you're probably paying between $15 and $25 per month to get on the Internet anyway.)

✦ $4.95 per month gives you a flat three hours of AOL a month — not much time! What can you do in three hours on the Internet? Hmmmmm... check your e-mail and your stocks in less than six minutes every day. Not likely. Besides, if you accidentally go over your three hour limit, you are billed at $2.50 for each additional hour. Not a safe option unless you have a LOUD alarm clock!

✦ $9.95 can give you a limited usage plan that allows five hours of AOL, including Internet access. This, too, would be a dangerous option at my house. Additional hours (accidental or otherwise) are charged at $2.95 an hour. It doesn't take too many term papers or Web searches to reach the financial stratosphere.

Acquiring and Installing AOL in Windows XP

When you first start Windows XP, you may find an AOL and Internet Free Trial icon on your desktop. Double-clicking this icon launches the AOL setup utility, which walks you through the paces of setting up your computer to use AOL's latest version.

If the AOL and Internet Free Trial icon *doesn't* appear on your desktop, don't feel slighted – it simply wasn't part of the manufacturer's deal for your particular computer. To get the files you need in order try give AOL a shot, follow the download procedure in the next section.

Downloading AOL

If you really want to try AOL, and you have no icon on your desktop and no AOL CD sitting underneath your coffee cup (wonder if they've worked out a deal with Starbucks yet?), you can download a free trial of the newest version from the AOL Web site. To download the trial version, follow these steps:

1. **Connect to the Internet.**

   Not sure how? Go back to Book IV, Chapter 1. Do not pass go, do not collect $200.

2. **Launch Internet Explorer.**

   Okay, okay, I know — it seems weird to launch IE to find out about AOL, but it's the shortest distance between two points.

3. **Type** www.aol.com **in the Address bar. Click Go.**

   The AOL Web page appears, as shown in Figure 1-1.

4. **Click the link that allows you to download the free trial.**

   AOL sends you the AOL software by mail, but you can also download it if you choose.

5. **When the File Download dialog box appears, click Save to save the file.**

   The Save As dialog box appears, and you can navigate to the folder in which you want to store the AOL software. The aolsetup.exe file is saved in the folder that you specified, and you can launch the setup utility any time you choose.

Go to www.aol.com to see what's going on.   Click here to try the new promo.

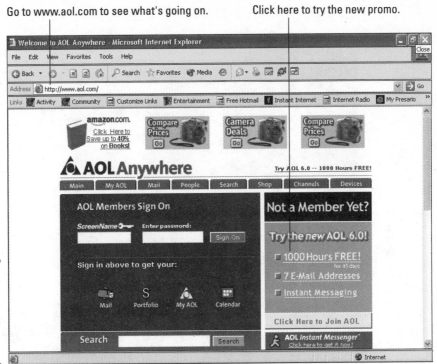

Figure 1-1:
When's the right time to jump? When you find a free offer.

Installing AOL

Whether you use the free trial placed on your Windows XP desktop or you download the latest version from AOL's Web site, the process for installing the program is simple:

✦ If you want to launch the free trial included with Windows XP, double-click the AOL and Internet Free Trial icon on your desktop.

✦ If you want to use a downloaded file that you saved on your hard disk, use Windows Explorer to navigate to the folder and double-click the `aolsetup.exe` file's icon.

The setup utility launches and walks you through the steps involved in setting up your system to log on to AOL. The program asks you for the information that it needs in order to find the closest access for you and set up your account (see Figure 1-2).

Choose any necessary calling options.   Click Next to complete setup.

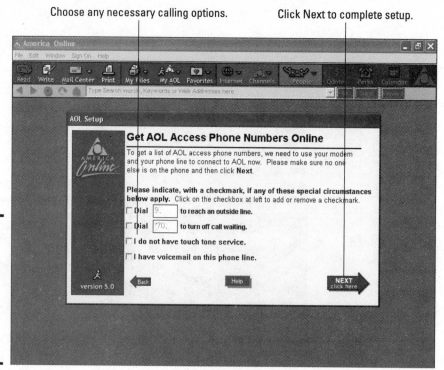

Figure 1-2:
AOL walks
you through
the process
and asks
for the
information
that it
needs.

Simply follow the instructions on the screen and click Next to continue through the process. Yes, answering all these seemingly trivial questions is a bit of a pain in the neck, but better now than later. You go through this only once, thank goodness — and then you are online with AOL.

Online with AOL

When the connection is finally made, the AOL window opens — and, right off the bat, you have the opportunity to work through a Quick Start that explains the high points of the program (see Figure 1-3). You can also create your Buddy List, which is a kind of AOL-version "contacts" list that lets you store the e-mail addresses of your favorite AOL buddies. From this point, you can begin your AOL adventure.

Canceling AOL

So what happens if you try using AOL for a week or so and you hate it? No harm done — especially if you signed up for the free 45-day trial. You can cancel your AOL account three different ways:

✦ You can call toll-free from inside the U.S. using 888-265-8008.

✦ Send a cancellation letter to America Online, P.O. Box 1600, Ogden, UT 84402-1600.

✦ Fax your letter to 1 801 622 7969.

Be sure that you have your screen name, full name, phone number, and address handy for the customer service rep. You may also need the last four digits of the charge card that you use for billing (for verification purposes).

You can learn more about AOL's cancellation policy by launching AOL, clicking Keyword, and typing **Cancel**.

America Online promises to cancel your account within 72 hours of your request, but be sure to check your charge statement regularly after your cancellation. A class-action suit is currently filed against AOL for overcharging after accounts have been canceled — so better to be safe than sorry.

Interested in an overview? The QuickStart leads you through program features.

You can click here to start a Buddy List.

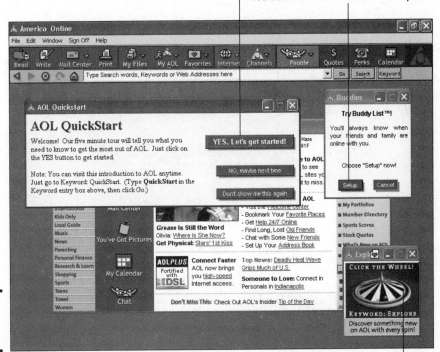

Figure 1-3:
Finally,
online!

The ever-present new feature pitch.

Starting AOL

Ready to have a go at it? AOL makes starting the program super easy for you, of course. To launch AOL from the menu, choose Start⇨All Programs⇨ America Online, and then click America Online (see Figure 1-4). You can also launch the program quickly by double-clicking the AOL icon in the system notification area, down near the clock on the right side of the Windows Taskbar.

After a moment, the AOL opening screen appears, followed by the Sign On window. In the Sign On window, simply click the Sign On button. AOL begins to dial the access number that you selected during setup and logs you on to AOL.

You never know when you may need another access number. For that reason, keeping a list of AOL access handy is a good idea, in case access gets blocked or a server goes down. To get the latest access numbers, click Access Numbers in the Sign On window. An AOL Setup window appears so that you can enter your area code and find access numbers in your area.

Click the program name to start.

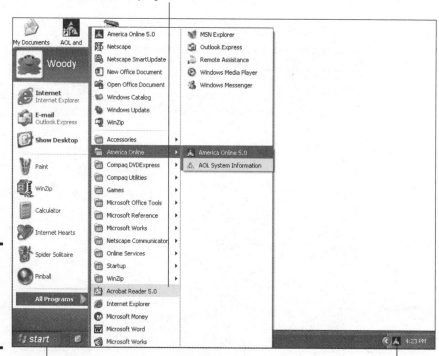

Figure 1-4: You can start AOL from the All Programs menu.

Choose Start ⇨ All Programs ⇨ America Online.

Launch quickly from the Taskbar.

A Good Screen Name Is Hard to Find

When you first installed AOL, the program asked you to choose a screen name for your account. You won't be able to delete this screen name as long as you have your AOL account, although you can rename it if you choose. Your screen name is the user ID that you use to log on to the service, and you can use it as your "handle" in chat rooms, newsgroups, and more. AOL enables you to use up to seven screen names for a single AOL account, which means that you could use one screen name for your business, one for fun, one for family, one for chat, and so on. It also means that each member of your family can have a different screen name — and you can set individual controls for each screen name, which means that you can set different access limits for each of your children if you choose.

Web safety for kids

Most of us are all-too-aware of the potential dangers that the Internet represents. Especially if you have small children at home, you may be concerned about this anonymous medium that enables anyone to contact almost anyone under a variety of guises. When you choose screen names for your children and make choices about how much access you want to allow, consider these guidelines:

- Don't use any derivative of the child's name. Don't use Susan (instead of Sue) or a nickname that is a familiar family name.

- Avoid using city names as part of the screen name. For example, *Indygirl* gives others too much information.

- Instruct your kids not to give personal information — names, addresses, cities, or phone numbers — to strangers, even if they seem friendly.

- Talk with your kids about ages on the Web. Kids usually assume that they are talking to other kids — and they usually assume that adults are talking to other adults. One of the big problems on the Internet is that easy

ways exist to keep children out of adult areas, but no simple ways exist to keep adults out of child areas. Make sure that your child knows to tell you about anything suspicious — including an adult (or a "kid" who sounds older) participating in a kids-only chat room.

- Think through AOL's Parental Controls. AOL offers a number of ways that you can limit access in a safe-but-still-fun way. See the "Who's in Charge Here?" section, later in this chapter, for more information.

- Know where your kids are. Wander through the room, ask questions, be interested. Know whom your kids are talking to and what sites they visit. It's not the Inquisition; it's just staying in touch with what's going on.

- Follow up with things that worry you. If you see or hear something that you find unsettling, don't hesitate to check it out. If you're still worried, send an e-mail to TOSGeneral@aol.com, a Community Action Team set up to deal with safety problems on AOL.

You may want to change your screen name, add new screen names, or delete a screen name that you already have. To get to the screen name area in AOL, click the Keyword button, type **screen name**, and click Go. The AOL Screen Names window appears, as shown in Figure 1-5.

Choose what you want to do.

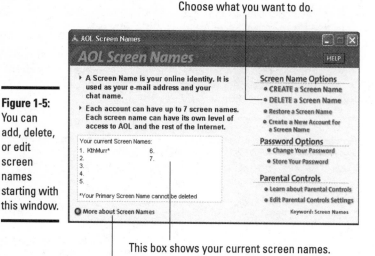

Figure 1-5:
You can add, delete, or edit screen names starting with this window.

This box shows your current screen names.

Want to find out more? Click here.

Adding a screen name

You can take care of all kinds of things from this window. To start the process, click Create a Screen Name. A pop-up message box appears, asking whether you are creating a screen name for a child. If you click Yes, a window with an "Important Note to Parents" appears. This window explains the basics of the Parental Controls function and offers suggestions for child safety on the Web. Scroll through the information and then click Continue to proceed.

If you know the new screen name that you want to use, you can enter it directly. Screen Names can be 3 to 16 characters; use letters, numbers, and spaces; and must have the first letter capitalized (with the remaining letters in any combination of uppercase and lowercase). Screen names cannot include special characters such as @, underscore (_), or question mark (?). Type the name in the Choose a Screen Name window and click Continue.

If your screen name is already being used by another subscriber, AOL displays this message:

```
The name you requested is already in use. Please try
another name.
```

Click OK to continue. When you click OK, AOL takes you back to the Choose a Screen Name. If you enter another screen name and that one's a bust as well, the Choose Another Screen Name appears, as shown in Figure 1-6.

AOL suggests a screen name if you enter three words that mean something to you. But if you want to be stubborn about it, click Try Another Screen Name and enter your next try.

TIP

Want to do your correspondents a big favor? Think about ambiguities when choosing a Screen Name. Try to avoid using the number 1 or the lowercase l, because they can be frequently and easily confused. Ditto for the number 0 and the letters O and o. Although many exceptions certainly exist — for example, Woody is a good Screen Name because the lowercase o's aren't likely to be misinterpreted as 0's — you can save your friends, family, and associates a whole lot of frustration by choosing a Screen Name carefully.

Sooner or later, you find a screen name that is available (or you give up and let AOL choose it for you). You feel a rush of accomplishment when you finally make it to the Choose a Password screen.

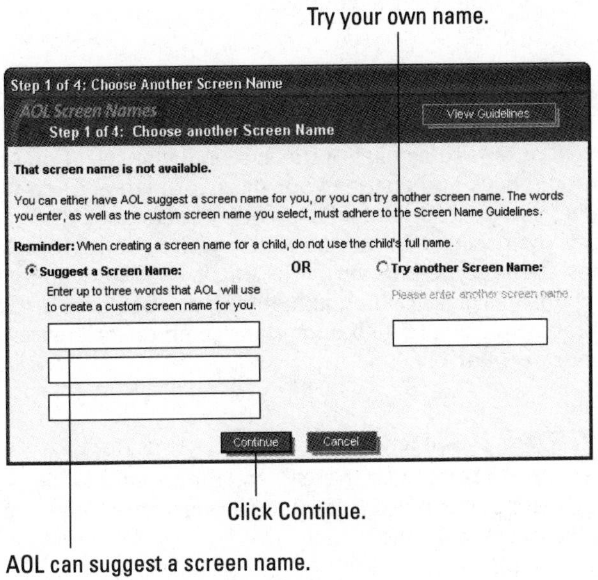

Try your own name.

Step 1 of 4: Choose Another Screen Name

AOL Screen Names
Step 1 of 4: Choose another Screen Name

View Guidelines

That screen name is not available.

You can either have AOL suggest a screen name for you, or you can try another screen name. The words you enter, as well as the custom screen name you select, must adhere to the Screen Name Guidelines.

Reminder: When creating a screen name for a child, do not use the child's full name.

Suggest a Screen Name: OR   Try another Screen Name:

Enter up to three words that AOL will use
to create a custom screen name for you.

Please enter another screen name.

Continue   Cancel

Figure 1-6:
Think again — that name is taken.

Click Continue.

AOL can suggest a screen name.

Deleting a screen name

After all your hard work, why would you want to delete a screen name? Perhaps you've found something that you like better, and you don't want a bunch of unused screen names cluttering up your name list. Maybe you have a Screen Name that's a magnet for every available piece of unwanted e-mail. (">>>Enlarge Your CRANIUM! Amazing NEW Process Guaranteed to ATRACT a MATE TODAY! FREE!!!!! BUT HURRY!!!!!!! ACT NOW!!!!!!!! WE'RE RUNNING OUT OF CAPITAL LETTERS!!!!!!!!!!! AND THE EXCLAMATION MARKS ARE GOING ON STRIKE!!!!!!!!!!!iii::::....") Whatever the reason, you can delete a screen name by following these steps:

1. **Launch AOL by clicking Sign On in the Sign On window.**

2. **In the main AOL window, click Keyword and type** Screen Names; **then click Go.**

3. **Click Delete a Screen Name in the right side of the AOL Screen Names window.**

   The following message box appears, asking you to confirm that you want to continue the deletion:

4. **Click OK to continue.**

   The Delete a Screen Name window appears, giving you a list of current screen names. Click the one that you want to delete and click the Delete button. A message box appears, telling you that the screen name has been deleted from your account.

Choosing, Changing, and Using Passwords

You choose a password as part of the screen name selection process, and you can also go back and change your password later. When you create a screen name, you see a Create a Password screen (see Figure 1-7). You simply enter the password that you want (*Hint*: AOL won't make this easy for you) and then retype it to verify the entry. If AOL doesn't give you the dreaded "D'oh! Message" (which actually says, The Password You Entered is Not Acceptable), you can finish up and move on to setting the parental controls for your account.

Change that password

After you're up and running with AOL, you may want to change your password to something that's easier for you to remember. If you want to make the change, follow these steps:

1. **Start AOL the usual way.**

2. **When you're connected, click Keyword, type** screen name, **and click Go.**

3. **In the AOL Screen Names dialog box, click Change a Password.**

4. In the Change Your AOL Password window, click the Change Password button.

The Change Password dialog box appears, as shown in Figure 1-8, asking you to enter your current password and then type the new password (twice).

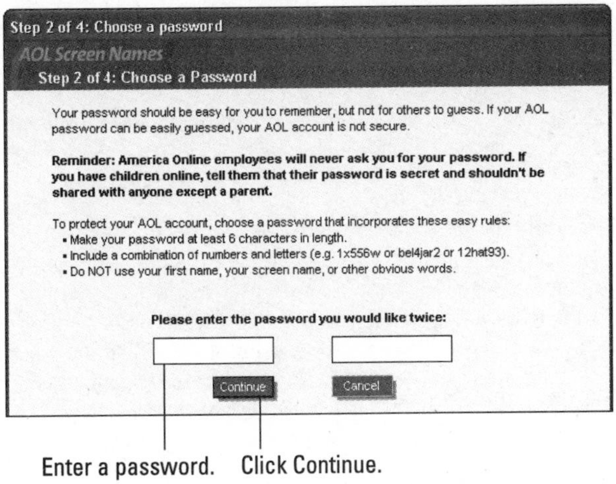

Figure 1-7:
Think this
looks
simple?
Think again!

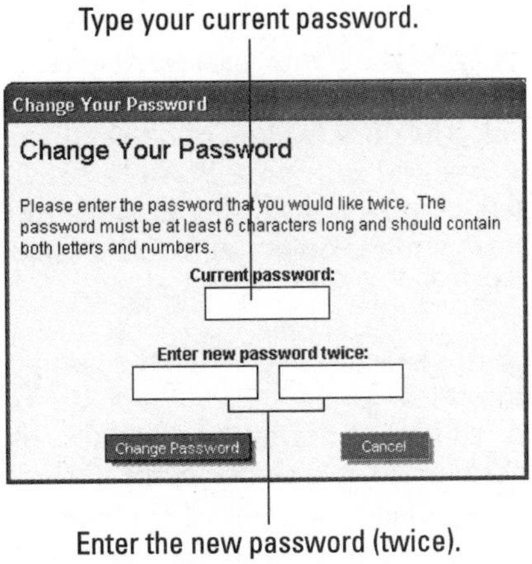

Step 2 of 4: Choose a password

AOL Screen Names
Step 2 of 4: Choose a Password

Your password should be easy for you to remember, but not for others to guess. If your AOL password can be easily guessed, your AOL account is not secure.

Reminder: America Online employees will never ask you for your password. If you have children online, tell them that their password is secret and shouldn't be shared with anyone except a parent.

To protect your AOL account, choose a password that incorporates these easy rules:
- Make your password at least 6 characters in length.
- Include a combination of numbers and letters (e.g. 1x556w or bel4jar2 or 12hat93).
- Do NOT use your first name, your screen name, or other obvious words.

Please enter the password you would like twice:

Continue   Cancel

Enter a password.   Click Continue.

Type your current password.

Figure 1-8:
Enter your
password –
again, and
again,
and again.

Change Your Password

Change Your Password

Please enter the password that you would like twice. The password must be at least 6 characters long and should contain both letters and numbers.

Current password:

Enter new password twice:

Change Password   Cancel

Enter the new password (twice).

Unfortunately, you face the same rules and regulations when you change your password that you encountered when you created it in the first place. When you find something that works, stick with it.

Password hints

It's hard to pass muster in AOL's password process. Because AOL is focusing so much on safety, it prompts (and, in some cases, forces) you to create passwords that follow these guidelines:

- Enter a password that is at least six characters long. The longer the better.

- Don't choose anything too easy or obvious. If you think you're being clever, you aren't: The most common password in the world is *password*, followed closely by *yourpassword*, birthdays, anniversary days, and the dates of major events (such as Pearl Harbor Day, which was very common a couple of decades ago).

- Don't use personal names — first or last.

- Don't even think about using your screen name.

- Choose something that you can remember but others won't be able to figure out. One of the favorite ploys of password crackers is to go through a dictionary, word by word, checking to see if any word fits. There's an entire subculture on the Web for the care and feeding of cracker dictionaries.

By the way, profanity is allowed for an AOL password — and it may be a necessary release by the time you find a password that works.

Here's a sure-fire method for picking passwords that you can remember: Choose two short words, and put a punctuation mark or digit between them: *go!boy* or *half/price* or *me4you* work great and they're easy to remember — although a purist would no doubt complain that they're easier to crack than random numbers and digits.

Even though your PC may offer to store your password and enter it automatically (which means that you don't have to type it in every time you log on to AOL), you are smart to pass the offer by. You don't want every Tom, Dick, or Harry — or anybody else who walks by your PC — to get your password. Remember, if some creep gets your password (I'd mention your ex-spouse by name, but never mind), everything you do on AOL is compromised — e-mail, secure transactions, the whole nine yards.

What? You think your password's safe if it's stored in the computer? Think again. Yes, the password may appear as stars (******) on the computer screen when Windows fills it out for you automatically. But behind the stars sit the password itself, and it's very easy for sufficiently advanced crackers to get your password, even if they can see only stars. No, I won't tell you how.

Avoid the temptation to write down your password, even in a place that is separate from all electronics... say, in your calendar or phone book, or on that little sticky note hidden underneath the dirty socks in your top dresser drawer. Snoopy people can bump into a seemingly innocuous note, put one and two together, and use your password to get onto AOL faster than you can say, "I'll have a double latte to go, extra foam." You're far better off to choose a password that you can remember.

At last count, I had 47 passwords floating around in my head — AOL, MSN, Windows XP logon, financial Web sites, subscription Web sites, and on and on. A friend of mine uses an ultra-secure Web site to store his passwords, so that he can look them up whenever he's online. Personally, I store all of my passwords in a single password-protected Word document. (In Word 2000, choose File⇨Save As⇨Tools⇨General Options; in Word 2002/XP, choose File⇨Save As⇨Tools⇨Security Options.) The password protection in Word 2000 and 2002, while hardly unbreakable, is still very, very good. I can carry the file with me, or I can e-mail it to myself whenever I'm traveling. As an added bit of obfuscation, I call the file Travel Notes.doc.

Storing your password

When you make a change to your password, AOL prompts you to store your password if you have included it in an automatic sign on feature (which enters your screen name and password for you).

Click Store Your Password. The Store Passwords window appears. To store your password, enter it in the Password box. If you want the password to be entered at sign-on, click the Sign-On check box. If you want to protect your Personal Filing Cabinet (the storage area online that keeps your preferences, mail, and more), click the PFC check box. Click OK to complete the process.

You can change your password while you're online with AOL by clicking Keyword, typing **Password**, and clicking Go.

Who's in Charge Here?

Earlier in this chapter, I talked a little bit about the onerous nature of the Web — and although the Internet (like the real world) has an overwhelmingly far greater number of child-friendly people than it has child predators, you're smart to think through the issue of access controls: How much do you want your children to do online? Using AOL's parenting controls, you can choose:

+ How long you want your child to be online

+ What types of sites your child can visit

+ Who your child can exchange e-mail with

+ Who can exchange Instant Messenger messages with your child

When you set up a screen name initially, you can choose parental controls for the screen name that you're creating. Figure 1-9 shows the window that appears when you first create a screen name. To choose the setting that you want, simply click it and then click Continue.

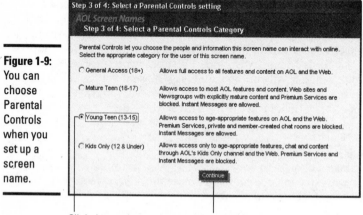

Figure 1-9:
You can choose Parental Controls when you set up a screen name.

Click the setting you want.   Click Continue when you're finished

Setting time limits

If you just can't stand the cries of "Awwwww, *Dad*," and you want AOL to automatically enforce the "AOL after homework" rule, you can use the Online Timing feature to set the boundaries for you. Online Timing gives you the flexibility to set time limits for one day, for every day, or for weekend use. You can create any schedule that works for you and your family.

To set time limits in parental controls, follow these steps:

1. **Launch AOL and click Keywords in the AOL window.**

2. **Type** screen name **and click Go.**

   The AOL Screen Names window appears.

3. **Click Edit Parental Control Settings.**

   The Parental Control window appears, showing you the control settings currently in effect.

4. **Click Online Timer.**

   The Custom Control Settings: Online Timer window appears (see Figure 1-10). The first screen shows you the current settings for Online Timer.

5. **To make changes, click Next. Choose the times when you want to allow access; then click OK.**

   AOL saves the control settings and you are returned to the Parental Control window.

6. **Click the Close box to return to the AOL Screen Names window; click the close box to return to the AOL window.**

Review the current timing settings.

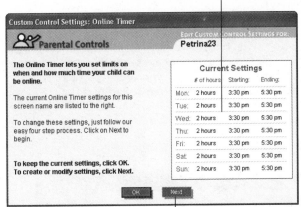

Figure 1-10:
You can choose daily controls or a specific time limit.

Click Next to make timing changes.

A little lesson in control

You can click the Learn about Parental Controls in the AOL Screen Names window to run a slide show to see more about parental controls in AOL. The slide show is called "Parental Controls: Empowering Parents," and it takes you through three lessons:

- Getting Started & Common Questions, which provides a list of Frequently Asked Questions about Internet safety issues and AOL controls.

- Recommend or Report Web Sites is an area that enables you to gather and send information about sites that you encounter — those you think other parents should see and stay away from.

- Discover the Online Timer explains how the online timer works and shows you how to set and change the choices you make.

To exit the slide show, click the close box in the top right corner of the window.

Editing parental controls

You can click Edit Parental Control Settings in the AOL Screen Name window to modify the general Parental Control settings that you've selected. AOL enables you to make changes for the following items:

✦ Online Timer

✦ Web Controls

✦ IM (Instant Messenger) Controls

✦ E-mail Controls

In the Parental Controls window (see Figure 1-11), you can review the settings currently in effect; if you want to make changes, simply click the category that you want to change. You are taken to another window with options related to the control that you selected. Make your choices and click OK; then click the close box to exit Parental Controls. Your changes immediately take effect.

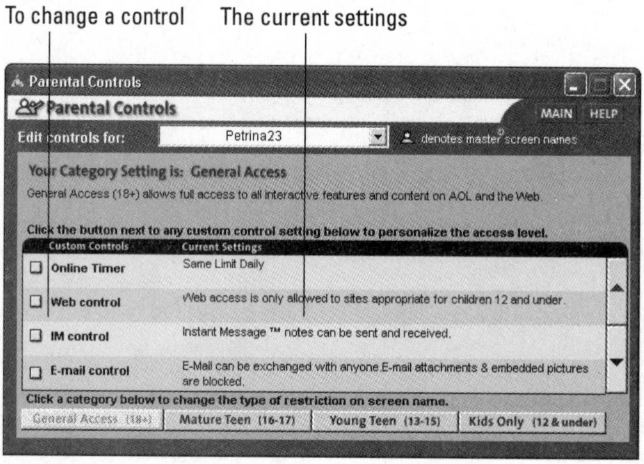

To change a control   The current settings

Figure 1-11: Click Edit Parental Controls to change the settings that you selected.

Setting Up Your Member Profile

Your member profile is the information that you show to the world — your name, personal information, and so on. To get your Member Profile going, follow these steps:

1. **Launch AOL, and when the AOL window appears, click Keyword.**

2. **Type** Profile **and click Go.**

   The Member Directory window appears, giving you the option of searching for another member's profile or clicking the My Profile button to see your own.

3. **Click My Profile.**

   The Edit Your Online Profile dialog box appears (see Figure 1-12).

Your member profile is where the security and privacy issues touch your life, Mom and Dad. Be sure that you don't put too much information out there in your member profile — no matter how proud you are of your occupation, how much you want to let people know what kind of profound messages you offer the world, or how interesting your hobbies may be. Members can and do read profiles to find out about others who have interests similar to their own, so if you enter hobbies such as *hamster juggling* and *sword swallowing,* you can expect to meet some, er, interesting online friends.

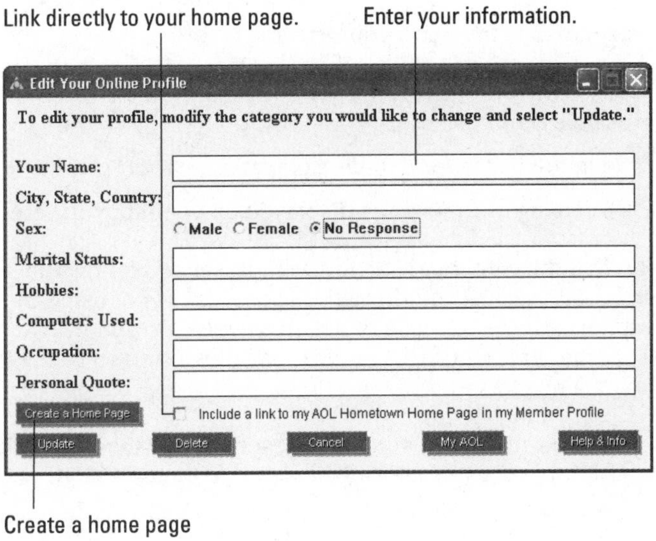

Link directly to your home page.   Enter your information.

Figure 1-12:
Your profile
is seen by
everyone
who is
interested —
so be
discreet.

> **Edit Your Online Profile**
>
> To edit your profile, modify the category you would like to change and select "Update."
>
> Your Name:
> City, State, Country:
> Sex: ○ Male ○ Female ● No Response
> Marital Status:
> Hobbies:
> Computers Used:
> Occupation:
> Personal Quote:
>
> Create a Home Page   ☐ Include a link to my AOL Hometown Home Page in my Member Profile
>
> Update   Delete   Cancel   My AOL   Help & Info

Create a home page

Enter your information by clicking in the fields that you want to add and typing the information. None of these fields is mandatory, so skip any that you're not sure you want to include. Remember, too, that you can update the information at any time, so you may want to test the waters with limited information. Enter that you're an unemployed itinerant sheep herder with a big-time lawyer brother who helps you file lawsuits against companies that send out spam. You can always go back and jazz up your story later, if you choose.

You can choose to create a home page right from the My Profile window. Might as well do it all at once. Click the Create a Home Page button, and AOL launches. In just a few simple steps, you have the basic design and text for your AOL Web page. When you're finished, click Save My Page and you return to the AOL Hometown page (which congratulates you for creating your home page). Click the Close box to return to your Profile window so that you can finish entering changes.

If you want to add a link in your profile to the home page that you just created, click the check box to the left of Include a Link to My AOL Hometown Home Page.

What Are Your Preferences?

While you're setting up your member profile, you may as well set up AOL to work the way you want it to. Click the My AOL button in the Edit Your Online Profile window to go to the My AOL window, where you can tell AOL how you feel about

✦ Personalizing the news you receive

✦ Setting up your daily calendar

✦ Tracking your stocks

✦ Linking to your favorite online places

✦ Customizing the shortcuts displayed on your startup screen

Simply click the category that you want to set and follow the instructions on-screen. AOL walks you through the process of choosing the features that you want to include for each of the areas you care about. When you're finished setting preferences, click the Close box to return to the Profile window.

You can review or modify your preferences at any time by clicking My AOL in the AOL toolbar or by clicking Keyword, typing **My AOL**, and clicking Go.

A Quick Look at the AOL Interface

The AOL window is built to be easy to use. Nothing too sophisticated here — unless you call big buttons sophisticated. When you first log on to AOL (after the initial Sign On screen), you see a window similar to the one shown in Figure 1-13.

Menu bar   Enter a URL.   Tool bar

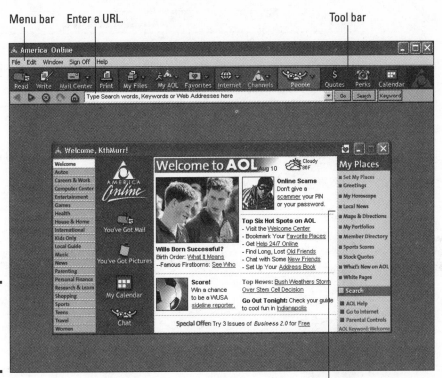

Figure 1-13:
The AOL
interface is
almost too
easy.

Links to more information

The items in the AOL window are familiar — even if this is the first time
you've worked with the program. The menu names are where they should
be — in the menu bar. The File menu includes commands that enable you to
create, open, save, and print files in AOL. The Edit menu houses the options for
cutting, copying, pasting, selecting, and editing information. The Window menu
enables you to organize, layer, and select open windows, and Sign Off gives you
the choice of choosing a different screen name or signing off altogether. Finally,
Help does what you expect Help to do — gives you options that provide more
information about the feature or process that's puzzling you.

The AOL toolbar is similar in function to the IE toolbar with which you're
probably familiar. The buttons all include labels — so you can never be *too*
wrong about what a button does — and some buttons have a down-arrow to
the right of the icon, showing that you have other options to select when
you click them. When you click a button with a down-arrow, a drop-down
submenu appears so that you can make your choice. Table 1-1 gives you an
overview of the various tools in the AOL toolbar.

Table 1-1	An AOL Tool Overview	
Button	*Name*	*Description*
	Read	Opens your mailbox so that you can read new mail
	Write	Displays the Write Mail window
	Mail Center	Opens the Mail menu so that you can choose a mail command or display your mailbox
	Print	Enables you to print the currently selected item
	My Files	Opens a submenu that gives you the option of working with your Personal Filing Cabinet or working with downloaded files or pictures
	My AOL	Displays a list of features that you can customize to suit your preferences
	Favorites	Enables you to choose and work with your favorite places on the Web
	Internet	Lets you access the Web and choose various Web features
	Channels	Displays a list of AOL channels that you can choose to move to the community you want to visit
	People	Gives you options for finding people, joining a chat, working with Instant Messenger, or visiting AOL member homepages
	Quotes	Displays the Personal Finance window so that you can track the stocks that you're most interested in
	Perks	Gives you a window full of perks available to use as an AOL subscriber

Button	Name	Description
	Calendar	Enables you to set up and enter items in an online calendar that AOL stores for you. The navigation bar, just beneath the AOL toolbar, includes everything you need in order to move around in AOL. You can choose to move forward or backward through Web pages, type a URL directly in the Address box, search for specific information, or use the Keyword button to navigate directly to items that you want to find within AOL.

REMEMBER

For more information on surfing the Web with AOL, see Book V, Chapter 3.

Chapter 2: You've Got AOL Mail

In This Chapter

- ✔ Write a little mail for me
- ✔ Ready, set, send!
- ✔ Addressing for fun and profit
- ✔ De-junking your inbox
- ✔ Autopilot e-mail

This chapter explains how to open, read, write, send, and throw away mail in AOL. From fun to functional, e-mail gives you the ability to stay in touch with those you love (as well as those you like, those you tolerate, and those you wouldn't want to deal with any other way). You find out how to send both simple messages and complex files. And you discover how to rid yourself of the scourge of junk mail and automate your mail delivery tasks so that e-mail fits your schedule both online and offline.

If you find e-mail a bit intimidating and off-putting, no need to sweat. It took my dad years to discover e-mail because he was convinced that it was too complicated and really not worth the effort. Now he sends messages to his kids and grandkids almost every day. When you get the hang of it, e-mail beats the socks off the telephone — and it's a whole lot cheaper, too.

My dad asked me to include a straightforward overview of e-mail, for all of you Dummies out there who are trying to convince your parents, spouses, co-workers, or poker buddies to get online. Here it is:

If you have AOL, using e-mail is simpler than using a TV remote. You type a letter — a message, as it's called — and tell AOL who should receive the message by using their e-mail address (something like woody@woodyswatch.com; it's like a telephone number). When you send it, the message gets routed to the recipient, anywhere in the world, within a fraction of a second. When AOL receives a message that's been sent to you, you hear, "You've got mail!" Click on the button, AOL sends the message to your PC, and you can read it. That's all there is to it.

Thanks, Dad. I couldn't have said it better myself.

Getting Mail

You've got mail!

When you first log on, if you've received a new e-mail message, the happy voice of the online greeter calls your attention to the arrival. The opening AOL page shows you that the flag on the trusty icon is up, which indicates visually (as if you could somehow miss the verbal cue) that mail awaits your attention.

For the future, I'd like to see AOL developers build in a customize-the-announcer option that enables us to choose different dialects, tones, and inflections for our mail announcements. Once, just once, I'd like to hear "Good grief — you've got *another* message!" or perhaps, in Ed McMahon's voice, "You're a winner!" And what I wouldn't give to hear Homer announce, simply, "D'OH!"

Opening the mail

To receive your mail, simply click the You've Got Mail! icon in the AOL main window. This opens your Mailbox, which lists the mail messages that are awaiting you (see Figure 2-1).

Open the message by double-clicking it or by selecting it and clicking Read. The message opens in a window on your screen. You can read through the content of the message (use the scroll bar if necessary to scroll down to read the entire message) and then do one of six things with it:

✦ **Close it.** When you click the Close box, AOL saves the message to the Old Mail section of your mailbox.

✦ **Delete it.** To get rid of the message, click Delete. It's that simple.

✦ **Reply to it.** Click Reply to send a return message to the person who sent *this* message to you. The address is entered automatically, so you don't have to enter the e-mail address in the Send To line. When you click Reply, AOL opens a new message window and you can simply type your message and click Send Now or Send Later. (See "Sending Messages" for details.)

✦ **Forward it to someone else.** If you get a message that includes a pearl of wisdom that you just *have* to share (it does happen once in a while), you can send it along to your favorite friends and relatives. Click Forward to start the process; then enter the e-mail addresses of those you'd like to share the message with. Finally, click Send.

Click to see mail you've sent.

Read messages are stored here.   Double-click to display the message.

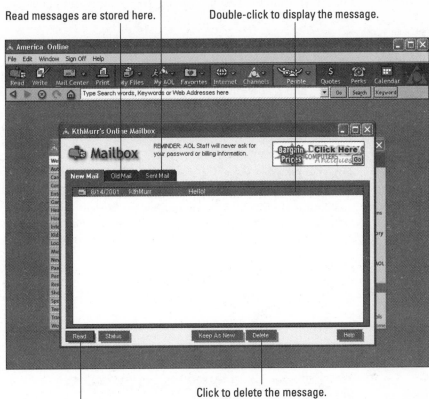

Figure 2-1:
Getting mail
with AOL.

Click to delete the message.

You can open the selected message by clicking Read.

✦ **Reply to all (if the e-mail was sent to multiple people).** Reply to All is available only if multiple people are on the recipient list. When you click Reply to All, the e-mail addresses of all the people who received the message initially are displayed in the Send To list. You can then type the text you want to add, if any, and click Send.

✦ **Add the Address of the sender to your Address Book.** When you click the Add Address button, AOL saves the sender's e-mail address in your AOL Address Book.

Of course, you can also get help if this e-mail thing confounds you. Just click Help to find out more.

After you finish reading your mail, close the Mailbox by clicking the Close button. You can then move happily to other AOL activities and check your mail again later whenever you like.

AOL gives you the option of automating your e-mail work by scheduling times for uploading and downloading mail. This means you can work *offline* — that is, while your computer is not connected to the Internet — creating and responding to mail. When you're ready, you can get back onto the Internet and send the old and receive the new all at once, which cuts down on your online time (and may help you organize your other activities, as well).

Going to the Mail Center

AOL puts all kinds of mail help at your disposal. The Mail Center is a kind of mail hub that pulls together a number of different options. You can open the Mail Center any time you are online with AOL. A whole list of mail options appears (see Table 2-1 for an overview of the different choices).

To display the Mail Center, click the Mail Center button in the AOL toolbar; then click the first option, Mail Center. The Mail Center window appears, giving you links to the things you are most likely to want to do with e-mail (see Figure 2-2).

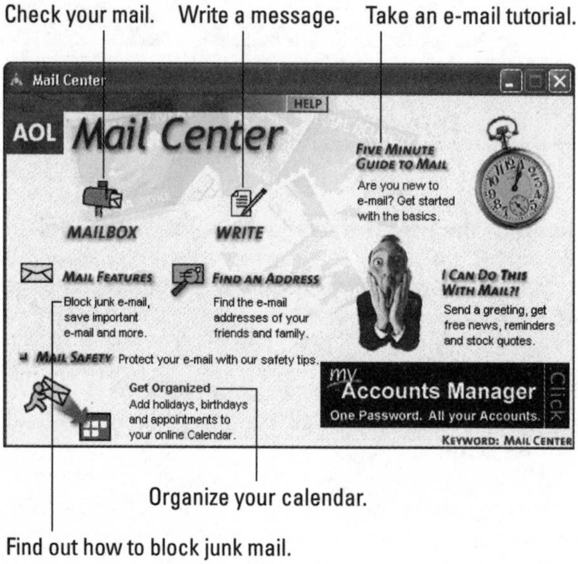

Check your mail.   Write a message.   Take an e-mail tutorial.

Figure 2-2:
The Mail
Center is a
central
access
point for lots
of mail
activities.

Organize your calendar.

Find out how to block junk mail.

Probably the best thing that the Mail Center has to offer you is convenience, while you're finding your way around the AOL mail system. After you get comfortable finding commands in the places where you are likely to use them most, you'll be less likely to need the Center to pull it all together for you.

To use any of the features in the Mail Center, simply click the link you want. Here's a brief description of where the links take you:

✦ **Mailbox** opens your mailbox, where you can read new, old, and sent mail.

✦ **Write** displays the Write Mail window, where you can compose a new message.

✦ **Five-Minute Guide to Email** takes you on an e-mail tour.

✦ **Mail Features** provide a list of features you can use, including blocking spam.

✦ **Find an Address** gives you the means to locate the address of another AOL member.

✦ **I Can Do This with Email?** Gives you e-mail extras, including the ability to send greeting cards, check news, and more.

✦ **Mail Safety** gives you suggestions for e-mail safety.

✦ **Get Organized** lets you use e-mail information in tandem with your online calendar.

Table 2-1	Mail Center Offerings
Option	*Description*
Mail Center	Displays the AOL Mail Center
Read Mail	Opens the Mailbox window
Write mail	Displays the Write Mail window so that you can write a new message
Old Mail	Shows you the mail you have received and read in the past
Sent Mail	Lists the mail you've sent from your AOL account
Recently Deleted Mail	Displays the mail you've deleted in the last 24 hours
Address Book	Opens the Address Book so that you can review, add, delete, or edit e-mail addresses and names
Mail Preferences	Displays a list of options that you can use to choose your preferences about the way in which mail is stored, formatted, and sent
Mail Controls	Enables you to set parental controls and block junk mail
Set up Mail Signatures	Opens a window so that you can add a digital signature to your messages

(continued)

Table 2-1 *(continued)*

Option	Description
Mail Extras	Displays the Mail Extras window so that you can add art, photos, sounds, and more
Set up Automatic AOL	Launches the setup program to help you automate e-mail tasks
Run Automatic AOL	Starts the Automatic AOL feature and gives you the option of forcing delivery
Read Offline Mail	Displays e-mail that you have written and saved using Send Later
Mail Waiting to be Sent	Shows the mail currently saved in your Personal Filing Cabinet

Creating Messages

E-mail has now been around long enough that you must have been sleeping in a castle surrounded by thorns and fierce dragons in order to have missed it. Chances are, with or without Prince Charming, you've used or at least seen e-mail in a number of different places, on different systems.

E-mail, like everything else in AOL, is oh-so-incredibly simple. Nothing mysterious here. Just click Write and the Write Mail window opens. This is the place where you compose and send the messages that you create (see Figure 2-3).

 Can't stand it anymore? You can turn off all sound in AOL (including the happy announcer's voice) by clicking the Mail Center button, choosing Preferences, clicking General Preferences, and clearing the Enable event sounds check box.

Addressing your message

The first step in the Write Mail window is to enter the address of the person to whom you want to send the message. Simply click in the Send To box and type the address. An e-mail address has three parts:

handle@server.com

The handle is the screen name or user name of the person to whom you're sending the e-mail. The @ sign divides the handle and the server on which the mail is stored. The server is usually the name of the online service providing the e-mail. For AOL users, e-mail addresses look like this:

Steve23@aol.com

 The most reliable way to enter a person's e-mail address is to select it from your AOL Address Book. See " A Well-Ordered Address Book" for the scoop on how to do that.

Click Write to start the process.

Enter the e-mail address you're sending to.

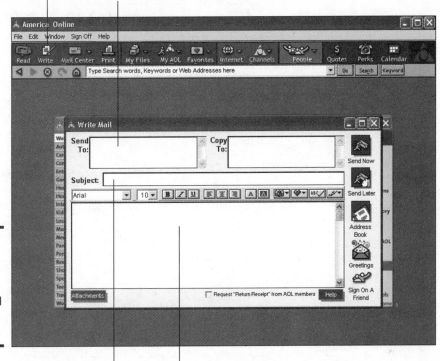

Figure 2-3:
Spill your
guts or
make your
case. E-mail
is easy with
AOL.

What's this all about?   Type your message here.

Choose your subject

The Subject line is like the title of your text; it tells readers at a glance what
the message will be about. To enter the subject of the message, just click in
the line and type the phrase. Remember to keep it short and to the point —
some e-mail programs display only the first 20 to 30 characters, and if you
drone on forever, the recipient may not have a clue what your message is
about.

Taking care of text

Just type your message in the text window. If you're more focused on sub-
stance than style, you don't need to worry about the formatting options
available to you. If you want to take an extra minute and make sure that
your words look the way you want them to, you can use some of the formatting tools to improve the aesthetics of your prose. Table 2-2 gives you an
overview of the various tools that you can use to work with the text of your
message.

Table 2-2	Tools You'll Use for E-Mail Composition	
Tool	**Name**	**Description**
Arial	Font	Allows you to choose the font for the text
10	Size	Lets you select the size of the text
B	Bold	Boldfaces selected text or text following the cursor position
I	Italic	Italicizes text or turns on the italic attribute
U	Underline	Underlines text or turns on the underline feature
≡	Left	Aligns text with the left margin
≡	Center	Centers text
≡	Right	Aligns text with the right margin
A	Text Color	Lets you choose text color
A	Background Color	Enables you to choose a background color for the message
📷	Insert a Picture	Inserts the picture that you select in the current message
♥	Insert Favorite Place	Adds a link to one of your AOL favorites
ABC✓	Spell Check	Checks the spelling of the current message
✎	Insert Signature File	Adds a signature to your message

Sending Messages

After you enter your message in the Write Mail window, you're ready to send. AOL gives you two choices for sending — now or later. If you click Send Now, AOL sends the message immediately and displays a small popup message box, telling you that the message has been sent. (You need to click OK to clear the message box and return to the AOL window.)

Don't send that virus warning

Every time a new virus appears, millions and millions of people take it upon themselves to forward virus warning messages to all of their friends, who dutifully forward the warnings to all of their friends, and so on. In several recent cases, the amount of damage done by well-intentioned people sending out warning messages to their friends actually exceeded the amount of damage done by the virus itself — the drain on systems around the world was so great.

To top if off, some of the warning messages are full of bogus information. Two recent bogus warnings advised people to delete perfectly legitimate files from their PCs, claiming the files were infected! A friend tells ten of her friends, who each tell ten of their friends, and all of a sudden people are self-inflicting far more damage than any mere virus could've done. Makes me wonder what would happen if you

started a chain letter advising people to stick a wad of chewing gum in their CD drives, to prevent the spread of the dread CD virus.

If you feel a real urge to warn all of your friends about the latest virus, don't forward a message to them, no matter how authoritive it may seem. Instead, pick up the phone or walk over to their cubicle, point them to a reputable news organization's Web site — www.cnet.com and www.cnn.com always have good virus coverage — and let them read the latest news for themselves.

And if a friend forwards you a virus warning in e-mail, do all of us a big favor. Send him the preceding paragraph, ask him to print it out and tape it to the side of his computer, and beg him to refer to it the next time he gets the forwarding urge.

Thank you.

 If you want to deliver the message later, click the Send Later button. A message appears telling you that your mail has been saved in the Mail Waiting to Be Sent folder of your Personal Filing Cabinet. You can schedule the time to send and receive mail by clicking Auto AOL (for more information on setting up a schedule, see "Autopilot AOL" later in this chapter).

 If you want to see the mail you saved, follow these steps:

1. **Click the My Files down-arrow.**

   The drop-down menu appears.

2. **Click Personal Filing Cabinet.**

   The Personal Filing Cabinet window opens (see Figure 2-4). The outgoing mail messages are saved in the Mail Waiting To Be Sent folder. You can view a message, if you want, by double-clicking the message that you want to see.

Save outgoing mail here.

Figure 2-4:
If you want
to wait to
deliver all
your mail
at one time,
you can
save it
in your
Personal
Filing
Cabinet.

View and edit the message by clicking Open.

Sending and Receiving Files

E-mail is not just for messages anymore. Luckily (especially for those of us who do our work in remote, ends-of-the-earth kinds of places), e-mail also allows us to send and receive files electronically. This means that the report can make it to the office on time, even though you're stuck in the Detroit airport. Or you can go ahead and take the kids to the Grand Canyon, even though you've got a research paper due the day after you get back.

Sending file attachments

The process of sending a file attachment is really creating an e-mail message, with one step added. Create your message as usual, entering the e-mail address, typing the subject, and adding the text that you want the recipient to read. Format as usual. Then, to add the file attachment, follow these steps:

1. **Click Attachments.**

The Attachments window appears.

2. **Click Attach.**

The Attach dialog box opens so that you can navigate to the folder where the file that you want to attach is stored.

3. **Select the file and click Open.**

The file is added to the Attachments window.

4. **Click OK to close the window.**

   The name of the attachment appears to the right of the Attachments window.

5. **Click Send Now or Send Later to send the message with the file attached.**

Want a receipt to make sure that your important file reaches its destination? Click the check box for Request "Return Receipt" from AOL Members.

Greetings, Earthlings! AOL wants to build in a little fun with the standard day-in, day-out tasks of creating and sending e-mail. By clicking the Greetings button in the Write Mail window, you can choose to send a variety of greetings, including e-mail art, banners, photos, smileys, and sounds.

Receiving files

Not only will you be sending other people e-mail messages with files attached; at some point, you'll no doubt be receiving such files yourself. The process of opening the file attachments (and saving them for later) goes like this:

1. **Connect to AOL.**

   You've got mail!

2. **Click Read in the AOL toolbar.**

   The Mail Center window appears.

3. **Double-click the message with the attachment.**

   The attachment appears as a smaller message icon to the left of the message's subject.

4. **Click Download Now.**

   The Download Manager window appears, displaying a warning that the attachment could be questionable if you don't know the person sending you the attachment. Click Yes if you want to continue.

Many viruses that you've read about in the newspapers — ILOVEYOU, Anna Kournikova, Sircam, and their ilk — travel as files attached to e-mail messages *from people you know*. These viruses are very crafty; they scan address books to make it appear as if the infected person sent you a file, when in fact, the virus sent the file. AOL does a very good job of scanning for infected messages, but it doesn't catch everything. You should never, ever, ever open a file that's sent to you unless you expect that specific file to be coming your way. If you have any doubts at all, shoot an e-mail message back to the sender and ask whether she intentionally sent you the file in question. If she didn't, chances are very good that she has the virus.

5. **Navigate to the folder in which you want to store the file. Click Save.**

A File Transfer window shows you the progress of the download. When the download is complete, the happy announcer says "File done!" and a message box appears, asking whether you want to view the downloaded file. If you do, click Yes; otherwise, click No.

A Well-Ordered Address Book

AOL's Address Book stores the names and e-mail addresses of people with whom you trade messages, whether you do it once or daily. When you are reading an e-mail message sent to you in the Read Mail window, you can click the Add to Address Book button to deposit the person's information in the book for later use. You can also enter names and addresses manually to create groups, delete names, and more. And when you're creating e-mail messages, you use the Address Book to choose names of the people whom you want to receive your messages.

Checking out the Address Book

To get started with the AOL Address Book, click Mail Center in the AOL toolbar. When the submenu appears, click Address Book. The Address Book window appears (see Figure 2-5).

Select the name to change an e-mail address.

Figure 2-5: The Address Book lists names of people with whom you trade messages.

Use these buttons to add the selected name

To add an Address Book entry.

The Address Book includes three different areas:

✦ The Name/Address list shows the names of all the people currently in your Address Book.

✦ The Add/Edit buttons enable you to create new entries and edit the ones you've already got.

✦ The Mail Command buttons let you choose the operation that you want to carry out using the selected recipient names.

Adding names to the Address Book

The more you e-mail, the more you discover new people you want to add to your Address Book. You can do this on the fly by clicking the Add to Address Book button when you're reviewing your new mail in the Read Mail window. That action adds the person automatically with no further action from you.

In some cases, however, you want to type in the information for a person without having received an e-mail message first. To add that person's data to the Address Book, click New Person. The New Person window appears, as shown in Figure 2-6.

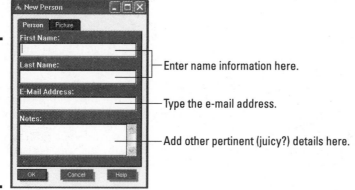

Figure 2-6: Add information for a new e-mail recipient in the New Person window.

Enter name information here.

Type the e-mail address.

Add other pertinent (juicy?) details here.

To enter the information, simply click in each of the fields, type the information requested, and then press Tab to move to the next field. When you're finished entering information, click OK. The New Person dialog box closes and you are returned to the Address Book window.

Creating a group of people enables you to send an e-mail message to a group of people all at once. You can create the list of addresses organized around a specific topic — for example, suppose that you write a weekly e-mail newsletter for all the music teachers in your district. If you create a music group in your AOL Address Book by clicking New Group and entering all the e-mail addresses that you want to include, you can send that one e-mail to all the teachers at once by simply clicking the group name and clicking Send To.

One thing that's sure about e-mail: Addresses are going to change. When you need to edit the e-mail address of a person already in your Address Book, simply select the name of the person and click Edit. The information is displayed in the Edit Person window. Simply make the changes you want and then click OK to save them.

Finally, you may have some people that you ultimately want to delete from your Address Book. Whether they have done something to fall from grace or they have simply changed e-mail addresses and moved along, you can delete their information easily by selecting the name in the Name/Address book and clicking Delete.

Using the Address Book

After you enter the information you need, you can use it in e-mails ad nauseum. Simply click the name that you want to use and then click one of the following buttons:

✦ **Send To** inserts the name in the Send To box in a blank e-mail message you're creating.

✦ **Copy To** adds the name to the Copy To box in a new e-mail message. Copy To simply sends a copy of the message that is sent to the primary recipient listed in the Send To box.

✦ **Blind Copy** puts the name in the BCC: box on the new e-mail message. This causes the message to be sent to the selected person without displaying the names of any other people listed in the BCC box.

✦ **Save / Replace** enables you to save a copy of your Address Book to use on another computer or replace your current Address Book with another.

Earn $25 by referring a friend to AOL. You can find out more by clicking Keyword and typing **Friend**; then click Go. You can also click Write and click Sign On a Friend in the Write Mail window.

Controlling Junk Mail

Get rid of junk mail — unwanted, unwelcome, uninvited mail. Junk mail, also called *spam*, clogs AOLs veins and slows down your wanted mail delivery. The AOL Mail Controls feature enables you to control the e-mail that you receive by netting out the mail you don't want. You can block specific screen names or Internet addresses, block exchanges of attached files or pictures in e-mail, and more.

Forward this message and save a poor child

Yes, it's true. Bill Gates will send you $10 for every copy of this e-mail message that you forward to a friend. I know. I asked Bill over coffee this morning. You can help a poor child survive a horrendous operation, because Intel will send ten cents to her for each copy of this message that you forward. I know. I asked Intel over coffee this morning. A bunch of hackers are going to start a riot on AOL next week, and they'll come after you if you don't send this message to ten of your AOL friends. I know. I scorched a hacker with hot coffee this morning. The President is about to impose a federal tax for every e-mail message you open. I know. I asked George Washington over coffee this morning. Your computer will die if you open any e-mail message with "It takes guts to say 'Jesus'" in the subject line. I know. I asked Jesus over coffee this morning. For the record, he likes low-fat lattes, half caffeine, extra foam, with a light dash of cinnamon.

Gimme a break, folks.

Virus myths flood the ether. If you send messages like those, you're only contributing to the problem. Bill isn't going to fork over ten bucks for mailing a message. George, er, the President doesn't have any way of counting how many e-mail messages you read. It takes guts to ignore chain letters, even when they come from people you know and otherwise respect.

Before you forward that improbable message and add to the deluge of bogus bits ricocheting around the information highway, drop by Rob Rosenberger's Virus Myths home page, www.vmyths.com. Rob doesn't have any particular axes to grind. He doesn't sell anti-virus software or spam scanners. He didn't make a mint from Code Red. He's a refreshing voice of sanity in this truly bizarre world. And he could keep you from making a really big fool of yourself.

1. **Connect to AOL.**

2. **Click Mail Center in the AOL toolbar. When the submenu appears, click Mail Controls.**

The Mail Controls window appears.

3. **Click Junk Mail.**

The Junk Mail window appears (see Figure 2-7), giving you three options:

- **Report Junk Mail** gives you the means to tell AOL about the mail you're receiving.

- **Mail Controls** provide choices that you can use to weed out unwanted mail.

- **Insider Tips** list suggestions for avoiding mail that you don't want.

4. **Choose the Mail Controls option.**

This action opens a window that leads you through the process of setting up blocking of the e-mail that you don't want.

Inbox filled with junk? Tell AOL about it.

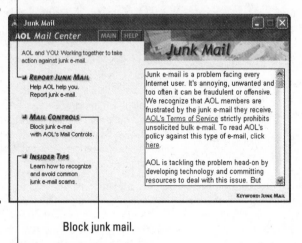

Figure 2-7:
AOL tries to
help you
weed out
the
messages
that you
don't want
by providing
mail-
blocking
controls.

Block junk mail.

How to avoid unwanted e-mail.

Autopilot AOL

Depending on the payment plan you've set up with AOL, you may or may not be worried about the amount of time you spend online. If you purchased an unlimited plan, you can stay online 24/7 if you choose (although your spouse and kids may object) with no additional charge. If you selected a plan that counts the minutes you are logged on, which means you get charged a premium for the time that you go over your allotment, you may be looking for a way to limit your actual online minutes without limiting the amount of work you can do (or fun you can have) on the Internet.

For just this reason, AOL created an Automatic feature that enables you to schedule the time when you send and receive mail. This keeps you from logging on and staying on all day, waiting for those next few e-mail messages. Now you don't have to run to your computer 14 times a day to wait hopefully to hear the happy announcer say, "You've got mail!" Your computer can do the checking for you, and you can create the e-mail messages that you want to send, click Save for Later, and trust that they will be delivered online when the time is right.

Not only can you send and receive e-mail messages all at once using Automatic AOL, but you can read and respond to newsgroup postings and download files that have been placed in the Download Manager.

There are two parts to working with Automatic AOL: setting the thing up; and letting it work. Setup begins with the Mail Center button in the AOL toolbar. You don't have to be online when you begin. Here are the steps for setting up:

1. **Launch AOL, if necessary.**

2. **Click the Mail Center button in the AOL toolbar.**

   The submenu appears.

3. **Select Set Up Automatic AOL.**

   This launches a setup utility that asks you whether you want AOL to automatically take care of the following things:

   - Retrieving files

   - Downloading files

   - Sending mail you've written offline

   - Downloading files saved in the Download Manager

   - Sending and receiving newsgroup postings

4. **Choose the screen names for which you want to set up automatic AOL.**

   You can choose to automate e-mail tasks for each name independently, if you choose. Enter the password for the screen name(s) you want to use; then click Continue.

5. **Select the days on which you want the process to be done.**

6. **Indicate how often you want the automated process to check for and download waiting mail.**

   You have several options, from every half hour to once a day.

7. **Choose the time when you want the process to occur.**

8. **Click OK, and you're scheduled!**

   The next time that clock clicks over to the appointed time, AOL (which must be left open in order for Auto AOL to work) logs on and checks e-mail for you automatically.

If you're too impatient to wait for your scheduled time, you can force the process by clicking the Mail Center button in the AOL toolbar and choosing Run Automatic AOL. When the Automatic AOL window appears, click the Sign Off check box if you want your computer to sign off after the download is complete. To start the Automatic process, click Begin.

Chapter 3: Beyond the Basics of AOL

In This Chapter

✔ Web surfing the AOL way

✔ News, up close and personal

✔ Writing and rants in AOL newsgroups

✔ Are you up for a little chat?

✔ Don't shoot the AOL Instant Messenger

*T*his chapter explains how to do those extra things that AOL offers — beyond e-mail and channel hopping. First, you go for a brief Web surf-and-search, using the easy-to-follow AOL interface. Next, you find out how to arrange to have news delivered to your mailbox so that you can see and read only the stories that you're most interested in (a handy feature in our time-crunched, information-glutted world). After you read up on current events, you can join a chatroom to discuss what you learned or — if you're feeling stout-hearted — lurk in a newsgroup to see what others are saying about your topics of interest. Finally, you find out a bit about the buzz around AOL Instant Messenger, enough that you can decide for yourself whether it's an added convenience or a massive time drain.

AOL Parental Controls are available for each of these various activities. If your kids are planning on surfing, using Instant Messenger, or chatting, revisit your filter settings to determine what you want to allow access to. To review your current settings and modify them if needed, click Keyword, type **Parental Controls**, and click Go.

Using AOL on the Web

If you've ever used another Web browser, you'll find it easy to move around on the Web in AOL. Nothing is too difficult about figuring out the address and navigation techniques. To get started on the Web, follow these steps:

1. **Start AOL as usual.**

   AOL starts and the Welcome! window appears (see Figure 3-1).

Not sure what you're looking for? Click Search.

Click here to display a list of common AOL Web sites.

Click and type the Web address here.

Figure 3-1:
Getting
Webby
with it.

2. **Click in the Address line, and type one of the following:**

   - **Search words.** Yes, that's right — you can just type **bugs** to search
     for bugs on the Web, no other tools needed.

   - **Keywords.** If you type a word that is one of AOL's keywords, such as
     parenting, the channel that corresponds to the keyword comes up.

   - **Web address.** If you know the address of the site that you want to
     see, enter it. For example, `www.aol.com` brings up AOL on the Web.

3. **Press Enter or click Go in the Web toolbar. Now you're surfing!**

Landing and looking around

When you get to the Web page you seek, you're charged with finding your
way around. It's pretty simple, really. The AOL Web toolbar includes a set of
five buttons that you can use to navigate:

- ✦ Click Previous to move to a previous page.
- ✦ Click Next to move to the next page.
- ✦ Click Stop to stop the page currently loading.
- ✦ Click Refresh to refresh the display of the current page.
- ✦ Click Home to move to the page you've specified as the default home page.

The Previous and Next buttons won't do anything until you've been surfing through a few pages. Until you have viewed other pages during your current work session, AOL has nothing to go backward or forward to.

When you find the site you're looking for, getting the information you seek is easy. As you would expect, the links that lead to more information appear as underlined text or as buttons on the Web page (see Figure 3-2). You can work with the Web window in the same way that you work with other windows; click the Maximize button to fill the AOL window with the Web window; click the close box to close the Web window.

A word about channels

AOL has a number of communities that you can join to share information about subjects that interest you. Whether your motives are professional or personal, you can find all kinds of information in the form of live chats, online articles, bulletin boards, and more. To move to one of AOL's channels, you can type the channel name directly in the Address line and press Enter, or you can click the Channels tool in the AOL toolbar to display the list of available channels. You can select from one of the following special-interest groups:

Autos	Music
Careers & Work	News
Computer Center	Parenting
Entertainment	Personal Finance
Games	Research & Learn
Health	Shopping
House & Home	Sports
International	Teens
Kids Only	Travel
Local Guide	Women

Use to navigate.   Click underlined links to move on.   Close Web window.

Web window

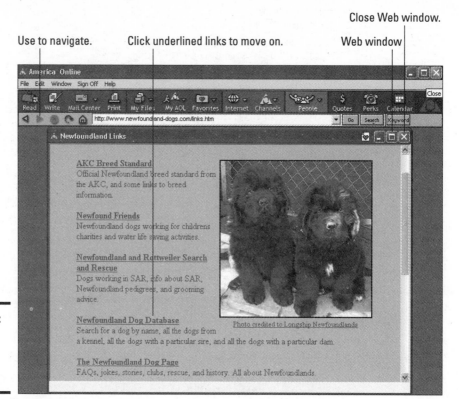

Figure 3-2:
Exploring
the Web,
the AOL
way.

Shooting fish in a barrel (AOL searching)

If you're not sure exactly which page you're looking for, you can search for
the page with AOL's built-in searching capability, using one of two methods:

✦ You can type the word or phrase that you're looking for in the Address
line and press Enter.

✦ You can click the Search button to display the Search window; then
enter your topic or phrase in the Search text box (see Figure 3-3).

After you enter the topic that you want to find, click Search or press Enter.
AOL displays a screen of links that match the setting you entered. To move
to the page with the information you seek, click the text link.

Enter what you are looking for.

Click a link to find information.

Narrow your search.

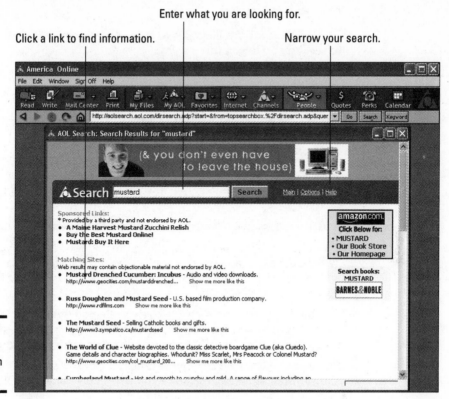

Figure 3-3:
Doing the AOL search thing.

Not sure about searching? You can click Help to find out how to narrow your search so that you're more likely to find what you want without too much wandering.

Receiving News the Way You Want It

Are you a news hound? If your morning isn't complete without seeing the latest headlines in your favorite areas of interest, you can have AOL serve up your daily helping of news while you sip your first cup of coffee. Using AOL's personalized news service, you can create a News Profile that tells AOL what you want to see so that AOL can deliver the news directly to your mailbox. To create a personalized news profile, follow these steps:

1. **Click My AOL in the AOL toolbar.**

A shortcut menu appears.

2. **Click News Profiles.**

   The My News wizard launches to help you customize the news you want to see. You do this in three steps:

   - Select the categories that you want to see.

   - Enter the search terms that you want AOL to look for.

   - Say, "Yes, I already *told* you — that's what I want!"

3. **Click Go to Step 1 to get things started.**

   AOL begins leading you through the process. A window appears, giving you a list of new categories. It's a can't-miss endeavor. Just click what you want to hear about, scroll down to the bottom of the page, and click Next Step.

4. **AOL then asks you to narrow the search to more specific categories.**

   For example, if you selected Media in the previous list, ask yourself "What am I most interested in seeing about the media?" If radio is your area of interest, both broadcast and webcast, you can enter **radio, broadcast, webcast** in the Required Terms box. Click Next.

5. **The final step shows you what you've selected, gives you the option of changing it, and lets you enter a name for your profile and choose the number of articles that you want to start with (see Figure 3-4).**

   When you finish entering your settings, click Preview Profile and AOL shows you a sample of the news you will receive in your AOL mailbox. To view the article, simply click the link.

Is there a subject that makes your skin crawl? You can tell AOL to block out any stories that have a certain topic by entering it in the "Do NOT deliver" box.

Joining Newsgroups through AOL

A *newsgroup* is a kind of discussion group on the Internet that takes place in the form of postings between individuals and the group. Newsgroups are a lot like the marathon talk sessions that you probably had in the dorm at college, where anybody can join in — and say just about anything that they like. In most newsgroups, facts rarely stand in the way of a good story.

Review your category and search choices.   Enter a profile name.

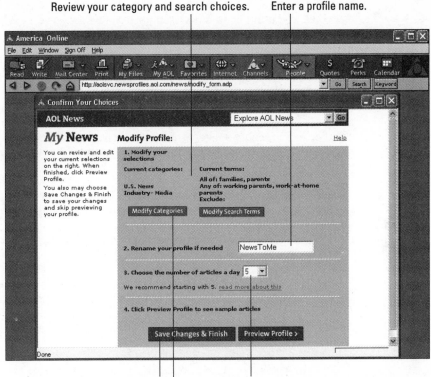

Figure 3-4:
News the
way you
want it.

Click here to save your choices.   How many articles do you want to see?

Click here to change your choices.

When you deal with newsgroups, make sure to leave your native-born non-sense detector set on "High." If somebody tells the group that Mnfsxlpt Corporation's stock price is about to double, consider the possibility that the person making the announcement may have a vested interest in it becoming a self-fulfilling prophecy. If somebody tells the group that Windows XP won't recognize more than 64 MB of memory, so you shouldn't buy any more memory, consider the possibility that the person offering advice may not know how to spell "Windows XP." (Don't laugh. I've seen it. For the record, any flavor of Windows since Windows 95 recognizes all the memory you can throw at it — at least 2 GB or 2048 MB. The 64 MB story is an urban legend, repeated a dozen times a day on various newsgroups around the Internet.)

Newsgroups require that you use a newsreader (which AOL provides) to view and respond to postings in the group.

Listserves are a little bit like newsgroups, but distributed messages are sent as e-mail. You don't need a newsreader to join a listserve — all you need is your regular, trusty e-mail program. But you do need a newsreader to read messages on a newsgroup.

Newsgroups are a bit controversial because their content is so varied. Depending on the newsgroup you visit, you may find lots of good information shared among people who have similar interests; but you also may find, as I did, almost all pornographic messages on an innocent-looking parenting site. For this reason, I suggest that you lurk a while before subscribing to any individual group so that you can see what they *really* talk about and see whether you want to join in.

Moderated newsgroups are groups in which a real person reads and allows the posting of messages to the list. These types of newsgroups tend to have more real information than their unmoderated counterparts. Why? Human nature, I guess — when the moderator's away, the cats will play.

Getting into newsgroups

Want to explore the strange world of newsgroups? If so, click Internet in the AOL toolbar and choose Newsgroups. (Or click Keyword and type **Newsgroups**; then click Go.) Figure 3-5 shows the Newsgroups window.

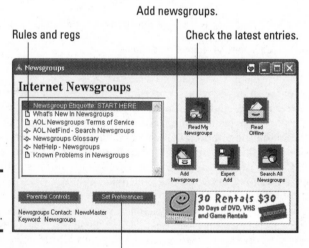

Figure 3-5: Launching Newsgroups.

Yippee! Filtering junk posts. When you first choose the Newsgroup option, a message appears telling you that AOL now provides the ability to filter out junk posts. You need to click the Set Preferences button on the newsgroups main form to enable the filtering option.

Whew — if ever a place needed parental controls, Newsgroups is it! When you get into the newsgroup listings, you see just about every subject under the sun . . . and then some. To keep unwanted topics away from your kids, click the Parental Controls button in the bottom of the Newsgroups dialog box. Choose the screen name to which you want to apply the parental controls, and click Edit. You can block all groups or block certain groups; but to really filter out all the messages that may not be suitable for young kids, you need to go into Preferences and enter the words you want to avoid. That's a lot of trouble just to gather a few stray bits of helpful info, in my opinion. I'd rather spend my time searching the Web.

Finding the newsgroups you want

In the Newsgroups dialog box, click Search All Newsgroups. When the Search All Newsgroups window appears, enter a word or phrase that you want to search for. Click List Articles and AOL displays a list of newsgroups related to the topic you entered (see Figure 3-6).

Enter the topic here.   Double-click your selection.

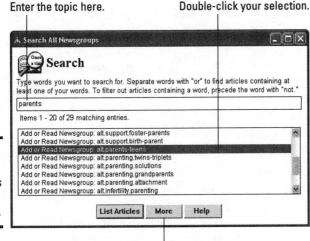

Figure 3-6:
Finding
newsgroups
that you
want to join.

Find groups that share your interest.

Getting help with newsgroups

AOL's Help isn't very helpful if you're a new user trying to find your way around a text-laden landscape in a click-the-button kind of world. Here are a few newsgroups that include information meant to help new newsgroup users find their footing:

✔ news.newusers.questions is a simple question-and-answer forum that helps new users find the answers they seek.

✔ news.announce.newusers is an active group that provides messages and resources for new users.

✔ news.answers provides FAQs (Frequently Asked Questions) on newsgroup-related topics.

If the newsgroup names don't make any sense to you, it may be because they are displayed in Internet-speak instead of English-style descriptions. You can change the way newsgroup names are displayed by clicking Set Preferences in the Newsgroups dialog box. In the Name Style column (on the Viewing tab, which should appear by default), click Descriptive newsgroup names; then click Save. When you search for newsgroups, the new names should better describe what you see. If you want to stick with the Internet-style names, however, you can always do as the natives do and learn to speak the language. Table 3-1 gives you a description of the basic newsgroup types and their identifiers.

Table 3-1	Making Sense of Newsgroup Categories
Category	*Description*
alt	alternative newsgroups
aol	America Online groups
bit	BITNET mailing lists
biz	business and commercial newsgroups
comp	computers and computer science
misc	miscellaneous groups
news	USENET newsgroup software & policies
rec	recreational and hobby newsgroups
sci	science and research newsgroups
soc	social issues (and socializing) newsgroups
talk	talk/debate and issues

To get a full list of newsgroup categories, go to www.zcu.cz/services/ news2www.

Before you subscribe to a newsgroup, click *List articles in newsgroup <name>* and read through the postings to see whether that's the group you're interested in. If you're not happy with the content, skip it by clicking the close box.

If you want to subscribe to the newsgroup, click *Subscribe to newsgroup <name>*. After a moment, a message box appears, telling you that the group has been added to your subscribed list.

Reading newsgroup postings

When you find a posting worth reading, simply click it to select it and then click the Read button. The message opens in a message window, similar in appearance to an e-mail message (see Figure 3-7). You then can do one of the following things:

+ Move to the previous subject in the posting list by clicking ← Subject.

+ Move to the previous message by clicking ← Message.

+ Move the message to your AOL personal filing cabinet by clicking Move.

+ Go to the next message by clicking Message →.

+ Go to the next subject in the list by clicking Subject →.

+ Mark the message as Unread (which enables you to view it again later).

+ Create a new message to post to the list by clicking New Message.

+ Reply to the current posting by clicking Reply.

+ Get Help on working with newsgroups by clicking Help.

Although you'll no doubt catch on to the lingo quickly if you spend any time at all in newsgroups, knowing a few of the common terms may be helpful:

+ **Flame:** A hateful, attacking posting directed at a newsgroup participant. Flaming messages are not allowed, but in an unmoderated newsgroup, who's to say? If you experience flaming on AOL, you can report it to the powers that be for the appropriate action.

+ **Lurk:** To hang out and read messages without posting anything yourself. Lurking is good. As a general rule, spend plenty of time lurking before you subscribe to a newsgroup, so that you can make sure that it's something you really want to join.

   ✦ **Posting:** The process of composing a message and sending it to the newsgroup. The message appears in the group list and is said to be *posted*.

   ✦ **Spam:** A name for annoying postings trying to sell participants something. Often used for get-rich-quick schemes, spam is also against the rules (which doesn't help much if nobody's watching).

Mark all the messages Read.

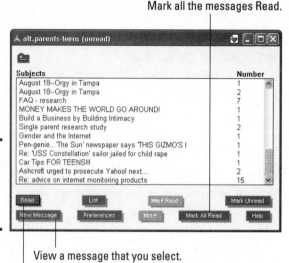

Figure 3-7:
Messages worth reading? Here's how.

View a message that you select.

Send a message to the group.

AOL Chat

You either love chat or you hate it. Chat is one of those real-time surrogates for actual human contact, enabling you to "converse" with other supposedly live people with the same spurts, starts, interruptions, and logic flaws that most human conversations contain. AOL has made good use of the chat phenomenon and has built communities around topics that are likely to have something for almost everyone.

Get Started with chat by clicking the Chat icon in the Welcome page or by clicking the People button in the AOL toolbar and clicking People Connection from the submenu. The People Connection window opens so that you can find the chat that you want to join (see Figure 3-8).

Locate a chat.   Take the chat tutorial or go to another live topic.

Search for a community.

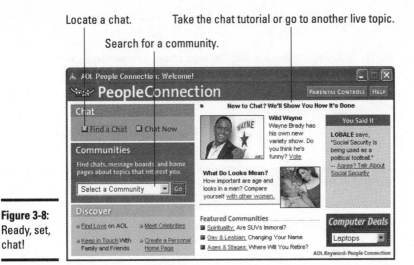

Figure 3-8:
Ready, set,
chat!

If you want to chat in one of the available communities (also called *channels* in AOL), click the Select a Community down-arrow and click Go. A list of channels appears. Click a channel and you move directly to the Web page that lists chats related to the topic that you're interested in.

AOL offers a tutorial that walks you through the paces of chatting in real-time. A link appears in the People Connection window; click it to start the tutorial.

If you're interested in celebrity chats — who can ever get enough Brittany Spears? — check out AOL Live. That forum lists the current and upcoming celebrity chats so that you can plan the times that you want to check back.

Finding a chat

If you just want to try chatting and any old room will do, you can jump right in with both feet by clicking the People button and then clicking Chat Now. Immediately, you are taken to the Town Hall, where a live chat is going on.

Until you become familiar with the different chats that AOL offers, however, you may want to try a sampling of different communities. To find a chat that interests you, you use AOL's Find a Chat feature. You can find a chat two different ways:

✦ Click People in the AOL toolbar, choose Find a Chat on the menu, and then choose Find a Chat in the People Connections dialog box.

✦ Click Chat in the Welcome window, and choose Find a Chat in the People Connections dialog box.

When you click Find a Chat, AOL opens the Find a Chat window (see Figure 3-9). To find a chat that is to your liking, follow these steps:

1. **In the left side of the Find a Chat window, choose the category of the chat you want to find.**

2. **Click the View Chats button to display the currently active chats in the category you selected.**

3. **Select the chat in the right side of the window that you think you want to look in on.**

4. **Click Go Chat to join the chat. The chat window opens and your attendance is announced to the list.**

See who's talking.

Go to where the chatting is.

Choose your category.

Select the chat.

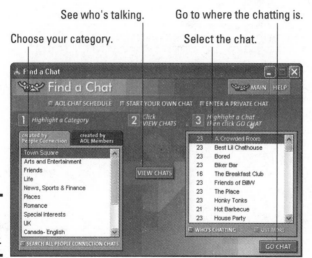

Figure 3-9:
Working the
chat locator.

You can find out what's scheduled in the various AOL communities by clicking AOL Chat Schedule in the Find a Chat window.

Checking out the chat window

Even if you've never chatted before, you figure out the chat window quickly as the conversation gets going. Individual chatters post their comments to the group, and remarks scroll up and off the screen as the talk continues. In the right side of the window, you find a pane that lists the number and screen names of current chatters. At the bottom of the chat window, you see a text entry box (that's where you type your words of wisdom), a Send button, a set of formatting tools (in case you want to get fancy with your thoughts), and other chat options (see Figure 3-10).

To participate in the chat, simply type your comment in the text box and click Send or press Enter. The note appears in the chat window. As other chatters answer you (or continue their earlier conversation), the text scrolls in the window.

If you want to change the format of your messages, click the font down-arrow and choose the new font. You can also change the style of the text by clicking one or more of the style buttons to the right of the font choice.

When you're ready to leave the chatroom, simply click the Close button. Of course, if you're concerned about chatiquette, be sure to say your good-byes first.

Conversations in progress   Screen names of participants

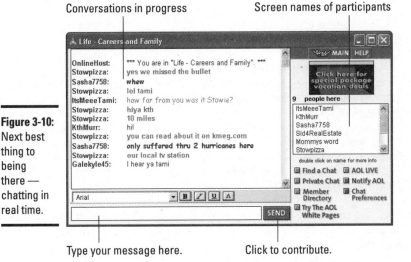

Figure 3-10:
Next best thing to being there — chatting in real time.

Type your message here.   Click to contribute.

Starting your own chat

Maybe you'll be so enamored with chat that you want to start your own online club. AOL simplifies creating your own chat — either public or private. Here are the steps:

1. **Click People in the AOL toolbar.**

2. **Click Start Your Own Chat.**

A dialog box appears, asking whether you want to start one of the following chats:

• Member Chat that other members can join (this is displayed publicly in the Find a Chat dialog box).

- Private Chat, which is a chat that is available only by invitation (you need to give other members the exact name of the group in order for them to join).

3. **Click your choice, double-click a category, enter a name for the group, and click Go Chat.**

   If you selected Member Chat, the group is listed in the Find a Chat listing. If you selected Private Chat, only those members to whom you give the group name will be able to find you.

After you create your chat, if you elected to create a public chat, the chat appears in the Created by AOL Members tab of the Find a Chat dialog box. To join the chat that you created, click the tab, select your chat, and click Go Chat. Yes, it's really that simple.

AOL Instant Messenger

Have you seen the ads for Instant Messenger? Have your friends and relatives started bugging you about how quick and easy it is to use? Well, everything they said is true. Instant Messenger (IM) is easy. It's fast. And it's addictive. I've found by experience that I can get so caught up in the fun of being online at the same time with friends (and friendly coworkers) that I don't do what I'm supposed to be doing — like researching this chapter. Before you know it, an hour or a day has passed and you've traded lots of trivia about last night's Letterman, but you haven't gotten much work done. So, be forewarned.

If you want to get the benefit of instant messaging without using signing up for AOL, you can download the AOL Instant Messenger program (known as AIM), from www.aim.com.

Sending a message

If you decide to test the power of your will and want to give IM a shot, you can follow these steps:

1. **Click People in the AOL toolbar.**

2. **Click Instant Message (or press Ctrl+I).**

   The Send Instant Message dialog box appears (see Figure 3-11).

3. **Type the name of the member that you want to contact in the To box.**

4. **Click Available? to see whether the other member is currently online.**

5. **Type your message in the message window.**

6. **Click Send.**

Enter the member's name.

Make it fancy if you want.

Figure 3-11:
Fast and
easy — and
distracting —
IM!

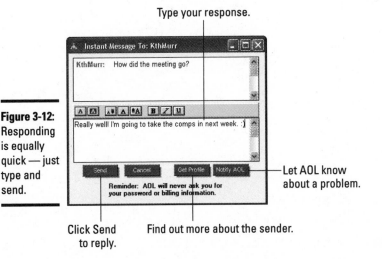

Type your
message.

Click Send to
contribute.

Click here to see
whether the member is online.

If you want to change the format of the message that you send, highlight the
text and click one of the formatting buttons above the text area.

Receiving a message

When an instant message comes in, AOL pops up a message box over your
current AOL window (see Figure 3-12). The message box tells you whom the
message is from and gives you the option of checking the profile of the other
user. It also gives you the means to reply to the message by typing your
response and clicking Send.

Type your response.

Figure 3-12:
Responding
is equally
quick — just
type and
send.

Let AOL know
about a problem.

Click Send
to reply.

Find out more about the sender.

See how easy? That's the great part. But no matter how self-disciplined you are, things can get hairy when you have 15 buddies online all at the same time, all sending you IM messages. For best results, ease into IM and Just Say No when you're really supposed to be working or doing something other than talking about Sam Donaldson's hair.

Sam, *put down that brickbat!* Sheesh. I didn't mean it personally. Really. Ping me on IM and we'll talk about it.

Index

Book VI

Connecting with Microsoft Network

The 5th Wave   By Rich Tennant

"Did you click 'HELP' on the MSN.com menu bar recently? It's Mr. Gates. He wants to know if everything's all right."

Contents at a Glance

Chapter 1: MSN Explorer for Busy People

In This Chapter

- ✓ MSN Explorer 101
- ✓ MSN versus AOL: Who's better?
- ✓ Getting started with MSN
- ✓ Signing off and checking out

This chapter explains how to set up and get moving with MSN Explorer, the new online service offering from Microsoft. Different from Internet Explorer, which is your standard Web browser, MSN Explorer includes all kinds of bells and whistles to play with, as well as friends to chat with along the way.

MSN Explorer is included as the service selected by default when you set up Internet services in Windows XP. However, if you bought your PC with Windows XP pre-installed, the PC's manufacturer may have had a, uh, slightly different opinion. It's all in a state of flux; courtroom dramas are unfolding, as of this writing anyway, as to how much MSN, Passport, and IE you'll see installed on your new systems that are set up to use Windows XP. So by the time you read this chapter — and depending on where, how, and when you purchased your computer — some of the details may be different. We're placing our bets, however, on the likelihood that MSN Explorer, Passport, and IE will all function basically the way they do today — albeit with varying limits about where and how they are offered to users.

What Is MSN Explorer?

Everybody wants an online community to belong to, don't they? After all, we're social animals. We want to chat, and learn, and laugh, and share. We want to buy and sell stocks in a way that makes us rich. We want to find games for our kids that don't cost us anything. We want to trade stories with other parents that make us feel better about the crazy things our kids did last night.

Tell me the important stuff: What's it gonna cost?

MSN Explorer is an online service that is of no charge to you if you can already get on the Internet. So if you are already paying $20 per month or so for access to the Internet and e-mail through an Internet Service Provider, you can simply dial in to the Internet as usual, and then launch MSN Explorer. Microsoft won't attempt to extract a pound of flesh. If you want to use MSN Explorer's Internet access, of course, Microsoft will be thrilled: You simply sign up for the monthly fee (not much different from the way AOL does it).

If you want to use MSN's Internet access, start the process by double-clicking the Signup for MSN Internet Access icon on your desktop.

A wizard launches that leads you through the signup process.

If you want to use MSN Explorer with your current Internet account, choose Start⇨Control Panel. In the Pick a Category window, click Network and Internet Connections. Under Pick a Task, click Set up or change your Internet Connection. When the Internet Properties dialog box appears, click the Setup button. This launches the New Connection Wizard, which leads you through the steps needed to use MSN Explorer on your computer. (For more detailed steps on setting up MSN Explorer, see "Getting Started with MSN Explorer," later in this chapter.)

MSN Explorer is Microsoft's answer to AOL, providing an instant online community, complete with e-mail, calendars, chat rooms, and more. It offers customizable news (the news you're interested in, delivered to your browser); local weather; simple search capabilities; shopping; music — whatever your interests and activities are, MSN provides some mind fodder for an hour or 10.

How MSN Explorer Compares to AOL

The last few chapters focused on AOL's vision of the online world, so if you want to see how AOL does it (and you're not an AOL member yourself), you can flip back through the last several pages and get a load of AOL's basic design and community strategy. But hey — that's a lot of trouble.

Basically, MSN Explorer is similar to AOL, packaged in kinder, gentler colors; presented with softer edges; and focused on *you*, which, depending on your trust level with Microsoft, may be either a good or a bad thing. For example, you have the option of creating an online calendar that tells you where to be and when to be there. Your Buddy List collects the names and addresses of your favorite people. Your mail is convenient and Web-based, which means you can read it from a friend's computer or an Internet kiosk at the mall. But it also means that all of these things are stored online and not on the hard drive of your own safe little system. No biggie? Maybe not. But giving away too much information makes some people nervous.

That being said, MSN Explorer is visually inviting and pretty easy to figure out. The buttons at the top of the window are large, colorful, and obvious. The names underneath save you from having to wonder what you're clicking (see Figure 1-1).

Home is the page displayed by default when you log on. If you get tired of the same old display, you can create a customized home page that is available whenever you sign in to MSN Explorer by clicking Help & Settings (in the MSN window title bar) and choosing Customize Content on Your Home Page.

E-mail in MSN Explorer is Web-based (similar to Hotmail), which means that you can read it online from anywhere. As usual, you can send and receive messages with attachments, pictures, and more. You also keep your address book online. And to keep those embarrassing errors to a minimum ("Looking forward to seeing you tomorrow!"), you can run the spelling checker automatically before you send.

**Book VI
Chapter 1**

**MSN Explorer for
Busy People**

Enter a Web address here.

Write and send e-mail.

Shop 'til you drop.

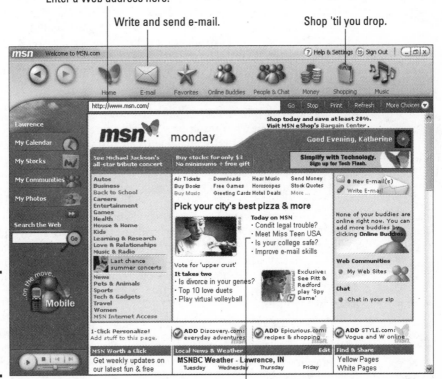

Figure 1-1:
A smooth,
sedate look
and feel
for MSN
Explorer.

Read about topics that interest you.

Both MSN and AOL have the familiar Favorites feature, which enables you to save the sites that you like so that you can return to them easily later. Favorites in MSN work pretty much the same as in AOL, but you have one additional perk: MSN makes it easy for you to copy your *other* Favorites from Internet Explorer into MSN Explorer.

Online Buddies is similar to the Buddy List on AOL; you can trade quick messages or talk with up to four people at once in the same message window, which is a pretty cool feature and something beyond AOL's offering.

Chat is chat is chat, with a few extras like creating your own Web sites. But, basically, you can do the same types of things here that you do with other services — find people of similar interests, strike up a conversation, and party online. Figure 1-2 shows the page displayed when you click People & Chat in the MSN Explorer toolbar — the screen lists the various interests you may have and suggests some possible routes for exploration.

MSN Explorer assumes that people are concerned about ways to manage their money online, and for that reason, it includes the Money tool right on the MSN toolbar. Choosing Money enables you to manage your finances through MSN. You can pay bills online, find a mortgage, track stocks, and more. Again, if you're having trust issues with Microsoft about how much information you want to provide online, this may or may not appeal to you.

Another difference that MSN Explorer has over AOL is that it makes some assumptions about what it thinks you're looking for. A Shopping tool on the toolbar takes you right into a page with all sorts of purchasing possibilities. The Music tool launches WindowsMedia.com — the same Web page that you see in Windows XP's Media Player — so that you can download songs, listen to streaming music, and generally avoid the after-lunch doldrums.

Finally, MSN Explorer makes sure to give you the flexibility that you probably want, offering up to nine different user accounts so that you can have different accounts for each of your family members and your pets. Each account can have its own home page, e-mail account, favorites list, and buddy list, too. MSN Explorer allows only one person to be the manager or administrator, however — so only that person is given the power to delete existing accounts.

S . . . L . . . O . . . W. One of my first experiences with MSN Explorer took a while to manifest. If you click a link to an article from the MSN home page during prime time (early evening), you may wait almost a full minute to see the results.

Enter the topic of your interest
to find a community fit.

Find a community organized around
a topic that interests you.

Go to a live chat.

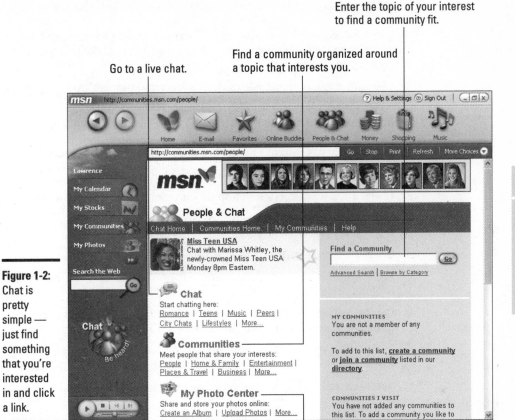

Figure 1-2:
Chat is
pretty
simple —
just find
something
that you're
interested
in and click
a link.

Show off and organized your pictures.

Getting Started with MSN Explorer

In Book IV, Chapter 1, I show you how to use the New Connection Wizard to set up your Internet access. During that process, you see an option to "Get online with MSN," which (surprise, surprise) sets up MSN as your Internet Service Provider.

If you have already run the New Connection Wizard and selected another option (for example, you may have connected to an Internet account with another Service Provider), you didn't pass up your chance to use MSN once and for all. No sireee Bob.

In fact, Microsoft offers you two different ways to use MSN Explorer:

✦ Use MSN as your Internet Service Provider (paying for the privilege, of course) *and* use MSN Explorer, complete with e-mail, Web communities, chat rooms, and more.

✦ Use MSN Explorer's nifty features for free, and pay for Internet access from another Internet Service Provider.

To start the process, follow these steps:

1. **Choose Start⇨Control Panel⇨Network and Internet Connections.**

The Network and Internet Connections window appears.

2. **Under Pick a Task, click Set up or Change your Internet Connection.**

The Internet Properties dialog box appears, with the Connections tab displayed.

3. **Click the Setup button.**

This launches the New Connection Wizard. You see a welcome screen. Ho-hum. Click Next.

4. **On the Network Connection Type page of the wizard, leave the default setting, Connect to the Internet. Click Next.**

5. **In the Getting Ready page of the wizard, leave the default set at Choose From a List of Internet Service Providers (ISPs). Click Next.**

6. **You then see two options that provide different results:**

• Get Online with MSN launches MSN Explorer.

• Select From a List of Other ISPs takes you to a page that displays folders or icons for AOL, Prodigy, Earthlink, MSN, or other ISPs.

When MSN Explorer first starts, the program asks you whether you want to get to the Internet and e-mail by using the Start menu. If you click Yes, the program adds MSN Explorer to the Internet and E-mail choices in the Start menu. Click Yes to add the items; otherwise, click No.

The Welcome to MSN Explorer screen appears and reminds you to make sure that your modem is connected to the phone line and "turned on." Of course, most modems are inside the system unit or laptop, but hey, humor them. Click Continue to start the steps for setting up MSN Explorer. Here are the steps in a nutshell:

1. **Choose your location by clicking the Country/Region down-arrow and scrolling to the name of your particular country. Click Continue.**

2. **Choose whether you want to use MSN Internet Access along with MSN Explorer. The choices are**

   - Sign up for MSN Internet Access and get a new e-mail address.
   - Sign up for MSN Internet Access but use your existing e-mail address.
   - Skip the MSN Internet Access offer.

3. **After you click Continue, the program asks you whether you have an MSN Internet Access account. Click Yes if you do or No if you've got something else. Click Continue.**

   MSN Explorer connects to the Internet and asks

   - Whether you have a hotmail.com e-mail address
   - Whether you have an msn.com e-mail address
   - Whether you just want to create a new e-mail address

4. **If you choose Create a New E-mail Address, MSN asks you for all the prerequisite information: Title, first name, last name. You know the drill. (You can keep your rank and serial number to yourself.)**

5. **Choose a name.**

   You may have to select from several names — or take one MSN offers. When you finally settle on a name, click Continue. The last page says Hello! and displays a happy button: Let's Login!

What's with these "secret questions"?

Okay, so most of us forget a password or two during our online life span. Knowing that we'll forget the password we've chosen, software manufacturers like Microsoft (and sometimes credit card companies) ask us to choose hints that jog our memories. MSN Explorer asks you, as part of the setup process, to choose a "secret question" that will give you a suggestion about the password you've entered. These secret questions are anything but secret. They include ho-hum prompts like these:

✔ What is your mother's maiden name?

✔ What is your favorite pet's name?

✔ What is your anniversary (mm/dd/yy)?

✔ What is your father's middle name?

✔ What is your favorite sports team?

If someone asked me (and nobody did), I'd give them some double-secret, nobody-can-answer-these questions. I'd choose things like, "In which side of the dresser drawer do I keep my socks?" or "What is my favorite snack?" or "How many accountants does it take to buy a pack of light bulbs?"

Figure 1-3 shows the MSN Explorer home page. I take you through the full screen tour in the next chapter.

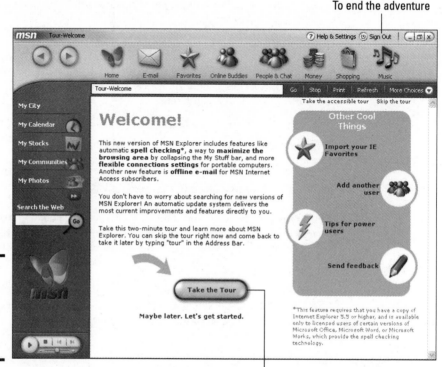

Figure 1-3: The big moment — MSN Explorer revealed!

To end the adventure

To explore the lay of the land

Over and Out

When you're ready to leave MSN Explorer (done with the fun *already?*), click Sign Out in the top right corner of the MSN window. A pop-up message box appears, asking whether you want to save the information you entered to your Windows user account. This enables you to sign in to all Passport-enabled sites from your current computer. Click Yes to save or No to not save.

The next time you sign out, you just hear the MSN Explorer happy voice say, "Goodbye!" If you are not using MSN Explorer as your Internet Service Provider, you are still connected to the Internet, so remember to log off before you turn in for the night.

Chapter 2: Taking MSN Explorer for a Spin

In This Chapter

✔ Checking out the MSN Explorer window

✔ Ready, set, surf!

✔ Get your passport to a better world

✔ Change that password

✔ Personalize your home page, your way

This chapter explains how to chart your Web course with MSN Explorer. You discover what the Web landscape looks like, and you find out about the pros and cons of Microsoft Passport. You also see how to do important, functional, and fun things such as change your password, choose security settings, and customize your MSN home page.

Checking Out MSN Explorer

Ready to take a spin with MSN Explorer? Good. Here's how:

1. **Choose Start⇨MSN Explorer.**

2. **If you're paying MSN for Internet service, your computer should connect directly.**

   If not, you may have to type in a user I.D. and password for your Internet Service Provider. Listen to the ping-ping-ping/scratch-scratch handshaking noise. The MSN login window appears.

3. **If you have created multiple accounts on your computer, choose your account, enter your password, and click the Sign In button.**

4. **MSN Explorer gets under way, and you are taken directly to your home page, which, until you customize it, is** www.msn.com.

Figure 2-1 shows you the basic elements on the MSN Explorer window that you use to surf, e-mail, chat, and jam on the Web.

"My Stuff"

Sign out

MSN toolbar

Access account information

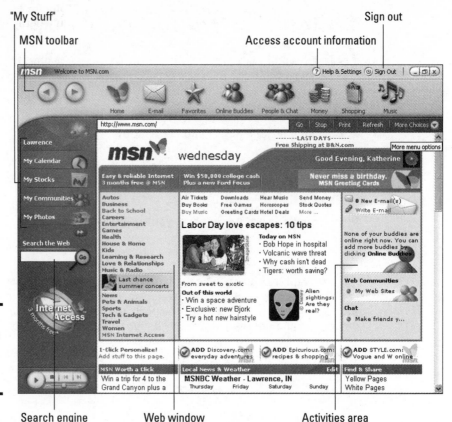

Figure 2-1:
Scoping the
MSN
Explorer
window.

Search engine

Web window

Activities area

If you've previously made a few trips around the Web using Internet
Explorer, AOL, or other online services, you'll be able to find your way
around easily in MSN Explorer. Here are the most important features:

✦ **Toolbar:** The MSN toolbar includes tools that give you quick access to the
various features and communities in MSN Explorer. Table 2-1 introduces
you to each of the tools.

✦ **Address Bar:** The Address Bar enables you to navigate around the Web,
find what you're looking for, and control your MSN account settings.

✦ **Web window:** This is the area in which the content of the Web page
appears — you find text, images, links, and more as you move from page
to page.

✦ **Activities area:** As part of your home page, MSN Explorer tells you
what's going on in your other areas of interest. If you have created a

Buddy List, MSN Explorer tells you whether any of your buddies are currently online. Additionally, this area shows you whether you have any new mail and gives you the option to write new mail.

✦ **My Stuff column:** This column on the left provides links to four areas that MSN thinks you'll want easy access to: My Calendar, My Stocks, My Communities, and My Photos.

✦ **Search:** No big surprise here — use the Search box to enter the topic that you want to find on the Web.

✦ **Media Player:** Your very own built-in sound system, placed conveniently in the bottom left corner of the MSN Explorer window. When you click Play, you are taken to the Music page so that you can select the type of music that you want to hear.

✦ **Help & Settings:** This selection, in the upper right corner of the MSN window, takes you to the Member Center, where you can customize your MSN Explorer settings.

Table 2-1		MSN Explorer Tools
Button	*Name*	*Description*
	Back	Displays the previous Web page
	Forward	Displays the next Web page in the sequence
	Home	Displays the home page you've set for MSN Explorer display
	E-mail	Launches Hotmail so that you can write, send, and read e-mail
	Favorites	Displays the sites that you have saved to your Favorites list
	Online Buddies	Opens the Buddies menu so that you can add, view, or talk with buddies through instant messaging
	People & Chat	Takes you to the People & Chat page so that you can start chatting
	Money	Launches the Money page, giving you all kinds of resources including My Money, Investing, Banking, Planning, Taxes, and Community areas
	Shopping	Takes you to a page with lots of shopping opportunities
	Music	Displays the Music site so that you can listen to music in 24 different categories

Surfing the Web with MSN

One of the features that distinguishes MSN Explorer from some of the other online services is something that you can easily miss — the way in which the Web is built seamlessly into all the activities in the service. You can see no real division between Web surfing and e-mail, Web work and chat, Web pages and shopping, managing your money or listening to music. It all works together transparently, without requiring much conscious thought.

Following links

Links on MSN Explorer look similar to the links that you see in other browsers. You find the following types of links in MSN:

✦ Text links appear underlined, often in a color different from regular text

✦ Buttons provide quick-click access to other pages

✦ Image links can be pictures of products, photos, or icons

How can you tell what's a link and what's just text or pictures? When you position the mouse pointer over a link, the arrow changes to a pointing hand. To follow the link, simply click the mouse button.

Navigating Web pages

Two of the primary navigational tools that you use to move around in MSN Explorer are actually part of the MSN Explorer toolbar:

 ✦ Click the Back button to return to the Web page that you were viewing previous to the current page.

 ✦ Click the Forward button to move to the next Web page in the current sequence. (*Note:* You have to go Back before you can go Forward. Er, if you have not previously used Back, Forward will not be available.)

You can find the rest of the tools and buttons that you use for working with Web pages in the Address bar. Table 2-2 gives you an overview of those tools.

Table 2-2	Deciphering the Address Bar	
Button	*Name*	*Description*
http://www.msn.com/	Address	Type the Web address of the page that you want to visit in this box; then press Enter or click Go
Go	Go	Click this command button to go to the page that you entered in the Address text box

Button	Name	Description
Stop	Stop	Interrupts the loading of the current page
Print	Print	Prints the current page
Refresh	Refresh	Updates the display of the current page
More Choices ▼	More Choices	Displays a menu of choices that you can use to work with the current page, including New Window, E-mail This Page, Find on Page, View Privacy Report, Cut, Copy, Paste, Select All, Help, Settings, and About MSN Explorer

**Book VI
Chapter 2**

Taking
MSN Explorer
for a Spin

When you find a page that you want to keep, click the Favorites tool in the MSN Explorer toolbar. A menu appears, giving you two options: Add to Favorites, and Organize Favorites. When you click Add to Favorites, a pop-up dialog box appears. Type a name for the page and click OK. MSN Explorer saves the page so that you can later access it by simply clicking the Favorites button.

How MSN Explorer Works with Passport

Microsoft Passport is one of the new features of Windows XP that has caused big reactions — some positive, most negative. Microsoft Passport is meant to (or so the corporate rhetoric goes) give you the utmost in online convenience, storing all your passwords, user names, credit information, and so on, in one handy *wallet* that you have with you whenever you surf the Web. In theory, carrying this passport enables you to log into all Passport-compatible sites with your single e-mail address and password.

The big benefits that Password advertises are these:

✦ **Convenience:** Enter information once; use it many times.

✦ **Shop:** Store your credit card numbers in one place, and whip them out easily for impulsive online purchases.

✦ **Control:** The Kids Passport enables you to set parental controls.

Microsoft promises that Passport is protected by cutting-edge security technology and a "strict privacy policy" (enforced by frowning Web matrons). However, many people feel slightly queasy at the thought of giving a large corporate entity any more personal information than absolutely necessary.

Until the last round of legal filings, Password registration asked users for all sorts of information — way beyond the routine basics. With the most recent ruling, Passport developers agreed to make only e-mail address and password a prerequisite for getting a Passport account, but industry insiders are still nervous. (If you're interested in a counter view on Microsoft's Passport strategy, check out the article by former Microsoft employee Joel Spolsky, at `joel.editthispage.com/stories/storyReader$139`.)

How does Passport work? When you sign into a "Passport participating site," you enter your e-mail address and password (the same information that you enter when signing into MSN Explorer) and the site checks the login information to verify it. When you're in, you're in — and you can surf, shop, and more, knowing that you don't have to stop and get additional information, even if you want to purchase something you find.

Want to find out more? The people at `www.passport.com` are glad to tell you all about it. Just be sure to check your wallet before you leave.

Which passport is which?

If you look around a bit, you find (at least!) four different names for Passport: Windows Passport, Microsoft Passport, MSN Passport, and .NET Passport. (That excludes just plain, old Passport, which tends to be my nomenclature of choice.) Just before Microsoft released Windows XP, it changed all the internal documentation — including the Help files — so that they no longer refer to "Windows Passport" but say ".NET Passport" instead. While that was going on, all of the Microsoft Web sites still referred to "Microsoft Passport." What's a Dummy to do?

All four (or five) terms refer to the same technology. Microsoft is constructing this giant database called Passport, and you're probably going to become part of it, one way or another. From the 'Softies point of view, they're building this wonderful new technology called Passport and offering it to the world at large to reduce the number of passwords that you need to remember and to make it simpler for you to buy things online. Which is true. But at its heart, Passport is a database. Microsoft may open up Passport to different, competing secure services — much as the banks' ATM systems started out as standalone, proprietary services, ultimately evolving into far-reaching multi-company amalgamations — but the devil is in the details, and the details at this point are sketchy.

One distinction does make a difference. As of this writing, Microsoft has two separate databases. Your *Passport Profile* contains your name, e-mail address, age, sex, ZIP code, and occupation. Your *Passport Wallet* contains credit card information and your shipping and billing address. Assuming that you gave Microsoft that information at some point, of course.

If you want to see some of the information that Microsoft has gathered about you, go to `www.passport.com`, and look under Member Services. What you see there is a tiny, tiny fraction of all the information that Microsoft has stored (see `www.woodyswatch.com/windows/archtemplate.asp?3-18` for some sobering examples).

Signing up for a Passport

You can sign up (or find out more about) Microsoft Passport by doing one of two things:

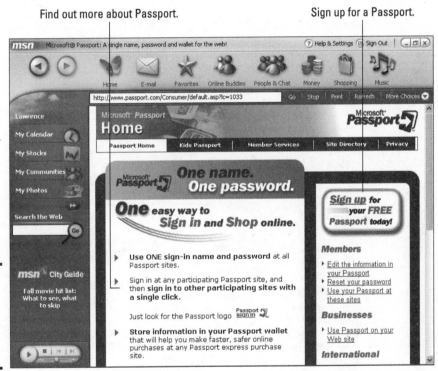

✦ Go to www.passport.com.

✦ Click the Microsoft Passport icon anywhere you see it.

The Microsoft Passport site appears, giving you lots of information about the passport idea and enabling you to sign right up (see Figure 2-2).

Find out more about Passport.

Sign up for a Passport.

Figure 2-2:
Want to store all those pesky numbers in one place?

Getting a Kids Passport

One of AOL's strengths is a well-developed parental controls system. One of the features totally missing in MSN Explorer is a parent's choice feature that enables parents to set controls to keep their kids safe. In fact, even in MSN's Online Safety area, the best they can do is offer parents some tips on how to keep their kids safe.

Perhaps Kids Passport is one attempt to provide a bit of a safety net for kids, but in my opinion, it's a bit lame. The idea is based on the regular Passport — collecting information so that you can use it when, where, and how you want. With Kids Passport, kids can't share information unless they have consent from a parent. Working through the Kids Passport system, permission is requested if a child starts to visit a site that requests more information than they have "clearance" to give.

If Microsoft's Kids Passport approach strikes you as, uh, underwhelming, welcome to the club. Kids Passport — at least in its current incarnation, as of this writing — doesn't hold a candle to AOL's parental controls, and MSN Explorer itself has absolutely no provisions for keeping kids safe.

If you're interested in finding out more about Kids Passport, take a look at its site (`kids.passport.com`). You can find out which sites are participating in the Kids Site Directory, visit the Parent area, or read through the Kids Passport FAQ (see Figure 2-3).

Go to kids.passport.com.   Click to get to the Microsoft Passport page.

Figure 2-3:
Kids
Passport
helps you
set up
parental
controls.

Setting and Changing Passwords

After you grow accustomed to MSN Explorer, you may decide that you want to change the password you originally selected. Piece of cake. Here's the process:

1. **Start MSN Explorer as usual.**

2. **Click Help & Settings.**

   The Member Center window appears (see Figure 2-4).

3. **Click Change Your Password.**

   The window appears so that you can enter the new password you want.

4. **Type the password that you currently use.**

5. **Type the new password in each of the two fields.**

6. **Click Change Now to save your changes.**

Book VI
Chapter 2

Taking
MSN Explorer
for a Spin

Change your password.

Display the Member Center.

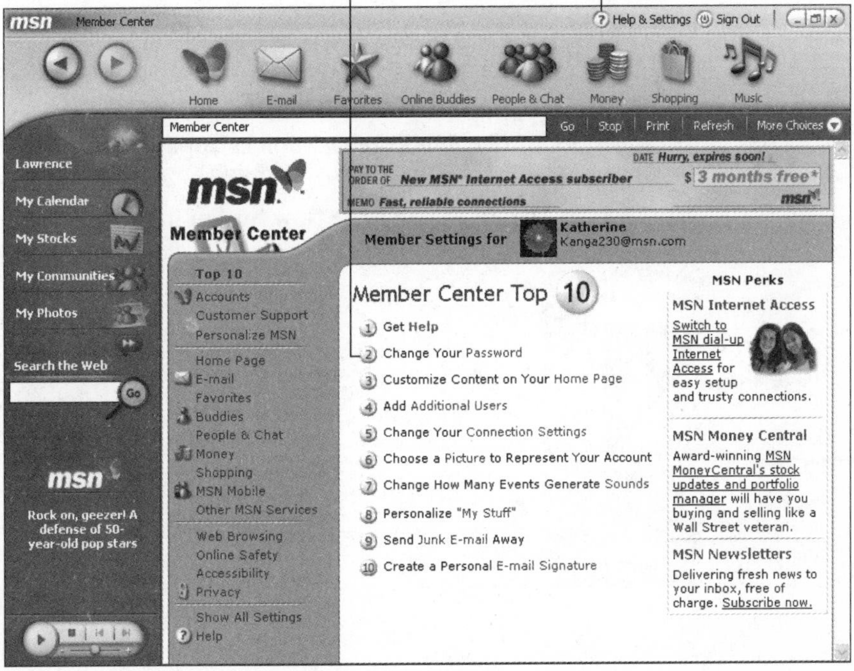

Figure 2-4: Modifying your password just takes a trip to the Member Center.

MSN Explorer enables you to create up to nine different accounts — with nine different passwords — on your system.

Your Home Page, Your Way

As you probably noticed, the MSN Explorer screen does not have a lot of room. If you want to control what kind of information is displayed in that limited space, you can call on MSN Explorer's personalization features. To customize your home page, follow these steps:

1. **With the MSN Explorer window open on your screen, click More Choices in the Address bar.**

   A submenu appears.

2. **Click Settings.**

   The Member Center window opens.

3. **Click Item 3, Customize Content on Your Home Page.**

   The Personalization window jumps into view, as shown in Figure 2-5.

4. **Enter your ZIP Code and choose your time zone to allow MSN to tailor local news to your location.**

   Don't be too surprised if that information ends up in your Passport.

5. **Click the topics in the left column that you want to see on your home page.**

   Descriptions of online content choices appear in the Web window. Scan through the list and click the Add check box to add the content.

6. **Click the Update Home Page Now button to update your page.**

Click the topics you're interested in seeing on your home page.

Enter your ZIP code for local news.

Customize your home page.

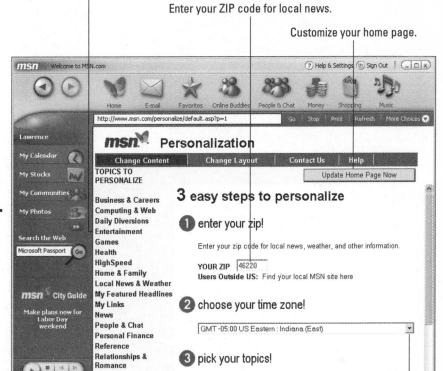

Figure 2-5:
On the Personalization screen, you can choose the items that you want to see on your home page.

Select your time zone.

Chapter 3: Advanced MSN Explorer

In This Chapter

✔ **The e-mail side of MSN Explorer**

✔ **Chat, schmat!**

✔ **Don't go in without a Buddy**

*T*his chapter explains how to receive, write, and send e-mail with MSN Explorer. And after you read your e-mail, what are you going to do about it? This chapter gives you the ins and outs for organizing the mail you want to keep and tossing the mail you don't want. And as you add to your bevy of online friends, you will no doubt want to add them to your Address Book. That's a simple task with MSN.

After you master e-mail basics, you may want to investigate some of the other offerings available to you as an MSN Explorer user. Chat is a simple point-click-and-type technique, and Online Buddies enable you to trade messages instantly with friends whom you may find online at any given moment.

Sending and Receiving E-Mail with MSN Explorer

The e-mail program that you use in MSN may be different from other e-mail programs that you have used. Microsoft has teamed up with Hotmail to provide a Web-based e-mail service in MSN Explorer. *Web-based* means that the mail isn't delivered to the Inbox on your computer; instead, it is stored online, waiting for you to open, view, and file it away when you're ready.

The following are some of the benefits of Web-based e-mail:

✦ You can access your e-mail anytime you can get to the Web.

✦ You can send and receive file attachments as normal.

✦ You don't have to use your own hard disk storage space for downloaded mail.

The downside of Web-based e-mail? Beyond the normal questions (such as "Do I want Microsoft to store my Address Book?"), the service has few real negatives. In earlier versions of Web-based e-mail, you couldn't save and store a message-in-progress; but in MSN Explorer, you can park a message in your Drafts folder and come back to it whenever the urge strikes.

Reading your mail

You know right away when you sign on to MSN whether you have e-mail or not. The E-mail button in the MSN Explorer toolbar shows a small number if new mail awaits your attention. Additionally, the notification in the top right side of the activities area of the MSN window tells you if you have new messages waiting.

 To read your mail, click either the E-mail tool in the toolbar or the 1 New E-mail link in the MSN Explorer Home page. As shown in Figure 3-1, the Hotmail window opens, displaying three different tabs:

✦ **My E-mail** displays your messages and enables you to file them or pitch them, whichever you prefer.

✦ **Write E-mail** gives you what you need to compose new messages.

✦ **Address Book** lets you add new contacts, organize existing contacts, or delete the contacts that you no longer need.

Open the e-mail window.

Lists your current e-mail messages

Add new contacts or delete old ones.

Compose a new message.

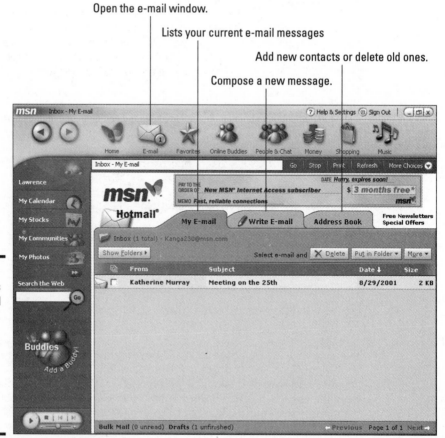

Figure 3-1: MSN offers Web-based e-mail, which means that you can access it no matter where you are.

To read a new message, simply click the text in the From or Subject column. The message opens in the Hotmail window (see Figure 3-2).

Add the sender's e-mail address to your Address Book.

To write back, click reply.

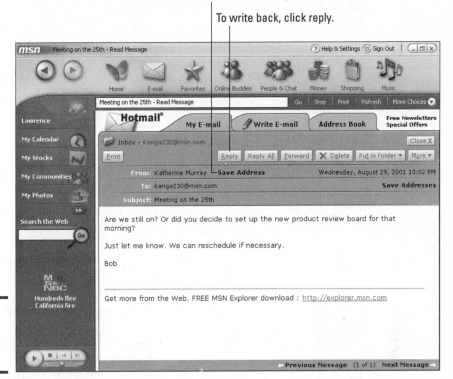

Figure 3-2:
Reading
a new
message.

What to do with your mail

After you open and read the e-mail message, what are you going to do with it? You have several options — you can print it, file it, reply to it, forward it to someone else, or delete it. Hotmail includes handy-dandy little buttons to help you finish off those tasks. Table 3-1 gives you an overview of the various tools in the Hotmail window. Here's a quick rundown of the steps involved in carrying out the various procedures:

✦ To print a message, click Print; choose whether you want to print the current frame (in which the e-mail message is displayed) or the whole screen; then click Print.

✦ To reply to a message, click Reply, type your message, and click Send. (Yes, it's really that simple.) If your message was sent to multiple recipients, click Reply All to send the same response to everyone on the recipient list.

✦ To forward a message to another person, click Forward, and enter the recipient's e-mail address or choose the recipient from your Address Book. Type any message that you want to insert at the top of the forwarded message and click Send.

✦ To file the message in a folder, click Put in Folder. A menu opens, giving you the option of saving the message either online or on your hard disk. The two options above the divider line (in the On MSN: section) enable you to put your message in the Trash or create a new folder online. The three options in the On My Computer: section give you the choice of saving the message in your Archived Mail, Trash, or Sent Messages folders on your hard disk.

If you want to create a new folder in which to store your saved e-mail messages, click [New] in the Put in Folder menu. The New Folder dialog box appears. Type the name for the new folder and click OK. The new folder name is added to the menu so that you can select it the next time you click Put in Folder.

✦ To delete the e-mail message, click Delete.

✦ To close the message, click Close. MSN Explorer leaves the message in your My E-mail folder until you choose to do something else with it.

Table 3-1		E-Mail Options
Button	*Name*	*Description*
Print	Print	Prints a copy of the current message
Reply	Reply	Opens a message so that you can reply to the current message
Reply All	Reply All	Opens a message that you can send to all recipients listed on the current message
Forward	Forward	Enables you to send the current message on to someone else
X Delete	Delete	Deletes the current message
Put in Folder ▾	Put in Folder	Displays a folder list so that you can save the message where you want it
More ▾	More	Displays additional e-mail options
Close X	Close	Closes the current message and leaves it in the My E-mail tab

Writing e-mail

Ready to compose a message? By now, you can probably guess the process. It's simple when you know what you want to say. Here are the steps:

1. **Launch MSN Explorer as usual.**

2. **Click the E-mail button in the toolbar.**

   The Hotmail window appears.

3. **Click the Write E-mail tab.**

   A blank e-mail window appears, listing your Address Book entries on the right side of the screen (see Figure 3-3).

4. **Click an entry in your Address Book to add the name to the To line or type the e-mail address directly in the line.**

5. **Click in the Subject line and type a heading or topic for your message.**

6. **If you want to change the default look of the text, you can change the Font, Size, color, style, and alignment options by clicking the tools that you want to use.**

7. **Type the message in the blank part of the message window.**

8. **Click Send.**

   MSN Explorer tells you that your message is being sent. When the operation is complete, you hear a chime, indicating that the task is completed.

Book VI
Chapter 3

Advanced
MSN Explorer

TIP

Many people — especially busy people — open an e-mail message only if they know what the message is about. So make sure that your Subject line is short, clear, and to the point. This helps to ensure that your message gets read.

Why fuss with e-mail options?

MSN Explorer also includes a handful of options that you can use to tailor your online e-mail experience to meet your needs. The options are actually helpful if you worry about things like blocking unwanted messages and protecting your privacy.

To display the e-mail options available with MSN Explorer, click the More button. (**Note:** Depending on the tab you are viewing, you see different options in the More menu.)

Block Sender(s) enables you to refuse messages from the person who sent the currently selected message. You may use this, for example, when you receive a solicitation that you don't want or an offer that you *can* refuse. Organize Folders enables you to rename your custom folders, view the number of messages stored, and check the memory allocated to each folder.

E-mail Settings enables you to choose further preferences, such as Inbox Protector, Mail Signature, and Mail Preferences. You can also use E-mail Settings to import Address Books from other computers or subscribe to Hotmail's online newsletters.

Select the person you're writing to.

Describe your message.   Click Send.

Text of your message   Select formatting.

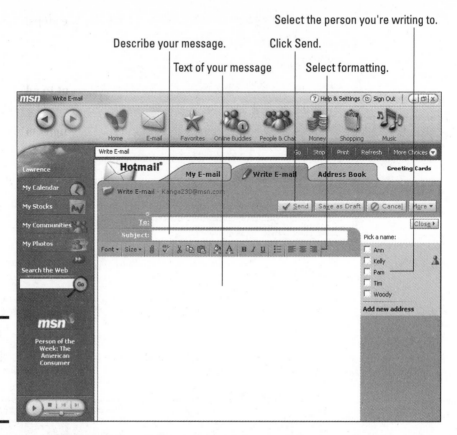

Figure 3-3:
Compose
and send
your
message
online.

If you want to think about the message before you send it, you can click Save as Draft to save what you've done so far. MSN tells you that the message will be saved in your Drafts folder. Click Yes to continue. Later, when you want to open the message to work on it, click the My E-mail tab, click the Show Folders button, and click Drafts.

Adding people to your Address Book

Unfortunately, MSN Explorer doesn't come with the names and addresses of your 5,000 closest friends already entered. That's up to you to do. Luckily, the Address Book feature is simple to use, and it's handy, too, if you don't mind storing all your information online.

To view the Address Book, simply click E-mail in the toolbar and then click the Address Book tab. The screen shown in Figure 3-4 appears.

To add a new entry in your Address Book, follow these steps:

1. **Click Add New Contact.**

The Add New Contact dialog box appears.

2. **Type the Nickname of the person whom you want to add.**

3. **Enter the e-mail address.**

4. **If you want the new contact to be available through Online Buddies, click the check box.**

5. **Enter the name and phone information, if applicable.**

6. **Click OK to save the entry.**

Hotmail adds the name to your Address Book, and the name is available the next time you begin to write a message or click the Address Book tab.

**Book VI
Chapter 3**

**Advanced
MSN Explorer**

Add the new e-mail address.

Type the name you want to show.

Click the Add New Contact button.

Click the Address Book tab.

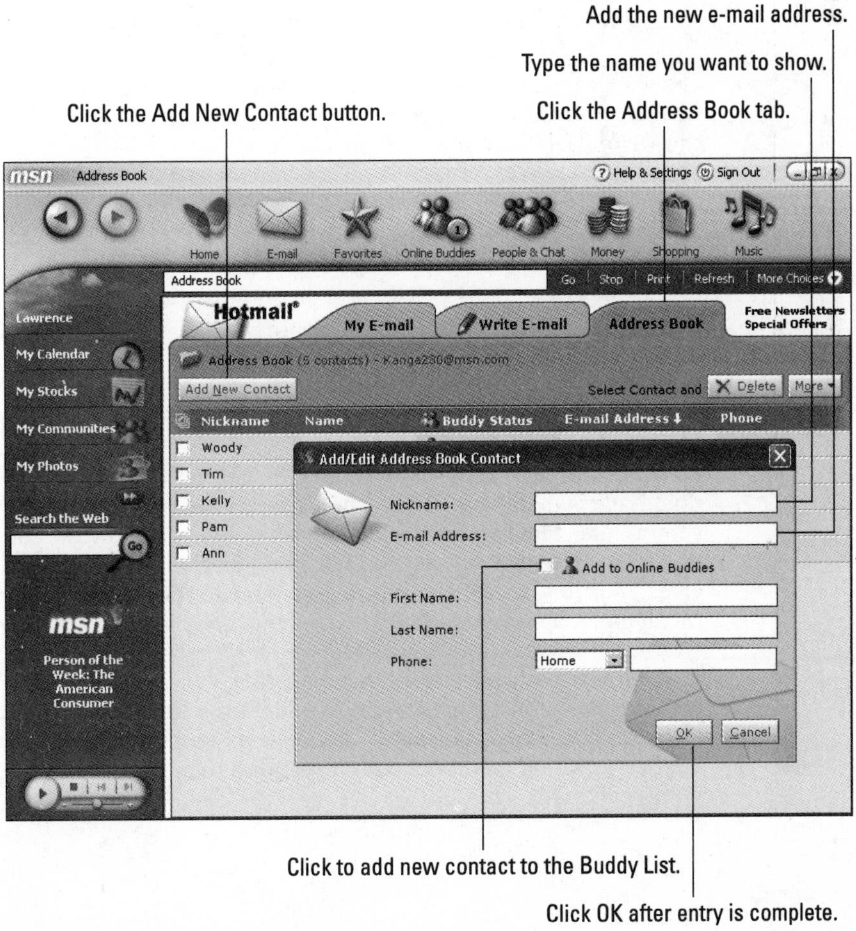

Figure 3-4:
Your online
Address
Book stores
names and
e-mail
addresses
of the
people you
write to.

Click to add new contact to the Buddy List.

Click OK after entry is complete.

Importing addresses

MSN Explorer lets you import the Address Book that you use in other e-mail programs for use in your MSN Explorer mail. To import an address book, follow these steps:

1. **Get online with MSN Explorer as usual.**

2. **Click E-mail to display the E-mail window. Click the More button on the right side of the screen. When the drop-down menu appears, click E-mail Settings.**

3. **On the Member Center page, click Import Address book.**

   Another page appears, explaining that you can import address books from Outlook Express or America Online. Click the Import Address Book link.

4. **Choose whether you want to import addresses from America Online and/or Outlook Express. Click OK to import the addresses.**

You can also add addresses on the fly: Click Save Address when you receive a new message from a sender whom you want to add to your Address Book. Or click Add New Address (shown at the bottom of the Pick a Name: list) in the Write E-mail window.

Chatting for Fun and Profit

Not a chatty person? Don't let it hold you back: Chat isn't just for extroverts anymore. MSN Explorer includes all sorts of online communities that are ready, willing, and eager to chat about whatever interests you.

Getting into Chat

To start chat with MSN, click People & Chat in the toolbar. The People & Chat page is displayed, listing the various chat categories that you can explore (see Figure 3-5). Click a Chat that you want to view and MSN takes you to a window in which you choose an MSN nickname for your chat. MSN gives you a few examples; type a nickname in the text box and click Register Nickname to continue.

A potential confusion here: When you click People & Chat, the displayed Web page lists both chats and communities, which are different things. Chat is a live, happening-as-you-type event; communities are message boards, in which members add or respond to messages that the whole group can read.

Communities provide additional ways to interact.

Here are the chat selections.

Click here to go to the Chat home page.

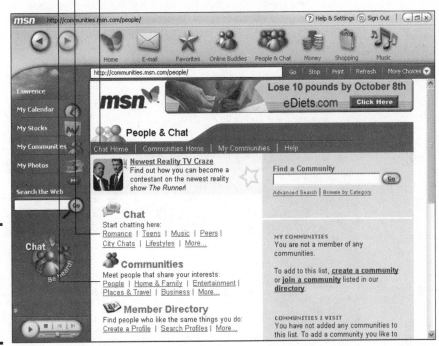

Book VI
Chapter 3

Advanced
MSN Explorer

Figure 3-5:
People &
Chat lists
your
choices for
online story
swapping.

If your nickname passes muster, you see a Confirmed! message, and you have the option to create a public profile or move right on into chat. You can do the profile later: Click Chat Now to start the process.

Click the category that you want to join, and MSN Explorer takes you to a listing of current chats in that subject area. Click the title of the chat that you want to join, and MSN Chat begins to download the necessary software for that chat. (*Note:* This happens only the first time you use chat.) After the software is loaded — hold on to your hat! — you're in.

If you find a chat room that you really like, you can save the chat for later by clicking Add to My Chats in the top right corner of the Chat window. The chat is then added to your my Chats list (and when the message box appears to tell you so, click OK), which means that you can select it from the MSN Explorer home page.

Know your chat room

Not all chat rooms are created equal. Some are fast and furious, with dozens of chatters and comments (civil and questionable) flying every which way. Others are more sedate and reserved. With some experience, you can find rooms that suit your style. When the chat room appears, you're ready for a little tour. Figure 3-6 shows a chat window with a conversation in progress.

The ongoing conversation   People participating in chat

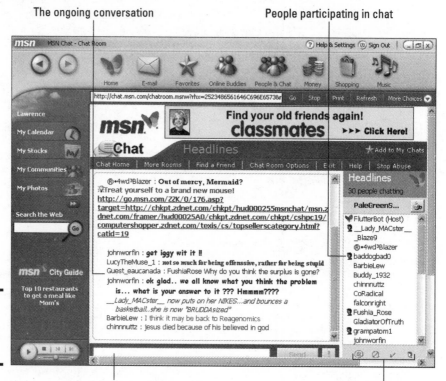

Figure 3-6: Exploring the Chat window.

Type your contribution here and click Send.   Control, block, or speak to other chatters.

The largest area of the Chat window is given to the continuing conversation. The entries are added quickly if you're in an active room, so you may have to continually click the down-arrow in the bottom of the vertical scroll bar to keep up with new lines.

What's in a profile?

The public profile is a collection of information about yourself that you may or may not choose to make available to the general population. You can enter all requested information, or you can enter only the items that you really want to share — it's totally up to you.

To create a public profile, click the Create a Public Profile button in the Chat window. The Member Directory window appears, listing basic name and contact info, your age, your marital status, and your occupation. You also have the option to share additional information, including a personal statement, your favorite things, your hobbies and interests, and your favorite quote.

You can also customize your profile by selecting a color scheme for the profile, adding a link to a Web photo, and adding the address of your personal home page. Click Save when you're happy with the information that you've elected to share. MSN creates the profile, and it becomes available to people who chat with you.

Just beneath the conversation area, you see the text-entry area, where you enter your contributions and click Send.

The people list tells you who is currently in the room and what their status is. The host of the chat is marked by a small MSN symbol (that colorful butterfly). Table 3-2 shows some additional tools and icons in the people list:

Table 3-2	Know Your Chat Tools
Tool	*Description*
💬	Whisper sends a message to one person without the rest seeing.
⊘	Ignore means that you are ignoring or blocking messages from the person you specify.
✓	Tagged means that you have tagged a person so that you can follow his or her comments.
👤	Profile means that the participant has created a public profile that you can view.
☕	Away means that the person is temporarily away from chat.

When you're ready to leave chat, simply click Exit. You are returned to the MSN Chat page (just in case you're interested in joining another chat).

Online Buddies: Where E-Mail Meets Chat

MSN Explorer certainly isn't the first service to offer instant messaging, but it makes the process easy — and free. Online Buddies are those MSN or Hotmail users who use MSN Messenger and can trade quick messages with you whenever you're online.

But you can't trade messages with your online buddies until you know who's online. Who is eligible for buddiness? Your other MSN and Hotmail companions or anyone who has signed up for a Passport. If you know someone who has an `msn.com` or `hotmail.com` e-mail address — or if you know the e-mail address of somebody who's signed up for Passport — you can invite those people to participate in instant messaging by following these steps:

1. **Click Online Buddies in the MSN Explorer toolbar.**

   The menu appears.

2. **Click Add New Buddy. In the Messenger Service window, type the e-mail address of the person you want to add.**

3. **Click Add Buddy.**

   This adds the person to your Buddy list and notifies you when the person is online.

Sending an instant message

When you're ready to send an instant message to an online buddy, follow these steps:

1. **Click Online Buddies.**

   The menu appears, showing you who is online and listing other options for adding and viewing users.

2. **Click the name of the buddy you want to contact.**

   The message window appears, as shown in Figure 3-7.

3. **Type your message and click Send.**

   The message appears in the top portion of the window. When the recipient begins entering a message, you see a descriptor telling you so in the bottom portion of the message window.

That's all there is to it! The conversation can continue as long as you wish, and you can spice it up with emoticons (smiley faces and more) and acronyms if you wish.

You can use Online Buddies even without having MSN Explorer open on your screen. If you look closely in the right side of the taskbar, you see a small buddies icon. (This is also the area where the buddy alerts appear when one of your buddies logs on or sends you a message.) Just click the icon to start an instant message or to reply to one you receive. Additionally, you can use this taskbar icon to sign in and out and find out who is currently online.

**Book VI
Chapter 3**

**Advanced
MSN Explorer**

Here's your conversation thread.

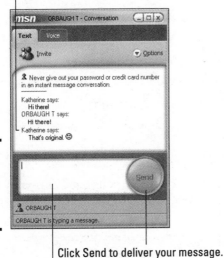

Figure 3-7:
Buddying
around with
instant
messaging.

Click Send to deliver your message.

Type your message here.

Instant batches of conversations

One feature that Online Buddies offers that other instant messaging services (such as AOL) do not offer is the ability to have a conversation with up to five different people at once. To include others in your conversation, click Invite and then click the names of the people whom you want to invite in. They can then participate in a sort of mini-chat-room session.

Controlling buddy access

Okay, so you're loving this instant messaging thing, but what happens when you've got a huge deadline and all your online buddies want to trade the latest Oprah news? You can tell your buddies that you're away, or busy, by choosing different options in the Online Buddies menu. Here are the steps:

1. **Click the Online Buddies tool in the MSN Explorer toolbar.**

   The menu appears.

2. **Click your name to display the submenu.**

   A list of options appears:

   - **Online** lets people know that you're available for chat.

   - **Busy** tells buddies that you can't talk right now.

   - **Be Right Back** says "Just a minute!"

   - **Away** lets people know that you're unavailable.

   - **On The Phone** encourages buddies to hang on for a minute.

   - **Out to Lunch** lets people know that you're not around.

   - **Appear Offline** makes you appear as though you're not online when you really are.

3. **Click the option that you want to apply.**

   The icon appears beside your name in your buddies' Buddy lists, so that they know what to expect when they prepare to contact you.

Buddies and Windows Messenger

As we went to press, Microsoft was busy changing and consolidating its various Messenger products. At this point, Windows XP Messenger and MSN Messenger apparently will receive a mutual makeover and become almost the same product. (Something else called .NET Messenger may or may not make it into the mess. Er, mix.)

At any rate, you can feel confident that just about any product from Microsoft with the word "Messenger" in it will work pretty much like MSN Messenger, as described in this chapter. Stay tuned to Woody's Windows Watch, www.woodyswatch.com, for details as they unfold.

Smileys and BTWs

As you get really good at this online communications thing, you'll want faster methods of letting people know what you think and feel. Emoticons and acronyms give you two quick ways to speed your communication.

Emoticons, or smileys, are small icons that you can use to communicate feelings to an online buddy or to people in a chat room. To produce smiley faces and other items in your instant communications, try these:

:)	Smiling face
:0	Yawn
:P	Tongue out
;)	Wink
:(	Frown
:S	Uncertain
:|	Bored

Acronyms are shorthand methods of saying often-used phrases. Here are some acronyms that you may want to use in your fast communication:

<G>	Grin
<EG>	Evil grin
AFK	Away from keyboard
BRB	Be right back
BTW	By the way
FWIW	For what it's worth
GMTA	Great minds think alike
IMHO	In my humble opinion
LOL	Laughing out loud
ROFL	Rolling on the floor laughing
TMI	Too much information
TTFN	Ta ta for now

**Book VI
Chapter 3**

**Advanced
MSN Explorer**

Index

Book VII

Adding and Using Other Hardware

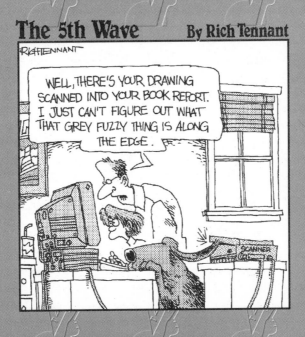

The 5th Wave   By Rich Tennant

WELL, THERE'S YOUR DRAWING SCANNED INTO YOUR BOOK REPORT. I JUST CAN'T FIGURE OUT WHAT THAT GREY FUZZY THING IS ALONG THE EDGE.

Contents at a Glance

Chapter 1: Finding and Installing the Hardware You Want

In This Chapter

✔ What's available

✔ How it works

✔ Stuff to avoid

✔ Stuff to die for

✔ How to install and use it

L et's face facts: You don't need all of the fastest, most expensive gadgets to get value out of your computer.

On the other hand, equipment that fits your needs can help you do more and better work in less time.

This chapter reviews the common computer accessories currently available to help you decide whether any of them would be valuable to you.

Understanding Hardware Types

Before you can make an informed decision about adding a new piece of hardware to your computer or network, you have to understand how hardware connects to your PC and what you need to make that sparkly new toy work.

Juggling internal and external devices

An *internal device* is one that goes inside your computer's case. An *external device* has its own case and is connected to your computer by a cable.

An internal device is more convenient to use. If you have to move your computer, the internal device goes right with it. There's no cable or separate power cord to get tangled and catch dust. But you have a physical limit on the number of internal devices you can cram into a box.

On the other hand, an external device is often more flexible. If you have more than one computer, you can move an external device from one to another as the need arises.

An internal device may be an *adapter card* that plugs into one of the *slots* on your computer's main board, or it may be connected to a *controller* by an internal cable. All external devices are connected to a controller.

The type of *interface* that a device has determines the type of controller it needs. (The next section explains interfaces.) A single controller can operate several devices with the same type of interface. Some types of controllers are built into the main board; others must be added as adapter cards.

Choosing an interface

Any device connected to your computer uses some type of *interface* to move data back and forth. The interface is just a physical connection — a plug, if you will. Many types of devices are sold with a choice of interfaces, and you need to know enough about the different interfaces to choose the right one for your needs.

Interfaces for adapter cards

Adapter cards — that is, computer cards that plug straight into the PC's motherboard — use one of three types of interfaces, corresponding to three types of slots on the main board. The names of the slots are pretty weird, but don't let the terminology put you off. There were reasons for the names, once upon a time, but they don't really mean much nowadays. Like, oh, "New York." Know what I mean?

The *PCI interface* gets the nod for most adapter cards. It's physically strong (so you'll have a hard time breaking the sucker when you stick a card in the slot), and lots of electrical contacts are inside. PCI supports *plug-and-play* operation, which means that Windows XP can detect the properties of an adapter card and do much or all of the software installation automatically. Most Windows computers have three, four, or five PCI slots.

The *AGP interface* is for video adapter cards only — that is, cards that slap stuff up on your screen. Video adapters with the AGP interface can offer better performance than those with the PCI interface. AGP is also a plug-and-play interface.

Not all Windows PCs have separate AGP slots, so check before you buy an AGP card, okay? An AGP card without an AGP slot is about as useless as a kite without a string.

The *ISA interface* is a much older interface, and is not plug-and-play. Most modern Windows computers have just one ISA slot or none at all.

Do not buy an adapter card with an ISA interface unless you need something unusual that is only made that way. If you buy an ISA card, expect to spend lots of hours wrestling with arcane topics such as IRQs, DMA channels, and base I/O addresses — all three of which were government plots designed to keep computers out of the hands of "normal" people. You have a hard time finding ISA cards nowadays for a reason. Let them die a well-deserved death.

IDE and EIDE interfaces

The *EIDE interface* controls the hard disk on most Windows computers. Often it controls the CD-ROM drive or DVD drive as well. All modern Windows computers have a built-in EIDE controller or two, sitting on the mother board, usually attached with wide ribbon cables to all the hard drives and CD drives in the PC.

The *IDE interface* is an ancestor of EIDE, and you still find hard disks that are designed to run with IDE. If your computer has an EIDE interface, you can probably plug an IDE hard drive into it, but we're talking slug city.

IDE and EIDE interfaces are rarely used for external devices because the length of the cable connecting the controller to the device is quite limited.

SCSI interface

The *SCSI* interface (pronounced *scuzzy*) is for fast devices such as high-performance disk drives and tape drives. It is used for both internal and external devices. The SCSI interface is the usual choice for external disk drives, including external CD and DVD drives.

Very few Windows computers have a SCSI controller built in. A controller must be installed in one of the slots on the computer's main board. Here's the reason why: Although SCSI is theoretically faster than EIDE, in practice very few people recognize much of a speed improvement when moving "up" from EIDE to SCSI. But SCSI is almost always (and sometimes quite considerably) more expensive than EIDE. Unless you have a crying need for SCSI speed, stick with EIDE.

USB interface

The *USB interface* is for slow- and medium-speed devices such as mice, printers, scanners, and digital cameras. All modern Windows computers have a built-in USB controller.

The USB interface is used only for external devices. It is the most flexible interface for such devices, and the easiest to use. You can plug in or remove a USB device without restarting your computer; Windows XP simply notices the device's presence or absence and adjusts itself accordingly. You can't do that with most other types of interfaces. In fact, you may damage the device or your computer if you try.

Serial and parallel interfaces

These two types of interfaces are used mainly for printers, scanners, and external dial-up modems. Both of them are much older than the other types of external interfaces described here. Parallel interfaces are 25-pin plugs, typically used to attach a printer to a PC. Serial interfaces are 9-pin plugs; you frequently see them used with external dial-up modems.

Almost all Windows computers have a parallel interface (good for one device), and most have one or two serial interfaces (good for one device each).

Many modern devices use the USB interface instead of the serial or parallel interface. Other things being equal, the USB interface is preferred because it is faster and easier to use.

Assuring Windows XP compatibility

Most types of devices raise the question of compatibility: Will this gadget work with Windows XP? You can dissect that question a thousand different ways, but the real acid test is a simple one: Is a good driver available for the hardware? (A driver is a program that allows Windows XP to interact with the hardware.)

You have the following three ways to get an answer to that question.

✦ The device may be on the Windows XP *hardware compatibility list* maintained by Microsoft. This means that Microsoft has tested the device with Windows XP and certifies that it works. Windows XP may have a built-in driver for the device.

Microsoft maintains the Windows XP compatibility list on its Web site. As of this writing, the list may be found through the page at www.microsoft.com/hcl. If you can't find it there, go to Microsoft's home page and use the Search dialog box to look for "hardware compatibility list."

✦ If the hardware isn't on the official hardware compatibility list, the company that makes the device may have a good, solid driver. (Some hardware manufacturers aren't overly fond of jumping through

Microsoft's hardware compatibility listing hoops.) If you're relying on the maker's driver, be sure that you get the driver for Windows XP, not just for some earlier version of Windows!

✦ Hard as it may be to believe, the new piece of hardware may require no driver at all because its interface to the computer is completely standardized, so that Windows XP can operate any device of the same type. Most (but not all!) keyboards, monitors, and mice work like this. Any such device may have unique features that are available only with an appropriate a driver, though.

Upgrading the Basic Stuff

You probably have a printer, but it may not suit your needs or may not fill all of your needs. Your monitor may have died — or you might've fallen in love with that gorgeous 17-inch flat hussy at your local Comput-O-Rama. Perhaps that giant 2 GB hard drive that you bought two years ago doesn't look so gigantic any more — particularly since the kids discovered how easy it is to print pictures taken on the digital camera.

Be of good cheer.

For the most part, basic upgrades under Windows XP go slick as can be.

Evaluating printers

Most modern printers come in one of two types:

✦ **Inkjet printers:** Work by spraying tiny droplets of ink on paper. Inkjet printers tend to be small, light, and inexpensive. They make less noise than laser printers and consume far less power.

✦ **Laser printers:** Work by fusing powdered toner onto the paper, essentially the same way a photocopier works. Laser printers tend to be larger and heavier than their inkjet cousins, and cost more. On the other hand, laser printers tend to be faster than inkjet printers, and any laser printer worth its salt produces much sharper results than an inkjet, at least on normal paper.

Choosing between inkjet and laser would be a reasonably simple chore, if it weren't for one big, fat variable: the cost of consumables.

Inkjet ink for some printers costs considerably more per page than laser toner does. This can make an inkjet printer cost more than a laser printer when you consider the cost of supplies over time.

Printers are available with USB, serial, and parallel interfaces. Many printers have more than one of these types. Some printers have Ethernet interfaces, and they can be connected directly to a network hub. In general, a USB interface is preferred for its speed and ease of use. For high-speed printers, an Ethernet interface also works well.

Printing photos

Most modern inkjet printers can print images in full color. Most of them print photographs well, and some are designed specifically for that task.

Color laser printers, on the other hand, are rare and expensive. The laser printing process does not deal well with areas of even tone or subtle variations in color. A few color laser printers claim to produce photo-quality output, but the majority of them are intended only for printing documents with solid-color features such as headings and charts. Like other laser printers, color laser printers are faster than color inkjet printers and are cheaper to operate

Dye sublimation printers produce the highest-quality photographic output, yielding results as good as a conventional photographic print or better. They are expensive, though, and they require special paper and dye ribbons, which are also expensive. The materials for a single print can cost several dollars. For this reason, dye sublimation printers are suitable only for photo printing, not for general printing.

Considering multi-function devices

Several companies sell *multi-function devices* that can do two or more functions, such as printing, photocopying, faxing, and scanning.

A multi-function device saves space and usually costs less than several separate devices. On the other hand, it is a compromise; it can't be designed to perform any of its functions as well as a single-purpose device would. Also, you must deal with the inconvenience of not being able to use more than one of the device's functions at a time, and you run the risk that a breakdown will take away your ability to do several things.

A multi-function device can be a real convenience if you use each of its functions lightly. If you use one function frequently, you're better off buying a dedicated device to perform that function.

Exploring exotic features

You can get printers that accept paper up to 11 inches wide. Wide-carriage inkjet printers cost a few hundred dollars extra; wide-format laser printers cost a thousand dollars or more extra. Even larger format printers are available from specialized suppliers (at specialized prices).

Many laser printers and some inkjet printers can print a page and then turn it over and print the other side. This is called *duplex printing*. It's a valuable feature if you print proposals or reports whose appearance is important, or if you mail a lot of documents and would like to save postage by reducing weight.

Some applications, notably Microsoft Word, include rudimentary support for duplex printing on a standard printer — if you don't mind taking a stack of printed pages out of the printer, flipping it over, and feeding it back in. The trick lies in figuring out which pages to print first (odd or even), whether they should be printed in normal order (pages 1-3-5 and so on) or reverse order (pages 5-3-1), and exactly how the stack needs to be flipped (face up, face down, rotated or not). With a bit of experimenting and a bit of time spent on the File➪Print dialog box, you can undoubtedly coax your standard printer into doing duplex.

An almost endless list of printers exists to meet specialized needs. For example, banner printers print on wide rolls of paper; drafting printers can print architectural drawings and similar documents on paper up to several feet wide; label printers can produce mailing labels one at a time; and more. If you need something unusual, look for it on the Web or ask people who deal with equipment for your business or hobby. Chances are that if you can imagine a printer with some specialized feature, somebody sells one.

Making a final decision

After a lot of years advising people and companies about printers, I've come to a handful of very simple conclusions:

✦ If you don't print a lot, get a good color inkjet printer from one of the major manufacturers. You won't go wrong with any of them.

✦ If you do print a lot — say, more than a dozen pages a day — get a laser. It costs less in the long run, although the initial expense is higher. For the occasional color print, find a company nearby that lets you run your pictures through their color inkjet.

✦ If you really, really need a color laser (or dye sub) printer, you'll know it as soon as you see a printout. Do the math, and hold onto your pocketbook.

✦ If you need to print color *and* a lot of black-and-white documents, consider getting both an inkjet printer and a laser printer. The laser printer still can pay for itself, and you won't have to compromise the quality of one type of output in order to get both.

Choosing a new monitor

Chances are good that the monitor you're using right now has a standard *CRT* (cathode ray tube) screen. Chances are also good that you've seen a flat-panel monitor that blew your socks off. Flat-panel displays are rapidly taking over the desktop, for good reason. So if you are thinking about replacing your monitor, the first hurdle you have to clear involves choosing between a standard screen and a flat-panel *LCD* (liquid crystal display) screen.

Evaluating CRT versus flat-panel monitors

Flat-panel LCD displays, long standard on laptop computers, have become popular as desktop monitors in the last few years. They have several inherent advantages over conventional CRT monitors:

✦ With no bulky CRT inside, they are much lighter and occupy less space.

✦ They use less power.

✦ The image is very sharp, straight lines always look perfectly straight, and color convergence is perfect.

✦ Because their images persist longer than those of a CRT, they don't flicker.

They also have some disadvantages, many of which aren't obvious at first blush:

✦ Although the prices keep coming down, LCD monitors cost considerably more than comparable CRT monitors, and the price discrepancy will probably be with us for a long time to come.

✦ Few LCDs have screens larger than 17 inches or resolutions greater than 1280 x 1024 (for details on screen resolution, see the next section).

✦ The manufacturing process frequently produces screens with *dead* pixels. A dead pixel shows up as a black spot (or some other non-matching color) in the image. Most manufacturers consider an LCD display functional if it has no more than three dead pixels, but a single dead pixel may drive you crazy, especially if it sits near the middle of the screen. If you look at a screen and immediately notice its dead pixel(s), pass it by.

If you buy a flat panel monitor and one or two or three pixels suddenly die, you have precious little you can do about it.

✦ An LCD can be difficult to read from certain angles, particularly far off the screen's axis. This can be a problem if several people have to watch the computer screen at once.

✦ LCDs tend to reproduce colors less accurately than CRTs, which makes them less suitable for working on photographs and movies.

✦ The longer image persistence that makes LCDs flicker-free has a down side: if you use applications that produce rapidly moving images, such as games and Windows Movie Maker, the movement tends to blur.

Picking the right screen size

The most obvious characteristic of a monitor is its screen size. Standard CRT monitors are made with screens that are nominally 15, 17, 18, 19, and 21 inches across the diagonal. Flat-panel LCD screens are generally smaller.

Manufacturers of standard CRT monitors (and television sets, for that matter) have a funny way of measuring the diagonal size of the screen — they frequently measure the size of the CRT itself, without regard to the fact that some of the screen is hidden by the plastic case, and therefore can't be seen. On a standard CRT monitor, if you measure the diagonal of the visible screen, it's as much as an inch less than the rated size of the screen. Some manufacturers come clean and tell you the actual visible area. Far too many do not.

A monitor's maximum *resolution* is at least as important as its screen size.

Resolution is the number of image-forming dots, or *pixels,* that the monitor can display horizontally and vertically. Standard CRT screens can vary the number of pixels shown on screen. Flat-panel displays cannot.

If you're working with flat-panel LCD screens, the resolution is fixed, typically at 1024 x 768 (although occasionally at 800 x 600). While it may be theoretically possible to change the resolution (from, say, 1024 x 768 down to 800 x 600), the results often leave much to be desired because the grid of dots in a flat panel display is fixed — the modified screen resolution is a sleight of hand, performed by interpolating between dots on the grid.

Standard CRT monitors have specified maximum resolutions, advertised by the manufacturer. The following are typical:

✦ 1280 x 1024 for a 15, 17, or 18-inch monitor

✦ 1600 x 1200 for a 19-inch monitor

✦ 1600 x 1200 or 1800 x 1440 for a 21-inch monitor

Some, uh, Dummies think that screen resolution has something to do with how sharp a picture appears on the monitor. It doesn't. As the resolution increases, the amount of information shown on the screen increases. The picture itself may be sharp or fuzzy, depending on how well the monitor works — a good monitor shows a sharp picture at 1600 x 1200, for example, while a lousy monitor may be so fuzzy at 1024 x 768 that you are forced to run at 800 x 600.

Book VII Chapter 1

Finding and Installing the Hardware You Want

I think the easiest way to understand the phenomenon is to consider the effect of screen resolution on a plain-vanilla Excel 2002 (which is to say, Office XP) spreadsheet:

✦ At 800 x 600 resolution, you can see cells A1 through L25 — or 30 cells — on a completely virgin spreadsheet.

✦ At 1024 x 768, you can see cells A1 through O34, or a total of 510 cells. That's 70 percent more usable cells than at 800 x 600.

✦ At 1280 x 1024 — the practical limit for detailed text work on any standard CRT screen, unless your eyesight is a darn sight better than my eyesight — Excel 2002 shows cells A1 through S50, for a grand total of 950 cells. That's 86 percent more cells than at 1024 x 768, and more than three times as many as 800 x 600.

Although you probably won't spend most of your time sweating over thousand-cell spreadsheets, this little comparison combined with a lot of experience leads me to a few simple generalizations:

✦ Any monitor you buy nowadays will handle 800 x 600 resolution just fine. At 800 x 600, you can see half a page in Word or Excel. For casual Windows users, that's good enough.

✦ Most 17-inch standard CRT monitors do well at 1024 x 768. Most flat panel LCD monitors run at 1024 x 768, too. If you move up to 1024 x 768, you can see about two-thirds of a page in Word. In Excel, you almost double the number of cells that you can see in a spreadsheet, compared to 800 x 600 resolution. Because of that, for most people, 1024 x 768 is well worth a small additional price and, for most people, a 17-inch (or larger) monitor makes sense.

✦ Resolutions above 1024 x 768 come in handy if you commonly need to work on more than one Word document at a time or if you're struggling with really hairy spreadsheets. Unfortunately, the screens that can handle really high resolution (for ordinary eyes, anyway) tend to be quite expensive. Before you shell out the bucks to reach to the resolution stratosphere, make sure you try some real-live work on the monitor of your choice at the resolution of your choice, and let your eyes be the judge.

Fighting flicker

Some people can't stand screen flicker, no way, no how, especially under certain kinds of fluorescent lights. If screen flicker really bugs you, get a flat-screen LCD monitor. They don't flicker. End of story.

Before you buy

"Quality" is hard to pin down, but it counts for a lot in a monitor. Don't just look at the specifications before you buy one. Look carefully at the image.

On a standard CRT monitor, look to see whether the image is sharp. (Check the corners!) Do the different colors that form the image converge properly all over the screen? Can you adjust the monitor so that straight lines near the edge of the screen look straight, or do they always bend outward or inward?

Will the monitor fit in your workspace? If you may have to move it, can you pick it up and carry it easily?

No matter what kind of monitor you're considering, you have to ask yourself: Does anything about the monitor bother you, such as a shiny screen that casts reflections into your eyes? If you have niggling doubts now, they'll turn into major headaches (literally and figuratively) after you've spent a thousand or two hours in front of the beast.

A standard CRT monitor's *refresh rate* is the number of times per second that it redraws the image on its screen. The refresh rate is measured in Hertz, abbreviated Hz, just like the frequency of a radio wave. At a refresh rate of 70 Hz, your monitor redraws the image 70 times per second.

If a monitor's refresh rate is too low, the image flickers. Most people cease to notice flicker at about 72 Hz, but this can be influenced by the monitor's CRT (cathode ray tube, or picture tube), the ambient lighting, and the sensitivity of your eyes. A refresh rate of 75 Hz looks flicker-free to almost everybody, and higher rates generally give no advantage.

A standard CRT monitor's refresh rate is variable, just as its resolution is. The maximum refresh rate typically is lower at higher resolutions: You can run 80 Hz refresh at 1024 x 768 resolution, say, but only 72 Hz at 1280 x 1024.

Before you buy a monitor, try it out at its highest resolution and see if the refresh rate is high enough to eliminate flicker. Be wary of really cheap monitors, which may have a maximum refresh rate as low as 60 Hz at their highest resolution.

Resolution and refresh rate are both controlled by your computer's video adapter: Your monitor may be capable of 1280 x 1024 at 80 Hz, but your video adapter has to be able to pump out a signal at that rate. The monitor's specifications determine whether the monitor can display the image that the video adapter produces. Thus, if you upgrade your monitor, you may have to upgrade your video adapter to take advantage of your new monitor's capabilities.

Checking and setting the resolution and refresh rate

Fortunately, Windows enables you to easily check and set the resolution and refresh rate that your monitor uses:

1. **Click Start➪Control Panel.**

2. **In the Control Panel, choose Appearance And Themes➪Display.**

Windows XP opens the Display Properties dialog box.

3. **Click the Settings tab.**

Figure 1-1 shows this tab. The Screen Resolution slider shows the display's current resolution.

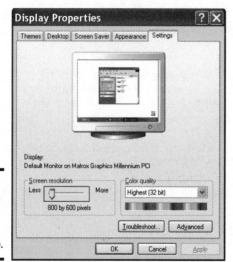

Figure 1-1:
The Display
Properties
dialog box,
Settings tab.

4. **If you want to change the resolution, move the slider to the setting you want. If you don't want to change the resolution, you may skip to Step 8.**

5. **Check the Color Quality dropdown list.**

If Windows XP set it to a lower value than you want when you moved the slider, you may have to upgrade or replace your display adapter. (See the section "Picking a video adapter.")

6. **Click the Apply button.**

Windows XP changes the display's resolution.

7. **If Windows XP opens a dialog box that asks if you want to keep the new settings, click Yes to keep the new settings or No to return to the old ones.**

   If the display disappears or becomes unreadable, press the Esc key to return to the old settings. (Or, if you wait 15 seconds, Windows XP returns to the old settings automatically.) This means that you chose a resolution that your monitor cannot display. You have to choose a lower resolution.

8. **When you're done, click OK to close the Properties dialog box.**

To check and set the refresh rate your monitor uses, follow these steps:

1. **Choose Start⇨Control Panel.**

2. **In the Control Panel, double-click Displays to open the Display Properties dialog box.**

3. **Click the Settings tab.**

4. **Click the Advanced button.**

   Windows XP opens another box that shows configuration settings for your video adapter.

5. **Click the Monitor tab.**

   Figure 1-2 shows this tab. The Screen Refresh Rate drop-down dialog box shows the display's current refresh rate.

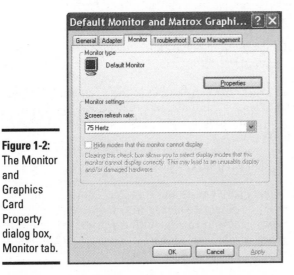

Figure 1-2:
The Monitor
and
Graphics
Card
Property
dialog box,
Monitor tab.

6. **If you want to change the refresh rate, select a different rate and click Apply.**

   Windows XP changes the refresh rate.

7. **If Windows XP opens a dialog box that asks whether you want to keep the new settings, click Yes to keep the new refresh rate or No to return to the old one.**

   If the display disappears or becomes unreadable, press the Esc key to return to the old refresh rate (or wait for Windows XP to return automatically). This means that you chose a refresh rate that your monitor cannot display at the current resolution. You have to choose a lower refresh rate or a lower resolution.

8. **When you're done, close both properties dialog boxes and the Control Panel.**

Picking a video adapter

You may want to replace your video adapter card to get higher resolution and a higher refresh rate, better performance, or additional features. Some graphics cards promise faster rendering of three-dimensional objects in several popular games. Many graphics cards fail to live up to their promises.

To produce a display with a given combination of resolution and refresh rate (see the discussion in the preceding sections), both your monitor and your video adapter have to be up to the challenge. If you buy a monitor that can run at 1800 x 1600 with 92 Hz refresh, you may also have to buy a more capable video card to keep up with it.

Alternatively, you could consider refinancing a third world country. This stuff doesn't come cheap, folks.

 Some computers have a video controller built in to the main board. If you add a video adapter card to such a computer, it usually disables the built-in controller automatically, so you shouldn't have a problem. The operative term, of course, is "shouldn't."

When you choose a new video adapter, consider the following points:

✦ Be sure that the card can display the highest resolution you want with a refresh rate high enough to eliminate flicker. Check the number of colors that the card can display at the resolution you want. If you work with video or photographs, you need at least 24-bit color (16 million colors), and preferably 32-bit color ("true color").

✦ If your computer's main board has an AGP adapter slot, get an adapter with an AGP interface. (See "Interfaces for adapter cards," earlier in this chapter.)

✦ Get an adapter designed to perform well with the types of applications you run. If you play video games a lot, you should get a *3D adapter,* which has special hardware to display game images quickly.

✦ If you want to watch TV on your computer, or use the computer to capture video from a TV signal, VCR, or video camera, choose a card that supports TV input and output. (See Book VIII, Chapter 2, for more information about video capture.)

✦ If you want to watch DVD movies on your computer, look for a video adapter with support for DVD decoding. (Without this feature, you can still play DVDs if your computer's CPU is fast enough, but DVDs take a lot of processing power and may reduce your ability to run other applications at the same time.)

✦ Be sure that the card you choose is fully supported in Windows XP. Some video card manufacturers are notoriously slow to provide support for new operating systems. (See "Assuring Windows XP compatibility," earlier in this chapter.)

In my experience, the single greatest source of frustration with Windows since its inception has been lousy video drivers. I've seen it happen year in and year out, in every version of Windows, with every video card manufacturer. Windows XP is no exception. It takes a long time for video card manufacturers to come out with decent drivers for their wares. If you buy a new video card, make sure you check the manufacturer's Web site for their latest Windows XP driver, prior to installing the card. And always keep your old video card, in case the new one simply won't work.

Most video adapters have built-in *video memory,* which they use to hold the image displayed on the screen. Some adapters let you add more video memory to get higher resolutions with more colors. Check out this option before you replace your card. If you can reach your goal by adding video memory, that's a cheaper and easier way to go.

Getting enough memory (RAM)

Random access memory, or *RAM,* is the type of memory that your computer uses to hold the programs it is running and the data they are working on. If a Windows XP system has too little RAM, it has to keep writing one piece of code or data to a *swap file* on your hard disk to make space to read in another. A little while later, it has to write something else to the swap file to make space to read the first item back in.

This situation can reduce your computer's overall performance, even to the point where the computer spends more time writing things to the swap file and reading them back than it spends doing useful work. Thus you may be able to increase your computer's performance by adding more RAM.

How much RAM you need depends on the types of applications you run, and to some extent on your working habits, such as how many different applications you tend to run at one time.

RAM is measured in *megabytes,* abbreviated MB. A megabyte is roughly a million bytes. A *kilobyte* (KB) is 1024 bytes. A *byte* is the basic unit of computer storage, commonly equated with one character, or eight bits. A *bit* is a one or a zero. If that has you confused, ask your eight-year-old niece. Trust me. She understands this stuff better than the guy at the computer shop.

As a rule, a Windows XP computer needs at least 128 MB to run well, particularly if you're using Microsoft Office. Applications that work with graphics, such as movie editors and drawing programs, often require 256 MB or even more.

To decide how much memory you need, look for recommendations in the documentation for the applications you run. Also observe your computer's behavior. If your computer tends to have fits of frantic disk activity while you're working with a file that's already open, more RAM may well be useful. The same is true if your computer uses the disk a lot when you switch from one open application to another.

Here's how to tell how much RAM your computer has now:

1. **Choose Start⇨Control Panel.**

2. **Click Performance and Maintenance and then click System.**

   Windows XP opens the System Properties dialog box.

3. **The General tab displays the amount of RAM in your system, as shown in Figure 1-3.**

Adding more RAM is reasonable if you just suspect you need it. RAM is not very expensive, and adding it can't hurt. If you do need it, it can help you a lot.

Different computers require different types of RAM. This is an issue of compatibility with the computer's main board, not with Windows XP. Be sure to buy memory that is compatible with your computer.

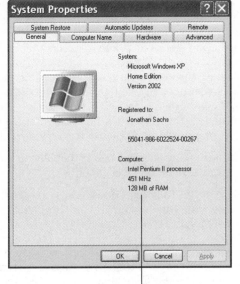

Figure 1-3:
The System
Properties
dialog box
displays the
amount of
RAM in your
system.

Amount of RAM

Upgrading keyboards

Face it. The keyboard that came with your computer wouldn't even make a decent boat anchor. Don't get me wrong. Those mushy, squishy, tinker-toy keyboards would make fine Cracker Jack prizes, and casual computer users can get by with them for years. I wouldn't look down *my* nose at your flimsy, somnambulant, ludicrous excuse for a keyboard. Sniff.

Seriously, if you spend more than a few hours a day at the computer, you're probably wondering why your fingers hurt, and why you make so many mistakes typing. There's a good reason why. That keyboard you're using probably cost a dollar. Maybe less. Getting a new one can make a big difference in how well you type and can speed up your computing enormously. You know. So you can get a life....

Several companies now make *ergonomic* keyboards, which are contoured to let you type with your hands in a position that (supposedly) reduces the stress on them. These keyboards take some getting used to, but some users swear by them. Personally, I swear at them. You can get a wireless keyboard. You can also get a keyboard with a built-in pointing device to replace the mouse. Heck, you can probably get one that *looks* like Mickey Mouse.

If you're serious about replacing your tin-can keyboard, keep these points in mind:

✦ Look for a keyboard that feels right. Some folks like quiet keys. I like 'em loud. Some prefer keys with short throws — ones you don't have to push very far. I like long throws. Some prefer minimal tactile feedback — when you push the key, it doesn't push back. I like lots of tactile feedback. Most current keyboards have a row of function keys across the top. I like mine on the left. Everybody's different, and the only way you're going to find a keyboard that you like is to try dozens of them.

✦ Expensive keyboards aren't necessarily better than cheap ones. Big-name keyboards aren't necessarily better than generics.

✦ Heavy keyboards are better than light ones, unless you're going to schlep your keyboard with you on your travels through Asia. Heavy keyboards with rubber feet stay put.

What keyboard do I use? The Avant Stellar, `www.cvtinc.com`, which is surely the Sherman Tank of the keyboard biz. The beast weights almost as much as a portable computer, and it costs just under two hundred bucks. It's ugly, it's retro, and it's decidedly un-hip. But it keeps goin' and goin' and goin' and goin'.

All keyboards designed for Windows computers are compatible with Windows XP. A keyboard may require a driver to operate its special features, though. Check its compatibility if this is a possible concern for you.

Choosing a mouse — or alternatives

Mice are probably available in more varieties than any other computer accessory. You can get mice with special ergonomic profiles, colored mice, transparent mice, special mice designed for kids, and on and on.

Among the most useful variations are optical mice. An optical mouse uses a light source and sensor to detect movement over a flat surface. It has no rolling ball to slip or stick, and it rarely needs to be cleaned. You may find this particularly helpful if you have furry pets, and your mouse tends to get clogged by their hair.

Some users prefer a *trackball* to a mouse. A trackball is a stationary device with a large ball resting in a cup on the top. You operate it by turning the ball with your palm.

Some users like to use a *graphics tablet* instead of a mouse, or in addition to a mouse. You control software with a graphics tablet by touching its surface with a special stylus. Unlike a mouse, the graphics tablet detects position, not motion, so you can literally point at the item you want. You can even write or draw with the stylus. Graphics tablets are popular with serious users of photo editors and other graphics software. Many of these applications have special graphics tablet support and can detect the amount of pressure you're applying to the stylus. Thus you can press hard to draw a wide line, for example, or lightly to draw a thin line.

A *touchpad* is similar to a graphics tablet, but you control it with your fingertip instead of a stylus. You "click" by tapping the pad. A touchpad is very convenient for moving the mouse around the screen, but because most people's fingers are less pointy than a stylus, it's not very good for drawing or writing. Touchpads usually are just a few inches long and wide, and cost $20 to $50, while graphics tablets are larger and cost $100 or more.

Touchpads are available with a serial interface, a USB interface, or the funny round plug used by most keyboards and mice (called a *PS/2 connector*). You can also buy a keyboard which has a touchpad built in, and which needs only the keyboard's usual connector.

All mice designed for Windows computers are compatible with Windows XP. Specialized devices such as graphics tablets may require special drivers; make sure the device you buy is Windows XP compatible.

Adding storage devices

You can add several types of storage devices to your computer: hard disk drives, CD and DVD drives, other types of disk drives, memory card readers, and tape drives.

Choosing a second hard disk

All Windows XP computers have a hard disk, but you can add a second one if you need more storage space.

Hard disk capacity is measured in *gigabytes,* abbreviated GB. One gigabyte is 1,000 megabytes, or 1,000,000,000 bytes.

It's also possible to replace your first disk with a larger one, but then you have to reinstall Windows XP, reinstall all of your applications, and transfer your data. (There are ways to transfer the operating system and applications intact, but they require special hardware or software.)

Be sure to buy a hard disk with the same type of interface as the disk controller in your computer. For most current Windows computers, that means an EIDE interface.

**Book VII
Chapter 1**

**Finding and
Installing the
Hardware You Want**

Picking CD-R or CD-RW drives

If you want to create CDs or CD-ROMs, you can replace your CD-ROM drive with a CD-R or CD-RW drive. Then you can do the following:

✦ Create custom CDs that contain your own choice of tracks copied from commercial CDs, Web sites, or other sources.

✦ Record your own or your friends' music.

✦ Back up your data on cheap, sturdy, reliable, media.

✦ Move large files from one computer to another on CDs.

A CD-R drive writes to CD-R media. These are CDs that you can write once. After a CD-R has been written, you cannot add to it or erase it.

A CD-RW drive can write to either CD-R or CD-RW media. CD-RW media are more expensive than CD-Rs, but they can be erased and reused many times. In fact, you can use CD-RW as you'd use a hard disk, erasing and rewriting individual files. (Any type of CD is a lot slower than a hard disk, though.)

As CD-RW drives become faster and cheaper, CD-R drives are becoming less common.

Most computers' CD-ROM drives can read CD-RW media, but audio CD players often cannot. CD players can read CD-R media recorded in a CD-RW drive, though.

The speed of a CD-R drive is measured by two numbers, such as "32x/12x." This means that the drive reads a CD 32 times faster than an audio CD player would, and it writes CD-R media at 12 times that speed. Similarly, the speed of a CD-RW drive is measured by three numbers, such as "32x/8x/12x." The third number is the speed at which the drive rewrites CD-RW media. The numbers aren't always given in the same order, but the largest number always is the read speed, the smallest is the CD-RW rewrite speed, and the middle one is the CD-R write speed.

The numbers don't tell the whole story. Drives with the same nominal speed may perform quite differently due to differences in their design or their drivers. Read product reviews and try out the drives, if possible, before you make a choice.

Using DVD drives

DVD drives can read DVD-ROM disks, which hold 4 GB to 16 GB of data, compared to about 650 MB for a CD-ROM. DVD-ROM disks are not yet a common medium for distributing software and data.

DVD drives can read CD-ROMs, so you can remove your CD-ROM drive when you install a DVD drive. If your video card does DVD decoding, they also can play conventional DVDs on your computer. (See "Picking a video adapter," earlier in this chapter, for information about DVD decoding.)

Writeable DVD drives are available, but they use one or more of several standards that have overlapping purposes and are more or less incompatible. Writing DVDs is a black art at this point, well beyond the scope of this book, made all the more treacherous by the lack of a single standard. If you're interested in the technology, research the latest information on the Web or consult a well-informed dealer.

Choosing a Windows-compatible device with the correct type of interface is important for DVD drives, just as it is for CD-R and CD-RW drives. See "Picking CD-R or CD-RW drives," above.

Understanding removable disk devices

You can buy an adapter kit that lets you "plug in" a hard disk drive by sliding it into a slot in your computer's front panel. If you equip two or more computers with such a kit, you can transfer your data from one computer to another simply by transferring the disk.

Removable drives require a moderate degree of care. The drives themselves are designed to be installed in a computer and left there, so they are liable to be damaged by rough treatment. Also, you must turn a computer off before you insert or remove a drive.

Several companies make disk drives that are designed to use removable disks (like a diskette drive) but have enough capacity and speed to be used like hard disks. These drives are also useful for moving data from one computer to another. Many people use them as a backup medium. Some models have a reputation for poor reliability, though, making them a questionable choice for backups.

Using memory card readers

A *memory card* is a small solid-state device that typically can hold a few dozen megabytes of data. Unlike most types of solid-state memory (for example, RAM) it doesn't require power to maintain its contents. This makes it an ideal storage medium for digital cameras, digital audio players, and other portable devices.

A *memory card reader* is a device that lets a computer read and write memory cards. To Windows XP, the reader appears to be a disk drive, and each memory card appears to be a removable disk.

Two widely used types of memory cards are SmartMedia (SM) and CompactFlash (CF). The two are not compatible, so which type you use may be determined by a device that you want or already own. The two work about equally well.

Readers for both types of memory cards are available in a variety of different forms. For the majority of users, the most convenient form is a small, freestanding device that plugs into the computer's USB port.

Backing up to tape

Tape is the medium of choice for backing up data on Web servers and other large computers. It's less popular on personal computers because tape drives tend to be expensive, but it has advantages that you shouldn't overlook. Tape is reliable, economical, and reusable, and it's the only backup medium with enough capacity to back up an entire hard disk at once — short of a second hard disk, anyway.

The low cost of tape makes it feasible to keep several generations of backups. If you need to refer to an old version of a file or recover a file that you deleted weeks or even months before, that can be life saver.

When you choose a tape drive, look for one with enough capacity to back up your entire hard disk on one tape and enough speed to do it in a time that you consider reasonable.

As with disk drives, choose a tape drive with a type of interface that is appropriate for your computer. Drives are available with EIDE, USB, and SCSI interfaces. Almost all high-capacity drives are SCSI only.

If you decide to buy an external tape drive, your choice of interfaces is limited to USB and SCSI. There's a particular reason why you may prefer an external drive: If your computer needs repair, you can more easily move an external drive to a loaner system to restore your data and resume your work. Tape drives are not standardized, so you can't necessarily read your tape on any loaner that has a type drive — even assuming that you can find any loaner that has a tape drive!

Unlike the various types of disks, a tape drive must be read and written by a special utility program. Several software publishers sell such backup utilities. Check with a given utility's publisher for information about what devices it supports.

USB Hubs

Your Windows computers probably has two USB connectors, but you can attach many more USB devices to it than that. In theory, you can attach

127 USB devices to one computer. If you keep that many devices, you probably have no space left to sit down!

To attach additional devices you need the USB equivalent of a power strip, to turn one connector into several. That device is called a *USB hub*.

A USB hub has one USB connector to attach it to a computer and several connectors to attach it to devices. Hubs most often have either four or seven device connectors.

You can plug one USB hub into another to attach more devices than a single hub can support.

The maximum length of a USB cable is not precisely defined, but the figure of 5 meters (about 16 feet) is widely accepted. This is the maximum length of a cable from a computer or a hub to a hub or a device. The maximum total length between the computer and any device is about 80 feet.

Beefing Up Communication

No computer is an island, unto its own. At least, not any more. With Windows XP, you have no excuse to remain isolated. Networking is part and parcel of the XP experience.

Establishing a network

The standard way to network several computers together is to put a network interface card, or *Ethernet adapter,* in each one. All of the Ethernet adapters are then cabled to a central *hub.* Other Ethernet-compatible devices, such as printers and high-speed modems, may also be attached to the hub. If a network has only two devices, it doesn't need a hub; the devices may be connected directly to each other with a special cable. (The most common type of two-device system consists of one computer and one high-speed modem. See "Running high-speed Internet access," later in this chapter.)

I talk about networking extensively in Book IX.

Many Ethernet adapters and hubs use a standard called *100BT* or *100BaseT* (pronounced *one hundred base T*), which theoretically can transfer data at 100 megabits (about 12 megabytes) of data per second. Realistic network speeds are some fraction of that.

Other Ethernet adapters and hubs use an older standard called *10BaseT,* which is ten times slower than 100BaseT but is still quite adequate for most small network users' needs.

You connect an Ethernet adapter to a nearby hub with a light, inexpensive *patch cable* that resembles the wire used to plug a telephone into the wall. Over longer distances (up to 100 meters, or about 330 feet), you must use special cable that is usually installed inside a wall or above a ceiling. This is a job for a professional installer.

Ethernet networking is a mature technology, and the devices are highly standardized. With few exceptions, you can mix different brands of hardware without compatibility problems. Just be sure that the adapters are on the hardware compatibility list.

Several companies now sell hardware for setting up a local area network by radio instead of cable. These make a lot of sense if you have computers in different parts of your home or office and want to avoid the expense of installing cables. Wireless networks are more expensive than conventional Ethernet networks, though, and usually are slower. They tend to use one of two different (and incompatible) standards, *WiFi* and *HomeRF.* Don't expect these two types of devices to work together. To be extra safe, don't expect any two brands of wireless networking devices to work together.

Running high-speed Internet access

Almost every current computer has a dial-up modem, which lets you access the Internet through a telephone connection to your *Internet Service Provider* (ISP). Under ideal conditions a dial-up modem can receive data at 53.0 Kb/second (53,000 bits, or about 5300 characters, per second) and send data at 33.6 Kb/second. In technical terms, the *downlink speed* is 53.0 Kb/second and the *uplink speed* is 33.6 Kb/second.

Several other types of connections offer much higher data rates. These types of connections have traditionally been sold to large organizations for hundreds or thousands of dollars per month, but over the last few years, they have become available to consumers for less than a hundred dollars per month — often much less.

DSL (digital subscriber line) is a special type of service provided over ordinary telephone lines, which allows much higher data rates: up to 6 Mb/second (6 million bits per second) for the downlink, and up to 600 Kb/second for the uplink.

DSL is not available in all areas. The telephone carrier's local switching station must be equipped for it, and your computer must be within 15,000 feet of the switching station, measured along the path of the telephone wires.

Many cable TV companies now offer Internet access through their cable systems. In areas where this service exists, it typically is available to anyone who has access to the cable. Speeds are typically in the range of 300 Kb/second to 3 Mb/second. Older systems handle only the downlink, requiring you to use a dial-up modem for the uplink. Most newer systems work both ways.

Fixed-station wireless Internet services are available in some areas, and they offer an attractive alternative where DSL and cable service do not go. This type of service uses a small antenna mounted on a roof or wall to communicate with a central relay station. Your distance from the station seldom matters, but your antenna must have a clear line of sight to it. Speeds are typically in the range of 500 Kb/second to 1.5 Mb/second for the downlink, and 50 to 250 Kb/second for the uplink.

Several services offer Internet access via satellite. These services tend to be more expensive than others, but are an option in many remote places where no other type of service is available. Some services provide two-way satellite communication; others are downlink-only, requiring you to use a dial-up modem and phone line for the uplink. Speeds are typically about 500 Kb/second for the downlink, and they range from dial-up speed up to about 150 Kb/second for the uplink.

All forms of high-speed Internet service tend to share certain characteristics. One is that uplinks are substantially slower than downlinks. This is not a serious limitation, because most users rarely uplink more data than they can type.

Although you can get high-speed Internet service by paying one bill, you usually get service from two different organizations: your ISP, which provides Internet access, e-mail service, and so on; and a *carrier,* which moves data between your computer and the ISP. This means that you may need to deal with two different customer service centers if you have a problem.

**Book VII
Chapter 1**

**Finding and
Installing the
Hardware You Want**

Firewalls

Most high-speed services connect your computer to the Internet whenever the computer is running. In technical terms, the connection is *always on.* This is convenient, because you can use the Internet at any moment without having to wait for a connection. It comes at a cost, though: Your computer is easier for a hacker to attack because it's always available, and it no longer is a moving target that appears on different Internet addresses at different times. For this reason, it's particularly important to install a *firewall* on your computer to protect it from attacks.

Windows XP comes complete with its own firewall, which you should install and use if you have an always-on Internet connection. I talk about firewalls extensively in Book IX.

All of these services require a special high-speed modem. This modem takes signals from the telephone line, cable, or antenna, and usually communicates with your computer by Ethernet. (See "Establishing a network," earlier in this chapter.) High-speed modems are not standardized as dial-up modems are; you must use the modem that your carrier provides or recommends.

Upgrading Imaging

Windows XP includes many exciting new features that may (finally!) lead you to install some new hardware that lets you capture and manipulate graphics.

Choosing a scanner

A scanner is a valuable accessory for many computer users. It works by scanning the image on a sheet of paper with a light sensor. It then digitizes the image and transmits it to your computer.

You can use an image captured by a scanner in many ways: You can attach it to an e-mail, include it in a document, publish it on a Web site, or use it as a starting point for artwork. *Optical character recognition* (OCR) software can "read" printed material from a scanner with some degree of accuracy and turn it into an editable document.

Scanners are available with USB, SCSI, and parallel interfaces. (See "Choosing an Interface" earlier in this chapter.) In most cases, the USB interface is preferred for its speed and ease of use.

Scanning paper items

Paper scanners for the consumer market fall into two categories. *Flatbed scanners* have a flat plate of glass covered by a hinged lid. You place the copy face down on the glass, close the lid, and the scanner moves the light sensor over the copy. *Path-through scanners* have a set of rollers that draws a sheet of copy past the sensor.

The two types of scanners cost about the same. Path-through scanners are more compact and convenient, but also more limited because they can scan only unbound sheets of paper. Flatbed scanners can handle books, magazines, and rigid material such as cardboard.

Most scanners do a creditable job of scanning black-and-white or color photographs or drawings as well as printed material.

A path-through scanner is sometimes called a *sheetfed scanner,* but that term also refers to a flatbed scanner with an automatic paper transport. The latter type is a relatively expensive gadget intended for high-volume work. There's an obvious potential for misunderstanding here.

Scanning photographic film

You can purchase an accessory for many flatbed scanners that lets you scan photographic negatives and transparencies. This accessory goes by various names like *transparency unit* or *transparency adapter.* Its essential purpose is to light negatives and transparencies from behind.

These units do an adequate job, but they have one big weakness: They can't increase a scanner's optical resolution. A resolution of 1200 DPI is plenty when you're scanning an 8½ x 11 inch page, but it doesn't go nearly as far when you're scanning a 1 x 1½ inch frame on a piece of film. If you enlarge that tiny image to a decent size, the individual pixels are likely to be visible.

You have several solutions to this problem:

✦ If you expect to scan a lot of negatives and transparencies, buy a *film scanner* — a scanner designed just for this purpose. Film scanners have much higher optical resolution than flatbed scanners in the same price range.

✦ If you need high-quality photographic scans only occasionally, send your film out to a service bureau to be scanned.

✦ If you need occasional photographic scans and don't need really top quality, have prints made and scan the prints. That way you can do the job yourself without having to buy any additional gadgets.

Picking a digital or video camera

A digital camera captures images in electronic memory, from which you can transfer them to a computer. A video camera does the same thing for movies.

Digital cameras and video cameras are more convenient than conventional cameras because you can see their images without waiting for film processing. They are less expensive to use because they record on reusable media, and you don't have to pay for processing.

An Internet camera, or *Webcam,* is a camera that connects directly to a computer and depends on computer processing to record an image. A computer can use one to capture either still pictures or video. Most Internet cameras use a USB interface.

Digital cameras, Video cameras, and Internet cameras are discussed further in Book VIII, Chapter 3.

Adding Audio

Windows XP's Media Player rocks 'n' rolls, but it doesn't do much unless your PC can play the tunes.

Choosing a sound card

A computer that can input and output sound has any number of interesting uses, such as:

✦ Playing CDs and DVDs

✦ Recording and playing back music with Windows Media Player or other applications

✦ Recording, editing, and viewing movies with Windows Movie Maker or other applications

✦ Gaming

✦ Internet telephony (making telephone calls through the Internet) and teleconferencing

✦ Voice recognition (converting speech into text, as input to a word processing application, for example)

✦ Composing electronic music

Many modern computers have sound hardware built into the main board. If your computer does not, you can add a sound card to give you the same capability.

For most users, selecting a sound card is easy. Just choose a card that is on Microsoft's hardware compatibility list. Be sure that the card plugs into a PCI slot. (See "Picking a video adapter," earlier in this chapter.)

If you want the best possible sound, things get more complicated. The sound hardware built into your main board probably won't satisfy you, and what you should look for depends on what you want to do.

For gaming, get a card that offers four-channel output. (You need four speakers or four-channel headphones, too.)

DVDs use a sound encoding system called *5.1 channel Dolby Digital*. To get the best possible sound, choose a sound card that supports this standard. (You also need five full-range speakers and a subwoofer. This runs into real bucks. Is the result worth it? That's up to you.)

If you're an audiophile or a musician, you'll appreciate a card that has a very broad, flat frequency response and has the specialized inputs and outputs used on high-end audio equipment, such as S/PDIF and optical S/PDIF.

The inside of a computer is a difficult place to process audio signals, because it is awash with all sorts of electromagnetic signals. A sound card needs good shielding to avoid picking up noise. The card's *signal to noise ratio* (SNR) measures its noise immunity. An SNR of 70 dB is so-so. An SNR of 90 dB is quite good.

Voice recognition is a particularly demanding application. If you plan to use this type of software, choose a card that is on the software publisher's hardware compatibility list as well as Microsoft's list. Consult the publisher for advice if in doubt.

MIDI sound generation (a technology developed for synthesizing electronic music) used to be a big deal, because many games used it to generate sound. Today, with CD-ROMs and big hard disks universally available, most games produce sound directly from digital soundtracks. MIDI is important only if you want to compose electronic music on your computer. In that case, look for a card with a large number of *voices,* that is, a card that can generate a large number of different sounds at the same time. Check the hardware compatibility list for the composing software you will use, and consult the software publisher for advice.

Hooking up speakers and headphones

To get sound out of your computer, you need either speakers or a set of headphones. Audiophiles spend a great deal of attention (and money) on these choices, but most folks do quite well with something considerably less, uh, precious. Here are a few pointers to help you choose something appropriate.

Decide how much quality you need. For casual gaming or music listening, almost any equipment will do. If sound quality is important to you, you need to be more selective, and the inexpensive speakers packaged with many computer systems probably won't satisfy you.

Look for the following things in a good speaker system:

✦ **Broad, flat frequency response for reproducing high and low frequencies accurately.** (Your sound card must have a comparable response, or the best speakers in the world won't help!)

✦ **Low total harmonic distortion (THD).** If the figure is below 1 percent, you won't notice any distortion at all unless your hearing is unusually sensitive.

✦ **More than enough power to produce the amount of sound you want.** A healthy surplus of power lets you avoid turning the volume all the way up, minimizing distortion.

✦ **Magnetic shielding.** If you intend to place speakers near your monitor, this prevents the speakers' magnets from distorting the monitor's image.

When you compare frequency response and harmonic distortion, try to get numbers from an impartial source — preferably all of the numbers from the same source. There are many ways to measure these things, so comparing measurements of different products that come from different places is not very useful.

A four-speaker system, often called *surround sound,* can give the sound a stronger feeling of coming from a particular place. Modern computer games make extensive use of this. When a race car whizzes by on the screen, the game designers make sure that you can *hear* it coming up on your left and speeding away to your right.

Surround sound can also make a significant impact in rock music recordings. For most other types of recordings, it makes less difference if it's used at all.

Many DVD movies use surround sound, but they follow a standard that works best with five speakers rather than four. (See "Choosing a sound card," above, for more information.)

A *subwoofer,* a separate speaker that produces very low frequencies, is another refinement. It adds to the effect of rock music and of many games, and to a smaller extent, of classical music.

Headphones are a good alternative to speakers for some users. Not only do they let you enjoy your music without disturbing your friends and neighbors; they also let you get primo quality sound for a lot less money than a set of top-of-the-line speakers.

If you go with headphones, decide whether you want *open-back* head-phones, which sit on your ears, or *closed-back* headphones, which enclose your ears in padded cups. Closed-back headphones shut out most ambient noise and tend to have better bass response, but are heavier, and for some users, less comfortable. If you want surround sound, look for headphones that are closed-back.

Choosing a microphone

You need a microphone for Internet telephony, teleconferencing, or voice recognition software.

For any of these purposes, a headset that combines a microphone with headphones is most convenient. For voice recognition, make sure that the microphone or headset you choose has been tested with your software and is known to produce good results.

The Microsoft Office XP Voice Recognition software recommends that you use a USB microphone for best results. Many experts in the field disagree. A standard noise canceling microphone that plugs into a good-quality sound card can produce results every bit as good as an all-electronic mike. Search the Woody's Office Watch archives, www.woodyswatch.com, for details.

Don't expect to find audiophile sound quality in a headset with a microphone. If you want that, buy one headset for listening to music and another for talking.

Picking a digital audio player

A digital audio player is a small gadget that stores music in digital form and plays it back, typically through earbud earphones. Call it an MP3 player if you like. You can carry it in your pocket or clipped to your belt. Thus it does the same job as a personal CD player or cassette player, but you can download music to it from your computer.

As of this writing, only a few digital audio players are compatible with Windows XP. The compatible players are named in Book VIII, Chapter 1. For updated information, see the current Windows XP hardware compatibility list.

When you choose a digital audio player, consider these factors:

✦ **Total capacity:** How many hours of music does the player hold?

✦ **Expansion:** Can you increase the player's capacity by adding a memory card? If so, what type of card? If you have other devices that use memory cards, does the player use the same type?

✦ **Convenience:** Is the player's design convenient for you?

✦ **Features:** Does the player have any special features that you want?

Choosing a Personal Data Assistant

A *personal data assistant,* or PDA, is a small computer that runs on batteries and can be held in one hand.

PDAs come in two forms. One is small enough to fit in your pocket. You enter information by touching a stylus to the LCD display. This type of device typically can read hand printing, although you may have to learn a special stylized version of the alphabet to use it. You may be able to buy a separate compact keyboard for entering larger amounts of text.

The other type of PDA is larger and has a full keyboard. Typically, the keyboard is smaller than the standard size but is large enough to make touch typing possible, if a bit, uh, contorted.

You should view a PDA as an electronic device in its own right, not as a tiny, limited computer. From this point of view, the lack of a keyboard is not necessarily a great disadvantage. Your particular needs may make a device with a keyboard more useful than a device that fits in your pocket, though.

When you choose a PDA, consider these factors:

✦ Does it fit in a pocket or not? Does it have a keyboard or not? If not, do you need a plug-in keyboard, and can you add one?

✦ What applications are built in? What applications can you add?

✦ What operating system does it run?

  • Some PDAs run a version of Microsoft Windows called *Windows CE,* which runs special, highly stunted versions of applications such as Microsoft Word and Excel. These PDAs provide a familiar environment that is highly compatible with your Windows XP system. You can move Word and Excel documents from your computer to your PDA and back, although you lose a lot in the translation.

  • Other PDAs run an operating system designed for portable computing from the ground up, most often the *Palm OS* from Palm, Inc. These devices can run applications equivalent to Word and Excel, but the applications are different and their compatibility is more limited.

✦ Does the device have a color LCD? Do you want one? Color LCDs use more power than monochrome LCDs, reducing the life of the batteries.

✦ What is the device's battery life?

✦ How much data can the device store? Does it have a slot for plugging in a memory card? If so, what type?

✦ What provisions does the device have for exchanging and synchronizing data with your Windows XP computer?

✦ What provisions does the device have for other types of communication? Does it have a built-in modem, or can you add a modem? What about a wireless modem?

✦ What special features or accessories do you need? Are they available?

How to Install New Hardware

Two fundamentally different approaches to installing new hardware exist. It amazes me that some people never even consider the possibility of doing it themselves, while other people wouldn't have the store install new hardware on a bet!

Have the store do it

When you buy a new disk drive or video card, why sweat the installation? For a few extra bucks, most stores will install what they sell. This is the easy, safe way! Instead of messing around with unfamiliar gadgets, which may be complicated and delicate, let somebody experienced do the work for you.

Different types of hardware present different levels of difficulty. It may make plenty of sense for you to install one type of device but not another.

At one end of the scale, installing a new video card or disk drive can be rather difficult and is best done by an expert. At the other end, speakers don't need any installation; you just plug them in and they work. The store can show you where the connectors go, but you have to plug them in yourself when you get home.

Here are some guidelines to help you judge how difficult an installation is likely to be:

✦ Any device that goes inside your computer is best left to the store unless you have experience with that specific kind of computer hardware.

✦ Any device that has a SCSI interface is best left to the store.

✦ A device with a USB interface is usually easy; nine times out of ten, you just plug it in and it works.

✦ A device with a serial or parallel interface is likely to be in between.

A high-speed modem should be installed by the communication carrier's technician if at all possible. The modem just plugs in, but the telephone line or cable may require configuration or rewiring to deliver the signal properly. Installing a wireless antenna is definitely a job for professionals. And configuring Internet applications to use the always-on connection can get complicated.

If you're unsure whether to install something yourself, ask the store what's involved. If you decide to try it, but the instructions confuse you or scare you when you read them, don't be embarrassed to go back and ask for help.

I do.

Do it yourself

If you decide to install a device yourself, the job is more likely to go smoothly if you observe these guidelines:

✦ **Don't just dive in — read the instructions first!** Pay attention to any warnings they give. Look for steps where you may have trouble. Are any of the instructions unclear? Does the procedure require any software or parts that appear to be missing? Try to resolve these potential problems ahead of time.

✦ **Back up your system before you start.** It's unlikely that your attempt to install a new device will disturb your system if it fails, but a backup is a good insurance policy in case something bad happens.

✦ **Write down everything you do in case you need to undo it or ask for help.** This is particularly important if you're opening up your computer to install an internal device!

✦ **If the device comes with a Windows XP driver, check the manufacturer's Web site to see if you have the latest version.** A company usually keeps drivers in one or more Web pages that you can find by clicking a link for Drivers, Downloads, or Support. If you discover a version that is newer than the one packaged with the device, download it and install it instead.

If you can't tell whether the version on the Web site is newer because you can't tell what version came with the device, you have two choices:

✦ Download and install the Web site's version just in case. It's unlikely to be older than the one that came with the device!

✦ Install the one that came with the device. Then check its date and version number. (See "Checking a driver's version," coming up next.) If the one on the Web site proves to be newer, download the newer one and install it. Read the instructions; you may need to uninstall the original driver first.

Checking a driver's version

To check the version number of a driver, follow these steps:

1. **Click Start➪Control Panel.**

2. **Click System.**

Windows XP opens the System Properties dialog box.

3. **Click the Hardware tab.**

4. **Click the Device Manager button.**

Windows XP opens the Device Manager window, as shown in Figure 1-4.

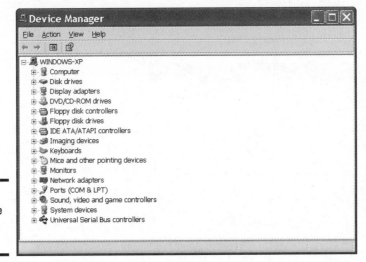

 5. **Click the plus sign next to the heading that contains the device you want to check.**

Windows XP expands that heading to show its devices, as shown in Figure 1-5.

You may have to try several headings to find the right one. If you guess wrong, just click again to collapse the heading you expanded.

6. **Double-click the device to open the Device Properties dialog box.**

7. **Click the Driver tab to display details about the driver, as shown in Figure 1-6.**

You should be able to identify the latest driver by its date, its version number, or both.

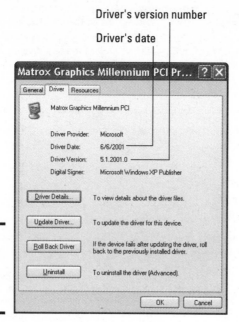

Driver's version number

Driver's date

Figure 1-6:
The Device
Properties
dialog box,
Driver tab.

If anything goes wrong

If your installation is unsuccessful, try these things in any order that makes sense to you.

+ Review the instructions. Look for a section with a title like "Troubleshooting" for suggestions on how to proceed.

+ Call or e-mail the manufacturer's technical support service for help. The manual or the Web site will tell you how.

+ Call the store, or pack everything up and take it in. If you happen to have a seven-foot-tall friend named Guido who drags his hairy knuckles on the ground, take him along with you. Moral support, eh?

If your computer no longer works correctly, restart Windows XP with the last known good configuration. (See the instructions in the next section.)

Restarting with the last known good configuration

When you install a new device driver, you change Windows XP's *configuration*. The next time you restart your computer, Windows XP tries to use the new configuration. If it succeeds, it discards the old configuration and makes the new one current.

Sometimes you install a new device driver, and everything goes to heck in a handbasket. If that happens to you, you need to restart Windows XP and tell it to use the "last known good configuration" — which is to say, Windows should ignore the changes you made that screwed everything up, and return to the state it was in the last time it started. That effectively removes the new driver from Windows XP.

1. **If your computer is operating, click Start⇨Turn Off Computer.**

   Windows XP opens the Turn Off Computer dialog box. Click the Restart button. Then skip to Step 3.

2. **If your computer isn't operating at all, press the power button to turn it off.**

   If that doesn't work, try pressing the button again and holding it in for several seconds. If that doesn't work either, pull the power cord out of the back of the computer; wait a few seconds, and then plug it in again. If you're working with a portable, you may have to remove the battery. Yes, it happens.

   Press the power button again to turn the computer back on. Then proceed to Step 3.

3. **Watch the display while your computer restarts. When the message** `Please select the operating system to start` **appears, press F8.**

   Windows XP displays a menu of special start-up options that you can choose.

4. **Use the up-arrow and down-arrow keys to move the menu's highlight to Last Known Good Configuration, and then press Enter.**

5. **Finish the start-up procedure as usual.**

If this procedure restarts your computer successfully, Windows XP discards the "new" screwed-up configuration and returns permanently to the last known good configuration.

Chapter 2: Working with Printers

In This Chapter

✔ Attaching a new printer to your PC or network

✔ Choosing the default printer

✔ Print queue problems

✔ Other troubleshooting

A h, the paperless office. What a wonderful concept! No more file cabinets bulging with misfiled flotsam. No more hernias hauling cartons of copy paper, dumping the sheets 500 at a time into a thankless plastic maw. No more trees dying in agony, relinquishing their last gasps to provide pulp as a substrate for heat-fused carbon toner. No more coffee-stained reports. No more paper cuts.

No more ... oh, who the heck am I trying to kid? No way.

Industry prognosticators have been telling us for more than a decade that the paperless office is right around the corner. Yeah, sure. Maybe around your corner. Around my corner, I predict that PC printers will disappear about the same time that *Star Trek* reruns go off the air. We're talking geologic time here, folks.

Windows XP has great printer support. It's easy once you learn a few basic skills.

For information about choosing a printer, see Book VII, Chapter 1.

Installing a Printer

You have three ways to make a printer available to your computer:

✦ You can attach it directly to the computer.

✦ You can connect your computer to a network and attach the printer to another computer on the same network.

✦ You can connect your computer to a network and attach the printer directly to the network's hub.

Connecting a computer directly to a network hub isn't difficult, if you have the right hardware. Each printer controller is different, though, so you have to follow the manufacturer's instructions.

At the time this book was written, a fourth method of attaching a printer to your PC was starting to emerge from the primordial Windows Ooze. It involves printing directly over the Internet, to a printer attached to the Internet. As you may imagine, there are a few, uh, logistical problems with this approach — I mean, if you think you get junk faxes now, wait till the spammers figure out how to shanghai your office printer to the tune of 40 pages per minute! Still, the technology may take hold, and you should keep your ear to the ground for it.

Attaching a local printer

So you have a new printer, and you want to use it. Attaching it locally — which is to say, plugging it into your PC — is the simplest way to install a printer, and the only way that makes sense if you haven't got a network.

First, physically connect the printer to your computer. If it uses a USB connector, simply plug the connector into your PC's USB port. If the printer uses a serial or parallel connector, turn your computer off, plug in the connector, and turn the computer back on.

After you connect your printer to the computer, you must make Windows XP recognize it. This is what "installing the printer" means.

If you have a USB printer, Windows XP may detect it and install it automatically when you turn the printer on. If you have a parallel or serial printer, Windows XP may detect and install it automatically when you restart the computer. If that doesn't happen, you have to haul out the big guns. Use this procedure:

1. **Choose Start⇨Control Panel.**

2. **In the Control Panel, click Printers And Other Hardware.**

   This opens the Printers And Faxes dialog box shown in Figure 2-1.

3. **In the Printer Tasks list, click Add A Printer.**

   This starts the Add Printer wizard and displays a Welcome page.

4. **Click Next.**

   The wizard displays the page shown in Figure 2-2. Click the Local Printer radio button.

   All USB printers are Plug and Play. Serial and parallel interface printers generally are not, although the printer's documentation may claim otherwise.

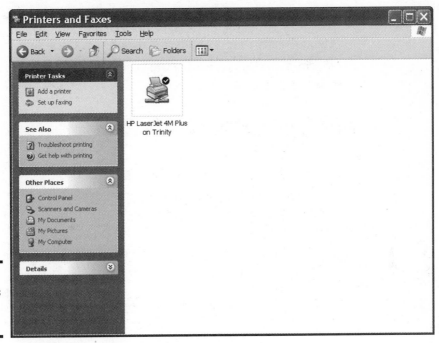

Figure 2-1:
The Printers
and Faxes
dialog box.

Figure 2-2:
Add Printer
Wizard,
Local or
Network
Printer?

5. **If you have a Plug and Play printer, check the Automatically Detect
And Install dialog box. Go to the head of the class, and click Next.**

The wizard tells you that it is searching for your printer. When it finds
the printer, it installs the driver for the printer. You can jump all the way
to Step 9.

6. **If your printer is not Plug and Play (or if you're back here because Windows XP couldn't automatically identify your printer), clear the Automatically Detect And Install dialog box. Click Next.**

   Windows asks you to identify which port your printer is connected to (see Figure 2-3).

Figure 2-3:
Add Printer
Wizard,
Select a
Printer Port.

7. **Select the appropriate port from the dropdown list, and then click Next.**

   Most Windows computers have one parallel port (the long oval one) and one or two serial ports (short oval ones). If your printer is connected to a parallel port, it is almost undoubtedly connected to the port named LPT1. If it is connected to a serial port, you must determine whether it is connected to the port named COM1 or COM2. The back of your computer may be stamped or etched with the names of the serial ports, but if you can't tell, tell the wizard that it's connected to COM1. If that doesn't work, shut down your computer, turn it off, and move the cable to the other serial port connector. Then you know it's in COM1. Probably.

8. **The wizard displays a page that prompts you to select your printer's brand and model, as in Figure 2-4. Select the brand and the model; then click Next.**

   If your printer's brand and model aren't in the lists, you can still install your printer if you have a diskette or CD-ROM with a Windows XP driver for it or if you can snag the driver on the printer manufacturer's Web site. Click the Have Disk button and follow the wizard's prompts.

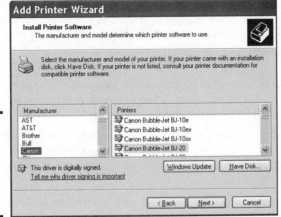

Figure 2-4:
Add Printer
Wizard,
Install
Printer
Software.

9. **The wizard prompts you to enter a name that Windows XP may use to identify this printer (see Figure 2-5). Accept the default name or enter another name that is short but meaningful to you.**

Short printer names (such as LJ4 or DJ930C) are easier to remember and harder to mistype.

You also must choose whether to make this printer your *default printer* — that is, the printer that a Windows XP application uses to print documents unless you explicitly tell it to use a different one. If this is the only printer on your system, the only meaningful choice is Yes.

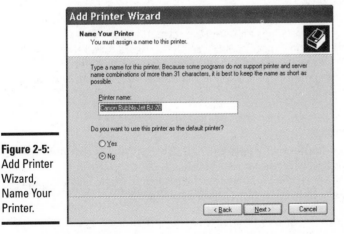

Figure 2-5:
Add Printer
Wizard,
Name Your
Printer.

If your computer is attached to a network and you have configured a network with the Home Networking wizard, the wizard asks whether you want to share the printer, as shown in Figure 2-6. "Sharing the printer" means that users of other computers on the network can see that this printer is attached to your computer, and can print documents on it.

10. **If you want to share the printer, click the Share Name radio button and enter a share name that other network computers may use to identify this printer. Click Next.**

If you are sharing the printer, the wizard asks you to enter the printer's location and comments about it. This information is optional, but it helps other network users understand where your printer is and how it ought to be used.

11. **Enter appropriate printer location and comments and click Next.**

The wizard asks whether you want to print a test page.

12. **Click the Yes radio button, and then click Next.**

The wizard displays a summary of information about your printer.

13. **Click the Finish button to print the test page.**

The wizard displays a dialog box that asks whether the test page was printed correctly.

14. **If the test page was printed correctly, click OK to end the wizard. If it was not, click Troubleshoot and follow the instructions that the wizard displays.**

Using a network printer

Windows XP networks work wonders. I talk (and talk and talk) about them in Book IX. If you have a network, you can attach a printer to any computer on the network and have it accessible to all the users on all the computers in the network. You can also attach different printers to different computers, and let the network users pick and choose the printer that they want to use as the need arises.

Sharing a printer

Before other computers on a network can use a printer, the printer must be officially shared. In order to share a printer, an Administrator has to go onto the *host* PC — that is, the PC to which the printer is physically attached — and tell Windows that the printer should be shared.

I talk about Administrators in Book I, Chapter 2. If you are using Windows XP/ Home, chances are good that you are an Administrator.

The procedure for sharing a printer depends on the operating system running on the host computer. This section describes the procedure for a host that runs Windows XP. Other versions of the Microsoft Windows operating system use very similar procedures.

1. **On the printer's host computer, choose Start⇨Control Panel.**

2. **In the Control Panel, click Printers And Other Hardware.**

    This opens the Printers And Faxes dialog box (refer to Figure 2-1).

3. **Right-click the icon for the printer that you want to share and click Properties from the menu.**

    This displays a Properties dialog box for the printer.

4. **Click the Properties dialog box's Sharing tab.**

    The Sharing tab looks similar to the one shown in Figure 2-6.

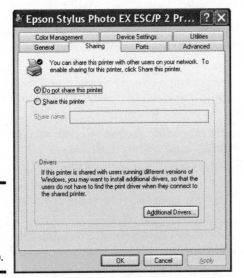

Figure 2-6:
A printer's
Properties
dialog box,
Sharing tab.

5. **Click the Share This Printer radio button.**

    Windows XP fills in a default share name for the printer. This is a name by which the printer will be known to other users of the network.

6. **If you like, you may enter another name that is more meaningful to your network's users. Then click the OK button.**

If you enter a name that is more than eight characters long or contains spaces or special characters, Windows XP warns you that MS-DOS computers will be unable to use the printer. That shouldn't give you any gray hair unless some of the computers on your network run MS-DOS instead of Microsoft Windows, or you plan on using some esoteric, ancient species of network administration software.

Installing a shared printer

Sometimes Windows XP is smart enough to identify printers attached to your network and install them right on the spot, and you don't have to lift a finger. When you look at a list of printers in WinXP, it identifies these automatically recognized printers as "Auto" printers — `Auto DJ930C on Thinkpad`, for example. Slick.

Sometimes (and for the life of me, I don't know why), WinXP doesn't automatically recognize all the printers on a network. For those special occasions, you need to install the printer manually on any PC that wants to use it:

1. **Make sure that the printer is installed on the host PC — that is, go over to the PC that the printer is attached to, and make sure that you can use it.**

   Try firing up a word processor and print a page. Something along those lines. If the printer doesn't work on the host PC, start at the beginning of this chapter, and get the printer going.

2. **Follow the steps in the preceding section to make sure that the printer is officially designated a shared printer.**

   At least 90 percent of the time, if you can't get a PC to recognize a printer attached to the network, either the printer itself isn't working on the host (see Step 1) or the printer isn't properly designated as a shared printer (see Step 2).

3. **On the computer that doesn't automatically recognize the printer, choose Start⇨Control Panel.**

4. **In the Control Panel, click Printers And Other Hardware.**

   This opens the Printers And Faxes dialog box (refer to Figure 2-1).

5. **Click Add A Printer to start the Add Printer wizard and display the Welcome page. Ho-hum.**

6. **Click Next.**

   The wizard displays the Local or Network Printer page (refer to Figure 2-2).

7. **Click the Network Printer radio button. Then click Next.**

   The wizard displays the page shown in Figure 2-7.

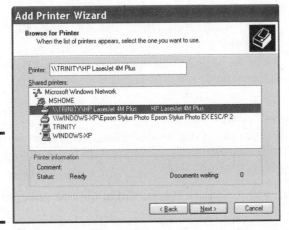

Figure 2-7:
Add Printer
Wizard,
Specify a
Printer.

8. **Click the Connect To This Printer radio button (the middle button). Leave the Name field empty. Click Next.**

   The wizard displays the Browse for Printer page, as shown in Figure 2-8. The Shared Printers dialog box displays the printers and computers in your workgroup.

Figure 2-8:
Add Printer
Wizard,
Browse for
Printer.

9. **Click the printer you want. Then click Next.**

   If the wizard does not display the printer that you want to install, you can install it anyway, but you must type its name into the Printer field above the Shared Printers dialog box. The name has this form:

   `\\host\printer`

For *host*, substitute the name of the host computer as it appears in the Shared Printers dialog box. For *printer*, substitute the share name of the shared printer. You get something like \\Dimension\LJ4. The section "Finding names of shared printers," later in this chapter, explains how to find the printer's share name.

10. **If the host computer requires you to log in to use its resources, the wizard displays a Connect dialog box, as shown in Figure 2-9. Enter a user name and password that are valid on the host computer, and then click OK.**

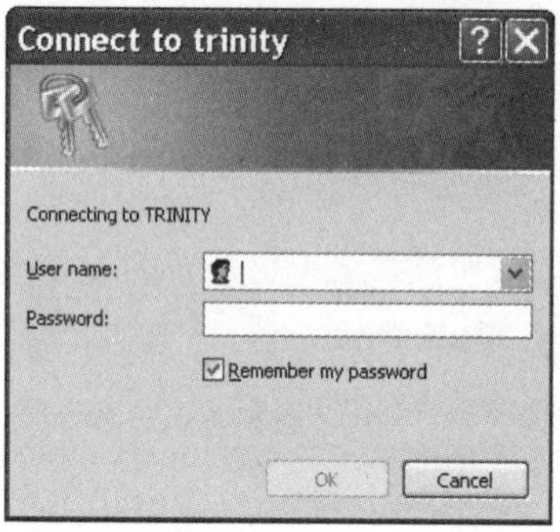

Figure 2-9: The Connect dialog box.

If you connect successfully, the wizard asks whether you want to make this printer your default printer: the one that an application uses unless you explicitly tell it otherwise.

11. **Click the Yes or No radio button, as appropriate, and then click Next to finish off the wizard.**

Finding names of shared printers

Occasionally, finding out the share names of shared printers on your local area network is useful, whether you have installed the printers on your own computer or not. Follow these steps:

1. **Choose Start⇨My Network Places, and in the task pane, click View Network Computers.**

2. **Double-click any host computer that you think may harbor a recalcitrant printer.**

If an officially designated shared printer is attached to the host computer, it shows up with a printer icon. The share name appears immediately to the right of the printer icon.

Selecting a Printer

If more than one printer is installed on your computer, either directly or through a network, you want to be able to choose different printers for different jobs. You may print ordinary documents to a laser printer, for example, and photographs to a color inkjet printer.

Changing the default printer

At any time, one of the installed printers is Windows XP's *default printer.* The default printer is the one that any application uses unless you tell it to use some other printer.

To see which printer is currently your default printer, follow these steps:

1. **Choose Start⇨Control Panel.**

2. **In the Control Panel, click Printers And Other Hardware.**

3. **Click View Installed Printers or Fax Printers.**

A checkmark appears next to the default printer, as shown in Figure 2-10.

Default printer

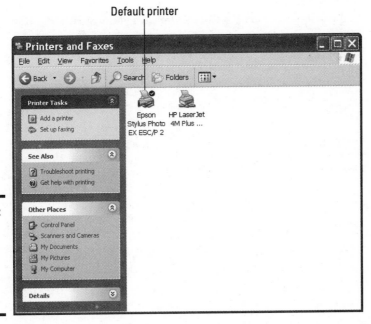

Figure 2-10:
A check-
mark
appears
next to the
default
printer.

If the icon is small, the checkmark may be hard to see. Choose a view that displays large icons, such as Icons or Thumbnails, by clicking View in the menu.

To change the default printer, right-click the printer that you want to make the default. Then click Set As Default Printer.

Changing the printer temporarily

If you want to print to a particular printer once, changing the default printer and then changing it back is inconvenient. In this situation, you can change the printer temporarily.

To change the printer temporarily:

1. Choose your application's Print command as you ordinarily would, usually by choosing File⇨Print.

The application opens a Print dialog box, as shown in Figure 2-11. The area labeled Select Printer lists the printers installed on your computer. The default printer is highlighted.

2. Click the printer that you want to use.

3. Print as usual.

The application uses the printer that you've just chosen.

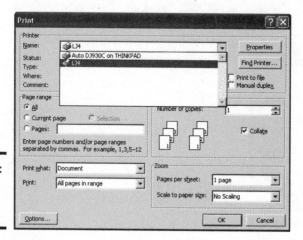

Figure 2-11: The Word 2002 Print dialog box.

A temporary printer change affects only the application in which you make the change; so if you switch printers in Word, for example, it won't change the printer in Excel. Some applications use the printer that you select for only one print operation; others remember it until you change it again.

TIP

If you're using an application that remembers the temporary printer, you can change it back the next time you print something. If you don't use the printer again for a while, though, you may easily forget to do so. It's a good idea to change back to the default printer as soon as you're done printing, while you're thinking about it. This Tip is brought to you by a guy who once printed a 50-page black-and-white brochure on a fancy, expensive color printer.

Using the Print Queue

You may have noticed that when you print a document from an application, the application reports that it is done before the printer finishes printing. If the document is long enough, you can print several more documents from one or more applications while the printer works on the first one. This is possible because Windows XP saves printed documents in a *print queue* until it can print them.

If more than one printer is installed on your computer or on your network, each one has its own independent print queue. The queue is maintained on the host PC — that is, the PC to which the printer is attached.

Windows XP uses print queues automatically, so you don't even have to know that they exist. If you know the tricks, though, you can control them in several useful ways.

Displaying a print queue

You can display information about the document that a printer is currently printing and about any other documents in its print queue:

1. **Get on the printer's host computer. Choose Start⇨Control Panel.**

2. **In the Control Panel, click Printers And Other Hardware.**

3. **Click the printer whose queue you want to display.**

4. **In the list of Printer Tasks over on the left, click See What's Printing.**

The Control Panel opens a printer queue window, as shown in Figure 2-12.

Epson Stylus Photo EX ESC/P 2

Printer Document View Help

Document Name	Status	Owner	Pages	Size	Submitted	Port
Printing tips.rtf	Printing	Jonathan...	1	592 bytes...	9:12:32 AM 8/16/2001	LPT1:
Print queue management.rtf		Jonathan...	1	628 bytes	9:13:04 AM 8/16/2001	
Select a Port.TIF		Jonathan...	1	585 KB	9:21:59 AM 8/16/2001	

3 document(s) in queue

Figure 2-12:
A printer
queue
window.

The jobs in the print queue are listed from the oldest at the top to the newest at the bottom. The Status column shows which job is printing.

You can close the Control Panel window and keep the print queue window open for later use. You can minimize the print queue window and keep it in the task bar. That can be very handy if you're running a particularly long or complex print job — Word mail merges are particularly notorious for requiring close supervision.

Controlling a print queue

You can use the print queue window, described in the preceding section, to exercise several types of control over the print queue.

If several users are printing documents to the same printer, Windows XP does not let them interfere with each other's work. Thus, you can control the documents that *you* placed in the queue; you cannot control other users' documents, nor can they control yours.

Pausing and resuming a print queue

When you *pause* a print queue, Windows XP stops printing documents from that print queue. If a document is printing when you pause the queue, Windows XP tries to finish printing that document and then stops.

Why would you want to pause the print queue? Say you want to print a page for later reference, but you don't want to bother turning your printer on to print just one page. Pause the printer's queue, and then print the page. The next time you turn the printer on, resume the queue, and the page prints.

Sometimes Windows has a hard time finishing the document — for example, you may be getting print buffer overruns (see "Troubleshooting," later in this chapter), and every time you clear the printer, it may try to reprint the overrun pages. If that happens to you, pause the print queue, and then turn off the printer. As soon as the printer comes back online, Windows is smart enough to pick up where it left off.

When you *resume* a print queue, Windows XP starts printing documents from the queue again.

To pause a print queue, choose the print queue window's File menu, then click the Pause Printing command. To resume the print queue, click the same command again. The Pause Printing command has a checkmark next to it when the queue is paused.

Depending on how your network is set up, you may or may not be able to pause and resume a print queue on a printer attached to another user's computer.

You can pause and resume the print queue in another way: Right-click the printer in the Control Panel's Printers and Faxes display, and then click the Pause Printing or Resume Printing command. Only one of these commands appears in the right-click menu at a time, depending on whether or not the print queue is paused.

Pausing, restarting, and resuming a document

Why would you want to pause a document? Say you're printing a Web page that documents an online order you just placed, and the printer jams. You've already finished entering the order, and you have no way to display the page again to reprint it. Pause the document, clear the printer, and restart the document.

Here's another common situation where pausing comes in handy. You're printing a long document, and the phone rings. To make the printer be quiet while you talk, pause the document. When you're done talking, resume the document.

When you *pause a document,* Windows XP is prevented from printing that document. Windows XP skips the document and prints later documents in the queue. If you pause a document while Windows XP is printing it, Windows XP halts in the middle of the document and prints nothing on that printer until you take further action.

To pause a document, select that document. Choose the print queue window's Document menu, and then click the Pause command. The window shows the document's status as Paused.

When you *restart a document,* Windows XP is again allowed to print it. If the document is at the top of the queue, Windows XP prints it as soon as it finishes the document that it is now printing. If the document was being printed when it was paused, Windows XP stops printing it and starts again at the beginning.

Book VII
Chapter 2

Working with Printers

Resuming a document is meaningful only if you paused it while Windows XP was printing it. When you *resume a document,* Windows XP resumes printing it where it paused.

To resume or restart the print document, select that document and choose the print queue window's Document menu, and then click the Resume or Restart command.

You have another way to pause a document: Right-click that document in the print queue window and choose the Pause command. To restart or resume the document, right-click the document and click the Resume or Restart command. (These commands appear in the menu only when the document is paused.)

Canceling a document

When you *cancel a document,* Windows XP removes it from the print queue without printing it. You may have heard computer jocks use the term *purged* or *zapped* or something totally unprintable.

Here's a common situation when document canceling comes in handy. You start printing a long document, and as soon as the first page comes out, you realize that you forgot to set the heading. Cancel the document, change the heading, and print the document again.

To cancel a document, select that document. Choose the print queue window's Document menu, then click the Cancel command. Or, right-click the document in the print queue window and click the Cancel command. Or, select the document and press the Delete key.

When a document is gone, it's gone. There's no Recycle Bin for the print queue.

Setting Printer Properties

Windows XP provides two means of controlling the properties of a printer: through the printer's Properties dialog box and through its Preferences dialog box. Both of these dialog boxes are accessible through the Control Panel. The Preferences dialog box is also accessible through an application's Print command.

In general, the Properties dialog box controls the printer's overall properties, and the Preferences dialog box controls properties that affect an individual document. The two groups of properties are not cleanly separated, though, and some properties may appear in both.

Using the Properties dialog box

To open a printer's Properties dialog box, follow these steps:

1. **Choose Start⇨Control Panel.**

2. **In the Control Panel, click Printers And Other Hardware.**

   This opens the Printers And Faxes dialog box (refer to Figure 2-1).

3. **Right-click the icon for printer and click Properties from the menu.**

   This displays a Properties dialog box for the printer, as shown in Figure 2-13.

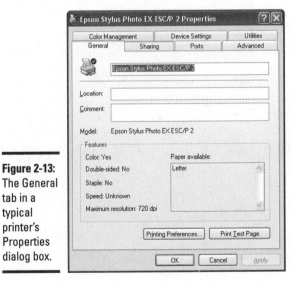

Figure 2-13:
The General tab in a typical printer's Properties dialog box.

The Properties dialog box has several tabs. The set of tabs, and in some cases their contents, depends on the features of your printer. Most of the tabs control technical aspects of printer operation and are best left at their default values. The following tabs contain information that you may want to inspect or change:

◆ **General tab:** Describes the printer's name, location, comments (see "Attaching a local printer," earlier in this chapter), and basic characteristics such as its color-printing capability and its resolution. You can change the name, location, and comments only.

◆ **Sharing tab:** Controls the printer's shared status and share name. (See "Sharing a printer," earlier in this chapter.)

◆ **Device Settings tab:** Controls features specific to this type of printer. (See Figure 2-14.)

On most printers, this tab lets you specify the size of paper, such as letter size, legal size, envelopes, and so on. If the printer can select among two or more paper sources, you can specify the size of paper for each. This allows Windows XP to select the right paper source for the paper size that you request when you print a document.

◆ **Utilities tab:** Gives you access to special operations that the printer can perform, such as nozzle cleaning for an inkjet printer.

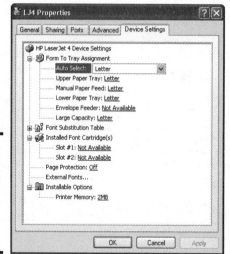

Figure 2-14:
The Device Settings tab in a typical printer's Properties dialog box.

Using the Preferences dialog box

Are you confused by all of this Properties/Preferences bull? Yeah, me too. I know the reason why you're so confused. Microsoft and the printer manufacturers aren't the least bit consistent in how they identify all of these printer settings. If you're using Windows XP and Office XP, and you play around with them a bit, you find all sorts of annoying anomalies.

My favorite: the HP LaserJet driver. If you right-click a LaserJet printer in Windows XP's Printers and Faxes list and pick Printing Preferences, you get the Preferences dialog box (which happens to be the subject of this section). Fair 'nuff. But if you go into an Office application, choose File➪Print, and click the Properties dialog box — note that I said *Properties*, not *Preferences* — you get a nearly identical Preferences dialog box. The only difference (see Figure 2-15) is that the Office dialog box sets preferences for one particular document, not default preferences for the printer in general.

Word 2002 File➪Print dialog box   The Properties button   Properties dialog box

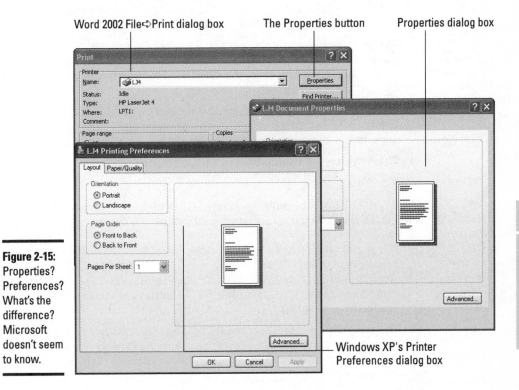

Figure 2-15: Properties? Preferences? What's the difference? Microsoft doesn't seem to know.

Windows XP's Printer Preferences dialog box

Anyway, here's how you open the Printing Preferences dialog box:

1. **Choose Start➪Control Panel.**

2. **In the Control Panel, click Printers And Other Hardware.**

3. **Right-click the icon for printer and click Printing Preferences from the menu.**

You get a dialog box similar to the ones in Figure 2-15.

Like the Properties dialog box, the Preferences dialog box has several tabs, and the set of tabs and their contents depend on the features of your printer. The most common tabs are the Layout tab, the Paper/Quality tab, and the Utilities tab.

The Layout tab controls the following options:

✦ **The orientation of printed output:** In *portrait* orientation, the document is printed so that the top and bottom of each page run along the short dimension of the paper. In *landscape* orientation, the top and bottom of each page run along the long dimension of the paper.

✦ **The page order of printed output:** Whether the document is printed from the first page to the last or from the last to the first. If you're tired of resequencing printout pages when they emerge from your printer, change this dialog box.

✦ **The number of pages per sheet:** If you select a number larger than 1, Windows XP reduces the size of each printed page in order to place more than one page on each sheet of paper.

✦ **The Advanced button:** Displays a dialog box of advanced properties that depend on the features of your printer.

The Paper/Quality tab, shown in Figure 2-16, which controls one or more of the following options, depending on your printer's features:

✦ **The paper source to be used:** In most cases, it's best to keep the default, Automatically select, and use the Print dialog box to choose the size of paper you want. Windows XP then selects the paper source that contains the right size, according to the settings you entered in the Properties dialog box.

✦ **The type of paper or other media in the printer:** Other media include copier paper, photo-quality paper, or overhead projector transparency film. (Some printers can adjust to produce optimum results on different types of media.)

✦ **The quality setting to use:** If your printer supports a choice of quality settings, you can choose among values such as Best, Normal, and Draft. Lower quality settings generally speed up printing and save ink.

✦ **Whether to print in color or black and white:** When you print documents that contain color but don't need it to be useful, you may choose black and white to conserve the relatively expensive color ink.

The Utilities tab presents the same utilities as the Utilities tab in the Properties dialog box.

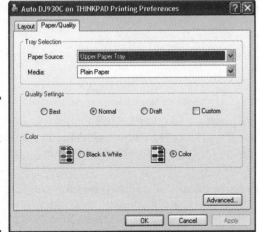

Figure 2-16:
The
Paper/Quality
tab is a
typical
printer's
Preferences
dialog box.

Troubleshooting

✦ *I'm trying to install a printer. I connected it to my computer, and Windows XP doesn't detect its presence.*

Be sure that the printer is turned on and the cable from the printer to your computer is properly connected at both ends. Check the printer's manual; you may have to follow a procedure (like push a button) to make the printer ready for use.

In general, Windows XP can detect the presence of a printer only if it is connected through a USB interface. If Windows XP cannot detect your printer, use the procedure described in the section "Attaching a local printer."

✦ *I'm trying to install a printer connected to another computer on my network, and Windows XP doesn't detect its presence. I know that the printer is OK; it's already installed and working as a local printer on that system!*

The printer may not be shared. See the section "Sharing a printer," earlier in this chapter.

If the host PC reports that the printer is shared, look at the computers attached to your network by choosing Start⇨My Network Places. If no computers show up, something is wrong with your network connection. If computers are shown but the printer's host is not among them, something is wrong with *its* network connection.

If the printer's host is visible on the network, you should be able to install the printer by typing in its name. The section "Installing a shared printer" explains how to do this.

✦ *I can't use a shared printer that I've used successfully in the past. Windows XP says it isn't available when I try to use it, or Windows XP doesn't even show it as an installed printer any more.*

This can happen if something interferes with your connection to the network or the connection of the printer's host computer. It can also happen if something interferes with the availability of the printer; for example, if the host computer's user has turned off sharing.

If you can't find a problem, or if you find and correct a problem but you still can't use the printer, try restarting Windows XP on your own system. If that doesn't help, remove the printer from your system and then reinstall it.

To remove the printer from your system, open the Control Panel's Printers and Faxes window, and then right-click the printer and choose the Delete command from the menu. Windows XP asks if you're sure you want to delete this printer. Click the Yes button.

To reinstall the printer on your system, use the same procedure that you used to install it originally. See "Installing a shared printer," earlier in this chapter.

✦ *I printed a document, but it never came out of the printer.*

Check the printer's print queue, over on the host PC (the one directly attached to the printer). Is the document there? If not, investigate several possible reasons:

✦ The printer isn't turned on. In some cases Windows XP can't distinguish a printer that is connected but not turned on from a printer that is ready, and it sends documents to a printer that isn't operating.

✦ You accidentally sent the document to some other printer.

✦ Some other user unintentionally picked up your document and walked off with it.

✦ The printer is turned on but not ready to print, and the printer (as opposed to the host PC) is holding your whole document in its internal memory until it can start printing. A printer can hold as much as several dozen pages of output internally, depending on the size of its internal memory and the complexity of the pages.

If your document is in the print queue but isn't printing, check the following:

✦ The printer may not be ready to print. See whether it is plugged in, turned on, and properly connected to your computer or its host computer.

✦ Your document may be paused.

✦ The print queue itself may be paused.

✦ The printer may be printing another document that is paused.

✦ The printer may be "thinking." If it is a laser printer or some other type of printer that composes an entire page in internal memory before it starts to print, it will appear to be doing nothing while it processes photographs or other complex graphics. Processing may take as long as several minutes.

   Look at the printer and study its manual. The printer may have a blinking light or a status display that tells you it is really doing something. As you become familiar with the printer, you get a feel for how long various types of jobs should take.

✦ On the other hand, the printer's status display may tell you that the printer is offline, out of paper, jammed, or unready to print for some other reason.

✦ *I tried to print a complex document, and only part of it came out. I got an error message that said something like "Printer Overrun," either on the last printed page or on the printer's status display.*

This can happen on laser printers and other printers that compose a whole page at a time in internal memory. The error occurs if a page is too complex for the amount of memory in the printer.

The following procedure corrects the problem in most cases, although details may vary with the type of printer you use:

1. **Press the printer's Reset control, or turn the printer off and then back on.**

2. **In Windows XP, open the printer's Properties dialog box and click the Device Settings tab. (See "Setting printer properties," earlier in this chapter.)**

3. **Look for a property named Page Protection. Its setting should be OFF for this problem to have occurred.**

4. **Click the Page Protection property.**

   The setting OFF is replaced by a dropdown list. Use the list to change the item's setting to ON. With Page Protection turned ON, the printer assembles each page in the printer's memory before printing it. With Page Protection OFF, the printer can start printing a page and get halfway through before discovering that it doesn't have enough memory to print the whole page. It happens, from time to time, with complex graphics.

Chapter 3: Getting the Scoop on Scanners

In This Chapter

- ✓ Installing a scanner in one — or two or three — easy steps
- ✓ Using a scanner
- ✓ Using scanners over your network
- ✓ Troubleshooting

A scanner is a device that "reads" an image from paper and creates a digital version of the image. It's like a copier that produces an image inside your computer instead of on another sheet of paper.

I've singled out scanners in this book for special treatment because scanners have so many potential uses. Combine a scanner and a printer to create a multitalented, powerful copier. Team a scanner with e-mail and a service like J2 (www.j2.com), and you can send and receive faxes to or from anywhere in the world at a fraction of the cost — without an extra phone line. You can use scanners with *optical character recognition* (OCR) software to convert printed text into editable document files. You can sit on the scanner's glass and create immoral, er, immortal images to send in e-mail or to post on your Web page for posterior ... er, posterity. Scanners certainly rate as versatile critters.

Book VII, Chapter 1 discusses how to choose a scanner. This chapter discusses how to set up and use a scanner.

Installing a Scanner

No doubt your new scanner comes with a fancy, big, printed sheet with step-by-step instructions for installing the beast and getting it running. I'd like to add a couple of points of emphasis, compliments of the Dummies School of Hard Knocks. To-wit:

1. **Find a place for your scanner that's going to work for you.**

   Scanners need extra room around the sides. You're going to try to scan a copy of the *Encyclopedia Britannica* some day, and it's gonna droop way over on the left, and then it's gonna droop way over on the right. If you cram your scanner into a teensy-tiny spot, you'll swear at it every time you want to scan anything bigger than a single sheet of paper.

2. **After you put your scanner in its place and remove all the plastic wrapping paper, cardboard, foam, and packing tape, and then clean off the sticky goo and heaven-knows-what, you have to unlock the lamp.**

   Look for the little sliding gizmo on the side or the back, probably with a picture of a lock on it. When you move the scanner around, you want to lock the lamp — that keeps it from getting knocked around and smashing up the insides of the machine. But before you can use the scanner, the lamp has to be unlocked.

3. **Plug in the power cord.**

   Yeah, I've forgotten to do that, too.

4. **If your scanner uses a USB interface, plug the data cable in to the scanner at one end, and plug it into the USB port on the other end. Turn the scanner on.**

   Windows XP should detect the scanner's presence and install it. Small pop-up windows describe the progress of the installation, as shown in Figure 3-1. At the end of the installation, you have a fully functional scanner. If Windows XP doesn't detect the scanner, mutter a few words of supplication to the WinGods, and skip to Step 6.

Figure 3-1:
Progress
of the
installation
for a Plug
and Play
scanner.

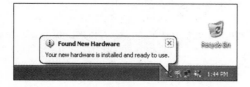

5. **If your scanner doesn't use a USB port, you have to turn off your PC and turn off the scanner, before you connect the data cable.**

   After the cable's connected, Windows XP turns on your scanner. If the scanner's mechanism moves when you turn it on, making a humming noise, wait until the noise stops. Then turn on your PC. If you're lucky, Windows XP detects the scanner, installs everything you need, and you're ready to roll. If you're unlucky, you end up at Step 6, too.

6. **So now that you know Windows XP didn't autoinstall your scanner, don't worry. Happens to the best of us. You need to get the Add New Hardware Wizard running, thusly: Choose Start➪Control Panel➪ Printers and Other Hardware. In the left pane, click Add Hardware.**

   Windows XP starts the Add New Hardware Wizard and displays a "welcome" page. Ho-Hum.

7. Click Next.

The wizard searches for hardware that has not yet been installed. If the wizard finds your scanner, it installs the scanner and tells you it is done.

8. Click the Finish button to close the wizard, which ends the procedure.

If the wizard doesn't find your scanner, it asks whether the hardware has been connected.

9. Click the Yes radio button, and then click the Next button.

The wizard displays a list of installed devices.

10. Check to see whether your scanner is in the list. If it is, click the Cancel button to close the wizard.

Your scanner is connected and working, even if you didn't think it was.

11. If your scanner is not in the list of installed devices, scroll to the end of the list, select Add A New Hardware Device, and then click the Next button.

The wizard asks whether you want to search for new hardware and install it automatically. Sheesh. If you get to this point, the wizard has already tried to find it and didn't succeed! Gimme a break.

12. Click the radio button labeled Install The Hardware That I Manually Select, and then click the Next button.

The wizard displays a list of common types of devices.

13. Click Imaging Devices, and then click the Next button.

The wizard displays a list of brands on the left and scanners on the right.

14. Click your brand, click your model, and then click the Next button. Answer any additional questions the wizard asks.

When you have answered all of the questions, the wizard installs the scanner and tells you it is done.

If your brand and model of scanner aren't in the Add New Hardware Wizard lists, you can still install your scanner if you have a Windows XP driver for it. The driver may come with the scanner on a diskette or CD-ROM, or you may be able to download it from the manufacturer's Web site. To install a scanner by supplying a driver, click the Have Disk button in the Add New Hardware Wizard and follow the wizard's prompts.

Sometimes a scanner's Windows 2000 driver works in Windows XP; sometimes it doesn't work. If no WinXP driver is available, try the Windows 2000 driver, if it exists — and if that's not possible, try a Windows NT driver.

Hewlett-Packard's ScanJet software, called HP Precision Scan, includes a driver that makes installing and using a scanner over a Windows XP network easy. To make an HP ScanJet scanner work on any computer on your network:

1. **Make sure you have the latest version of HP Precision Scan by checking the HP Web site,** `www.hp.com`.

2. **Attach the scanner to a PC on the network (called the "host" PC); then install the scanner on the host PC normally, using the instructions for the Precision Scan software.**

3. **Make sure that the HP Precision Scan LAN Host program is running. If it is, you see an icon shaped like a scanner in the notification area of the Windows Taskbar — down near the clock. If it isn't, choose Start➪Programs➪HP ScanJet Software➪HP ScanJet Utilities➪ Share Scanner.**

4. **Install the HP Precision Scan software on any PCs on the network that you want to be able to use the scanner. The PCs automatically detect the shared scanner on the scanner's host computer.**

When the HP Precision Scan LAN Host program is running, and Precision Scan is installed on a networked PC, scanning from that networked PC is as simple as scanning on the host.

Getting the Most from a Scanner

Windows XP's Scanner and Camera Wizard performs basic scanning tasks with any type of scanner.

Your scanner may come with software that has features the wizard lacks. Check your scanner's manual for information. Unless the manufacturer's scanning software has a feature that you really, really need — such as network sharing, discussed in the preceding section — you're probably much better off to stick with the Windows XP native software.

Scanning with the Wizard

To use the Scanner and Camera wizard:

1. **Click Start➪Control Panel.**

   Windows XP opens the Control Panel window.

2. **Click Printers and Other Hardware, and then click Scanners and Cameras.**

   Windows XP opens the Scanners and Cameras window.

3. **Double-click the icon that represents your scanner.**

   Windows XP opens the wizard and displays a "welcome" page.

4. **Click the Next button.**

   The wizard displays the Choose Scanning Preferences dialog box, shown in Figure 3-2.

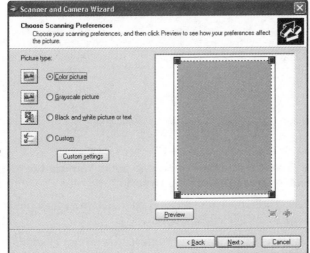

Figure 3-2:
The wizard's
Choose
Scanning
Preferences
dialog box.

5. **Click the radio button for the type of copy you are scanning.**

   In the Scanning Preferences dialog box, note that the Black and White Picture button applies to line drawings, which do *not* have shades of gray. They are, quite literally, black and white.

   The Preview button lets you zoom in to a specific portion of the picture. See the section "Using the Preview button," later in this chapter, for details.

   The Custom Settings button lets you control brightness, contrast, and resolution. See the section "Using the Custom Settings button" for details.

6. **Click Next.**

   The wizard displays the Picture Name and Destination dialog box, shown in Figure 3-3.

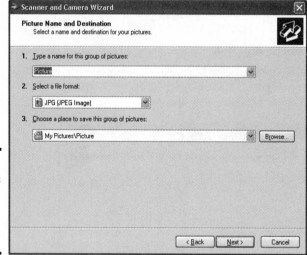

Figure 3-3:
The wizard's
Picture
Name and
Destination
dialog box.

7. **In the Type A Name field, enter the name you want to give the file to be created from the item you're scanning.**

   If you use the same name for several items, the wizard adds numbers to the name to make each one unique.

   The Select a File Format field controls the format in which the file is saved. JPG is suitable for color pictures. TIF is preferable for grayscale and black and white.

   The wizard automatically stores the scanned images in the My Pictures folder, in a sub-folder with the name you entered. If you entered "Meeting notes," for example, it stores the images in *My Pictures\Meeting notes.* If you want a different folder, you can choose one with the Browse button or the Choose a Place drop-down list.

8. **Click Next.**

   The wizard displays the Scanning Picture dialog box, shown in Figure 3-4, while it scans. When the wizard finishes scanning, it displays a dialog box that asks you what you want to do next. This dialog box is designed for pictures downloaded from a digital camera and isn't very useful for scanner copy.

9. **Click the Cancel button to close the wizard.**

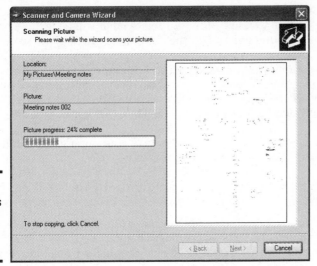

Figure 3-4:
The wizard's
Scanning
Picture
dialog box.

Using the Preview button

In the section "Scanning with the Wizard," Step 4 of the Scanner and Camera Wizard brings up the Choose Scanning Preferences dialog box (refer to Figure 3-2). If you click the Preview button, your scanner performs a quick preview scan of the copy and displays the image in the preview pane, as in Figure 3-5.

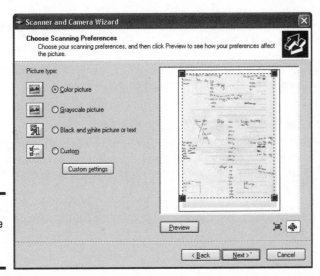

Figure 3-5:
Effect of the
Preview
button.

Notice the rectangle composed of dotted lines with little solid squares in the corners. That dotted line outlines the area that will be included in the scan. Initially, the dotted line covers the entire image area of the scanner.

If you need only part of the image, you can move the selection's borders to contain just the part you need. Drag each of the selection's corner boxes to the place where you want that corner to be. You can also move a single side of the selection by dragging the dotted line that marks that side.

Why is it useful to scan a selected part of your copy? Why not just scan the whole thing? Here are a couple of reasons:

+ The size of an image file is roughly proportional to the area being scanned. You can save disk space by scanning only the area you need.

+ The time required to complete a scan depends on how far the scanning lamp must move while scanning. That is, it depends on the height of the scan area you have chosen. Even if the scanner must move down the page to the start of the selection, it can do that faster than it would if it had to scan the whole way.

Both of these factors become more significant when you increase the resolution of the scan. For details, see "Using the Custom Settings button" later in this chapter.

 After you set up the scan area, you can make the wizard show an enlargement by clicking the "enlarge" button. This lets you see more detail so that you can be sure that you set the scan area correctly.

 To reduce the preview image so that the entire image area is shown again, click the "entire page" button.

When the selection is set the way you want it, click the Next button. The wizard scans only the part of the image that you have chosen.

Using the Custom Settings button

In the section "Scanning with the Wizard," Step 4 of the Scanner and Camera Wizard brings up the Choose Scanning Preferences page (refer to Figure 3-2). If you click the Custom Settings button, you have a chance to control the details of the scan.

Click Custom Settings, and the wizard displays a Properties dialog box like the one in Figure 3-6.

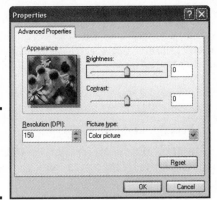

Figure 3-6:
The Custom
Settings
properties
dialog box.

This dialog box lets you adjust the appearance of the scanned image. Within
limits, you can correct shortcomings in the copy you're scanning.

✦ **Brightness control:** Adjusts the brightness of the image. Move the
   control to the right to brighten the image; move it to the left to darken
   the image.

In a black-and-white image (without grays), darkening the image is
helpful if the copy is very light, making letters and lines appear thin and
broken. Lightening the image is helpful if the background is not clean,
creating dark speckles all over the image.

✦ **Contrast control:** (Present only for color and grayscale images.) Adjusts
   the contrast of the image — that is, changes the image to increase or
   decrease the sharpness of the transition between bright and dark parts of
   the picture. Move the slider right to increase the contrast (to sharpen the
   transition between light and dark); move it left to decrease the contrast.

✦ **Picture Type list:** Lets you choose the type of scanned image to create:
   color, grayscale, or black and white.

✦ **Resolution field:** Lets you set the resolution of the scan in dots per inch
   (DPI). The default value is suitable for medium-resolution images with
   most types of copy. A higher value yields an image with more detail but
   makes the scan go more slowly and produces a larger image file. A lower
   value yields an image with less detail but makes the scan go faster and
   produces a smaller image file. See the sections called "Choosing a resolution best for your work" and "Choosing a resolution best for your
   scanner."

✦ **Reset button:** Resets all of the Custom Settings to their default values.

**Book VII
Chapter 3**

**Getting the Scoop
on Scanners**

Choosing a resolution best for your work

Here are some suggestions to help you choose the best resolution for scanning a given type of work. If two conflicting suggestions apply to your work, try a range of values to see what works best.

✦ **Scanning documents for record-keeping purposes (where reasonable legibility is sufficient):** 150 to 200 DPI.

✦ **Scanning documents for best quality:** 250 to 300 DPI.

✦ **Scanning documents for optical character recognition (OCR):** 400 to 500 DPI, or as recommended by the OCR application.

✦ **Scanning printed text:** 400 to 500 DPI.

✦ **Scanning text and photographs in glossy magazines:** 250 to 300 DPI.

✦ **Scanning photographic prints:** 250 to 300 DPI.

✦ **Scanning line art (black and white images):** 250 to 300 DPI.

✦ **Images to be printed:** Choose a value no more than ⅓ the resolution of the printer. For example, if the printer's resolution is 600 DPI, scan at no more than 200 DPI. A setting higher than 300 DPI generally does not improve the results in any case.

✦ **Images to be displayed on a monitor:** 72 DPI.

In each case, if the image will be enlarged, increase the resolution in proportion. For example, if the image will be printed or displayed three times the size of the original, multiply the recommended resolution by three. Remember one exception to this rule: text and photographs in glossy magazines. The recommendation of 250 to 300 DPI is based on the size of the dots that form in images in the original copy. Increasing the resolution generally does not improve the results.

Choosing a resolution best for your scanner

To get the best results, you must not only consider the resolution that's best for your work, you also need to pick a resolution that your scanner will treat with some care. You are best to choose a resolution that divides evenly into your scanner's optical resolution. For example, if your scanner's optical resolution is 1000 DPI, 200, 250, or 500 DPI is a good resolution to use. If your scanner's optical resolution is 1200 DPI, use 200, 240, 300, 400, or 600 DPI.

If your scanner's optical resolution is different in the horizontal and vertical dimensions, use the lower number.

You can find your scanner's optical resolution by consulting its manual or by displaying its Properties dialog box like this:

1. **Choose Start➪Control Panel.**

   Windows XP opens the Control Panel window.

2. **Click Printers and Other Hardware, and then click Scanners and Cameras.**

   Windows XP opens the Scanners and Cameras window.

3. **Right-click the icon that represents your scanner and choose Properties.**

   Windows XP displays the scanner's Properties dialog box, as shown in Figure 3-7. In this example, the Properties dialog box shows that the scanner's optical resolution is 1000 DPI.

Figure 3-7:
A scanner's
Properties
dialog box.

If you check the manual, look for the scanner's *optical resolution* or *hardware resolution*. Don't be misled by the "maximum resolution" or "interpolated resolution," which is usually much higher. Using a resolution greater than the scanner's optical resolution generally does not improve the results.

Scanner Skullduggery and Useful Tricks

The following couple sections go over some handy things to know when it comes to the art of scanning.

Printing a scanned image

One way to print a scanned image is to open it with Windows Paint, and then choose File➪Print.

Another way is to use the Photo Printing Wizard, which is described in the section Book VIII, Chapter 3.

Many scanners come with a photocopier utility that scans and prints an image in one step. This is a more efficient way to make a paper copy with a scanner. Some photocopier utilities have features that are available on only very expensive copiers.

Programming your scanner's action buttons

Many scanners have buttons to perform specific actions, such as starting a scan and making a photocopy. These buttons are a convenience; after you put copy in the scanner, you can simply press a button instead of going back to your computer to run a program.

You can control the functions of your scanner's action buttons with the scanner's Properties dialog box:

1. **Choose Start➪Control Panel.**

Windows XP opens the Control Panel window.

2. **Click Printers and Other Hardware, and then click Scanners and Cameras.**

Windows XP opens the Scanners and Cameras window.

3. **Right-click the icon that represents your scanner and choose Properties.**

Windows XP displays the scanner's Properties dialog box.

4. **Click the Events tab (see Figure 3-8).**

The Select An Event dropdown list names the events that your scanner can generate (that is, the action buttons it has). To see the function of an action button, select that button from the list.

To change the function of the action button, click one of the radio buttons in the Properties dialog box's Actions group.

- **Start This Program** lets you select a program to run when the button is pushed.

- **Prompt For Which Program To Run** tells Windows XP to prompt you to select a program when you push the button.

- **Take No Action** disables the button.

Figure 3-8:
The
Properties
dialog box,
Events tab.

Some action buttons do not allow all of these possible actions. If you choose a button that does not allow some actions, the corresponding radio buttons are disabled.

5. **Click the OK button to apply your changes and close the Properties dialog box, or click the Apply button to apply your changes and leave the dialog box open.**

Troubleshooting

Here's a quick list of things that can go wrong and what you can do about them:

✦ *My scan came out blank!*

Make sure you remembered to put the document in the scanner, facing the right way. Repeat after me: D'OH!

✦ *My scanned document is dark gray on light gray, instead of black on white.*

The image type is probably set to Color or Grayscale. Set it to Black and White.

✦ *My scanned photograph is all black and white; no grays, no color.*

The image type is probably set to Black and White. Set it to Color or Grayscale.

✦ *My scans always seem to come out a little crooked.*

When you put the copy on the scanner's glass plate, align the edges of the copy with the frame around the plate. This is easiest if you push the copy right into a corner of the frame. On most scanners the upper right corner is the one to use.

Aligning copy is particularly hard when you're scanning a newspaper article. You usually have to fold the newspaper to make it fit in the scanner, and then the copy has no edges that are likely to be square with the text. In this case, you should try to fold the newspaper back on itself so that you can see at least one edge of the individual page you're scanning.

✦ *I tried to scan, but the wizard said that "the current picture could not be copied."*

To test the scanner's electronics and its connection to the computer, close the Scanner and Camera Wizard; then right-click the icon for the scanner and choose Properties. In the Properties dialog box (refer to Figure 3-7), click the Test Scanner button. If Windows XP reports that the scanner failed the test, look for a problem in the connection. If the connection appears to be okay, look for a problem with the scanner.

If Windows XP reports that the scanner passed the test, try to scan again. Be sure to click the Preview button before performing the scan. For some reason, this often makes the problem go away. At least, it does for me.

✦ *I tried to scan a picture from a magazine, and it came out with light and dark bands all over the surface.*

This effect is called a *Moiré pattern.* It happens when one pattern of image elements is superimposed on another, and the two patterns are almost (but not quite) aligned. In this case, the first pattern consists of the dots that make up the picture you're scanning, and the second pattern consists of the pixels in the scanned image.

Try again with a slightly lower resolution. Keep reducing the resolution a little at a time until the Moiré pattern disappears.

Index

Book VIII

Joining the Multimedia Mix

The 5th Wave   By Rich Tennant

@RICHTENNANT

"Well, well! Guess who just lost 9 pixels?"

Contents at a Glance

Chapter 1: Jammin' with Windows Media Player

In This Chapter

- What's playing now?
- Media Guide: The world-wide program schedule
- Copying music from a CD
- The Media Library: Where your music is kept
- Radio Tuner
- Copying music to a CD or digital audio player
- Changing Media Player's appearance
- Customizing Media Player

WMP da *MAN*. Er, uh. Wait a sec. Let me start over. Windows Media Player sucks. No that's not what I meant. Hold on. I've got this loud thud coming from my speakers, the Water Ambience visualization looks like smoke in Godzilla's eye, while Trent Reznor screams "you can't take it away from me." Lemme turn the volume down. There. Yeah. That's better.

What I meant to say is that Windows Media Player (or WMP) sucks you in from the moment you start it. As Windows XP's built-in boom box, it plays CDs, of course, but it also lets you play, organize, and generally enjoy any kind of music stored on your computer, whether the tunes came from CDs, the Internet, or your buddy down the hall. It also plays video and lets you tune into the nascent Internet radio market.

If you have a CD writer, Windows Media Player creates CDs that contain any combination of tracks you want. If you have a digital audio player, WMP copies music to the player, so that you can hip and/or hop, as circumstances dictate, wherever you go.

Windows Media Player can even do a chameleon act, changing its *skin* — its appearance on your screen — to suit your whims.

Windows Media Player is useful to you only if your computer has a sound card and a headphone or a set of speakers. The little speaker inside the box that goes "Beep" when you start the computer won't cut the mustard. If your computer doesn't have sound hardware, you have to get some or forget about using Windows Media Player.

Windows Media Player's normal appearance is a little unusual. If you use skins, it can get downright weird. You've been warned.

Starting with the Media Guide

To start Windows Media Player, choose Start⇨All Programs⇨Accessories⇨ Entertainment⇨Windows Media Player. (If you have run WMP recently it's in the Start menu's short list, and you can much more easily choose Start⇨ Windows Media Player.) Click the Media Guide button on the left side of the WMP window. The application now should look something like the version shown in Figure 1-1.

To control WMP   To see menu   Recommended download speeds   To minimize and close windows

Figure 1-1:
Windows Media Player looks like this when it starts.

Windows Media Player looks like the application shown in Figure 1-1 if you have a continuous connection to the Internet, or if the application can make a connection. That is because its initial display is actually a Web page — www.WindowsMedia.com, which you can view with any Web browser.

If Windows Media Player can't connect, it shows a warning that says The page cannot be displayed. This warning looks just like the message that Internet Explorer would display in this situation, because this part of Windows Media Player really *is* Internet Explorer, with an odd-looking border around the edges, and without the navigation tools you're accustomed to.

The Media Guide hooks into www.WindowsMedia.com, which is owned and operated by — you guessed it — a little company in Redmond, Washington that also makes PC operating systems. The www.WindowsMedia.com site features clips from new music and videos, entertainment news, and other information that may interest users of WMP. Many of the pages have links that allow you to buy the products described.

Windows Media Player really, really, really wants to be connected to the Internet whenever it runs. If it can't connect, you can still use it to perform offline operations, such as playing stored music and writing CDs, but be ready to put up with constant complaints about Web sites that Windows Media Player can't access. Microsoft Web sites, of course.

Notice that Windows Media Player has no menu bar. Well, actually it does, but often the menu bar is hidden. Most of the time, you can use the application just fine without the menu bar, but when you need an operation that is only accessible through the menu bar, you can make it visible. Simply click the button shown near the upper left corner of the window in Figure 1-1. Click the button again to make the menu bar go away.

When the menu bar is hidden, a Windows application's Minimize and Close boxes appear in the upper right corner of the Windows Media Player window. They may look rather faint, but they work just as they do when they appear in their usual places.

You control Windows Media Player with the row of buttons that runs down the left side of the window.

Playing with Now Playing

The first control button on the left edge of WMP is named Now Playing. When you click it, WMP displays the Media Playlist, as shown in Figure 1-2.

The right side of the window displays a *playlist,* which is just a sequence of tracks. The left side displays details of the first track. When the track is playing the area below the details shows either a picture of the album cover or a psychedelic *visualization* of the music.

To select a different playlist, choose one from the dropdown list of playlist names. When you do, WMP behaves just as a CD player does when you put in a CD: It starts playing the first track, then it plays the second one, and so on until it reaches the end.

To select a different track from the current playlist, double-click the track down in the list of playlist contents.

Author
and title

Way cool,
dude

Name of
current playlist

Contents of
the playlist

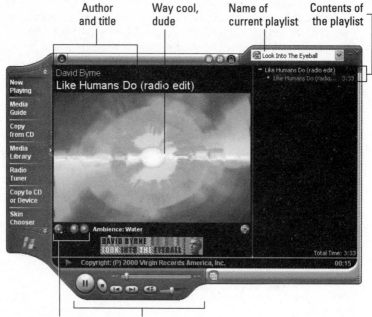

Figure 1-2:
The Media
Playlist
display.

Change the picture   Playback buttons

Playback buttons

The buttons along the bottom of the window control Now Playing. They are
very similar to the buttons on a conventional CD player:

 ✦ The first button pauses the playing.

When playing is paused, the button looks like this. Click it again
to make playing resume.

 ✦ The second button stops the playing.

Click the first button to start playing again. Unlike Pause/Resume,
Stop/Start returns to the start of the track. To start a different track,
double-click that track over in the playlist.

 ✦ The third button skips to the start of the previous track. From the
first track in the playlist, it skips to the beginning of the last track
on the playlist.

 ✦ The fourth button skips to the start of the next track. From the
last track in the playlist, it skips to the first.

+ The fifth button mutes (silences) the sound. Click the button again to restore the sound. Unlike the Pause button, the Mute button does not halt playing. If you mute the sound for ten seconds, you miss hearing ten seconds of the track. If you mute Snoop Doggy Dog for ten seconds, you get unwrapped (hardy har har).

+ The little slider to the right of the buttons controls volume.

+ The big slider above the buttons shows WMP's position in the current track. As the track progresses from beginning to end, the slider moves from the left to the right. While WMP is playing a track, you can shift it to any point in the track by clicking that point on the track, or by dragging the slider control to that point.

That's about all you need to know to play music from a playlist. Rocket science.

Playing a CD

Want to play a CD? That's hard, too. Here's how:

1. **Take the CD out of its plastic case, if it's in one.**

2. **Wipe the pizza stains off the shiny side (don't worry about the other side).**

3. **Stick the CD in the PC's drive and close it.**

If WMP isn't running already, it starts all by itself. Then you wait a few seconds (well, quite a few seconds, especially if you're afflicted with a slow Internet connection), and WMP starts playing the first track.

You can use the control buttons the same way for a CD as you do for a playlist — to pause and resume playing, select different tracks, and so on.

To WMP, the CD *is* a playlist. The tracks on the CD appear in the playlist area on the right side of the window. Look at the drop-down list of playlists in the upper right corner of the window; the name of the CD appears as the selected item.

How does WMP know what's on the CD? After it identifies the CD from information encoded along with the recorded tracks, it gets the CD's description and track titles through the Web, from a database at www.WindowsMedia. com maintained for that purpose. Now you know why WMP takes so long before it starts playing the first track.

**Book VIII
Chapter 1**

**Jammin' with
Windows
Media Player**

If a CD is quite obscure — or really good — it may not be in Microsoft's database. Then WMP can display only the information it finds on the CD itself: the number of tracks and the playtime of each track (see Figure 1-3).

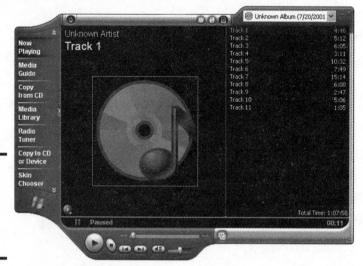

Figure 1-3:
This CD is
not in the
Windows-
Media
database.

Changing the graphic area

The three buttons below the graphic area, er, visualizations screen, change its contents.

✦ Click the first button to display a list of options. The first option is Album Art. The others are different groups of abstract visualizations of the music.

✦ Click the second button to cycle through the selected group of visualizations backward.

✦ Click the third button to cycle through it forward. (These buttons disappear when you select Album Art. You only get one Album Art per album.)

The coolest visualizations have to be the Plenoptics. I'm particularly partial to Smokey Circles. Reminds me of Bill Clinton's college days.

Changing the size of the window

In its initial form, WMP occupies a substantial chunk of real estate on the Desktop. To make it smaller, drag a corner of the window to the desired location, as you do with any other window. But note that when the menu bar is not visible, the only corner you can drag is the lower-right one.

When you make the window small, the window may not have enough room for all of the buttons that run down on the left side. Use the double arrows above and below the buttons to scroll them so that you can reach them all.

Copying from a CD

Click the Copy From CD button on the left edge of the WMP screen to copy tracks from a CD to your computer.

If the CD is already in your PC when you click Copy From CD, WMP simply presents a list of tracks, like the display shown in Figure 1-4.

Figure 1-4:
The Copy From CD display.

If you select Copy From CD first and then insert the CD, WMP automatically starts playing the first track. Click the Stop button at the bottom of the window to make it stop or, if you remember, hold down the Shift key when Windows starts reading the CD. The Shift key tells Windows "don't try to run this CD, or play these songs; I just want to look at what's on the stupid CD."

Unless your WMP window is very wide, it won't show all of the information in the track list. You can use the scroll bar at the bottom of the track list area to display the columns that initially don't fit in the window.

See the column of check boxes down the left side of the track list? They indicate which tracks are selected for copying to your computer.

✦ To copy all of the tracks, just leave the boxes alone.

✦ To exclude a few tracks, clear those tracks' check boxes.

✦ To copy only a few tracks, clear the check box at the top of the column, level with the column titles. This clears the whole track list. Now check the check boxes for the tracks that you want to copy.

Copying a track takes a significant fraction of the track's play time. Select just a few tracks so that you can see how the copying process works, without having to wait all day.

When you've chosen the tracks that you want to transfer to your PC, click the Copy Music button. (It's above the playlist, roughly in the middle of the screen.) Watch the track list's Copy Status column; it shows your computer's progress as it copies the selected tracks.

Where can you find the copied music in your computer? In a playlist, of course. WMP creates a new playlist with the same name as the album and puts the copied tracks in it. If you switch to Now Playing and look at the playlist drop-down box, you see the CD's title with a playlist icon next to it (see Figure 1-5). That's where your copied tracks live.

Figure 1-5:
The newly
copied CD's
playlist.

The music itself is stored in the My Music folder. WMP makes a folder for each artist, and inside the artist's folder, it makes a sub-folder for each album. The music tracks go into the album's folder. If you use the Copy From CD command, WMP stores all the associated information — track titles, album cover art, artist — along with the music. That's handy because WMP can pick up the info from the files and folders when it needs to, without having to run to www.WindowsMedia.com.

Organizing Your Media Library

WMP uses the Media Library to organize sound tracks. When you understand how the Media Library works, you'll be able to organize your music just the way you want.

WMP constructs the Media Library on the fly, using all the entries in your My Music folder and the shared My Music folder for the PC, if one exists.

Leafing through the Media Library

Click the Media Library button to display the Media Library. WMP displays a window split into left and right panes, with the Media Library's structure on the left and the contents of the selected item on the right, as shown in Figure 1-6.

Figure 1-6:
My Media
Library.

The Media Library is organized into folders, just like the Windows XP file system. Unlike the file system, the Media Library has a fixed set of folders:

✦ **Audio:** Contains audio tracks, such as those you have copied from CDs.

- **All Audio:** Contains all of the sound tracks in the Media Library.

- **Album:** Contains all of the albums in the Media Library.

    An album is "in" the Media Library if you have copied at least one track from that album with the Copy from CD operation.

    Click the plus sign next to Album to expand Album into a list of albums, as shown in Figure 1-7.

Figure 1-7:
All of the albums in the Media Library.

Click an album to display that album's tracks in the right pane.

- **Artist:** Contains all of the artists known to have tracks in the Media Library.

  Click the plus sign next to Artist to display a list of artists under the Artist folder. Select an artist to display tracks known to be by that artist.

- **Genre:** This item works just like Artist, except that it organizes tracks by genre (rock, classical, and so on) instead of by artist.

✦ **Video:** Video recordings, discussed in Book VIII, Chapter 2.

- **All Clips:** Contains all of the video clips in the Media Library.

- **Author:** Contains authors who have video clips in the Media Library. This item works just like the Artist sub-folder in the Audio folder: You can expand the item into a list of authors by clicking the plus sign, and you can select an author to display a list of that author's video clips.

✦ **My Playlists:** Playlists that you create or that come with Windows XP. Click the plus sign to expand the item into a list of playlists, and select a playlist to see the audio tracks or video clips it contains.

✦ **Radio Tuner Presets:** Lists streaming audio providers on the Web that you have stored as *presets* (see "Radio Tuner," later in this chapter).

✦ **Deleted Items:** Items you have deleted from the other folders. Deleted Items serves the same function that the Recycle Bin does for files: It lets you restore a deleted item if you change your mind.

Finding the tracks you want

The Media Library folders are powerful tools for keeping your recordings organized, because they offer so many different ways of looking at the same information.

Want to know what albums contain recordings by a given artist? That artist's entry in the Artist folder tells you. Want to look at one of those albums to see what else is on it? The album's entry in the Album folder tells you.

Sorting

You can sort a list in the right pane by the contents of any column. For example, click the All Audio folder to display a list of all of your audio tracks. Now click the heading of the Artist column to sort the list of tracks by artist. Click the heading of the Album column to sort the list by album. Click a heading twice in a row to sort the list backwards on that column. If your collection of recordings is large, sorting the list in different ways can help you find items you want.

Searching

You can search the Media Library for items that have certain words in their titles or for artist names, album names, or genres. When your collection of recordings becomes too large to inspect easily, this is a convenient way to find things in it.

To search the Media Library, click the Search button, located just above the panes of the window. WMP displays the Search Media Library dialog box, as shown in Figure 1-8.

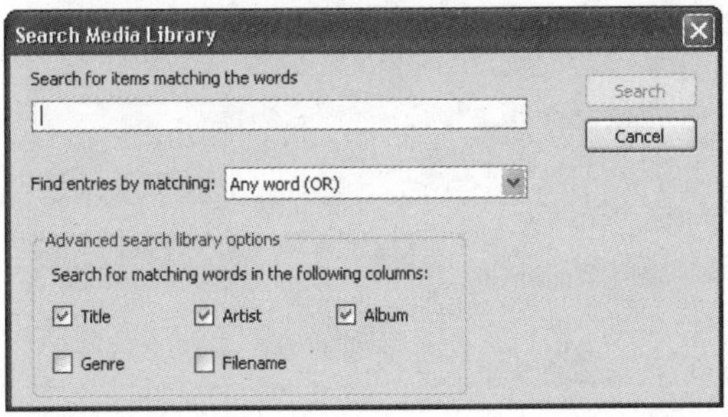

Figure 1-8:
The Search Media Library dialog box.

Enter a word that appears in at least one track title, artist name, or album name in the Media Library. Click the Search button. WMP searches the library and displays a larger version of the same dialog box, as shown in Figure 1-9.

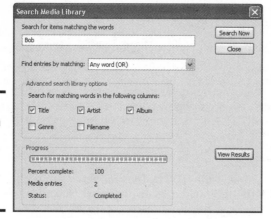

Figure 1-9:
The Search
Media
Library
dialog box
after the
search.

Click the View Results button to close the Search Media Library dialog box.
Notice that a new playlist is named Search Results; it's selected, and it contains, logically enough, the tracks that were found in the search. Figure 1-10
shows such a result list.

Figure 1-10:
The Search
Results
playlist.

The Search Results playlist is just like any other playlist, except that the
contents of the list — the matching tracks — are changed every time a
Search is run. You can keep a Search Results playlist around for a long time.

Look at the Search Media Library dialog box carefully, and you see that it lets you perform the search in several different ways:

✦ If you enter more than one word in the "Search for..." dialog box, you can search for items that match the words in several different ways, including items that contain *any* of the words, items that contain *all* of the words, and items that contain the *exact phrase* you entered.

✦ You can search any combination of several properties (title, artist name, and album name among them).

The next time you use the Search button:

✦ You must enter the word(s) to be searched for again.

✦ You must select the type of matching (items containing any word, items containing all words, and so on) again.

✦ The properties that you chose to search for matches are remembered and used again, unless you change them.

✦ The items previously in the Search Results playlist are removed, and the new search results are added.

Playing tracks in the Media Library

You can play a track directly from the Media Library. Just select the track and click the Start button at the bottom of the WMP window.

You can even play a group of tracks by selecting the group. To play all of the songs by a given artist, for example, select that artist under the Artist folder and click Start.

Nailing "Track 6, Unknown Artist, Unknown Album"

You probably already know that if you copy a track from a really obscure CD, the Windows Media Web site may not be able to provide the track name, artist, and so on. In that case, the Media Library lists the track number as the track name and shows the artist, album, and genre as "Unknown."

Blech.

If you have many such files, they aren't very useful, because you can't tell them apart. Fortunately, you have a way to add the missing information.

**Book VIII
Chapter 1**

Jammin' with
Windows
Media Player

Display the track in the right pane of the window. To fill in one of the Unknown fields, right-click that field and click the Edit command. WMP selects the field and places a caret at the end. Now you can replace or edit the contents of the field, just like any other piece of text. When you're done, press Enter or simply click somewhere else.

Each piece of information that you enter is added or updated in the appropriate folders. For example, if you fill in the album name, it is added to the Album folder. If you fill in the Artist name, it is added to the Artist folder, if necessary, and the track is added to it there. WMP remembers the information, so you only have to enter it once.

Managing playlists

Er, maybe that should be *mangling* playlists.

WMP gives you all sorts of control over which songs you hear, and it does so through playlists. Did you ever want to rearrange the order of the songs on the Beatles' *White Album*? My son just about croaked when he found out he could burn a CD that plays *Oops... I Did It Again* immediately after Eminem's homage *Oops... The Real Slim Shady Did It Again.* You've got the power. Hmmm. That's a catchy tag line, isn't it?

Media Library lets you create your own playlists, and you can modify them to your heart's content.

Creating a new playlist

If you have a favorite set of tracks that you like to hear in a particular order, and the tracks are in the Media Library, you can build a playlist that gives you precisely what you want. It's like being able to create your own custom CD.

In fact, you can use a playlist to make your own custom CD. Nothing to it. The section "Copy to CD or Device" explains how.

To make your own playlist, click the New Playlist button on the left side of the Media Library window. WMP opens a dialog box that prompts you to name the new playlist (see Figure 1-11).

Figure 1-11:
Enter the
new playlist
name.

Enter a name for the list and click OK.

If you look at the dropdown list of playlist names above the right pane of the window, your new playlist is there (see Figure 1-12).

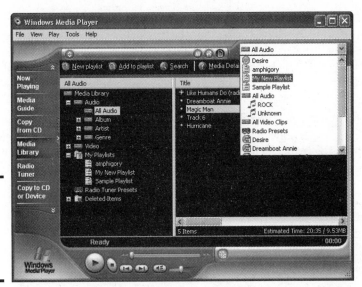

Figure 1-12:
Your new playlist is in the dropdown list.

That's how hard it is to create a new playlist.

Adding a track to a playlist

In the Media Library, you can add a track to any playlist, at any time:

1. **Select any folder or folder item that contains that track, so that the track appears in the right pane of the window.**

2. **Click the track to select it.**

3. **Click the Add to Playlist button (which is next to the New Playlist button, in the upper left).**

   WMP displays a dropdown list of playlists.

4. **Click the playlist that you want.**

   If you have a lot of playlists, WMP displays only the first few of them in the drop-down list. If the one you want isn't there, click the last list item, Additional Playlists. This opens a scrolling list of all playlists. Click the one you want, and then click OK.

5. **WMP adds the track to the playlist and closes the scrolling list.**

You can add the same track to any number of playlists. Just use the "Adding a track to a playlist" procedure again, specifying a different playlist.

You can even add a track to a playlist from a different playlist, using the same procedure. Pick the Playlist with the desired track on the left. Click the track on the right, and click Add to Playlist. Voilà.

Don't worry about using up storage space. No matter how many playlists you add a track to, the Media Library maintains just one copy of the track. Playlists are like headings in a library catalog: No matter how many headings a particular book is indexed under, there's still just one copy of the book.

Renaming and deleting playlists

To delete a playlist, right-click the playlist and click the Delete command from the resulting menu, as shown in Figure 1-13. Or you can just select the playlist and press the Delete key.

Figure 1-13:
How to delete a playlist.

A deleted playlist goes into the big digital bit bucket in the sky. Actually, it goes into the Media Library's Deleted Items folder. To get it back, display the contents of that folder; then right-click the playlist and click the Restore command.

To change a playlist's name, right-click the playlist and click the Rename command from the resulting menu.

Managing the contents of playlists

Just as you can manage playlists, you can manage the contents of a playlist.

To make any type of change to a playlist, first select the playlist in the left pane of the Media Library to display its contents in the right pane.

To delete a track from the playlist, right-click the track and click the Delete From Playlist command, or select the track and press the Delete key.

When you delete a track from a playlist, the track does not appear in the Deleted Items folder. That's because you haven't actually deleted the track; you've only deleted a reference to the track.

To change a track's position in the playlist, just drag the track to the position you want.

Deleting tracks from the Media Library

If you've been reading about the Media Library, you know that no matter how many playlists a track is added to, the Media Library still contains just one copy of the track. The reverse is just as true: even if you delete a track from every playlist that contains it, the Media Library still contains one copy of the track.

It's possible to delete a track from the media library, though. You can do this in a couple of ways.

The first way is to select the All Audio folder, or an appropriate item under the Album, Artist, or Genre folder, so that the track appears in the right pane of the window. Then right-click the track and click the Delete From Library command, as in Figure 1-14. Or, select the track and press the Delete key.

The second way is to select a playlist that contains the track. Then right-click the track and click the Delete From Library command. (In this case, pressing the Delete key does not work; it simply deletes the track from the playlist.)

Take care not to delete a track from the Media Library when you intend to delete it only from a playlist. When you right-click a track in a playlist, the Delete From Library command and the Delete From Playlist command are right next to each other! It's easy to choose the wrong one.

If you do delete a track from the Media Library by accident, you can always get it back by restoring it from the Deleted Items folder. You must add it back to the playlists yourself, though. When you delete a track from the Media Library, WMP automatically deletes it from every playlist that contains it, and when you restore the track, its playlist memberships are not restored.

Figure 1-14:
How to
delete a
track from
the Media
Library.

Working with files and Web sites

WMP can play more than tracks from CDs or the Media Library. It can play any sound recording that is accessible to you from a file on your computer, through your local area network, or through the Internet.

This opens up all sorts of possibilities. You can trade soundtracks with your friends through e-mail. Or, you can download tracks from conventional Web sites.

Playing a file

To play a file that contains a sound recording, make sure that WMP's menu bar is visible. Choose File➪Open. This opens a file choosing dialog box. Use it to find and open the file. When you click the Open button, WMP plays the file.

If you don't have any sound recordings outside the Media Library, you can try this with a bunch of sound recordings that come with Windows XP. These files contain the sounds that you hear when you log on, log off, and so on. Go to C:\Windows\Media and try opening any of the media files you find there.

Playing a Web site

To play a Web site, choose File➪Open URL. Type the Web site's address (a URL such as www.chriscalloway.net/minni.mp3) and click OK.

Because the addresses of files on the Web are often long and difficult to type, copying the address is easier than typing it. Here's one way to do it:

1. **Use Internet Explorer to navigate to a Web page that contains a link to the sound recording.**

2. **If you clicked the link, Internet Explorer would play the recording. Don't do that now; instead, right-click the link and click the Copy Shortcut command.**

3. **Return to WMP, click the File/Open URL command, and paste the URL (the "shortcut") into the dialog box.**

Adding a file or Web site to the Media Library

This process is very similar to playing a file or a Web site, as discussed in the preceding section. To add a file to the Media Library, follow these steps:

1. **Show the menu bar (if it isn't visible) by clicking the toggle button in the upper-left corner of the WMP screen (refer to Figure 1-1).**

2. **Choose File⇨Add to Media Library.**

   This opens a submenu.

3. **Click the Add File command, click the file, and click the Open button.**

   WMP adds the file to the Media Library as an entry in the All Audio folder.

To add a Web address to the Media Library, follow the steps above, but in Step 3 choose Add URL

Note that when you add a file or a Web site to the Media Library, you're not storing a copy of the sound recording in the library; you're just storing a *reference* to it. When you play the recording through the Media Library, WMP actually plays the original copy, wherever it happens to be stored.

If you add a file to the Media Library and then delete or move the original file, the entry for the file still appears in the Media Library, but WMP can't play the file. The same is true if you add a Web site to the Media Library and then the Web site moves it, deletes it, or goes out of service.

In many cases, you have a choice between downloading a file from a Web site and adding it to the Media Library or simply adding its address to the Media Library. Each approach has advantages.

Advantages of downloading the file and adding it to the Media Library are:

✦ You have your own copy of the recording. You don't risk losing access to it if it becomes unavailable through the Web.

Book VIII
Chapter 1

Jammin' with
Windows
Media Player

✦ You don't have to be concerned about whether you can download the recording fast enough to play it without pauses. If your Internet connection is slow or the Internet is busy, the download may take a long time, but when it is over you can play the file continuously. This is the only way that you can play high-quality recordings without constant interruptions.

Advantages of adding a Web site address:

✦ It consumes virtually no space on your disk. Sound recordings, on the other hand, tend to be large. So if you download a lot of files, they consume a lot of disk space.

✦ Adding the Web site address may be your only option. Many Web sites let you play music directly from their site but won't let you download files, because they don't want to distribute free copies of their intellectual property.

Some sound recordings are stored in formats that WMP can't read. These may be proprietary formats for which you are legally required to purchase a special player from an independent source. If you try to play a file or Web site that is recorded in one of these formats, WMP displays a message that says it cannot play the file.

Radio Tuner

Microsoft controls the appearance of the WMP Radio Tuner from its bunkers located thirteen stories below ground level at a secret location underneath a heavily fortified parking lot on 156th Street in Redmond, Washington. Okay, okay. That's not quite accurate. Still, Microsoft can change the appearance and the function of the Radio Tuner at any moment, simply by changing a Web site. That means the detailed instructions and screen shots that you see here may or may reflect what you actually get when you crank up the Radio Tuner. If you're having a hard time getting the radio to work, follow along here because the functions that you need to perform — setting preset lists, picking channels, and so on — will be the same, no matter what whim strikes the fancy of the Windows Media Web designers this week.

Bet you never imagined that Windows XP has a radio hidden inside it.

Actually, that's very close to the truth. Many Web sites offer *streaming audio,* which is essentially broadcast sound (radio) over the Internet. Many AM and FM radio stations offer their own programming through their own Web sites. Other organizations provide streaming audio that isn't available over the air waves at all. WMP lets you listen to all of these.

If you click the Radio Tuner button on the left side of the screen, and you're connected to the Web, WMP presents the display shown in Figure 1-15.

Figure 1-15:
The Radio
Tuner
display.

The Radio Tuner doesn't look much like a conventional radio, but you control it in a very similar way.

The right half of the window does the job of a radio's tuning dial. It lets you find *stations* (streaming audio sources) through a search service provided by Microsoft's Windows Media Web site, www.WindowsMedia.com.

The left half of the window lets you set up and select your favorite stations more easily, like a radio's preset buttons.

Listening to a station

The simplest way to tune in to a station is to select it from one of the lists of presets in the left half of the window. There are three lists there, titled Featured Stations, My Stations, and Recently Played Stations. Initially, only the Featured Stations list is displayed.

You can see more information about a station by clicking either its name or the double arrowhead to the right of the name. The Radio Tuner expands that station's listing as shown in Figure 1-16.

**Book VIII
Chapter 1**

**Jammin' with
Windows
Media Player**

Figure 1-16:
More
information
about a
station.

To tune in to this station click the Play or the green arrowhead next to it. (You can also click the green arrowhead next to the station's name, whether you display the station information first or not.) Wait a few seconds (well, actually, quite a few seconds, particularly if you have a slow Internet connection), and WMP starts playing the station.

At least, WMP starts playing the station if everything goes right. Streaming audio is still an immature medium, though, and many things may go wrong:

✦ The Web site that provides the station that you chose may be out of order or may have gone "off the air."

✦ The Web site may be so busy that it can't deliver data as fast as your computer plays it, yielding snatches of audio with pauses between them.

✦ The Internet itself may be busy, yielding the same result.

✦ The Web site or the Internet may be so busy that WMP can't receive the station at all, so it just displays a message box that talks about "insufficient bandwidth."

This isn't a complete list of potential problems, and you can't do much about any of them. The point is, be patient with the Radio Tuner. If you can't get the station you want, try another, or try again later. Like in ten years.

Many stations open one or more browser windows to tell you what great stations they are, or to ask you to give them free information, or to try to sell you stuff. If you don't like a station's advertising policy, vote with your feet — uh, your mouse.

The first few times you try to tune in a new station you're liable to get a message box that asks whether you want to install a "codec," a "Java Virtual Machine," or some other arcane nonsense. Figure 1-17 shows an example of such a box.

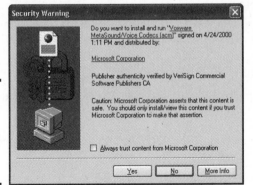

Figure 1-17:
The "Do
you want
to install...?"
message
box.

Don't be scared by "Security Warning." This type of message is normal, and is not as dangerous as it appears.

Here's what it means: Many radio stations encode their programming in ways that require WMP to have a special piece of decoding software. With this box Windows XP tells you that WMP has to download the decoding software from a Web site, and asks whether it should be allowed to go ahead.

What's the security warning for? Windows XP says that because certain nasty Web sites use this technique to download software that does mischief in your computer.

In general, you should click No when this box appears if you have any doubts about the reliability of the software in question. When the software is distributed by a reputable source, though, you can be pretty sure it's safe.

In this case the source is identified as Microsoft Corporation, and an independent verification service confirms that the source really *is* Microsoft Corporation, not some pirate pretending to be Microsoft. If you trust Microsoft not to sabotage your computer, go ahead and click Yes. (If you don't trust Microsoft not to sabotage your computer, you shouldn't be using Windows!)

Radio stations use a variety of encoding techniques which require different decoding software. Therefore you're likely to encounter this message box repeatedly. You only need to download each piece of software once, though, so these interruptions should become rare after a while.

Kvetching about streaming speed

Streaming speed refers to the speed at which a station ideally delivers the data that Windows Media Player converts to sound. By assuming that it can deliver data at a higher speed, a station can provide better sound quality. If

**Book VIII
Chapter 1**

**Jammin' with
Windows
Media Player**

your computer can't actually get data that fast, though, it must pause after playing a segment of data while it waits to receive the next segment. This gives the sound a disjointed character that can be just as irritating as poor audio quality.

The trick is to know how fast your computer can receive data and listen to stations that don't try to deliver it too fast. The Station Finder shows the speed of each station in thousands of bits per second.

+ The lowest common speed, 28K (28,000 bits/second), is adequate for speech, but hopeless for music.

+ The next speed, 32K, is quite good for speech and passable for music. If you connect to the Internet through a dial-up modem, this is probably the highest speed you can use consistently.

+ The next speed, 56K, yields very good sound indeed. It is suitable for use with all types of broadband connections. It also works well with a dial-up connection if you have a high-speed modem and the quality of the connection is close to ideal.

+ The highest common speed, 100, is comparable to the quality of a good CD. It is suitable for use with many types of broadband connections.

Saving a station in the Media Library

You can save a station setting in the Media Library along with your sound recordings, as well as in a preset list. When a station setting is in the Media Library, you can include it in playlists. (Why would you *want* to? You'll find out when you get to the section "Switching skins," later in this chapter.)

To store a station in the Media Library, make sure that WMP's menu bar is visible. (Remember: If it is not visible, click the round button in the upper edge of the frame, near the upper left corner.) Tune in the station by whichever means you prefer. Then choose File⇨Add to Media Library. This command opens a submenu; select Add Currently Playing Track.

After you add a station to the Media Library, you can select the Media Library tab and see the station in the All Audio folder.

Some stations don't let WMP play their sound streams directly; they make it open a separate Internet Explorer window from which you can play their sound streams. This type of station can't be added to the Media Library. Inconvenient, but true.

Copy to CD or Device

If your computer has a CD writer, you can copy sound recordings from the Media Library directly to CDs. If you own a digital audio player that is compatible with Windows XP, you can copy sound recordings from the Media Library to your player.

In either case, you can't copy live feeds such as programs from radio stations. Such programs are broadcast for listening only, so recording them would often violate the intellectual property rights of the radio station or of others.

You also can't copy files that use certain recording techniques, indicated by a file's extension. As of this writing, the only types of files that you can copy to a CD are Windows Media files (`.wma` extension), MP3 files (`.mp3`), and Wave sound files (`.wav`).

See my rant about showing filename extensions in Book I, Chapter 2.

Understanding CD-Rs and CD-RWs

There are two types of writeable CDs: CD-Rs and CD-RWs.

CD-R is short for *CD read.* This is a CD that you can write once. After a CD-R has been written, you cannot add to it or erase it.

CD-RW is short for *CD read-write.* This is a CD that you can erase and rewrite many times.

A CD-R writer can write only CD-Rs. A CD-RW writer generally can write either CD-Rs or CD-RWs.

You generally can play a CD-R on a conventional CD player or on a computer's CD-ROM drive (or a CD-R drive, or a CD-RW drive). As a rule, only a computer's CD-ROM drive can play a CD-RW.

You can find a detailed discussion of CD-Rs and CD-RWs in Book I, Chapter 5.

WMP cannot add data to a partially recorded CD-RW. Before you can reuse a CD-RW, you must erase it, like this:

1. **Put the CD-RW in the CD writer.**
2. **Choose Start⇨My Computer.**
3. **Select the CD writer.**
4. **Click Erase CD-RW.**

Burning a CD

In this section, "CD" refers to both CD-Rs and CD-RWs.

The process of writing data to a CD is called *burning*. WMP enables you to burn a CD very, very easily. Here's how:

1. **Choose Start⊅Windows Media Player to start Windows Media Player.**

(If for some reason WMP isn't visible when you click Start, use Start⊅ All Programs⊅Windows Media Player.)

2. **Click the Copy to CD or Device button.**

WMP displays the window shown in Figure 1-18. The left pane of the window, Music to Copy, shows the tracks currently available to copy to the CD.

Figure 1-18:
The Copy to CD or Device window.

3. **If the left pane is not empty, select all of the tracks and delete them.**

This deletes the tracks only from the window — not from the Media Library. The right pane of the window, Music on Device, shows the device to which Windows Media Play is set to copy, and what is on the device. Your CD writer should be shown in the dropdown list at the top of the pane.

4. **If your CD writer is not shown in the list, click the drop-down list and select it.**

5. Select the tracks that you want to copy to the CD. Start by clicking the Media Library tab.

6. To copy an individual track, display the track that you want in the right pane of the window. Then right-click the track and click Copy to Audio CD.

WMP returns to the Copy to CD or Device window and displays the track in the Music to Copy pane.

7. To copy another track, return to the Media Library and do it again.

8. To copy several tracks at once from a playlist, display the contents of the playlist in the Media Library's right pane. Select the tracks with either shift-click or control-click, and then right-click any one of the selected tracks and click Copy to Audio CD.

9. After you collect all of the tracks that you want to copy to the CD, consider the order of the tracks.

WMP records them on the CD in the order that they appear in the Music to Copy pane. If that isn't what you want, drag each track to the desired position.

If you see a track in the Music to Copy pane that you don't want to copy, you can delete it from the pane, or you can clear the check box to its left. Only items whose check boxes are checked will be copied.

10. Put a blank CD in the CD writer and close the door.

Wait a few seconds, and the message `Copy...to drive` appears above the Music to Copy pane.

11. Look at each track's status, shown in the Status column.

All statuses should say "Ready to copy." If some say "Will not fit," the total play time of the tracks is greater than the recording capacity of the disk. If you write the CD anyway, the tracks that "Will not fit" will not be copied to it. You probably want to remove some tracks so that the whole list will fit.

12. Click the Copy Music button, above the Music on Device pane, to begin the copying operation.

WMP makes two passes through the list of tracks to copy. In the first pass, it prepares each track for copying and changes the track's status from "Ready to copy" to "Converted." In the second pass, it writes the tracks to the CD and changes each track's status to "Copying to CD" and then to "Complete" when it is done.

13. When the last track's status changes to "Complete," the CD is done, and WMP ejects it from the drive.

Book VIII Chapter 1

Jammin' with Windows Media Player

The copying process takes a substantial fraction of the time it would take to play the copied tracks, the exact time depending on the speed of your CD writer.

It is best not to use your computer for other tasks while writing a CD. If another task's activity prevents WMP from writing a continuous stream of data, the CD will be spoiled.

If you interrupt the writing process by clicking the Cancel button, or by removing the CD from the writer before it is complete, WMP goes bananas and the whole process stops. If you screw up a CD-RW, you must erase it before you can reuse it. A fried CD-R ain't good for anything but a coaster.

Instead of copying individual tracks to the Music to Copy pane, you can copy an entire playlist in one step.

Go to the Media Library and select the playlist (double-click it). WMP starts playing the playlist; click the Stop button at the bottom of the window to stop it. Then click Copy to CD or Device. The entire contents of the playlist appear in the Music to Copy pane.

When you copy an entire playlist to the Music to Copy pane in this way, you are copying the playlist itself — not the tracks in the playlist. If you then delete a track from the Music to Copy pane, that track will be deleted from the playlist!

Copying to a digital audio player

The "Device" in "Copy to CD or Device" refers to a digital audio player: one of those nifty little gadgets that you can carry around with you and use to play music out of electronic memory. People will forgive you if you call it an MP3 player. The folks at Microsoft call it that.

Here's how to get your tunes onto your MP3 player:

1. **Attach your player to one of your computer's USB ports and turn it on.**

2. **Select WMP's Copy to CD or Device tab.**

3. **If your player is not selected in the Music on Device pane's dropdown list, click the list and select it.**

If you click the list and don't see your device there, a couple of things could be wrong:

✦ WMP may not have noticed that you have attached the player to the computer. To fix this problem, quit and restart WMP.

✦ Windows XP may not support your particular player. To fix this problem, you may need a new bank account.

The rest of the copying process is essentially the same as burning a CD, which I discussed in the preceding section: Build a list of tracks in the Music to Copy pane, click the Copy Music button, and wait for the process to complete.

Some differences in the process reflect differences between a digital audio player and a CD writer:

✦ You can add tracks to a digital audio player that already has tracks stored on it.

 ✦ You can delete tracks from your digital audio player. To delete a track, click the track and then click the button labeled with an "X" at the top of the Music on Device pane.

Skin Chooser

A *skin* is a little file that changes WMP's appearance. I'm not talking subtle changes here; I'm talking complete transformation. A skin can make WMP look like a 1950's juke box, a Star Trek phaser, a funny face, or Bill G's trampoline room.

If you like intriguing visual effects, skins are for you.

Skins have a practical advantage, too: Most of them make WMP occupy less screen space in *skin mode* than it does in its normal *full mode*. Skins do this by presenting only WMP's most frequently used functions; but if those are the only functions you need, why should you mind? You can always switch back to full mode when you need a function that your preferred skin doesn't provide.

Switching skin modes

 Getting WMP into skin mode is easy. Click the Switch to Skin Mode button in the bottom frame, to the right of the volume control slider. Or use the shortcut **Ctrl+2**.

What does skin mode look like? Well, that depends on the skin. The skin that WMP displays out of the box looks like the one shown in Figure 1-19.

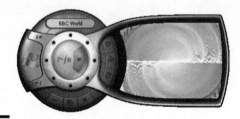

Figure 1-19:
WMP's
initial skin.

Using the anchor window

Notice that the skin has two parts. The big part is the WMP skin itself, the part that controls the music. The little part in the lower right corner, called the *anchor window,* controls the skin.

The anchor window does not vary from skin to skin. It has a minimize button that minimizes both the anchor window and the skin, and a close button that closes both. The grayed-out outline of a maximize button is there too, but it doesn't do anything.

If you click anywhere in the lower part of the anchor window it pops up a menu of frequently performed functions, as shown in Figure 1-20.

Figure 1-20:
The anchor
window's
popup
menu.

The first menu item is very important; it's how you make WMP return from skin mode to full mode. The other items largely duplicate operations that you can perform from full mode.

You can also switch WMP back to full mode with the shortcut **Ctrl+1**. That should be easy to remember: **Ctrl+2** for skin mode, **Ctrl+1** for full mode.

Switching skins

Each skin looks and behaves like nothing but itself, so you have to learn to use a particular skin by playing with it. Still, skins are similar enough that it's helpful to examine one in detail.

Let's switch to a skin that shows up better in this book's screen shots, and work with it:

1. **Click the button in the center of the Anchor Window and choose Select A New Skin.**

    WMP displays the Skin Chooser window, as shown in Figure 1-21. Now you can see that the initial skin's name is Windows XP. Who would have guessed?

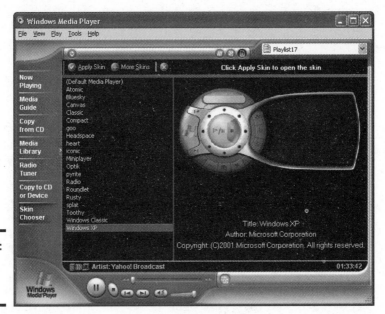

Figure 1-21: The Skin Chooser window.

Book VIII Chapter 1

Jammin' with Windows Media Player

You can also display this window from full mode (without ever entering skin mode) by clicking the Skin Chooser tab.

2. **Choose a different skin — Toothy is a nice one; it reminds me of a boss I once had — and click the Apply Skin button above the list of skin names.**

    You're back in skin mode, but now your skin is Toothy instead of Windows XP. A portrait of Toothy appears in Figure 1-22.

Minimize and close

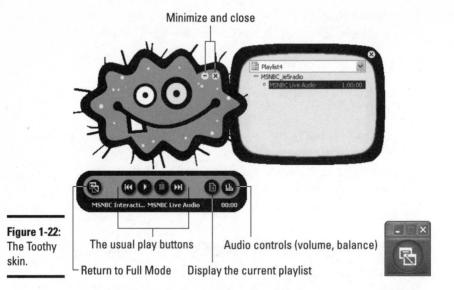

Figure 1-22:
The Toothy
skin.

The usual play buttons

Audio controls (volume, balance)

Return to Full Mode

Display the current playlist

Toothy is a more-or-less typical skin, as skins go. The controls below the face work exactly the way you think they would.

TIP

If you're playing a radio station, the current playlist contains the radio station. If you have several stations that you like to listen to, use the instructions in the section called "Saving a station in the Media Library" to save each in its own playlist. That enables you to switch among them easily.

REMEMBER

How could you possibly be expected to figure out which facial features are controls, much less what they do? As long as Windows XP's Balloon Help feature is turned on, it's easy. Just let the mouse cursor hover over a part of the face or the control bar, and if it's a control, Windows XP pops up a little box that tells you what the control does.

You can also right-click a skin to pop up a menu of common operations. These operations cover most of the things you're likely to want to do in skin mode — including the switch back to full mode.

More skins!

The list of skins that you saw in the Skin Chooser is not the end of the story. You can find even more skins by clicking the More Skins button near the top of the Skin Chooser window.

The More Skins button opens Internet Explorer and displays the skins download page at www.WindowsMedia.com (yep, that's Microsoft's site, the same one that provides information about artists, albums, and radio stations).

It's odd that the Media Guide and Radio Tuner both use WMP as an ersatz Internet Explorer shell, whereas the Skins chooser doesn't — the chooser brings in Internet Explorer in all its glory. Oh well. Microsoft works in mysterious ways.

I won't describe this Web site in detail, because its appearance is liable to change at any time, and its content changes regularly. All you need to know is this: When you click a link that represents a skin, the browser window downloads the skin file to your computer. After it's done, the new skin appears in the Skin Chooser's list of skin names.

If the list of skin names gets too long to display in the window, it scrolls.

When you get tired of a skin, you can delete it from the list by selecting it and clicking the Delete button, right next to the More Skins button. Be cautious about this, though. If you later want to get a skin back, you may find that the skins download page has changed, and that skin is no longer available.

Customizing WMP

You can customize WMP in a large number of ways. Most of them are accessible through the Tools menu's Options command. This command displays a tabbed dialog box for customizing many aspects of WMP's behavior:

+ The *Player* tab controls general aspects of WMP's behavior, such as whether the anchor window is visible in skin mode.

+ The *Copy Music* tab controls aspects of the copying process, such as the amount of data compression to apply when copying a CD. (More compression makes the copied tracks occupy less space, but reduces sound quality.) It also controls the folder to which music is copied (by default the My Music folder, which is the folder that the Media Library uses).

+ The *Devices* tab lists available devices that WMP can use (such as CD drives and digital audio players) and lets you control certain aspects of their behavior.

+ The *Performance* tab lets you control how WMP handles streaming media.

+ The *Media Library* tab controls access to the Media Library by other applications and other sites on the Internet.

+ The *Visualizations* tab lets you choose the visualization that WMP displays when it plays sound tracks.

✦ The *File Types* tab lets you select file types, such as .wav and .mp3, for which you want WMP to be the default player. (Double-click one of these files in a folder and its default player — whatever application that may be — plays it.)

✦ The *Network* tab lets you select the network protocols that WMP may use to receive streaming media. It also lets you control *proxy settings,* which you may have to change if your computer is on a local area network protected by a firewall.

Many of these options can't be understood without technical background, and a detailed discussion of them is beyond the scope of this book. It's a good policy to change one of the options only if you understand it well and keep careful notes so that you can restore the original setting if anything goes wrong.

There's no harm in *looking* at the options, though. You can learn a lot by clicking the Help button on each tab of the Options dialog box.

Understanding Digital Licenses

You know about copyrights. The law says that the creator of a written work (including a sound recording) has a right to fair compensation for the copying and use of the work. With some very limited exceptions, it's illegal to deprive the copyright owner of these rights... for example, by e-mailing copies of the work to 50 of your closest friends.

Copyright has always been difficult to enforce where computers are involved, because copying data is so easy. WMP supports a concept called *digital licensing*, which helps to protect the rights of copyright owners.

Acquiring a license

Here's how digital licensing works. The owner of the copyright in a sound recording can encode the recording in a Windows Media Audio (.wma) file and lock the file so that no one can play it without digital license. Then the owner (called a *content provider* in this context) can publish the file in any manner, such as putting it on a public Web site. Anyone can download the file, but no one can use it without first obtaining a license.

How do you get a license? That's entirely up to the content provider! If the content provider is a record company, it typically sells you a license. Thus the content provider gets its money and you get a useable copy of the recording, just as if you bought one in a store.

What can you do with a licensed file after you get the license? Not, as you may suppose, anything you want! In particular, you can't e-mail copies of the file and the license to 50 of your closest friends. If you try this, your friends will get a useless file, because your license is good only on your computer. (Your friends are free to get their own licenses, of course, and then they can play the file.)

Here are the important restrictions that a digital license may carry:

✦ The license is valid only on your computer.

✦ The license may expire at some point, requiring you to obtain another. (Whether a license expires, and when, is up to the content provider.)

✦ The license may prevent you from using the file in certain ways, for example, by copying it to a digital audio player.

Using digital licenses

It's important to back up your computer's digital licenses. If you ever have to restore your copy of Windows XP because of a hardware or software failure, you have to restore your digital license backup to use your licensed files. If you have no backup, you would have to obtain each license again from its issuer. That would be troublesome, time consuming, and probably expensive.

Similarly, if you move your operations to a new computer, you must restore your digital license backup to the new computer to use your licensed files.

Windows XP allows you to restore backed-up digital licenses a total of four times.

Backing up a license

To back up your digital licenses:

1. **In Windows Media Player, choose Tools⇨License Management.**

   This displays the License Management dialog box, as shown in Figure 1-23.

2. **Click the Browse button. Select the device or folder in which you want to store the backup, and then click OK.**

3. **After you choose a location for the backup, click the Backup Now button.**

   WMP backs up your licenses in the specified location and then displays the message Transfer complete. Click OK.

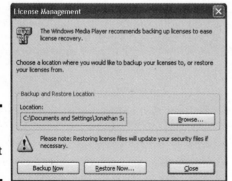

Figure 1-23:
The License
Management
dialog box.

Microsoft recommends backing up the licenses to a diskette. This has the advantage of preserving the licenses if your computer's hard disk crashes, or if the computer itself is lost or damaged. Diskettes are not a very reliable storage medium, though, so if you use this option, always back up in duplicate. A safer medium for backups would be a CD or a file that you keep on another computer or in a secure file area provided by your ISP.

How often should you create an updated backup of your licenses? Ideally, you should do it whenever you acquire a new license. Realistically, you should do it on a regular schedule, the frequency depending on how often you tend to acquire digital licenses.

Restoring the licenses

The procedure for restoring the licenses is very similar to the procedure for backing them up.

1. **Ensure that your latest backup is available to your computer.**

   If it is on a CD, for example, put the CD in your computer's CD drive.

2. **In Windows Media Player, choose Tools⇨License Management.**

3. **Click the Browse button and select the device or folder in which the backup is located. Click OK.**

4. **Click the Restore Now button.**

   WMP restores your licenses from the specified location.

If you try this process just to see how it works, *don't click Restore Now.* Remember that Windows XP allows you to restore your license backup only four times.

Getting free licenses

If the license for a licensed file is free and does not require you to register with the content provider, WMP can download it for you automatically when you download the file. In that case, you aren't even told that the file is licensed unless you check to see.

To control the automatic downloading of licenses, choose Tools⇨Options, and on the Player tab, check or uncheck the Acquire Licenses Automatically box.

Licensing a file and then giving it away is not as pointless as it may seem because it enables the content provider to exercise some control over how the licensed file may be used. The content provider can also build a free mailing list by requiring you to register for your free license, but in that case the license isn't downloaded automatically. WMP requires you to register yourself, letting you choose whether to go ahead or not.

Viewing a license

Does a particular audio file have a license, and if so, what are its terms?

To find out, display the file in the right pane of the WMP window; for example, by selecting the Media Library and clicking the album that contains the file. Right-click the file and click the Properties command. WMP opens a tabbed dialog box that displays the file's properties. If the file has a license, the dialog box has a License Information tab. Click this tab to see a description of the license.

Protecting CDs with licensing

WMP gives you the option of placing license protection on tracks that you copy from a CD to the Media Library. By protecting these tracks, you can help prevent the misuse of copyrighted material.

If license protection is enabled, WMP generates a license automatically when it copies a track from a CD. Like any other digital license, this license is valid only on your computer. If the track is copied to another computer, it cannot be played. You can write the protected track to a CD, and you can copy it to many (not all) types of digital music players.

By default, WMP gives copied CD tracks license protection. You can disable and enable protection with the Protect Content check box in the Tools⇨ Options dialog box's Copy Music tab.

**Book VIII
Chapter 1**

Jammin' with
Windows
Media Player

Chapter 2: Lights! Action! Windows Movie Maker

In This Chapter

✓ Recording and editing video

✓ Using still pictures as titles

✓ Bringing in narration and background sounds

✓ Organizing your clips

Windows Movie Maker brings a full-featured video-editing workshop to your PC. You can use it to create anything from a few seconds of action — say, to dress up an e-mail message — to a full-length documentary about your kid's first birthday party. Get the sound synchronization right, and you could even toss together a decent music video, sell it to Hollywood, and turn into an overnight sensation.

Just remember where you got the idea, huh?

Windows Movie Maker isn't going to drive George Lucas out of business any time soon, and it's definitely still an "in progress" application. You don't want to bet your company or your reputation on it. But for casual stitching together of home movies, it works great.

What You Need to Create Movies

Movie making requires a lot of hardware. Obviously, you need some type of video camera. But you need a lot of computer, too. Microsoft recommends the following as a minimum:

◆ A 300 MHz Pentium II or equivalent

◆ At least 64 MB of RAM

◆ A sound card or equivalent hardware on your computer's main board

◆ At least 2 GB of free disk space

Depending on the type of camera you have, you may also need a special kind of video card to pull recorded video into your computer. If you're going with a full-fledged digital video camera, with direct feed into your PC, plan on using at least a 600 MHz Pentium, with 128 MB of memory, and acres (and acres) of free hard disk space. Video goes through disk space like Orville Redenbacher goes through corn.

Introducing Windows Movie Maker

Windows Movie Maker doesn't look much like other Microsoft applications: It's specially built for the task at hand and doesn't make many bones about that fact. If you start Windows Movie Maker (choose Start⇨All Programs⇨ Accessories⇨Windows Movie Maker), you see the window shown in Figure 2-1.

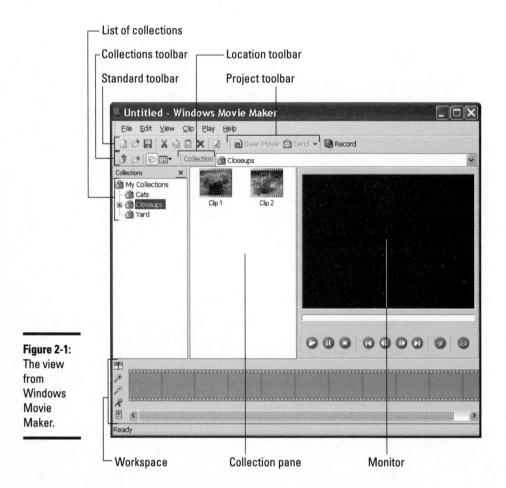

Figure 2-1: The view from Windows Movie Maker.

Take a moment to become familiar with the parts of the window. The central part is divided into three panes. The one on the left shows *collections* of movie clips. A collection is a group of related movie clips with a name. You can use collections to organize your movie clips, much as you use folders to organize other types of files.

The middle pane is called the *collection pane*. If one of the collections is selected (if there is a *current collection*), the collection pane shows the clips stored in it. You can play movie clips in the right pane, which is called the *monitor*.

Below the three panes is the *workspace*. As you assemble movie clips into a whole movie, this area displays the state of your work and lets you control it.

 Up at the top of the window, you see a menu bar, and below it are a couple of toolbars. The upper toolbar controls the operation of Windows Movie Maker. The small lower toolbar controls the appearance of the left and middle panes. The most useful button in the lower toolbar is the one on the right, which controls the appearance of the collection pane.

Recording and Editing Video

Before you can edit video, you must get it into your computer. If you want to reuse (and slice and dice) existing video, head for the Web: Any MPEG or AVI file can import directly into Windows Movie Maker.

If you want to work on your own video, in videospeak, you must *capture* it. That can get complicated, because capturing video may require additional hardware, and the procedure you use depends to some extent on what hardware you use.

Choosing a camera

Video hardware comes in four major types:

+ **Analog video camera:** This is the traditional type of video camera. Its recordings are essentially of the same quality as regular TV. You capture the video with an analog video capture card — the type of card that you can use to display TV on your computer.

+ **Digital video camera:** This type of video camera produces the highest-quality results. To capture digital video without loss of quality, you must connect the camera to an *IEEE 1394* card (also called a *FireWire card*) installed in your computer. You can use an analog video capture card instead, but you lose some of the digital video quality.

✦ **Video cassette recorder (VCR):** You can capture video from a VCR by cabling its Video Out connector to your analog video capture card. You can capture either recorded video or live TV.

✦ **Internet camera (Webcam):** Capturing video from an Internet camera requires no additional hardware. Just plug the camera into your computer's USB port, let Windows XP install the appropriate driver, and get to work.

If your Internet camera has a built-in microphone, Windows Movie Maker can capture both image and sound from it. If not, you must have a separate microphone in order to capture sound. Plug the microphone into your computer's microphone input jack.

If you don't have all the gadgets you need — or don't know how to operate them — ask your dealer for assistance.

Recording video

Windows Movie Maker makes recording video a snap:

1. **Plug in the camera.**

If you're capturing video from a recording, connect the camera or VCR to your computer and prepare it to play back the recording. If you're recording from an Internet camera, make sure that the camera is plugged in and pointed at something interesting.

2. **Click the Record button in Windows Movie Maker's Project toolbar.**

Windows Movie Maker opens the Record dialog box, as shown in Figure 2-2. The controls in the left half of the dialog box determine what Windows Movie Maker will record. The Record drop-down list lets you record video and audio together, video only, or audio only.

3. **For now, select Video and Audio.**

Video only and audio only are useful for recording an image and sound track separately.

4. **Video Device and Audio Device, listed near the top of the Record dialog box, show the devices from which Windows Movie Maker is set to record. If these are not the right devices, click the Change Device button to change them, and then click OK**

This button opens the Change Device dialog box, as shown in Figure 2-3.

The Video and Audio drop-down lists choose the devices through which your computer captures video and audio. The Line list selects the type of source that originates the audio signal. In most cases, Windows Movie Maker sets Line correctly when you select the audio capture device.

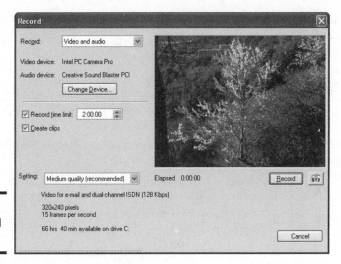

Figure 2-2:
The Record
dialog box.

Figure 2-3:
The Change
Device
dialog box.

The Change Device dialog box closes and you return to the Record
dialog box (refer to Figure 2-2).

5. **To record, click the Record button.**

   Windows Movie Maker may take a few seconds to get started. When it
   does, the Record button is relabeled Stop and the elapsed time starts
   counting. The image being recorded is shown in the Record dialog box's
   monitor window.

6. **If you're recording from a video tape in a camera or VCR, roll the
   tape as soon as Windows Movie Maker starts recording. Record
   enough material to include at least a few different shots.**

   If you're recording from an Internet camera, quickly cover and uncover
   the lens with your hand a few times. (I'll explain why in a moment. For
   now, just *do* it!)

7. **When you're ready to stop recording, click Stop.**

   Windows Movie Maker opens a Save dialog box that prompts you to
   enter a name for the material you've just recorded.

8. **Enter a name and click Save.**

   Windows Movie Maker saves the material and closes both the Save dialog box and the Record dialog box.

   Look at the left pane in Windows Movie Maker's main window: the pane that lists collections. You see a new collection with the name you entered in the Save dialog box. This collection contains the video you just recorded.

9. **Click the collection that you just recorded to display its contents in the collection pane.**

   You should see several clips named Clip 1, Clip 2, and so on. These contain the individual shots from the recorded video. If you recorded from an Internet camera, they contain the "shots" you created by covering the lens with your hand.

How does Windows Movie Maker know where one shot ends and another begins? It looks for a complete change in the image between two consecutive frames of the recording. Whenever it observes that, it closes the video clip that it was recording and starts a new one. This separates your recording into smaller, logically divided segments.

Look back at the Record dialog box in Figure 2-2. See the check box labeled Create Clips? That check box controls the behavior you just saw. If you clear that box, Windows Movie Maker stores an entire recording in one clip.

Assembling a movie

A *project* is a file that contains your work on a movie. In effect, a project *is* a movie, either completed or in development. A *clip* is a piece of a movie. In the preceding section, I showed you how to create clips with a camera or VCR. When the clips are ready, you assemble the clips to create a project.

Here's how to put together a project, er, a movie:

1. **Choose File⇨New⇨Project.**

   These menu selections create a new project, which means that they start a new movie.

2. **Choose a clip from one of your collections and drag it to the workspace at the bottom of the window.**

   An image of the clip appears at the beginning of the workspace.

3. **Drag one or two more clips to the unoccupied part of the workspace.**

   An image of each one appears in the workspace. The workspace now looks like the one shown in Figure 2-4.

Figure 2-4:
The
workspace
with some
clips.

You can insert a clip between two existing clips. Just drag it into the workspace at the boundary between the two clips.

4. **When a clip is in the workspace, you can move it to a different position. Click the clip, drag it to the place where you want to insert it, and release.**

When you need to move a clip a long way, dragging can be clumsy and error-prone; cutting and pasting is more convenient. To cut and paste, right-click the clip that you want to move and click the Cut command. Then right-click the clip *before which* you want to place this clip, and click the Paste command.

To delete a clip from the workspace, right-click the clip and click the Delete command.

5. **To save your project, choose File⇨Save.**

The first time you save a project, Windows Movie Maker opens a Save dialog box to let you give the project a name. Congratulations. You're well on your way to becoming a film legend.

**Book VIII
Chapter 2**

Lights! Action!
Windows Movie
Maker

Playing a clip or a movie

Have you wondered how you're supposed to tell which clip is which from the tiny images in the collection pane? It's actually easy because you can see what's in any clip by playing it in the monitor.

To play a clip, select it either in the collection pane or in the workspace. Then click the play button under the monitor. When you've seen enough, click the pause button to stop the playback. (See Figure 2-5.)

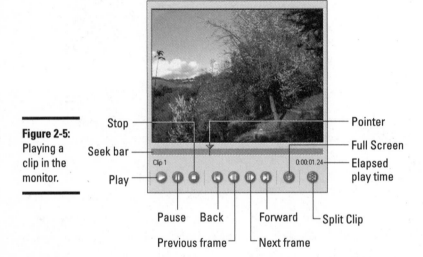

Figure 2-5:
Playing a
clip in the
monitor.

As you play a clip, the pointer on the *seek bar* moves across the bar to show how far the monitor has progressed through the clip. The number near the monitor's lower right corner shows the elapsed play time to the nearest 0.01 second.

The other buttons below the monitor are as follows:

✦ **Stop:** Stops playing the clip and deselects the clip.

✦ **Back:** Selects the preceding clip.

✦ **Previous Frame:** Positions the monitor to the previous frame (use after Pause).

✦ **Next Frame:** Positions the monitor to the next frame (use after Pause).

✦ **Forward:** Selects the following clip.

✦ **Full Screen:** Expands the monitor to fill the whole screen. The seek bar and control buttons are not visible. While in full screen, you can control the monitor with these keys (they work in the normal display mode, too):

- **Play or Pause:** The space bar
- **Stop:** The period key
- **Back:** Ctrl+Alt+Left Arrow
- **Previous Frame:** Alt+Left Arrow
- **Next Frame:** Alt+Right Arrow
- **Forward:** Ctrl+Alt+Right Arrow
- **Leave Full Screen Mode:** Esc
- **Split Clip:** Ctrl+Shift+S

✦ **Split Clip:** Splits a clip in two (see "Splitting and combining clips").

You can also play your entire movie on the monitor. Choose Play⇨Play Entire Storyboard/Timeline.

Viewing storyboard and timeline

The storyboard and the timeline are two different ways of viewing a movie.

The *storyboard* view represents each clip in the movie with a thumbnail image, as shown in Figure 2-6. Storyboard view is useful for assembling and rearranging clips.

Figure 2-6: The storyboard view of the workspace.

Book VIII Chapter 2

Lights! Action! Windows Movie Maker

The *timeline* view represents each clip with a thumbnail image set in a space whose width is proportional to the clip's length, as shown in Figure 2-7. A timeline above the thumbnails helps you judge the playing time of each clip. Timeline view is useful for trimming the beginnings and ends of clips.

To switch between the storyboard and timeline view, click the topmost icon in the group of five icons to the left of the workspace.

Figure 2-7:
The timeline
view of the
workspace.

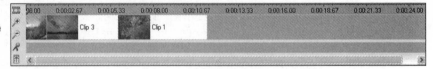

Trimming a clip

Windows Movie Maker lets you *trim* individual clips — hack away pieces at the beginning or end of the clip, to make it shorter. You can trim a clip in either storyboard or timeline view, but in most cases you want to do it in timeline view because the workspace shows what you're doing.

To trim either end of a clip, follow these steps:

1. **Select the clip in the workspace.**

The first frame of the clip appears in the monitor.

2. **Move the monitor's seek bar to the point where you want to trim the clip. You can choose from several ways to do this:**

- Click the play button, and then click the pause button when the clip reaches the right point.

- Drag the seek bar's pointer to the right position. The monitor displays the frame at the spot in the clip where you release the pointer.

- Click the previous frame and next frame buttons to move the pointer (and the monitor) backward and forward one frame at a time.

3. **When the seek bar's pointer is correctly positioned, choose Clip⇨ Set Start Trim Point to trim the start of the clip to that point. Choose Clip⇨Set End Trim Point to trim the end of the clip to that point.**

When you trim a clip, the remaining part expands to fill the entire seek bar. If the workspace is in timeline view, the clip contracts in the timeline so that only the trimmed part is shown.

4. **If you trim too much from a clip, choose the Clip menu's Clear Trim Points command to display the entire clip again and start over.**

If you drag a clip from the collection pane to the workspace and trim it, and then you drag the same clip into the workspace again, the second copy is *not* trimmed. You can trim it differently if you want to.

Try another way to trim a clip: In timeline view, drag the clip's *trim handles* to the points where you want to trim. Figure 2-8 shows the trim handles.

The monitor display and the seek bar's pointer track each trim handle as you drag it. Hold the mouse button down until you're sure you have the handle in the right spot.

Left trim handle   Right trim handle

Figure 2-8: A clip in timeline view, with trim handles.

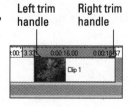

If you trim a clip too far, choose Clip⇨Clear Trim Points. This moves the trim points back to the beginning and end of the clip, and you can start over.

The timeline view's trim handles give you a more precise remedy. Drag either trim handle outward (away from the clip) to move the corresponding trim point back toward the start or end of the clip. You can drag a handle as far as it will go, or just a little way.

When you undo trimming by dragging a trim handle, the clip is left *overlapping* the adjacent clip. If you leave the clips in this state, the overlapping parts of the clips are superimposed when you play the movie. (See "Fading," coming up next.) To remove the overlap, drag the right overlapping clip to the right. Any clips to the right of that one move along with it.

To see more detail in the timeline view, click the *zoom in* icon. To see a larger span of time in less detail, click *zoom out*.

Fading

A *fade* is a transition where one clip fades out while the next one fades in.

To create a fade, the workspace must be in timeline view. Select the second clip (the one that will fade in) and drag it to the left so that it partially overlaps the first clip (which will fade out). The amount of overlap determines the length of the fade.

To plan a fade, study the two clips and use the monitor's time display to find the points where you want the fade to start and end. After you trim the two clips appropriately, use the workspace's timeline to judge the proper amount of overlap.

Splitting and combining clips

You can split or combine clips in two ways: In the workspace and in the collection pane. When you split or combine clips in the workspace, the effect is similar to trimming a clip: Only that use of the clip is affected. When you split or combine clips in the collection pane, you actually split or combine the files that store the clips. This affects all projects that use the clips, now or in the future.

Splitting a clip in the workspace is useful if you want to insert a still picture or another clip in the middle of a clip. Combining clips in the workspace is not as common as splitting a clip, but it is possible if you want to do it.

Splitting/combining clips in the workspace

To split a clip in the workspace, follow these steps:

1. **Click the clip you want to split.**

2. **Set the monitor's seek bar pointer to the position where you want the split to occur.**

 3. **Click the monitor's split button.**

   The first part of the clip retains the clip's name. The second part becomes a new clip with same name followed by a number in parentheses. For example, if you split a clip named *Blowing out the candles,* the first part retains that name, and the second part becomes a new clip named *Blowing out the candles (1).*

These clip names have meaning only in the workspace; the clip in the collection is not affected.

To combine two or more consecutive clips in the workspace, hold down the Shift key and click the first and last of the clips. Then right-click any of the selected clips and click the Combine command.

Splitting/combining clips in the collection pane

Splitting and combining clips in the collection pane is useful for organizing your clips. For example, you may need to split a clip because Windows Movie Maker failed to start a new clip between shots when recording. You may need to combine clips because Windows Movie Maker started a new clip where a new shot did not begin.

To split a clip in the collection pane, select the clip in that pane. Move the seek bar's pointer to the split point that you want, and click the monitor's split button.

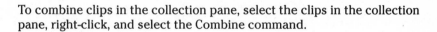

To combine clips in the collection pane, select the clips in the collection pane, right-click, and select the Combine command.

You can combine clips only if they were recorded consecutively or were previously split from a single clip.

Finishing the movie

After you edit a movie to your satisfaction, you probably want to show it to other people. Windows Movie Maker stores the movie as a project that can be watched only in Windows Movie Maker. If you want your friends to be able to view it, either they have to run Windows Movie Maker, or you have to convert the movie into a form that other folks can use. The .WMV extension (for *Windows Media Video*) works well with the Windows Media Player, and Windows Movie Maker uses WMV format as its "final" recording format of choice.

To let others view your movie, follow these steps:

1. **Choose File⇨Save Movie.**

Windows Movie Maker opens the Save Movie dialog box shown in Figure 2-9.

Figure 2-9:
The Save
Movie
dialog box.

Save Movie	☒

Playback quality

Setting: High quality

Profile: Video for broadband NTSC (256 Kbps)

Video Profile: 320x240 pixels
30 frames per second

File size: 564.0 KB

Download time: 0:02:44 28.8 Kbps (modem)
0:01:24 56 Kbps (modem)
0:00:36 128 Kbps (high speed)

Display information

Title:

Author: Jonathan Sachs

Date: 8/ 6/2001

Rating:

Description:

OK   Cancel

2. **Choose the quality setting most appropriate for this movie.**

Higher quality makes the movie file larger, which may be a problem if you plan to write the movie to a CD, send it in e-mail, or put it on a Web site.

Profile describes the uses appropriate for each quality setting. File Size shows how much space your movie will occupy if saved with the selected quality setting.

3. **Fill in the display information to describe your movie.**

   When Windows Media Player lists your movie in its Media Library, it displays the information you enter here.

4. **Click OK.**

   Windows Movie Maker opens a Save dialog box to let you choose a name and location for the movie file.

   By default, a movie has the name of its project file (with the file extension .WMV) and is saved in the My Videos folder. You can name it whatever you want and save it wherever you want.

   I recommend saving movies to some folder other than My Videos. Otherwise, they are hard to distinguish from your clips, which are stored in the My Videos folder, and also use the file extension .WMV.

5. **Click Save.**

   Windows Movie Maker displays a progress bar while it saves the movie to the file. After the file is saved, Windows Movie Maker opens a dialog box that asks whether you want to watch the movie now.

6. **If you click Yes, Windows Media Player opens and plays the movie.**

Anyone running Windows can view the movie later by double-clicking on the file. This starts Windows Media Player and plays the movie.

To add a movie file to Windows Media Player's Media Library, choose File➪Add to Media Library➪Add File. Windows Media Player opens a file choosing dialog box. Select the movie file that you want to add to the Media Library, and click the Open button. Now the movie appears in the Media Library's Video folder under both All Clips and Author (provided you filled in the author's name when you created the movie file).

You can place a movie file on a Web site for others to download, or attach it to an e-mail message and send it to your friends.

Windows Movie Maker also lets you save and distribute a movie in a single step. To save and distribute a movie, choose the File➪Send Movie To➪ E-mail or Web Server. Windows Movie Maker leads you through the process of saving and distributing the movie by the method you chose. (See Book VIII, Chapter 3, for more information about uploading files to Web sites.)

Using Still Pictures in Movies

Still pictures can be useful in a movie both as titles and as clips that do not require motion. Windows Movie Maker accepts still picture files in most formats (including JPEG, GIF, and BMP, but surprisingly not in PNG). You can also capture a still picture from a video source such as a live TV feed, a video camera, or a video recording.

Here's how to grab a still:

1. **Use the steps outlined in the "Recording video" section, earlier in this chapter, to display the incoming image on Windows Movie Maker's monitor. If you're using a video camera's recorded tape, a VCR, or some other source that lets you stop on a single frame, set the source to the frame you want to capture.**

   If you're using a camera, a live TV signal, or an Internet camera, be ready to capture the picture at the right moment.

2. **Click the toolbar's Record button to open the Record dialog box (refer to Figure 2-2). Select the appropriate capture device, if necessary.**

3. **To capture the picture, click the button with the camera icon, next to the Record button.**

   Windows Movie Maker opens a Save dialog box.

4. **Choose a name and location for the picture and click the Save button.**

   Windows Movie Maker stores the picture in the file and adds it to the current collection.

5. **After Windows Movie Maker saves the picture, it returns to the Record dialog box. You can capture another picture or click Cancel to close the dialog box.**

When a still picture is in a collection, you can use it in a project just as you use a video clip: Drag it to the desired point in the workspace.

How long does a still image play in a movie? That's up to you. By default, it plays for five seconds. You can reduce its duration by trimming the picture, just as you can trim a video clip. You can increase its duration by dragging the picture's trim handles outward, just as you would to correct excessive trimming.

To change the five-second default for a still picture's appearance in a movie, select View⇨Options, change the value in the Default Imported Photo Duration dialog box, and then click OK. This change affects the default duration of only newly captured pictures. After a picture has been captured, you can't change its default duration.

Using Sound Clips

You can record narration (or any other type of sound clip) for use in your movies. Windows Movie Maker stores the sound clip on your disk as a .WAV file and inserts it in the current collection. When it is in a collection, you can add it to the workspace much as you add a video clip or a still picture.

Recording a sound clip

Choose from two techniques for recording a sound clip. One is used specifically for narration, which has to be synchronized with the movie. The other is more convenient for recording background sound and other types of material where synchronization isn't as crucial.

To record a narration, follow these steps:

1. **Open the project in which you want to use the recording and select the collection to which you want to add it.**

2. **When you're ready to record, choose File⇨Record Narration.**

Windows Movie Maker opens the Record Narration Track dialog box, as shown in Figure 2-10.

Figure 2-10:
The Record
Narration
Track
dialog box.

3. **Device and Line display the device and line through which Windows Movie Maker will record. If you need to change them, click the Change button. Use the Record Level slider to set the recording level.**

If the video clips have a sound track of their own and you don't want to be distracted by it, check the Mute Video Soundtrack check box.

4. **Click the Record button to start recording.**

Windows Movie Maker plays the movie as you record so that you can synchronize your narration with it.

5. **When you're done, click the Stop button (which replaces the Record button while you're recording).**

   Windows Movie Maker opens a Save dialog box. Choose a filename and location for the recording and click the Save button. Windows Movie Maker saves the file and adds it to the current collection. After Windows Movie Maker saves the file, it returns to the Record dialog box.

6. **You can make another recording or click Cancel to close the dialog box.**

You can't synchronize narration with a single clip selected in the workspace. To get the same effect, create a separate project that contains the clip, and synchronize the narration to it.

Material other than narration usually doesn't have to be recorded to synchronize with the movie. Such material can be recorded just like video:

1. **Click the toolbar's Record button to open the Record dialog box.**

2. **Use the Record dropdown list to select Audio Only.**

3. **Click the Change Device button if necessary to select the input device and line for your computer's audio input.**

   Normally, the device should be your sound card, and the line should be Mic Volume for a microphone; Line In for a radio, tape deck, or other external device; or CD Audio for your computer's CD-ROM drive.

4. **Proceed as you would to record video and audio.**

   Windows saves your sound clip in a Windows Media Audio (.WMA) file.

Adding a sound clip to a movie

To add a sound clip to a movie, drag the sound clip from the current collection to the appropriate point in the workspace. This is essentially the same operation as adding a video clip, but note the following differences:

✦ Sound clips are visible only in timeline view and can be added or managed only in timeline view.

✦ Sound clips appear below video clips, as shown in Figure 2-11.

✦ You can't leave spaces between video clips in the timeline, but you can leave spaces between sound clips. This lets you set each sound clip's exact position relative to the movie's video clips.

You can play a sound clip by selecting it and clicking the monitor's play button, just as you would play a video clip. You also can trim a sound clip the same way you would trim a video clip. Click the sound clip, and then use the monitor or the trim handles in the workspace's timeline.

Figure 2-11:
Sound clips
are shown
below video
clips in the
workspace.

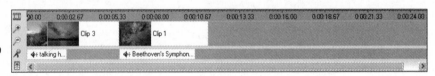

Importing Clips from Other Sources

You can use video clips, sound clips, and still pictures from other sources in your movies. For example, you can use pictures captured with the Scanner and Camera wizard (see Book VIII, Chapter 3) or sound tracks recorded from a CD by Windows Media Player (see Book VIII, Chapter 1). You also can download all three types of material from sources on the Web.

To import a clip or still into Windows Movie Maker, it must reside on your computer. If the clip is on the Web, you must download it first.

If you plan to distribute your movie publicly or use it for commercial purposes, you cannot use copyrighted material without the copyright holder's permission. If in doubt, see your attorney for guidance.

When you have the file, here's how to put it in your movie, er, project:

1. **Choose File⇨Import.**

2. **Find and select the file that you want to import, and then click the Open button.**

Windows Movie Maker adds the file to the current collection.

3. **When the clip or still is in the current collection, you can click and drag away.**

The only technical restriction on importing clips is that they must be in one of the recording formats that Windows Movie Maker knows how to handle. Here is a list of the more common formats that work:

✦ **Video clips:** .AVI, .WMV, .MPEG, .MPG, .MP2, and .WMV.

✦ **Audio clips:** .WAV, .WMA, and .MP3.

✦ **Still pictures:** .BMP, .JPEG, .JPG, and .GIF.

Organizing Your Clips

When you make movies, you tend to accumulate a lot of clips. A single project may use dozens or even hundreds of them. It's important to organize your clips so that you can find them easily.

Whenever you record a clip, add descriptive information to it.

Here's how to attach descriptive information to a clip:

1. **In Windows Movie Maker, right-click the clip and click the Properties command.**

Windows Movie Maker opens the Properties dialog box shown in Figure 2-12.

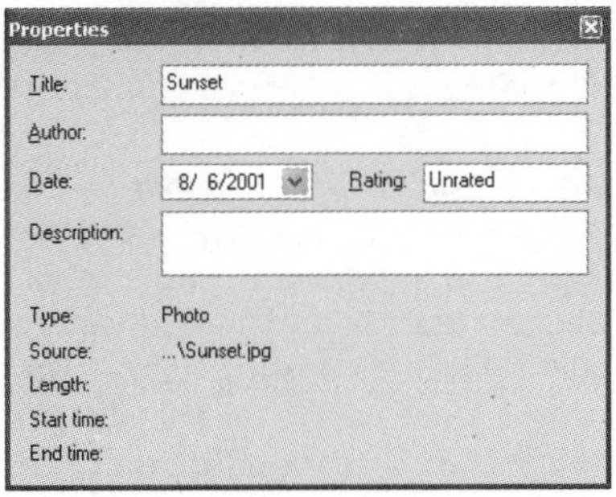

Figure 2-12: A clip's Properties dialog box.

2. **Replace the clip's default title with something descriptive and fill in the other fields as appropriate.**

3. **When you're done, close the Properties dialog box by clicking its close button or pressing the Esc key. (This dialog box has no OK button.)**

The collections that Windows Movie Maker creates when you record clips are rarely useful for organizing them. Create additional collections to support the type of organization that suits your needs, and move your clips into them. After you have emptied a collection that Windows Movie Maker created for you, you may delete it.

To create a new top-level collection, follow these steps:

1. **Click the My Collections icon in Windows Movie Maker's collection list.**

2. **Choose File➪New➪Collection.**

This creates a new collection named New Collection.

3. **Type an appropriate name to replace New Collection and press the Enter key.**

Windows Movie Maker lets you put collections inside other collections, just as the Windows file system lets you put folders inside other folders. To put collection X inside collection Y, drag the icon for X on top of the icon for Y. To create a new collection inside collection Z, select collection Z, and then create the new collection.

To delete a collection, right-click it and click the Delete command.

Similarly, to rename a collection, right-click it and click the Rename command.

Although Windows Movie Maker lets you put clips and collections in other collections, that type of organization is not represented on your disk by files and folders in other folders. All of the clip files created by Windows Movie Maker go in the My Videos or My Audios folder; when you import clips, you may put them anywhere. Collections are represented not by folders, but by data in a special collections file that Windows Movie Maker maintains.

If the collections file is damaged, Windows Movie Maker "loses" some or all of your collections and clips. The clips may be right where they always were, but Windows Movie Maker can't find them. I had a lot of problems working with the collections backup feature and strongly suggest that you not rely on it for anything important. Your clips are safe — they're sitting in files that you can see and copy and store wherever you like. Your projects are safe, too. But, until Microsoft gets its act together, don't bet the farm on your collections. They may disappear on you one day.

Chapter 3: Discovering Digital Cameras and Video Devices

In This Chapter

✔ Choosing a Camera

✔ Photo Printing

✔ Windows Movie Maker

✔ Customizing Media Player

✔ Troubleshooting

*W*indows XP stands light years ahead of Microsoft's earlier operating systems in its ability to handle images. Most of its capabilities aren't really new, but XP makes many things easy that used to require a lot of technical knowledge and a lot of work.

In this chapter, you discover everything you need to know to choose a camera, hook it up with your PC, and move pictures from the camera to the PC, where you can store, edit, and print them, with just a couple of clicks.

Choosing a Camera

Before you can have fun with your images, of course, you need to get them into your computer. The following are several ways to do that:

✦ You can use a *conventional camera* to record images on film and then request the film processor to return the images to you on computer media. When I talk about conventional cameras in this book, I'm talking about the kind that produce images on regular, ol' everyday film. Silver halide.

✦ You can use a *digital camera* like the one in Figure 3-1 to record images in electronic memory and then transfer them into your computer. When I talk about digital cameras in this book, I mean a camera that produces images as files, one image at a time, and stores the files inside the camera.

Figure 3-1:
The 5.24 megapixel DSC-F707 Cybershot® digital camera from Sony, with Carl Zeiss™ Vario-Sonnar lens, Hologram AF laser focus assist, Multi-pattern metering and TTL pre-flash exposure control. Courtesy of Sony Electronics, Inc.

✦ You can use an *Internet camera* (a "Webcam") like the one in Figure 3-2 to feed live images directly into your computer and capture them as either still frames or movie clips. When I talk about Internet cameras here, I'm talking about the ones that have to be tethered to a computer. They have no capability to store images.

✦ You can use an analog or digital *video camera* (a "camcorder") like the one in Figure 3-3 to record movie clips on tape and then feed them into your computer from the camera or from a playback device. When I talk about video cameras in this book, I'm talking about the kind that internally store moving images.

Strictly speaking, Internet cameras are digital cameras. So are many video cameras. Then again, strictly speaking, Dummies are smart. But I digress.

Figure 3-2:
The SiPix iQuest DualCam is a full-featured USB video camera, video-conferencing camera, and digital camera all in one.

Understanding digital cameras

You use a digital camera just like a conventional one, but it records images in electronic memory, not on film. Instead of sending a roll of film to be processed and printed, you simply copy the images into your computer. Then you can erase the camera's memory and use it again.

Digital cameras have sorted themselves roughly into four categories:

✦ **Point-and-shoot cameras:** The simplest and least expensive type. Most point-and-shoot cameras have inexpensive lenses, often made of plastic, and often with no means of adjusting the focus. They're good for casual photography and for taking pictures to use on your personal Web site.

Figure 3-3:
CCD-TRV98
Sony Hi8™
Handycam™
Camcorder.
Courtesy of
Sony
Electronics,
Inc.

+ **Advanced viewfinder cameras:** More capable than point-and-shoots, and more expensive. Their design is essentially the same, but they have more features and use higher quality parts. For example, advanced viewfinder cameras have more sophisticated all-glass lenses and generally focus the lens automatically.

+ **Zoom-lens reflex (ZLR) cameras:** These cameras have a zoom lens that is permanently attached. The viewfinder's image is formed by the same lens that takes the picture, rather than by a separate optical system. Because these cameras are designed for advanced amateur photographers and professionals, they tend to offer better quality and more features than advanced viewfinder cameras.

+ **Single-lens reflex (SLR) cameras:** The most capable kind. And the most expensive. These cameras work like the ZLR cameras, but they feature interchangeable lenses. Many of them are based on conventional SLR cameras, adapted to use digital imaging instead of film.

This brief summary should give you a good idea of which type of camera is most appropriate for you, but it doesn't begin to cover the variety of features that camera makers have developed. Becoming a fully informed buyer in this market takes weeks of research.

Unless you enjoy learning obscure technical details, seek advice from a well-informed friend or a retailer whom you trust.

Resolution

A digital camera forms its image on a sensor that contains a square grid of tiny light-sensing areas called *pixels. Resolution* refers to the number of pixels the sensor has. The more pixels, the more detail the camera can record. The more detail, the larger a print you can make without the individual pixels becoming noticeable.

Here's a good rule to remember: A sensor with about 1 million pixels is good for a 5 x 7" print. At 2 million pixels, you can make a good 8 x 10" print. At 3 million pixels, you can make an 11 x 14" print.

Having more resolution than you need gives you leeway to crop out the unimportant parts of an image and still get a good quality print. Those extra pixels cost money, of course.

Zoom lens

A *zoom lens* lets you vary the angle of view that your camera takes in by increasing or decreasing the lens's magnification. Most advanced viewfinder cameras have this feature, as do all ZLRs and SLRs. The better ones cover a wider range. Most point-and-shoot cameras do not have a zoom lens.

The zoom lens feature is also known as *optical zoom.* Many cameras offer *digital zoom,* which simply enlarges an image by making each pixel bigger. Digital zoom isn't very useful. You can get the same result by enlarging the final image.

Focusing

Many point-and-shoot cameras have a lens with one or a few fixed focus settings that give reasonably good results over a range of distances. If you're looking at a camera with one setting for close-ups and another for general shots, you are dealing with a fixed-focus camera.

Better cameras adjust the focus automatically — they *auto-focus* — to give the sharpest result at any distance. Auto-focusing cameras generally can be held closer to the subject than fixed-focus ones: sometimes down to a few inches, which can be useful if you want to photograph small objects like flowers or coins.

As an added feature, some advanced cameras let you deal with special photo situations — where the auto-focus just doesn't work very well — by adjusting the focus manually. Typically, auto-focus has problems when the subject of the shot isn't at the middle of the picture; when the subject is very bright, very dark, or low-contrast; when you're taking the picture through glass or water; or when you want to emphasize a small part of a picture by giving it the sharpest focus — a small flower standing quite some distance in front of a face, for example.

Exposure control and flash

All digital cameras adjust the exposure automatically to suit different light levels. The better ones have more sophisticated circuits that produce good results under a wider range of conditions. Better cameras also give you some control over exposure, either by taking a picture that's lighter or darker than what the camera thinks is ideal, or by allowing you to set the exposure controls (the aperture and shutter speed, for those technically inclined) yourself.

Many cameras have a built-in electronic flash that fires automatically when needed. Better cameras have more powerful and flexible flashes, and offer you various types of control. You may be able to turn off the built-in flash and attach a separate electronic flash of your choice, for example.

Digital cameras are notorious for overly powerful or utterly wimpy flash systems — and far too frequently the same flash is too powerful under one set of lighting conditions and doesn't work worth squat under slightly different conditions. If you're willing to schlep around a standalone flash unit (called an *external flash*), look for a camera that has a *synchro-flash terminal* — a place to plug in and control a standalone flash. Using an external flash with simple techniques like bouncing (aiming the flash at a white ceiling or wall) can make a world of difference in the quality of your pictures, and in most cases the camera does all the work.

Image storage and transfer

Really inexpensive cameras store images in built-in memory. When the memory is full, you must transfer the images to your computer to make room for more. If you're at Grand Canyon and your computer is at home, this can be, uh, awkward.

Better cameras use removable memory media, often shaped like little cards. When one memory card fills up, you just pull it out and insert a new one. Different cameras use different types of memory cards; all of them work about equally well.

Most recent cameras have a USB interface for transferring images to your computer. USB is easy and fast, but the whole setup can be clumsy, especially if you want to plug your camera into the wall to avoid draining the batteries during file transfers.

If you buy a camera that uses memory cards, spend an extra $40 or so for a card reader that plugs into your computer's USB port. You can then slide the camera's memory card into the reader and treat it like any other disk drive. Or you can plug the camera's memory card into the reader, then plug the reader into a USB port or PCMCIA slot, and Windows XP will identify it immediately.

Plugging your camera's memory card into a USB or PCMCIA reader virtually eliminates compatibility problems (see the next section). More than that, you don't have to worry about the dog tripping over the camera's power cord or USB cable, knocking the camera off your desk. I know. My Beagle broke my Nikon Coolpix that way, and it cost hundreds of dollars to get it fixed. Blecch!

Compatibility

Windows XP provides direct support for many digital cameras, but not for all of them. If you happen to own a camera that Windows XP doesn't support, it's not a big deal; you may have to use the application provided with the camera to move pictures onto your PC, instead of the Scanner and Camera Wizard built in to Windows XP itself. If you're buying a new camera, though, direct support in Windows XP is a feature you should consider.

The cameras supported in Windows XP are identified in the Windows XP *hardware compatibility list.* I talk about compatibility extensively in Book VII, Chapter 1.

Look and feel

Yeah, cameras have look and feel, just like computer applications do. And it's important. The best camera in the world won't do you much good if you can't use it easily. If you're always pushing controls the wrong way, or you can't quite find a comfortable way to hold the camera when you're taking a shot, that camera isn't for you.

It's always wise to try out a camera in a quiet, unpressured environment before you buy it. And in case you miss something important, buy from a dealer who will let you exchange your purchase if you change your mind. For these reasons, buying from a reputable local dealer can be a good move, even if a discounter on the Web offers you a better price.

Using conventional cameras

If you don't want to buy a digital camera, you can take pictures with a conventional film camera and have the photofinisher digitize them. The photofinisher may return the digitized images to you on a CD-ROM or may post them on a secure Web site from which you can download them.

If you're a casual picture taker, this approach lets you get your pictures online without buying a new camera. If you're an advanced user, it may be attractive because the best film cameras still produce better results than the best digital cameras. By having the photofinisher do the digitizing, you get the best of both worlds: digital images for their ease-of-use, and negatives/positives for the highest quality results.

On the other hand, digitizing with a photofinisher is relatively slow, because you have to wait for the film to be processed. It is expensive, because you have to pay for film, processing, and digitizing. And you may have to change photofinishers to get the service.

Plugging Internet cameras

An Internet camera (also called a *Web camera* or *Webcam*) is like a little video camera designed to work only while attached to a computer. All Internet cameras nowadays come with USB interfaces.

Some people use Internet cameras to publish a continuous live video feed through a Web site. Popular feeds include pictures of fish in a tank, waves on a shore, burglars breaking into houses, and... uh, let's just leave it at that. Other popular uses are video conferencing and recording still pictures or short movie clips to include in e-mail.

Internet cameras are generally less expensive than digital picture-taking cameras, but are also more limited because they only work when plugged into an operating computer. Their resolution is low: typically 320 x 240 pixels (about 77,000 pixels, compared to 1 million pixels for a typical point-and-shoot camera). The better ones can go up to 640 x 480 pixels (about 300,000 pixels). The lens, image quality, and color accuracy are adequate for the camera's intended purpose, but may be poorer than a point-and-shoot camera.

If you want to get images into your computer quickly and easily, and you don't need high quality, an Internet camera may be just the thing for you. They're pretty darn cheap, to boot.

Consult the Windows XP hardware compatibility list before you buy an Internet camera. Windows XP may be unable to work with a camera that is not on the list. See the section "Compatibility" in this chapter for details.

Panning video cameras

If you have a video camera, you can transfer its recordings onto your computer. Depending on the type of camera you have, you may need additional hardware to connect the camera.

A video camera is an ideal tool for recording video that you will edit with Windows Movie Maker. It is less suitable for capturing still images. A video camera's resolution is much less than that of a comparable digital camera.

Moving Images to Your Computer

How you transfer images to your computer depends on the type of camera you're using.

If you're using a conventional camera and your images were scanned by the photofinisher, transferring images is easy: Simply put the CD-ROM in a handy CD drive and copy the files, or go to the photofinisher's Web site and follow its directions. Rocket science.

If you're using a video camera, the procedure depends on the type of camera and interface you use. There are so many different permutations and combinations, I won't try to cover them all here. If you're looking for answers, start with the camera manufacturer's Web site. See Table 3-1.

Table 3-1	Major camera manufacturer's Web sites
Manufacturer	*U.S. Web site*
Canon	www.canon.com
Intel	www.intel.com
Kodak	www.kodak.com
Logitech	www.Logitech.com
Minolta	www.minolta.com
Nikon	www.nikon.com
Olympus	www.olympus.com
Panasonic	www.panasonic.com
Philips	www.Philips.com
Sony	www.sony.com

You can use any one of three procedures to bring images from digital cameras and Internet cameras into your PC:

✦ With Internet cameras and digital cameras supported by Windows XP, the Windows XP Scanner and Camera Wizard is the simplest way.

✦ With any digital camera, you can use the file transfer application provided with that camera.

✦ With any digital camera that uses memory cards, you can transfer images by putting the card — most likely a SmartMedia or CompactFlash card — in a memory card reader.

Use the Scanner and Camera Wizard to transfer images stored in the memory of a digital camera to your PC or to capture still images from an Internet camera.

1. **Plug the camera into the appropriate port on your computer.**

If it's a digital camera, turn it on. You may have to move the camera's controls to some particular setting; consult the camera's instructions for transferring images.

2. **The Windows Scanner and Camera Wizard may start automatically at this point. If it doesn't, choose Start⇨My Pictures to display the contents of the My Pictures folder in Windows Explorer.**

When you start Windows Explorer this particular way, it displays some special *task lists* in its left pane, as shown in Figure 3-4.

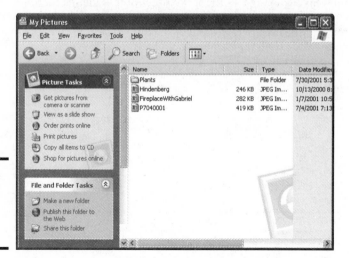

Figure 3-4: Windows Explorer with task lists.

3. **From the Picture Tasks list, choose Get Pictures from Camera or Scanner.**

This opens the dialog box shown in Figure 3-5. Select the icon that represents your camera, and then click OK. The wizard displays a welcome box.

4. **Click Next to display the dialog box shown in Figure 3-6.**

If you're connected to an Internet camera, the Preview panel shows the live image captured by the camera. Each time you click the Take Picture button, the wizard captures a still image. The images appear in the Pictures panel.

Figure 3-5:
The Select
Device
dialog box

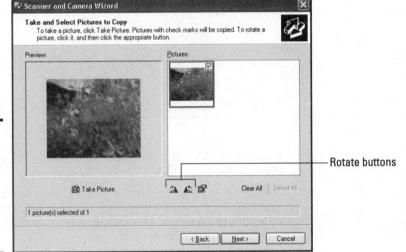

Figure 3-6:
Scanner
and Camera
Wizard,
Take and
Select
Pictures to
Copy.

Rotate buttons

If you're connected to a digital camera, the process is very similar, but the Pictures panel shows the pictures stored in the camera's memory.

If any of the pictures are not right-side up, you can rotate them. Click a picture to select it, and then click one of the "rotate" buttons under the Pictures pane to rotate the picture a quarter turn right, a quarter turn left, or a half turn.

Notice the small check box above each picture. Check the boxes for the pictures that you want to save and/or clear them for the pictures you don't want to save. You can use the Clear All and Save All buttons for convenience.

**Book VIII
Chapter 3**

Discovering Digital
Cameras and
Video Devices

5. **Click Next.**

   The wizard displays the dialog box shown in Figure 3-7.

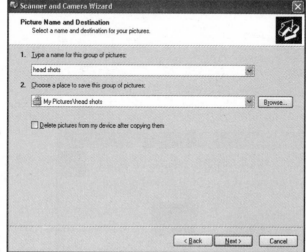

Figure 3-7:
Scanner
and Camera
Wizard,
Picture
Name and
Destination.

6. **In the Type a Name field, enter the name you want to give the first picture you're saving.**

   If you're saving several pictures, the wizard gives each one a unique name. For example, if the name you enter is "head shots" and you're saving three pictures, the wizard names the pictures "head shots," "head shots 001," and "head shots 002."

   The wizard automatically stores the pictures in the My Pictures folder, in a sub-folder with the name you entered. If you entered "head shots," for example, it stores the pictures in My Pictures\head shots. If you want a different folder, you can choose one with the Browse button or the Choose a Place drop-down list.

   Notice the check box labeled "Delete pictures from my device after copying them." If you're using a digital camera, this box deletes the pictures from the camera's memory. It deletes only the pictures that it transferred — that is, the ones you check marked in the wizard's previous box.

   If you're using an Internet camera, the camera has no memory, but the wizard gets the same result by keeping copies of the pictures itself. If you don't check the check box, the next time you use the wizard, the pictures you saved will still be in the Pictures pane. If you do check the check box, the next time you use the wizard, the pictures you saved will not be there.

7. **Click Next.**

   The wizard copies the pictures to the folder you chose and displays the dialog box shown in Figure 3-8.

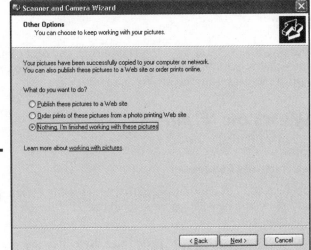

Figure 3-8:
Scanner
and Camera
Wizard,
Other
Options.

8. **Click the radio button for the operation you want to perform next. Then click Next.**

   The wizard displays a "farewell" screen.

   If you don't want to publish pictures or order prints now, you can still do those things at a later time.

9. **Click Finish.**

   The wizard closes itself and opens a Windows Explorer window showing the folder in which you just saved your pictures.

If Windows XP doesn't recognize your camera, the least-hassle alternative, by far, is a memory card reader. These cheap little devices plug into your computer's PCMCIA card slot or USB port. Simply stick your camera's memory card (probably a SmartCard or a Compact Flash card) into the card reader, and Windows XP thinks you have a new hard disk drive. Files on the camera's memory card are treated just like any picture files in Windows.

You may also want to try the software that shipped with the camera to transfer images from the camera to your PC. Most digital cameras come with such an application. Install the application and follow its instructions. Good luck.

If Windows XP *does* support your camera directly, you may still want to take a look at the camera's file-transfer application anyway. Many of these applications have additional functions that Windows XP does not provide, such as remotely setting some of the camera's controls.

Printing Pictures

Windows XP provides several ways to print photos and other images. If you have a photo-quality printer, you can use Windows XP's Photo Printing Wizard to print pictures from the My Pictures folder.

Printing with the Wizard

To use the Photo Printing Wizard:

1. **Choose Start⇨My Pictures.**

   This opens a copy of Windows Explorer with the My Pictures folder in the right pane and task list commands in the left pane (refer to Figure 3-4).

2. **Select the picture you want to print, and then click the wizard's Print This Picture command.**

   This starts the Photo Printing Wizard. "Print This Picture" replaces "Print Pictures," the command shown in Figure 3-4, when you select a picture. The wizard displays a "welcome" page. Ho hum.

3. **Click Next.**

   The wizard displays thumbnails of the pictures in the folder, as shown in Figure 3-9. Above each picture is a check box. The picture you selected has its box checked, indicating that this picture will be printed. You can check additional pictures to make the wizard print more than one at a time.

4. **Click Next.**

   The wizard displays a panel of printing options, as shown in Figure 3-10.

   This panel lets you select the printer to use (if you have more than one printer). The Printing Preferences button opens a dialog box that lets you set options such as the type of paper you're printing on, the level of print quality you want, and whether to print in black-and-white or color. The options displayed depend on the type of printer you have.

5. **Click Next.**

   The wizard displays a page that lets you select a layout and set the number of times to print each picture (see Figure 3-11).

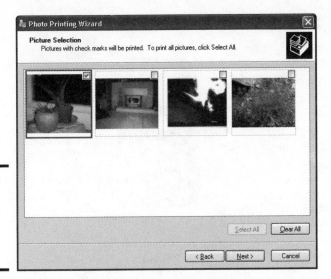

Figure 3-9:
Photo
Printing
Wizard,
Picture
Selection.

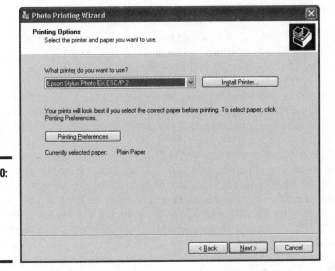

Figure 3-10:
Photo
Printing
Wizard,
Printing
Options.

You can choose among a full-page layout (one print per page) and several options that put two or more smaller pictures on a page. The latter options are useful if you selected several images or told the wizard to print a picture more than once.

6. **Click Next.**

The wizard displays a panel with a progress bar while it prints and then displays a panel that says it is finished.

Figure 3-11:
Photo
Printing
Wizard,
Layout
Selection.

7. **Click Finish to close the wizard.**

The Windows Explorer View menu lets you select several different views of your pictures. The Thumbnails view and the Filmstrip view are particularly useful. Try both to see which you prefer.

The plain old Details view is not quite so plain in the My Pictures folder. It displays some additional information that you may find useful: the date each picture was taken, if recorded, and the dimensions of the picture in pixels.

When your pictures are in the My Pictures folder, you can organize them any way you want. For example, you can put them in one folder for "Vacations," one for "The Kids," one for "Blackmail" (just kidding), and so forth. You can create two or more levels of folders if you want. As long as you keep your folders inside the My Pictures folder, they inherit the My Pictures folder's task lists, and they show the same additional information in the Details view.

If you want to share a bunch of pictures across your network, put them in a separate folder and drag them to the Shared Pictures folder.

Advanced printing software

The Photo Printing Wizard is okay for making an unmodified print of an entire picture. But suppose you want to print just part of a family portrait to omit the rude gesture one of your kids was making? Or suppose the light in your back yard made Aunt Gertrude's face look a little green, and you want to make the color balance more flattering? Want to chop your ex's head off? It's easier than you think.

The wizard can't do those things, but many commercial photo printing programs can. If you're interested in capabilities like these, look into programs like Adobe PhotoShop (the professional's choice), Microsoft Picture-It, PaintShop Pro, MGI Software's PhotoSuite, and Ulead PhotoImpact. See Table 3-2 for some URL listings.

Table 3-2	Commercial Photo Printing Programs
Program	*URL*
Photoshop	www.adobe.com/products/photoshop/main.html
Picture-It	http://pictureitproducts.msn.com/default.asp
PaintShop Pro	www.jasc.com
PhotoSuite	www.photosuite.com
Ulead PhotoImpact	www.ulead.com/pi/runme.htm

Printing via the Web

You can send your pictures to a service that makes prints on standard photographic paper and mails them back to you. The convenience is unbeatable, and the quality of the prints can be better than a photo-quality printer provides. And some services can do things that a photo-quality printer can't — such as printing poster-size pictures, or printing on coffee mugs.

Such services predate Windows XP, but Windows XP adds a new level of convenience: You can access a service right from Windows itself.

To see how this works:

1. **Choose Start⇨My Pictures.**

2. **Open a sub-folder that contains some pictures you want to print.**

   If you don't want to print pictures now, open any sub-folder. You can explore the process without committing yourself or spending any cash.

3. **Click the Order Prints Online command in the Picture Tasks list.**

   This starts the Online Print Ordering Wizard. The wizard first displays a Welcome dialog box.

4. **Click Next to display the dialog box shown in Figure 3-12.**

   The dialog box in Figure 3-12 lists the pictures in the folder you chose. A check box next to each picture's name indicates whether you want to order prints of that picture.

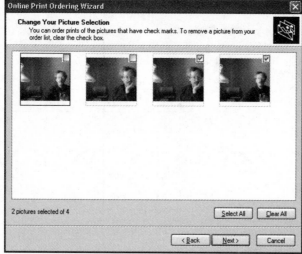

Figure 3-12:
Online Print
Ordering
Wizard,
Change Your
Picture
Selection.

5. **Check and clear the boxes to select the pictures that you want to print. Then Click Next.**

   The wizard displays the dialog box shown in Figure 3-13. This dialog box lists companies whose printing services are now available through the wizard.

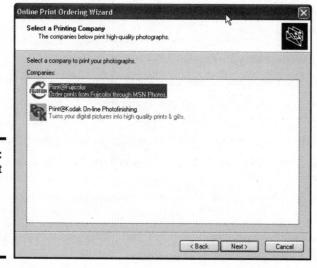

Figure 3-13:
Online Print
Ordering
Wizard,
Select a
Printing
Company.

6. **Select the company that you prefer and click Next.**

   At this point, the printing service's Web server takes over, so the details of the process depend on which service you chose. Each of them leads you through a sequence of pages in which you select the services you want, give your address, and arrange to pay.

Sharing Your Pictures with Others

When you have some nice pictures on your computer, naturally you want to share them with other interested people. You can share in several ways.

E-mail

People frequently send picture files as *attachments* to e-mail. See your mail reader's documentation for instructions on how to do this. If you use a Web-based mail service, check the Web site's help pages.

If you're using Outlook Express, you can find full details in Book III, Chapter 2.

Many Internet service providers and Web-based mail services limit the amount of data that you may attach to a message. The limits vary but are typically in the range of half a megabyte to a few megabytes. Most single picture files are small enough to send, but such a limit may restrict the number of pictures you can attach to one message.

CD-ROM

If you have a CD writer, you can easily copy pictures to CDs. A CD has enough space to hold several hundred or even thousand pictures.

To burn pictures on your CD-R or CD-RW drive, see Book I, Chapter 5.

In a pinch, you can use diskettes for lower-quality pictures. Don't expect to get more than a handful of pictures on one diskette, though — fewer if you have high-quality shots. Remember that a floppy can hold only 1.44 MB of data.

A Web site

Many Internet service providers maintain Web sites where their subscribers can post personal material. You can use such a Web site to "publish" your pictures. Anyone who knows where to look can see them, of course, which you may or may not consider a good thing.

Check your service provider's Web site for information about its file hosting policies and instructions for uploading files.

You can also find independent services that provide Web hosting services at little or no cost. One of the free ones is at `http://familyinternet.about.com`.

Photo-hosting Web sites

Some organizations don't necessarily offer Internet access, but make a business of publishing other people's files for them on the Web. Different organizations offer different types of service.

One of the most interesting services is photo hosting. A photo hosting service typically lets you upload your pictures to a private area on its Web site. You then can choose the people who may have access to your area.

Most photo hosting services are inexpensive or free. They count on making money from some combination of advertising and selling photo printing services to the people who come to look at your pictures.

Three such services you can check out are at:

✦ Microsoft's own `www.msn.com`

✦ `www.myfamily.com`

✦ `www.webshots.com`

The Windows Web Publishing Wizard

Windows XP has a wizard for uploading pictures and documents to Microsoft's Web site `www.msn.com` (and certain other Web sites). If you choose `www.msn.com` as your photo hosting service, the wizard is a particularly convenient way to upload your photos.

Funny thing about that.

To use the uploading wizard, choose Start⇨My Pictures (refer to Figure 3-8), find the File and Folder Tasks list (below Picture Tasks), and click the Publish File to the Web command. The wizard prompts you to select the file(s) you want to upload and then the service provider to which you want to upload them. When you select the service provider "MSN" for the first time, it requires you to register. There's no charge for this, but Uncle Bill's MSN will want information about you.

Setting a Picture as Desktop Background

The Desktop background is the picture that Windows XP displays when no other windows are open. See Book II, Chapter 1, for details.

Setting your own picture as the Desktop background is easy. First, click the picture in the My Pictures folder. Then, from the Picture Tasks list, choose Set as Desktop Background. You won't see anything happen, but the next time you expose the desktop, your picture will be there.

If your picture's dimensions (in pixels) are no more than half those of the screen, Windows XP tries to fill the screen with as many copies of the picture as necessary. This technique is called *tiling*. Otherwise, Windows XP stretches or shrinks the picture to fit the Desktop.

Setting the background with Paint

Windows Paint can make a picture the Desktop background too, and it gives you the option of tiling a small picture or fitting a single copy of it to the Desktop. Here's how:

1. **Choose Start⇨All Programs⇨Accessories⇨Paint to start Windows Paint.**

2. **Choose File⇨Open. Use the Open dialog box to display the folder that contains the picture you want to use. Hold the mouse cursor over the entry for the picture until a popup appears displaying the picture's dimensions, type, and size. Note the type and then open the picture.**

   If the picture's type is Bitmap Image, skip to Step 5. Otherwise, proceed to Step 3.

3. **You must save the picture as a bitmap image. Choose File⇨Save As.**

   Paint opens a Save As dialog box.

4. **From the Save As Type drop-down list, choose one of the Bitmap options, depending on the number of colors you want your Desktop background to have. Click Save.**

   Paint saves the picture in a new file with the filename extension `.bmp`.

5. **To fit a copy of the picture to the Desktop, choose File⇨Set As Background (Centered). To tile the picture, choose File⇨Set As Background (Tiled). Note that if you tile a picture that is bigger than the Desktop, the Desktop will display only part of it.**

Don't delete the .bmp file as long as you're using that picture as background. Windows XP needs it to display the background.

A tiled background picture looks best if its dimensions go evenly into the display's dimensions. For example, a tiled background on a 1280 x 1024 display might use a 640 x 480 picture (2 x 2 tiles) or a 320 x 240 picture (4 x 4 tiles).

Book VIII
Chapter 3

Discovering Digital
Cameras and
Video Devices

Most commercial picture editors allow you to change a picture's dimensions. Windows Paint can do this too, although the procedure is awkward:

1. **Start Paint and choose File⇨Open command. Use the Open dialog box to display the folder that contains the picture you want to use. Hold the mouse cursor over the entry for the picture until the popup appears. Note the dimensions and then open the picture.**

2. **Choose Image⇨Stretch/Skew. This command opens the dialog box shown in Figure 3-14, which lets you change the picture's dimensions.**

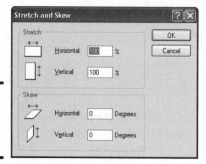

Figure 3-14:
The Stretch
and Skew
dialog box.

Stretch/Skew asks you to enter the *percentages* by which you want to change the picture's dimensions. For example, suppose the picture's current dimensions, which you noted from the popup, are 800 x 600, and you want the picture to fit a 320 x 240 tile. To reduce the horizontal dimension from 800 to 320 you must change it to 320 / 800 = 0.4, or 40 percent. To reduce the vertical dimension from 600 to 240 you must change it to 240 / 600 = 0.4, or 40 percent.

3. **Enter the percentage changes for the horizontal and vertical dimensions. Do not enter anything in the "skew" part of the dialog box. Click OK.**

4. **Use File⇨Save As to save the file as a bit map, as in the first procedure in this section. If the file is already a bitmap, change the file's name to avoid losing the old file when you save the new one.**

    If the file's type is Bitmap Image you *can* use File⇨Save instead of File⇨Save As, but this is not recommended. Reducing the size of a Bitmap Image reduces the amount of detail it contains, and if you later increase the size again, the lost detail is not recovered. A similar loss may occur if you increase the size of the file, then later reduce it again.

5. **Choose one of the File⇨Set As Background commands, as in the first procedure in this section.**

Setting the background with the Control Panel

Using the Control Panel to set the background has the advantage of letting you set any of Microsoft's predefined backgrounds or no background at all (an unadorned white screen):

1. **Choose Start➪Control Panel.**

2. **Choose Appearance and Themes; then pick the task marked Change the Desktop Background.**

3. **Select the Desktop tab. It looks like Figure 3-15.**

Figure 3-15:
The Display
Properties
dialog box,
Desktop tab.

4. **Click the background you want. To choose a plain white background, scroll to the top of the list and click None. To choose a picture of your own, click Browse. Use the Browse dialog box to select the picture you want; then click OK.**

5. **Use the Position drop-down list to select the way you want to position the picture on the desktop.**

The Desktop tab gives you *three* positioning choices. *Center* actually centers the image on the Desktop; if the image is smaller than the Desktop, it is surrounded by borders in the background color. (Set the background color with the Color dropdown list.) *Tile* tiles the images. *Stretch* stretches the image to fit the Desktop.

6. **Click OK.**

7. **Close the Control Panel window.**

Windows Movie Maker

Don't neglect Windows Movie Maker (see Book VIII, Chapter 2) as a picture tool.

You can import your still pictures into Windows Movie Maker with the File menu's Import command for use in movies. You also can use it to capture a still picture from an Internet camera or from the images recorded in a video camera for use in movies or for any other purpose.

Troubleshooting

Here are some suggestions to try if you have a problem with one of the procedures described in this chapter:

✦ *I plugged my camera into the computer, but the Scanner and Camera Wizard doesn't believe it's there.*

Be sure the cable is secure at both ends, the camera is turned on, and its batteries are charged.

If your camera's controls must be set a certain way to permit a transfer, be sure they are set.

If you haven't used this camera with Windows XP before, be sure it's on the Windows XP hardware compatibility list. If it isn't, install and use the file transfer application provided with the camera.

✦ *I displayed the My Pictures folder in Windows Explorer, but the left pane doesn't show the Picture Tasks list — just the usual map of my folders.*

Exit Windows Explorer and start it again directly from the Start menu. (Choose Start⇨My Pictures.) This is the easiest way to make it display the Picture Tasks list.

✦ *My pictures look pretty good on the screen, but when I print them they look awful.*

The quality of many color inkjet printers leaves a lot to be desired, but there are some things you can do that may help.

Use the highest quality settings available: Superior will produce a much better image than Normal.

Use an appropriate paper. Paper formulated for printing photos on inkjet printers is best. Any coated (glossy) paper is likely to work better than ordinary printer paper. Photo quality paper produces the best results of all.

Be sure you have a photo printer. Many older color inkjet printers are designed for printing things like business charts, with large areas of solid color. They can't handle the subtle gradations of a photograph very well.

✦ ***This is fascinating, and I want more information about one of the topics you discussed.***

See the answer to the next question.

✦ ***I'm totally confused!***

Lots of information about digital photography is available on the Internet.

 One good place to start looking is www.zdnet.com. Enter a topic like "digital camera" in the Search dialog box and see what the site comes up with. For easy-to-read background information, look for the "Quick Start guides." You can also pick up the latest edition of *Digital Photography For Dummies* (published by Hungry Minds, Inc.).

 You can find more sources of information through your favorite Web search engine by searching on keywords like "digital photography tutorial." If you don't have a favorite search engine, try www.google.com.

Index

Book IX

Setting Up a Network with Windows XP

The 5th Wave   By Rich Tennant

"We take network security very seriously here."

Contents at a Glance

Chapter 1: Those Pesky Network Things You Have to Know

In This Chapter

✔ Why you really *do* want a network, at the office and at home

✔ Client/server (domain) and peer-to-peer (workgroup) networking

✔ What you need to get started

✔ Networking for Neanderthals

W hen business people talk to each other, it's called networking.

When computers talk to each other, it's called pandemonium.

This chapter tries to distill 25 years of advances in computer pandemonium, er, networking into a succinct, digestible, understandable synopsis. I think you'll be pleasantly surprised to discover that even the most obnoxiously inscrutable networking jargon — much of which has made its way into Windows XP — has its roots in simple concepts that everyone can understand.

Understanding Networks

Not long ago, networks were considered esoteric and intimidating, the province of guys in white lab coats, whose sole purpose in life was to allow you to print on the company's fancy laser printer or share that super-fast Internet connection but keep you from seeing your boss's personnel file or the company's budget. Those same guys (and they were always guys, it seems) often took it upon themselves to tell you what you could and couldn't do with your PC — what software you could use, how you could use it, where you could put your data, and so much more. They hid behind a cloak of mumbo-jumbo, initiates in the priesthood of "systems administration."

That's changed a lot. With Windows XP, a network is something that your 13-year-old can throw together in ten minutes. Mine did. (Your results may vary!)

The terminology doesn't help. Ask a network geek — or computer store salesperson — about the difference between a LAN and a WAN, and you'll provoke a tirade of inscrutable acronyms so thick that you need a periscope to see out.

Let's cut through the bafflegab.

What a network can do for you

Do you need a network?

The short answer: yes. If you have two or more computers, with one running Windows XP and the other running Windows 98 or later, a network is well worth the hassle. You don't need a fancy one. But you do need one. Consider these facts:

✦ If you have a network, just about any piece of hardware attached to one computer can be used by the other. That CD-ROM drive on your desktop, for example, can be used by your portable, the same way as if it were connected directly. A printer or scanner attached to one computer can be shared by all computers.

✦ All of your computers can use one, single Internet connection. With *ICS* (Internet Connection Sharing), you don't need to pay for two Internet accounts or run two connections (over the phone, or via DSL or cable modem) at the same time. If everybody is downloading huge files at the same time, you'll feel the performance hit, of course, but in most normal circumstances you won't notice at all. And, yes, ICS works well in Windows XP. Very well.

✦ You can use Windows XP's features on data from other machines, regardless of whether they're running XP. For example, with Windows XP's Explorer, you can view pictures stored on a networked computer as a slide show, even if the pictures are stored on a computer running Windows 98. You can burn a CD with XP's built-in CD burning support, using data from any computer on your network. Even the Windows XP Media Player can work with sounds and video clips from other machines.

✦ The easiest, fastest, most reliable way to back up data is to copy it from the hard drive on one machine to the hard drive in another machine on the network.

✦ You can share documents, pictures, music — just about anything — between the networked computers, with practically no effort. Although very few applications allow you to share individual files simultaneously — Word won't let two people on two different machines edit the same document at the same time, for example — sharing data on networked machines is still much simpler.

TECHNICAL STUFF

What's a LAN?

So much baffling terminology is floating around that any excursion outside of this book is bound to leave your head reeling. It's a jungle out there. One acronym you hear over and over again is *LAN*, short for *Local Area Network*. What's a LAN? Well, it's a ... network. Just a plain, old everyday network — the kind that the computer geeks put together at the office, or the kind you build with Windows XP. The kind I talk about in this chapter.

You can hook together more than one network and give the resulting paired-up network a different name, such as *WAN* (a *Wide Area Network*) or *VLAN* (a *Virtual Local Area Network*). A few years ago that kind of distinction made some sense, because the hardware boxes that you needed in order to hook together two (or more) networks were a little bit different from the plain-vanilla network boxes. But, over time, the differences are fading and the linguistic distinctions start sounding like William Safire arguing with himself.

Forget the terminology. A network is a network is a network. If you hook together computers, you have a network. If you unhook 'em, you don't. Whether you have a LAN, a VLAN, a WAN, a VPN, an Intranet, or a DUN connection to an L2TP-tunneled RAS server running IP over a hot-switched router doesn't really make much difference when you're sitting behind a PC, trying to get your work done.

How a network networks

All you really need to know about networks you learned in kindergarten:

✦ Good computers talk to each other over a network. If your computer is on a network, it can play with other computers on the same network. If your computer is not on a network, it can only sit in the corner and play by itself.

✦ You can see all the computers on your network by looking at Mr. Roger's... uh, at Start⇨My Network Places.

✦ Every computer in a network has its own name — actually, it's a number called an *IP address* — and all the names (er, numbers) are different. That's how computers keep track of each other.

✦ You can share stuff on your computer. You have two different ways to share. The way you share depends on how the network — uh, kindergarten class — is organized:

  • If you have a really mean teacher (called a *network administrator*), she decides what can be shared. When other kids want to borrow your stuff, they usually have to ask the teacher. I don't talk about this kind of network very much, because the teacher makes most of the decisions. Details are in the next section, "Organizing Networks."

- On the other hand, if the kids are in charge of sharing, each kid can share his stuff in one of two ways. He can put the stuff that he wants to share in a special place that's called *Shared* (such as Shared Documents or Shared Music); or he can tell the computer to just go ahead and share the stuff (using a shared folder, shared drive, or a shared printer).

✦ Your network can share with other networks, just like kids in your class can share with kids in other classes. The Internet is the biggest class of all. Yippie!

✦ Unfortunately, some creeps are in other classes, and they may want to take things from you or share something that will hurt you. You have to protect yourself.

When you run into trouble, the advice you hear over and over again (especially in the Windows XP Help and Support Center) is "talk to your teacher" uh "contact your system administrator." That advice is every bit as useless now as it was when you were five.

When networks work right — which they do about 90 percent of the time in Windows XP — they really are simple.

Organizing Networks

If you want to understand an abstract computer concept, nothing works better than a solid analogy. I use lots of them in this book: A document is like a sheet of paper; a CPU is like a car engine; a modem is like a high-tech hearing aid with a pronounced stutter set to "max" at a Nine Inch Nails concert. You know what I mean.

That's the problem with networks. No really good analogies exist. Yes, you can say that a server is like a gatekeeper, or a hub is like a collection of tap-dancing monkeys at a hyperactive organ-grinder's convention, but all of the analogies fall flat in short order. Why? Because networks are different from what you experience, day to day.

So without benefit of a good analogy, let's forge ahead.

Understanding servers and serfs

There are two fundamentally different kinds of networks. They both use the same basic kind of hardware — cables, boxes, interface cards, and so on. They both talk the same basic kind of language — Ethernet and something called TCP/IP, usually, but a few renegades speak in tongues. They differ primarily on a single, crucial philosophical point.

In one kind of network, a leader, a top-dog PC, controls things. The leader is called (you guessed it) a *server*. I still get shivers down my spine at the Orwellian logic of it all. In this kind of network, the lowly serf PCs are called *clients*. Thus, this type of network gets the moniker *client/server*. If you've ever wondered how in the realm of the English language a "client" could be all that much different from a "server," now you know: In the topsy-turvy world of PC networking terminology, a server is really a master.

In the other kind of network, all the pigs, er, PCs are created equal. No single PC dominates — perhaps I should say *serves* — all the others. Rather, the PCs maintain an equal footing. This kind of network is called, rather appropriately, *peer-to-peer*, which sounds veddy British to me. Eh, wot?

Introducing client/server

Client/server networks have one PC, called a server, that's figuratively "on top" of all the others. Figure 1-1 shows a logical diagram of a client/server network. It's important that you not take the diagram too seriously: It only shows the way client PCs are subservient to the server. It doesn't show you how to hook up a network.

Client PCs have some autonomy in a client/server network, but not a whole lot. And a bit of leeway exists in how much security a specific network or server enforces — some less-secure networks may allow Guest accounts, for example, that don't require passwords. But by and large, client/server networks are set up to be secure. They exist to allow computers (and users and peripherals) to talk to each other. But strict limits are rigorously enforced on what individual users can do, where they can go, and what they can see.

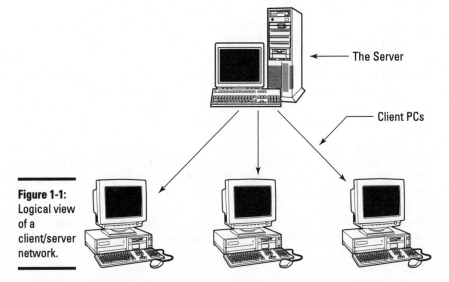

The Server

Client PCs

Figure 1-1:
Logical view
of a
client/server
network.

Microsoft introduced a new umbrella security system in Windows 2000 Server called Active Directory. It's designed to put control of all client/server security activities in one place. Active Directory is a very complex program — a world unto its own. If you have trouble talking to your network administrator in simple English, you may take some solace in the fact that he has to talk to Active Directory, and the translation can be challenging. The African "click" languages pale in comparison.

In general, you want to use Windows XP/Pro if you're on a client/server network. Yes, you can set up an XP/Home computer to work on a client/server network. No, it isn't worth the effort — or added expense.

In this book, I don't talk about client/server networks (Microsoft calls them *domains*) very much, simply because you don't have much control over them. If you use a client/server network, chances are good that somebody else in your company made the decision to go with client/server. They probably installed your copy of Windows XP — most likely XP/Pro — or bought a new machine rigged to their specifications and configured it to work with your company's network. They also get to fix things when your network connection goes bump in the night. Poetic justice, sez I.

I have to talk about client/server from time to time, though, for three big reasons:

✦ You may have an existing client/server network that you want to convert to peer-to-peer. Many Dummies (I'll raise my hand here) installed Windows NT or Windows 2000 client/server networks in their homes or offices, and they're tired of the constant hassles. They need to understand enough about client/server to get rid of it.

✦ You may actually need some of the features that client/server offers and not know it. In that case, you are better off to bite the bullet now and get client/server going, instead of struggling with peer-to-peer as an unintentional stopgap.

✦ Client/server is the original form of networking (at least in the business environment; we can argue about academia some other time). As such, many networking concepts — and much of the obscure terminology — originated in the client/server cauldron.

Administrator accounts on client computers can make major changes to the client PC in question, but the real action is on the server. If you really want to change things around, you need an Administrator account on the server. That's the seat of power in the client/server milieu.

In a client/server network, the network's Internet connection is (almost) always controlled through the server, using the following:

✦ **Windows Proxy Server:** A *proxy server* is a program that allows all the people on a network to share one Internet connection and, at the same time, acts as a *firewall*. A firewall monitors data as it passes between your network and the Internet, acting as a security barrier.

✦ **Microsoft Internet Security and Acceleration Server:** This is a souped-up, extra-charge proxy server.

✦ **Other proxy servers:** Many proxy servers are made by companies other than Microsoft. Ositis Software's WinProxy, for example, is used in many companies to protect their client/server networks. (See www.winproxy.com. WinProxy works on peer-to-peer networks, too.)

Introducing peer-to-peer

On the other side of the networking fence sits the undisciplined, rag-tag, scruffy lot involved in peer-to-peer computing. In a peer-to-peer environment, all computers are created equal, and security takes a back seat to flexibility.

I like peer-to-peer (see Figure 1-2). Could you tell?

At different times, in different places, Microsoft calls peer-to-peer networks by the following names:

✦ Workgroups and/or workgroup networks

✦ Small office networks and/or small business networks

✦ Home networks

The Windows XP Help and Support Center also, on occasion, refers to peer-to-peer networks as, uh, peer-to-peer networks. They all mean the same thing.

Traditionally, client/server networks (see the preceding section) dangled all of the shared peripherals off the server. Five years ago, your office's big laser printer was probably connected directly to the server. The massive bank of two-gigabyte hard drives no doubt lived on the server, too. Even today, you hear reference to *print servers* and *file servers* in hushed tones, as if only the server itself were capable of handling such massive processing demands.

Nowadays, you can buy a laser printer out of petty cash — although you better have a line in the budget for toner and paper — and 100 gigabyte hard drives fit on the head of a pin. Well, almost.

Peer-to-peer networks dispense with the formality of centralized control. Every authorized Administrator on a particular PC — and most users are Administrators; see Book I, Chapter 2 — can designate any drive, any folder, or any piece of hardware on that PC as shared, and thus make it accessible to anyone else on the network.

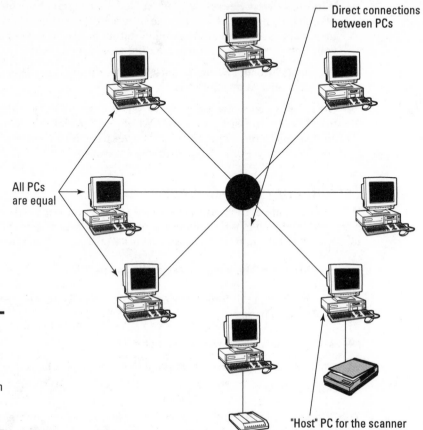

Direct connections between PCs

All PCs are equal

"Host" PC for the scanner

Figure 1-2:
Peer-to-peer networks don't rely on a single super-PC.

In a peer-to-peer network (a *workgroup*), any Administrator on a given PC can share anything on that PC. If you're the least bit concerned about security, that fact should give you pause, high blood pressure, and intense anxiety attacks. Not to mention apoplexy. Say you set up a home office network using the standard XP/Home settings. The network that is installed is a peer-to-peer network, with no passwords. That means anyone can walk up to a Welcome sign-on screen, click one of the user names, and immediately designate every drive as shared. The entire process would take less than 30 seconds. From that point on, anybody who can get to any of the computers on the network would have full control over all of the files on the shared drive — anybody can read, change, even delete them permanently, without the benefit of the Recycle Bin.

The primary distinguishing factor among PCs in a peer-to-peer network lies in the shared hardware hanging off an individual PC. Refer to Figure 1-2, for example, and you see that only one PC has a scanner attached to it.

Although you may be tempted to call this machine "The PC with the Scanner Hanging off of It," in general parlance you hear the PC referred to as the scanner's *host*.

Peer-to-peer networks are far more adaptable (computer nerds would say "more robust") than their client/server cousins because they don't rely on any single PC to keep running. In a peer-to-peer network, if the laser printer's host PC breaks down, you only need to schlep the printer over to a different PC and install it. You can immediately begin using the printer from any PC in the network. (If auto detect kicks in properly, it's particularly simple: You only need to change the printer in the File⇨Print dialog box.) In a client/server network, if the server PC breaks down, you can probably kiss your weekend goodbye.

For many people, *Internet Connection Sharing* (ICS) alone pays for the expense of setting up a network. With ICS, only one PC in the peer-to-peer network connects directly to the Internet, and that one connection is shared, equally and transparently, among all the PCs on the network. The ICS host takes care of all the details.

To the outside world, ICS appears as if you have just one PC connected to the Internet — and it sits behind a big, scary firewall to fend off would-be attackers. To little Johnny, who's using the PC in his bedroom to download massive full-color pictures of anatomically correct Pokemon figures, his Internet connection works just like it always did: slow and cantankerous, with frequent dropped connections and unexplained outages. But at least everybody in the family gets bumped off the Internet at the same time.

At various times in various places, Microsoft calls the PC running Internet Connection Sharing an *ICS host* and/or a *gateway*. Both names mean the same thing. Microsoft also insists on (sporadically) calling certain computers *ICS clients* if they're connected to an ICS host via a peer-to-peer network, even though the term *client* means something quite different in client/server networking. Like I said, networking terminology is all over the map.

Comparing the p-pro's and c-con's

If you need to decide between installing a client/server network (Microsoft calls it a *domain*) and a peer-to-peer network (*workgroup* in MS-speak), you should read the two preceding sections for an overview of how each works, and then weigh each of these factors:

✦ The *C* in client/server stands for complicated, cumbersome, and costly. You, or someone you hire, will spend a lot of time setting up a client/server network. If you have a small network with few employees and one or two applications, you know precisely what machines will be performing which tasks, and you know who needs access to what information and where it's stored, a real pro with extensive Active Directory experience can probably set up your client/server network in half a day. Beyond that, the sky's the limit — and plan on getting your network consultant's home telephone number, because you're going to need it every time you get a new employee, install a new computer, or maybe even begin using a new application.

✦ Client/server networks can handle enormous volumes of data. High-end servers can juggle hundreds (or even thousands) of client PCs, with data transmission speeds that would bring tears to a lowly peer-to-peer network's eyes. The server can take on additional functions, such as handling e-mail for the entire network (most likely using Exchange Server, another cantankerous Microsoft product that's chock full of features). Data backup and other maintenance tasks that would be a nightmare to coordinate over a peer-to-peer network are all localized. In some client/server networks, applications (such as Microsoft Office) run from the server, so upgrades involve only one copy of the application, not hundreds of copies.

✦ The *P* in peer-to-peer stands for powerful, painless, and potentially embarrassing. You can have your network up and running in hours — and most of that time will be sweating over cables, interface cards, and other hardware that doesn't work right the first time. When it's up, the network will be reliable and easy to use — and as exposed as a lobster in a glass tank. Unless you go to the trouble of setting up passwords and protecting folders with sensitive data (using the techniques described in Book I, Chapter 2), anybody who can sit down at a PC can make all of the PC's contents available to anyone on the network, at any time.

✦ If you try to install and maintain a client/server network yourself — even with helper tools such as Microsoft's Small Business Server — be aware of the fact that it's not nearly as simple as the marketing brochures would have you believe. Many Dummies, this one included, feel that installing and maintaining your own client/server network rates as a low-benefit, high-commitment time sink of the first degree.

Someday, secure networks will be easy to set up and use. That day hasn't arrived yet. Although peer-to-peer networking in Windows XP (specifically XP/Home) has made simple networking a reality, truly secure networks — and really big networks — are still the province of guys in white lab coats.

Making Computers Talk

Getting computers to talk to each other can be as simple as buying a box and some cables and plugging it all together like you do with telephones — or as painful, expensive and hair-challenging (as in pulling it out by the roots) as any computer pursuit you've ever encountered.

In this section, I step you through the details of setting up a simple, traditional peer-to-peer network with interface cards in each PC, a *hub* (which is an incredibly dumb switch), and a bunch of cable.

After you see the basics, I step you through some of the newer technologies. I don't go into depth on any of the new technologies for three reasons:

✦ As of this writing, none of them work very reliably. That will change, although it isn't yet clear which technologies are going to iron themselves out and which are going to die on the vine.

✦ As of this writing, they're all quite expensive. That, too, will change.

✦ Every manufacturer does things differently. You have to *RTLM* (Read The Lousy Manual — that's a technical term, folks) to get it to work right.

For details on actually assembling a network — choosing hardware components, installing and testing them, and then getting Windows XP to recognize the network — see Book IX, Chapter 2.

Understanding Ethernet

The easiest, fastest, cheapest, most reliable, and most secure way to hook up a peer-to-peer network is also the oldest, least flexible, and most boring. If you want sexy, look somewhere else. If you want an old workhorse, hey, have I got a horse for you: It's called *Ethernet* (see Figure 1-3), and it works like a champ.

Ethernet really isn't that complicated. In the early 1970s, Bob Metcalfe came up with an interesting new way to connect Xerox Alto computers. He called the technique *EtherNet*. The name stuck, give or take a capital *N*. So did the technology. By modern standards, Ethernet isn't very sophisticated:

✦ All the PCs on a network watch messages going over a wire.

✦ When PC *A* wants to talk to PC *B*, it shoots a message out on the wire, saying something like, "Hey, B, this is A," followed by the message.

✦ PC *B* sees the message on the wire and retrieves it.

Hard to believe, but with a few minor tweaks — like what happens when two PCs try to send messages at the same time, so that they're talking over the top of each other — that's really all there is to Ethernet.

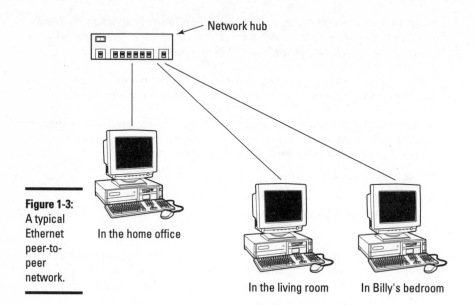

Network hub

Figure 1-3:
A typical
Ethernet
peer-to-
peer
network.

In the home office

In the living room   In Billy's bedroom

Even harder to believe: PCs using plain, old Ethernet can send and receive messages at the rate of 10 Mbps, or 10,000,000 bits per second. (By comparison, a 56K modem, under the best possible circumstances, receives data at 56,000 bits per second.) Things slow down if many PCs are trying to talk to each other at the same time — they start talking over the top of each other — but for a typical peer-to-peer network, 10 Mbps (also called 10Base-T) works great.

Ethernet relies on a hub — a box — and cables running from the hub to each PC. The PCs need network cards, so you have a place to stick the cables. The PCs can be using Windows 98 (any flavor), Windows ME, or Windows 2000. Plug it all together, run the Windows XP Home Networking Wizard on your XP machine(s), run a special program that XP sticks on a floppy on the other machines, and your network is ready to use.

That's the theory, anyway. Surprisingly, at least 90 percent of the time, it works. I go into all the details in the next chapter.

A faster version of Ethernet (called, uh, Fast Ethernet, or 100Base-T) works at 100 Mbps. If you're tying together newer PCs, chances are good that Fast Ethernet won't cost much more than UnFast Ethernet. The only significant advantage I've seen to Fast Ethernet occurs when you have a fast Internet connection that's shared by the PCs on your network. If a lot of people are using the Internet at the same time, 100 Mbps can make a significant difference.

Oh. I should also mention... An even faster version of Fast Ethernet is called Gigabit Ethernet. (They shoulda called it Faster Ethernet, but there's a dearth of humor at these higher speeds.) Gigabit Ethernet runs at 1,000,000,000 bits per second.

Adding wireless

What's the biggest problem with Ethernet? The cables. Unless your office or home has been wired with those big eight-wire Ethernet cables, you have to string them across the floor or under the rug, run them up and down staircases, or hang them out the window and pray they don't blow away. Don't laugh. I've done all of that and more.

Wireless networking relies on radio transmitters and receivers in place of Ethernet's cables. You need a wireless hub (which goes by a lot of different names), and wireless network adapters connected to each PC. Usually you buy the wireless hub with one or two bundled network adapters:

✦ The wireless hub typically uses a standard Ethernet cable (with RJ-45 connectors) to connect to an Ethernet hub, although many other options exist, depending on the manufacturer.

✦ The network adapters may be internal adapters (which have to be installed inside your PC), or they may run off one of the ports (typically a USB port).

If you're going to try to pump a lot of data through your wireless network, try to avoid using the USB port for the network adapter, especially if you want to use USB for anything else. Wireless network adapters are notorious for sucking up all of the USB's available data-shuffling capability, leaving other USB devices in the dust.

As of this writing, the most likely survivor in the Ethernet wireless knock-out wars is a technology best known by its user-friendly name, 802.11b, or WiFi. That name refers to a transmission and receiving standard that allows PCs to communicate with the hub at about 11 Mbps (or 11,000,000 bits per second; for comparison, standard Ethernet is 10 Mbps and Fast Ethernet is 100 Mbps).

802.11b wireless is limited to about 300 feet indoors; the PC and the hub can't be much farther apart than that, and if you are in an electrically "noisy" area, or one with lots of walls, you may not have much luck at even lesser distances. Some cordless phones have been known to cause havoc with WiFi connections.

Hijacking phone lines for HPNA

Home Phoneline Network Adapter (or HPNA) technology uses the telephone line that's already installed in your office or home. Conceptually, the HPNA adapter steals a portion of the telephone line and squeezes in computer data. You plug each of your PCs into the phone jack, and the HPNA adapter handles the rest.

HPNA is not a modem! The telephone line is just a convenient wire. HPNA doesn't work like a modem and doesn't act like a modem.

As of this writing, HPNA was advertised as being capable of carrying 10 Mbps — about the same amount of data as a standard Ethernet link.

As of this writing, HPNA is widely regarded as a technological dog. It works, after a fashion, but it's expensive, it's limited to telephone lines (which may or may not exist in the same locations as your computers), and it isn't that much better than simply running Ethernet cable. There are also potential interference problems with the Intercom capabilities of some telephones. Unless you're absolutely convinced that HPNA manufacturers have over-come the problems inherent in the technology, go for 802.11b Wireless WiFi.

Chapter 2: Building Your Network

In This Chapter

✔ Everything you need to get your network going

✔ What to buy

✔ How to hook it together

✔ Convincing Windows XP that your network works

✔ Using one Internet connection for the whole network

Sharing a printer. Transferring files. Freeing up a phone line. Saving money. Those are great reasons for setting up a network. Snoooooooooore.

I know you really want to get your office or house computers networked so that you can blister your co-workers at Half Life or War Craft. Maybe you want to spend some quality time with your son one Sunday afternoon spraying demons in Diablo. Splat! Don't worry. I won't tell anybody.

So you read Book IX, Chapter 1, and you're convinced that you want to assemble your own network. Good. About 90 percent of the time, in my experience anyway, it's pretty easy to put it all together if you know the tricks. Windows XP really does make networking simple. In this chapter, I show you how.

Planning Your Network

Yeah, you have to plan your network. Sorry.

You have a choice of lots and lots (and lots and lots) of ways to put together networks. The way I show you in this chapter is the way I recommend for all first-time networkers. It ain't cool. It ain't sexy. It ain't state of the art. But it works.

In case you haven't had enough of the arcane terminology yet, this chapter shows you how to put together a *100Base-T Ethernet peer-to-peer network*. There. Now you can impress your friends and neighbors. Harrumph.

Follow the next sections in order, and you'll have your network up and networking in no time.

Blocking out the major parts

To set up a network, you need only a handful of parts:

✦ Each PC needs a network adapter.

✦ If you're going to have three or more computers in your network, you need a box called a *hub*. I talk about hubs in Book IX, Chapter 1.

If you want to network only two computers, you don't need a hub. All you need is a special kind of cable called a *crossover cable*. You can buy one — and you only need one — at any store that sells networking cables; just tell them you want an RJ-45 crossover cable to network two PCs. Plug one end of the cable into the network adapter on one PC, and the other end of the cable into the network adapter on the other PC, and you're ready to run the Windows XP Home Networking Wizard. It's that easy.

✦ You need cables to connect each PC to the hub. Take a cable. Plug one end of the cable into the PC's network adapter and the other end into an open slot on the hub. Repeat for each PC. Sounds like the instructions on a shampoo bottle, eh?

A few tricks lurk in the dark corners, as you may imagine, but all in all, if you stick to the simple, old-fashioned (cheap!) equipment, you'll be fine.

Making sure your PCs are good enough

Before you run out and buy networking equipment, double-check and make sure that the PCs you're going to connect are up to the rigors of networking. As a certified (and certifiable) graduate of the Dummies School of Hard Knocks, I have five hard and fast rules when choosing PCs to put on a network:

1. Any PC currently running Windows XP will do fine on a network.

2. At least one of the PCs on your network should be running Windows XP. It makes your life much simpler.

3. If you're going to share an Internet connection on your network (through a modem and a telephone line, DSL, cable, two-way satellite, or psychic connection), make sure that the machine directly connected to the Internet is running Windows XP.

4. Any PC currently running Windows 98, Windows ME, or Windows 2000, that works reasonably well — it doesn't crash all the time or run like a slug — is a good candidate for your network, too.

5. Any other PC (specifically one running Windows 3.1 or 95, or Windows NT 4 or earlier) should be considered only if you already have a network adapter installed on the PC, and you know for an absolute fact that the network adapter is working properly.

Don't violate the last rule. That way lies madness. With rare exceptions, you spend more time and money getting a new network adapter to work on an old Windows 95 machine than you would pay to throw the slacker PC away (or donate it to a worthwhile charity) and buy a cheap new machine.

Why is it so hard to get network adapters to run properly on Windows 95 and NT 4 machines? Millions of analyst hours have been spent pondering that question (both computer analyst and psychiatric analyst, I assure you). It all boils down to a fundamental difficulty in making the network adapter cooperate with the PC. Network adapters make two big demands on PCs: something called an *IRQ* (an internal line for sending information into and out of the PC) and a *base address* (a location inside the PC for the network adapter to stick the information that's coming and going). Both the IRQ and the base address must be unique; the network adapter won't share either with any other part of your computer. If you find yourself in the disastrously unenviable position of trying to get a network adapter card to work in an older PC, do yourself a favor and give up. Life's too short. Have to make it work? Hire an old geezer at a computer shop to wrestle with the problems. I'm an old geezer. I know whereof I speak.

Some folks would have you believe that Macs and Linux PCs will participate in a Windows XP network, with nary a hitch. Sorry, but I don't buy it. Some Macs seem to work well on an XP network, but others can curl your hair. I don't claim to know why. And Linux is ... well, Linux is Linux, if you know what I mean. If you can get a network adapter to work with Linux, I salute you.

Adding network adapters

Armed with the warnings in the preceding section, you now know which PCs you want to connect to the network.

Each of those PCs has to have a network adapter — basically, a place to plug the network cable. When you shop for network adapters, consider these four points from the Dummies School of Hard Knocks, Graduate Division:

✦ Your PC may already have a network adapter, and you may not know about it. Believe me, stranger things have happened in the world of network connections. Examine the back of your computer for a receptacle that looks like a place to plug in a telephone, only it's wider. That's an RJ-45 jack. It's the kind you want (see "Selecting cables," later in this chapter, for details).

Unfortunately, some PCs have "dead" RJ-45 jacks. (Don't believe it? I'll introduce you to my IBM Thinkpad some day.) Some manufacturers put jacks in all their machines — presumably that cuts costs — but don't hook up a network adapter unless you pay for one. The only way to tell for sure if a suspect RJ-45 jack is dead or alive is to plug it into a hub, and turn on both the hub and the PC. If the light on the hub shows that the PC is online, the RJ-45 jack is alive. No light, no adapter.

✦ If you need to buy a network adapter for your PC, your first choice should be a PCMCIA card — one of those gizmos that's about the size of a credit card, only thicker. Check to see if your PC has room for a PCMCIA card. If it does, buy a cheap name-brand card that can handle Fast Ethernet (it says 100 Mbps or 100Base-T or something similar). PCMCIA cards rate number one with me because they're reliable, easy to install, cheap, don't have as many conflict problems as USB network adapters, and invariably work right the first time.

✦ Your next choice — if your PC doesn't have a free PCMCIA slot — is a USB network adapter. Again, you want one that's rated for Fast Ethernet (equivalently, 100 Mbps or 100Base-T).

Sometimes USB network adapters interfere with other USB devices. I have a portable, for example, that works fine with a USB network adapter and works fine with a USB mouse, but starts acting like a jilted lover when I put the two together. The only solution I've found is to use the network or use the mouse, but don't even try to use both at the same time.

✦ Your absolute last resort for a network adapter? The traditional *Network Interface Card*, or NIC (pronounced *nick*). I do believe that a ring in Dante's Hell is reserved for NICs, somewhere below the seventh. You want a NIC that works with Fast Ethernet (= 100 Mbps = 100Base-T). To install a NIC, you have to crack open your PC's case and wield an unforgiving screwdriver. Modern Plug 'n Play NICs usually go in easily and work right the first time. But when they don't....

If you insist on installing a NIC all by yourself, allow around half an hour to put it in your PC, and another half an hour for troubleshooting. Follow the manufacturer's instructions religiously. If you can't get the card to work within an hour, stick it back in its box and return it to the retailer. No doubt the retailer (or manufacturer) will tell you that the problem you're encountering is unique, must be caused by your PC, has to be listed in the troubleshooting database on the manufacturer's Web site, could've arisen only because you made a mistake, must in any case *surely* be due to something wrong with Windows. What, you're using Windows XP? Oh! *That's* the problem. Windows XP is full of these horrible bugs. The retailer will go on to say that the problem absolutely, positively has nothing to do with the card itself. Yeah, right. If it's so easy, the retailer should install it for free, yes?

It's important that all of the network adapters on your network run Fast Ethernet (or 100 Mbps or 100Base-T). If you have just one adapter card on the entire network that's only capable of regular Ethernet speeds (10 Mbps or 10Base-T), the whole network will run at the lower speed, unless you sink a lot of money into a hub that side-steps the differences. Fast Ethernet adapters are cheap. Use 'em.

Choosing a hub

A *hub* is nothing more than a box that connects together all the wires in all the cables that are plugged into it.

If you have a DSL or cable Internet connection, the DSL or cable company may have a hub that goes along with the Internet service. That kind of hub is usually called a *residential gateway.* Or something equally obscure. As long as the hub, er, residential gateway, allows you to have more than one PC connected to the Internet simultaneously — without being clobbered by extra charges — use the DSL or cable company's hub. No need to buy an extra one.

If your Internet Service Provider wants to charge you extra for having more than one PC connected simultaneously, though, be aware of the fact that you have two good options:

✦ Windows XP's *Internet Connection Sharing* (ICS) turns one PC in your network into an Internet Mother Hen. (That's a technical term.) The anointed ICS PC interacts with the Internet. All the other PCs on the network interact with the ICS PC. To the outside world, you have only one connected PC. But all of the other PCs in your network think they're on the Internet, too, thanks to the Mother Hen. Clever. And effective.

✦ *IP Address Sharing* relies on a special kind of hub (sometimes called a Router, an IP Sharing Device, or a Gateway) that's specifically designed to look like a single PC to your Internet Service Provider, but acts just like a regular hub in all other respects. You attach a modem or a phone line or the DSL or cable company's wire to this kind of hub, and plug in your PCs normally. The IP Address Sharing hub acts like the Mother Hen. (See the sidebar called "Sharing IP addresses.") I don't recommend IP Address Sharing for most Dummies simply because Internet Connection Sharing is simpler and cheaper, but IP Address Sharing has advantages that you may want to consider.

Your DSL or cable Internet Service Provider may get hot under the collar if it discovers that you're using Internet Connection Sharing or IP Address Sharing to allow more than one person on your network to use the Internet at the same time. Such inappropriate behavior may circumvent their obscene, extortionate billing policies, and the ISP may demand that you ante up. Aside from the sheer audacity of it all — you should tell 'em to take a flying leap, as far as I'm concerned — technically, you only have one computer connected to the Internet. Whether it's a PC running Windows XP Internet Connection Sharing or the little computer inside an IP Address Sharing hub, only that one, single computer is talking to your Internet Service Provider's computer. That may provide little solace if the ISP has a monopoly in your area and you have to play by their rules. But it's a fact, nonetheless.

If you're in the market for a hub, shopping for one couldn't be simpler. You want the following:

✦ A hub that uses Fast Ethernet — the advertising will say 100 Mbps, 100Base-T, or something similar.

✦ Eight RJ-45 slots. See the next section on "Selecting cables" for a description of RJ-45, but it's the kind of slot that you (almost) always find on a network hub. If you expect to have more than six PCs on your network, get 12 RJ-45 slots. If you expect to have more than ten PCs on your network, go for 16 RJ-45 slots, and please consider adding me to your will.

Get a cheap, name-brand hub. Make sure that you can return it to the store if it doesn't work straight out of the box.

I've seen a lot of claims about a lot of hubs, but I've never seen anything that a normal Dummy could use — in an office, or at home, on a peer-to-peer network — that justified spending an extra dime.

Selecting cables

To get your network running, you have to connect each PC to the hub with cables. Ethernet — the kind of network that you're building — can run over many different kinds of cables. I won't tell you about all of the different options, because I want you to get one, specific kind of cable.

There's a problem, though, and it all comes down to networking's lousy terminology. This specific kind of cable goes by five (or six or seven) different names. It looks a bit like a telephone cable. Telephone cable has four wires in it, but this particular kind of Ethernet cable has eight wires inside.

The ends of the cable have little plastic snap-in connectors, much like telephone wire connectors, except they're wider (they have to hold eight wires instead of four, eh?). The connectors on the end are called RJ-45 connectors, and that's the easiest way to reliably talk about the kind of cable you want — tell anyone trying to sell you cable that you want good quality network cable with RJ-45 connectors.

The cable itself is frequently called "RJ-45 cable" (in honor of the connectors at the ends), but you may also find that it's called 10Base-T cable (or 100Base-T or even 10/100Base-T cable), Twisted Pair Ethernet ("twisted pair" being old-fashioned telephone lingo for the innards of a common phone line, although it sounds considerably more interesting), TPE, Unshielded Twisted Pair (UTP) 10Base-T, IEEE 802.3 UTP cable, Category 5 cable, and heaven only knows what else.

Sharing IP addresses

Every computer connected to a network — at least the kind of networks I'm talking about in this book — has to have a number. A lot of mumbo-jumbo is involved, but basically the number is called an IP Address, and it uniquely identifies the computer. Every computer on a network has an IP Address, and every IP Address is different. Easy, right?

Well, not so easy, for a number of reasons, but I'd like to concentrate for the moment on the problem of getting an IP Address when you're connected to the Internet. Your Internet Service Provider gives you an IP Address. Depending on the kind of Internet connection you have, that IP Address may be assigned to you permanently (commonly the case with DSL or cable modems), or you may be assigned a new IP Address every time you connect to the Internet.

If you have a permanent Internet connection, you pay for one IP Address. In the not-so-good old days, that generally meant you could connect exactly one computer to the Internet: one computer, one IP Address, one Internet connection, one bill. If you and your daughter shared a dial-up Internet account, chances are pretty good that both of you couldn't be online at the same time. Your daughter would dial up and get an IP Address assigned; but if you dialed up and tried to get a second IP Address assigned at the same time, the Internet Service Provider probably prohibited it. (Some ISPs would hand out more than one IP Address to a particular account simultaneously, but they were pretty few and far between, and you paid for the privilege!)

Ultimately, the question of billing for Internet access hinges on IP Addresses — who gets an address, and when, and how much they have to pay for it.

That's why IP Address Sharing is so popular. With Windows XP's Internet Connection Sharing, all of the PCs on your network share a single IP Address: The PC that's running the Internet Connection Sharing program takes care of all the details. With IP Address Sharing hubs (or routers or gateways or whatever you want to call them), all of the PCs on your network share a single IP Address, and a little computer inside the hub (or router or gateway) takes care of keeping things coordinated. As far as your Internet Service Provider knows, you only have one computer connected to the Internet — after all, the ISP has only doled out one IP Address.

If you have more than one computer that needs to get onto the Internet at the same time, IP Address Sharing is a no-brainer. Your big choice: whether to use Windows Internet Connection Sharing, or whether to use a hub (router, gateway) to share IP Addresses. My personal preference is for ICS — it goes in easy and fast, and with Windows XP it (finally!) works well. Many of my friends, though, swear by their IP Address Sharing hubs. The hubs are a bit more difficult to install (follow the instruction manual carefully!), but they don't rely on any particular PC, and will thus keep on chugging (er, sharing) even when Windows crashes or a PC breaks down. And they aren't all *that* much more expensive than a plain-vanilla hub.

Category 5 refers to the quality of the cable. If you're offered Category 3 cable, don't bother. It costs about as much as Category 5, but may not be able to handle the blazing speeds that I'm having you install.

You need one piece of RJ-45 cable for each PC in your network. The cable has to be long enough to stretch from the PC to the hub. When in doubt, overshoot: A cable that's too long can be stuffed behind a desk; a cable that's too short can be painted black and studded with sharp steel spikes to make a stylish necklace.

Or so I'm told.

Scoping out the installation

Measure twice, cut once.

That's awfully good advice, even in the electronic era.

If you've been following along so far in this chapter, you should be armed with a concrete idea of what pieces you need to make your network network. Now it's time to figure out exactly where those pieces go. Physically. In meatspace. Keep these tips in mind:

✦ If you're going to share one Internet connection across the network, the PC that's connected to the Internet must be running Windows XP. In meatspace terms, that means you need to have a pretty hefty machine located next to a telephone jack, your DSL, or your cable modem.

✦ If you're going to burn CDs on a CD-R or CD-RW drive, you'll thank your lucky stars if that machine is running Windows XP. Plan on attaching your CD burner to an XP machine.

✦ Other than those two provisions (Internet connection and CD-R/RW placement), I've found no particular reason to stick a specific peripheral on a specific PC. A networked printer, for example, works fine whether it's attached to a Windows XP machine or a Windows 98 machine.

✦ The hub can go anywhere. Once in a blue moon you may want to watch the lights on the panel dancing, just to make sure that all of your machines are talking to each other, but you really don't need to put the hub on your desk. If you want a light show, get a flashlight. It's cheaper and marginally more interesting.

 There's a theoretical limit to the length of the RJ-45 cable connecting the hub to a networked PC: 100 meters, or about 330 feet. If you go much farther than that, you may have problems with the whole network crashing. When you figure out where your hub is located, keep that in mind — and the fact that I'm talking about the length of the cable itself, not distances "as the crow flies." If you get stuck, talk to your friendly local hardware purveyor about something called a *repeater*. I don't recommend them, but if you have to go more than 100 meters, a repeater can make a big difference.

Installing Your Network

You have your PCs ready to go — network adapters installed and waiting. The hub's sitting in a box on the floor. All of that cable makes quite a mess, and your spouse is starting to wonder, out loud, just what in the Sam Hill you expect to do with all of it.

Yep. You're ready.

Here's a simple, 15-step process for getting your new network up and running with a minimum of fuss and hassle:

If you are trying to convert an existing network to a Windows XP-style peer-to-peer network, beware of a few additional wrinkles. Follow the instructions in the "Troubleshooting" section at the end of this chapter.

1. **Set up each of the PCs. Get the network adapters installed, but don't plug in the network cables (the RJ-45 cable) just yet. Connect the peripherals. Test each machine to make sure that it's working.**

   In particular, if you're going to be sharing an Internet connection through one PC, get that PC connected to the Internet, and make sure everything is working fine.

2. **Turn off all of the PCs.**

   Yeah, that sounds weird, but do it. Put the hub where it's going to go, and connect all the RJ-45 cables, both at the hub and at each individual PC. Plug in the hub and make sure that it's running.

3. **Pick a PC and turn it on.**

   Don't turn on the others. Just this one. Verify that the light on the hub for that PC comes on — in other words, make sure that the network adapter and cable for that PC are working okay. Now's the time to sort out connection problems: if the light doesn't go on, chances are good that a cable is loose or a NIC isn't installed correctly. Fix the problem now. When the light comes on at the hub, this PC's done — put a fork in it ... er, shut this PC down, and move on to the next one.

4. **It's time for the main event. Turn off everything. Unplug all of the connections to the outside world — modems, cable modems, ISDN boxes, DSL boxes, satellite boxes.**

5. **Turn on everything — your PCs, peripherals, the hub, the whole nine yards.**

   Make sure that all the peripherals attached to the PCs are working — print test pages on the printers; slap CDs in CD drives and make sure they're working. If you're using an IP Address Sharing box (see sidebar "Sharing IP addresses"), make sure that it's up and working, and that you've followed the instructions that came with the box to set up all the

PCs on your network. Anything that you want to share on the network should be up and running.

6. **If you plan to use Internet Connection Sharing (ICS), go over to the PC that will be used for ICS, and do whatever you need to do to connect it to the Internet — plug in the modem, attach the box, and so on.**

   Verify that the ICS PC's Internet connection is working by bringing up Internet Explorer and pointing it at a favorite site. (Bonus points if it's funny.) Leave Internet Explorer running, and leave the Internet connection on until you finish adding *all* of the PCs to the network. You're ready to start building your network by adding your first PC.

7. **If you're going to use Internet Connection Sharing, go over to the PC that will be connected to the Internet. If you aren't going to use ICS, pick a Windows XP machine at random. Choose Start⇨Accessories⇨Communications⇨Network Setup Wizard.**

   You see a Welcome screen. Ho-hum. Click Next. You see a reminder screen. Ho-hum. Click Next.

8. **In the Network Setup Wizard's Select a Connection step (see Figure 2-1), you have three choices:**

   • Click the first button if you want to set up Internet Connection Sharing on the network and you want Windows to use this PC for the connection. The PC better be connected to the Internet. (See Step 6.)

   • Click the second button if you already have Internet Connection Sharing set up on your network or if you have an IP Address Sharing box installed on the network. In either case, the Internet connection better be up and working. (See Step 6.)

   • Click the last button if neither of the first two situations applies. Most frequently, that happens if you have an oddball PC on your network that should use its own modem to connect to the Internet, or if you really don't want to use Internet Connection Sharing or an IP Address Sharing box.

9. **Click Next.**

   If you told Windows XP that you wanted to set up Internet Connection Sharing and you wanted it to connect through this PC, you see a dialog box like the one shown in Figure 2-2. This one's a little confusing because it lists your network adapter in addition to your potential Internet connection(s). Rest assured that Windows hasn't gone totally bonkers — you just need to pick your modem or other Internet connection out of the proffered list.

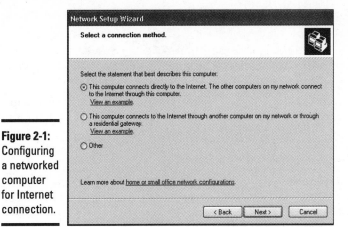

Figure 2-1:
Configuring
a networked
computer
for Internet
connection.

Figure 2-2:
Choose the
Internet
connection,
not the
network
adapter.

10. **Click Next.**

The Wizard asks you to fill out a name for the computer and a description (see Figure 2-3). The description doesn't mean much; it shows up in
the Start⇨My Network Places dialog boxes, and that's about it. The computer name, on the other hand, is used behind the scenes for a hundred
different purposes. That's why it has to be unique on the network — no
two computers can have the same name.

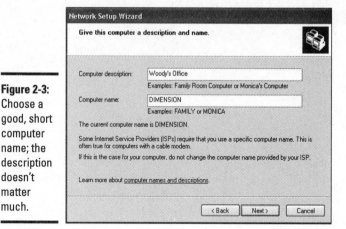

Figure 2-3:
Choose a
good, short
computer
name; the
description
doesn't
matter
much.

Keep your computer names short and simple. You may find yourself typing the name from time to time. Although you're theoretically allowed to use periods in the name, along with slashes, dollar signs, underscores, and a handful of additional oddball characters — I keep expecting to see amulets and chicken entrails to appease the WinGods — you're best to stick with simple letters and numbers.

11. **Click Next.**

The Wizard asks for a network name, suggesting MSHOME (see Figure 2-4). Unless you have a very, very good reason for changing the network name, leave it alone.

Figure 2-4:
Use
MSHOME
for the
network
name,
unless you
absolutely
must
change it.

12. **Click Next.**

The Wizard tells you what it's going to do (see Figure 2-5). Buried in the details, you may discover that Windows XP takes it upon itself to install a firewall, to protect you from malicious attacks over the Internet. That's good. Very good.

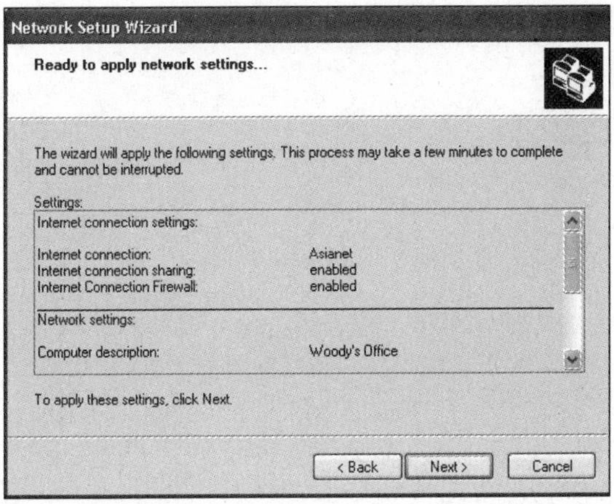

Figure 2-5:
Final
warning
before the
network
connections
are
established.

13. **Click Next.**

It may take forever, but by the time your PC comes back up for air, the network will be ready — on this PC. If you are installing Internet Connection Sharing and this PC will provide the connection, the Wizard installs the ICS program, other programs that are necessary for sharing the Internet Connection (see the sidebar "What's a DHCP and other imponderables"), as well as the firewall that sits between your network and the Internet. The Wizard also sets up the Shared Files folders for every user on the PC and shares all of the printers attached to the PC. As the Wizard says (see Figure 2-6), you're almost done, but you have one crucial last step.

14. **If all of the PCs that you're going to connect to your network are running Windows XP, you're home free — you can check Just Finish the Wizard; I Don't Need to Run the Wizard on Other Computers, then click Next, and you're done.**

On the other hand, if any one of the PCs on your network is *not* running Windows XP, the easiest way I know to get a non-XP PC hitched up to the network is via the Windows XP-generated Network Setup Disk. So if you have any non-Windows XP PCs on your network, check Create a Network Setup Disk, and click Next. Windows XP takes you through the steps to put the XP Network Setup program on a diskette.

What's a DHCP and other imponderables

In my experience, about 90 percent of the time, Windows XP/Home's Network Setup Wizard works like a champ. If you're in the minority 10 percent, though, you're in for some interesting times. The folks who don't get away with a click-click-click network installation experience find themselves immediately confronted with the most ornery, complex, raw computer gobbledygook ever to hit a fan. A big fan.

It would take a book this big to go into the details about what can go wrong with Windows networking, and how to fix the things that go bump in the night. I can't possibly dig through all that offal in this space — and even if I could, I wouldn't know where to start. I list the three most common problems that I've encountered (and, I hope, their solutions) in the section called "Troubleshooting." For the other 10,000,000 things that can go wrong, I wanted to give you my sympathy — and a little guidebook.

Each PC in a peer-to-peer network has a unique number. It's called an IP Address, just like the IP Addresses that I discuss in the sidebar "Sharing IP addresses," except that this IP Address is used to identify the PC on the network. (When I talk about sharing IP Addresses in that other sidebar, I'm referring to the IP Addresses used on the Internet. In this sidebar, I'm talking about IP Addresses used on your network. Confused yet?)

When you write down an IP Address, you usually write down four numbers, separated by periods: 192.128.33.117, for example. The IP Addresses used on Windows XP peer-to-peer networks go from 192.168.0.1 to 192.168.0.254, so if you get tossed into the belly of the beast and see a number such as 192.168.0.3 or 192.168.0.5, you can bet that the number you're looking at is the IP Address of one of the PCs on your

peer-to-peer network. If you have a PC set up to handle the Internet connection for Internet Connection Sharing — a so-called ICS host — the host PC always has an IP Address of 192.168.0.1.

In a client-server network (see Book IX, Chapter 1), the server assigns IP Addresses to all the PCs on the network. That's pretty easy. In a peer-to-peer network, though, it isn't so simple: No single PC is in charge, so no computer is around to make sure that everybody has a different number. Windows XP peer-to-peer networking gets around this conundrum in one of three ways:

- You can tell a PC to use a specific IP Address. It's kind of a manual override. You have to be careful that you don't give the same IP Address to two different computers on the network. This is the approach that's sometimes taken to make IP Address Sharing boxes work — it's an extra, relatively complicated step that you'll no doubt be instructed to take when installing the IP Address Sharing box.

- If the network is set up for Internet Connection Sharing, the PC that runs the connection — the ICS host — is put in charge. It assigns IP Addresses.

- Otherwise, every time Windows XP starts on a PC, it takes a guess at an IP Address, and immediately checks all the other PCs on the network to see if anybody else has already grabbed the address. If it finds a conflict, Windows XP chooses a different address and canvasses the neighborhood again. Sooner or later, it finds a number that isn't being used.

One acronym that you see when your eyes are bleary and your head can't take it any more: *DHCP*. That may sound like a cabalistic curse, but... come to think of it, DHCP *is* a cabalistic curse, but I digress. DHCP stands for Dynamic Host Configuration Protocol, but it's really just a fancy term for "the program that doles out IP Addresses."

When you install Windows XP, or certain pieces of hardware, you may be asked about DHCP, or you may be asked for an IP Address (or a subnet gateway mask or a DNS domain name). If you're ever confronted by those kinds of questions, consider this analogy:

You walk into Starbucks. You say, "I would like a venti non-fat latte to go, please."

The clerk responds by saying, "Certainly, sir. What bonding sequence would you prefer for the carbon chains in the caffeine molecules for that order, sir?"

Some day, the people who design networks and network installation software will be smart enough to understand "venti non-fat latte to go." Until that time, you may have to slog through DHCP settings, subnet gateway masks, and other worse-than-senseless things.

So here's my advice. If you get stuck with a setup program that starts asking questions so complex that no rational human could ever understand them, first do nothing: Click Next or OK or Yeah, Go Ahead and Do Whatever You Think Is Right, You Stupid Machine. If that doesn't work, read the manual, follow it precisely, and pray that it's written in some remotely decipherable variant of English. If that doesn't work, call the manufacturer and scream really loud. Demand your money back and find a simpler solution.

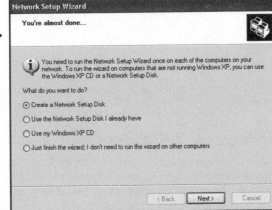

Figure 2-6:
If any PC on your network will not be running Windows XP, create a Network Setup Diskette.

15. **After you complete the preceding steps for the first PC, the others go quickly. Hop over to the next PC on the network:**

   • If the PC is running Windows XP, choose Start⇨Accessories⇨ Communications⇨Network Setup Wizard. Run through the Network Setup Wizard again, beginning with Step 7, with two exceptions. In

Step 8, do not choose the first button. And in Step 14, choose Just Finish the Wizard; I Don't Need to Run the Wizard on Other Computers.

- If the PC is running any other version of Windows, put the Network Setup Disk in the diskette drive, choose Start⇨Run, type **a:\netsetup.exe**, press Enter, and follow the instructions. If you run Network Setup on Windows ME, for example, you see the dialog boxes shown in Figure 2-7. Click Yes, and you're home free, give or take a couple of whirring hard drives and a restart or two.

Figure 2-7:
The Windows XP Network Setup Disk, run under Windows ME.

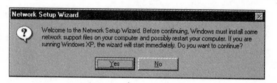

Repeat Step 15 for every computer on your network. When you're done, you're, uh, done. The network should be networking. Try choosing Start⇨My Network Places and make yourself at home. Try printing on a networked printer. Betcha bucks to buckaroos that it sets itself up just that easily.

Troubleshooting

I've encountered three general types of problems — or should I say opportunities? — while working with Windows XP peer-to-peer networks.

Using cable modems, DSL, and ISDN

Many people get bamboozled by their Internet Service Providers when it comes to any form of Internet connection other than plain, old simple modem. Depending on the company, the prevalence of pricing/marketing predators, and the type of technology involved, you may be presented with several expensive alternatives. Most commonly, you are asked to buy a fancy residential gateway, er, hub, uh, router that takes the place of a regular, cheap network hub (see Figure 2-8). You may get socked for the price of an expensive gateway/router. You may even get socked with additional charges for each PC that's plugged into the gateway/router.

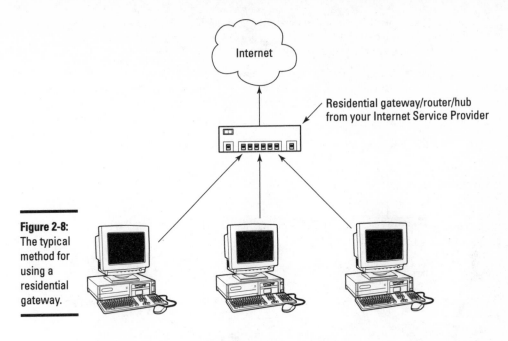

Figure 2-8:
The typical
method for
using a
residential
gateway.

You have a good alternative: Windows XP's built-in Internet Connection
Sharing. Consider the redesigned network shown in Figure 2-9. It has one big
advantage: only one PC is connected to the residential gateway/router/hub,
and that may make a big difference in your bill. The PC that's running
Internet Connection Sharing needs two network adapters — one plugs into
the plain, old everyday networking hub. The other plugs into the box from
the Internet Service Provider.

Which approach will work better for you? Hard to say. It's primarily a question of money. Your ISP may want to charge you extra for using Internet
Connection Sharing on the attached PC.

Installing peer-to-peer over client/server

If you already have a network, and you want to install Windows XP networking, I congratulate you on an excellent choice. Did the same thing, myself. I
had a Windows 2000 client/server network running on my office machines,
and it was such a headache. Oy! I could tell you such stories.

Anyway, I found a sequence of steps that works very well if you're trying to
install a Windows XP peer-to-peer network over the top of an existing
Windows 2000 (or presumably Windows NT) client-server network. The
clients can be running any flavor of Windows, from version 95 on up. Of
course, you won't be able to get the Windows 2000 (or NT) server working
on the network, but you can get any other networked computers to switch
over to peer-to-peer quite easily.

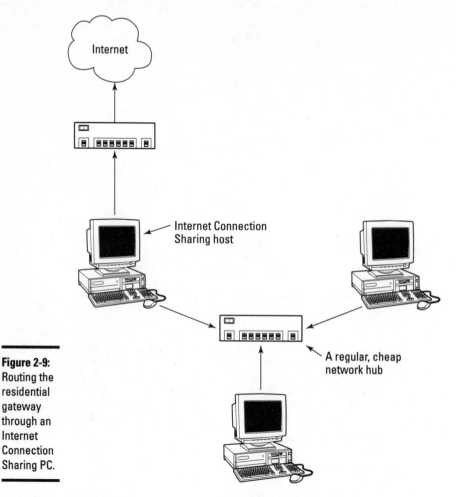

Figure 2-9:
Routing the residential gateway through an Internet Connection Sharing PC.

Here's what I did:

1. **Shut down all the machines on the network. Dead cold.**

2. **Start a Windows XP machine.**

   If you're going to use Internet Connection Sharing, start the ICS host. Otherwise, pick a Windows XP machine at random.

3. **Start one — and only one — of the PCs on the existing network.**

   (Note that this cannot be the server. It won't convert to peer-to-peer unless you completely replace the operating system.)

4. **On the Windows XP machine, follow the steps mentioned in the section called "Installing Your Network" to get the new network going. Make sure that you generate a Network Setup disk.**

5. **Take the Network Setup diskette to the "old" network machine and run it. Restart the "old" network machine. It should be connected to the peer-to-peer network.**

6. **Repeat Step 5 on every machine that you want to move from the "old" to the new peer-to-peer network.**

When you're done, the PCs on the new peer-to-peer network will still be able to access shares (folders, drives, and printers) on the old client/server network, although you have to supply a valid user I.D. and password when you try to access them. To find the old network's resources, follow these steps:

1. **Choose Start⇨My Network Places.**

2. **In the Network Tasks pane, pick View Workgroup Computers.**

3. **In the Other Places pane, pick Microsoft Windows Network.**

Similarly, PCs on the old client/server network can find shares on the new peer-to-peer network. On Windows 98, ME, NT 4, or 2000 computers, double-click the My Network Places icon on the Desktop, and choose Entire Network. Again, you may be required to supply a valid user I.D. and password when you try to access the shares.

You may be able to bypass the user I.D./password requirement for shares on a Windows XP machine if you activate the Guest account on that machine. To do so, see Book I, Chapter 2.

Networking on the road

Most of the time when I travel, I need to hook together two PCs. Guess it's the writer in me, but I've spent hours — days, weeks — trying to get PCs paired up in the field. Direct cable connect. Laplink. USB-to-USB adapters. A dozen other hardware and software kludges. I've resorted to e-mailing files to myself more times than I care to admit.

Suddenly, with Windows XP peer-to-peer networking, it's easy. I mean, really easy.

If you're on the road and you need to plug your PC into a "foreign" network, there's absolutely nothing to it, as long as your portable and the foreign network are running Windows XP peer-to-peer networks. Plug an RJ-45 cable into the portable's network adapter, plug the other end into an available slot on the hub, turn on the portable, and ba-da-boom-ba-da-bing, the whole operation takes maybe 30 seconds.

More than that, though, if I'm carrying two portables that I need to network, all it takes is a crossover cable. (For a discussion of crossover cables — basically, an RJ-45 cable with one pair of wires crossed — see "Blocking out the major parts" earlier in this chapter.)

Whenever I pack two portables, I carry a little one-meter long crossover cable. If I need to network the portables, I plug one end of the cable into the network adapter on one portable, the other end on the other portable, and suddenly my Windows XP peer-to-peer network is right there with me. Everything I can do on the "big" network in my office works precisely the same way on the road.

Absolutely phenomenal.

Chapter 3: Protecting Your Network and Your Privacy

In This Chapter

✓ Viruses and Trojans and Worms, oh MY!

✓ How to keep from getting infected

✓ Care and feeding of your firewall

✓ Identifying and avoiding hoaxes

✓ Cookies on the half shell, and other mixed metaphors

✓ Protecting your privacy

*I*t's a jungle out there. On the one hand, these guys (and they're almost always guys) in black hats keep churning out bad programs that crash systems, erase drives, clog the Internet with millions of bogus messages, and bring down major Web sites with amazing ease.

On the other hand, these companies (and they're almost always companies) keep tons of information about you and your online habits, manipulating and collating and slicing and dicing the information to turn yet another cyberbuck.

I think it's fitting that the last chapter in this book tackles the single most important problem facing Windows XP users: security. It's a problem that has dogged us since the earliest days of computing. It's a problem that will not go away.

You need to understand how you, your computer, and your network fit into the grand scheme of things so that you can avoid security problems in the first place and identify and correct problems should something go awry. You also need to understand how to protect yourself in the networking jungle. It ain't easy.

Understanding the Hazards

Not long ago, most PC viruses planted themselves on diskettes. People spread infections by passing around infected diskettes. Machines got infected when they started — booted — with infected diskettes in the drive.

Infected machines subsequently put copies of the virus on every diskette that had the misfortune of being stuck in the PC's diskette drive. Although they had a bit of competition from other types of viruses, so-called Master Boot Record viruses ruled the PC roost for several years. The most famous — er, infamous — boot record virus, Michelangelo, received an enormous amount of media publicity in early 1992. If you were around at the time, you recall that Michelangelo fell flat on its face, putting egg on the face of more than a few self-appointed "experts" who predicted the Demise of Computing as We Know It.

You'll find that's a recurring theme.

One day in the summer of 1995, somebody wrote a little virus using WordBasic, the macro programming language that came embedded within Microsoft Word. The virus didn't work very well. Matter of fact, it's a wonder it worked at all. But by the end of August 1995, a very large percentage of all the PCs on Microsoft's Redmond campus were infected with the Winword.Concept.A virus. Microsoft called it a "prank macro" at the time and downplayed its significance. Boy howdy, what a prank!

Note: Do you know who wrote Concept.A? I'd love to hear the whole story! Drop me a line at talk2woody@woodyswatch.com. If I get the low-down, you'll see it first in my free newsletter, Woody's Office Watch, www.woodyswatch.com.

Winword.Concept.A spawned an entire industry. Two of them, in fact: the virus writers (whom I generally call "the guys in black hats" or, equivalently, "cretins"), and the anti-virus software folks ("the guys in white hats"). Many of the best-known Internet-borne scares of today — the Melissas, the ILOVEYOUs, and their ilk — work by using the programmability built into the computer application itself, just like good ol' Concept.A.

Windows XP includes some very heavy-duty tools for protecting your PC and your network. It also includes some very heavy-duty capabilities — particularly related to networking — that make it all the more imperative that you protect yourself and the other people on your network.

We've come a long way, baby.

Identifying types of attacks

People in the press tend to call every kind of software with malicious intent a *virus*. That's a bit like calling every TV personality Sam Donaldson. (No, Sam, I'm not making jokes about your hair again. Honest.)

In fact, there are many different kinds of bad software — *malware,* if you will — and no two anti-virus experts agree completely on definitions. In general, and very loosely, the following definitions apply:

♦ **Trojan (or Trojan horse):** Like its namesake, looks like a program that you want to run, but ends up doing something you don't expect. For example, a friend may send you a program that shows a fireworks display, without realizing that the same program is jiggering some of your Windows settings.

♦ **Virus:** Replicates by attaching itself inside another file, such as a Word document or Excel spreadsheet. Viruses generally focus their efforts on infecting many files on the same PC. They travel from PC to PC when an infected file — such as an infected Word document — goes from PC to PC.

♦ **Worm:** Replicates itself, like a virus, but it doesn't use another file to do the replicating. Worms tend to push themselves from PC to PC, most commonly as infected attachments to e-mail messages. Because of that unholy urge to procreate via e-mail, worms tend to travel much faster than viruses.

As far as I'm concerned, you can call a Trojan a virus, you can call a virus a worm, and you can call a worm a three-toed tree sloth. You can even call me late for dinner. But please, please, please don't call any of these ornery critters *bugs*. They aren't bugs. A bug is a mistake in a program. Many Trojans, viruses and worms have bugs — the cretins who write them aren't the brightest lights on the tree, know what I mean? — but that doesn't mean that they *are* bugs. Many computer geeks have mangy mutts. Got it?

Rather than splitting hairs about whether a particular piece of malware is really a virus, a Trojan, or a worm, I think it's more important for you to understand how malicious software can attack you and your system:

♦ Old-fashioned viruses still make the rounds attached to Word documents, Excel spreadsheets, even PowerPoint presentations and Adobe Acrobat documents. The virus typically starts spreading when you open an infected file.

♦ Destructive software often arrives in the form of a file attached to an e-mail message. You open the file and the malware kicks in, sending out hundreds of messages with infected attachments to people in your e-mail contacts list and burying some sort of payload that will hurt you at some point in the future.

You don't stand a snowball's chance of protecting yourself from bad e-mail file attachments if Windows XP hides filename extensions from you. Those three little letters at the end of a filename, after the period, make all the difference. Read and follow the advice on showing filename extensions in Book I, Chapter 2.

♦ More and more cretins are finding ways to put bad programs inside Web pages and formatted e-mail messages. Once upon a time, conventional wisdom had it that merely looking at a Web page or viewing (or previewing) a formatted e-mail message couldn't get you infected. Conventional Wisdom has been knocked down a notch or two.

✦ Direct network infectors are getting more sophisticated. If one PC on your Windows XP network gets infected, these bloodthirsty worms reach out to all the PCs on the network to infect them, too. Protection against malware is a group effort. Everybody on your network has to be careful.

✦ Your Windows XP machine can be turned into a zombie. That sounds like voodoo, I know, but it's true. The basic idea is pretty simple: people (actually, their automated henchmen) roam the Internet, looking for PCs that are easy to break into. When they find a PC with its front door unlocked, they stick a program on the PC and then move on without leaving much of a trace. At the appointed hour, all of the PCs — hundreds or even thousands of them with their zombie programs — start bombarding a single Web site. The Web site can't handle all the traffic, and it's brought to its knees. The process is called a *Distributed Denial of Service,* or DDoS, attack.

✦ Of course, if your front door is unlocked, DDoS may be the least of your worries. Anybody smart enough to turn your PC into a zombie can figure out how to wreak havoc on you, directly.

If you are using a dial-up Internet account, your exposure to the last two types of attacks — zombie and simple break-in — is minimal: Every time you dial into your Internet Service Provider, you get a different address, so would-be attackers won't be able to track you for very long. But if you have a persistent Internet connection — DSL or cable modem — the latter two types of attacks present a very real threat.

Protecting against attacks

With all the threats floating around, you may be tempted to toss Windows XP in the trash. All that great networking and Internet connectivity comes at a price, eh?

Nawwww. Yes, you need to be cautious. No, you don't need to throw the baby out with the XP bathwater. Here's a very short checklist of all the protection that you really require:

✦ Buy, install, update, and religiously use one of the major antivirus software packages. It doesn't matter which one — they all work well. As long as you update the signature files regularly by connecting to the manufacturer's Web site, and you use the product precisely the way the manufacturer recommends, you'll be protected from most nasties.

You may think that anti-virus packages target viruses, viruses, viruses, and that's the extent of it. Not so. All of the major anti-virus packages these days protect against many different kinds of malware, from traditional viruses (and worms and Trojans) to bad Web pages (see Figure 3-1) to infected e-mail message attachments.

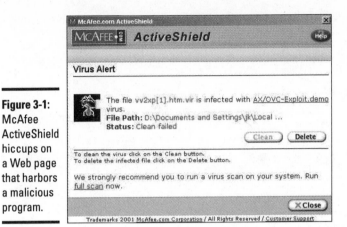

Figure 3-1:
McAfee
ActiveShield
hiccups on
a Web page
that harbors
a malicious
program.

✦ Don't open files attached to e-mail messages until you do the following:

- Contact the person who sent you the file and verify that he did, indeed, send you the file.

- After you verify that the sender actually sent the file, save the file on your hard drive and run your anti-virus software on it to make absolutely certain that it passes muster.

Open the file only after you've jumped through both of those hoops.

✦ Run Windows XP's Internet Connection Firewall on any PC that's directly connected to the Internet.

A *firewall* is a program that insulates your PC (or network) from the Internet. At its heart, the firewall keeps track of requests that originate on your PC or network. When data from the Internet tries to make its way into your PC or network, the firewall checks to make sure that one of your programs requested the data. Unsolicited data gets dropped. Requested data comes through. That way, rogues on the Internet can't break in.

If one of your PCs uses Internet Connection Sharing, make sure that it's using the XP Internet Connection Firewall. If any other PC connects directly to the Internet — perhaps you have a portable that usually gets to the Internet via your Windows XP network using Internet Connection Sharing, but occasionally uses a dial-up connection — make sure that connection gets protected by the Internet Connection Firewall as well.

Windows XP protects specific Internet connections. If you have two different dial-up connections, for example, you have to make sure that both of the connections have Internet Connection Firewall enabled. Here's how to make sure that a specific Internet connection has the Internet Connection Firewall in place:

1. **Choose Start➪Connect To➪Show All Connections. Click the connection that you want to protect.**

2. **In the Network Tasks pane, choose Change Settings of This Connection.**

3. **Click the Advanced tab.**

You see a Properties dialog box, like the one shown in Figure 3-2.

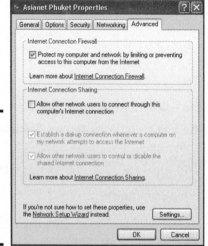

Figure 3-2:
Enable
Internet
Connection
Firewall
from the
Advanced
tab.

4. **Check the box marked Protect My Computer and Network by Limiting or Preventing Access to this Computer from the Internet. Click OK and the Internet Connection Firewall activates itself the next time you use the connection.**

If you access the Internet through your network using only Internet Connection Sharing, you need to set up the Internet Connection Firewall only on the PC that hosts Internet Connection Sharing.

Keep the Windows XP Firewall updated! Even if you bypass Windows Automatic Updates for everything under the sun (see Book I, Chapter 6), it's important that your firewall have all the latest fixes. Why? Because it's the number-one target of online cretins: More PCs run the Windows XP Internet Connection Firewall than all other firewalls combined. That makes it a huge draw for people who like to break things. Don't turn your system into cannon fodder.

Recovering from an attack

Every day I get e-mail messages from people who are convinced that their PC has been clobbered by a virus. Almost invariably, the problems have nothing to do with viruses — intermittently bad hardware, an aberrant program, maybe a flaky Internet connection can cause all sorts of grief, and malware has nothing to do with it.

If you think a virus or worm has hit you, you should do three things immediately. Actually, this is one thing you *shouldn't* do, and two things you should do:

✦ **DON'T REBOOT YOUR COMPUTER.** This is particularly important advice with Windows XP, because of the way it takes snapshots of "last known good" system configurations. If you get infected, reboot, and Windows XP mistakenly thinks your infected system is "good," it may update the "last known good" configuration information incorrectly. Resist the urge to hit the Reset button until you've exhausted all possibilities.

✦ **Follow your anti-virus software manufacturer's instructions.** If you threw away your copy of the manual, beg, borrow, or steal another PC and log onto the manufacturer's Web site. All the major anti-virus software manufacturers have detailed steps on their Web sites to take you through the scary parts.

✦ **If you aren't running anti-virus software, kick yourself.** No, kick yourself twice. Then pick one of the major anti-virus software sites (such as McAfee at `www.mcafee.com` or Norton at `www.symantec.com/avcenter`) and follow the instructions there to download a demo version of their software.

The days of self-diagnosing and manually removing viruses and other malware have long past. Nowadays that's akin to do-it-yourself brain surgery. Rely on the professionals. Get help.

Avoiding hoaxes

Tell me if you've heard this one:

✦ A virus will hit your computer if you read any message that includes the phrase "Good Times" in the subject (Late 1994). Ditto for any message entitled "It Takes Guts to Say 'Jesus'" or "Win a Holiday" or "Help a poor dog win a holiday" or "Join the Crew" or "pool party" or "A Moment of Silence" or "an Internet flower for you" or "a virtual card for you" or "Valentine's Greetings," and so on.

✦ A deadly virus is on the Microsoft [or put your favorite company name here] home page. Don't go there or your system will die.

✦ If you have a file called [put a filename here] on your PC, it contains a virus. Delete it immediately!

They're all hoaxes. Not a breath of truth in any of them.

The hoaxes hurt. Sometimes when real worms hit, so much e-mail traffic is generated from warning people to avoid the worm, that the well-intentioned watchdogs do more damage than the worm itself! Strange but true.

Do yourself a favor. Me, too. If somebody sends you a message that sounds like the following examples, just delete it, eh?

✦ A horrible virus is on the loose that's going to bring down the Internet.

✦ Send a copy of this message to ten of your best friends and for every copy that's forwarded, Bill Gates will give [pick your favorite charity] $10.

✦ Forward a copy of this message to ten of your friends, and put your name at the bottom of the list. In [pick a random amount of time] you will receive $10,000 in the mail, or your luck will change for the better, or your eyelids will fall off if you don't forward this message.

✦ Microsoft [Intel, McAfee, Norton, Compaq, whatever] says you need to download something, or not download something, or go to a specific place, or avoid a specific place, and on and on.

If you think you've stumbled on the world's most important virus alert, via your uncle's sister-in-law's roommate's hairdresser's soon-to-be-ex boyfriend, (remember, he's the one who's a *really smart* computer guy, but kind of smelly?), count to ten twice, and keep three important points in mind:

✦ Chances are very good — I'd say, oh, 99.9999 percent or more — that you're looking at a half-baked hoax that's documented on Rob Rosenberger's Virus Myths site, `www.vmyths.com`. Check it out.

✦ If it's a real virus, all of the major news agencies will carry reports that (even if they're inaccurate!) are far, far more reliable than anything you get in e-mail. Check out `www.cnn.com`, `www.cnet.com`, or your favorite news site before you go way off the deep end.

✦ If the Internet world is about to collapse, clogged with gazillions of e-mail worms, the worst possible way to notify friends and family is via e-mail. D'OH! Pick up the phone, walk over to the water cooler, or send out a carrier pigeon, and give your intended recipients a reliable Web address to check for updates. Betcha they've already heard about it anyway.

Try hard to be part of the solution, not part of the problem, okay?

Defending Your Privacy

I continue to be amazed at Windows users' odd attitudes toward privacy. People who wouldn't dream of giving a stranger their telephone number fill out their mailing addresses for online service profiles. People who are scared to death at the thought of using their credit cards online to place an order with a major retailer (a very safe procedure, by the way) dutifully type in their social security numbers on Web-based forms.

Windows XP — particularly through its ancillary services, such as .NET Passport and MSN Explorer — gives you unprecedented convenience. Enter your credit card information once in .NET Passport, for example, and you can order a book at Amazon.com or buy all of page 32 in the Victoria's Secret Christmas catalog with a couple of mouse clicks.

That convenience comes at a price, though: Everything you do with .NET Passport or MSN — or just about any commercial site on the Web, for that matter — ends up stored away in a database somewhere. And as the technology gets more and more refined, your privacy gets squeezed.

Do you have zero privacy?

"You have zero privacy anyway. Get over it."

That's what Scott McNealy, CEO of Sun Microsystems, said to a group of reporters on January 25, 1999. He was exaggerating — Scott's been known to make provocative statements for dramatic effect — but the exaggeration comes awfully close to reality. (Actually, if Scott told me the sky was blue, I'd run outside and check. But I digress.)

Consider. With Windows XP, you're forced to activate (no personal information collected); persistently urged to register (lots of personal info there); confronted with in-yer-face prompting to sign up for a Passport (hey, you need it for Hotmail and Windows Messenger); and given an, uh, opportunity to enter your credit card info in Passport to simplify ordering in the future. When you crank up the Windows Media Player, you're immediately connected to a Microsoft Web site, where you're offered the opportunity to order music from the Mother $hip. When you're in My Pictures you're offered the opportunity to order prints.

Marketing, marketing, marketing.

Privacy concerns extend beyond the Microsoft Marketing Marvel, of course. A lot of money can be made in collating, filtering, and dishing out personal information, in any usable form. To date, Microsoft isn't the worst offender. Not by a long shot.

Understanding Web privacy

Windows XP in general, and Internet Explorer 6 in particular, give you an unprecedented level of control over your privacy on the Web. One key capability: the Platform for Privacy Preferences (P3P) privacy policy.

P3P technology allows Web designers to tell you what they're going to do with the information that they collect from you. That information is stored in a uniform, machine-readable way. P3P Web sites give specific answers to nine questions:

- ✦ Who is collecting the data?
- ✦ Exactly what information is being collected? Can the information be traced to a specific individual?
- ✦ For what purposes? Why does the site need it?
- ✦ Which information is being shared with others?
- ✦ Who are these data recipients?
- ✦ Can users make changes in how their data is used?
- ✦ How are disputes resolved?
- ✦ What is the policy for retaining data?
- ✦ Where can the detailed policies be found in human-readable form?

Most commercial Web sites have set up formal P3P statements. If you ever want to see a Web site's privacy policy, follow these steps:

1. **Bring up Internet Explorer (choose Start⇨Internet Explorer) and navigate to the site.**

2. **Choose View⇨Privacy Report.**

   You see a list of all the files that go into making up the current Web page (see Figure 3-3).

   Note that many Web pages use advertisements that originate on other Web sites. You may be surprised to learn that an ad appearing on www.abc123.com came from www.def456.com, and www.def456.com may not have the same privacy policy as www.abc123.com. For example, a recent look at www.WindowsMedia.com — the Microsoft Corporation Web page that you see when you start the Windows XP Media Player — revealed numerous ads from doubleclick.net, an advertising company with a P3P policy that's very different from Microsoft's.

3. **Select the site that interests you, and press Summary.**

   The site's P3P statement appears.

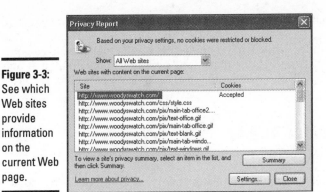

Figure 3-3:
See which
Web sites
provide
information
on the
current Web
page.

4. **Click the underlined text to look at any statements that concern you.**

   Some of the statements are quite innocuous. Others may give you
   pause. Figure 3-4, for example, shows the P3P statement for `msads.net`,
   the site that provides advertising for many Microsoft Web pages, including `www.msn.com`.

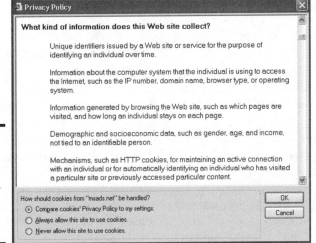

Figure 3-4:
Privacy
statement
from `msads.
net`, a
Microsoft
Web site.

Although you have every reason to expect that a Web site will live up to its
stated P3P policy, you have no absolute guarantee.

TIP

If you find yourself sitting on a Web site that doesn't have a privacy policy, write to webmaster@ the site (for example, webmaster@woodyswatch.com) and complain. Loudly. While P3P technology is hardly infallible, it's a good step in the right direction — one that's long overdue, in my opinion — and Webmeisters who balk at implementing it should be convinced of the error of their ways.

Keeping cookies at bay

So what's a cookie, anyway? Inquiring Dummies want to know.

A cookie is a text file that a Web site stores on your computer. Why would a Web site want to store a file on your computer? To identify you when you come back. It's really that simple.

Let's consider the case of D. Dummy, D. Dummy's computer, and a Web site that D. Dummy visits — let's pick my hometown newspaper, www.phuketgazette.net . The Phuket (say *poo-KET*) Gazette uses cookies to keep track of when readers last visited their Web site, so readers can click on a button and see what's happened since the last time they looked at the site. Nifty feature.

Here's how cookies come into the picture:

1. D. Dummy decides he wants to look at the Phuket Gazette's site, so he types www.phuketgazette.net in Internet Explorer and hits Enter.

2. D. Dummy's computer starts talking to the Web site. "Howdy y'all!" (Did I mention that D. Dummy's computer comes from Texas? Details, details.) "I'm D. Dummy and I'd like to take a look at your main page."

3. The Phuket Gazette site, www.phuketgazette.net, starts talking back to D. Dummy's computer. "Hey, D. Dummy! Have you been here before?" (Actually, the Phuket Gazette's site is a whole lot more polite than that, but you get the idea.)

4. D. Dummy's computer runs out to its hard drive real fast and looks for a text file called — bear with me here — DDummy@www.phuketgazette.txt. It doesn't find a file, so D. Dummy's computer says to the Web site: "Nope. I don't have any cookies here from y'all."

5. The Phuket Gazette site pulls off its shoes and socks, starts counting fingers and toes, and then says to D. Dummy's computer, "Fair enough. I figure you're user number 1578462. Store that number away, wouldja, so I can identify you the next time you come back here? And while you're at it, could you also remember that you were last here at 11:36 AM on December 14?"

6. D. Dummy's computer runs out, creates a new file called `DDummy@www.phuketgazette.txt`, and puts the number 1578462 and 11:36 AM on December 14 in it.

The Phuket Gazette site's main page starts to come up on the screen, D. Dummy scans the headlines, and then heads off to do some shopping. Two hours (or days or weeks or months) later, dear old D. Dummy goes back to `www.phuketgazette.net`. Here's what happens:

1. D. Dummy types `www.phuketgazette.net` in Internet Explorer and hits Enter.

2. D. Dummy's computer starts talking to the Web site. "Howdy y'all! I'm D. Dummy and I'd like to take a look at your main page." Texans.

3. The Phuket Gazette site, `www.phuketgazette.net`, says to D. Dummy's computer. "Hey, D. Dummy! Have you been here before?"

4. This time, D. Dummy's computer runs out to its hard drive and finds a file called `DDummy@www.phuketgazette.txt`. D. Dummy's computer says to the Web site: "Gee willickers. I have a cookie from you guys. It says that I'm user number 1578462 and I was last here at 11:36 AM on December 14."

5. That's all the Phuket Gazette Web site needs to know. It flashes a big banner that says, "Welcome back D. Dummy!" and it puts together a button that says "Click here to see everything that's happened since 11:36 AM on December 14."

Note that the Phuket Gazette site could also keep track of user 1578462 — stick an entry in a database somewhere — and accumulate information about that user. (They don't, but they could.)

No doubt you've been told that cookies are horrible, evil programs lurking in the bowels of Windows that will divulge your credit card number to a pimply teenager in Gazukistan and then slice and dice the data on your hard drive, shortly before handing you over, screaming, to the Feds. In fact, your uncle's sister-in-law's roommate's hairdresser's ... and so on probably told you so himself. Well, guess what? A cookie is just a text file, placed on your hard drive by a Web page. Nothing sinister about it.

A cookie can be retrieved only by the same site that sent it out in the first place. So the Phuket Gazette can put cookies on my hard drive, but only the Phuket Gazette can read them. There's a trick, though. See the sidebar "The doubleclick shtick" for details.

To understand how cookies can pose problems, you have to take a look at the kind of information that can be accumulated about you, as an individual, and how big a squeeze that puts on your privacy.

When you visit a Web site, the site can automatically collect a small amount of information about you:

✦ Your computer's address. (Actually, the IP Address; see Book IX, Chapter 2 for details.) If you use a dial-up Internet connection, the computer's address changes every time you dial up. But if you have a permanent Internet connection — with DSL, or a cable modem — your address probably doesn't change. That means a sufficiently persistent data mining program can (at least in theory) track your activities over long periods of time.

✦ The name of the browser that you're using, its version number, and the name of your operating system — in other words, the Web site will know that you're using Internet Explorer 6 and Windows XP. No biggie.

✦ The address of the Web page that you just came from.

That isn't a whole lot of information, but it comes along for the ride every time you visit a Web site. You can't do anything about it. When you're on a site, of course, the site can keep track of which pages you look at, how long you spend on each one, what buttons you click, and so on.

In addition, the site you're visiting can ask you for, quite literally, anything: size of your monthly paycheck, mother's maiden name, telephone numbers, credit card numbers, social security numbers, driver's license numbers, shoe sizes, and your dowdy Aunt Martha's IQ. If you're game to type in the information, the Web site can collect it and store it.

That's where things start getting dicey. Suppose that you go to one Web site and enter your e-mail I.D. and credit card number and then go to another Web site and enter your e-mail I.D. and telephone number; if those two sites share their information — perhaps through a third party — it's suddenly possible to match up your credit card number and telephone number. See the sidebar "The doubleclick shtick" to see where we're all headed.

Microsoft, of course, gathers an enormous amount of information about you in its Windows XP registration database, its Passport database, the MSN user database, and on and on. As of this writing, it doesn't appear as if Microsoft has attempted to correlate the data in those databases. Yet.

Windows XP and Internet Explorer 6 give you the tools to clamp down on unnecessary cookies. They're tied directly to the P3P policy published by conscientious Web sites (see the section "Understanding Web privacy"). To set higher hurdles for cookies, follow these steps:

1. **Start Internet Explorer by choosing Start⇨Internet Explorer.**

2. **Choose Tools⇨Internet Options, and then click the Privacy tab.**

   You see the Internet Privacy dialog box, shown in Figure 3-5.

Figure 3-5:
Windows
XP/Internet
Explorer 6's
cookie
handling is
tied directly
to Web
sites' P3P
policies.

3. **Adjust the slider up or down, to allow more or fewer cookies to be placed on your PC.**

   If a cookie gets blocked, a small icon appears at the bottom of the Internet Explorer screen. Click on it to see which cookie was blocked, and why.

4. **If you want to block all the cookies on a particular site — or allow all the cookies on a specific site, for that matter — click the Edit button and enter your manual overrides on the Per Site Privacy Actions dialog box, as shown in Figure 3-6.**

For in-depth, knowledgeable updates on cookie shenanigans, drop by `www.cookiecentral.com`.

Encrypting e-mail

Bill G. does it. George W. does it. Even Arthur C. Clarke, basking in a shack in Sri Lanka, does it. Maybe you should, too.

Very nearly all the e-mail in the world goes out "in the clear." Just about anybody with a passing interest can look at your messages, re-route them, snoop to their heart's content. If they're smart, you'll never even know it happened.

Figure 3-6:
If you want
to block all
the cookies
from a
particular
site,
Windows
XP/Internet
Explorer 6
makes it
easy.

The simplest way to protect your mail from prying eyes is by using encryption. And the simplest form of encryption comes in your e-mail program:

✦ If you use Outlook 2002 (which comes with Microsoft Office XP), Outlook 2000 (from Office 2000), or Outlook Express (from Windows XP and Internet Explorer 6), choose Tools⇨Options, bring up the Security tab, and check the box marked Encrypt Contents and Attachments for All Outgoing Messages. Follow the instructions to create a digital certificate and you'll be in business.

✦ If you don't use any flavor of Outlook — or you'd rather not rely on the most commonly used e-mail encryption routines — check out Pretty Good Privacy at web.mit.edu/network/pgp.html. It's free for personal use.

Protecting personal privacy

A few more important privacy points, which all good Dummies should follow:

✦ In the US, with very few exceptions, anything you do on a company PC at work can be monitored and examined by your employer. E-mail, Web site history files, even stored documents and settings, are all fair game. At work, you have zero privacy anyway. Get over it.

Why use your company e-mail ID for personal messages? C'mon. Drop by www.yahoo.com or www.hotmail.com or any of dozens of other Web sites for a free e-mail ID.

The doubleclick shtick

A Web site plants a cookie on your computer. Only that Web site can retrieve the cookie. The information is shielded from other Web sites. Billboard.com can figure out that I like Nine Inch Nails. WindowsMedia.com knows that I buy CDs. But a cookie from Billboard can't be read by Microsoft's WindowsMedia.com, and vice versa. So what's the big deal?

Enter Doubleclick.com. As of this writing, both Billboard.com and WindowsMedia.com include ads from a company called Doubleclick.com. Don't believe it? Use Internet Explorer 6 to go to each of the sites, and choose View⇨Privacy Report. Unless Billboard or Microsoft has changed advertisers, you see Doubleclick.com featured prominently in each site's Privacy Report.

Here's the trick. You surf to a Billboard.com Web page that contains a Doubleclick.com ad.

Doubleclick kicks in and plants a cookie on your PC that says you were looking at a specific page on Billboard.com. Two hours (or days or weeks) later, you surf to a Windows Media.com page that also contains a Doubleclick.com ad — a different ad, no doubt (I found ads for the National Kidney Foundation and the National Child Abuse Hotline) — but one distributed by Doubleclick. Doubleclick kicks in again and discovers that you were looking at that specific Billboard page two hours (or days or weeks) earlier.

Multiply that little example by ten, a hundred, or a hundred thousand, and you begin to see how cookies can be used to collect a whole lot of information about you and your surfing habits. There's nothing illegal or immoral about it. Just realize that Big Brother Doubleclick may be watching, no matter where you go online.

Internet Explorer saves copies (in a *cache*) of Web pages that you've accessed, to make things faster if you look at the same page again. IE also maintains 20 days' worth of history, listing the sites you've visited. Clear them both by starting Internet Explorer (Start⇨Internet Explorer), choosing Tools⇨Options, and choosing the appropriate buttons under the General tab.

✦ You can surf the Web anonymously. It's easy. Check out `www.anonymizer.com`. Be aware of the fact, though, that surfing anonymously still leaves a trail on your PC. To get rid of the trail, follow the Tip above to clear the history and cache.

✦ You can send e-mail anonymously, too — nobody will be able to trace it back to its source. Look at `www.gilc.org/speech/anonymous/remailer.html`. It's particularly valuable for journalists. Whistle-blowing friends of mine inside a, uh, certain company in Redmond use it all the time.

Keep your head low and your powder dry!

Index

Index

O

P

S